The Routledge Handbook of Gender Politics in Sport and Physical Activity

This progressive and broad-ranging handbook offers a comprehensive overview of the complex intersections between politics, gender, sport and physical activity, shining new light on the significance of gender, sport and physical activity in wider society.

Featuring contributions from leading and emerging researchers from around the world, the book makes the case that gender studies and critical thinking around gender are of particular importance in an era of increasingly intolerant populist politics. It examines important long-term as well as emerging themes, such as recent generational shifts in attitudes to gender identity in sport and the socio-cultural expectations on men and women that have traditionally influenced and often disrupted their engagement with sport and physical activity, and explores a wide range of current issues in contemporary sport, from debates around the contested gender binary and sex verification, to the role of the media and social media, and the significance of gender in sport leadership, policy and decision-making.

This book is an authoritative survey of the current state of play in research connecting gender, sport, physical activity and politics, and is an important contribution to both sport studies and gender studies. It is fascinating reading for any student, researcher, policy-maker or professional with an interest in sport, physical activity, social studies, public health or political science.

Győző Molnár is Professor of Sociology of Sport and Exercise at the University of Worcester, UK.

Rachael Bullingham is Senior Lecturer at the University of Gloucestershire, UK.

The Routledge Handbook of Gender Politics in Sport and Physical Activity

Edited by Győző Molnár and Rachael Bullingham

LONDON AND NEW YORK

Cover image: © Getty Images

First published 2022
by Routledge
4 Park Square, Milton Park, Abingdon, Oxon OX14 4RN

and by Routledge
605 Third Avenue, New York, NY 10158

Routledge is an imprint of the Taylor & Francis Group, an informa business

© 2022 selection and editorial matter, Győző Molnár and Rachael Bullingham; individual chapters, the contributors

The right of Győző Molnár and Rachael Bullingham to be identified as the authors of the editorial material, and of the authors for their individual chapters, has been asserted in accordance with sections 77 and 78 of the Copyright, Designs and Patents Act 1988.

All rights reserved. No part of this book may be reprinted or reproduced or utilised in any form or by any electronic, mechanical, or other means, now known or hereafter invented, including photocopying and recording, or in any information storage or retrieval system, without permission in writing from the publishers.

Trademark notice: Product or corporate names may be trademarks or registered trademarks, and are used only for identification and explanation without intent to infringe.

British Library Cataloguing-in-Publication Data
A catalogue record for this book is available from the British Library

Library of Congress Cataloging-in-Publication Data
Names: Molnar, Gyozo (Sport studies teacher), editor. | Bullingham, Rachael, editor.
Title: The Routledge handbook of gender politics in sport and physical activity / Edited by Győző Molnár and Rachael Bullingham.
Other titles: Handbook of gender politics in sport and physical activity
Description: Abingdon, Oxon ; New York, NY : Routledge, 2022. | Series: Routledge international handbooks | Includes bibliographical references and index.
Identifiers: LCCN 2021060992 | ISBN 9780367555221 (hardback) | ISBN 9780367555245 (paperback) | ISBN 9781003093862 (ebook)
Subjects: LCSH: Sports--Sex differences--Finland. | Sex discrimination in sports--Finland--History. | Sports--Finland--Political aspects. | Sports--Finland--Sociological aspects. | Exercise--Finland--Political aspects. | Exercise--Finland--Sociological aspects.
Classification: LCC GV706.5 .R675 2022 | DDC 796.094897--dc23/eng/20220406
LC record available at https://lccn.loc.gov/2021060992

ISBN: 978-0-367-55522-1 (hbk)
ISBN: 978-0-367-55524-5 (pbk)
ISBN: 978-1-003-09386-2 (ebk)

DOI: 10.4324/9781003093862

Typeset in Bembo
by KnowledgeWorks Global Ltd.

We dedicate this anthology to those who have struggled, and will continue to do so, with and within the overarching multitude of Western binary systems and whose views, desires and identities have been marginalised, excluded and vilified.

Contents

List of Contributors   xi
Acknowledgements   xv

1 Connecting Gender, Politics, Sport and Physical Activity:
An Introduction   1
Győző Molnár and Rachael Bullingham

Part I
Gendered History   17

2 Gender Equality, Sport Media and the Olympics, 1984–2018:
An Overview   19
Aneta Grabmüllerova and Hans Erik Næss

3 Sex Verification and Protected Categories in Sport: Binary or Bust?   29
Pam R. Sailors and Charlene Weaving

4 The Politics of Positions of Sport Leadership: The Subtexts of
Women's Exclusion   38
Annelies Knoppers and Ramón Spaaij

5 Gendered Transformations: Conflict and Resistance in the
Regulation of Female Athlete Eligibility in International Sport   47
Ekain Zubizarreta and Madeleine Pape

6 Analysis of Government Policy Relating to Women's Sport   59
Julia White and Jean McArdle

7 Gender and Strength: Representation in Strength and Conditioning   70
Yvette L. Figueroa and Emily A. Roper

Part II
Gender Binary Troubles 81

8 Patriarchy and Its Discontents 83
Eric Anderson

9 Atrophying Masculinity within Professional Road Cycling: Contesting 'The Male' Through a (Re)scripting of the *Anti*-Male 94
James J. Brittain

10 Rainbow Dancing and the Challenge of Transgender Inclusion in Finland 105
Anna Kavoura and Santtu Rinne

11 The Politics of Minority Ethnic Women's Leisure Time and Physical Activity in Denmark 115
Adam B. Evans, Sine Agergaard and Verena Lenneis

12 Patriarchal Politics of Women Footballers in Australia: Changing the Narrative from Welfare to Women Saving Men's Football 126
Michael Burke, Matthew Klugman and Kate O'Halloran

13 A Gendered Focused Review of Sports Diplomacy 137
Verity Postlethwaite, Claire Jenkin and Emma Sherry

14 Gender Politics in British University Sport: Exploring Contemporary Perceptions of Femininity and Masculinity 149
Amelia Laffey and Stuart Whigham

15 The Gender Politics of Sex Integrated Sport: The Case of Professional Golf 160
Ali Bowes

16 Reclaiming Women's Voice in Masculine Competitive Sports Cultures: Playing to Win? 169
Adi Mohel

17 Towards Equality in Women's Sport, Exercise and Physical Activity: Complexities and Contradictions 180
Claire-Marie Roberts

Part III
Intersecting Gender 191

18 Postcoloniality, Gender and Sport: A Snapshot of the Literature and Insights from Fiji 193
Yoko Kanemasu and Atele Dutt

19 From Disability to "Adaptivity": Bethany Hamilton in Sean
    McNamara's *Soul Surfer* (2011)   203
    Tatiana Prorokova-Konrad

20 Women's Parasport Experiences of Sacrifice, Conflict, and Control:
    Always Tilting   212
    Nancy Spencer, Eri Yamamoto and Bobbi-Jo Atchison

21 Muslim Women and Sport: Obstacles and Perspectives in
    Socio-Political Contexts   224
    Fabrizio Ciocca

22 The Politics of Passing for Trans and Non-Binary People in Physical
    Activity in the UK: "Yeah, Congratulations! You Look like a Cis
    Person, Well Done!"   234
    Abby Barras

Part IV
Gender, Politics, Sport and Physical Activity Case Studies   247

23 Gender Politics of Social Media: A Case Study of Megan Rapinoe   249
    Connor MacDonald and Jamie Cleland

24 Gender and the Politics of Patriarchy in Zimbabwean
    Football Administration   259
    Tafadzwa B Choto and Manase Kudzai Chiweshe

25 Women in Golf: Policy and Progress   270
    Niamh Kitching

26 Narratives of Women Surfers: Rethinking Pre-constructed Gender Bias   281
    Aimee Vlachos and Nuria Alonso Garcia

27 Fitness Practitioners' Overcoming of Self-objectification: The Problem
    with 'Legs, Bums and Tums'   291
    Hannah Kate Lewis

28 Sex Integration and the Potential of Track-and-Field: A New Norm   301
    Anna Posbergh

29 Gender Justice and Women's Football: A Macro and Micro Analysis
    of the Game in England   312
    Hanya Pielichaty

Contents

30 Gender Participation in Decision Making Positions of Sport
    Federations   323
    Amalia Drakou, Popi Sotiriadou and Dimitris Gargalianos

31 Mamanet: Empowering Mothers Towards Sport   334
    Riki Tesler, Kwok Ng, Daniel Gelber and Elina Hytönen-Ng

32 A Strategy to Promote Gender Equality: The Number and
    Status of Women in Leadership and Decision-making Positions
    in Finnish Sport   344
    Matti Hakamäki, Salla Turpeinen and Kati Lehtonen

Index   *354*

Contributors

Sine Agergaard is a Social Anthropologist and Professor at the Department of Health Science and Technology at Aalborg University, Denmark.

Eric Anderson is Professor of Sport, Health and Masculinities at the University of Winchester, UK.

Bobbi-Jo Atchison is the owner of Equality Fitness & Recreation and an Instructor in the Faculty of Kinesiology, Sport and Recreation at the University of Alberta, Canada.

Abby Barras has recently submitted her PhD at the University of Brighton, UK, and works as a researcher for the charity Mermaids (www.mermaidsuk.org.uk).

Ali Bowes is Senior Lecturer in the sociology of sport at Nottingham Trent University, UK.

James J. Brittain is Professor in the Department of Sociology and faculty member of the Social and Political Thought graduate program at Acadia University in Wolfville, Nova Scotia, Canada.

Michael Burke is an academic at Victoria University, Australia.

Manase Kudzai Chiweshe is Senior Lecturer in the Sociology Department, University of Zimbabwe.

Tafadzwa Blessing Choto is Lecturer in the Department of Community Studies at the Midlands State University in Gweru, Zimbabwe, and a PhD Student in the Department of Sociology at the University of Zimbabwe.

Fabrizio Ciocca is a sociologist, and he is currently completing his PhD fellowship at Sapienza University of Rome, Italy.

Jamie Cleland is Senior Lecturer in Sport and Management at the University of South Australia.

Amalia Drakou is teaching Human Resources and Rhythmic Gymnastics at the Department of Physical Education & Sport, Aristotle University of Thessaloniki, Greece.

Atele Dutt is a PhD candidate in Sociology at the University of the South Pacific, Fiji.

Contributors

Adam B. Evans is Associate Professor in sociology of sport at the University of Copenhagen, Denmark.

Yvette L. Figueroa is Assistant Professor in the Department of Kinesiology at Sam Houston State University, USA, and specialises in strength and conditioning, fitness assessment and female athletes.

Nuria Alonso García is Professor in Global Studies and Secondary Education at Providence College, USA, and directs the M.A. in Global Education & TESOL and the M.Ed. in Urban Teaching.

Dimitris Gargalianos is Associate Professor of Sport Management at the Department of Physical Education & Sport Sciences, Democritos University of Thrace, Greece.

Daniel Gelber is active in research within the Department of Public Administration and Policy, School of Political Science at the University of Haifa, Israel.

Aneta Grabmüllerova is a PhD Candidate in Sport Management and Media Studies at Kristiania University College, and at the University of Bergen, Norway.

Matti Hakamäki is Senior Researcher at the School of Health and Social Studies, JAMK University of Applied Sciences, Jyväskylä, Finland.

Elina Hytönen-Ng is a docent at the University of Turku, Finland.

Claire Jenkin is Senior Lecturer in Sports Development at the University of Hertfordshire, UK.

Yoko Kanemasu is Associate Professor in Sociology at the University of the South Pacific, Fiji.

Anna Kavoura is a postdoctoral fellow at the School of Sport and Service Management at the University of Brighton, UK.

Niamh Kitching is Lecturer in Physical Education at Mary Immaculate College, University of Limerick, Ireland.

Matthew Klugman is a Research Fellow at the Institute for Health & Sport, Victoria University, Australia.

Annelies Knoppers is Emeritus Professor at the Utrecht School of Governance, Utrecht University, the Netherlands.

Amelia Laffey recently completed an MA by Research in the Department of Sport, Health Sciences and Social Work, Oxford Brookes University, UK.

Kati Lehtonen is Senior Researcher at the School of Health and Social Studies, JAMK University of Applied Sciences, Jyväskylä, Finland.

Verena Lenneis is Assistant Professor at the Department of Health Science and Technology at Aalborg University, Denmark.

Contributors

Hannah Kate Lewis is a PhD researcher at Queen Mary, University of London, UK.

Jean McArdle is Programme Leader on a BSc in Sports Coaching and Performance in the Waterford institute of Technology, Ireland.

Connor MacDonald is a postgraduate student at the University of South Australia in the School of Business.

Adi Mohel is a group facilitator, lecturer and program writer in the field of gender mainstreaming and leadership development of female athletes in Israeli sports.

Hans Erik Næss is Associate Professor in Sport Management, Department of Leadership and Organization at Kristiania University College, Norway.

Kwok Ng is Adjunct Professor of Health Promotion and Adapted Physical Activity at the University of Jyväskylä, Finland, and is affiliated with the School of Educational Sciences and Psychology, University of Eastern Finland.

Kate O'Halloran is an award-winning journalist and academic.

Madeleine Pape is a sociologist and Postdoctoral Researcher at the University of Lausanne, Switzerland.

Hanya Pielichaty is Associate Professor at the University of Lincoln, UK.

Anna Posbergh is a doctoral candidate in the Department of Kinesiology at the University of Maryland-College Park, USA.

Verity Postlethwaite is an independent researcher based in the United Kingdom and working between academic and industry contracts.

Tatiana Prorokova-Konrad is a postdoctoral researcher at the Department of English and American Studies, University of Vienna, Austria.

Santtu Rinne is a licensed psychologist in integrative psychotherapy training and is also a professional dance teacher and Rainbow trans dancer in Finland and abroad.

Claire-Marie Roberts is Senior Research Fellow at University of the West of England, Bristol, UK.

Emily A. Roper is Professor and Interim Dean for the College of Health Sciences at Sam Houston State University, USA.

Pam R. Sailors is Professor of Philosophy and Associate Dean at Missouri State University in Springfield, Missouri, USA.

Emma Sherry is Professor at Swinburne University and Department Chair for Management and Marketing in the Swinburne Business School, Australia.

Contributors

Popi Sotiriadou is Associate Professor of Sport Management at the Griffith Business School, Australia.

Ramón Spaaij is a Professor in the Institute for Health and Sport at Victoria University, Australia. He also holds a Special Chair of Sociology of Sport at the University of Amsterdam, the Netherlands.

Nancy Spencer is Associate Professor in the Faculty of Kinesiology, Sport and Recreation at the University of Alberta, Canada.

Riki Tesler is Senior Lecturer in the Department of Health Systems Management at Ariel University, Israel.

Salla Turpeinen is Researcher at the School of Health and Social Studies, JAMK University of Applied Sciences, Jyväskylä, Finland.

Charlene Weaving is Professor and Chair of the Human Kinetics Department at St. Francis Xavier University in Antigonish Nova Scotia, Canada.

Aimee Vlachos is Teaching Professor at the University of New England, Australia.

Stuart Whigham is Senior Lecturer in Sport, Coaching and Physical Education in the Department of Sport, Health Sciences and Social Work, Oxford Brookes University, UK.

Julia White is a PE Teacher with an undergraduate degree from the University of Limerick and Masters Degree (Research) from Waterford Institute of Technology, Ireland.

Eri Yamamoto is the project leader for the Nippon Foundation Paralympic Support Center.

Ekain Zubizarreta received his PhD in Sport Sciences in 2021 from the Université Paris Nanterre, France.

Acknowledgements

As editors, we wish to express our thanks to Routledge, especially to Simon Whitmore, who supported and guided this project especially at its embryonic stage. We are also grateful to Simon Whitmore and Rebecca Connor at Routledge for their support and much needed guidance during the production phase. We would like to express our gratitude to the authors for agreeing to write chapters, for the contribution they have made to our understanding of the intersection of politics, gender and sport and for their positive attitudes towards our seemingly never-ending editorial requests. We would also wish to extend our thanks to our academic Institutes at both the University of Worcester and the University of Gloucestershire. And, last but not least, we wish to note all those politicians and political activists whose actions and views lit and fuelled the fire for the production of this volume. We are grateful for the copious amount of material which we could include and critique.

1
Connecting Gender, Politics, Sport and Physical Activity
An Introduction

Győző Molnár and Rachael Bullingham

It is our main aim in this introduction and, in fact, throughout this Handbook to reveal and demonstrate to what extent and in what ways various forms of political power and related agendas have the tendency to intersect with gender, sport and physical activity (PA). In doing so, we aim to make a case for the significance of including politics into our socio-cultural analysis and the need to critically read the ever-shifting and complex political landscape as it relates to sport and PA. Through illustrative examples, we describe a way through which, we think, the areas focused on in this anthology may be effectively connected. We will pay particular attention to how populist political sentiments and movements have been impacting gender studies and marginalising challenges to traditional gender binarism. To acknowledge that gender studies have been contested globally, we deploy examples from the UK, Central Europe, the US and Brazil to illustrate our case. We will also argue that it is possible to detect connections between some aspects of populist politics and certain feminist perspectives. In doing so, we revisit the idea of gender-related biological rationale and its connection to political power to analyse and explain concerns with some mainstream feminist arguments, which have the tendency to reduced gender views to the biological barebones. To labour this point around biological determinism, we briefly discuss men's controversial position in the feminist movement, which, in many instances, also rest on biological rationale-based exclusion and suspicion. Along these lines, we explore the case of Emma Raducanu (professional tennis player) to showcase the arbitrary, self-serving nature of a selection of dominant narratives of nationhood that have been used to reinforce primordial ideas around national sporting success in a populist right political context. Our main aim here is to explain that nationhood, similar to gender, sexuality, 'race,' etc., is socially constructed and frequently used (or abused) to serve dominant ideological needs. In so doing, we draw clear links between populist right and political power and tease out how ideologies around representation of nationhood and gender, in our case, have been modified and distorted to serve certain political agendas, e.g., to decide who is British and who is not or who is a woman and is not. Given our critique of bio-medical approaches to understanding and categorising people's gender (and people in general), we propose a closer alignment with gender critical and decolonial feminist perspectives which show discontent with dominant Western approaches and aim to unpack and redress issues that surround capitalism and its cultural offshoots.

While the analysis, by and large, that is put forward here may seem sombre in relation to the future development of the connection between politics, gender, sport and PA, we also briefly explore some emerging generational trends in terms of understanding and practice of gender. We note that Gen Z and the Millennials seem to be demonstrating more fluid attitudes to gender and more liberal political sentiments in comparison to older generations. In particular, Gen Z and the Millennials appear to be questioning and challenging many aspects of the still dominant binary gender system, which can be perceived as a degree of hope in relation to the current polarisation of gender and political trends. To what extent such views may work their way through to mainstream sport and PA remains to be seen, but the chapters included in this Handbook offer a broad range of examples, sports and cultural perspectives to guide further explorations in the area of gender politics and demonstrate, among other things, that there are multiple and complex intersections between the key foci of the anthology and that it is pertinent to consider politics as an analytical angle.

Connecting gender, politics, sport and PA

The idea for this Handbook was borne out of pre-COVID-19 times and began in a campus café without masks, social distancing rules and plexiglass dividers. Little we suspected that the casual, close-proximity, face-to-face ambiance that we took for granted was to be traded for a different, more restrictive type of social setting. We had no inkling as to how COVID-19 was to transform the landscape of social life across the globe and further add to the long list of social anxieties and divisions. In COVID-19 times, we experienced an elevated level of apprehension when someone stands or sits too close to us or when a person does not wear a mask indoors or we may take nervous glimpses at someone who dares to utter a cough. We have also witnessed the emergence of yet another divisive social narrative that revolves around the presence and utility of fast-tracked COVID-19 vaccines. Under these new-born moral panics, one might think that discussing gender and other culturally generated categories such as 'race' and sexuality have somewhat lost their merit; that the ideas behind this Handbook we conjured up in our heavily caffeinated discussions have lost some of their relevance as we have other immediate and pressing matters to tend to, as the end of the COVID-19 era is still not in sight we are writing this introduction.

To the contrary, we argue that, if anything, COVID-19 has further illuminated the multiplicity of social inequalities, divisions and to what extent people living, loving and gendering on the margins of societies have been neglected and often left to their own devices to cope with some of the greatest cultural, social, environmental and economic challenges of our times. In fact, at the time of writing, of the 5.2 million (this number continues to increase) global deaths from COVID-19, Alison Phipps (2020, p. x) argues, many 'have been from oppressed groups: people marginalised by disability, race, and/or class; migrant and displaced populations; people who were incarcerated.' In addition to the ever-widening gap between the 'haves' and 'have nots,' there is a continued and growing resurgence of conservative, right-wing political sentiments in Western countries, which have not been quelled by COVID-19, with a clear agenda to keep the marginalised on the social periphery and/or to attempt to exclude them completely. Such resurfacing of 'fascistic habits,' as explained by Natasha Lennard (2019, p. 14), which relate to behaviours formed out of desire to dominate, oppress and obliterate the other, has become evident.

Fascistic habits are intricately connected to the idea and manifestation of necropolitics (Mbembe 2003), which is essentially being in the position and/or having the power to decide over who or what will live or die. Such political strategy became explicit in the UK in 2020 when Dominic Cummings, then chief adviser to the Prime Minister Boris Johnson, was reported to have said that the initial government strategy for handling COVID-19 was: 'herd immunity, protect the economy and if that means that some pensioners die, too bad' (cited in Shaw 2020). By practicing necropolitics, the needs of certain social strata are marginalised or completely ignored (e.g., disregarding food deserts, maintaining ableist environments, etc.) by withdrawing essential services (e.g., healthcare, education, etc.), erecting fences across made-up borders (e.g., Ceuta and Melilla in Spain), threatening to turn people seeking refuge away from our shores, refusing to globally share resources (e.g., distributing COVID-19 vaccines to the countries of the Global South) and muting dissident voices (e.g., sexual dissidence and gender activism). These are all political manoeuvres to protect the interest of the (mostly) Western dominant and subjugate other types of society and social practices.

Gender studies and subversive thinking around normative gender perspectives have long been subjected to necropolitics. Feminist scholars and gender activists, along with gender- and minorities-focused research, have experienced a tough reception from a range of social interest groups. Such groups often purport to maintain gender binary, heteropatriarchal status quo and white sovereignty. An example of such oppressive voices and related outcomes is the Hungarian populist, right-wing government, led by Victor Orbán, expressing their less than unenthusiastic views towards gender studies programmes offered at Hungarian universities. What is particularly alarming here is that the Orbán government did not stop at verbally lashing out at gender studies but withdrew their university accreditation and central funding in October 2018. It was widely reported in the global media how the Hungarian government rationalised their decision. Zsolt Semjén, Deputy Prime Minister, expressed in an interview that gender studies have no place at universities because it is 'an ideology not a science' and added that 'No one wants to employ a gender-ologist.' It is not without irony that Semjén holds a PhD in religious studies, which reveals a discernible favouritism to one ideological system over another. In addition to abolishing genders studies, in 2021, the Orbán government also targeted the LGBTQ+ movement and ratified legislation that prompts the exclusion of LGBTQ+ content and identities from education materials and TV programmes for people under the age of 18 (Rankin 2021). Similar legislation was also present in the UK between 1988 and 2003, known as Section 28 of the Local Government Act, which prohibited the promotion of homosexuality.

To support the structure of heteropatriarchy, Orbán has gone beyond mortal moral technologies and has sought divine support for his gender ideology. After meeting Pope Francis in September 2021, the Hungarian Government released a soundbite from a radio interview with Orbán in which he explains that like him, Pope Francis (a controversial and complex public figure in relation to gay rights and gay marriage) disagrees with the European Union (EU)-informed relativist family model and notes that: 'The family is a father, a mother, children and full stop' (https://www.facebook.com/kormanyzat/videos/146507091010458). This dominant heteropatriarchy and strong sentiment towards the retention of traditional family unit and gender roles which are underpinned and informed by a Judaeo-Christian belief system leave no room for misunderstanding that gender critical thinking, queer couples and families are not welcome in Hungary.

While this is a cautionary example of the state curbing academic freedom and impinging on the liberties of queer people to serve the ideological needs of the dominant, the ascendancy of populist right-wing political views in Hungary is not an isolated incident. In fact, attacking gender studies, LGBTQ communities and critical thinking around established, binary gender norms has been growing globally. Other recent examples demonstrate that rising conservative, right-wing sentiments and voices are taking formidable actions against any rhetoric that questions the "naturality" and dominance of traditional, binary acceptance of gender and gender roles. An example of this is the increasing legislation across the United States that curb the rights of LGBTQ communities. Ronan (2021) notes that '2021 has been a record-breaking year for the passage of anti-LGBTQ and specifically anti-transgender legislation, with 25 anti-LGBTQ bills having been enacted, including 13 specifically anti-transgender laws across 8 states.' Ronan (2021) adds that 'more than 250 anti-LGBTQ bills have been introduced across 33 states… including more than 130 specifically anti-transgender bills.' Furthermore, in 2017, Judith Butler, a well-known gender scholar, was burnt in effigy in São Paulo, Brazil to protest her ideas on gender, which were perceived as undermining people's gender identities and traditional (predominantly Judaeo-Christian) values. The current far-right, openly homophobe Prime Minster of Brazil, Jair Bolsonaro, had made his discontent with gender studies and the concept of gender official by eradicating references to feminism, homosexuality and violence against women from textbooks. Furthermore, he restructured university funding in an attempt to abolish educational programmes not in line with his government agenda, namely humanities and social sciences (Barasuol 2020). Both actions demonstrate his ultimate goal to undermine feminism and discredit gender studies, leading to a direct return to an antiquated heteropatriarchal society.

Similar examples can be seen emerging across Europe, which, we argue, is aligned with the continuous growth of populist right-wing political parties. The intensification of populism in European politics is evidenced by the expansion of such right-wing populist parties that have been gaining momentum in Spain, Greece, Italy, Germany, the Netherlands and Sweden, amongst others. Examples of right-wing populism include the election of President Donald Trump in the US, the success of the 'Leave' campaign in the 2016 British referendum on EU membership, the unexpected popularity of the Brexit Party in the 2019 UK European Elections and the growing presence of the Vox party in the Spanish parliament. The direct connection between populist right and attacks on gender studies could be also seen in 2016 by Jarosław Gowin, Minister of Science and Higher Education in the Morawiecki cabinet in Poland. Gowin suggested that some gender studies journals, as well as those focusing on gay and lesbian issues, should be stripped of their official status and not receive central funding. Furthermore, the Alternative for Germany, a right-wing populist party, views gender studies as an illegitimate academic discipline that unnecessarily challenges traditional/natural gender dichotomy. Similar assaults on gender studies and more broadly women and LGBTQ rights have been observed in Russia, US and Italy. For instance, the American now ex-president, Donald Trump, has become infamous for his objectifying attitudes, behaviour and comments towards women. In 2016, The New York Times released an unedited version of the dialogue between Trump and Billy Bush (American radio and television host) in which the now notorious comment 'Grab 'em by the pussy' by Trump appears (https://www.nytimes.com/2016/10/08/us/donald-trump-tape-transcript.html). Considering the above evidence in unity, it is credible to argue that there seems to be a growing personal as well as political discontent with problematising gender and gender studies, questioning and critiquing norms embedded in heteropatriarchy that many populist right-wing parties and their representatives would consider part of their core values.

Informed by the above, we argue that this is an opportune time for gender studies to formulate strategic responses to such politically motivated attacks, reinforce the significance of its value and challenge dominant socio-cultural narratives around gender binary sentiments. This is of particular importance in the fields of sport and PA where the reasons for clearly separating genders are historical and ongoing. There are numerous sources that speak to the socio-historical interconnectedness of gender binary and sport/PA and to what ways and extent (some) men have been privileged and (many) women marginalised (see e.g., Hargreaves 1994, Birell 2000,

Burton and Leberman 2019). Therefore, arguably, sport and PA are two pertinent social spheres where the binary gender logic has been and still is engrained. As per that logic, we still have the tendency to gender divide and associate certain practices and activities with men and others with women. In such a gender-restrictive climate, both women and men can, and do, experience the consequences when attempting to erase the set contours of Western femininity and masculinity. For instance, women may experience identity issues and social ostracism when they have high levels of desire to build muscle (Edwards, Molnár and Tod 2021). On the other hand, men may socially and emotionally suffer from dominant masculinist expectations placed on them, which they feel they have not met or cannot meet (Edwards, Molnar and Tod 2017). These examples, and many others, reveal that the rigid cultural subscription of gender norms can harm anyone with bodies, feelings and behaviours out of bounds, and reinforce the need to continue to interrogate gender to make critical sociological sense of the sport and PA spheres, which consist of a broad range of people from different backgrounds and with divergent experiences.

In other words, despite the progress that has been made in terms of drive for equality and balancing the gender scales in sport and PA, the structure of sport remains (and it seems will remain) specifically useful to reinforce gender binary, as in most sports, men and women compete separately and crossover is either not allowed or leads to enormous controversy (it is, however, to note that in some sports, such as darts, gender crossover has happened, but predominantly on an individual level and not on a wholesale basis). In 2019, various mass and social media platforms were replete with discussions and often strong opinions around transgender athletes and their potential contribution to the demise of women's sports exclusively. Here a cacophony of voices and opinions clash, which varyingly focus on protecting women's sport, principles of inclusivity, biological/sex differences and advantages as well as gender identities and fairness. It is in this particular debate around transgender athletes that we see the interlocking of some feminist trends with narratives of heteropatriarchy and necropolitics. The approach taken by feminists might be referred to as trans-exclusive feminism, mainstream feminism or 'lean-in' feminism (Phipps 2020). To shed light on this type of discourse around transgender athletes, especially in relation to male-to-female transformation, we revisit one of the historic pillars of women's marginalisation in sport, i.e., physiology-based exclusion.

In the sport literature and in dominant, longitudinal discourses, different rationales for excluding women from sport include social, aesthetic and biological (see Kay and Jeanes 2010, Molnar and Kelly 2013). Biological rationale refers to the exclusion and/or marginalisation of women from certain activities based on their physiological make up. In essence, the argument purports that women have slighter, more fragile bodies that are not suited for the heavy physical demands of sport and PA. Thus, women should be kept out of activities that might endanger their supple flesh and breakable bones as well as their reproductive potential. Of course, today, few people would give serious attention to such an argument and there are just as many outstanding female athletes as male ones in every sport and PA imaginable. Therefore, to put the argument forward that women's biology does not permit them to participate in activities that are associated with heavy physical demand would not excessively challenge contemporary gender orthodoxy. Yet, when it comes to transgender athletes, it appears that the previously challenged and discredited biological rationale for identifying and categorising gender is resurrected. Here, this rationale is used to 'protect' women from the possibility of male infiltration, unwanted male gaze and unexpected penises (#NoUnexpectedPenises). Being a man and a woman is again reduced to the biological barebones while identities as well as socio-cultural factors are ignored and/or marginalised. The issue here is that being a man or a woman, or somewhere between, is so much more complex than participating in genetic lottery dishing out Y and X chromosomes. Instead, we argue that seeing gender as a binary, an either-or, is an aspect of perverse, zero-sum capitalist and colonial enterprise that ignores individual identities and the complexity of everyday life. As we noted earlier, such sentiments are magnified through the binary logic and system of sport. According to Anzalúda (1987, p. 19), thinking of gender as an absolute binary is a 'despot duality [that] says that we are able to be only one or the other.' This 'despot duality,' many feminists have fought to dismantle, is now used again to redraw traditional gender lines which have been blurred by narratives of multiplicity and possibility. This type of trans-exclusive feminism is essentially using the masters' tools, as Lorde (2003) put it, to support a system that marginalises anyone who is different. Building on Lorde (2003), Ahmed (2017, p. 242) also argues that the 'master's tool will never dismantle the master's house.' Furthermore, Phipps (2020, p. 127) notes that 'saying "fuck the patriarchy" is hardly radical when this is followed by calling on patriarchal disciplinary power' to maintain status quo. We argue that this heteropatriarchal disciplinary toolset is deployed when trans-exclusive feminism is engaged. Such an approach has the tendency to reinforce a traditional gender binary and related social division and neglect the reality that gender is more complex and extensive meaningful discussions are essential for re-evaluating existing sporting structures.

The issue here is not simply the resurgence of a biological rationale to exclude people from traditional gender categories as and when they don't fully comply with set binary criteria, but also that such biological determinism is arbitrarily applied, often when it suits the needs of people endeavouring to maintain their status and privilege. Biological rationale has been and still is used extensively to justify racism and to perpetuate the privilege of one 'race' over another. This is despite that since completion of the human genome project in 2003 (https://www.genome.gov/human-genome-project), we have scientific proof that all humans belong to the same race, homo sapiens, and that 'race' – as it applied to social discriminatory practices – is a mere social construction such as gender. Jablonski and Chaplin (2020) state that 'race is a historical contingency, not a state of nature' and 'any subdivisions erected between people [based on genetics] are essentially meaningless.' Yet, racism is alive and well, and so is sexism and biological gendering. The inconsistency in the application of biological rationale (not that it should be applied at all!) becomes conspicuous when this thinking is accepted in some socially constructed categories, such as 'race' and gender, but not in others, such as nationality. Let's turn our attention to how a biological-rationale informed thinking might be applied in a sport setting through the example of 'British' professional tennis player Emma Raducanu.

Raducanu received extensive global media attention when she won the US Open without dropping a set in 2021. Her victory was followed by an outpour of accolades from the national media, calling her a 'British sensation' and 'British superstar.' All in all, her achievement was a great British or Great British triumph. And, technically, she is British, but she was born in Canada to a Chinese mother and to a Romanian father. So, 'did she win because she is an immigrant?' as the question was posed by Radio Two show host Jeremy Vine on 13th September 2021 (https://www.bbc.co.uk/programmes/m000zm17) or are there other factors to consider? If we applied a biology-driven approach (which clearly informed and informs anti-EU and anti-migration narratives in the UK, see Molnar and Whigham 2021, Molnár forthcoming) to Raducanu's nationality – a concept also socially constructed similar to gender and race – that would resonate with a 'primordialist' approach to the concept of nationhood. Primordialist nationalism emphasises the importance of long-term historical roots linked to socio-biological factors such as ethnicity and bloodline (Van den Berghe 1978), i.e., connecting land and blood (Lennard 2019). This moves towards an ethnically-rooted notion of the nation that manifests itself in the 'cultural backlash' thesis, triggering a recurring reaction from historically dominant groups in a given nation to the progressive cultural value changes prompted by the growing presence of multicultural and open immigration policies (Inglehart and Norris 2016). Inglehart and Norris (2016, p. 6–7) note that 'populist discourse typically emphasizes nativism or xenophobic nationalism, which assumes that the 'people' are a uniform whole, and that states should exclude people from other countries and cultures.' Primordial nationalism, thus, is concerned with threats of mass immigration and a move towards 'ethno-traditional nationalism' to protect the historic preponderance of ethnic majorities through limited immigration. In this sense, Raducanu's victory cannot and should not be celebrated as British as it is not primordially British. Yet, this contradiction did not seem to trouble many of the British media outlets, previously subscribing to primordial nationalist tendencies, to celebrate Raducanu's win as a national success. In relation to this example, the inconsistency of applying cultural narratives and categories is blatantly obvious, and not without a healthy dose of irony. For instance, the front page of the Daily Express (09/09/2021) hailed Raducanu's achievement by calling her a 'history maker' and, right next to that celebratory note, declared that 'MIGRANTS WILL BE TURNED BACK TO FRANCE.'

The above is necropolitics par excellence. It demonstrates how decisions are made about who is accepted or not, who is welcome or not, who is celebrated or who is demonised based on dominant political agendas and beliefs. In turn, with the arbitrary application of socially constructed categories which are portrayed as 'natural,' biology-informed divides are revealed. Similarly, in relation to the case of Caster Semenya, Wheaton et al. (2020, p. 120) observed that:

> Past and present control of sportswomen's sexed bodies have illustrated the ways governance of femininity and femaleness has been embedded within West versus East geopolitical conflicts, for example, during the Cold War, and Global South and North colonial relations.

Spracklen (2008) also notes that sport has the tendency to be and has been normalising scientific racism, thereby reproducing a Western narrative around the concept and practice of 'folk genetics' of Black athletic physicality. Kanemasu and Molnar (2013, 2017) have made similar observations regarding Pacific Islander rugby players and military personnel in relation to their Western-perceived 'natural' physical flair that makes them exceptional athletes and soldiers. These are further examples of collapsing cultural and biological boundaries, i.e., the (Western) biological is used to explain and/or exclude the cultural other.

Biological rationale-informed arguments have also been put forward around the extent to which men should (or should not) be involved in feminist work, which is a recurring debate in feminist literature (e.g., Adu-Poku 2001; Holmgren and Hearn 2009; Van Der Gaag 2014). Men who actively engage with feminism can find themselves in a precarious position where they are criticised by both men and women. For instance, when supervising male students entering the field of gender studies, we have conversations with them about how they, and their work, may be received within academia, to make them aware of potential challenges they may face. It can indeed be precarious to male and feminist. Feminist men may be perceived by other men as social anomalies, 'gender traitors' (Bartky cited in Digby 1998, p. xii) or betrayers of hegemonic masculinity (Adu-Poku 2001). Women may look at them with suspicion as they represent the very oppressive power women fight against. Holmgren and Hearn (2009, p. 408) explain that 'normal within the context of feminist movement is being defined as a woman and thereby being the subject of subordination in a patriarchal social structure whereas being a male indicates deviance.' Again, following this biology-informed logic, Caitlin Moran (2012, p. 79–80), British journalist and author, offers a 'self-check' to determine if someone is a feminist:

Put your hand in your pants.

a   Do you have a vagina? And
b   Do you want to be in charge of it?

If you said 'yes' to both, then congratulations! You are a feminist.

Moran, similar to other biology-driven feminist outcries such as Jessica Valenti's famous Twitter post in 2014 in which she donned a t-shirt displaying that she *bathed in male tears*, expresses a form of misandry which is reflective of a mainstream (white) feminist attitude to men. While we agree with feminists calling out oppression enacted by white males or males of any colour, it is also pertinent to note that feminists can and have used their own tears to deflect. Phipps (2020, p. 71) writes that: 'White women's tears are powerful, the ultimate symbol of femininity.' This refers to the power of (white) women's emotions that can be and has been used to privilege some and disadvantage the cultural other.

To what extent white women's tears have been used for achieving and/or maintaining white, Western privilege is debatable (even Phipps acknowledges that white tears in relation to the #MeToo movement were genuine), but we think that a similarly important question to raise is: what about male tears and tears of transgender women? This question points to the need to carefully examine the socio-cultural manifestations and individual consequences of zero-sum feminism and feminist gender fatalism. Whilst we understand the source(s) of and motivation for misandry and more recently emerging issues around transgender women, we are inclined to support feminist views that are less embedded in the idea of gender fatalism and are carried forward by gender critical and decolonial feminist perspectives. Specifically, decolonial feminism is focused on 'the deconstruction of racism, capitalism and imperialism' (Vergés 2019, p. 5), all of which have, in unity, contributed to the privilege of both white men and women. In particular, arguments which recognise that by using a biological rationale, a gender fatalistic sentiment (Ahmed 2017) is embraced and buys into a zero-sum capitalist model and adopts a 'boys-will-be-boy' gender logic require critical scrutiny. This approach essentialises men as the source of every social evil and oppression. Ahmed (2017, p. 25) writes that the 'will be' in "boys will be boys" acquires the force of prediction. The prediction becomes a command. When you have fulfilled the command… you have lived up to an expectation.' Such gender-informed expectations with long historical roots have been impressed upon people, regardless of their gender, in many cultures. Gendered cultural beliefs have been (op)pressing both women and men by moulding them into a socio-cultural bulk. 'Something pressed is something caught between or among forces or barriers which are so related to each other that jointly they restrain, restrict or prevent the thing's motion or mobility' (Frye 1983, p. 54). Men and women (and people gendering between those ends of the spectrum) are all caught between and within traditional, socio-cultural gender forces that hinders and sometimes completely stops their mobility and vision for an alternative arrangement. In fact, we argue that the cultural forces of gender can be so powerful that they shape, (op)press people to accept their lot in the existing structure. The cultural expression of such forces may indeed prevent people to see or imagine alternatives, or question to what extent gender is natural and unchangeable, or, as per Bolsonaro, Orbán and the Pope, divinely ordained (for a definition of power, see Lukes 2005).

Consequently, while we are not negating the existence of physiological differences between men and women, we argue for the importance of recognising the (op)pressive power of social settings in which we operate and the articulation of cultural categories that are borne out of such settings. Our biology, like our bodies, doesn't exist in a social vacuum (Turner 2008). Boys don't 'just' become boys and neither do girls. Ahmed (2017, p. 14) explains that 'no feminism worthy of its name would use the sexist idea "women born women" to create the edges of feminist community.' On the contrary, becoming and being a man as well as a woman is a taught behaviour (Katz 2013). Butler (1988) referred to gender and gender identity as performative individual social act informed by cultural standards and expectations. In other words, we are not born with our gender, we learn to perform it as per socio-cultural standards and expectations. Performing and having gender is part and parcel of our rich socio-cultural tapestry and, as noted above, historical contingencies. Therefore, to distil a person's gender identity (and other identities) to the bare biology is reductionist at best, ignorant of the complexity of human identity formation and inconsiderate towards recognising the potential for dissonance between the body, culture and identity.

As we have tried to demonstrate, an area where such dissonance can also be continuously and distinctly observed is sport and PA. In these areas, we have not effectively come to see or imagine an alternative way of doing and managing gender. Consequently, we argue that not being beholden to gender essentialism is of particular importance in sport and PA, given that gender binaries are persistent in such contexts and the whole system is embedded in and informed by male-female dichotomy, male physical superiority and the 'boys will be boys' doctrine. As Fink et al. (2016, p. 1317) observe: 'sports are typically sex-segregated… [and provide] an especially powerful reinforcement of this gendered hierarchy as… [they offer a] context in which visible 'evidence' of male supremacy is constantly emphasised.' Consequently, within sport and PA, a traditionally masculinist and gender bifurcated arena, there is a pertinent need to continue to engage with ongoing and emerging debates around gender, sex, sexuality, identity and surrounding power matrices.

Generational change

Given the complexity and significance of politics and gender interconnection, a sensible, and perhaps straightforward approach for many may be to buy into the mantra of populist right-wing parties and, for instance, agree with the views of the Orbán and Bolsonaro governments that people are either born male or female and no gender alternatives should be recognised. Or to advocate that men and women are (or should be) solely defined by their binary-coded visible biological features, all of which helps to maintain the dominance of heteropatriarchy and existing gender order. In this politically exclusionist climate that attributes primordial approaches to understanding gender and sex, we argue, the role of gender studies and gender activism is of exponential importance.

Nevertheless, generational differences have surfaced in this shift to populist right-wing politics. Kaplan (2020, p. 417) writes: 'One report noted that Millennials are outraged by politicians whose rhetoric and actions embolden extremist views.' The UK's EU referendum clearly showed a generational difference between remain and leave voters, with the majority of the young electorate strongly leaning towards remain. Equally, the UK election in 2015 showed generational disparities with the right-wing conservative vote becoming more prominent through each age group. YouGov polls in 2015 show that the difference between 18–19-year-olds compared to the 50–59 age bracket were a mirror image of voting patterns between Conservative and Labour. Moreover, Gen Z (born between 1996–2010) are keenly aware of key social movements and are considered the 'woke' generation, ready to make cultural changes and challenge traditional forms of inequality (Kaplan 2020).

In addition to differences in voting patterns, generational shifts have also been noted in the area of gender identities. Young people are more likely to ascribe to differing labels (e.g., non-binary and pansexual) than older generations, thereby acknowledging generation shifts in sexual and gender fluidity. Additionally, shifts can be seen within sexuality data trends, particularly challenging the binary nature of sexuality. A YouGov poll in 2019 found that 18–24-year-olds were twice as likely (16% compared to 8%) to identify as bisexual compared to 25–34-year-olds. Similarly, 48% of 18–24-year-olds identify as 'somewhere in the middle' on the Kinsey scale of sexuality compared with just 11% of over 55-year-olds. In America, the Pew Research Center asked different generations if they had heard about the use of gender-neutral pronouns, Gen Z respondents indicated that 32% had heard this many times, 42% a few times and 25% not at all (https://www.pewresearch.org/social-trends/2019/01/17/generation-z-looks-a-lot-like-millennials-on-key-social-and-political-issues/). When comparing Gen Z with Baby Boomers, (born between 1946 and 1964) who on the same scale scored just 13% many times, 37% a few times and 49% not at all, it is safe to note that there is a clear shift in terms of identity transformations and increasing openness towards extending the boundaries of traditional gender binarism. In essence, Gen Z are challenging cultural norms around traditional gender binary and it is, therefore, pertinent to consider how Gen Z view the interplay between gender, sport and PA.

The gender and sexuality fluidity that this generation is exhibiting will have the potential to challenge the binary notions that have been deeply ingrained within sport and PA. There are also signs to suggest that this shift away from binary thinking and behaving has been causing change that will, in the long run, benefit not only those identifying outside the traditional norms but everyone. For instance, new leisure facilities having changing villages rather than gendered changing rooms help non-traditional as well as traditional families. Any parent might have encountered difficulties with the binary changing room system dominant in many leisure centres when taking their child/children to a class that requires the use of such facilities. It has been a recurring dilemma whether a father should take his young daughter to the male or female changing room and vice versa. Furthermore, many newly merging sports have principles of gender inclusion embedded within their structure from the outset, such as Roller Derby or Quidditch. With QuidditchUK.org noting on its website, 'Irrespective of age, experience, ability, or gender; quidditch is for everyone - including those from an LGBTQ+ background and who identify within the trans or non-binary community' (https://quidditchuk.org).

Gen Z are seen as the woke generation that are challenging the status quo and combat inequalities. The Pew Research Center notes that 59% of Gen Z believe that official forms in which individuals are asked to self-identify should offer more than the binary options, compared to just 37% of Baby Boomers (https://www.pewresearch.org/social-trends/2019/01/17/generation-z-looks-a-lot-like-millennials-on-key-social-and-political-issues/). This can be seen within student actions in high schools and colleges. As previously mentioned, while Texan lawmakers are becoming increasingly restrictive with the legislature around LGBTQ+ rights, younger generations are increasing their efforts to make a stand for equality. For instance, in Temple, Texas, in September 2021, high school students walked out in support of a transgender girl allegedly being stopped from using the female bathroom (Funk, 2021). Arguably, Gen Z are emerging to be protesters and activists across a broad range of social issues.

Additionally, there are examples within mainstream culture where discussions around the multiplicity of gender and/or sexuality are beginning to be embedded in popular discourses, indicating a shift in society. Examples include, but not limited to, the portrayal of pansexuality by one of the main characters (David Rose) in Schitt's Creek (a popular Netflix Canadian sitcom). Throughout the series, various conversations note that David is pansexual; they define pansexuality through a dialogue while buying wine, in which David explains his sexuality by saying: 'I like the wine, not the label.' David's pansexuality is completely accepted by the family members and wider community and is part of his identity rather than being portrayed as the master identity of his character. Changes to portrayal of sexual fluidity can also be seen in the BBC drama Vigil, which was watched by over 13 million people. Here the main character is shown to have previously been in relationships with a man prior to entering into a relationship with a female co-worker. Again, the language of the TV series shows the limitation of (lack of need for) traditional labels and normalises sexual fluidity, and the idea that we should care more about the wine than the label.

Social media has also shown to have generational differences in terms of platform use. Gen Z have moved away from Facebook and onto platforms like TikTok, Instagram and SnapChat, which focus on photographs rather than text (Levak and Šelmić 2018). The use of social media has provided female athletes the opportunity to present themselves to the world without the constraints of the traditional media outlets, frequently owned by men. As Toffoletti and Thorpe (2018, p. 28) note: 'Existing research into the depiction of female athletes has indicated that while they remain under-represented across traditional and online media outlets, social media is a potential tool for female athletes to redress this lack of coverage, and even contest and rework normative gender and sexual identities in sport.' In essence, the traditional gatekeepers of the mainstream media outlets are side-lined, which has allowed athletes to develop their own brands, to gain sponsorship and reach more people than they could via standard mass media outlets. Yet, there remain gendered elements to the use of social media. Female athletes have the tendency to receive unwanted messages and online abuse directed at their gender identity, while still having to conform to traditional femininity including sexually suggestive posts (Geurin 2017).

What has become clear is that Gen Z and the Millennials are challenging many aspects of the binary status quo, thereby offering a degree of hope in relation to the current polarisation of political trends. Gen Z and the Millennials appear to see and embrace diversity and are going beyond the established cultural contours as a positive impact on society unlike previous generations (https://www.pewresearch.org/social-trends/2019/01/17/generation-z-looks-a-lot-like-millennials-on-key-social-and-political-issues/). Consequently, both Millennials and Gen Z are frequently criticised by their seniors for being 'woke,' but they are clearly softening boundaries and binaries to be more inclusive across the intersectional spectrum. Older generations have also labelled Millennials, in particular, as being the 'snowflake' generation and are seen as not fit for work within the competitive environment while being easily offendable. This observation appears to be somewhat ironic given that baby boomers also have a good measure of potential for being offended when the existing system and their privileges within that are challenged. For example, the Pew Research Center notes that 61% of Gen Z approved of the taking the knee protests in the NFL compared to just 37% of baby boomers (https://www.pewresearch.org/social-trends/2019/01/17/generation-z-looks-a-lot-like-millennials-on-key-social-and-political-issues/). As a generation, Gen Z appear more flexible in their attitudes, are able to voice their opinions through social media and protest cultural and political sentiments that they see as unjust and discriminatory. It is hoped that this generation can and will provide the groundswell and the chance to challenge the right-wing veil that is currently sweeping across the world. However, this hope is hinging on thoughts, ideas and observations transformed into actions and active cultural resistance, the prospect of which has been questioned (Schaillée et al. 2021).

Handbook's content and structure

One of the challenges when editing a book is finding a sensible balance between our imagination, as editors, of what chapters should be like and what contributors see as appropriate and relevant. We have done our best to offer constructive comments to authors while maintaining an open mind and a supplicant learner attitude. We are grateful to contributors for working hard at meeting our incessant demands and responding to our queries and comments in a timely fashion. By engaging with the broad range of sports, geographic locations, theoretical perspectives and viewpoints encompassed by this anthology, we significantly broadened our own gender research-related horizons and understanding. We are pleased to be able to afford this rich content to the reader to experience a similar learning trajectory.

It is perhaps worth noting at this juncture that to actively and effectively combine all aspects of this Handbook's focus was a challenging task. It was especially true of the integration of politics into analyses and narratives. This might have been the case as in the field of sport scholarship, we have a long history of artificially separating sport and politics. There is a resounding echo coming from a range of sources and agents, and reverberates through history, that sport and politics don't and shouldn't mix or that sport politics exclusively mean sport policy. While we agree that policies are connected to politics and, in fact, policies are often a result of political agendas, there is more to politics (as we demonstrated at the outset of this Introduction) than policy formation and implementation. However, scholarly analyses that consider sport from a critical political perspective, aside from a few notable examples (see work by Alan Bairner, Stuart Whigham and John Kelly), are still limited. It is also true of accounts that explore the politics, sport and gender intersection, which is one of the key rationales behind producing this anthology. We believe that the chapters presented in this book capture various angles of the complex intersections between gender, politics, sport and PA in their own idiosyncratic way. These connections might be revealed through connecting historical events, engaging theoretical perspectives and/or offering critical interpretation of primary data from people, from a board range of societies and social strata, who have, in some shape or form, been influenced by the exertion of some form of political power which was targeted at their (assigned and/or achieved) gender and sport/PA involvement.

Part I of this anthology offers a range of historical accounts that demonstrate the longitudinal interconnections between politics, gender, sport and PA. The chapters highlight the importance of approaching gender from a historical perspective, thereby revealing extensive temporal connections between social attitudes to gender and related cultural activities such as sport and PA. Here we have chapters offering a review of research on sport media coverage and gender equality related to the Olympic Games between 1984 and 2018 and exploring the controversial history of gender verification. Chapters also question the long-term effectiveness of the principle and practice of gender diversity as there remains resistance to women in leadership positions and demonstrate via policy analysis that, by and large, governments pay only lip service to gender equity in central positions. Chapters also focus on specific areas, such as strength and conditioning coaching, that are still deeply associated with traditional masculine values and are exceptionally slow to find gender equilibrium.

While finding and achieving gender equilibrium in sport and PA (and beyond) can be considered a key segment of ongoing debates around gender, so is questioning the relevance and utility of gender binaries. As we noted earlier, we sustain that gender is performed and socially constructed. Such social constructions, to some extent and in some instances, privilege one gender over another. Gender-informed privileges can be and have been advantageous and constraining for men and women, depending on the socio-cultural circumstances. Chapters in Part II trouble the gender binary by challenging mainstream feminist arguments around patriarchy, questioning contemporary society's optimum male aesthetic via cycling and arguing for the significance and effectiveness of more gender fluid inclusivity in dancing. Chapters then explore gender-segregated swimming spaces in Denmark in relation to Muslim and Danish cultures, critique phallocentric narratives that continue to inform policies and practices of Australian women's football and analyse gendered understandings in academic literature and their applications of contemporary Australian and British sports diplomacy. Contributions also unpack the impact of contemporary perceptions of 'femininity' and 'masculinity' on the experiences of female university athletes, present critical discussions around gender politics at play during sex-integrated professional golf tournaments and highlight conflicts between women's athletic experiences and hegemonic masculine discourses in the context of 'competing with' versus 'competing against.'

Exploring complex connections between genders and in what ways and to what extent women and men (and people gendering between those nodes of the spectrum) continue to relate to each other is the very focus of this anthology. Nevertheless, we must recognise that academic explorations around gender politics as they relate to sport and PA need to also consider how gender intersects with other socio-cultural experiences. People can, and do, have different encounters with and give dissimilar meanings to sport and PA depending on their own circumstances. For instance, geographic location, social class, sexual orientation, experiencing disability, 'race,' etc. feed into sporting and PA-related discourses. Consequently, chapters in Part III explore intersections between gender and other social categories and thereby tease out the socio-political trajectories of postcolonial communities, and how those shape and are shaped by gendered relations of power in the sporting arena. Furthermore, contributions examine the intersection of disability and gender, and unfold that adaptivity not only foregrounds disability as a legitimate, 'normal' condition, but also communicates gender as an important aspect in athletes' professional career. Then, chapters turn to analyse the stories of athletes at the intersections of gender and disability in sport by drawing on critical literature addressing empowerment in parasport and feminist disability studies and highlight some of the key issues related to Muslim women in sport, and how political transition towards populist and conservative positions affects their involvement in PA. Finally, the complex intersections between our gendered bodies and the gendered spaces are discussed, which can often be difficult to navigate when gender is viewed as non-conforming.

Part IV of this Handbook offers a range of case studies to further demonstrate the value and importance of gender focus across a broad array of settings, sports and issues. Chapters in Part IV discuss the paradoxes and privileges associated with Megan Rapinoe as a successful white woman actively engaging on social media platforms, analyse the politics of patriarchy in Football administration in Zimbabwe and examine the role of the Royal and Ancient (R&A) – a global golf governing body – in promoting women in golf. Chapters also unfold key segments of gender equality in surfing through interviews, problematise issues with the diet and fitness industry's role in promoting self-objectification among women and discuss the conflicting ideologies of sport and sex integration in male and female track-and-field. Contributions also reveal the extent to which football in England has traditionally been guarded by male gatekeepers, tease out issues around gender participation in leadership positions within sport federations and introduce the growing cultural presence of Mamanet (a team sport based on Newcomb Ball) as the fastest growing sport among Israeli women. Last but not least, there is a report on the development of the legal basis and policies of gender equality promotion in Finnish sport since the 1990s.

While the chapters included in this collection cover a broad range of issues, sports, geographic areas and aspects that revolve around gender politics, we also see other cultural spheres through which links between politics, gender, sport and PA may be further explored but not included here. Given that the concept and cultural manifestation of gender and related roles have fundamental effects on both men and women, and anyone in between, adhering to them may not, in the long run, be logical, sensible and sustainable. For instance, marginalising women from PA and exercise throughout their lives, but expecting them to take up PA after the age of 60 so they would reduce the burden on healthcare services is not a sustainable, neither is it a sensible approach. In addition, expecting men and women to accessorise according to their gender and spend sometimes exorbitant sums of money on engineering their culturally expected gender, which can range from paying for beauty treatments to surgical body modifications, may not be socially and economically sustainable approach in the long run. Another area where the relationship between gender and sport may also become troubling and unsustainable is our food culture. Whilst our Western societies are obsessed with meat production and consumption, and the professed benefits of that, there are rapidly emerging concerns around the socio-cultural as well as environmental sustainability of such practices. One of the key issues here is that meat and its consumption has the tendency to be associated with performance enhancement, especially muscle generation, and, thus, considered to be a staple diet for many athletes and exercisers. Meat is also a cultural signifier of masculinity and it is often perceived in Western societies that men hunt, barbeque and eat meat. There is evidence to suggest that it is and has been culturally often acceptable for women to eat vegetables, but not for men. In fact, throughout history, men advocating vegetarianism were often ridiculed and considered feminine. In this sense, meat is a cultural gender signifier, the consumption of which now goes beyond the confinement of gender and reaches the sphere of environmental concerns around our planet. Through examining various issues connecting gender-related cultural practices and sustainability, we wish to point out the multiple reaches of gender that go beyond the cultural, incorporating the historical, social, political and environmental dimensions, which intersect with sport and PA. Against this backdrop, by recognising the long-term and continuous complex interplay between politics, culture, gender, sport and PA, we propose to reinforce the contemporary importance and essence of gender studies and their potential for offering a critical outlook on residual, dominant and emerging cultural discourses. We also encourage scholars focusing on gender research around sport and PA to consider adding politics to their repertoire to interpret the ever-more increasing complexity of contemporary gender discourses.

REFERENCES

Adu-Poku, S. (2001) 'Envisioning (Black) Male Feminism: A Cross-Cultural Perspective', *Journal of Gender Studies*, 10(2): 157–167.
Ahmed, S. (2017) *Living a feminist life*. Georgia: Duke University Press.
Anzalúda, G. (1987) *Borderlands/la frontera: The new mestiza*. San Francisco: Aunt Lute Books.
Barasuol, F. (2020) Academic feminists beware: Bolsonaro is out to crush Brazil's 'gender ideology'. *The Loop*, accessed on 17/09/2021 at: https://theloop.ecpr.eu/academic-feminists-beware-bolsonaro-is-out-to-crush-brazils-gender-ideology/
Birell, S. (2000) Feminist theories in sport. In J. Coakley and E. Dunning (eds.), *Handbook of sport studies*. London: Sage, pp. 61–77.
Burton, L.J. and Leberman, S. (eds.) (2019) *Women in sport leadership: Research and practice for change*. London: Routledge.
Butler, J. (1988) 'Performative Acts and Gender Constitution: An Essay in Phenomenology and Feminist Theory', *Theatre Journal*, 40(4): 519–531.
Digby, T. (1998) *Men doing feminism*. London: Routledge.
Edwards, C., Molnar, G. and Tod, D. (2017) 'Searching for Masculine Capital: Experiences Leading to High Drive for Muscularity in Men', *Psychology of Men and Masculinity*, 18(4): 361–371.
Edwards, C., Molnár, G. and Tod, D. (2021) 'Searching for Ontological Security: Women's Experiences Leading to High Drive for Muscularity'. *Qualitative Research in Sport, Exercise and Health*. DOI: 10.1080/2159676X.2021.1969995

Fink, J.S., LaVoi, N.M. and Newhal, K.E. (2016). 'Challenging the Gender Binary? Male Basketball Practice Players' Views of Female Athletes and Women's Sports'. *Sport in Society*, *19*(8–9): 1316–1331.

Frye, M. (1983) *The politics of reality: Essays in feminist theory*. Berkley: Crossing Press.

Funk, K. (2021) 'Texas students protest after trans student allegedly denied use of high school facilities'. *Newsweek*, accessed on 7/11/2021 at: https://www.newsweek.com/texas-students-protest-after-trans-student-allegedly-denied-use-high-school-facilities-1633987

Geurin, A.N. (2017) 'Elite Female Athletes' Perceptions of New Media Use Relating to Their Careers: A Qualitative Analysis'. *Journal of Sport Management*, *31*(4): 345–359.

Hargreaves, J. (1994) *Sporting females: Critical issues in the history and sociology of women's sport*. London: Routledge.

Holmgren, L.E. and Hearn, J. (2009) 'Framing 'Men in Feminism': Theoretical Locations, Local Contexts and Practical Passings in Men's Gender-conscious Positionings on Gender Equality and Feminism', *Journal of Gender Studies*, *18*(4): 403–418.

Inglehart, R. and Norris, P. (2016) Trump, Brexit, and the rise of populism: Economic have-nots and cultural backlash. *HKS Working Paper No. RWP16-026. Available online at*: http://dx.doi.org/10.2139/ssrn.2818659.

Jablonski, N.G. and Chaplin, G. (2020) 'We need to unpack the word "race" and find new language'. *Conversation*, accessed on 19/09/2021 at: https://theconversation.com/we-need-to-unpack-the-word-race-and-find-new-language-138379

Kanemasu, Y. and Molnar, G. (2013) 'Pride of the People: Fijian Rugby Labour Migration and Cultural Identity'. *International Review for the Sociology of Sport*, *48*(6): 720–735.

Kanemasu, Y. and Molnar, G. (2017) 'Private Military and Security Labour Migration: The Case of Fiji'. *International Migration*, *55*(4): 154–170.

Kaplan, E.B. (2020) 'The Millennial/Gen Z Leftists are Emerging: Are Sociologists Ready for Them?'. *Sociological Perspectives*, *63*(3): 408–427.

Katz, J. (2013) *Tough Guise 2: Violence, manhood and American culture*. Media Education Foundation Production.

Kay, T. and Jeanes, J. (2010) Women, sport and gender inequity. In B. Houlihan (ed.), *Sport in society*. London: Sage, pp. 130–154.

Lennard, N. (2019) *Being numerous: Essay on non-fascist life*. London: Verso.

Levak, T. and Barić Šelmić, S. (2018) 'Escaping the 'Virtual Promenade': New Trends in Use of Social Networks by Members of Generation "Z"'. *Media, Culture and Public Relations*, *9*(1-2): 37–55.

Lorde, A. (2003) The master's tools will never dismantle the master's house. In R. Lewis and S. Mills (eds.), *Feminist postcolonial theory*. Edinburgh, UK: Edinburgh University Press, pp. 25–28.

Lukes, S. (2005) *Power: A radical view* (2nd ed.). London: Red Globe Press.

Mbembe, A. (2003) 'Necropolitics'. *Public Culture*, *15*(1): 11–40.

Molnar, G. and Kelly, J. (2013) *Sport, exercise and social theory*. London: Routledge.

Molnar, G. and Whigham, S. (2021) 'Radical Right Populist Politics in Hungary: Reinventing the Magyars through Sport', *International Review for the Sociology of Sport*, *56*(1): 133–148.

Molnár, G. (forthcoming) Sport, labour and migration. In L. Wenner (ed.), *Oxford handbook of sport and society*. Oxford: Oxford University Press.

Moran, C. (2012) *How to be a woman*. Croydon: Ebury Press.

Parker, K., Graf, N. and Igielnik, R. (2019) 'Generation Z looks a lot like Millennials on key social and political issues'. *Pew Research Center*, accessed on 14/11/2021 at: https://www.pewresearch.org/social-trends/2019/01/17/generation-z-looks-a-lot-like-millennials-on-key-social-and-political-issues/

Phipps, A. (2020) *#Me too, not you: The trouble with mainstream feminism*. Manchester: Manchester University Press.

Rankin, J. (2021) 'Hungary passes law banning LGBT content in schools or kids' TV'. *The Guardian*, accessed on 17/09/2021 at: https://www.theguardian.com/world/2021/jun/15/hungary-passes-law-banning-lbgt-content-in-schools

Schaillée, H., Derom, I., Solenes, O., Straume, S., Burgess, B., Jones, V. and Renfree, G., 2021. 'Gender inequality in sport: perceptions and experiences of generation Z', *Sport, Education and Society*, *26*(9), pp. 1011–1025.

Ronan, W. (2021) 'Texas Senate passes anti-transgender sports ban bill'. *Human Rights Campaign*, accessed on 29/09/2021 at: https://www.hrc.org/press-releases/texas-senate-passes-anti-transgender-sports-ban-bill-2

Shaw, M. (2020) '"Herd immunity and let the old people die" – Boris Johnson's callous policy and idea of genocide'. *Discover Society*, accessed on 29/09/2021 at: https://archive.discoversociety.org/2020/03/23/herd-immunity-and-let-the-old-people-die-boris-johnsons-callous-policy-and-the-idea-of-genocide/

Spracklen, K. (2008) 'The Holy Blood and the Holy Grail: Myths of Scientific Racism and the Pursuit of Excellence in Sport'. *Leisure Studies*, *27*(2): 221–227.

Toffoletti, K. and Thorpe, H. (2018) Female Athletes' Self-representation on Social Media: A Feminist Analysis of Neoliberal Marketing Strategies in 'Economies of Visibility'. *Feminism and Psychology*, *28*(1): 11–31.

Turner, B.S. (2008) *The body and society: Explorations in social theory* (3rd ed.). London: Sage.

Van den Berghe, P. (1978) Race and Ethnicity: A Sociobiological Perspective. *Ethnic and Racial Studies*, *1*(4): 401–411.

Van Der Gaag, N. (2014) *Feminism and men*. London: Zed Books.

Vergés, F. (2019) *Decolonial feminism*. London: Pluto Press.

Wheaton, B., Mansfield, L., Caudwell, J. and Watson, R. (2020) Caster Semenya: The surveillance of sportswomen's bodies, feminism and transdisciplinary research. In C.A. Taylor, C. Hughes and J.B. Ulmer (eds.), *Transdisciplinary feminist research*. London: Routledge, pp. 116–123.

Part I
Gendered History

2
Gender Equality, Sport Media and the Olympics, 1984–2018

An Overview

Aneta Grabmüllerova and Hans Erik Næss

Introduction

In 1935, Pierre de Coubertin – the founder of the International Olympic Committee (IOC) – claimed that women's roles at the Olympic Games 'should be above all to crown the victors' (Coubertin and Müller, 2000, p. 583). This idea of the Olympic competitions as a male domain would remain largely unchallenged until the 1984 Olympics in Los Angeles, which 'provided it with a new cultural template that would keep the Olympics relevant in the twenty-first century' (Llewellyn et al., 2015, p. 1). This template included a renewed focus on media, commercialization and female athletes. Even though only 1,700 of the 7,500 athletes at the 1984 Olympics were female, and only 73 of the 226 events were for women (Vecsey, 1984), it still represented a shift in the gender patterns of mega-events (Llewellyn et al., 2015). This shift was subsequently encouraged by the IOC's decision that any new sport in the Olympics must include women in 1991 (Koenigsberger, 2017). Subsequently, a variety of commissions to support women's participation were introduced, including the IOC Gender Equality Review Project in 2017 (IOC, 2018a). Consequently, the number of female participants in the Olympics has grown steadily. While women represented only 21% of the participants in the 1976 Games, that proportion increased to 34% at the 1996 Atlanta Games before reaching 45% in the 2016 Rio Olympics (Nunes, 2019).

While the increase in female athletes' Olympic mass media coverage was observed between 1984 and 2018, the statistics on gender ratio reveal only part of the story. This chapter, therefore, offers a review of research linking media, the Olympic Games and gender equality. It opens with a brief explanation of the data and methods underpinning this review and offers three chronologically ordered sections on media and gender representation in the Olympics. Due to the dramaturgical opportunities sports offer media to exploit, we focus on findings related to 'what facts to include, what kind of story to tell, what kind of wording to use to describe the event and the athlete, and what pictures to use in order to underline the message' (Hartmann-Tews, 2019, p. 268). Finally, a brief discussion of five key patterns in these findings precedes our summary of the practical implications and further research directions of this review.

DOI: 10.4324/9781003093862-3

Data and methods

Data for this chapter was gathered through the Oria search engine, which contains 70 international and Norwegian scientific databases, including Web of Science, and resources of the Olympic World Library in Lausanne, Switzerland. From April 2020 to January 2021, we searched those databases and resources for documentation on the development of the IOC's gender equality initiatives and gender-related research on media portrayal since the 1984 Olympics till the 2018 Winter Olympics. By using English search keywords such as 'media', 'coverage', 'portrayal', 'Olympic(s)' and 'gender', we accumulated an English-based sample of 88 articles. As mediatization processes and gender equality initiatives in sport go conjointly in the selected period (e.g., Bruce, 2013; Djerf-Pierre, 2011), we chose to conduct a descriptive review of sources identified to explore existing interpretable patterns in the body of information (Paré et al., 2015). In contrast to other review forms, such as integrative (Torraco, 2005) and systematic (Xiao and Watson, 2019), the benefit of a descriptive review is its overview of how research has addressed the construction of gender in Olympic media coverage across a range of disciplines (e.g., sociology, sport management, gender studies, communication and media studies). This form of review, therefore, contributes to discussion about why some forms of representation and stereotypes persist and others do not, in a way which is less bound by the disciplinary traditions which are necessary to consider, for example, in a systematic review. Finally, drawing upon the analytic dualism, mentioned by Loy et al. (2009), between equity and legitimacy, our overview is presented as a timeline with an emphasis on how sportswomen have struggled to achieve equality with their male counterparts ('equity') and to overcome stereotypes related to their participation ('legitimacy').

1984–1996: Almost exclusive male dominance

In this period, most of the research was concentrated on the American television company NBC, as it became the exclusive broadcaster of the Olympics in the USA from 1988 onwards (Armour, 2014). At this time, men competed in nearly twice as many events and, in terms of *equity*, received more coverage and name mentions (Eastman and Billings, 1999). NBC also used more male experts, and most announcers were men (Tuggle and Owen, 1999). Positively, in the Australian TV, the amount of airtime for the 1988 and 1992 Olympics was distributed proportionally to the number of men and women on the national team, and interestingly, the most watched sports (swimming, gymnastics and track and field) were the ones that offered the most gender-equal representation (Toohey, 1997).

Two longitudinal studies showed that until the 1980s, sportswomen were inadequately portrayed in the Olympic coverage (King, 2007; Urquhart and Crossman, 1999), but with their increasing participation, the media attention devoted to them increased as well (Pfister, 1987). Women became well represented in the coverage of gender-appropriate sports (Vincent et al., 2003), and men remained overrepresented in sports that emphasize strength, endurance and risk (Lee, 1992). These sports are perceived by the society as more masculine, while sports that require aesthetics are seen as feminine. This is a result of 'gendertyping', which is a process in the social practise of gender that influences the segregation of sports (Sobal and Milgrim, 2019). In terms of *legitimacy*, the trend was to focus on other gender differences such as first-name calling (Messner et al., 1993) or sexualization (Higgs et al., 2003). Sportswomen also received more stereotypical comments and remarks about their appearance (Shields et al., 2004). Even though media started to notice female athletes and devote more airtime to them, their sporting achievements were still under communicated.

1996–2006: The more (sportswomen), the merrier (coverage)

During the 2000 Summer Olympics, it seemed that the issue around *equity* of female vs male athletes was starting to even out with fairer depiction of gender balance in athletes' name mentions. Yet, NBC devoted more prime-time coverage to men (Billings and Eastman, 2002), while most of the coverage of sportswomen remained confined to feminine sports only (Tuggle et al., 2002). Male announcers, speakers and experts also continued to dominate mass media platforms (Capranica and Aversa, 2002).

Confirming this trend, female athletes received greater headline coverage in the British news during the 2004 Summer Olympics (King, 2007) and outnumbered males in the Australian News Online (Jones, 2006). Bruce et al. (2010) performed a content analysis of the 2004 Olympics coverage across 18 countries. The results showed that women generally received less coverage than their male counterparts; however, in most cases, the amount was related to their participation and/or to success. Similarly, NBC prime-time coverage of the 2004 Olympics mirrored men's greater participation and medal success and, as result, they received the majority of the coverage time and name mentions (Billings, 2008). Also, Italian television coverage was closely related to the proportion of Italian athletes in 2000 (Capranica and Aversa, 2002), and national success overrode gender in 2004 (Capranica et al., 2008). However, NBC persisted in employing fewer female journalists (Tuggle et al., 2007). British media continued to trivialize female athletes by depicting them only in feminine sports and located female athletic achievements in the latter pages of the sports section (King, 2007). At this point, it is interesting to note that while the media coverage of the Summer Olympics, in general, began including sportswomen more equitably, the coverage of Winter Olympics did not display any change in longitudinal terms and women still remained as underrepresented as in previous iterations (Billings and Eastman, 2003).

At the same time as the gender patterning of media coverage remained the same, national differences began to occur. In terms of *legitimacy*, studies of newspapers in European countries (Belgium, Italy, Denmark, France, Sweden and Finland) concluded with fair representation of sportswomen corresponding with their participation and number of events (Capranica et al., 2005; Laine, 2016). However, while in Sweden, women were portrayed as serious athletes, Finnish newspapers trivialized and sexualized their sportswomen. In a similar vein, analysis of NBC's coverage of ice-hockey revealed that men are often referred to as role models for women players who are often compared to them (Poniatowski and Hardin, 2012). Furthermore, female athletes continued to be characterized according to their domestic roles and presumed emotional states (Daddario and Wigley, 2007). Billings (2007) revealed that associating women with emotions and domestic roles happens more frequently in sports that are based on aesthetic performances which are judged by individuals (e.g., gymnastics) than in sports with objective assessment (e.g., track and field).

2008–2018: New media, new vistas?

The *equity* of female athletes and women's sports did not initially change much in traditional mass media outlets in this period. Male athletes received more prime-time in the NBC coverage of the 2008 Olympics (Davis and Tuggle, 2012), more performance descriptors in Slovenian coverage (Ličen and Billings, 2013) and the majority of the stories in Australian, British, Canadian and American online news (Jones, 2013). Furthermore, in traditional media, female athletes remained underrepresented in Serbia (Stojiljković et al., 2020), Turkey (Ayvazoglu, 2017), Sweden (Hedenborg, 2013), Great Britain, USA, Australia, Brazil, China and Kenya

(Eagleman et al., 2014). Interestingly, at the same time, NBC devoted more time to women's beach volleyball despite the fact that both American men and women won gold medals (Smith and Bissell, 2014).

In terms of *legitimacy*, women were less likely to be depicted in action. Instead, the attention remained on their roles as wives and mothers (Jones, 2013). A significant portion of the media coverage remained ambivalent, and sportswomen were stereotyped, infantilized, genderized and sexualized (Xavier, 2014). For example, men's gymnastics was described in the US news in more technical language while women's coverage focused on their physical appearance (Eagleman, 2015). Only a French newspaper, *L'Equipe*, placed emphasis in their coverage on success rather than gender (Delorme and Testard, 2015).

Despite these setbacks from a gender equality perspective, both equity and legitimacy issues related to female athletes were challenged at the 2012 London Olympics (Arth et al., 2018; Boykoff and Yasuoka, 2015). For the first time, NBC devoted more airtime and name mentions to women (Billings et al., 2014). An improvement was also noticed in media coverage of sportswomen competing in more masculine sports (Delorme and Testard, 2015). For the first time in the history of the Winter Olympics, women were featured more prominently than men during NBC's broadcast in 2014 (MacArthur et al., 2016). Also, in the two following Olympics in 2016 and 2018, NBC continued to increase airtime for women's sports (Billings and Angelini, 2019; Coche and Tuggle, 2017). Yet, a pattern of national preferences persists. For instance, Chinese broadcasts devoted more coverage to male athletes in three most prominent winter sports in China despite women's greater success (Xu et al., 2019), and its gymnastic coverage gave men more airtime and name mentions even during women's events (Xu et al., 2018).

A key characteristic of this era was the emergence and growing influence of social media, such as Twitter (launched in 2006) and Facebook (launched in 2007). Consequently, we can observe a shift in academic research and new opportunities for fairer gender representation in sport. The ramifications of this shift, however, remained insignificant until around 2016. Nevertheless, towards the end of this era, social media outlets have transformed sports coverage into an interpersonal, intercultural and global public domain (Creedon, 2014), exposing many of the offensive remarks made by television commentators and newspaper headlines (Villalon and Weiller-Abels, 2018). With the rapid development of social media, Olympians gained their own voice, and their communication came under extensive scrutiny. Again, the impression is mixed. Litchfield and Kavanagh (2019) analysed social media accounts of the Australian team and Team GB. Despite some prevailing stereotypes, the British coverage offered fair representations of gender, but Australian women remained underrepresented on the Australian Olympic Team Twitter site (@AUSOlympicTeam). Xu (2019) analysed gender portrayal in the online Olympic Channel, an over-the-top Internet television operated by the IOC, over 16 months from 2016 to 2018, revealing that 60.1% of pictures of news stories were devoted to men with greater focus on masculine sports, and that women only received 39.9% of the coverage. Despite the IOC's efforts to enhance the gender representation, sportswomen continue to be underrepresented not only in media but also in IOC's own communication.

Discussion

Our examination of existing research reveals a gradual increase and a more balanced portrayal both in terms of equity and legitimacy of sportswomen's coverage in the Olympics between 1984 and 2018. However, the development is cluttered with reservations, and research findings are sometimes contradictory. For example, Arth et al. (2018) claimed that women received more coverage than men for the first time during the Winter Olympics in 2018, but MacArthur et al. (2016) claimed that this had already happened in 2014. Consequently, the development in women's media portrayal can be and has been interpreted in different ways, which means that our findings on the Olympics (1984–2018) represent gender-significant portrayal patterns rather than an exhaustive list of themes and development trajectories. Below we discuss five mass media portrayal patterns that are essential in unfolding the gender-media-sport interconnection.

The first pattern centres around the development of media coverage of Olympic sports and is characterized by *ambivalence* as it 'incorporates representations that oscillate between valorizing female sporting prowess and undermining or trivializing it' (Bruce, 2013, p. 130). As an example of this ambivalence, an Australian online news coverage study of the domestic Sydney 2000 Olympics indicates an increase in the proportion of coverage dedicated to female athletes and the range of sports. However, it notes the retention of stereotyping of female athletes as emotionally vulnerable and dependent adolescents (Jones, 2004). Metcalfe (2019) analysed how such ambivalent coverage is interpreted and understood by the audience. All interviewees, but one, said that they expected male athletes to receive more coverage. Since unconsciously accepting social signals fails to challenge masculine hegemony, media-generated gender stereotypes prove to be detrimental for many young people (Metcalfe, 2019).

The second pattern concerns *market demand*. While the coverage of sportswomen and sportsmen competing in different sports will differ and the sports media industry remains men's territory, both male and female journalists argue that the media are responding to audience interests (LaVoi et al., 2019; O'Neill and Mulready, 2015). Evidently, sports media often decide with reference to only their own opinion what will appeal to an audience that they see as mainly male (Dashper, 2018; Villalon and Weiller-Abels, 2018), even though women spend similar amounts of time watching the Olympics (Tang and Cooper, 2012). The issue with Olympic broadcasting appears to be that the rights often belong to one media company for decades (e.g., NBC in the USA) and the audience has no choice but to follow the Olympics through their lens. The majority of the audience watches the Olympics in long, continuous segments, not selectively. Consequently, they are 'ultimately becoming immersed in the frames employed by NBC gatekeepers' (Billings and Eastman, 2003, p. 583), who are largely men (Billings, 2009).

The third pattern regards the *production of content*. Previous research identifies the decision-making processes in editorial sports departments as mainly masculine (Hardin, 2013). Billings (2009) found that the NBC Olympic producers feel they set a fair agenda; however, content analysis proved otherwise. Xu's (2019) study with the Olympic Channel personnel revealed that individuals have substantial impact while claiming considerate agency and autonomy, with their own personality and perspective influencing production, challenging the prevalent ideology of 'gender neutrality' in sports newsrooms. Therefore, the lack of knowledge of women's sports might lead to a more generic and plain coverage (Dashper, 2018). According to O'Neill and Mulready (2015), who interviewed UK journalists during the 2012 Olympics, sport organizations play an important role in the co-creation of sports coverage. The respondents in their study criticized sport governing bodies for not utilizing their female athletes in a way which promoted women's sport.

The fourth pattern concerns the role of *nationalism and success*. The strong nationalistic fervour ignited by the Olympics seems in some instances to override gender bias (Capranica et al., 2005; Wensing and Bruce, 2003). The amount of coverage dedicated to certain sports and events corresponds with national medal expectancies, success and participation, and, therefore, gender may not be the most crucial matter for media coverage of mega events (Billings and Angelini, 2019; Capranica et al., 2005; Delorme, 2014, p. 201; Jakubowska, 2017; Markula et al., 2010; Toohey, 1997; Wehden and Schröer, 2019). But medal success is not the only indicator (Hedenborg, 2013; Pfister, 2010). Some sports are also more complex than others and have, as a result of their rules and time limits, a structural advantage that yields greater coverage times (Wehden and Schröer, 2019). For example, while some events last seconds (e.g., sprint swimming or track and field), others stretch over longer timeframes (e.g., tennis, ice-hockey). Related to this, the cultural background must be considered as regional differences in media coverage depend on local sport preferences (Capranica et al., 2005). For example, in the case of snowboarding, the amount of viewing of men's or women's events directly influenced the perceptions of the sport as either more masculine or more feminine (Jones and Greer, 2012).

The fifth pattern concerns *methodology*. Research often looks at the coverage of the Olympics as whole, seeking parity, while there are sports and events women did not take part in. Therefore, the same amount of coverage devoted to female and male can hardly be expected. Delorme (2014) re-analysed 18 academic articles that investigated coverage of female and male athletes at Summer Olympics from 1984 to 2008 and revealed methodological irregularity and lack of consideration of other factors affecting the coverage. He suggests that the number of participants and events on both international and national level should be considered when quantitatively analysing media coverage. Considering this view, women were underrepresented in 24.24% of cases. Furthermore, Eastman and Billings (1999) suggested that only medal events attract viewers and, therefore, there should be parity in name mentions. However, in the analysed Olympics, women won the most medals despite their lower participation on the US team. Based on this logic, women should have received more coverage but that was not the case. For that reason, not only participation but other aspects such as nationalism, success and culture need to be considered in studies of gender in the Olympics before drawing any conclusion.

Conclusion

Our review of research on gender equality, sport media and the Olympics from 1984 to 2018 reveals that while male and female athletes in the Olympics have become nearly equal in participation ('equity'), there are still great differences in their respective media coverage ('legitimacy'). Although both quantitative and qualitative sources point towards less gender-based stereotyping and prejudice, contradictory aspects of this development also generate new questions, especially around what factors cause progress or setbacks when it comes to gender representation in sport media. Specifically, there is one main question that is worth pondering upon: is the progress we have observed so far the effect of the IOC's own initiatives? To answer such question, special attention should be given to the IOC Gender Equality Review Project (IOC, 2018a), mentioned in the introduction. It contains 25 action-oriented recommendations within five themes, among them some related to 'Portrayal' – i.e., balanced representation of both genders, communications partnerships and organizing committees. So far, its actions have had limited effect, and research has shown that the IOC struggles with translating its goals into action (Matthews et al., 2019). For researchers as well as the IOC, it is, therefore, pertinent to consider the entire media coverage process, including the gender ideologies of media production and the IOC's role and not only to evaluate the results and theorize about the effect it can have on female athletes.

REFERENCES

Armour, N. (2014) *NBC Universal pays $7.75 billion for Olympics through 2032*. Available at: https://www.usatoday.com/story/sports/olympics/2014/05/07/nbc-olympics-broadcast-rights-2032/8805989/ (Accessed 31 August 2020).

Arth, Z., Hou, J., Rush, S. and Angelini, J. (2018) '(Broad)casting a Wider Net: Clocking Men and Women in the Primetime and Non-Primetime Coverage of the 2018 Winter Olympics', *Communication & Sport*, 7(5), pp. 565–587. doi: 10.1177/2167479518794505.

Ayvazoglu, N. (2017) 'The Coverage of Female Athletes at London 2012 Summer Games in Turkish Sports Media', *The Anthropologist*, 27(1-3), pp. 49–57. doi: 10.1080/09720073.2017.1311688.

Billings, A. and Angelini, J. (2019) 'Equity Achieved? A Longitudinal Examination of Biological Sex Representation in the NBC Olympic Telecast (2000–2018)', *Communication & Sport*, 7(5), pp. 551–564. doi: 10.1177/2167479519863652.

Billings, A.C. (2007) 'From Diving Boards to Pole Vaults: Gendered Athlete Portrayals in the "Big Four" Sports at the 2004 Athens Summer Olympics', *Southern Communication Journal*, 72(4), pp. 329–344. doi: 10.1080/10417940701667563.

Billings, A.C. (2008) 'Clocking Gender Differences: Televised Olympic Clock Time in the 1996—2006 Summer and Winter Olympics', *Television & New Media*, 9(5), pp. 429–441. doi: 10.1177/1527476408315502.

Billings, A.C. (2009) 'Conveying the Olympic Message: NBC Producer and Sportscaster Interviews Regarding the Role of Identity', *Journal of Sports Media*, 4(1), pp. 1–23. doi: 10.1353/jsm.0.0027.

Billings, A.C. and Eastman, S.T. (2002) 'Selective Representation of Gender, Ethnicity, and Nationality in American Television Coverage of the 2000 Summer Olympics', *International Review for the Sociology of Sport*, 37(4), pp. 351–370. doi: 10.1177/1012690202037004023.

Billings, A.C. and Eastman, S.T. (2003) 'Framing Identities: Gender, Ethnic, and National Parity in Network Announcing of the 2002 Winter Olympics', *Journal of Communication*, 53(4), pp. 569–586. doi: 10.1111/j.1460-2466.2003.tb02911.x.

Billings, A., Angelini, J., MacArthur, P., Bissell, K. and Smith, L. (2014) '(Re)Calling London', *Journalism & Mass Communication Quarterly*, 91(1), pp. 38–58. doi: 10.1177/1077699013514416.

Boykoff, J. and Yasuoka, M. (2015) 'Gender and Politics at the 2012 Olympics: Media Coverage and Its Implications', *Sport in Society: Gender, Media, Sport*, 18(2), pp. 1–15. doi: 10.1080/17430437.2013.854481.

Bruce, T. (2013) 'Reflections on Communication and Sport: On Women and Femininities', *Communication & Sport*, 1(1-2), pp. 125–137. doi 10.1177/2167479512472883.

Bruce, T., Hovden, J. and Markula, P. (2010) *Sportswomen at the Olympics. A Global Content Analysis of Newspaper Coverage*. Rotterdam: Sense Publisher.

Capranica, L. and Aversa, F. (2002) 'Italian Television Sport Coverage During the 2000 Sydney Olympic Games: A Gender Perspective', *International Review for the Sociology of Sport*, 37(4), pp. 337–349. doi: 10.1177/101269020203700309.

Capranica, L., D'Artibale, E., Cortis, C., Tessitore, A., Casella, R., Pesce, C. and Camilleri, E. (2008) 'Italian Women's Television Coverage and Audience During the 2004 Athens Olympic Games', *Research Quarterly for Exercise and Sport*, 79(1), pp. 101–115. doi 10.1080/02701367.2008.10599465.

Capranica, L., Minganti, C., Billat, V., Hanghoj, S., Piacentini, M., Cumps, E. and Meeusen, R. (2005) 'Newspaper Coverage of Women's Sports During the 2000 Sydney Olympic Games', *Research Quarterly for Exercise and Sport*, 76(2), pp. 212–223. doi: 10.1080/02701367.2005.10599282.

Coche, R. and Tuggle, C. (2017) 'Men or Women, Only Five Olympic Sports Matter', *Electronic News*, 12(4), pp. 199–217. doi 10.1177/1931243117739061.

Coubertin, P. and Müller, N. (2000) *Pierre de Coubertin 1863-1937. Olympism. Selected Writings*. Lausanne: International Olympic Committee.

Creedon, P. (2014) 'Women, Social Media, and Sport', *Television & New Media*, 15(8), pp. 711–716. doi 10.1177/1527476414530476.

Daddario, G. and Wigley, B.J. (2007) 'Gender Marking and Racial Stereotyping at the 2004 Athens Games', *Journal of Sports Media*, 2(1), pp. 29–51. doi: 10.1353/jsm.0.0003.

Dashper, K. (2018) 'Smiling Assassins, Brides-to-be and Super Mums: The Importance of Gender and Celebrity in Media Framing of Female Athletes at the 2016 Olympic Games', *Sport in Society*, 21(11), pp. 1739–1757.

Davis, K.K. and Tuggle, C.A. (2012) 'A Gender Analysis of NBC's Coverage of the 2008 Summer Olympics', *Electronic News*, 6(2), pp. 51–66. doi: 10.1177/1931243112452261.

Delorme, N. (2014) 'Were Women Really Underrepresented in Media Coverage of Summer Olympic Games (1984-2008)? An Invitation to Open a Methodological Discussion Regarding Sex Equity in Sports Media', *Mass Communication and Society*, 17(1), pp. 121–147. doi: 10.1080/15205436.2013.816740.

Delorme, N. and Testard, N. (2015) 'Sex Equity in French Newspaper Photographs: A Content Analysis of 2012 Olympic Games by L'Equipe', *European Journal of Sport Science*, 15(8), pp. 757–763. doi: 10.1080/17461391.2015.1053100.

Djerf-Pierre, M. (2011) 'The Difference Engine', *Feminist Media Studies*, 11(1), pp. 43–51. doi: 10.1080/14680777.2011.537026.

Eagleman, A., Burch, L. and Vooris, R. (2014) 'A Unified Version of London 2012: New-Media Coverage of Gender, Nationality, and Sport for Olympics Consumers in Six Countries', *Journal of Sport Management*, 28(4), pp. 457–470. doi: 10.1123/jsm.2013-0151.

Eagleman, A.N. (2015) 'Constructing Gender Differences: Newspaper Portrayals of Male and Female Gymnasts at the 2012 Olympic Games', *Sport in Society*, 18(2), pp. 234–247. doi: 10.1080/17430437.2013.854509.

Eastman, S. and Billings, A. (1999) 'Gender Parity in the Olympics', *Journal of Sport and Social Issues*, 23(2), pp. 140–170. doi: 10.1177/0193723599232003.

Hardin, M. (2013) 'Want Changes in Content?: Change the Decision Makers', *Communication & Sport*, 1(3), pp. 241–245. doi: 10.1177/2167479513486985.

Hartmann-Tews, I. (2019) 'Sports, the Media, and Gender', in: *The Business and Culture of Sports: Society, Politics, Economy, Environment*. Farmington Hills, MI: Macmillan Reference USA, pp. 267–280.

Hedenborg, S. (2013) 'The Olympic Games in London 2012 from a Swedish Media Perspective', *The International Journal of the History of Sport*, 30(7), pp. 789–804. doi: 10.1080/09523367.2013.773889.

Higgs, C.T., Weiller, K.H. and Martin, S.B. (2003) 'Gender Bias in the 1996 Olympic Games: A Comparative Analysis', *Journal of Sport and Social Issues*, 27(1), pp. 52–64. doi: 10.1177/0193732502239585.

International Olympic Committee (2018a) *IOC Gender Equality Review Project*. Lausanne, Switzerland: International Olympic Committee. Available at: https://stillmed.olympic.org/media/Document%20Library/OlympicOrg/News/2018/03/IOC-Gender-Equality-Report-March-2018.pdf (Accessed 31 August 2020).

Jakubowska, H. (2017) 'Framing the Winter Olympic Games: A Content Analysis of Polish Newspapers Coverage of Female and Male Athletes', *Polish Sociological Review*, 197(1), pp. 67–81.

Jones, A. and Greer, J. (2012) 'Go "Heavy" or Go Home: An Examination of Audience Attitudes and Their Relationship to Gender Cues in the 2010 Olympic Snowboarding Coverage', *Mass Communication and Society: Olympics, Media, and Society*, 15(4), pp. 598–621. doi: 10.1080/15205436.2012.674171.

Jones, D. (2004) 'Half the Story? Olympic Women on ABC News Online', *Media International Australia*. 2004;110(1):132–146. doi:10.1177/1329878X0411000114

Jones, D. (2006) 'The Representation of Female Athletes in Online Images of Successive Olympic Games', *Pacific Journalism Review*, 12(1), pp. 108–129.

Jones, D. (2013) 'Online Coverage of the 2008 Olympic Games on the ABC, BBC, CBC and TVNZ', *Pacific Journalism Review: Te Koakoa*, 19(1), pp. 244–263. doi: 10.24135/pjr.v19i1.248.

King, C. (2007) 'Media Portrayals of Male and Female Athletes: A Text and Picture Analysis of British National Newspaper Coverage of the Olympic Games since 1948', *International Review for the Sociology of Sport*, 42(2), pp. 187–199. doi: 10.1177/1012690207084751.

Koenigsberger, A.A. (2017) 'Gender Equality in the Olympic Movement: Not a Simple Question, Not a Simple Answer', *Journal of the Philosophy of Sport*, 44(3), pp. 329–341. doi: 10.1080/00948705.2017.1359616.

Laine, A. (2016) 'Gender Representation of Athletes in Finnish and Swedish Tabloids: A Quantitative and Qualitative Content Analysis of Athens 2004 and Turin 2006 Olympics Coverage', *NORDICOM Review: Nordic Research on Media and Communication*, 37(2), pp. 83–98. doi: 10.1515/nor-2016-0012.

LaVoi, N., Baeth, A. and Calhoun, A. (2019) 'Sociological Perspectives of Women in Sport', in: *Routledge Handbook of the Business of Women's Sport*, pp. 36–46. doi: 10.4324/9780203702635-4.

Lee, J. (1992) 'Media Portrayals of Male and Female Olympic Athletes: Analyses of Newspaper Accounts of the 1984 and the 1988 Summer Games', *International Review for the Sociology of Sport*, 27(3), pp. 197–219. doi: 10.1177/101269029202700301.

Ličen, S. and Billings, A.C. (2013) 'Cheering for "Our" Champs by Watching "Sexy" Female Throwers: Representation of Nationality and Gender in Slovenian 2008 Summer Olympic Television Coverage', *European Journal of Communication*, 28(4), pp. 379–396. doi: 10.1177/0267323113484438.

Litchfield, C. and Kavanagh, E. (2019) 'Twitter, Team GB and the Australian Olympic Team: Representations of Gender in Social Media Spaces', *Sport in Society*, 22(7), pp. 1148–1164. doi: 10.1080/17430437.2018.1504775.

Llewellyn, M., Gleaves, J. and Wilson, W. (2015) 'The Historical Legacy of the 1984 Los Angeles Olympic Games', *The International Journal of the History of Sport*, 32(1), pp. 1–8. doi: 10.1080/09523367.2014.990892.

Loy, J.W., McLachlan, F. and Booth, D. (2009) 'Connotations of Female Movement and Meaning: The Development of Women's Participation in the Olympic Games', *Olympika: The International Journal of Olympic Studies*, 18, pp. 1–24.

MacArthur, P., Angelini, J., Billings, A. and Smith, L. (2016) 'The Dwindling Winter Olympic Divide Between Male and Female Athletes: The NBC Broadcast Network's Primetime Coverage of the 2014 Sochi Olympic Games', *Sport in Society*, 19(10), pp. 1556–1572. doi 10.1080/17430437.2016.1159193.

Markula, P., Bruce, T., & Hovden, J. (2010) 'Key Themes in the Research on Media Coverage of Women's Sport', in: *Sportswomen at the Olympics*, pp. 1–18. doi: 10.1163/9789460911071_002.

Matthews, J., D'Amico, L, Jimoh, R. and Jimoh, S. (2019) 'Gender, sport and the politics of in/equality: The IOC Gender Equality Review', *Frontiers in Sociology*. ISSN 2297-7775 (In Press)

Messner, M.A., Duncan, M.C. and Jensen, K. (1993) 'Separating the Men from the Girls: The Gendered Language of Televised Sports', *Gender and Society*, 7(1), pp. 121–137.

Metcalfe, S.N. (2019) 'The Development of an Adolescent Sporting Gendered Habitus: Young People's Interpretation of UK Sports-Media Coverage of Rio 2016 Olympic Games', *European Journal for Sport and Society*, 16(4), pp. 361–378. doi: 10.1080/16138171.2019.1693145.

Nunes, R.A. (2019) 'Women Athletes in the Olympic Games', *Journal of Human Sport and Exercise*, 14(3), pp. 674–683. doi: 10.14198/jhse.2019.143.17.

O'Neill, D. and Mulready, M. (2015) 'The Invisible Woman?: A Comparative Study of Women's Sports Coverage in the UK National Press Before and After the 2012 Olympic Games', *Journalism Practice*, 9(5), pp. 651–668. doi: 10.1080/17512786.2014.965925.

Paré, G., Trudel, M., Jaana, M. and Kitsiou, S. (2015) 'Synthesizing Information Systems Knowledge: A Typology of Literature Reviews', *Information & Management*, 52(2), pp. 183–199. doi 10.1016/j.im.2014.08.008.

Pfister, G. (1987) 'Women in the Olympics (1952—1982): An Analysis of German Newspapers (Beauty Awarded vs. Gold Medals)', in: Kidane, F. *The Olympic Movement and the Mass Media*. Canada: Hurford Enterprises Ltd.

Pfister, G. (2010) 'Women in Sport – Gender Relations and Future Perspectives', *Sport in Society*, 13(2), pp. 234–248. doi: 10.1080/17430430903522954.

Poniatowski, K. and Hardin, M. (2012) '"The More Things Change, the More They …": Commentary During Women's Ice Hockey at the Olympic Games', *Mass Communication and Society*, 15(4), pp. 622–641. doi: 10.1080/15205436.2012.677094.

Shields, S., Gilbert, L., Shen, X. and Said, H. (2004) 'A Look at Print Media Coverage across Four Olympiads', *Women in Sport and Physical Activity Journal*, 13(2), pp. 87–99.

Smith, L.R. and Bissell, K.L. (2014) 'Nice Dig: An Analysis of the Verbal and Visual Coverage of Men's and Women's Beach Volleyball During the 2008 Olympic Games', *Communication & Sport*, 2(1), pp. 48–64. doi: 10.1177/2167479512467771.

Sobal, J. and Milgrim, M. (2019) 'Gendertyping Sports: Social Representations of Masculine, Feminine, and Neither-Gendered Sports among US University Students', *Journal of Gender Studies*, 28(1), pp. 29–44. doi: 10.1080/09589236.2017.1386094.

Stojiljković, N., Randjelović, N., Živković, D., Piršl, D. and Stanišić, I. (2020) 'Analysis of Reporting on Male and Female Athletes in Serbian Media During the Olympic Games in London 2012', *Facta Universitatis, Series: Physical Education and Sport*, pp. 491–505.

Tang, T. and Cooper, R. (2012) 'Gender, Sports, and New Media: Predictors of Viewing during the 2008 Beijing Olympics', *Journal of Broadcasting & Electronic Media*, 56(1), pp. 75–91. doi: 10.1080/08838151.2011.648685.

Toohey, K. (1997) 'Australian Television, Gender and The Olympic GAMES', *International Review for the Sociology of Sport*, 32(1), 19–29. doi: 10.1177/101269097032001003.

Torraco, R. (2005) 'Writing Integrative Literature Reviews: Guidelines and Examples', *Human Resource Development Review*, 4(3), pp. 356–367. doi: 10.1177/1534484305278283.

Tuggle, C.A. and Owen, A. (1999) 'A Descriptive Analysis of NBC's Coverage of the Centennial Olympics: The "Games of the Woman"?', *Journal of Sport & Social Issues*, 23(2), pp. 171–182. doi: 10.1177/0193723599232004.

Tuggle, C.A., Huffman, S. and Rosengard, D.S. (2002) 'A Descriptive Analysis of NBC's Coverage of the 2000 Summer Olympics', *Mass Communication and Society*, 5(3), pp. 361–375. doi: 10.1207/S15327825MCS0503_7.

Tuggle, C.A., Huffman, S. and Rosengard, D. (2007) 'A Descriptive Analysis of NBC's Coverage of the 2004 Summer Olympics', *Journal of Sports Media*, 2(1), pp. 53–75. doi: 10.1353/jsm.0.0004.

Urquhart, J. and Crossman, J. (1999) 'The Globe and Mail Coverage of the Winter Olympic Games: A Cold Place for Women Athletes', *Journal of Sport & Social Issues*, 23(2), pp. 193–202.

Vecsey, G. (1984) *Sports of the Times; the Women's Olympics*. Available at: https://www.nytimes.com/1984/08/04/sports/sports-of-the-times-the-women-s-olympics.html (Accessed 27 May 2020).

Villalon, C. and Weiller-Abels, K. (2018) 'NBC's Televised Media Portrayal of Female Athletes in the 2016 Rio Summer Olympic Games: A Critical Feminist View', *Sport in Society*, 21(8), pp. 1137–1157. doi: 10.1080/17430437.2018.1442206.

Vincent, J., Imwold, C., Johnson, J. and Massey, D. (2003) 'Newspaper Coverage of Female Athletes Competing in Selected Sports in the 1996 Centennial Olympic Games: The More Things Change the More They Stay the Same', *Women in Sport and Physical Activity Journal*, 12(1), pp. 1–21.

Wehden, L.-O. and Schröer, N. (2019) 'Golden News? Analysis of Summarizing Coverage of the Olympic Winter Games 2018 on German TV', *MedienJournal*, 43(1), pp. 101–121. doi: 10.24989/medienjournal.v43i1.1795.

Wensing, E. and Bruce, T. (2003) 'Bending the Rules', *International Review for the Sociology of Sport*, 38(4), 387–396. doi: 10.1177/1012690203384001.

Xavier, R. (2014) *Olympic Values and Sports Journalism Ethics: The International Press Coverage of the 2012 Olympics*. PhD. Autonomous University of Barcelona.

Xiao, Y. and Watson, M. (2019) 'Guidance on Conducting a Systematic Literature Review', *Journal of Planning Education and Research*, 39(1), pp. 93–112. doi: 10.1177/0739456X17723971.

Xu, Q. (2019) *Challenging The Gender Dichotomy?: Examining Olympic Channel Content, Production, and Audiences Through A Gendered Lens*. Ph.D. The University of Alabama.

Xu, Q., Billings, A. and Fan, M. (2018) 'When Women Fail to "Hold Up More Than Half the Sky": Gendered Frames of CCTV's Coverage of Gymnastics at the 2016 Summer Olympics', *Communication & Sport*, 6(2), pp. 154–174. doi: 10.1177/2167479517695542.

Xu, Q., Billings, A., Wang, H., Jin, R., Guo, S. and Xu, M. (2019) 'Women, Men, and Five Olympic Rings: An Examination of Chinese Central Television's Broadcast of the 2018 PyeongChang Winter Olympics', *International Review for the Sociology of Sport*, 55(6), 747–766.

3
Sex Verification and Protected Categories in Sport
Binary or Bust?

Pam R. Sailors and Charlene Weaving

Introduction

International Olympic Committee (IOC) and World Athletics policies are based on the rationale that the main justification to have sex-segregated sport is the discrepancy in athletic performance between men and women. But the question of whether sport should be sex-segregated is more complex than often recognized and not easily answered. It is simply untrue that all women are athletically inferior to all men (there are areas of overlapping capability), and the degree of difference depends in large part on the sport. For example, the degree of difference is much lower in archery than in boxing. Still, the preservation of the protected category for women is important because it guarantees women the opportunity for competitive success, presents successful female athletes as role models and conveys the message that women in general are not inferior to men as a class (Sailors 2014; 2016). Unfortunately, the binary categorizations prompt expectations regarding femininity and heterosexuality, creating problems around how the categories and binary configurations of men and women are regulated and enforced. Sex verification was originally put into place to protect women's sport from men who were imagined would masquerade as women in order to dominate women's sports (Pieper 2016). However, sex verification ultimately became a process to police women's bodies, which was and continues to be framed in the notion of 'fair play.' Additionally, some argue with Pielke (2017) that the problem with sex verification is that biological sex does not always divide into two distinct categories because it is complex and cannot be determined by any single characteristic or combination of characteristics. Society struggles with women athletes who don't fit the pervasive restrictive societal ideals and norms and consequently, much debate about sex verification has arisen amongst academics, sport policy makers and athletes. This chapter takes direction from Judith Butler (2009, para 5), who suggests we think 'about the standards for participation under gender categories that have the aim of being both egalitarian and inclusive.'

Segregation

Why have sex segregated sport? Why not simply have all athletes compete together? One answer, discussed by Jane English more than 40 years ago, is that women athletes need role models, but are unlikely to see them without the presence of a protected category for women. As English noted, the most popular and visible sports were created by men to reward physiological traits possessed by men. 'Speed, size, and strength seem to be the essence of sports. Women *are* naturally inferior at "sports" so conceived' (English 1978, p. 276). English's prescription stemming from this is for the creation of new sports, ones that would reward the physiological traits more commonly possessed by women, e.g., balance, buoyancy and flexibility. Unfortunately for this suggestion, in the cases where such sports, like rhythmic gymnastics and synchronized swimming, have been created, they have often failed to take hold of the public's interest. Instead, these women's sports have been marginalized and belittled as not "real" sports (Simon, Torres and Hager 2015). But if English (1978) is correct about the importance of role models, the negatives that follow from the absence of them extends beyond young women and girls who are interested in sports.

According to English, sport confers both basic benefits and scarce benefits. The basic benefits are ones that are available to all participants: 'health, the self-respect to be gained by doing one's best, the cooperation to be learned from working with teammates and the incentive gained from having opponents, the "character" of learning to be a good loser and a good winner, the chance to improve one's skills and learn to accept criticism—and just plain fun' (English 1978, p. 270). Everyone is equally entitled to these benefits. To the contrary, only those who have the exceptional sporting skills to attain a level of success in athletic performance are entitled to scarce benefits, which are those that come with fame and fortune. However, English (1978) also believes that the self-esteem of all members of a group is bolstered or damaged by the success or failure of members of the group as compared to other groups. That is, if one group almost invariably attains a lower level of success than another group, the self-esteem of all the individuals in the unsuccessful group will be negatively affected. It is, therefore, reasonable to argue that since the group 'women' would not have the same athletic success as men if they competed against one another, all women would consider themselves, and be considered by others, to be inferior. Given this negative, and far-reaching, effect of mixed-sex sport, it would seem imperative that the women's category be retained and protected.

Still, some have argued that women can in fact compete successfully against men, and carefully chosen examples would seem to support this claim. During her career in the late 1980s through the early 2000s, ultrarunner Ann Trason was second overall finisher at the Western States Endurance Run twice, third overall finisher three times, and in the top ten 13 times. She had similar success at the Leadville Trail 100-mile race, and was the outright winner of the National Track and Field 24-hour Championship, the Silver State 50-Mile Trail Run, the Quicksilver 50-Mile Trail Run, the Sri Chinmoy 100-Mile run and the Bay Area 12-Hour Run. Women ski-jumpers have also had great success relative to men, perhaps in part because the sport requires adjustments in ski-length based on the weight of athletes. Anecdotal evidence like this has led to calls for the abolishing of sex-segregated competition. Mary Jo Kane, for example, argues that:

> Although, given current conditions, it is certainly the case that most elite male athletes can beat most elite female athletes in sports that privilege men, it does not automatically follow that *every* elite male can outperform *every* elite female in these same sports. Yet this is precisely what we are trained to believe because it is one of the cornerstones of the oppositional binary. And it is because of this socially constructed and rigidly maintained sport structure that females are truly at a disadvantage in sports, not because of biology.
>
> (Kane 1995, p. 201)

Kane would replace the binary with a continuum, situating all athletes at points along it, regardless of sex. Foddy and Savulescu (2011, p. 1187) argue similarly, concluding that 'once we recognize that gender is not a binary quantity, sex segregation in competitive sport must be seen as an inconsistent and unjust policy.'

Although superficially persuasive, in addition to a problematic slippage between 'gender' and 'sex,' this position cannot easily be maintained in the face of increasing empirical evidence that male physiology confers athletic performance advantage. The physical changes that come with male puberty result in a roughly 10–12% general sporting advantage, increasing to 30% for strength sports (Tucker 2019). While this may not seem like a vast difference, it becomes clearer when the performance differential is illustrated with actual results. Jamaican Shelly-Ann Fraser-Pryce is one of the fastest female sprinters in history, with a personal best of 10.70 seconds in the 100 meters event. In only the 2020 season, 14 high school boys in the state of California alone ran faster times. If women and men competed against one another at elite level, the fastest woman would not even make the finals, thus resulting in the invisibility of women athletes, loss of women sporting role models and the strengthening of the perceived inferiority of women.

Of course, it is crucially important to remember that sports are not all the same, and various sports cover a wide variety of skills. There are individual sports and team sports; sports where athletes compete directly against one another and ones where athletes face the same challenge (against, say, a clock or a target), but not directly against one another; contact sports and non-contact sports; and amateur and professional sports. We might also pay attention to whether a sport involves a non-human element, as in automobile racing or equestrian sports where it is already the case, at least sometimes, that competition is not sex-segregated, even if still dominated by males. Whether it is advisable or even possible for women and men to compete against one another depends, in some cases to a determinative degree, on the sport in question (Sailors 2014, 2016). In sports where it is unlikely or impossible for women to succeed against men, the loss of success, and the resulting lack of role models, provides a strong case for continuing to protect the women's category, especially since success itself emerged from a patriarchal system and, thus, functions to protect male advantage. 'If people are to identify themselves with a sex, draw role models from their particular sex and place themselves in a societal context with reference to their sex, it would indeed be regrettable if a whole sex…should lose sporting role models' (Coggon, Hammond and Holm 2008, p. 9). Thus, we conclude that the current notion of success ensures that the preservation of separate sex categories is essential to the success, and even participation, of women in sport. Unfortunately, however, the binary categories have their own set of problems.

Binaries

According to Blithe and Hanchey (2015), sex verification is entangled with binaries. 'Modern testing relies on a series of intertwined assumptions: the gender binary of woman/man, the sex binary of female/male, and the mapping of the first onto the second… Such binary divisions implicitly rely on a slippage between sex and gender' (Blithe and Hanchey 2015, p. 487). Unfortunately, binary categorizations prompt expectations regarding femininity and heterosexuality, creating problems around how the categories and binary configurations of men and women are regulated and enforced. Creating binaries in sport is inherently problematic because gender is not binary and gender and sex are not interchangeable. Mapping gender onto sex legitimizes sex binaries. According to Pielke (2017, p. 680): 'It is of course true that biological sex often corresponds to gender identification across societies, but this is not always the case because neither biological sex nor socially constructed gender fall into neatly delineated categories.' Lock (2003) refers to Butler's 'heterosexual matrix' in her essay on compulsive heterosexuality and the doping ban. Lock (2003, p. 399) interprets the matrix in the following manner:

> the hegemonic belief in the relationship connecting sex, gender, sexual practice and desire. Each element of the matrix is fundamental to the intelligibility of gender and likewise gender is fundamental to the intelligibility of sex, sexual desire and practice. For example, masculinity and femininity are understood as genders because there are the biological sexes of males and females to which they can be attached. If there were no differences demarcated between males and females it would be difficult to imagine the performance of gender at all.

Lock (2003) argues that women who do not appear feminine and heterosexual are demonized and considered to be masculine. Even though Lock (2003) examines doping and gender, her analysis of the heterosexual matrix applies also to the binary categories prominent in sport. For Lock (2003, p. 399), 'Thus, the promotion of femininity as *the* legitimate aesthetic, and the criticizing and effacement of non-feminine women, also has the effect of policing non-heterosexual gender expressions of women.' The binary in sport reinforces heterosexuality and stereotypes.

Lock (2003, p. 405) analyzes past doping cases like the Chinese women swimmers and describes how the women athletes were considered to be masculine because of not looking feminine and heterosexual:

> In these instances, the accused or tested dopers are insulted because of their muscularity. They are either suggested to be ugly or like men, and in heterosexual discourse, looking like a man means one is ugly for a woman. Being accused of looking like a man is said as if it is the gravest insult there is for a woman. What these kinds of insults reveal is that femininity is aligned with heterosexual attractiveness and one is read as ugly when one's muscularity is close to that of a man's. The lack of difference renders one unattractive to the heterosexual gaze.

In 2014, Davis and Edwards analyzed the new (at the time) IOC and International Athletics Association Federation (IAAF) policies (now World Athletics). Their argument is similar to Lock's (2003) claims of women athletes, fitting ideals and binaries:

> And since heterosexuality itself is key to what Butler has called the 'heterosexual matrix' of sex, gender, heterosexual femininity and appearance, to be heterosexually unsuccessful is to fail at being a woman. And again, given the preceding staunch binary opposition which respectively conflates physical, psychological and social qualities, to be at once be a woman who fails to be a woman is culturally alarming, since one exposes that the constituents of the female side of the binary are not superglued but can instead be disaggregated.
> (Davis and Edwards 2014, pp. 46–47)

It is necessary to assert that, in addition to the gender binary in sport reinforcing traditional masculine and feminine ideals, the binary also exemplifies racist views of Black women's bodies. Pieper (2014, p. 1559), via a historical analysis of political sex/gender in relation to the IAAF and sex verification, argues that:

> The binaries established by the colonial/modern gender system shaped the history of sex testing/gender verification in elite sport; yet, much of the scholarship on the topic does not

consider the intersections of race, gender and sexuality. Instead, many scholars focus on the significance of the Cold War context in the establishment of sex/gender controls.

For Pieper, binary ideals developed in the eighteenth and nineteenth century. To illustrate the intersections of 'race' in sporting binaries, we begin with the case of Florence Griffith Joyner (better known as Flo Jo), whose muscularity and power, according to Lock (2003), were overshadowed by her heterosexual feminine appearance. Flo Jo was glamourous—stylish running uniforms, loose hair flowing and long painted fingernails. We refer to Flo Jo to make the case that she was accepted and celebrated in track and field even though many suspected she was doping. Flo Jo was accepted because she fit the constraints of the binary. However, when Black women do not look the part, they are critiqued. For example, in the last decade when South African runner Caster Semenya became a force on and off the track—it becomes more apparent that non-white, muscular bodies struggle to fit the binary. According to Munro (2010, p. 390), Semenya's embodiment as an elite athlete is embedded with 'race':

> The legacy of imperialism and slavery, and how it has shaped the figuration of the Black women, seems to be being re-pixelated, if you will, through the global media circus over Semenya... For South Africans, the questioning of Semenya's sex... brings to mind apartheid's categorizations of people into racial groups—a traumatic and chaotic process that involved the inspection of people's bodies on a nationwide scale.

Douglas (2019) examined the cases of tennis athlete Serena Williams and basketball athlete Brittney Griner's perceptions and 'blackness' in elite sport, and claimed:

> In addition to their colleagues, the public and media have described both of these athletes as possessing an unnatural physicality and embodying masculine traits that give them an "unfair advantage." Consequently, I consider how the athletic performance/excellence of these two Black female athletes interacts with the presumed obviousness of the un/intelligibility of their race-sex-gender-sexual difference to elicit a "high anxiety" that reveals the "ongoing problem of Black exclusion from social, political and cultural belonging; our abjection from the realm of the human."
> (Sharpe 2016, p. 14, cited in Douglas 2019, p. 331)

Both Griner and Williams possess muscular and powerful bodies and simply do not fit the binary ideals. Douglas (2019) maintains that there is a denial of Black female subjectivity in sport. Douglas refers to examples of how Griner and Williams have been portrayed in the media. For instance, 'Serena Williams is half man, half gorilla! I'm sure of it' (Douglas 2019, p. 337). Similarly, Griner has been described as: 'What are you? #man? #ape?' (Fagan 2013b, cited in Douglas 2019, p. 342). Framing Black individuals as primates is a racist practice derived from 'racial' stereotyping which is connected to social stacking and emphasizes the racialized sport institution.

Our point is that the sex binary is so engrained in the institution of sport and has morphed into sexist and racist views of women's bodies, ideals and expectations. For Blithe and Hanchey (2015, p. 499): 'Athletic female bodies challenge ideals of femininity, a tendency that seems to be exacerbated by factors relating to gender expression, 'race' and nationality. Most of the athletes suspected of not truly being female over the courses of the tests somehow provoked Western anxieties.' Additionally, Blithe and Hanchey (2015) argue that sex verification is not simply an issue of sex; sex verification diminishes the possibility of breaking down the binary between male and female, and all the variations in between. MacKinnon (1987, p. 119) argued, over 30 years ago, regarding women, self-possession and sport that: 'If a woman is defined hierarchically so that the male idea of a woman defines womanhood, and if men have power, this idea becomes reality. It is therefore real. It is not just an illusion or a fantasy or mistake. It becomes *embodied* because it is enforced.' For MacKinnon (1987, p. 120, italics in original), being a woman and being an athlete is 'socially contradictory,' and is reinforced in the sport binary categories.

The binary in sport perpetuates strict heterosexual feminine and masculine ideals and whiteness. Society struggles with women athletes who don't fit the pervasive, restrictive societal ideals and norms and, consequently, much debate about sex verification and binaries has arisen amongst academics, sport policy makers and athletes.

Rehabilitating the binary

In this section, we cover alternatives to sex verification in sport. In order to balance equity and inclusion, we start with Butler's (2009) arguments on the infamous case of Caster Semenya, sex verification and binaries. Butler (2009, para 5) argued that instead of trying to 'figure out' what sex Semenya or any competitor is:

> Why don't we think instead about standards for participation under gender categories that have the aim of being both egalitarian and inclusive? Only then might we finally cease the sensationalist witch hunt antics of finding anyone's "true sex" and open sports to the complexly constituted species of human animals to which we belong.

As outlined in the previous sections, because so many do not conform to the standards established by the binaries, and yet having categories is necessary in sport, finding other ways to decide who can compete under what category is key.

Given that the crux of the philosophic debate about sex verification and inclusion has rested on hormone levels, specifically testosterone (Jordan-Young and Karkazis 2019), an option is to categorize competitors based on testosterone levels. As outlined by Butler (2009, para 5):

> One cannot exceed certain levels of testosterone to play in women's sport, then a competitor could still be a 'woman' in a cultural and social sense and, indeed in some biological senses as well, but she would not qualify to compete under those standards. Conversely, a 'man' in a cultural sense may not qualify to compete in men's sport according to the same standard, but does qualify for women's sports- why should that be a problem?
>
> (Butler 2009, para 2)

In the above scenario, one does not have to first decide the sex to determine which category one should compete in. The standards for qualifications do not have to be the same as final determinations about sex. As Young (2005, p. 17) argued about the importance of the lived body experience: 'The idea of the lived body thus can bring the physical facts of different bodies into theory without the reductionist and dichotomous implications of the category of "sex."' The concerns around proceeding with categorization based on testosterone levels are as follows and emphasize genetic advantages: What would be the testosterone threshold? What is fair? For instance, Ross Tucker (2019) asserts: 'Fundamentally, the difference between the men's world champion and the women's world champion in any given event is "androgenization" or virilization that drives a set of secondary sex characteristics including higher muscle mass, lower fat mass, greater strength, increased cardiovascular capacity and function, more haemoglobin, different skeleton.' The primary androgen in males is testosterone. Thus, Tucker (2019) claims:

> If you have the Y chromosome, and the testes, and the testosterone, and you can use the testosterone, then you have a huge advantage compared to a woman who has all the same other attributes, but not those. So if you really want to get rid of regulation and separation based on "natural genetic advantages", then you should just as well throw all humans into one race, and crown the "World's fastest human", and see how women get on!

Defining gender based solely on testosterone levels ignores the complexity of gender and sex. So, the strategy of categorization based on testosterone levels is contentious to such a degree that other criteria should be considered.

If the method for categorization is that sport be separated into categories based on the physical traits most closely connected to success in specific sports, the main concern is that women would be further disadvantaged. For example, the length of one's arms (wingspan) is related to success in swimming: the longer the wingspan, the faster one can swim (Mortenson, 2022). However, if swimming was organized around wingspan, instead of sex, women would still almost certainly lose to men. Olympic swimmers Missy Franklin and Ryan Lochte have almost identical wingspans, but her best time in the 200-m backstroke is a full nine seconds slower than his. In a race where each swam their best times, Franklin would have finished half a lap behind Lochte. 'In a world in which competitors were categorized by height and wingspan—or just height or just wingspan—instead of sex, Franklin would not have had a world record; she would not have been on the podium; in fact, she would not have made the team. In those circumstances, we might not even know her name' (Coleman 2018, p. 90). Consequently, it is not ideal to categorize sports via sport-specific traits.

Another option involves a more utopian idealization, where competitors would self-declare the category into which they 'fit.' Among those who have proposed this idea, Bruce Kidd (2011, slide #9) provided an example of what a self-declaration would look like:

> I understand that the XXX is a women's sports organization, and that by being a competitor on a XXX league I attest to the fact that I am placing myself in the appropriate category according to my sex, gender, or identity. If, at some point in the future, I find that I no longer belong in a women's sports organization due to changes in my sex, gender, or identity, I will remove myself from the position of competitor. If I am found to be wilfully disregarding this policy my league has the right to revoke my status as a competitor.

At a surface glance, self-declaration may work. Historically, there have been no cases of men who attempted to masquerade as women in order to participate in the women's category of sport, and there is no reason to expect that such a practice would spring up. Although some might object by pointing to Dora Rajten, Pieper (2016) notes that Rajten, a high jumper who finished fourth at the 1936 Olympics, was born a woman but may have been intersex. Yet, self-declaration raises concerns for fairness, in light of transwomen and athletes with Differences of Sexual Development (DSD) who possess physiological advantages over most female competitors (Knox, Anderson and Heather 2019; Sailors 2020; Tucker 2019). Remembering the importance of the separate women's category for role models for young girls and self-respect of women in general, it is imperative not to accept sports policy that would endanger these accomplishments.

Conclusion

We conclude that, at the time of writing this chapter and based on the arguments reviewed here, we have not been able to identify an optimal method for maintaining the binary without also preserving the accompanying harmful stereotypes. We are encouraged, however, by the potential of a more athlete-centred approach to policy development (as, for example, in the newly-formed Women's Sport Policy Working Group, who claim as their task finding a way to balance inclusion and fair competition in sport, while protecting the women's category). The inclusion of voices of a large number of diverse athletes, rather than ceding the decision-making role to medico-scientific boards with no sport experience, strikes us as essential. As Kidd (2018, p. 782) puts it:

> I also agree that there must be some way of defining who is male and who is female for purposes of competition. But should the medical and scientific commissions have a monopoly on these issues? Humans are not the sum of our hormones, and an understanding of human biology and biochemistry is insufficient for a complete understanding of human sexuality and human societies. Both the definition of gender and considerations of fairness in sport require social scientific, legal and ethical considerations as well as biophysical ones… The IOC and the international federations should remove the responsibility for these issues from the medical and scientific commissions and transfer any responsibility for gender definition to the women's and athletes' commissions, and for 'fairness' to the athletes' and ethics commissions.

The worst option is any method that involves increased surveillance of women's bodies and gender boundaries, especially given the difficulties in establishing such boundaries. The lack of consensus on how to draw the boundaries provides an argument for continued debate and discussion, not reanimation of historically intrusive and harmful practices. It would be disingenuous to ignore, however, that the nature of sport, at least as it has always been practiced, requires binary categories. As Dreger (2010, p. 23, italics in original) argued: 'Humans like their sex categories neat, but nature doesn't care. Nature doesn't actually have a line between the sexes. If we want a line, we have to draw it *on* nature.' Sport requires us to draw this line, to preserve a binary classification, to ensure the sporting success of women in their own category, but it can be done in a way that respects the value of inclusion. There is still much work to be done to ensure fair, equitable and inclusive environments for women in sport. However, to progress and create change, we insist that a feminist lens and inclusion of diverse women's voices ought to be a key starting point.

REFERENCES

Blithe, S.J. and Hanchey, J.N. (2015). 'The discursive emergence of gendered physiological discrimination in sex verification', *Women's Studies in Communication*, 38(4), pp. 486–506.

Butler, J. (2009). 'Wise distinctions', *London Review of Books Blog*. Available at: https: www.lrb.co.uk/blog/2009/november/wise-distinctions (Accessed 10 February 2021).

Coggon, J., Hammond, N. and Holm, S. (2008). 'Transsexuals in sport – fairness and freedom, regulation and law', *Sport, Ethics and Philosophy*, 2(1), pp. 4–17.

Coleman, D.L. (2018). 'Sex in sport', *Law and Contemporary Problems*, 80(63), pp. 63–126.

Davis, P. and Edwards, L. (2014). 'The new IOC and IAAF policies on female eligibility: Old emperor, new clothes?', *Sport, Ethics and Philosophy*, 8(1), pp. 44–56.

Douglas, D. (2019). 'Dis'qualified! Serena Williams and Brittney Griner: Black female athletes and the politics of the im/possible', in P. Farquharson, K. Pillay and E.J. White (eds.) *Relating worlds of racism dehumanisation, belonging, and the normativity of European whiteness*. London: Palgrave MacMillan, pp. 329–355.

Dreger, A. (2010). 'Sex typing for sport', *The Hastings Center Report*, 40(2), pp. 22–24.

English, J. (1978). 'Sex equality in sports', *Philosophy & Public Affairs*, 7(3), pp. 269–277.

Foddy, B. and Savulescu, J. (2011). 'Time to re-evaluate gender segregation in athletics?', *British Journal of Sports Medicine*, 45, pp. 1184–1188.

Jordan-Young, R.M. and Karkazis, K. (2019). *Testosterone: an unauthorized biography*. Cambridge, MA: Harvard University Press.

Kane, M.J. (1995). 'Resistance/transformation of the oppositional binary: Exposing sport as a continuum', *Journal of Sport & Social Issues*, 19, pp. 191–218.

Kidd, B. (2011). 'The intersex challenge to sport', *Play the Game*. [PowerPoint.] Available at: https://www.playthegame.org/fileadmin/image/PTG2011/Presentation/Wednesday/Kidd_Bruce_The_intersex_challenge_to_sport.pdf (Accessed 10 February 2021).

Kidd. B. (2018). 'Towards responsible policy-making in international sport: Reforming the medical-scientific commissions', *Sport in Society*, 21(5), pp. 773–787.

Knox, T., Anderson, L.C. and Heather, A. (2019). 'Transwomen in elite sport: Scientific and ethical considerations', *Journal of Medical Ethics*, 45, pp. 395–403.

Lock, R. (2003). 'The doping ban: Compulsory heterosexuality and lesbophobia', *International Review for the Sociology of Sport*, 38(4), pp. 397–411.

MacKinnon, C.A. (1987). *Feminism unmodified: discourses on life and law*. Cambridge, MA: Harvard University Press.

Mortenson, J.P. (2022). 'What makes the Perfect Swimmer's Body?', *Swimming World*. Available at: https://www.swimmingworldmagazine.com/news/what-makes-the-perfect-swimmers-body/ (Accessed 18 February 2022).

Munro, B. (2010). 'Caster Semenya: Gods and monsters', *Safundi: The Journal of South African and American Studies*, 11(4), pp. 383–396.

Pielke, R. Jr. (2017). 'Sugar, spice and everything nice: How to end "sex testing" in international athletics', *International Journal of Sport Policy and Politics*, 9(4), pp. 649–665.

Pieper, L.P. (2016). *Sex testing: gender policing in women's sports*. Champaign, Il: University of Illinois Press.

Pieper, L.P. (2014). 'Sex Testing and the Maintenance of Western Femininity in International Sport' *The International Journal of Sport History*. https://doi.org/10.1080/09523367.2014.927184

Sailors, P.R. (2014). 'Mixed competition and mixed messages', *Journal of the Philosophy of Sport*, 41(1), pp. 65–77.

Sailors, P.R. (2016). 'Off the beaten path: Should women compete against men?', *Sport in Society*, 19(8-9), pp. 1125–1137.

Sailors, P.R. (2020). 'Transgender and intersex athletes and the women's category in sport', *Sport, Ethics and Philosophy*, 14(4), pp. 419–431.

Simon, R.L., Torres, C.R. and Hager, P.F. (2015). *Fair play: the ethics of sport*. Boulder, CO: Westview Press.

Tucker, R. (2019). 'On transgender athletes and performance advantages', *The Science of Sport*. Available at: https://sportsscientists.com/2019/03/on-transgender-athletes-and-performance-advantages/ (Accessed 7 February 2021).

Young, I.M. (2005). *On female body experience: "throwing like a girl and other essays."* Oxford: Oxford University Press.

4

The Politics of Positions of Sport Leadership
The Subtexts of Women's Exclusion

Annelies Knoppers and Ramón Spaaij

Introduction

Sport organizations have begun to employ a rhetoric of equality and equal opportunity in their organizational goals and policies, often by highlighting their efforts to increase the number of women athletes. The percentage of women in positions of sport leadership, such as coaching and board membership, however, continues to be lower than that in other sectors (Elling, Knoppers and Hovden, 2019; Evans and Pfister, 2020). The purpose of this chapter is to discuss how resistance to women in positions of leadership in sport manifests itself in implicit ways and, thus, subtly continues to keep women out despite a rhetoric of equity and equality. We first briefly summarize the findings of research about the underrepresentation of women in positions of leadership in sport. Subsequently, we argue that although this research points to many dynamics that may contribute to an unbalanced gender ratio, less attention has been paid to how implicit resistance to the presence of women in coaching and on voluntary sport boards works to keep women out of these positions, despite a rhetoric of equality and opportunity often espoused by sport organizations. We foreground this implicit resistance in our analysis.

In this chapter, we specifically focus on the subtexts of three discursive practices used by sport organizations and analyse how they contribute to the continuation of the relatively low gender ratio in positions of leadership: (1) the construction of gendered qualifications for coaching positions in men's and women's sports; (2) the determination of the size and demographic constitution of the quota in sport governance; and (3) the misogyny embedded in homonegative language and gendered hierarchy in sport that materially and ideologically devalues what women do. We conclude that although gender diversity is framed as a valuable goal by sport organizations, this frame will remain an empty ideology unless the ways prevailing discursive practices in sport that are supported by gendered subtexts are recognized, addressed, and radically changed.

Research on the underrepresentation of women in leadership positions in sport

The explanations for the underrepresentation of women in leadership positions have often been attributed to women themselves, such as insufficiently qualified in skills and/or experience, responsibilities for child and household care, failure to apply for positions, stereotypes about women, and a lack of interest in these positions (Evans and Pfister, 2020). Such research tends to focus on women as a political category and rarely looks at men as also constituting a political category. The role of those currently holding positions of leadership play in keeping many women out or on the periphery is often ignored and is rarely framed as explaining the overrepresentation of men in positions of leadership in sport (Knoppers, Spaaij and Claringbould, 2021). Rarely does this research accentuate how men and the qualities associated with them, often described as practices of desirable masculinity, have become the seemingly implicit standard for required abilities/skills and ways of working in these leadership positions in sport. Recently, however, researchers have begun to look at resistance to women's inclusion by current board members of sport organizations and at the lived experiences of women coaches. Such scholarship suggests that although sport organizations profess the need for more women in positions of leadership, they have relatively little interest in actively changing the gender dynamics of leadership (Spaaij, Knoppers and Jeanes, 2019; Knoppers, Spaaij and Claringbould, 2021). In the following sections, we reveal several ways in which this lack of interest and resistance manifests itself by looking at the discursive gender subtexts of organizational dynamics (Bendl, 2008).

Conceptual framework

We draw on the notion of discursive gendered subtexts to explore resistance to women in positions of leadership in sport (Bendl, 2008; Benschop and Doorewaard, 2012). Subtexts are implicit or hidden processes that are part of the procedures that keep many women out of positions of leadership by reproducing constructed gender differences. For example, much of the research on women's relative absence cited above reinforces women as a political category. This suggests that men's normative ways of doing gender in sport are seen as gender neutral and taken for granted although they are in plain sight (Fink, 2016). These normative practices form the gendered subtexts of many sport organizational processes. Subtexts, therefore, refer to an organization's hidden arrangements – that is, the principles, measures, routines, and ways organizations do, in this case, gender (Piggott and Matthews, 2020). These subtexts are not passive or static but are situated within agentic power relations that include resistance and counter-resistance (Bendl, 2008). Although organizations may emphasize their equal opportunities and policies that purport to enhance gender diversity, their ideas about the "ideal leader", for example, may be constructed as gender neutral while implicitly they are based on assumptions about the congruency between leadership and practices of desirable masculinity (Acker, 1990). Women have to enact leadership behaviors that are defined and shaped by ideas about desirable masculinity such as being competitive, fearless, and self-confident. Women must, however, also enact a form of acceptable femininity, i.e., they have to be nice, compliant and not be seen as strident (Shaw and Hoeber, 2003; Knoppers et al., 2021). These assumptions contribute to what Acker (2006, p. 443) calls "inequality regimes" that are "loosely interrelated practices, processes, actions, and meanings that result in and maintain class, gender, and racial inequalities within particular organizations". Unmasking a regime includes an exploration of the ideology that is used to legitimate it. We argue that subtexts reflect this ideology. In the following sections, we will examine the gendered subtexts of selection of coaches of women's and men's sport, the quota policies for sport board membership, and the use and approval of homonegative speech acts in sport and will reveal how each of these aspects individually as well as jointly have systematically gendered subtexts that reproduce inequality regimes while purporting to be gender neutral.

Gendered qualifications for coaching positions

Sport has been a field not only populated by men but is also a site built on a binary gendered subtext that assumes the superiority of males in all domains and that makes male sporting excellence and the practices of masculinity surrounding it the norm for women (Anderson, 2009). This constructed gender hierarchy has been quite resistant to change and permeates all of organized sports including access to allocation of resources, media attention, distribution of power, leadership, etc. This gender hierarchy is entrenched in ideologies about the needed attributes coaches should possess and enact, such as physicality, assertiveness, a sport autobiography, and dominance associated with desirable masculinities (Hovden, 2000, 2010; Schull and Kihl, 2019). As a result, men tend to be systematically privileged over women in selection or choices made in the hiring for coaching positions (Kane and LaVoi, 2018; Norman, Rankin-Wright and Allison, 2018). Schaeperkoetter, Mays and Bass (2017, p. 100) examined gender differences in the evaluation of coaches of elite athletes and concluded that "simply being a man results in obtaining social and cultural capital unavailable to women, and provides a distinct advantage in the [sport] marketplace".

A gendered subtext about coaching assumes heterosexual men are better coaches than women because these men "naturally" or inherently know more about sport (Messner and Bozada-Deas, 2009; Norman, Rankin-Wright and Allison, 2018; Knoppers, et al., 2021). This assumed naturalness of knowledge extends to men coaching in both women and men's sport, although men have not participated as athletes in women's sport. For example, Knoppers et al. (2021) found that although elite women football/soccer coaches had grown up participating in football with boys and later played on national women's teams, they were assumed to be less knowledgeable about women's football than men. Men were presumed to be better coaches for, and more knowledgeable about, women's football even though they had never participated in it or did not have the necessary coaching qualifications or experience. This assumption meant that men tended to be considered for positions in the coaching of women's elite football, even though women applicants were more qualified and had a history of participating in high-performance football. Maleness was equated with in-depth knowledge and experience in football. Paradoxically, women coaches were assumed not to be qualified to coach elite men because women had not competed at the elite men's level. This difference was seen as normal and as an implicit truth. Similarly, Clarkson, Cox and Thelwell (2019) found that women coaches were subject to a greater scrutiny of behavior and skills than their male colleagues. Women athletes have also internalized this hierarchy, often preferring male coaches to female coaches (Schull, 2016). Attempts to increase the number of women coaches through recruitment and coach education will do little if this gender hierarchical subtext that frames men as superior to, and more knowledgeable than, women coaches is not addressed (Norman, Rankin-Wright and Allison, 2018).

This subtext about "women coaches" has another problematic dimension. Except for research on lesbian coaches (e.g., Norman, 2013), policies and studies that address the lack of women coaches tend to frame "women" as a universal political category and often ignore minority women and women of colour (Knoppers, McLachlan, Spaaij and Smits, 2021). Various scholars (e.g., Rankin-Wright and Hylton, 2020; Rankin-Wright, Hylton and Norman, 2019; Walker and Bopp, 2011) contend this lack of attention to intersectionality in research on gendered coaching practices meaning that the voices and contributions of Black and minority ethnic (BME) women coaches and the inequality regimes they experience and encounter have been systematically hidden and ignored. However, in this chapter, we focus on the white heterosexual subtext about the lack of women coaches and the subsequent lack of attention to intersectionality by policy makers and scholars throughout this chapter.

Size of quotas

Sport leadership does not only consist of administrators, managers, and coaches but also of boards of directors that exercise their authority and power purportedly according to the stated mission of the organization (Dowling, Leopkey and Smith, 2018). They govern sport organizations and are ultimately responsible for the selection and recruitment of coaches. Similar to coaching, board members of sport organizations have tended to be men, especially at national and international levels. While the dominance of males in sport management (administrators and coaches) is often deemed not to need structural intervention, the gender ratio of members of sport boards has become a political issue in the last decade requiring such interventions.

Since power has rarely been voluntarily redistributed, quotas have been instituted to ensure women are represented on sport boards (Hovden, Elling and Knoppers, 2019; Sisjord, Fasting and Sand, 2017). Quotas are seen as structurally efficient measures that change institutional barriers to board membership for women, and that eliminate the possibility of boards appointing only token women. Quotas are assumed to distribute power more evenly across a board and transform board culture. The percentages of mandated women board members usually range from 30% to 40% of members. The creation of quotas for a board often begins with the institution of gender ratios and are accompanied by voluntary compliance. Spain and Norway, for example, initially required that women represent minimally 40% of sport board members, while the percentage for England was 30% (Sisjord, Fasting and Sand, 2017; Piggott and Matthews, 2020; Valiente, 2020). This voluntariness generally seemed to have had relatively little effect, which has led these countries to institute penalties for non-compliance, such as fines (England and Spain) or loss of charter (Norway). The size of the desired quota is rarely contested, however.

The justification for setting the desired ratio or quota at 30–40% in sport is often tied to the percentage of women participants in a specific sport and/or to the notion of the relationship between critical mass and change in board culture. Some policy makers, for example, have suggested that the percentage of women participants in a sport should serve as a target or quota (Adriaanse and Schofield, 2014; Elling, Knoppers and Hovden, 2019). However, using this figure as a quota can do little to change the status quo in those sports in which male participants form a significant majority, such as football or cricket. The use of this criterion of percentage of women athletes in a sport seems to overlook the possibility that a reason for male numerical dominance in that sport may be the lack of women on sport boards. In contrast, more women board members might mean more women-friendly policies and, thus, lead to an increase in women members/participants. Other scholars, including those focusing on quotas in non-sport organizations, have suggested basing the quota percent on the number of women board members needed to create a critical mass of three or more women, which is often around 30–40% (Konrad, Kramer and Erkut, 2008). The size of a critical mass that is specific to the number of board members has often served as a basis for determining the size of a quota on sport boards (Elling, Knoppers and Hovden, 2019).

However, these percentages based on a critical mass often have a gendered subtext. Implicitly, they can serve as a target or ceiling for recruiting women after which efforts to increase the number of women members cease (Claringbould and van Liere, 2019; Piggott, 2019). In addition, the overrepresentation of male members is ignored. This subtext of equating targets with quotas and ignoring men as a political category and their overrepresentation is rarely questioned. An exception is Norway, which has set a limit of 60% on the percentage of members of each gender on sport boards (Sisjord, Fasting and Sand, 2017). Since 40% of board members must be male, and 40% must be female, no gender can comprise more than 60% of the membership. The advantage of this approach of limiting both genders is that it makes men, just like women, visible as having gender and constituting a political category.

All in all, the use of quotas has had an effect in terms of gender diversity on board memberships. Currently, there are few sport boards and occupations that consist only of men (Elling, Knoppers and Hovden, 2019). The subtext that the presence of a critical mass and quotas will transform board culture has, however, been challenged (Sisjord, Fasting and Sand, 2017). Women still form a minority if they comprise about or less than a third of the board members; they may also be selected based on their perceived fit with the current organizational culture. This minority status suggests that men can continue to dominate a board, even when that board is in compliance with gender representation rules. The presence of a critical mass of women may therefore do little to change the institutional and socio-cultural context that excluded or resisted their presence in the first place.

Possibly then, a critical mass or a quota that keeps women as a minority group on a board may not bring about desired or transformational change; yet, its size is rarely questioned. We contend that a quota policy needs to reflect the gender ratio in society. Specifically, a democratic way of setting quotas that may begin to bring about transformational change is basing quotas on the percentage or ratio of women and men in a general population. As such, a 50–50% ratio or quota constructs both genders as political categories instead of only women (Dahlerup and Freidenvall, 2005; Hovden, Elling and Knoppers, 2019). We contend that keeping quota size at 30–40% suggests an implicit general agreement that men may continue to dominate sport governance. It therefore needs to change.

Similar to actions meant to increase the number of women coaches, another subtext that contributes to inequality regimes on sport organizations' boards underlies the use of quotas as well. To whom does "women" as a group refer? To those marked as white heterosexual majority women? The literature on quotas and critical mass rarely addresses its intersectional subtext that seems to imply that women form a homogenous demographic group that consists of white heterosexual able-bodied women. Rarely do quota policies ensure that quotas for women and men are based on demographic diversity. Specifically, discussions about quotas seldom include a focus on other social power relations that intersect with gender, such as "race", ethnicity, sexuality, transgender, (dis)ability, and class. Political science research shows that even the aforementioned parity claim advocating a 50% gender quota does not necessarily open the door to a more intersectional feminist politics; in reality, gender quotas can be a considerable obstacle to intersectional politics (Lépinard, 2013). Further research is needed to identify what factors shape the relationship gender quota policies has with intersectional issues in sport governance. In doing so, we recognize that inclusion of a diversified group of board members does not automatically change a board culture that reinforces inequality regimes; however, it may provide role models and give a voice to those who have been invisible. The question remains if that voice is heard and taken seriously.

Homonegative speech acts

In the legitimation of gendered hiring practices for coaches and appointments/elections for board members, the focus is often on the (in)adequacy and qualifications of women and, in contrast, on the outstanding qualifications of men (Sotiriadou, De Haan and Knoppers, 2017; Knoppers, et al., 2021). Such research is categorical, focuses on gender as an identity and, as we argued above, ignores intersecting inequality regimes. Less attention has been paid, however, to subtexts associated with the policing of gender enactment of those in positions of leadership that are part of inequality regimes. The standards for behavior in sport continue to be practices associated with desirable sporting heteromasculinities (Adams, 2013). The binary gender hierarchy means heteronormative masculinity serves as a subtext for desired behavior although its practices are often constructed as gender neutral. These practices of masculinity include symbolic and physical violence directed towards what is associated with femininity (Kimmel, 1997). Consequently, women coaches and board members need to enact behaviors associated with heterosexual men in sport such as authority, assertiveness, and heroic individualism (Hovden, 2010; Schull, 2016; Madsen, Burton and Clark, 2017; Madsen and McGarry, 2016). So-called feminine skills of communication and nurturing are often discursively valued as well (Enderstein, 2018). While women are assumed to possess those skills naturally, men attend courses to learn such skills. Women are required to use these skills and enact manners associated with heterosexual femininity in addition to performing the "desirable masculine" behaviors noted above. If they do not do so or are seen as too tough, they may be labelled "bitch" (Shaw and Hoeber, 2003). Discussions about the dominance of this heteromasculine discourse that results in a double bind for women, however, rarely mention the misogyny and the devaluation of markers of femininity that are embedded in this dominance. Specifically, little attention has been paid in scholarship that focuses on sport leadership as to how this masculinity is policed through a repudiation of the feminine (Bridges and Pascoe, 2014). Labelling someone's behavior as effeminate is considered an insult, especially in men's sport. To be marked as a "sissy", especially in sport, is worse than to be constructed as a "tomboy".

Heterosexual masculinity is valorized while practices associated with femininity are disdained and seen as abject, which explains why fans use homonegative language against opposing teams. Magrath (2017), for example, found that fans at football games used homonegative language against opponents to try to gain an advantage for their own team whenever they perceived a weakness or mistake. Smits, Knoppers and Elling-Machartzki (2020) found that athletes and referees were called "fags" when they were accused of making mistakes, losing a game or were seen as showing inadequate skills during football matches and practices. Those who were seen as enacting these inadequacies and what is associated with a gay aesthetic such as the way they walked, ran, gestured, etc., were mocked for their "effeminacy". This gendered subtext of sport leadership embedded in homonegative language and its possible relation to inequality regimes that jointly contribute to the underrepresentation of women is rarely addressed.

We contend that a subtext about the negativity assigned to femininity creates an abject femininity (Smits, Knoppers and Elling-Machartzki, 2020). Ideologically this language systematically devalues femininity and links it to weakness/mistakes and abjectness (Bridges and Pascoe, 2014). Richardson (2009) has called this disdain for, or fear or devaluation of, femininity, femmephobia (see also Adams, 2013; Hoskin, 2019, 2020). This subordinated status of femininity is a regular feature of men's sport, especially football, and is used to shame, motivate and embarrass boys and men participants (Fink, 2016; Caudwell, 2017). The role of abject femininity or femmephobia in sport in the framing of incompetence has, however, received relatively little scholarly attention (Schippers, 2007). In addition, with few exceptions (see e.g., Walker and Bopp, 2011; Rankin-Wright and Hylton, 2020), an intersectional analysis of the construction of women as incompetent in positions of leadership has rarely been conducted. For example, does the subtext of femmephobia differ when attached to women of colour than to white women? Serano (2012) has argued that this femmephobia is also reflected in practices of trans-misogyny because trans-misogyny also has a subtext of the inferiority of femaleness and femininity to maleness and masculinity. In sum, the devaluation of constructions of femininity may play various roles in inequality regimes that keep "women" out of positions of leadership in sport regardless of their positioning in social relations of power.

Hoskin (2020) argues that research and policy making should focus on ways femininity is implicitly and explicitly devalued and constructed. We argue that sport is a major site for this devaluation. The subtext of devaluation of women's qualifications for coaches and board members, the femmephobia underlying homonegative language, and how femmephobia acts as a regulatory power to maintain gendered hierarchies, have rarely been addressed in sport (see also Fink, 2016). Smits, Knoppers and Elling-Machartzki (2020, p. 16) contend that this notion of abject femininity/weakness/inadequacy that is associated with women, "may partially help to explain the difficulties in increasing the gender ratio in positions of leadership such as governance and why men are preferred as coaches for high-performance sport". The responsibility for exclusion of or resistance to women in positions of leadership can therefore be placed on "women" enacting (abject) femininity. They need to learn to act like men, although as we argued above, they also need to act "nice". This resistance tends to consist of invisible practices or subtexts that ignore intersectionalities and consequently contribute to and strengthen inequality regimes.

Conclusion

In this chapter, we have argued that although gender diversity is framed as a valuable goal by sport organizations, this frame largely remains an empty ideology. In part, this lack of change may be ascribed to the subtexts of discourses about "ideal" coaches and the problematic size of quotas for sport boards and their embeddedness in hidden inequality regimes. These practices not only need to be identified but future research also needs to explore how seemingly gender-neutral notions of an "ideal" coach and of appropriate quota size continue to contribute to inequality regimes. This relative lack of women leaders is exacerbated by prevailing discursive practices in sport that construct women and some of the behaviors or practices associated with femininity as inadequate or inferior. Successful efforts to increase the number of women in positions of leadership may therefore do little to change sport culture unless behaviors and practices that rely on femmephobia and contribute to inequality regimes are unmasked, named, addressed and changed to value what has been constructed as abject femininity.

REFERENCES

Acker, J. (1990). 'Hierarchies, jobs, bodies: A theory of gendered organizations'. *Gender & Society*, 4, pp. 139–158.

Acker, J. (2006). 'Inequality regimes: Gender, class, and race in organizations'. *Gender & Society*, 20(4), pp. 441–464.

Adams, M. L. (2013). 'No taste for rough-and-tumble play: Sport discourses, the DSM, and the regulation of effeminacy'. *GLQ: A Journal of Lesbian and Gay Studies*, 19(4), pp. 515–543.

Adriaanse, J., and Schofield, T. (2014). 'The impact of gender quotas on gender equality in sports governance'. *Journal of Sport Management*, 28(5), pp. 485–497.

Anderson, E. (2009). 'The maintenance of masculinity among the stakeholders of sport'. *Sport Management Review*, 12(1), pp. 3–14.

Bendl, R. (2008). 'Gender subtexts–reproduction of exclusion in organizational discourse'. *British Journal of Management*, 19, pp. S50–S64.

Benschop, Y., and Doorewaard, H. (2012). 'Gender subtext revisited'. *Equality, Diversity and Inclusion: An International Journal*, 31, pp. 225–235.

Bridges, T., and Pascoe, C. (2014). 'Hybrid masculinities: New directions in the sociology of men and masculinities'. *Sociology Compass*, 8(3), pp. 246–258.

Caudwell, J. (2017). 'Everyday sexisms: Exploring the scales of misogyny in sport', in Kilvington, D., and Price, J. (eds.) *Sport and discrimination*. London: Routledge, pp. 73–88.

Claringbould, I., and Van Liere, M. (2019). 'The Netherlands: Transformations but still a great deal to be done', in Elling, A., Hovden, J., and Knoppers, A. (eds.) *Gender diversity in European sport governance*. New York: Routledge, pp. 94–104.

Clarkson, B. G., Cox, E., and Thelwell, R. C. (2019). 'Negotiating gender in the English football workplace: Composite vignettes of women head coaches' experiences'. *Women in Sport and Physical Activity Journal*, 27(2), pp. 73–84.

Dahlerup, D., and Freidenvall, L. (2005). 'Quotas as "fast track" to equal representation for women'. *International Feminist Journal of Politics*, 7, pp. 26–48.

Dowling, M., Leopkey, B., and Smith, L. (2018). 'Governance in sport: A scoping review'. *Journal of Sport Management*, 32(5), pp. 438–451.

Elling, A., Knoppers, A., and Hovden, J. (2019). 'Meta analysis: Data and methodologies', in Elling, A., Hovden, J., and Knoppers, A. (eds.) *Gender diversity in European sport governance*. New York: Routledge, pp. 179–191.

Enderstein, A. M. (2018). '(Not) just a girl: Reworking femininity through women's leadership in Europe'. *European Journal of Women's Studies*, 25(3), pp. 325–340.

Evans, A., and Pfister, G. (2020). 'Women in sports leadership: A systematic narrative review'. *International Review for the Sociology of Sport*. doi: 1012690220911842

Fink, J. S. (2016). 'Hiding in plain sight: The embedded nature of sexism in sport'. *Journal of Sport Management*, 30(1), pp. 1–7.

Hoskin, R. (2019). 'Femmephobia: The role of anti-femininity and gender policing in LGBTQ+ people's experiences of discrimination'. *Sex Roles*, 81(11–12), pp. 686–703.

Hoskin, R. A. (2020). '"Femininity? It's the aesthetic of subordination": Examining femmephobia, the gender binary, and experiences of oppression among sexual and gender minorities'. *Archives of Sexual Behavior*, 49, pp. 2319–2339.

Hovden, J. (2000). 'Gender and leadership selection processes in Norwegian sporting organizations'. *International Review for the Sociology of Sport*, 35(1), pp. 75–82.

Hovden, J. (2010). 'Female top leaders–prisoners of gender? The gendering of leadership discourses in Norwegian sports organizations'. *International Journal of Sport Policy and Politics*, 2(2), pp. 189–203.

Hovden, J., Elling, A., and Knoppers, A. (2019). 'Meta-analysis: Policies and strategies', in Elling, A., Hovden, J., and Knoppers, A. (eds.) *Gender diversity in European sport governance*. London: Routledge, pp. 179–191.

Kane, M. J., and LaVoi, N. (2018). 'An examination of intercollegiate athletic directors' attributions regarding the underrepresentation of female coaches in women's sports'. *Women in Sport and Physical Activity Journal*, 26, pp. 3–11.

Kimmel, M. S. (1997). 'Masculinity as homophobia: Fear, shame and silence in the construction of gender identity', in Gergen, M. M. and Davis, S. N. (eds.) *Toward a new psychology of gender*. London: Routledge, pp. 223–242.

Knoppers, A., De Haan, D., Norman, L., and LaVoi, N. (2021). *'Elite women coaches negotiating and resisting power in football'*. *Gender, Work and Organization*. Early view. doi.org/10.1111/gwao.12790.

Knoppers, A., McLachlan, F., Spaaij, R., and Smits, F. (2021). 'Subtexts of research on diversity in sport organizations: Queering intersectional perspectives' *Journal of Sport Management, Early view*. doi.org/10.1123/jsm.2021-0266

Knoppers, A., Spaaij, R., and Claringbould, I. (2021). 'Discursive resistance to gender diversity in sport governance: Sport as a unique field?' *International Journal of Sport Policy and Politics*, 13(3), pp. 517–529. doi: 10.1080/19406940.2021.1915848

Konrad, A., Kramer, V., and Erkut, S. (2008). 'The impact of three or more women on corporate boards'. *Organizational Dynamics*, 37(2), pp. 145–164.

Lépinard, E. (2013). 'For women only? Gender quotas and intersectionality in France'. *Politics and Gender*, 9, pp. 276–298.

Madsen, R., Burton, L. and Clark, B. (2017). 'Gender role expectations and the prevalence of women as assistant coaches', *Journal for the Study of Sports and Athletes in Education*, 11, pp. 125–142.

Madsen, R., and McGarry, J. E. (2016). '"Dads play basketball, moms go shopping!" Social role theory and the preference for male coaches.' *Journal of Contemporary Athletics*, 10(4), pp. 277–292.

Magrath, R. (2017). '"To try and gain an advantage for my team": Homophobic and homosexually themed chanting among English football fans'. *Sociology*, 52(4), pp. 709–726.

Messner, M. A., and Bozada-Deas, S. (2009). 'Separating the men from the moms: The making of adult sex segregation in youth sports'. *Gender & Society*, 23, pp. 49–71.

Norman, L. (2013). 'The concepts underpinning everyday gendered homophobia based upon the experiences of lesbian coaches', *Sport in Society*, 16(10), pp. 1326–1345.

Norman, L., Rankin-Wright, A. J., and Allison, W. (2018). '"It's a concrete ceiling; It's not even glass": Understanding tenets of organizational culture that supports the progression of women as coaches and coach developers'. *Journal of Sport and Social Issues*, 42(5), pp. 393–414.

Piggott, L. (2019). *Gender, leadership, and organisational change in English sport governance*. Unpublished PhD Thesis, University of Chichester, UK.

Piggott, L., and Matthews, L. (2020). 'Gender, leadership, and governance in English national governing bodies of sport: Formal structures, rules, and processes'. *Journal of Sport Management*, 35(4), pp. 338–351. doi: 10.1123/jsm.2020-0173

Rankin-Wright, A. J., and Hylton, K. (2020). 'Black women, intersectionality and sport coaching', in Bradbury, S., Lusted, J., and van Sterkenburg, J. (eds.) *'Race', ethnicity and racism in sports coaching*. London: Routledge, pp. 128–144.

Rankin-Wright, A. J, Hylton, K., and Norman, L. (2019). 'Negotiating the coaching landscape: Experiences of Black men and women coaches in the United Kingdom'. *International Review for the Sociology of Sport*, 54(5), pp. 603–621.

Richardson, N. (2009). 'Effeminophobia, misogyny and queer friendship: The cultural themes of Channel 4's "Playing It Straight"'. *Sexualities*, 12(4), pp. 525–544.

Schaeperkoetter, C., Mays, J., and Bass, J. R. (2017). '"When there was no money in it, there were no men in it": Examining gender differences in the evaluation of high performance coaches'. *International Sport Coaching Journal*, 4(1), pp. 95–100.

Schippers, M. (2007). 'Recovering the feminine other: Masculinity, femininity, and gender hegemony'. *Theory and Society*, 36(1), pp. 85–102.

Schull, V. (2016). 'Female athletes' conceptions of leadership: Coaching and gender implications', in LaVoi, N. (ed.) *Women in sports coaching*. New York: Routledge, pp. 126–138.

Schull, V., and Kihl, L. (2019). 'Gendered leadership expectations in sport: Constructing differences in coaches'. *Women in Sport and Physical Activity Journal*, 27, pp. 1–11.

Serano, J. (2012). Reclaiming femininity, in Enke, F. (ed.) *'Transfeminist perspectives in and beyond transgender and gender studies'* (pp. 170–183). Temple University Press.

Shaw, S., and Hoeber, L. (2003). '"A strong man is direct and a direct woman is a bitch": Gendered discourses and their influence on employment roles in sport organizations'. *Journal of Sport Management*, 17(4), pp. 347–375.

Sisjord, M. K., Fasting, K., and Sand, T. S. (2017). 'The impact of gender quotas in leadership in Norwegian organised sport'. *International Journal of Sport Policy and Politics*, 9(3), pp. 505–519.

Smits, F., Knoppers, A., and Elling-Machartzki, A. (2021). '"Everything is said with a smile": Homonegative speech acts in sport'. *International Review for the Sociology of Sport*, 56(3), pp. 343–360. doi: 1012690220957520.

Sotiriadou, P., De Haan, D., and Knoppers, A. (2017). *Understanding and redefining the role of men in achieving gender equity in sport leadership*. Lausanne, Switzerland: The Olympic Studies Centre.

Spaaij, R., Knoppers, A., and Jeanes, R. (2019). '"We want more diversity but…": Resisting diversity in recreational sports clubs'. *Sport Management Review*, 23(3), pp. 363–373.

Valiente, C. (2020). 'The impact of gender quotas in sport management: The case of Spain'. *Sport in Society*. doi: 10.1080/17430437.2020.1819244

Walker, N. A., and Bopp, T. (2011). 'The underrepresentation of women in the male-dominated sport workplace: Perspectives of female coaches'. *Journal of Workplace Rights*, 15(1), pp. 47–64.

5

Gendered Transformations

Conflict and Resistance in the Regulation of Female Athlete Eligibility in International Sport

Ekain Zubizarreta and Madeleine Pape

Introduction

The regulation of female athlete eligibility in international sport has re-emerged in recent years as one of the most divisive and widely debated issues in global gender politics. In 2019, the Court of Arbitration for Sport (CAS) in Switzerland determined that World Athletics — the international governing body for athletics, formerly International Athletics Association Federation (IAAF) — could proceed with implementing their most recent iteration of eligibility regulation, focused on women's middle-distance running (from the 400m to the mile) and targeting women deemed to have 'unfair' levels of naturally occurring testosterone. More specifically:

> [It] is up to [World Athletics] to decide, based on a careful consideration of the available evidence (including the scientific evidence of the extent of the performance advantage that such elevated testosterone levels confer), what conditions (if any) need to be placed on (…) the female classification in order to preserve fair and meaningful competition.
> (World Athletics, 2019)

The protagonist, South African Olympic champion Caster Semenya, may no longer compete in her favoured events unless she medically lowers her testosterone levels, an outcome that has been met with outrage in many women's sport and LGBTQ+ circles and has made Semenya an icon of resistance for women of colour in Global South nations (see e.g., South African Government Department of Women, 2019). Adding to the outrage, a report released by the Human Rights Watch (HRW) in 2020 detailed the traumatic experiences of numerous Global South women in recent years. HRW (2020) noted:

> [T]he human rights violations that such [gender] testing involves have taken place under the veneer of purportedly evidence-based policies that sport governing bodies have presented as necessary to ensure fairness in competition, even though the science behind them is contested.
> (Human Rights Watch, 2020)

Yet, World Athletics — and certain advocates of women's sport — have remained firm in their commitment to the notion that women considered to have high testosterone must be excluded, regardless of the consequences, to achieve a so-called 'level playing field' for (certain) elite women athletes (Coleman, 2019; World Athletics, 2018). Interestingly, cisgender male athletes experience no such regulation, despite there being great variation in their testosterone levels (Travison et al., 2017).

The issue of female athlete eligibility regulation has attracted several decades of rigorous feminist scholarship, carefully documenting the flawed scientific reasoning that has underpinned such regulations since their formal introduction in the late 1950s (see e.g., Bohuon, 2015; Erikainen, 2019; Kane, 1995; Pieper, 2016). Key to this scholarship is the notion that change over time in these regulatory regimes — from gynaecological examinations (or 'nude parades'), to the Barr body or sex chromatin test of the 1970s and 1980s, to the more recent focus on testosterone levels — has not brought sports regulators closer to defining 'sex itself' once and for all. Rather, the evolving scientific grounds that have been relied upon to exclude certain women from competing reveal the inherent complexity of embodied variation, the elusiveness of a clear definition of the female body and the ways in which efforts to know the body are always shaped by social and political context (Henne, 2014). Indeed, the very organization of sports competition in terms of a female/male binary is revealed as far from given.

Building on this insight, we ask: how can changes over time in the regulatory approach of sports governing bodies be explained? More specifically: how have these governing bodies navigated conflict and arrived at redefining their meaning of the legitimate female athlete body, though without abandoning their commitment to regulating inclusion? To answer these questions, we compare and contrast two specific periods of contestation that have produced changes in the regulatory technologies relied upon by sports governing bodies: first, the debates between scientists and the International Olympic Committee (IOC) during the 1970s and 1980s over the IOC's use of sex chromatin testing; and second, public and legal challenges to World Athletics' reliance on testosterone to determine eligibility, from 2014 to 2019. The former period culminated in the IOC abandoning its use of the Barr body test as its preferred regulatory technology, only for regulations to be reimposed in the form of a testosterone limit. The latter period is still unfolding, but there have been several important changes to where and how World Athletics deploys testosterone levels to achieve the exclusion of certain women.

We begin this chapter with an overview of our theoretical framework, in which we bring a feminist perspective to bear on a *pragmatic sociology of transformations*: an approach that focuses on 'key moments of argumentation' — and the network of actors, arguments and arenas implicated therein — to explain the trajectory of a regulatory or policy issue (Chateauraynaud, 2009; Chateauraynaud, 2011). In our analysis, we use a range of textual materials to explore and contrast how contestation unfolded in the two periods of interest to our project. We show that the former constituted an epistemic challenge to the regulation of eligibility, characterized by debate over the scientific basis of regulation but without any challenge to the necessity of regulating inclusion in women's sport. By contrast, in the latter period, we are witnessing an existential challenge in which the act of regulation itself is being called into question. We conclude by proposing that it may be an opportune time for those seeking to overturn existing regulatory regimes to decentre their own emphasis on science and pursue lines of resistance that emphasize an alternative vision of 'fairness' in women's sport.

Theorizing gendered transformations

In this section, we develop the theoretical framework of *gendered transformations* as a jointly sociological and critical feminist approach to explaining change over time in the trajectory of a regulatory or policy conflict in which gender politics are at stake. We take the pragmatic sociology of transformations proposed by Francis Chateauraynaud as our starting point, in which the author invites us to approach 'intensive moment[s] of argumentation' as 'key frames for understanding the turning points in a long series of disputes and mobilizations' (2009, p. 41). Such moments of destabilization can see an issue evolve from being a (scientific) 'controversy' (discussions within a specific epistemic community), to 'scandals' (confrontations brought to trial by one of the parties) or to other different configurations of confrontation (Chateauraynaud, 2011).

Critical to Chateauraynaud's pragmatic approach is attention paid to not only the actors themselves and how their particular institutional location grants them varying degrees of influence and resources, but also to: (a) the 'argumentative regimes' or kinds of arguments actors make in an effort to realize their desired course of action (Chateauraynaud, 2009, p. 42); (b) the arenas or settings within which a conflict unfolds; and (c) the longer-term trajectory or temporal dimensions of a given policy or regulatory issue. In the case of female athlete eligibility regulation, then, explaining the current state of the issue requires attention to how confrontation moments have unfolded over time, the different athletes, scientists, sports governing bodies and other actors that have been involved, and how the terms of argumentation have been enforced, resisted and changed in the context of the specific settings within which debate has proceeded.

Chateauraynaud is primarily interested in regulatory or policy conflicts in which science and/or technology play a central role, such as the place of genetically modified organisms in European agriculture or nanotechnologies in France. Absent from Chateauraynaud's approach, however, is a critical feminist lens for explaining the gendered terrain upon which the trajectory of policy and regulatory issues unfold.

The production and application of scientific knowledge is far from neutral with respect to gender. Scholars aligned with feminist science studies have carefully documented how scientific claims about the female body, and sex-related variation more broadly, are shaped by the gendered assumptions of researchers, which influence the questions that are deemed worth asking, how studies are designed and the analysis and interpretation of data (Haraway, 1988; Richardson, 2013; Martin, 1991). For example, Joan Fujimura has shown how geneticists need to overlook 'awkward surpluses' of data that undermine the definitiveness of a female/male binary in order to affirm *SRY* and *DAX-1* as so-called sex-determining genes (2006, p. 74). Far from being a binary form of embodied variation, feminist scholars and biologists have revealed the complexity, dynamism and indeterminacy of 'sex', including the inconclusive role of testosterone and other hormones (Hyde et al., 2019; Jordan-Young and Karkazis, 2019). Similarly, feminist critiques of the clinical response to intersex variation — defined as reproductive or sexual anatomy that doesn't seem to fit the typical definitions of female or male (Intersex Society of North America, 2018) — have been particularly important in demonstrating the considerable work that medical practitioners undertake in order to affirm binary narratives of sex (Fausto-Sterling, 2000; Kessler, 1990).

Practices of eligibility regulation in elite women's sport offer fertile ground for such feminist work. In more recent years, sport has also served as an important institutional domain for analysing the entanglement of race and nation within ideologies of binary sex difference, including how this relationship has shifted over time (Henne and Pape, 2018; Karkazis and Jordan-Young, 2018; Magubane, 2014). According to Anais Bohuon, female athlete eligibility regulation has moved from an 'East/West antagonism' of the 1970s and 1980s — during which time the regulation of eligibility was marked by Western fears about the supposed muscularity of Eastern bloc women — to the 'North/South antagonism' that characterizes the current era, under which women of colour from Global South nations are over-represented amongst those female athletes singled out for scrutiny (2015, p. 965; see also Beamish and Ritchie, 2007; Karkazis and Jordan-Young, 2018).

Against this background, we propose a gendered theory of transformations according to which change over time in the regulation of female athlete eligibility — including which changes have and have not been possible to realize — can only be explained by accounting for the gendered ideologies that pervade sport as an institutional terrain. These privilege particular ontologies and epistemologies of the female body: most notably, as having discrete biological boundaries that can be confirmed and policed with the aid of science. In turn, the axiom that *science can and should define the terms of participation in women's sport*, and that this is necessary in order to achieve the so-called 'level playing field' — itself a highly contested construct — has dominated and indeed constrained trajectories of change. It limits how actors engage one another, which arguments become possible to advance and where and how debate unfolds. As we will show, it is the dominance of this axiom that differentiates the former period of conflict from the latter, and which requires further resistance if eligibility in women's sport is to be re-defined.

'Barring' participation: Scientific conflict from 1968 to 1991

The period of sex chromatin testing, from the late 1960s until the early 1990s, constitutes the longest-standing testing approach in the history of female athlete eligibility regulation. While both World Athletics and the IOC deployed this mode of testing, our analysis focuses on the actions of the IOC (1968–1991) as archival materials from the IOC's Medical Commission enable a close examination of where and how various members of the scientific community sought to influence this regulatory approach. The key technology was the Barr body test: a sex chromatin test that in practice took the form of a buccal smear cytological analysis of mucus. The purpose was to identify the presence of the Barr body, or inactive X chromatin, which was then taken by the IOC as 'proof' of a female athlete's sex (Henne, 2014, p. 799). Called 'femininity control', all female athletes were required to undergo testing and obtain a 'gender certificate' before they were eligible to compete (Pieper, 2016).

As early as 1972, a group of Danish researchers released a memorandum calling on the IOC to stop their use of the sex chromatin test for the purposes of femininity control, arguing that the method was 'open to criticism for scientific as well as for medical and ethical reasons' since sex chromatin testing was 'a coarse way of getting information about chromosomal sex' (Danish Olympic Committee, 1972). The concern was that the test was excluding women who had chromosomal variations but in every other way resembled a 'normal' female athlete. Such critiques intensified in the late 1970s, with British researcher and medical doctor Elizabeth Ferris writing to the IOC on several occasions. In 1979, the lead publication of the IOC — the *Olympic Review* — even featured an article by Ferris, in which she argued that 'women with rare, anomalous chromosome conditions have been the unfortunate victims of this weeding-out process' (1979, p. 338). Responding to Ferris' concerns in 1981, however, IOC member Dr Eduardo Hay explained that while the Barr body test was an imperfect testing method, some form of femininity control was necessary 'to protect the woman athlete in competitions reserved for female competitors' (Hay, 1981, p. 1).

Throughout the 1980s, outspoken geneticist Dr Albert de la Chappelle challenged the IOC's use of sex chromatin testing on many occasions, including in professional forums such as the Journal of the American Medical Association (de la Chapelle, 1986). He urged 'the IOC to accept that the present screening method is scientifically unfounded, nearly totally ineffective and sometimes harmful' (de la Chapelle, 1984, p. 1). Of particular concern to de la Chappelle was the inability of the Barr body test to identify XX females with 'male-type body build and muscles' (de la Chapelle, 1982, p. 6). In other words, he did not oppose the principle of regulating eligibility *per se*, but wanted to see the IOC 'find the right way' by engaging the input of experts in the fields of genetics and endocrinology (de la Chapelle, 1983, p. 2). Various scientific organizations located in North America, Europe and Australasia similarly lobbied the IOC to replace the Barr body test with a more accurate method of screening of competitors. For example, in 1987, the Endocrine Society and Lawson Wilkins Paediatric Endocrine Society both called on the IOC to 'develop more appropriate and sensitive criteria of female gender verification for use in athletic competition' (Endocrine Society, 1987). The American Society of Human Genetics similarly urged the IOC to 'better define the purpose of screening' and 'identify optimal methods for achieving that purpose' (American Society of Human Genetics, 1987, p. 1). Arne Ljungqvist, member of both the IOC and IAAF's medical commissions, wrote in 1988 that 'almost daily I receive letters from various scientific societies urging IOC (and IAAF) to abandon the present sex testing procedure' (Ljungqvist, 1988, p. 2).

With the overall goal of 'femininity control' unchallenged, the IOC continued to resist calls to abandon the Barr body test. For example, responding to de le Chappelle in 1983, Dr Hays stated that while 'we know the procedure is not an absolute safe method… it is a practical and economical one' (Hay, 1983, p. 3), prompting de la Chappelle to claim that 'the Medical Commission of the IOC is closing its ears to the voices of the entire scientific community' (de la Chapelle, 1987, p. 2). Under this pressure, however, the IOC did establish an ad hoc committee to review the existing approach and explore alternative techniques for regulating eligibility. Only in 1999 did the IOC finally abandon chromosome-based testing, more than 25 years after scientific concerns were first expressed (Ljungqvist, 1999). Eligibility regulation disappeared from public view by becoming a discretionary rather than mandatory testing procedure and, as we explore in the following section, surfaced again only when South African champion Caster Semenya became the focus of such scrutiny.

Where were impacted women athletes during the period of the Barr body test? The most notable athlete to resist the use of this technology was Spanish hurdler Maria José Martínez Patiño, who wrote to IOC President Juan Antonio Samaranch in 1987 to appeal her exclusion from women's competition. In her words:

> I passed the worst moments of my life, as a result of shame and especially of the loss of friends. I have never seen my best male friend since… From the bottom of my heart … I appeal to your humanity to help me.
>
> (Martínez Patiño, 1987, pp. 1–2)

With the assistance of Arne Ljungqvist, Martínez Patiño did indeed have her license reinstated in 1988 (Martínez-Patiño, 2005). But unlike athletes in more recent years, Martínez Patiño did not challenge the existence of regulations *per se*: 'Sir, I am not asking for any rule to be changed; I am only asking for justice and, if I have no sports advantage, for permission to run' (Martínez Patiño, 1987, pp. 1–2). As we will show below, this constitutes a fundamental axiological difference between the Barr body conflict and recent resistance to testosterone-based testing. The legitimacy of the sex chromatin test as a method of female athlete eligibility regulation was contested on scientific grounds, but not in principle. With debate largely limited to private correspondence between IOC members and scientists, or to the publications and fora of professional scientific communities, female athlete eligibility regulation remained an epistemic conflict rather than one that attracted wider public interest and debate.

Testosterone regulations: Existential conflict from 2014 to 2019

We turn now to the 2014–2019 period of regulation, focused on naturally occurring testosterone levels, which at the time of writing is still unfolding. Caster Semenya, for example, lodged an appeal against her exclusion from elite competition to the European Court of Human Rights (ECHR) in February 2021 (Olympic Channel, 2021). In contrast with the earlier period examined above, the current conflict has been transformed from an internal scientific debate into a legal and public interest issue, largely as a result of Caster Semenya's decade-long struggle to compete without restriction. While the IOC has remained part of the story, here our focus is on the actions of World Athletics as they have been at the centre of recent debate and legal activity. In a further break from the previous period, the act of regulation itself is now being openly called into question. Even so, and for reasons that we will show, World Athletics has for the time being succeeded in continuing to define the regulation of eligibility as a scientific matter.

The terrain of testosterone-based eligibility regulation has moved quickly since the public fallout of World Athletics' mishandling of the 2009 World Athletics Championships, during which time they subjected 18-year-old Caster Semenya to unprecedented scrutiny by announcing to the world that they intended to investigate her biological make-up. Two years later, World Athletics introduced formal 'Hyperandrogenism Regulations', which established a limit to the amount of naturally occurring testosterone allowed in female athletes (10nmol/L) (IAAF, 2011). Characterizing this and subsequent versions of this regulatory approach are the following: those women found to have testosterone in excess of the designated limit are required to medically lower it or otherwise compete in men's competitions; only those women deemed to be suspicious by designated medical officials are singled out for testing; and, in an effort to sidestep the conflict of earlier decades, World Athletics maintains that their goal is not to determine an athlete's 'gender', but rather to focus on 'physical advantage', the pursuit of a so-called 'level playing field' and the respect of 'fairness' in competitions (Bohuon and Giménez, 2019). In many ways, however, decision-makers at World Athletics have had to adapt how they deploy testosterone to regulate eligibility due not only to concerned scientists, but also pressure from affected athletes and an interested public.

In 2014, Indian athlete Chand brought World Athletics' regulations before the CAS. For the first time, World Athletics had to justify in a legal setting the rationale behind and arguments for their regulatory approach, including the scientific evidence on which it relied. In addition to building a scientific case, Chand and her legal team attempted to broaden the terms for debating the legitimacy of eligibility regulation, emphasizing in particular the harms and human rights violations that had marked Chand's experience. The athlete argued, for example, that 'she felt abandoned, insecure and helpless' and experienced 'severe distress… as a result of the ensuing media speculation about her gender, which humiliated and "shamed" her and her family' (CAS, 2015, p. 108). However, the ruling focused first and foremost on whether World Athletics had appropriate scientific data on the performance-related effects of testosterone. While the adjudicating panel did not side with Chand *per se*, they ultimately concluded that World Athletics lacked the scientific evidence to exclude women with high testosterone, resulting in a two-year suspension of the Hyperandrogenism Regulations to allow World Athletics to find the data to support their thesis (CAS, 2015, p. 158).

In the ensuing years, World Athletics did indeed pursue the required evidence to re-introduce testosterone-based regulations, spurred on by the success of Caster Semenya — and two other women athletes of colour from Global South nations — at the 2016 Rio Olympic Games. In 2018, World Athletics released their 'Eligibility Regulations for the Female Classification'; this time applying only to races of distances between 400 meters and one mile. Reactions followed immediately, with some scientists attacking World Athletics' so-called evidence for relying on 'highly dubious' data (Pielke Jr., Tucker and Boye, 2019, p. 25). So, too, did the logic of the revised regulations fail to add up. Data concerns aside, World Athletics researchers found the strongest correlation between testosterone and performance in the hammer throw and pole vault (Bermon and Garnier, 2017), yet these events were *not* included in the revised regulations. By contrast, events for which no correlation was found — the 1500 metres and mile — *were* included in the regulations. In taking a new appeal to the CAS, Semenya and her legal team argued that this — amongst other factors — illustrated the fact that the regulations were 'arbitrary', lacked 'a sound scientific base' and were aimed explicitly at excluding her (CAS, 2019, p. 2).

While Semenya primarily sought to challenge World Athletics on scientific grounds, her case also sought to frame these 'unfairly discriminatory, arbitrary and disproportionate' regulations as violating 'universally recognized fundamental rights' (CAS, 2019, pp. 2–3). This, she claimed, was 'borne out by what is now known about how physically, emotionally and socially destructive the past practices of sex testing have been', including the 'long-term harmful consequences to the health and wellbeing of athletes' (CAS, 2019, pp. 23–24). At one point in her witness statement, Semenya noted that her case 'is not just about the right to participate in sport. It is about the right to be human' (CAS, 2019, p. 18). In response, World Athletics claimed that it was not 'subject to human rights instruments such as the United Nations Declaration of Human Rights (CAS, 2019, p. 74). That is, World Athletics preferred to limit the discussion to scientific questions.

Under the guise of science, however, they sought to re-categorize women with high testosterone as 'biological males with 5-ARD (and other 46 XY DSDs)', whom they explicitly contrasted with 'biological females' (CAS, 2019, pp. 72–73), thereby transforming eligibility regulation into a determination of sex after all. The CAS elected to uphold the regulations in a controversial and non-unanimous ruling, describing them as 'discriminatory', but 'necessary, reasonable and proportionate' (CAS, 2019, p. 160). While they noted that the issue involved 'a complex collision of scientific, ethical and legal conundrums' (CAS, 2019, p. 119), and recognized the testimony of experts who rejected the evidence relied upon by World Athletics, the panel concluded that it was not in their mandate to question the rule-making approach of World Athletics.

More recently, however, the ascendancy of 'science' as the arbiter of female athlete eligibility regulation has begun to look less certain, with human rights critiques gaining momentum. In November 2019, while the panel was considering Semenya's appeal, the German TV-channel ARD aired a report on the harms endured by numerous women athletes under World Athletics' regulatory regime, all of them women of colour from Global South nations (ARD, 2019). The United Nations High Commissioner for Human Rights (UNHCHR) has since openly criticized World Athletics (UNHCHR, 2020), as has HRW (2020). The World Medical Association (WMA), too, has called for the testosterone-based regulation of women athletes to be abandoned on the grounds that the procedures they impose cannot be medically justified (WMA, 2019).

In contrast with earlier conflict, then, the key issue has changed from the epistemological question of *how* to conduct eligibility regulation to the existential one of *whether* to conduct it at all, given the high personal costs to affected women. While for the time being, World Athletics remains stubbornly committed to its regulatory approach, the ground appears to be shifting. Critically, athletes' appeals have modified the configuration of the confrontation, forcing the issue to shift from 'scientific controversies' to a 'public scandal' that implicates diverse concerns beyond science (Chateauraynaud, 2011). Importantly, wider public interest and debate has not been resolved by juridical assessments of scientific credibility.

Discussion

Clear differences exist in the periods of conflict that have shaped the trajectory of female athlete eligibility regulation in recent decades and years. In the former period, scientific resistance to the IOC's regime did not challenge the overarching logic for regulating inclusion in the female athlete category; rather, the basis of the conflict was epistemic — *what form of scientific knowledge should sports governing bodies rely upon to define the female athlete category* — and left intact the notion that certain women ought to be excluded. The issue took the form of an epistemic controversy, with discussions implicating scientific communities and largely limited to private correspondence, but also including some professional forums and publications, where scientific expertise and credibility were primarily at stake. In the latter period, resistance became existential; scientific resistance did not disappear, but was redirected to target the very existence of regulatory practices.

This has in large part been due to the role of athletes, activists and some institutions legally and publicly challenging the legitimacy of the regulations (see, for example, Mitra, 2020), transforming the issue into a (public) 'scandal' (Chateauraynaud, 2011, p. 39). Most notably, the monopoly of scientific experts has been challenged, with human rights starting to gain ground as a legitimate basis upon which to judge the legitimacy of eligibility regulation. The image and reputation of sports governing bodies is now in question on a broader public level.

Sports governing bodies have not abandoned their commitment to regulate the 'fair' boundaries of women's bodies (but not men's) since they created their first policies. However, the different challenges faced throughout these gendered transformations have shaped the strategies available to them to navigate conflict. During the first period, the IOC resisted calls to abandon the Barr body test until the 1990s, when it adopted a new technique and then a new strategy by making tests non-compulsory. Scientific criticism towards regulation diminished considerably during this period of covert regulation, although it did not disappear. In the last decade, both the IOC and World Athletics have rooted their new regulations in a new set of arguments. The objective became to regulate 'physical advantages' in order to preserve 'fairness' or a 'level playing field' in sport, instead of 'regulating gender/sex' (Henne, 2014). This discursive shift can be seen as a strategy to avoid the criticism received in the former period, as some social researchers suggest (Pieper, 2016; Schultz, 2019). Yet, the overarching objective of the policies has remained the same.

World Athletics has continued to claim a scientific approach to 'fairness' and rely on the CAS as a quasi-legal forum for affirming the legitimacy of their approach (Pape, 2019). Outside of the CAS, however, diverse authorities including the WMA and leading international human rights organizations have challenged the reduction of eligibility regulation to questions of (dubious) science alone. While World Athletics has sought to dodge the question of human rights, it is clear that these organizations have succeeded in *beginning* to shift the argumentative frame of the debate (Chateauraynaud, 2007, 2011). Notably, after the first regulations were suspended by the CAS, the IOC opted not to develop a new policy, in effect delegating this responsibility to each of the international federations. However, they have not opposed the principle of excluding certain women from competing, indicating the diffuse nature of these regulatory practices and the diverse ways that sports governing bodies can participate in their legitimation.

At the beginning of 2021, confrontation regarding gender eligibility regulations seems far from being over; regulations are still in force, but scientific debates carry on and public/existential challenges remain unresolved as athletes and activists pursue possible new actions. They are also doing so in new forums, with human rights instruments being tested from Ontario to Europe (see, for example, Brown, 2015). As we advanced at the beginning of the chapter, it may be an opportune time for those seeking to overturn existing regulatory regimes to pursue lines of resistance that emphasize an alternative vision of 'fairness' in women's sport. This is not to say that science does not have a role; the significantly limited scope of current regulations (applying to only a handful of women's track events), which came about as a direct result of the evidence bar being raised by the Dutee Chand appeal, shows that scientific argumentation can be leveraged to hold sports governing bodies to account, at least to some degree. However, a scientific approach is insufficient for the project of removing eligibility regulation altogether and, moreover, does not reflect the degree of public interest in human rights and gender recognition as legitimate concerns.

The choice of the IOC to delegate responsibility to the international federations and World Athletics' recent efforts to limit appeals and avoid debates on human rights suggest that although recent public scandals may not have succeeded in revoking gender eligibility regulations, they have meaningfully impacted the public image of sports governing bodies and destabilized eligibility regulation as an accepted practice, leading hopefully towards a gendered transformation.

Archival references

Letter from Danish National Olympic Committee to Monique Berlioux, 18 February 1972. OSC Archives, IOC Medical Commission, reference number CIO AH B ID04 MEDIC.

Letter from Dr. Eduardo Hay to Dr. Elizabeth Ferris, 4 March 1981, p. 1. OSC Archives, IOC Medical Commission, reference number CIO-AH B-ID04-MEDIC.

Letter from Albert de la Chapelle to Dr. Eduardo Hay, 9 May 1983, p. 1. OSC Archives, IOC Medical Commission, reference number CIO-AH B-ID04-MEDIC.

Letter from Albert de la Chapelle to Prince Alexandre de Mérode, 17 August 1982, p. 6. OSC Archives, IOC Medical Commission, reference number CIO-AH B-ID04-MEDIC.

Letter from Albert de la Chapelle to Dr. Eduardo Hay, 9 May 1983, p. 2. OSC Archives, IOC Medical Commission, reference number CIO-AH B-ID04-MEDIC.

Endocrine Society. Resolution on Gender Verification of Female Athletes, June 10–12, 1987, p. 1.

American Society of Human Genetics. A Resolution on Gender Verification of Female Athletes, 9 October 1987, p. 1.

Letter from Arne Ljungqvist to the IOC Medical Commission, 18 March 1988, p. 2. OSC Archives, IOC Medical Commission, reference number CIO-AH B-ID04-MEDIC.

Letter from Arne Ljungqvist to the members of the gender verification fax club, 23 June 1999. Malcolm Ferguson-Smith Papers, reference number UGC188/8/34.

Letter from Dr. Eduardo Hay to Dr. Albert de la Chappelle, 25 April 1983, p. 3. OSC Archives, IOC Medical Commission, reference number CIO-AH B-ID04-MEDIC.

Letter from Dr. Albert de la Chappelle to Professor Hans Howald, 22 December 1987, p. 2. OSC Archives, IOC Medical Commission, reference number CIO-AH B-ID04-MEDIC.

Letter from María José Martínez Patiño to Juan Antonio Samaranch, 24 October 1987, pp 1–2. OSC Archives, IOC Medical Commission, reference number CIO-AH B-ID04-MEDIC.

REFERENCES

ARD (2019) *Annet Negesa - How the IAAF fails to ensure human rights*. Available at: https://www.youtube.com/watch?v=Af4CIrCL3D0 (Accessed: 6 April 2021).

Beamish, R. and Ritchie, I. (2007) 'Totalitarian regimes and Cold War sport: Steroid "Übermenschen" and "ball-bearing females"', in Stephen Wagg and David Andrews (eds.) *East Plays West: Sport and the Cold War*, pp. 11–26. Abingdon: Routledge.

Bermon, S. and Garnier, P.-Y. (2017) 'Serum androgen levels and their relation to performance in track and field: Mass spectrometry results from 2127 observations in male and female elite athletes', *British Journal of Sports Medicine*, 51(17), pp. 1309–1314. doi: 10.1136/bjsports-2017-097792.

Bohuon, A. (2015) Gender verifications in sport: 'From an East/West antagonism to a North/South Antagonism', *International Journal of the History of Sport*, 32(7), pp. 965–979. doi: 10.1080/09523367.2015.1037746.

Bohuon, A. and Giménez, I. (2019) 'Performance sportive et bicatégorisation sexuée: Le cas de María José Martínez Patiño', *Genèses*, 2(115), pp. 9–29. doi: 10.3917/gen.115.0009.

Brown, A. (2015) 'Worley's case to proceed in Human Rights Tribunal', *Sports Integrity Initiative*, 15 September. Available at: https://www.sportsintegrityinitiative.com/worleys-case-to-proceed-in-human-rights-tribunal/ (Accessed: 10 February 2020).

de la Chapelle, A. (1986) 'The use and misuse of sex chromatin screening for "gender identification" of female athletes', *The Journal of the American Medical Association*, 256(14), pp. 1920–1923. doi:10.1001/jama.1986.03380140090028.

Chateauraynaud, F. (2007) 'La contrainte argumentative. Les formes de l'argumentation entre cadres délibératifs et puissances d'expression politiques', *Revue Européenne Des Sciences Sociales*, (XLV-136), pp. 129–148. doi: 10.4000/ress.93.

Chateauraynaud, F. (2009) *Public controversies and the pragmatics of protest toward a ballistics of collective action*. Available at: http://gspr.ehess.free.fr/documents/FC-Public%20controversies%20and%20the%20Pragmatics%20of%20Protest.pdf (Accessed: 1 February 2021).

Chateauraynaud, F. (2011) *Argumenter dans un champ de forces. Essai de balistique sociologique*. Paris: Editions PÉTRA.

Coleman, D. (2019) 'A victory for female athletes everywhere', *Quillette*, 3 May. Available at: https://quillette.com/2019/05/03/a-victory-for-female-athletes-everywhere/ (Accessed: 10 February 2020).

Court of Arbitration for Sport (2015) '*CAS 2014/A/3759 Dutee Chand v. Athletics Federation of India (AFI) & The International Association of Athletics Federations (IAAF)*'. Ruling. Available at: https://www.doping.nl/media/kb/3317/CAS%202014_A_3759%20Dutee%20Chand%20vs.%20AFI%26%20IAAF%20%28S%29.pdf (Accessed: 6 April 2021).

Court of Arbitration for Sport (2019) '*CAS 2018/O/5794 Mokgadi Caster Semenya v. International Association of Athletics Federations*'. Ruling. Available at: https://www.tas-cas.org/en/jurisprudence/recent-decisions/article/cas-2018o5794-mokgadi-caster-semenya-v-international-association-of-athletics-federations-cas-2.html (Accessed: 6 April 2021).

Erikainen, S. (2019) *Gender Verification and the Making of the Female Body in Sport: A History of the Present*. Abingdon: Routledge.

Fausto-Sterling, A. (2000) *Sexing the Body: Gender Politics and the Construction of Sexuality*. Basic Books.

Ferris, E. (1979) 'Sportwomen and medicine', *Olympic Review*, 140, 332–339.

Fujimura, J. (2006) 'Sex genes: A critical sociomaterial approach to the politics and molecular genetics of sex determination', *Signs*, 32(1), pp. 49–82. doi: 10.1086/505612.

Haraway, D. (1988) 'Situated knowledges: The science question in feminism and the privilege of partial perspective', *Feminist Studies*, 14(3), pp. 575–599. doi: 10.2307/3178066.

Henne, K. (2014) 'The "science" of fair play in sport: Gender and the politics of testing', *Signs*, 39(3), pp. 787–812. doi: 10.1086/674208.

Henne, K. and Pape, M. (2018) 'Dilemmas of gender and global sports governance: An invitation to Southern theory', *Sociology of Sport Journal*, 35(3), pp. 216–225. doi: 10.1123/SSJ.2017-0150.

Human Rights Watch (2020) '"They're chasing us away from sport": Human rights violations in sex testing of elite women athletes'. Available at: https://www.hrw.org/sites/default/files/media_2020/12/lgbt_athletes1120_web.pdf (Accessed: 6 April 2021).

Hyde, J.S., Bigler, R.S., Joel, D., Tate, C.C. and van Anders, S.M. (2019) 'The future of sex and gender in psychology: Five challenges to the gender binary', *American Psychologist*, 74(2), pp. 171–193. doi: 10.1037/amp0000307.

IAAF (2011) '*IAAF regulations governing eligibility of females with hyperandrogenism to compete in women's competition*'. Available at: https://www.sportsintegrityinitiative.com/wp-content/uploads/2016/02/IAAF-Regulations-Governing-Eligibility-of-Females-with-Hyperandrogenism-to-Compete-in-Women%E2%80%99s-Competition-In-force-as-from-1st-May-2011-6.pdf (Accessed: 1 February 2021).

Intersex Society of North America (2018) '*What is intersex?*'. Available at: http://www.isna.org/faq/what_is_intersex (Accessed: 14 November 2020).

Jordan-Young, R. and Karkazis, K. (2019) *Testosterone: An Unauthorized Biography*. Cambridge: Harvard University Press.

Kane, M.J. (1995) 'Resistance/transformation of the oppositional binary: Exposing sport as a continuum', *Journal of Sport and Social Issues*, 19(2), pp. 191–218. doi: 10.1177/019372395019002006.

Karkazis, K. and Jordan-Young, R. (2018) 'The powers of testosterone: Obscuring race and regional bias in the regulation of women athletes', *Feminist Formations*, 30(2), pp. 1–39. doi: 10.1353/ff.2018.0017.

Kessler, S.J. (1990) 'The medical construction of gender: Case management of intersexed infants', *Signs*, 16(1), pp. 3–26. doi: 10.1086/494643.

Magubane, Z. (2014) 'Spectacles and scholarship: Caster Semenya, intersex studies, and the problem of race in feminist theory', *Signs*, 39(3), pp. 761–785. doi: 10.1086/674301.

Martin, E. (1991) 'The egg and the sperm', *Signs*, 16(3), pp. 485–501. doi: 10.1080/00497878.2011.537986.

Martínez-Patiño, M.J. (2005) 'Personal account: A woman tried and tested', *The Lancet*, 366(Suppl 1), p. S38. doi: 10.1016/S0140-6736(05)67841-5.

Mitra, P. (2020) 'In search of a safer playing field and gender justice in sport', *Human Rights Defender*, 29(2). Available at: https://issuu.com/humanrightsdefender/docs/volume_29_issue_2/s/10850366 (Accessed: 9 April 2021).

Olympic Channel (2021) 'Caster Semenya appeals to the European Court of Human Rights', *Olympic Channel*, 25 February. Available at: https://www.olympicchannel.com/en/stories/news/detail/caster-semenya-appeal-european-court-human-rights/ (Accessed: 6 April 2021).

Pape, M. (2019) 'Expertise and Non-binary Bodies: Sex, Gender and the Case of Dutee Chand', *Body & Society*, 25(4), pp. 1–26. doi: 10.1177/1357034X19865940.

Pielke Jr., R., Tucker, R. and Boye, E. (2019) 'Scientific integrity and the IAAF testosterone regulations', *The International Sports Law Journal*, 19(1), pp. 18–26. doi: 10.1007/s40318-019-00143-w.

Pieper, L.P. (2016) '"Preserving la difference": The elusiveness of sex-segregated sport', *Sport in Society*, 19(8–9), pp. 1138–1155. doi: 10.1080/17430437.2015.1096258.

Richardson, S.S. (2013) *Sex Itself*. Chicago: University of Chicago Press.

Schultz, J. (2019) 'Good enough? The "wicked" use of testosterone for defining femaleness in women's sport', *Sport in Society*, 24(4), pp. 607–627. doi: 10.1080/17430437.2019.1703684.

South African Government Department of Women (2019) '*Department of Women supports Caster Semenya*', 20 February. Available at: https://www.gov.za/speeches/department-women-20-feb-2019-0000# (Accessed: 20 November 2020).

Travison, T.G., Vesper, H.W., Orwoll, E., Wu, F., Kaufman, J.M., Wang, Y., Lapauw, B., Fiers, T., Matsumoto, A.M. and Bhasin, S. (2017) 'Harmonized reference ranges for circulating testosterone levels in men of four cohort studies in the United States and Europe', *The Journal of Clinical Endocrinology and metabolism*, 102(2), pp. 1161–1173. doi: 10.1210/jc.2016-2935.

United Nations High Commissioner for Human Rights (2020) '*Intersection of race and gender discrimination in sport*'. Available at: http://www.mitpressjournals.org/doi/abs/10.1162/itgg.2008.3.2.189 (Accessed: 1 February 2021).

World Athetics (2018) '*IAAF introduces new eligibility regulations for female classification*', 26 April. Available at: https://www.worldathletics.org/news/press-release/eligibility-regulations-for-female-classifica (Accessed: 30 October 2020).

World Athetics (2019) '*Eligibility regulations for the female classification*'. Available at: https://www.iaaf.org/download/download?filename=0c7ef23c-10e1-4025-bd0c-e9f3b8f9b158.pdf&urlslug=IAAF%20Eligibility%20Regulations%20for%20the%20Female%20Classification%20%5BAthletes%20with%20Differences%20of%20Sex%20Development%5D%20in%20force%20as%20from%201st%20November%202018 (Accessed: 1 February 2021).

World Medical Association (2019) '*WMA urges physicians not to implement IAAF rules on classifying women athletes*', 25 April. Available at: https://www.wma.net/news-post/wma-urges-physicians-not-to-implement-iaaf-rules-on-classifying-women-athletes/ (Accessed: 1 February 2021).

6
Analysis of Government Policy Relating to Women's Sport

Julia White and Jean McArdle

Introduction

Sport in Ireland, as in many other countries, is an integral part of society (Rouse 2015; Sport Ireland 2018b). In the most watched Irish TV programmes of 2019, sports featured seven times on the top ten list (RTÉ [Raidió Teilifís Éireann] 2019). Gender remains one of the most discriminating variables within sport, leading to many studies examining gender inequality and stereotypes (Koivula 1995; Schmalz and Kerstetter 2006). Liston (2014) argued that, similar to developments internationally, females have gradually increased their participation in sports and physical activities in Ireland over the past 20 years. Two in five Irish girls between the ages of 12–17 play sport and 33% of Irish male adults and 23% of Irish female adults play sport (Lidl 2017). However, while research carried out by Liston (2001; 2014) and Lidl (2017) provide valuable data on women's participation rates in sport in Ireland, there is a dearth of research on sport policy. This research gap is confirmed by a recent study that explores the gender data gap in talent development (Curran, MacNamara and Passmore 2019). Perhaps, because of this, policy relating to women in sport (WIS) in Ireland has not been analysed, nor have the experiences of female athletes in Ireland been extensively investigated. The purpose of this chapter is to examine sports policy in Ireland that relates specifically to WIS.

In 1997, the Irish Government authorised the establishment of a Taskforce on Women in Sport, and to this day, there is no clarity as to why the Taskforce was established. The Taskforce received more than 100 submissions 'from interested parties on key issues related to female participation in sports and physical activities' (Oireachtas 2004, p. 38), including: individual sports people, National Governing Bodies (NGBs) and other associations involved in sport (Oireachtas 2004, p. 13). Examples included: the Physical Education Authority of Ireland (PEAI), the Irish Female Rugby Football Union, Irish Squash, the National Coaching and Training Centre, and the Olympic Council of Ireland, to name but a few (Oireachtas 2004). This showed an appetite for change in Ireland, echoing developments that were happening around the world in sports policy; such as the Brighton Declaration (International Working Group 1994). In 1998, the Taskforce produced a lengthy report for the Oireachtas (Irish house of Parliament) that provided impetus for change, suggesting several realistic and actionable policies to increase females' involvement in sport at all levels (Oireachtas 2004). However, to date that report remains unpublished, and while 23 recommendations were proposed, our research has shown that few were implemented. In fact, since 1998, changes in the landscape of WIS in Ireland have only occurred after 2018, and many of the proposed policies from the 1998 report remain relevant to this day.

In 2003/4, the Joint Oireachtas Committee on Arts, Sport, Tourism, Community, Rural and Gaeltacht Affairs considered that it was both a political and socially opportune time to examine the situation of Irish females and their participation and involvement in sport and recreational activities (Oireachtas 2004). The Joint Committee initiated the investigation as 'Irish females have demonstrated a passion for spectating and being involved (from recreational to elite level) in sports and physical activities, though this involvement has generally not been acknowledged in the same way as male involvement in sport' (Oireachtas 2004, p. 11). The aims were clear: 'it is hoped that it can provide further impetus to those who are genuinely motivated to promote female sports in Ireland as well as providing an up-to-date and informed discussion of relevant issues in this area' (Oireachtas 2004, p. 11). In July 2004, Women in Sport Report (WISR) was published, providing an extensive review of female sport in Ireland and the challenges it faced. The Joint Committee were 'strongly of the view that women should have a central, rather than a potentially marginal role in all sporting activities from leisure based to elite' (Oireachtas 2004, p. 1). The report proposed 23 recommendations to be implemented to enhance the positioning of WIS in Ireland. Subsequent to its release was a WIS conference in 2004. The first WIS funding stream to be issued by the Irish Sports Council was announced in 2005. The stage seemed set for change, or for increased votes. The Irish Sport Council (ISC) acknowledged the absence of national data relating to females in sport and indicated that it was a necessary prerequisite for good planning in relation to females' involvement in sport (Oireachtas 2004, p. 17). However, there has been no research investigating if any of the recommendations of the report had ever been fulfilled. Liston (2014) found that there was an absence of critical discourse in the proceedings that followed.

This chapter offers an analysis of the organisation of socio-political and socio-cultural values that relate to the development and structures in women's sport in Ireland. The chapter explores how the lack of policy relevant to women's sport in Ireland has influenced areas of funding, media, corporate investment and attitudes and interest towards WIS. Changes and successes have been reflected by the Irish Women's National Hockey Team in the 2018 Women's Hockey World Cup (becoming the first Irish team ever to reach a World Cup final in any sport) and the ever-increasing success of Katie Taylor (boxing). These achievements aligned with the formation of a Women's Gaelic Players Association (WGPA) in 2015 to represent the elite female players in Irish indigenous sports. In 2018, almost in conjunction with the WGPA was the launch of a social media campaign entitled '20x20', which focused on increasing media coverage of, participation in and attendance at, women's sports and events by 20% by the year 2020 (20x20). All culminated in the publication of the Sport Ireland Policy on Women in Sport (SIPWIS) in March 2019, with the formation of a new Women in Sport Steering Committee in the same year.

Methodology

The role of policy was that women athletes were beginning to be viewed more positively, especially as they develop to a higher level, and increase in number (McClung and Blinde 2002). However, any analysis of WIS shows that female athletes continue to be subordinate in sports, thereby perpetuating the idea that sports continue to be a masculine domain

(Fink 2016; Wilde 2007). This gender inequality can be connected to patriarchy as well as continuous resistance to it by encouraging girls and women to be physically active, involved in sports at all levels, and willing to confront traditional female stereotypes (Wilde 2007). Bell-Altenstad and Vail (1995) previously stated that for those who are committed to changing women's inferior status in sports, government policy is significant to encourage change.

Policy by its very nature is an ambiguous and difficult term to conceptualise (Houlihan 2002). Here, policy documents are defined as written documents that contain strategies and priorities, define goals and objectives, and are issued by a section of the public administration. Wilde (2007) recognised that women's sport has rarely been a priority for policy makers and emphasised the necessity of policy in the quest to transform sport for the benefit of every woman and girl. Wilde (2007) believed that it is only through policy that women would continue to make headway in sports. Many gender policies have been implemented as a result of political pressures (Hovden 2012; Kay 1996; Shaw and Penney 2003). While an organisation may be committed to gender equality, individuals within it can and do interpret this in different ways (Hoeber and Frisby 2001; McKay 1997; Slack and Parent 2006). Therefore, policies may be formulated with no strategy or programme applied in order to implement it (Stewart et al. 2004), influencing their impact. Policies are also constrained by laws and regulations of parent organisations, umbrella organisations, regulatory bodies, community expectations, government policy and legislation (De Bosscher et al. 2008).

Highlighting the lack of focus given to this topic by previous governments, very few policy documents are in existence in Ireland on WIS. Only documents that were government based or from organisations that can influence change were considered for analysis. The main document chosen for analysis was the WISR (Oireachtas 2004). Each policy document was assessed under key headings which provided structure and a framework to this stage of the research:

- Consultation and development process;
- Time frame;
- SMART (specific, measurable, achievable, realistic and time specified) objectives;
- Evaluation and funding.

The research questions focused on using a macro-meso frame analysis, which was a useful way of studying the transition of a policy from high-level idea to programme in action (De Bosscher et al. 2008). The content analysis (Bowen 2009; Caldwell and Mays 2012) of the WISR, the National Sport Policy (NSP) and the SIPWIS were then explored under macro (how policy will help to inform the future) and meso (changes that have been implemented since 2004) levels of analysis. The chapter focuses on the 2004 report, while alluding to the content of the NSP and the SIPWIS reports, which have made claims to undertake many of the same recommendations.

Content analysis enables the analysis of data to be structured and may be used in both qualitative and quantitative studies (Neuendorf 2002). A content analysis of the WISR (Oireachtas 2004), the NSP (Sport Ireland 2018b), and the SIPWIS (Sport Ireland 2019b) was carried out by means of document analysis, a systematic, qualitative research method for thematically reviewing documents. This analysis can be helpful in contextualising one's research within its subject or field and ensure research is critical and comprehensive by pointing to questions that need to be asked or to situations that need to be observed (Bowen 2009). Examples of document analysis focusing on policies relating to sport include: Bekker and Finch (2016), O'Gorman (2011) and Strittmatter et al. (2017).

Policy consultation and development process

A breakdown on consultation processes, a key component of the primary stage of any policy formation, shows the following: the WISR used a pre-established 1998 Taskforce report as its baseline along with existing research data from 1996 (Department of Education and Health Promotion Unit), 1999 (Department of Health and Children and Health Promotion Unit) and 2001 (Liston) surveys on participation by females in sport, recreation and physical activities. This suggests governmental interest in implementing change for WIS. However, the 2004 report recognised that very few of the recommendations of the 1998 report were met (Oireachtas 2004). Liston (2020, p. 3) notes that: 'There appeared to be more interest in writing the report and in its timing and release than its content'. While there appears a link between the 1998 and 2004 reports, no discernible progress was made in many of the areas highlighted.

Policy timeframes

For policies to be effective, a timeframe of works to be completed is imperative. Analysis showed that the WISR contained no specific timeframe for implementation of the recommendations. While positions were put in place for some key staff to be employed within the Irish Sports Council and funding was provided to help develop some projects (for example, Golf for Woman – including six free golf lessons), the 23 recommendations became just that. With no expectation of evaluations or impact assessment put in place, there was no level of accountability for the WISR. Today in Ireland, evaluation and impact assessment are key components of policy directives and the National Sports policy (2018–2027). Other policies that have been published since have included broad time frames of ten years with a 'vision' for Irish Sport in 2027.

The following is an example of why the absence of a timeline is worrying for WIS in Ireland. A recommendation from the 2004 report stated that the ISC were to appoint a full-time Women's Development Officer with specific responsibility for the implementation of the Brighton Principles across the structures of legislative and voluntary sports organisations. May 2019 was the first time that a full-time, permanent 'Women in Sport Lead' was appointed, meeting one of the objectives of the 2004 report, 15 years (!) after the initial recommendation. The fact that this recommendation is one of the only recommendations from the 2004 report fulfilled to date is a great cause for concern.

Policy SMART Objectives

SMART objectives are imperative to the success of any policy. Implementing change and the development of policy should lead to specific measurable goals. While very few recommendations were realised from the ones proposed in 2004, in the foreword of the more recent publication of a national sports policy (NSP), the then Minister stated that:

> Given that girls are more likely to give up sport during the adolescent years and that those who play a combination of individual and team sports are more likely to sustain their involvement beyond the school years, this provides a compelling argument for increasing our investment in sport and physical activity programmes.
>
> (DTTAS 2018, p. 4).

It is unclear as to why the 'compelling argument' does not include increasing investment in specific female targeted sport and physical activity programmes and the statement is inconsistent in nature with many others. The same policy also acknowledged that:

> Stemming the withdrawal of young girls, from structured participation in clubs during their teenage years is particularly challenging and recognising that issues around body image and self-confidence can influence behaviour in these formative years, we will consider interventions to mitigate this challenge such as improved changing facilities.
>
> (DTTAS 2018, p. 31).

All worthy points; however, there was no specific action assigned. In fact, most actions relating to WIS and improving gender gradients are merely mentioned within actions targeting numerous other minority groups and not specifically women. Something that seems to be continuously reiterated in national policy on WIS since 2004. Close analysis showed that these actions would also not be 'realistic' or 'achievable' as there are too many gradients being focused on and there is a significant hazard that the case for the female minority would be lost and diluted by the others. 'Progress towards greater gender balance in board membership of funded sports bodies' (DTTAS 2018, p. 20) was also cited as a key performance indicator for the policy, with a 30% minimum on each board by 2027. However, the reluctance of the policy to make this an 'action' suggests the commitment of the policy makers to achieving this goal was muted.

The SIPWIS (2019) seems to repeat many of the recommendations of the WISR report (2004), without acknowledging that said recommendations have not been implemented. Out of the 11 actions outlined in SIPWIS to achieve the objectives of the four target areas, none of them are time specific. There are also no details as to how each action will be measured, and many are vague in nature. For example, one such action is to 'require female athletes in receipt of funding to give back as ambassadors for sport' (Sport Ireland 2019b, p. 15). There is no mention of exactly what type of funding would qualify female athletes to do this or in what way they must 'give back'. Most of the actions relate to investment in different areas related to WIS; however, the amount/type/source of the investment is not summarised anywhere in the report.

Policy evaluations of implementation and funding

This work is the first time that the 2004 report has ever been evaluated and/or monitored. What was promoted as a 'way forward' for women ended up filling a shelf in government buildings. Liston, in conversation, discussed how it has been a continual source of frustration to her that this 2004 report was not drawn upon in any meaningful way by the ISC (now Sport Ireland) or other bodies, given her key role in the development. During the process of evaluating the recommendations made in 2004, it was discovered that 78% were never implemented. Only five out of the 23 recommendations have been met with any real assurance and the quality to which they have been implemented lacks consistency. For example, regarding recommendation 11 (to examine the role that the media must play in the promotion of WIS), while a national survey of the Irish public's interest in female sports coverage has been carried out (Lidl 2017), it was not done by any government body or by Sport Ireland. Dunne (2017, cited in Liston and O'Connor 2020) has acknowledged a dearth of research, particularly in relation to analysis of gender and media coverage of sport in Ireland.

In relation to other recommendations that were made in 2004, no longitudinal research project was carried out by the ISC or Sport Ireland to establish the depth, breadth, types and content of media coverage of female sports and no research project was carried out by print, radio and visual media producing empirical data on the sporting interests of their consumers. An Irish Women's Sports Foundation (WSF) does not exist today, thereby rendering fulfilment of three specific recommendations incomplete. Essentially, there has not been 'a coordinated focus on females and sport by government research agencies' and therefore it has been impossible to develop 'coherent policies with realistic targets and measurable outcomes' (Oireachtas 2004, p. 14).

Review, monitoring and evaluation – current policies

Three of the most important aspects of any well-functioning policy or plan is to review, monitor and evaluate effectiveness (De Bosscher et al. 2008). Metrics become the way in which we measure success and need for change. The NSP contains a chapter entitled 'Implementation, Monitoring and Review' (DTTAS 2018, p. 97), which proposes that a Sports Leadership Group (SLG) be established within three months of the publication of the policy to agree a prioritised Action Plan. In December 2018, the SLG was announced (Department of Tourism, Culture, Arts, Gaeltacht, Sport and Media 2019). Co-chaired by current government ministers, the SLG represents a broad spectrum of relevant Government Departments, Sport Ireland, the wider sports sector, Local Government, the Leisure Sector and the Volunteer Sector, who are all key stakeholders in this process. The SLG has committed to oversee the implementation of the Action Plan and report biannually on progress to the Cabinet Committee on Social Policy. A full mid-term review of the policy will be undertaken in 2023. Unfortunately, the SIPWIS (2019), similar to the WISR (2004), incorporates no such information pertaining to the implementation, monitoring and evaluation of the policy. As no evaluation of the WISR was suggested, the ISC/Sport Ireland and other stakeholders could afford to abide by very little of the recommendations and not be held accountable, as is evidenced above.

Funding

Funding is heralded as the 'fix all' of women's sports, and cries around the lack thereof have always been loud and continuous. In 2005, the ISC launched the €0.75 million Women in Sport Initiative, and in 2013, Sport Ireland announced an investment package of €0.71 million for the Women in Sport programme. From 2016 to 2018, the allocation of funding for the Women in Sport programme fell to €0.6 million (Gleeson 2019). Because there are no documents available providing information on how each of the recommendations of the WISR were to be funded, it appears that the figures mentioned above invested in the 'Women in Sport' programme were due to be responsible for the implementation of all 23 of the 2004 recommendations. Consequently, coupled with the lack of review and evaluation structures put in place, so few of the recommendations were fulfilled successfully. The consistent message that emerged was that 0% of the reports and policies analysed specifically mentioned the funding needs of females.

Recently, the doubling of Government investment in sport, from the previous annual figure of €111 million to €220m, was one of the standout objectives of the new NSP when it was announced by the Government in July 2018. In January 2019, the Department of Sport announced the allocation of almost €6.9 million for sports clubs and community projects under the Sports Capital Programme for 170 projects (Dublin People 2019). The announcement seemed indicative of appropriate funding being allocated to the specific actions in the NSP. However, it emerged that projects in two Irish ministers' constituencies would account for 5% of the total allocation of State funding, while projects in the Minister for Sports constituency were allocated a total of €325,200, which accounted for 4.7% of the total amount of funding (Gleeson 2019). A combined 10% of funding going to the constituencies of the policy makers and funding allocators does not bode well for the distribution of funding for other areas of the policy. This alludes again to the use of WIS as a promotional tool to endorse individual political aspirations as opposed to realistic plans to improve the state of play.

As promised by the NSP, in September 2019, Sport Ireland announced details of a multi-year investment of over €3m in NGBs through the re-launched Women in Sport Programme (RTÉ 2019). Bringing Sport Ireland's investment in WIS for 2019 and 2020 to €3,277,000 after €265,000 was also allocated to 26 Local Sports Partnerships (LSPs) countrywide earlier this year (€8,400 for each LSP representing an increase of 130% from €115,000 in 2018 in this particular sector) (O'Riordan 2019; Sport Ireland 2019c). Chair of the Sport Ireland Women in Sport Steering Group, Lynne Cantwell, says the funding will bring policy for women's sport to life and will tackle more than simply participation, and it is hoped that NGBs will embrace projects focused on developing leadership opportunities and pathways to coaching and officiating (RTÉ 2019). The rewarding of sporting bodies who achieve greater gender diversity at board level is a key element of the new SIPWIS (2018) policy.

While the Sport Ireland Sport Investment document (Sport Ireland 2019c) provides details of allocated funding to all NGBs in 2018 and 2019, more clarity and transparency around exactly how much funding each NGB received for females only, and why, would be beneficial. Despite the many developments and changes in the WIS landscape, it is challenging to decipher how funds are disseminated. Furthermore, it could be construed as ironic that women in Ireland still have to be afforded access to specific funding because the NGBs do not provide them with enough themselves, possibly as a result of the lack of policy surrounding this area.

Conclusion

It is a glaring anomaly that women's lack of involvement in sport in Ireland has, until very recently, been more or less unchallenged, in political, academic and public spheres (Liston 2017). The findings presented in this chapter prove the accuracy of this statement, that the world of WIS in Ireland is by no means at an equal level with males. The findings of this study are supported by those of the State of the Nation Report (Lidl 2017, p. 25), which found that men's sport is still taken more seriously than women's in Ireland. In fact, that many women still have far fewer opportunities than men to turn any participation they may have in physical activity into social, cultural or economic capital is deplorable (Shilling 2012, p. 147). The under-representation and marginalisation of Irish sportswomen in a major broadsheet newspaper (less than 4% of sports images were of women) still shows a bias towards coverage of certain sports. The overall effect of this proves that WIS in Ireland are continually undervalued (Liston and O'Connor 2020).

The findings by Wilde (2007), which recognised that women's sport was rarely a priority for policy makers, still rings true today. Therefore, the publication of SIPWIS (Sport Ireland 2019b) and NSP (DTTAS 2018) are undoubtedly welcome additions to the WIS (2004) report in the Irish sports policy landscape. These policies committing to improving women's experiences in sport have been long overdue, arriving later than many others (IWG 2012; Ottesen et al. 2010; Puig, Martinez and Garcia 2010). The policies also come 15 and 16 years, respectively, after the WISR (Oireachtas 2004). The setting up of the Women in Sport Steering Committee, the appointment of the Women in Sport Lead and the recent announcement of extra funding allocated to facilitate the actions are just a few of the practical and productive outcomes of the Sport Ireland policy (2019a). These effects offer a significant cause for optimism surrounding the future implementation of other targets and the continuation of strides taken in this area. However, correlation is not causation, and multiple variables are at play in the complex sport policy field (Liston and O'Connor 2020).

Indeed, the implementation of the actions related to WIS (2004) would be the greatest markers of success of any recent policy. However, it is also a source of concern, given the extremely poor completion rate of those recommendations. Proper evaluation and implementation strategies must be considered to combat the complex process of implementing gender equity sports policy (Hoeber and Frisby 2001; McKay 1997; Shaw and Frisby 2006; Slack and Parent 2006). Particular omissions in recent policies could suggest that policy could be merely an act of tokenism and a strategy by the government to appear to improve the cause of WIS in Ireland. It is possible that the policies were not published as a result of political pressures, as has been the case for many gender policies (Hovden 2012; Shaw and Penney 2003; Kay 1996). Questions that have been asked about political pressure relate to things like gender quotas. Liston and O'Connor (2020) have questioned what sportive diplomatic channels were clearly activated, which led to the relative silencing of a Minister who sought to apply a 'kick under the table' to NGBs regarding quotas. Furthermore, considering international developments around gender mainstreaming, why had neither the government in Belfast or Dublin, nor the two state-funded sports bodies (Sport Ireland and Northern Ireland), formalised a policy position regarding gender equality or equity? (Liston and O'Connor 2020).

Symposiums facilitating discussions exploring gender equity in sport through research – policy – practice dialogue could be an effective way of avoiding hollow policies being formed (Griffith University 2019). This, in turn, could aid the encouragement of engagement of industry and government with academic researchers and the sharing of insights that could support innovative government directions addressing gender equity in sport. Brooke-Marciniak and de Varona (2016) suggest that, perhaps, as a result of inconsistencies in policy formation and implementation, sustained equal funding for women's sport has failed to occur in many countries and sporting organisations, despite funding being absolutely paramount for elite success. Based on findings presented here, Ireland seems to be guilty of this over the past number of years. While the new funding announced in September 2019 to support effective implementation of the SIPWIS (Sport Ireland 2019c) should aid the completion of some of the shorter-term targets, it is critical that adequate funding and the newly introduced compliance measures for NGBs are maintained on a regular basis to avoid the policies becoming 'toothless tigers' (Bell-Altenstad and Vail 1995).

It is also clear that change is happening and growth is evident for WIS in Ireland. A previously mentioned social media campaign (i.e., 20x20) showed what corporate investment alongside a lack of government or structured policy could cause: a 13% increase in female participation in sport at all levels, a 17% increase in attendances at women's games and events, a 3–5% increase in coverage of women's sport in print media, a 4–6% increase in coverage of women's sport online, 86% more awareness of women's sport that was taking place on a day-to-day basis, and a 7–18% increase in television audiences of women's sport in 2018–2019. Hence, when surveyed, three quarters of the general population believed that sponsors should invest in both versions of sport and should support women's sport. This questions how effective national policy is if a media campaign can produce these results! More women are needed in sports leadership positions, as are male feminists, before a more cohesive and concerted challenge can be made to male-dominated organisational cultures. Such an alternative future would also require further research on the complexities of participation by women and girls in sports in Ireland and a greater understanding of the views of the range of stakeholders in the women's sports sector (representative groups, academics, sports organisations and service delivery providers, policy makers, and private interest groups) (Liston and Lane 2019). However, equal possibilities, pay inequality, discrimination, stereotyping, cultural barriers and promotion of the women's game are all still incumbent within women's sport. Policy should be the bringer of change yet consistently seems to fall short.

REFERENCES

Bekker, S. and Finch, C.F. (2016) 'Too Much Information? A Document Analysis of Sport Safety Resources from Key Organisations', *BMJ Open*, 6(5), p. e010877.

Bell-Altenstad, K. and Vail, S. (1995) 'Developing Public Policy for Women in Sport: A Discourse Analysis', *Canadian Woman Studies*, 15(4), pp. 109–112.

Bowen, G. (2009) 'Document Analysis as a Qualitative Research Method', *Qualitative Research Journal*, 9(2), pp. 27–40.

Brooke-Marciniak, B.A. and de Varona, D. (2016) 'Amazing things happen when you give female athletes the same funding as men', *World Economic Forum*, 11 July. Available at: https://www.weforum.org/agenda/2016/08/sustaining-the-olympic-legacy-women-sports-andpublic-policy/ (Accessed: 14 July 2018).

Caldwell, S.E. and Mays, N. (2012) 'Studying Policy Implementation Using a Macro, Meso and Micro Frame Analysis: The Case of the Collaboration for Leadership in Applied Health Research and Care (CLAHRC) Programme Nationally and in North West London', *Health Research Policy and Systems*, 10(1), p. 32.

Curran, O., MacNamara, A. and Passmore, D. (2019) 'What About the Girls? Exploring the Gender Data Gap in Talent Development', *Frontiers in Sports and Active Living*, 1(3), pp. 1–7.

De Bosscher, V., Bingham, J., Shilbi, S., Bottenburg, M., and Knop, P.D. (2008) *The global sporting arms race: An international comparative study on sports policy factors leading to international sporting success*. Aachen: Meyer and Meyer.

Department of Education and Health Promotion Unit (1996) A National Survey of Involvement in Sport and Physical Activity. Available at: https://www.lenus.ie/handle/10147/242227 (Accessed: 23 June 2019).

Department of Health and Children and Health Promotion Unit (1999) *The National Health and Lifestyles Survey*. Available at: http://www.nuigalway.ie/hbsc/documents/slan03pdf.pdf (Accessed: 23 June 2019).

Dublin People (2019) 'Sports clubs in grants bonanza', *Dublin People*, 29 August. Available at: http://www.dublinpeople.com/news/southside/articles/2019/02/02/4168362-sports-clubs-ingrants-bonanza/ (Accessed: 5 March 2019).

Fink, J.S. (2016) 'Hiding in Plain Sight: The Embedded Nature of Sexism in Sport', *Journal of Sport Management*, 30(1), pp. 1–7.

Gleeson, C. (2019) 'Department of Sport announces €6.9m funding through Sports Capital Programme', *The Irish Times*, 5 May. Available at: https://www.irishtimes.com/news/socialaffairs/department-of-sport-announces-6-9m-funding-through-sports-capital-programme1.3761823 (Accessed: 8 April 2019).

Government of Ireland Department of Transport, Tourism and Sport (2018) *National Sports Policy 2018 – 2027*. Dublin: Stationary Office. Available at: http://www.dttas.ie/sites/default/files/publications/sport/english/national-sports-policy-2018- 2027/national-sports-policy-2018.pdf (Accessed: 3 February 2019).

Government of Ireland Department of Tourism, Culture, Arts, Gaeltacht, Sport and Media (2019) *Sport Action Plan*. Dublin: Stationary Office. Available at: https://www.gov.ie/en/publication/c03e26-sport-action-plan/# (Accessed: 25 July 2019).

Griffith University (2019) *Women in Sport III: Collaborating for change: Addressing gender equity in sport through research-policy-practice dialogue*. Available at: https://www.griffith.edu.au/griffith-centre-social-cultural-research/women-in-sport-symposium (Accessed: 21 September 2019).

Hoeber, L. and Frisby, W. (2001). 'Gender Equity for Athletes: Rewriting the Narrative for This Organisational Value', *European Sport Management Quarterly*, 1(3), pp. 179–209.

Houlihan, B. (2002) *Sport, policy, and politics: A comparative analysis.* Hove: Psychology Press.

Houses of the Oireachtas (2004) *Joint Committee on Arts, Sport, Tourism, Community, Rural and Gaeltacht Affairs Fifth Report Women in Sport.* Dublin: Stationary Office. Available at: http://uir.ulster.ac.uk/21611/1/Women-In-Sport.pdf (Accessed: 3 January 2017).

Hovden, J. (2012) 'Discourses and Strategies for the Inclusion of Women in Sport - The Case of Norway', *Sport in Society,* 15(3), pp. 287–301.

International Working Group on Women and Sport (IWG) (1994) *Brighton Declaration on women and sport.* Available at: http://www.iwg-gti.org/iwg/brighton-declaration-on-womenan/ (Accessed: 21 March 2017).

International Working Group on Women and Sport (IWG) (2012) *Analysis and review of International Working Group* on Women and Sport progress reports 1994 – 2010, vol. 2012. Available at: https://iwg–gti-org-bin.directo.fi/ (Accessed: 20 May 2017).

Kay, T. (1996) 'Just Do It? Turning Sports Policy into Sports Practice', *Managing Leisure,* 1(4), pp. 233–247.

Koivula, N. (1995) 'Ratings of Gender Appropriateness of Sports Participation: Effects of Gender Based Schematic Processing', *Sex Roles,* (33), pp. 543–557.

Lidl (2017) *State of the Nation: Teenage Girls and Sport Quantitative Report.* Available at: https://ladiesgaelic.ie/lidl-research-highlights-benefit-sport-young-girls/ (Accessed: 16 October 2017).

Liston, K. (2001) 'Power at Play: Sport, Gender and Commercialisation', *JSTOR,* 90(359), pp. 251–265.

Liston, K. (2014) 'Revisiting Relations between the Sexes in Sport on the Island of Ireland', in Landini, T. and Depelteau, F. (eds.) *Norbert Elias and Empirical Research.* London: Palgrave Macmillan.

Liston, K. (2017) 'Women who participated in other traditional "male" sports used to be regarded as some sort of sexual deviants', *Irish Independent,* 6 August. Available at: https://www.independent.ie/sport/rugby/other-rugby/women-who-participated-in-othertraditional-male-sports-used-to-be-regarded-as-some-sort-of-sexual-deviants-36003724.html (Accessed: 14 June 2019).

Liston, K. and Lane, A. (2019) 'Sports, Gender, and Representation: The Women's Gaelic Players' Association', in Maguire, J., Falcous, M. and Liston, K. (eds.) *The Business and Culture of Sports.* Vol 3. USA: Macmillan, pp. 399–412.

Liston, K. and O'Connor, M. (2020) 'Media-Sport, Women and Ireland: Seeing the Wood for the Trees', in Free, M. and O'Boyle, N. (eds.) *Sport, the Media and Ireland: Interdisciplinary Perspectives.* Cork: Cork University Press, Forthcoming.

McClung, L. and Blinde, E. (2002) 'Sensitivity to Gender Issues: Accounts of Women Intercollegiate Athletes', *International Sports Journal,* 117–133.

McKay, J. (1997) *Managing gender: Affirmative action and organisational power in Australian, Canadian, and New Zealand sport.* Albany: State University of New York Press.

Neuendorf, K.A. (2002) *The content analysis guidebook.* Thousand Oaks, CA: Sage.

O'Gorman, J. (2011) 'Where is the Implementation in Sport Policy and Programme Analysis? The English Football Association's Charter Standard as an Illustration', *International Journal of Sport Policy,* 3(1), pp. 85–108.

O'Riordan, I. (2019) 'Sport Ireland to appoint new full-time Women in Sport Lead position', *The Irish Times,* 7 March. Available at: https://www.irishtimes.com/sport/other-sports/sport-irelandto-appoint-new-full-time-women-in-sport-lead-position-1.3817806 (Accessed: 7 March 2019).

Ottesen, L., Skirstad, B., Pfister, G. and Habermann, U. (2010) 'Gender Relations in Scandinavian Sport Organizations - A Comparison of the Situation and Policies in Denmark, Norway and Sweden', *Sport in Society,* 13(1), pp. 657–675.

Puig, N., Martinez, J. and Garcia, B. (2010) 'Sport Policy in Spain', *International Journal of Sport Policy,* 2(3), pp. 381–390.

Rouse, P. (2015) *Sport and Ireland: A history.* Oxford: Oxford University Press.

RTÉ (2019) *Sport Ireland announces €3m Women in Sport investment.* Available at: https://www.rte.ie/sport/other-sport/2019/0905/1074114-sport-ireland-announces-3m-womenin-sport-investment/ (Accessed: 6 September 2019).

Schmalz, D.L. and Kerstetter, D.L. (2006) 'Girlie Girls and Manly Men: Children's Stigma Consciousness of Gender in Sports and Physical Activities', *Journal of Leisure Research,* 38(4) pp. 536–557.

Shaw, S. and Frisby, W. (2006) 'Can Gender Equity Be More Equitable? Promoting an Alternative Frame for Sport Management Research, Education, and Practice', *Journal of Sport Management*, 20(4), pp. 483–509. doi:10.1123/jsm.20.4.483.

Shaw, S. and Penney, D. (2003) 'Gender Equity Policies in National Governing Bodies: An Oxymoron or a Vehicle for Change?', *European Sport Management Quarterly*, 3(2), pp. 78–102.

Shilling, C. (2012) *The body and social theory*. London: Sage.

Slack, T. and Parent, M.M. (2006) *Understanding sport organizations: The application of organization theory*. 2nd edition. Champaign, Il: Human Kinetics.

Sport Ireland (2018a) *Performance Planning*. Available at: https://www.sportireland.ie/High_Performance/High_Performance_Unit/Performance_Planning/P erformance_Planning.html (Accessed: 3 February 2019).

Sport Ireland (2018b) *Sport Ireland Announces 2018 National Governing Body and High Performance Funding*. Available at: https://www.sportireland.ie/Media/Latest_News/Sport%20Ireland%20Announces%20 2018%20N ational%20Governing%20Body%20and%20High%20Performance%20Funding.html (Accessed: 3 February 2019).

Sport Ireland (2019a) *Sport Ireland Launches New Women in Sport Policy*. Available at: https://www.sportireland.ie/Media/Latest_News/Sport%20Ireland%20Launches%20New%20Wo men%20in%20Sport%20Policy.html (Accessed: 8 March 2019).

Sport Ireland (2019b) *Sport Ireland Policy on Women in Sport*. Available at: file:///C:/Users/julia/AppData/Local/Packages/Microsoft.MicrosoftEdge_8wekyb3d8bbwe/TempS tate/Downloads/Sport%20Ireland%20Women%20in%20Sport%20Policy%20(1).pdf (Accessed: 8 March 2019).

Sport Ireland (2019c) *Sport Ireland Sport Investment 2019*. Available at: https://www.sportireland.ie/Media/Latest_News/2019%20Sport%20Ireland%20Investment.pdf (Accessed: 6 February 2019).

Sport Ireland (2019d) *Women in Sport Survey*. Available at: https://www.sportireland.ie/Media/Latest_News/Women-in-Sport-Survey.html (Accessed: 7 May 2019).

Stewart, B., Nicholson, M., Smith, A. and Westerbeek, H. (2004) *Australian sport: Better by design?* London: Routledge.

Strittmatter, A.M., Stenling, C., Fahlen, J. and Skille, E. (2017) 'Sport Policy Analysis Revisited: The Sport Policy Process as an Interlinked Chain of Legitimating Acts', *International Journal of Sport Policy and Politics*, 10(4), pp. 621–635.

Wilde, K. (2007) *Women in sport: Gender stereotypes in the past and present*. Athabasca University. Available at: http://wgst.athabascau.ca/awards/broberts/forms/Wilde.pdf (Accessed: 19 May 2018).

7

Gender and Strength

Representation in Strength and Conditioning

Yvette L. Figueroa and Emily A. Roper

Introduction: Muscularity and women

Given that strength, power, and muscularity have long been recognized as essential aspects of masculinity, women entering a profession that focuses specifically on building muscle and strength goes against gendered expectations (McGrath and Chananie-Hill 2009). The ideal feminine and masculine body has varied to reflect the aesthetic standards of historical eras. In modern Western societies, White women's body ideal has moved from a larger, well-rounded shape during times of food scarcity to one that is thinner in a society where food is abundant (Choi 2003; Grogan et al. 2004). Male body perceptions have also experienced historical variance and, according to American societal standards, the current ideal male body has a muscular mesomorphic build, in contrast to the current female (usually White) ideal that emphasizes thinness (Steinfeldt et al. 2011). D'Alonzo and Fischetti (2008) found that Hispanic and Black women in their study viewed their bodies distinctly different from White women. Bledman (2011) suggests that some Black women do not view being thin as healthy or attractive. However, research has also suggested that some Black women feel pressured to conform to White body standards (D'Alonzo and Fischetti 2008). While more research is needed around the area of "race", body perception and sports intersection, it is safe to note that regardless of "race" or ethnicity, females are often discouraged from having a muscular physique across Western cultures.

The female body has long been a site of constant self as well as external scrutiny. While the cultural acceptance of physical exercise as a desirable lifestyle behaviour has been influential – it is no longer sufficient to be thin; a woman must also be firm and well-toned, but not muscular. Markula (1995) described the confusing contradiction that women are expected to understand and work towards. There are boundaries placed on the extent of muscularity that is deemed acceptable for women; the female muscular body is generally considered unattractive because it symbolizes masculinity in its strength and size. Dworkin's (2001) study examining American women in gyms found that approximately 75% of the women she interviewed were conscious of the "upper limit" in terms of their muscularity and adjusted their training accordingly. Some purposefully elected not to train with weights, while others trained with lighter weights or would "back off" (Dworkin 2001, p. 341) if they felt they were approaching what they referred to as the glass ceiling. Despite the increasing acceptance of women's participation in physical activities and sport, perceptions of athleticism and femininity continue to remain contradictory, and physically strong women still represent a resistance to archetypal femininity (Bordo 1990; Choi 2003).

Athletes represent a population for whom muscularity may serve a function, as opposed to simply representing a body type. Many female athletes face the challenge of needing a degree of muscularity yet endure social pressures of femininity (Krane 2001; Krane et al. 2004; Mosewich et al. 2009; Steinfeldt et al. 2011). As Choi (2003, p. 545) noted: "the paradox becomes particularly difficult for female athletes who exist essentially in two worlds (i.e., sport and social circles) that constantly collide". Therefore, female athletes often report a contradiction between the cultural ideals of femininity and their athletic, muscular body (Krane 2001; Russell 2002; Krane et al. 2004; Ross and Shinew 2008; Steinfeldt et al. 2011). Such contradiction between expected appearance and femininity has been a historical feature of strength and conditioning (S&C) coaching which exists in a context and culture where the construction and training of bodies is central (Brace-Govan 2004). This next section, therefore, offers a brief examination of the historical disconnect between muscle and femininity with a specific focus on the emerging S&C context.

History of strength and conditioning in the United States

In the United States, it was not until the 1970s that S&C would become a way to not only complement athleticism, but to prevent and safely return from injury. It can be argued that the field of S&C began when Bob Devaney hired Boyed Epley as the first S&C coach for the University of Nebraska. Nebraska went on to win back-to-back national championships in 1970 and 1971 (Epley 2019). Much of this success was attributed to Epley's contribution through strength training. Throughout the 1970s, other universities looking to maintain or develop their competitive edge decided that having a S&C coach was an integral part of the team. Soon, intercollegiate athletic football programs across the nation began hiring strength coaches to aid the development of their athletes (Siff 2003). In 1975, Nebraska hired their first Women's Athletic Director, Dr Aleen Swofford, who asked Epley to work with all women's teams on strength training (Epley 2019, p. 45).

Since Epley's era, S&C has grown exponentially (Bishop et al. 2019). Initially, S&C coaches were former football players who had become injured or given up the sport and subsequently transitioned to the weight room. Head football coaches leaned towards hiring strength coaches with prior football experience and who "looked the part" by being muscular and strong. Given the emphasis on muscular physique and prior experience of playing football, female S&C coaches were historically marginalized from the S&C profession. Homologous reproduction operates within an organization when those in power maintain their influence by allowing access to only those who have similar characteristics (e.g., gender, race, sport experience, etc.) (Whisenant et al. 2002; Acosta and Carpenter 2014; Darvin and Sagas 2017). The male gatekeepers responsible for recruiting and hiring in S&C have historically engaged in homologous reproduction (Darvin and Sagas 2017). As such, women have historically been at a disadvantage when applying for S&C positions or when they seek advancement in their careers (Thomas et al. 2021). Today, depending on local circumstances, S&C coaches may be responsible for servicing anywhere between one to 15 sport teams (Laskowski and Ebben 2016). Thus, we have seen an increase in gender representation across sports, although male S&C coaches continue to dominate football and men's basketball, both high status revenue sports that garner the most resources and prestige in intercollegiate sport (Chalabaev et al. 2013).

The National Strength and Conditioning Association (NSCA) was founded in 1978 by a group of male strength coaches who wanted to create opportunities for networking and professional development (NSCA 2021). As the organization gained recognition, the Certified Strength and Conditioning Specialist (CSCS) accreditation was created in 1985 to allow its members to set themselves apart and establish the field as a reputable branch of athletic enhancement (Baechle and Earle 1992). The Collegiate Strength and Conditioning Coaches Association (CSCCa) serves a similar role and was established in 2000 when coaches felt there was a need for an organization that addressed the specific needs and unique environment of intercollegiate athletics (CSCCa 2021).

As the field of S&C has evolved and increased in popularity, the academic background and job training related to athletic performance has also changed. In the early years of the profession, strength coaches only needed to have prior sport and training experience, and often experience in American football was coveted. Such experiences certainly help to explain the overrepresentation of male S&C coaches historically. While this can still be the case today, most S&C coaching positions require a strong foundation in exercise science/kinesiology. The shift to requiring academic training in exercise science/kinesiology is a way in which S&C can move towards a more equitable field in terms of gender representation.

Nevertheless, the NSCA Board of Directors presently (in 2021) has three women out of eight members and CSCCa's Board of Directors has three women out of 13 members – all its advisors are male. Currently (as of 2021), the NSCA has a Women's Committee whose purpose is to "encourage and promote the strength training and conditioning profession for women…by providing a forum for discussion of current issues and dissemination of information" (NSCA 2021). To promote evidence-based practices in S&C, the *Journal of Applied Sport Science Research* (changed to *Journal of Strength and Conditioning Research* in 1993) released its first issue in 1987. Its editorial board currently consists of 47 senior associate editors, four of which are female, and 131 associate editors, 23 of which are female. While women are present in all aspects of S&C and their number is increasing, there is still an overarching dominance of men in the field.

Responsibilities of strength and conditioning coaches

Intercollegiate S&C coaches occupy various roles in athletic departments dedicating anywhere from 10 to 12 hours a day performing numerous responsibilities. The most important is establishing and maintaining the physical well-being of the student-athlete population (Massey and Vincent 2013). However, S&C coaches often find themselves performing day-to-day operations outside of coaching and the job description (e.g., coordinating conference travel, renewal of professional organization memberships, obtaining office supplies, community outreach efforts, helping to clean the weight room) (Nuzzo 2014; NSCA 2018). A recent review by Hartshorn et al. (2016) reported that S&C coaches work 60–64 hours per week when their primary sport assignment is in-season. This increased to 71–75 hours per week during the off-season, almost twice as many hours as a typical full-time job.

History of women's representation in strength and conditioning

Historically, S&C coaches have been identified as a relatively homogenous group of professionals who are primarily men, White, and similarly educated (Brooks et al. 2000; Martinez 2004; Lapchick et al. 2020). The imbalance is even greater in leadership positions (e.g., head or director S&C coach) and with revenue-generating sports (e.g., men's basketball and football).

While professional interest in S&C has increased exponentially, women employed in the profession have not followed suit (O'Malley and Greenwood 2018). In 1991, Todd et al. (1991) reported that 99% of head S&C coaches of National College Athletic Association (NCAA) Division I (DI) schools were male. When examining the educational background, experience, and duties of DI S&C coaches working specifically with football, Pullo (1992) found only one female working in all DI athletics. In 2004, Martinez compared his research with the work of Pullo (1992) and reported that for all three NCAA subdivisions, 98–100% of head S&C coaches were men. Brooks et al. (2000) examined leadership behaviour and job responsibilities of NCAA DI S&C coaches, eight of which were women (all assistant coaches) and 45 men (27 head coaches and 18 assistant coaches). The UK Strength and Conditioning Association (UKSCA) reported having 750 accredited coaches – only 7% of those were women (Medlin-Silver et al. 2017).

Acosta and Carpenter (2014) reported that DI has the highest percentage of S&C coaches, and the highest percentage of schools with at least one female strength and coaching coach. Forty-four percent of DI, when considered as a whole, have at least one female S&C coach, up from 34.6% in 2012. More recently, Laskowski and Ebben (2016) reported approximately one-third of all S&C positions of surveyed NCAA DI universities were held by women. Of the 43 participants in their study, 27 held the title of assistant S&C coach, 12 held some sort of director or associate director role within their department, and one did not list her job title. Thirty-eight participants were employed full-time and five were part-time. Lapchick et al. (2020)'s Racial and Gender Report Card identified that 86.1% of all S&C coaches employed are male. This high percentage of male S&C coaches has remained largely unchanged since the 2005/2006 season. Consequently, although still a predominantly White, male field, S&C staff are increasing in female representation. Gender bias, however, remains a pervasive barrier for women's access to and advancement in the profession.

Barriers to strength and conditioning

The dearth of female S&C coaches cannot be understood without positioning it within the wider context of sexism that exists within sport. The attributes commonly associated with sport – power, strength, dominance, competitiveness, and aggression – are socially defined as masculine qualities (Clément-Guillotin et al. 2012). Researchers have studied the barriers facing female professionals in athletic training (Mazerolle and Eason 2016), sport coaching (LaVoi and Dutove 2012), sport psychology (Roper 2002, 2008; Roper et al. 2005), and sport administration (Taylor and Wells 2017).

Women working in the sport domain report organizational constraints including gender stereotyping (Grappendorf et al. 2008; Burton et al. 2009) and the "good old boys" network in which men support and promote other men (Whisenant et al. 2002; Acosta and Carpenter 2014; Darvin and Sagas 2017). The lack of female mentors/role models in sport has also been well documented across various sport professions (Roper 2008; Mazerolle and Eason 2016). In athletic training, Mazerolle and Eason (2016) found that women in the field were not often mentored by female athletic trainers in leadership positions, sending the message that women cannot succeed in the role or do not want the role altogether. Female students and young professionals in the sport domain need not only recognize that female professionals exist but can openly discuss any unique issues and concerns being faced as a female within their respective field.

Motherhood has also been described as a barrier to career advancement in sport given the long, unstructured hours and travel (Inglis et al. 2000; Kamphoff 2013; Mazerolle and Eason 2016). Mazerolle and Eason (2016) found that the time constraints and demands of athletic training severely limited the time and energy available to take care of one's family and personal needs. Similarly, being childless was a catalyst for female head athletic trainers' upward mobility in the DI setting (Mazerolle and Eason 2016); successful navigation of the role of head athletic trainer was possible because women could manage the time-consuming aspects of the job and did not need to care for their families. Similarly, Roper (2008) found that women working in applied sport psychology, most with elite level athletes and teams, described travel as the hardest part of the job. The travel, much of which was international, was difficult due to the strains it placed on their role as mothers and sport psychologists. Some of the participants purposefully reduced their travel to lessen that burden, but also recognized the resultant loss of experiences and opportunities. Like the athletic trainers in Mazerolle and Eason's (2016) study, the participants that were mothers in Roper's (2008) study acknowledged a distinct difference in their productivity before they were mothers. Likewise, Kamphoff (2013) found that some sport coaches perceived conflict between motherhood and coaching, perceiving that female sport coaches with children were viewed as being distracted by motherhood.

While there has been an increase in women employed as S&C coaches in intercollegiate sport, in leadership roles, there remains a large discrepancy. History indicates that authority and leadership roles have been occupied by men in sport (Whisenant et al. 2002). Much of the gain in gender diversity has come at entry-level and mid-level management positions, with much smaller increases in senior leadership and executive-level positions (Hindman and Walker 2020). One potential reason for many leadership positions being held by men is because leadership skills are often constructed in terms of masculinity whereby females are excluded from jobs that hold leadership duties (Hovden 2000; Connell and Messerschmidt 2005). As women have been stereotyped as less capable leaders than males (Embry et al. 2008), there has been a normative, gendered social order established (Greenwood et al. 2008) that institutionalized male sport leaders (Eagly and Karau 2002). That is, there are perceptions that male coaches are inherently more knowledgeable and experienced than female coaches (Darvin and Sagas 2017; Schull and Kihl 2019), and, consequently, women are less likely to be hired for leadership positions than equally qualified male candidates (Burton et al. 2011; Burton 2015).

In S&C, physical appearance is another unique factor to consider. Edmonds (2018) noted that it was not uncommon for S&C coaches to be hired based solely on their physical appearance; a muscular appearance was described as a signal of expertise and knowledge, regardless of one's qualifications. Such perceptions can harm women's access to positions where muscularity and a large physique are considered fundamental. Male and female athletes in Shuman and Appleby's (2016) study indicated that their perceptions of female S&C coaches were changed when the female strength coaches had proven that they could perform in the weight room. The need to "look the part" or even prove oneself in terms of strength as a female S&C coach is yet another example of the institutional biases that restrict and limit women's access to and mobility within the profession (Mullin and Bergan 2018). As Thomas et al. (2021, p. 2) asserted: "it can be argued that women entering the field of S&C are transgressing, not only through sport but also muscle, both of which are still considered to be quintessential components of Western masculinity".

Experiences of women in strength and conditioning

While there is limited research examining women's experiences in the profession of S&C, female S&C coaches have reported remarkably high job satisfaction (Massey and Vincent 2013; Laskowski and Ebben 2016). Although job satisfaction was high among most of the participants, they did identify common stressors including time pressures associated with their position, heavy workloads when in season, early mornings, keeping sport coaches happy, wanting their athletes to be healthy, and associated challenges with boundaries and balancing motherhood and a career (Massey and Vincent 2013; Sartore-Baldwin 2013; Laskowski and Ebben 2016).

The importance of maintaining proper professional boundaries as female S&C coaches was noted by the participants (Massey and Vincent 2013). It was suggested that female S&C coaches needed to establish clear professional boundaries to maintain authority and ensure respect. While professional boundaries are critical of any S&C coach regardless of gender, the recommendation made specifically to female S&C coaches is of importance to address. In sport, due to male domination, women's presence is often questioned and viewed as a transgression (Hindman and Walker 2020). In a study investigating female sport managers, Hindman and Walker (2020) found that women's motives for working in sport were under a cloud of suspicion regarding whether they have, or might in the future, engage in a sexual relationship with an athlete. Female athletic trainers, as Burton et al.'s (2009) study indicated, were told that they were a distraction to the male athletes. Female professionals working in the sport domain are often viewed as a threat to established male privilege and gender order, and thus, women's attempt to access or progress in S&C may still be perceived as trespassing and outside of certain cultural bounds (Banwell et al. 2019). It is, therefore, quite common within the sport context for women to be recognized for their sex appeal rather than for their talent, experiences and capabilities (Roth and Basow 2004).

Female S&C coaches also noted a "glass ceiling" that impeded women's advancement to leadership roles in the profession (Massey and Vincent 2013). The glass ceiling is a long-standing metaphor for the intangible systemic barriers that prevent women from professional progression (Johnson 2017). The participants perceived that as they progressed through their career, there would be fewer opportunities for advancement, compared to men (Massey and Vincent 2013; Laskowski and Ebben 2016). For progress to occur within the profession of S&C, White male S&C coaches as well as other White, male leaders need to advocate for equitable representation within the field. Men in positions of power and privilege must not continue to flood the profession with those who hold the same experiences and identities regarding social status, gender, race, and sexual orientation (Thomas et al. 2021).

Many researchers have suggested that one of the most critical aspects of advancing women in leadership is through mentoring (Bower 2009; Sartore-Baldwin 2013; LaVoi et al. 2019). When asked about the factors that led them to their current positions, the women all mentioned a significant male or female mentor who led them to the career and helped guide them through their development. These types of relationships are central to all developing professionals but are especially important for women in sport (Hartzell and Dixon 2019). O'Malley and Greenwood (2018) noted that given the lack of women S&C mentors available, novice S&C coaches may find that as a barrier for pursuing and progressing in the field.

Gender preferences

A small group of researchers have examined gender preferences of S&C coaches among athletes (Magnusen and Rhea 2009; Shuman and Appleby 2016). Whereas Magnusen and Rhea (2009) found that male intercollegiate athletes preferred male S&C coaches and female athletes had no preference based on gender, Shuman and Appleby (2016) found no preference relative to gender among male and female intercollegiate athletes. Rather, knowledge, a reciprocated level of respect, professionalism on the part of the S&C coach, support from the S&C coach, and the S&C coach's ability to assist the student-athlete in increasing their personal performance were found to contribute to the preference of an S&C coach (Shuman and Appleby 2016). These findings are especially optimistic as they represent factors unbiased by gender that would influence one's attitude towards an S&C coach.

A consistent trend in the job analysis of major collegiate female S&C coaches in North American universities is the hiring of female S&C coaches to work specifically with female athletes (Massey and Vincent 2013). There is a pervasive stereotype that female S&C coaches are most effective with only female athletes, and vice versa for male S&C coaches and male athletes. Yet, findings from Magnusen and Rhea (2009) discount this argument. Several studies have indicated female S&C coaches' frustration with the belief that female S&C coaches are better prepared to work with female athletes and specifically not prepared to work in football (Massey and Vincent 2013; Laskowski and Ebben 2016).

Conclusions

Historically, S&C has received limited research attention regarding gender. While there have been improvements in women's representation in S&C over the past 30 years, the field predominantly remains a White, male profession (Thomas et al. 2021). Like other sport professions (e.g., journalism, sport coaching, etc.), S&C is a site where men and their perceived skills and knowledge are privileged. As scholarly work has brought attention to women's S&C experiences and representation (Sartore-Baldwin 2013; Thomas et al. 2021), it is vital that the field pays heed to the findings. In doing so, the field of S&C should initiate an overhaul of the culture that has been historically plagued by excessive male domination. It would require an extensive rework of the recruitment, hiring, advancement, and retention of employees.

A deeper understanding of women's experiences in the profession is needed to explore the ways in which the profession can advance and move forward and create a more equitable and inclusive environment (Scraton and Flintoff 2013; Kane and LaVoi 2018). The culture and environment of the profession – taxing work schedules and heavy team commitments – disproportionally undermines women. While male S&C coaches are also negatively impacted by the work schedules and commitments, the social and cultural expectation of heterosexual women to serve as the primary caregiver at home conflicts with the demands of the profession and subsequently holds women back from potentially accessing the field, and certainly advancing within the profession. We do not see similar disadvantages for male S&C coaches who are also parents. There are also cultural expectations surrounding the strength coach in terms of appearance and background (Edmonds 2018). There is a perception that women strength coaches must prove their physical abilities because of their gender. In contrast, the assumption is that male strength coaches have inherent knowledge and abilities because of their gender. The landscape of women's sport has significantly changed, yet societal barriers, stereotypes, and expectations continue to restrict women's participation and experiences in sport. Having more female representation in S&C is one way in which to challenge and debunk that misperception.

REFERENCES

Acosta, R.V. and Carpenter, L.J. (2014) *Women in intercollegiate sport: A longitudinal national study thirty-seven-year update. 1977-2014* [Online]. Available at: www.acostacarpenter.org (Accessed: 27 September 2021).

Baechle, T. and Earle, R. (1992) "Survey: Does being C.S.C.S. certified make a difference?," *National Strength and Conditioning Journal*, 14, pp. 23–27.

Banwell, J., Stirling, A. and Kerr, G. (2019) "Towards a process for advancing women in coaching through mentorship," *International Journal of Sports Science & Coaching*, 14(6), pp. 703–713. doi: 10.1177/1747954119883108.

Bishop, C.J. *et al.* (2019) "Advertising paid and unpaid job roles in sport: An updated position statement from the UK Strength and Conditioning Association," *British Journal of Sports Medicine*, 53(13), pp. 789–790. doi: 10.1136/bjsports-2018-099047.

Bledman, R. (2011) *The ideal body shape of African American/Black college women*, dissertation, University of Missouri. doi: 10.32469/10355/14193.

Bordo, S. (1990) "Reading the slender body," in Jacobus, M., Keller, E.F. and Shuttleworth, S. (eds.) *Body/politics: Women and the discourse of science*. New York: Routledge, pp. 83–112.

Bower, G.G. (2009) "Effective mentoring relationships with women in sport: Results of a meta-ethnography," *Advancing Women in Leadership Journal*, 29(3). doi: 10.18738/awl.v29i0.268.

Brace-Govan, J. (2004) "Weighty matters: Control of women's access to physical strength," *The Sociological Review*, 52(4), pp. 503–531. doi: 10.1111/j.1467-954X.2004.00493.x.

Brooks, D.D. *et al.* (2000) "Leadership behavior and job responsibilities of NCAA Division 1A strength and conditioning coaches," *The Journal of Strength and Conditioning Research*, 14(4), pp. 483–492. doi: 10.1519/1533-4287(2000)014<0483:LBAJRO>2.0.CO;2.

Burton, L.J. *et al.* (2009) "'Think athletic director, think masculine?': Examination of the gender typing of managerial subroles within athletic administration positions," *Sex Roles*, 61(5–6), pp. 416–426. doi: 10.1007/s11199-009-9632-6.

Burton, L.J. (2015) "Underrepresentation of women in sport leadership: A review of research," *Sport Management Review*, 18(2) pp.155–165. doi: 10.1016/j.smr.2014.02.004.

Burton, L.J., Grappendorf, H. and Henderson, A. (2011) "Perceptions of gender in athletic administration: Utilizing role congruity to examine (potential) prejudice against women," *Journal of Sport Management*, 25(1), pp. 36–45. doi: 10.1123/jsm.25.1.36.

Chalabaev, A. *et al.* (2013) "The influence of sex stereotypes and gender roles on participation and performance in sport and exercise: Review and future directions," *Psychology of Sport and Exercise*, 14(2), p. 136–144. doi: 10.1016/j.psychsport.2012.10.005.

Choi, P.Y.L. (2003) "Muscle matters: Maintaining visible differences between women and men," *Sexualities, Evolution & Gender*, 5(2), pp. 71–81. doi: 10.1080/14616660310001632554.

Clément-Guillotin, C., Chalabaev, A. and Fontayne, P. (2012) "Is sport still a masculine domain? A psychological glance," *International Journal of Sport Psychology*, 43, pp. 67–78.

Collegiate Strength and Conditioning Coaches Association (CSCCa). (2021) *About the CSCCa*. https://cscca.org/about.

Connell, R.W. and Messerschmidt, J.W. (2005) "Hegemonic masculinity," *Gender & Society*, 19(6), pp. 829–859. doi: 10.1177/0891243205278639.

D'Alonzo, K.T. and Fischetti, N. (2008) "Cultural beliefs and attitudes of Black and Hispanic college-age women toward exercise," *Journal of Transcultural Nursing*, 19(2), pp. 175–183. doi: 10.1177/1043659607313074.

Darvin, L. and Sagas, M. (2017) "An examination of homologous reproduction in the representation of assistant coaches of women's teams: A 10-year update," *Gender Issues*, 34(2), pp. 171–185. doi: 10.1007/s12147-016-9169-2.

Dworkin, S.L. (2001) "'Holding back': Negotiating a glass ceiling on women's muscular strength," *Sociological Perspectives*, 44(3), pp. 333–350. doi: 10.1525/sop.2001.44.3.333.

Eagly, A.H. and Karau, S.J. (2002) "Role congruity theory of prejudice toward female leaders," *Psychological Review*, 109(3), pp. 573–598. doi: 10.1037/0033-295X.109.3.573.

Edmonds, S. (2018) "Bodily capital and the strength and conditioning professional," *Strength & Conditioning Journal*, 40(6), pp. 9–14. doi: 10.1519/SSC.0000000000000356.

Embry, A., Padgett, M.Y. and Caldwell, C.B. (2008) "Can leaders step outside of the gender box? An examination of leadership and gender role stereotypes," *Journal of Leadership & Organizational Studies*, 15(1), pp. 30–45. doi: 10.1177/1548051808318412.

Epley, B. (2019) *The golden age of strength and conditioning*. Indian Trail, NC: The Core Media Group.

Grappendorf, H. et al. (2008) "Gender role stereotyping: A qualitative analysis of senior woman administrators' perceptions regarding financial decision making," *Journal of Sport Management*, 25, pp. 36–45.

Greenwood, R. et al. (2008) *Handbook of organization intuitionalism*. London: Sage.

Grogan, S. et al. (2004) "Femininity and muscularity: Accounts of seven women body builders," *Journal of Gender Studies*, 13(1), pp. 49–61. doi: 10.1080/0958923032000184970.

Hartshorn, M.D. et al. (2016) "Profile of a strength and conditioning coach: Backgrounds, duties, and perceptions," *Strength & Conditioning Journal*, 38(6), pp. 89–94. doi: 10.1519/SSC.0000000000000255.

Hartzell, A.C. and Dixon, M.A. (2019) "A holistic perspective on women's career pathways in athletics administration," *Journal of Sport Management*, 33(2), pp. 1–14. doi: 10.1123/jsm.2018-0127.

Hindman, L.C. and Walker, N.A. (2020) "Sexism in professional sports: How women managers experience and survive sport organizational culture," *Journal of Sport Management*, 34(1), pp. 64–76. doi: 10.1123/jsm.2018-0331.

Hovden, J. (2000) "Gender and leadership selection processes in Norwegian sporting organizations," *International Review for the Sociology of Sport*, 35(1), pp. 75–82. doi: 10.1177/101269000035001006.

Inglis, S., Danylchuk, K.E. and Pastore, D.L. (2000) "Multiple realities of women's work experiences in coaching and athletic management," *Women in Sport and Physical Activity Journal*, 9(2), 1–26. doi: 10.1123/wspaj.9.2.1.

Johnson, H.L. (2017) *Pipelines, pathways, and institutional leadership: An update on the status of women in higher education*. Washington, DC: American Council on Education.

Kamphoff, C. (2013) "Bargaining with patriarchy," *Research Quarterly for Exercise and Sport*, 81(3), pp. 360–372.

Kane, M.J. and LaVoi, N. (2018) "An examination of intercollegiate athletic directors' attributions regarding the underrepresentation of female coaches in women's sports," *Women in Sport and Physical Activity Journal*, 26(1), pp. 1–33. doi: 10.1123/wspaj.2016-0031.

Krane, V. (2001) "We can be athletic and feminine, but do we want to? Challenging hegemonic femininity in women's sport," *Quest*, 53(1), pp. 115–133. doi: 10.1080/00336297.2001.10491733.

Krane, V. et al. (2004) "Living the paradox: Female athletes negotiate femininity and muscularity," *Sex Roles*, 50(5), pp. 315–329. doi: 10.1023/B:SERS.0000018888.48437.4f.

Lapchick, R.E. et al. (2020) *The 2021 Racial and Gender Report Card TM Major League Baseball*. Available at: www.tidesport.org.

Laskowski, K.D. and Ebben, W.P. (2016) "Profile of women collegiate strength and conditioning coaches," *Journal of Strength and Conditioning Research*, 30(12), pp. 3481–3493. doi: 10.1519/JSC.0000000000001471.

LaVoi, N.M. and Dutove, J.K. (2012) "Barriers and supports for female coaches: An ecological model," *Sports Coaching Review*, 1(1), pp. 17–37. doi: 10.1080/21640629.2012.695891.

LaVoi, N.M., McGarry, J.E. and Fisher, L.A. (2019) "Final thoughts on women in sport coaching: Fighting the war," *Women in Sport and Physical Activity Journal*, 27(2), pp. 136–140. doi: 10.1123/wspaj.2019-0030.

Magnusen, M.J. and Rhea, D.J. (2009) "Division I athletes' attitudes toward and preferences for male and female strength and conditioning coaches," *Journal of Strength and Conditioning Research*, 23(4), pp. 1084–1090. doi: 10.1519/JSC.0b013e318199d8c4.

Markula, P. (1995) "Firm but shapely, fit but sexy, strong but thin: The postmodern aerobicizing female bodies," *Sociology of Sport Journal*, 12(4), pp. 424–453. doi: 10.1123/ssj.12.4.424.

Martinez, D.M. (2004) "Study of the key determining factors for the NCAA Division I head strength and conditioning coach," *The Journal of Strength and Conditioning Research*, 18(1), pp. 5–18. doi: 10.1519/1533-4287(2004)018<0005:SOTKDF>2.0.CO;2.

Massey, C.D. and Vincent, J. (2013) "A job analysis of major college female strength and conditioning coaches," *Journal of Strength and Conditioning Research*, 27(7), pp. 2000–2012. doi: 10.1519/JSC.0b013e31827361a9.

Mazerolle, S. and Eason, C. (2016) "A longitudinal examination of work-life balance in the collegiate setting," *Journal of Athletic Training*, 51(3), pp. 223–231. doi: 10.4085/1062-6050-51.4.03.

McGrath, S.A. and Chananie-Hill, R.A. (2009) "'Big freaky-looking women': Normalizing gender transgression through bodybuilding," *Sociology of Sport Journal*, 26(2), pp. 1–11. doi: 10.1123/ssj.26.2.235.

Medlin-Silver, N., Lampard, P. and Bunsell, T. (2017) "Strength in numbers: An explorative study into the experiences of female strength and conditioning coaches in the UK," in Milner, B. (ed.) *Women in sports: Breaking barriers, facing obstacles*. ABC-CLIO, pp. 125–150. Available at: https://www.researchgate.net/publication/318987795.

Mosewich, A.D. et al. (2009) "Exploring women track and field athletes' meanings of muscularity," *Journal of Applied Sport Psychology*, 21(1), pp. 99–115. doi: 10.1080/10413200802575742.

Mullin, E.M. and Bergan, M.E. (2018) "Cultural and occupational barriers facing women professionals in the field of strength and conditioning," *Strength & Conditioning Journal*, 40(6), pp. 15–20. doi: 10.1519/SSC.0000000000000379.

National Strength and Conditioning Association (NSCA). *National Strength and Conditioning Association's Coaches Survey: A Note of Caution and Confidentiality* (2018). Published online: Employers Council. Available at: https://www.nsca.com/contentassets/d101681d8bfa4f8d8c33b04e99ad9529/2018-nsca-coaches-salary-survey-complete-report.pdf (Accessed: 22 October 2021).

National Strength and Conditioning Association (NSCA). (2021) *Who is the NSCA?* Available at: https://www.nsca.com/about-us/about-us/.

National Strength and Conditioning Association (NSCA). (2021) *NSCA Committees*. Available at: https://www.nsca.com/membership/volunteer-leadership-opportunities/committee/.

Nuzzo, J.L. (2014) "Commercial and noncommercial strength and conditioning practices in the United States," *Strength & Conditioning Journal*, 36(2), pp. 66–72. doi: 10.1519/SSC.0000000000000042.

O'Malley, L.M. and Greenwood, S. (2018) "Female coaches in strength and conditioning—Why so few?," *Strength & Conditioning Journal*, 40(6), pp. 40–48. doi: 10.1519/SSC.0000000000000401.

Pullo, F.M. (1992) "A profile of NCAA Division I strength and conditioning coaches," *Journal of Strength and Conditioning Research*, 6(1), pp. 3481–3493. doi: 10.1519/00124278-199202000-00009.

Roper, E.A. (2002) "Women working in the applied domain: Examining the gender bias in applied sport psychology," *Journal of Applied Sport Psychology*, 14(1), pp. 53–66. doi: 10.1080/10413200209339011.

Roper, E.A. (2008) "Women's career experiences in applied sport psychology," *Journal of Applied Sport Psychology*, 20(4), 408–424. doi: 10.1080/10413200802241840.

Roper, E.A., Fisher, L.A. and Wrisberg, C.A. (2005) "Women's experiences working in the field of sport psychology: A feminist standpoint approach," *The Sport Psychologist*, 19, pp. 32–50.

Ross, S.R. and Shinew, K.J. (2008) "Perspectives of women college athletes on sport and gender," *Sex Roles*, 58(1–2), pp. 40–57. doi: 10.1007/s11199-007-9275-4.

Roth, A. and Basow, S.A. (2004) "Femininity, sports, and feminism," *Journal of Sport and Social Issues*, 28(3), pp. 245–265. doi: 10.1177/0193723504266990.

Russell, W.D. (2002) "Comparison of self-esteem, body satisfaction, and social physique anxiety across males of different exercise frequency and racial background," *Journal of Sport Behavior*, 25(1), pp. 74–90.

Sartore-Baldwin, M.L. (2013) "The professional experiences and work-related outcomes of male and female Division I strength and conditioning coaches," *Journal of Strength and Conditioning Research*, 27(3), pp. 1–11. doi: 10.1519/JSC.0b013e31825c2fd3.

Schull, V.D. and Kihl, L.A. (2019) "Gendered leadership expectations in sport: Constructing differences in coaches," *Women in Sport and Physical Activity Journal*, 27(1), pp. 1–11. doi: 10.1123/wspaj.2018-0011.

Scraton, S. and Flintoff, A. (2013) "Gender, feminist theory, and sport," in Andrews, D.L. and Carrington, B. (eds.) *A companion to sport*. Oxford, UK: John Wiley & Sons, Ltd, pp. 96–111. doi: 10.1002/9781118325261.ch5.

Shuman, K.M. and Appleby, K.M. (2016) "Gender preference? National Collegiate Athletic Association Division I student-athletes and strength and conditioning coaches," *Journal of Strength and Conditioning Research*, 30(10), pp. 2924–2933. doi: 10.1519/JSC.0000000000001384.

Siff, M.C. (2003) "A short history of strength and conditioning." Available at: https://physicalculturestudy.com/2019/09/11/dr-mel-siff-a-short-history-of-strength-and-conditioning-dolfzine-2003-2/.

Steinfeldt, J.A. et al. (2011) "Muscularity beliefs of female college student-athletes," *Sex Roles*, 64(7–8), pp. 543–554. doi: 10.1007/s11199-011-9935-2.

Taylor, E.A. and Wells, J.E. (2017) "Institutionalized barriers and supports of female athletic directors: A multilevel perspective," *Journal of Intercollegiate Sport*, 10(2), pp. 157–183. doi: 10.1123/jis.2016-0041.

Thomas, G., Guinan, J. and Molnár, G. (2021) "'It's not particularly P.C., you know…' Women coaches' performing gender in strength and conditioning," *Women in Sport and Physical Activity Journal*, 29(2), pp. 1–11.

Todd, J., Lovett, D. and Todd, T. (1991) "The status of women in strength and conditioning profession," *Strength and Conditioning Journal*, 13, pp. 35–38.

Whisenant, W.A., Pedersen, P.M. and Obenour, B.L. (2002) "Success and gender: Determining the rate of advancement for intercollegiate athletic directors," *Sex Roles*, 47, pp. 485–491. doi: 10.1023/A:1021656628604.

Part II
Gender Binary Troubles

8
Patriarchy and Its Discontents

Eric Anderson

An institution controlled by men will benefit…

Linguistically, the term 'patriarchy' originates from Greek and has been widely adopted in modern social sciences. It was mostly used in the study of cultural anthropology as a descriptor to label the family structure in which the male patriarch makes decisions – similar to its first usage. It has, however, been overly and incorrectly used ever since as, I argue, patriarchy is a concept, not a theory. For something to be a theory, it should be testable, empirical, and capable of making predictions. It should also be falsifiable. I argue that patriarchy, as either previously or currently used, is none of those things. Today, the term patriarchy is used within social sciences, more broadly, and particularly in gender studies, to denote the framework by which men are advantaged as a group in society. Holmes (2007, p. 2), for example, defines it as 'a social system in which men have come to be dominant in relation to women.' This is an inadequate definition because scholars have made the mistake of assuming that because something is controlled by men, it must also always favour men. Yet, *controlled by* is not the same as *controlled for*.

A salient example of this comes from maritime laws, which have historically been written by men. Throughout the 20th Century, it was men who sailed the ships, and the male work force of captains who controlled all decision making on their vessels. Yet, when the Titanic hit an iceberg, the patriarchal system aboard that ship (as with all other sinking ships of the century) benefited women, not men. As a result of the maritime industry's organisational patriarchy, 74% of women on board the ship were saved, compared to 18% of men (Barhoom et al. 2019). This was not a statistical reflection of the White Star Cruise Line employees being mostly men either as 91% of female staff survived compared to 21% of males. Arguably, the men who controlled maritime policies – the men with power – used that power to favour the saving of women's lives, over men. I argue that if women had been included in the making of maritime policy, it is unlikely they would have viewed men's lives as being equal to their own. This suggestion is made because the Titanic sank in 1912, and there was no movement of women calling for their draft into the Great War in 1914. Conversely, some women handed out white feathers to military-aged males on the streets as a mark of shame and cowardice (Gullace 1997).

Another patriarchal organisational structure is the United States Military, which, as of this writing, are on their 46th consecutive male leader. Yet, when the nation's liberties were either attacked, as in World War Two, or perceived to be under threat (rightly or wrongly) in the following decades, it was patriarchy that drafted men into selective services to fight and die against their will. Nobody would deny that many men and some women also volunteered. Equally, nobody would deny that if there is such a thing as a patriarchal structure, the military would be it. However, it is only boys and men alone, who have been conscripted into its service.

There are other patriarchal institutions that benefit women over men. Doerner and Demuth (2012) use data from the United States Sentencing Commission (2001–2003) to examine the role of gender in the sentencing of defendants in federal courts. Overall, they found that female defendants receive more lenient sentences, even when extra-legal factors are considered. Similarly, Fluharty-Jaidee et al. (2018) use data collected from the now disbanded South Carolina Sentencing Commission (1982–2003) where women were consistently sentenced more leniently than men for similar charges (see also Richards et al. 2016). Likewise, in juvenile justice systems, results again indicate that girls were more likely to be sentenced to group homes and boys were more likely to be sentenced to correctional facilities in Los Angeles County for first-time offences (Tam et al. 2016).

Part of this is likely attributable to the powerful arguments made by feminist criminologists that incarceration has particularly damaging experiences for women, given that prisons were originally devised solely for men (Carlen 1990). Yet, this is not how patriarchy is analysed among feminist scholars. They tend to see females as victims. I argue that they never have been, and are not now. Gender, power, and inequality are much more complicated than that. This should not be mistaken for a platform of suggesting that men should solely control organisations or society at large. It, however, does say that when one is ruled by an unequal gender balance, that imbalance will not always favour the majority. That is, the concept of patriarchy is unhelpful to the social sciences and, ultimately, politics of equality.

Patriarchy as commonly used

As noted above, patriarchy is not a theory. Nor is it any longer just a descriptive term for a society in which men make formal decisions. I argue that it is not definable, nor provable. It has adherents who believe that patriarchy controls everything, and detractors who argue patriarchy is an illusion. I recognise that patriarchy exists – increasingly less – in a numerical way. Men dominate numerically in the decision making for the formal structures of politics, laws, business, church and other important institutions. However, because men control these institutions, they are not always advantaged by them. Neither do men make decisions that favour women. I argue that patriarchy, thus, exists more as an ontology than an empirically demonstrable social fact.

The philosophy of patriarchy

When sociologists discuss patriarchy, it is normally understood as the social structures which are primarily controlled by men. The operation of patriarchy has formed the basis for a broad range of academic work. Gerda Lerner's (1986) book, *The Creation of Patriarchy*, situates the concept of patriarchy in family systems organised around the primacy of the father in 19th Century anthropological studies. Seeing its evolution (and with each generation it has decreased specific meaning), Weber (1947) used the concept to refer to a system of government in which men dominated societies through their position as heads of households. Either way, the idea among those who use the term is that men used their positions to disproportionately distribute wealth to males over females.

Wealth can be material, power and/or rights. Thus, women in the 19th Century were denied the right to vote (in what is a rather complex history having much to do with land ownership and recognising that some women did vote, and some men did not), oftentimes to work, or to make their own decisions about marriage and family. Sport is certainly one arena where women were historically denied equality. Feminist activism and liberalising attitudes have, however, seen the repeal of oppressive laws and women being granted the same rights as men in many Western societies. Genital mutilation (of females but not males) is illegal, women can divorce for any reason, they can fight in combat in many countries (if they choose to) and have all the legal rights in modern democracies that men do. Women today not only have the right to a state-sponsored education, but they graduate from university at higher rates than men, according to HESA (the Higher Education Statistics Agency) (2021) data from 2015 to 2020. It is important to recognise these progressive changes, while simultaneously highlighting the real cultural issues that persist. Some of these cultural issues affect women negatively, others affect men negatively (Anderson and Magrath 2019). Basic patriarchal argument maintains that if these institutions are dominated by men, they will – intentionally or not – serve to benefit men more than women. Evidence of this, however, only exists in the representation of men in these positions; there is no systematic evidence showing that the state disproportionally discriminates against women compared to men, and there is considerable evidence that the reverse is sometimes true (Anderson and Magrath 2019).

Feminist views of patriarchy

To explain how some feminists often view patriarchy and its reproduction, I turn to Sylvia Walby's (1989) influential book, *Theorizing Patriarchy*. Walby (1989) argues that there are six structures which restrict women's freedom in society and reproduce male dominance: paid work, household production, culture, sexuality, violence and the state. Here, I do not engage with each of these in detail; rather I provide a simple overview of each structure, with varying detail as some continue to be more relevant than others.

Feminism has helped bring about positive change toward human equality, but many influential feminists do not find the concept of patriarchy helpful. Acker (1989, p. 235) highlighted that patriarchy was applied by radical feminists in a manner that saw it as a 'universal, trans-historical and trans-cultural phenomenon.' Even in 1975, Rubin argued that patriarchy had been used too broadly, applied to most societies, and as such lost its utility (similarly, feminism may no longer be helpful in achieving human equality). One interesting framing of gender inequality beyond patriarchy is to consider gender as a social structure (Risman 2004). A social structure, or social institution, is central to how a society is ordered and used by individuals to process their experiences and go about their lives. A social structure is also held to be systematic – change is difficult to achieve as structures are bolstered by social norms and rituals. A similar term to gender as a social structure is 'gender regime.'

I think this kind of framing is more sophisticated than patriarchy, principally because it enables an understanding of how gender impacts upon both men and women. As Rubin (1975) argued, patriarchy *presumes* men's dominance over women and does not allow for social change. We need a theory that allows for men and women to be advantaged and disadvantaged and to critically analyse the social structures that lead to gender being so damaging. The idea of gender regime permits an understanding of how men are harmed by gender too. Consequently, I argue that the philosophy of feminism has run its useful course. It is a dated view of gender and equality. Its very label favours females over male and non-binary (trans and others), and its very loud social media adherents make it hostile to engage with. I argue that we need a movement of *gender equality activist*. This term indicates that what one desires is equality in law and culture for any and all genders. Who can disagree with that?

Paid work

Walby's (1989) paid work clause has largely been watered-down, replaced, by claims of unequal pay in the workforce – the gender pay gap. There is limited merit in suggesting that, in some sectors, women and men do the same task under different titles, with varying pay. However, the concept of the gender pay gap is the suggestion that women make 70% of what men make, for the same job, is not true. It is, in fact, illegal to pay women less than men for the same job. What the gender pay gap does is to examine an entire industry, and all the roles within, to then average the pays. Take airlines, where there is a gender pay gap differential that needs further analysis; men are pilots and women cabin crew, and nobody is going to argue that pilots be paid the same as cabin crew. This makes the gender pay gap an illusion of patriarchy. What counts is not the gender pay gap, but the question: are women paid the same for the same level of education, experience, and competency as men? If they are not, a lawsuit surely awaits.

This is not to suggest that women (as a whole in any industry) earn the same as men. In many industries, they do not. A meta-analysis of the gender pay gap literature, however, shows that this is not a matter of discriminatory policy as the first wave of feminists fought against. It is mostly a reflection of the fact that more women than men take time away from their careers when they have children (Bishu and Alkadry 2017).

Nevertheless, there are certain industries in which equal pay for equal work becomes more problematic to control and people are not paid for their volume of work, but their ability to draw clients, fans or consumers (e.g., sport). In most sports, professional male athletes make more money than professional female athletes. This reflects their bargaining power in an industry that is far more profitable for males than for females. Women in these sports are free to demand equal pay, but salary negotiation is depending upon the sporting organisations' abilities to pay those demands. Conversely, tennis players in the Wimbledon competition are paid equally for winning the male and female categories, despite the fact that women play fewer sets in the event.

Household production

The second area where men have traditionally been advantaged concerns how men have maintained economic control over the household, limiting how women can spend family income. Walby (1989) argues that family men benefit from women's unpaid labour. For Walby, instead of the family being a source of rich-support, security, and equality for women, it is instead '…central to women's lives and to the determination of gender *inequality*' (1989, p. 61). Similarly, functionalist sociologists (see Parsons and Bales 1955) had argued the family was a place of nurturing and support for men. Yet, Walby argued that while this was often the case (many people have loving families), the family was also a place of gender inequality. This is a long-standing feminist proposition: patriarchy begins at home. Arguments for this not only concern economic agency, but the fact that studies, then and now, continue to show that women do most of the housework and childcare, in heterosexual relationships (Hochschild 1989). Many of these studies do not, however, examine the amount of outdoor labour men do at home. Such studies depict men lying around waiting for women to serve them without having served women by making the household's money. However, much has changed for women since Walby wrote this. Today, most heterosexual couples work and they pay to export much of the household labour: the grocery store delivers food, they pay to have their houses cleaned, and they put their children into nurseries or they get state-funded nursery vouchers.

Sexuality

Walby (1989) is not referring to sexual minorities or sexual orientation when she uses the word; instead, she uses sexuality as a node of power that structures experience. Hence, I note that since Walby's writings, LGBTQ social and legal equality have emerged. I also note that, to my knowledge, gay and lesbian couples have not been examined for patriarchy in the domestic sphere. That is because studies of those families would show that everybody works, in one way or another, to keep the household running. In essence, the study of patriarchy is also heterosexist.

Walby (1989) highlights that women's bodies are objectified in multiple cultural capacities, including the workforce, and that this serves the pleasure of men while simultaneously undermining the talent of women in the workplace. No place is this more salient, Walby (1989) argues, than in pornography. She argues that pornography is a central site for debates about the regulation of sexual expression in society. One needs only think of the word 'porn' and imagine ways in which, despite its prominence, society tends to view it negatively. In the 1970s and 1980s, feminists developed a critique of pornography that claimed it perpetuated social issues, such as rape and wider gender inequality. Porn was seen as equivalent to violence against women. Perhaps none were more famous/infamous for their activism than Dworkin (1978), who seemed to know no limits to her claims of the evils of pornography, even titling a book: *Pornography: The New Terrorism*. Yet, this provoked heated debate among feminists with arguments against this position (see Rubin 1993). Indeed, a broad body of academic research continues to focus on the negative effects of pornography (see Flood 2009). There is hysteria around porn; it is blamed for all forms of social ills, even when the evidence for this is weak, easily refuted or non-existent (Grubbs et al. 2018).

Pornography has radically changed since Walby's time; no longer is pornography just male on-top of female. There is now a democratisation of the porn industry which is diminishing rapidly, as free pornography and user-made pornography dominates (Anderson 2012). This is a democracy with equal opportunity to click, shoot, and post resulting in major porn websites having varying categories, so we can all find what we desire.

Violence

Walby (1989) argues that violence against women is a form of male privilege and male control over women. Male violence against women comes in numerous forms, including rape, sexual assault, domestic violence, sexual harassment in the workplace, etc. Although there is a global trend of decreasing violence (Pinker 2011), there is still a gender issue in regard to recognizing violence by men, over women. Indeed, if we take a look at the statistics accompanying some of these issues, almost all indicate how women are far more likely to be the victim of certain types of violence. In the UK, for example, the Office for National Statistics (ONS) estimated in 2019 that there are approximately 1.6 million female victims of domestic abuse a year, compared with 786,000 male victims, who may also be less likely to report violence.

Statistics for sexual violence illustrate a similar trend. In 2017, ONS showed that one in five women in the UK between the ages of 16 and 59 have experienced some form of sexual abuse since turning 16 (ONS 2017). Elsewhere, in a study from 2000–2018, the World Health Organization (WHO) estimate that one in three women throughout the world will experience physical and/or sexual violence by either a partner or non-partner (WHO 2021). I argue that the broader trends here are generalizable since these statistics were first collected, i.e., the number of women murdered by (male) partners or ex-partners is far greater than the reverse. It is important, of course, to remember that these statistics may also reflect an under-reporting of crimes (for both sexes), and depending on the questions, it might reflect an under-reporting by one sex over another.

Women are, statistically, more likely to be victims of sexual abuse in the US and across most other Western nations. Though, men are more likely to be physically assaulted or murdered. There is no doubt that men far outnumber women in terms of stranger-assault, and murder. There is no doubt that men far outnumber deaths in war than women. A mainstream feminist argument here is that these issues are less important because it is also men doing the damage.

A salient example of this trope comes from Suzanna Danuta Walters (2018), who is the editor of the highest ranked feminist journal of gender studies, *Signs*. She wrote in an opinion piece in the Washington Post on June 8, 2018, titled, *Why Can't We Hate Men?*:

> So men, if you really are #WithUs and would like us to not hate you for all the millennia of woe you have produced and benefited from, start with this: Lean out so we can actually just stand up without being beaten down. Pledge to vote for feminist women only. Don't run for office. Don't be in charge of anything. Step away from the power. We got this. And please know that your crocodile tears won't be wiped away by us anymore. We have every right to hate you. You have done us wrong. #BecausePatriarchy. It is long past time to play hard for Team Feminism. And win.

In this proclamation, Walters blurs the line between academic and activist, and selectively ignores the problems of men, while promoting both misandry and total matriarchy. Her call, however, evades the complexity of the issue: on violence, some women are perpetrators, and many women are victims. More men are perpetrators, and many men are victims. Again, a binary account of gender is inadequate.

The state

Walby (1989) defines 'the state' as a specific set of social institutions which maintain social cohesion and control. Evidence of patriarchy here is the exclusion of women from a direct presence in the state and a lack of power to influence the state. 'Women are excluded from access to state resources and power as part of a patriarchal system' (Walby 1989, p. 224). However, this is hyperbole today as women are not denied access to any state resource, and they are free to vote more women into office. However, women choose not to run for public office in disproportionate numbers to their gender (i.e., less than 50%), and when they vote, they tend to vote for men over women. Pew Research (Pew 2018) shows that women turn out, on average, in 4% larger numbers to vote than men. If they voted for female candidates over male, Hillary Clinton would have been the 45th President of the United States. Instead, they chose an inexperienced politician, known for right-wing ideology, promotion of violence, and downright mockery of women over one of America's most seasoned female politicians. If there was ever a figure that symbolised 'patriarchy,' it is Donald Trump, and women voted him into office. Thus, if state-run patriarchy exists, it is partially the wilful result of American women's choice. Nevertheless, I wish to highlight that women are increasingly running for and being elected to office. In 1989, Walby noted that only 6% of Members of Parliament in the UK were female; similar statistics were true in the US Congress. Today, about 32% are female in the UK Parliament, 20% of the US Congress is female, and 21% of the American Senate are women.

Patriarchy and sport

The argument I make is: feminism explicated patriarchy on these distinct disadvantages. Those disadvantages have been hard-fought and won. Women today have legal equality with men. Issues that remain in Walbys' list are more complicated. Where Walby went wrong, however, was to avoid the examination of patriarchy in sport. Sport was founded as an institution that was run by men and for the promotion and benefit of men. To prove the contrary, I have spent much of my academic career (e.g., Anderson 2005) showing that the foundation of sport as a male enterprise was not purely about giving men access to another form of income, or access to play fun games. I have shown that the promotion of organised, competitive sport emerged only in the 19th Century as a result of the fear that men were becoming too soft, too gay, too feminine. Instead of viewing sport as a socio-positive institution, I view its origins as an attempt to control men's bodies, and uniformly shape their gendered belief system into sacrificing for the sake of family, corporation, and country. I highlight (Anderson 2005) that the institution emerged after the growing awareness of homosexuality, the industrial revolution, and the Great War. I show that organised sport was a political project to assure that young boys would volunteer for war and to follow the orders of older males. Sport encouraged males to sacrifice life and limb in coal mines and factories and was utilised to 'produce' heterosexual young boys. This is not what privilege looks like. Still, as gender is complicated, in the actual playing of sport, and profiting from it, there are some uniquely male advantages today.

To elaborate on male advantages, I highlight two categories: the first concerns biological advantages. Here, men have the advantage of urinating while standing, not having menstruation, and not having to carry children. There are both medical and social actions we can take to lessen these advantages: more toilets in women's restrooms, medicine to relieve symptoms of menstruation, not taxing tampons, and parental leave policies in the workforce. Still, there will be advantages that remain, particularly in sport. The list of the male advantage in sport is huge. But let's not get stuck into testosterone wars, or explaining how male osteology promotes performance, or how men maintain greater aerobic capacities, etc. Instead, let us just examine one thing that never gets analysed: men have bigger bladders than women (Haylen et al. 1989). Anyone who has ever run a marathon will know the value of that. The other advantages are mostly the result of how societies are organised, which then relate to sport. These include men being seen (by both men and women) as better leaders, having some advantages in employment, and also having their interests represented because men are over-represented in most influential institutions. It is this latter advantage that some call patriarchy. I choose three advantages to examine that, peripherally or directly, relate to sport: medical advantages, leadership advantages, and sporting profits.

Men's Advantages

Medical advantages

In 1992, Eichler, Reisman and Borins (1992, p. 62) argued that 'medical research displays the same types of gender bias as have been documented for the social sciences.' Here, women have historically been excluded from being subjects in toxicological and biomedical research. Resulting in the development of modern medicine has largely been for the benefit of men: a medical gender bias. This bias has its roots in the requirements of science, which necessitates that extraneous variables are held constant to examine a drug's effect. Thus, the bias is not intentional, but rather a requirement of science. Women's bodies have higher rates of shifting hormones, as part of their monthly menstruation cycle, and therefore men's bodies are easier subjects for medical studies (Regitz-Zagrosek 2012). This is why most lab studies on animals are also done on male animals (Kooti et al. 2015).

Another reason for the removal of women from drug trials concerns the thalidomide crisis of the 1960s. Here, pregnant women taking the drug had children with serious birth defects. This had the obvious impact of reminding researchers that women taking experimental drugs might also mean that developing children were, too. Not wanting to harm children with experimental drugs, men's bodies are rationally preferred for medical trials (Scaffidi, Mol and Keelan 2017). Once the efficacy of a drug has then been established, it is then prescribed to women on a prorated basis, according to, for example, body weight. This could be mistaken as an advantage for women: being in drug tests is risky and can cause serious harm, so the men who do so are at extra risk. Yet, comparing at a *group* level, the biological differences between men's and women's bodies and variations in how they respond to drugs means that men are now structurally advantaged in the availability of medication. We are learning that dosages of medicine for men (controlled by body weight) may not be right for women (see Krystal and Attarian 2016). These, and other unknown reasons, are why in 1993, the National Institute of Health mandated that women (and certain minority groups) should be included in any government-funded health research. The problem is that most drug development funding comes from pharmaceutical industries and not government grants, meaning the problem persists. The only way around this is that women will have to be subjected to drug trials as well.

By examining an advantage that most have not previously considered, men's medical research and resultant care, I relate it to sport performance because medicine and sport sciences have worked together to promote sporting performance. While I mainly detail the impact of gendered medicine on general wellbeing, one can assume that the same is true of medical interventions in the realm of sport. How much cortisone to inject? How might concessive tests vary for women to men? I have not done extensive research here on these questions; I pose this as a medical issue in which it seems logical that there will be some ramifications in sport medicine, as well. At least it remains an open question.

Leadership advantages

In terms of progression and promotion of those coaching/training athletes, I also argue that men are assumed to be more competent leaders than women, a finding that has emerged in multiple countries studied, including China, Japan, the UK, US, and Germany (Schein et al. 1996). Culturally, we might point towards claims of male dominance in coaching positions to the fact that a key 'trait' of masculinity is that men possess and exhibit greater assertiveness than women. Women are, instead, culturally expected to possess 'traits' such as subservience and emotionality. Norman (2010) identifies ways that female leaders in sport are viewed as less competent and patronised by males in the profession. There might be some form of evolutionary advantage that males, particularly tall males, have, too. Hamstra (2014) shows that tall men have an advantage in getting into management roles and are also generally perceived to be more successful in those roles than shorter people. And because of the morphological differences between men and women, this provides another explanation for men's dominance.

Other factors also help create leadership as male terrain. For instance, childcare responsibilities also hinder the ability of heterosexually-married or single women to engage in the long days and nights required to progress – to achieve success. Women must, naturally, take more time out than men from work when having a baby. Yet, the predominance of early years' childcare, and the burden placed on a heterosexual family, is social and up to that individual family. Linking back to paternal leave, heterosexual families must make decisions about who takes how much time off or reduces work capacity. Social policy has, until recently, presumed that it is women and not men who will take this caring role.

Regardless of the explanations for this dominance, the simple fact is: men continue to dominate top managerial, coaching, team ownership, and other stakeholder positions in sport. Men tend to be assumed as better leaders than women, thus giving men significant advantage over women. It is for this reason that, generalising to the whole sporting industry, the key positions of sport are currently occupied by about 86% men in the Anglo-American world (Anderson and White 2017).

Sporting profits

Sport itself is also deeply gendered, because it flows from sexed differences in the mean averages of male and female bodies. Hence, if one adds up the strength of 100 18-year-old men, they will be stronger than 100 18-year-old women. The same would occur for speed explosiveness, power and jumping distances. This, in turn, means that sportsmen are usually paid more than sportswomen: because elite men are unquestionably better at performing the sports that we socially value. In football, for example, the average weekly wage for a Premier League player – the most elite men's league in the UK – exceeds £50,000. For the comparative league in women's football, the average salary is £26,752 *a year*(!). In this capacity, a very few – the elite of the elite – male athletes make considerably much more money than the very few – the elite of the elite – female athletes. Of course, there are some exceptions: male and female tennis players earn the same prize for winning the annual Wimbledon Tennis Championships, even though there is no evidence that female tennis is equally or more popular than male tennis, and even though women at Wimbledon only play three sets, compared to the men's five. Also, in late 2017, Norway became the first country in the world to pay its male and female footballers the same salary.

There may be various extenuating circumstances as to why men are paid so much more money for playing these sports. Even a cursory glance at sporting salaries reveals just how large the disparity is, and some female athletes aren't even professional. But athletes – whether male or female – are participating at their absolute physical limits. This entire process is a vicious circle. Men's sports are far more popular than women's (in terms of those listed above), because elite male athletes outperform elite female athletes and some deem it less exciting resulting in less media coverage. It is hard to see how women's sports will be granted equal pay to men's sports, unless women's sports bring in as much money as men's sports, or if men's sports subsidise women's. It is evident that women will not compete to the same degree of performance as men, at least without chemical intervention, and this suggests that women are at a biological disadvantage in earning a living, or becoming wealthy, from sporting prowess. Walby missed this institution, a major source of employment, in her analysis. And unlike her other mentions, this one has not progressed. It has not progressed because it stems mostly from biological variance, and some existing cultural inequality. There does not seem to be progress in changing this, either because sport is funded through capitalism, and people seem to be far more willing to pay, or pay more, to watch men compete over women.

Still, the industry is under threat. Sport exists as a bifurcated system. In recent years, transgender, intersex, gender queer, and non-binary individuals have questioned and demanded change to the system. This has divided feminists. For example, should transgender males competing in sport against cisgender women be able to win medals and be rewarded financially? If so, should they have to have medical or surgical alteration? Or is gender a matter of the brain, and self-identity is all that counts? These athletes (and non-athletes) contest what it means to be male or female in the first place. Do trans males count as part of the patriarchal order? How about gay males? Are those who appear to be male but identify as female equally as culpable? When prominent feminist, academic, and journal editor Suzanna Danuta Walters decries that it's okay to hate men, just who is she talking about? This is a highly complicated, hostile, and complex terrain that requires further exploration and debate (see Anderson and Travers 2017).

REFERENCES

Acker, J. (1989) The problem with patriarchy. *Sociology, 23*(2), pp. 235–240. https://doi.org/10.1177/0038038589023002005

Anderson, E. (2005) *In the game: Gay athletes and the cult of masculinity*. SUNY Press. New York.

Anderson, E. (2012) *The monogamy gap: Men, love, and the reality of cheating*. Oxford University Press. Oxford.

Anderson, E. and Magrath, R. (2019) *Men and masculinities*. Routledge. London.

Anderson, E. and Travers, A. (eds.) (2017) *Transgender athletes in competitive sport*. Taylor and Francis. London.

Anderson, E and White, A. (2017). *Sport, Theory and Social Problems A Critical Introduction* (2nd Ed). London: Routledge.

Barhoom, A.M., Khalil, A.J., Abu-Nasser, B.S., Musleh, M.M. and Naser, S.S.A. (2019) Predicting Titanic survivors using artificial neural network. *International Journal of Academic Engineering Research, 3*(9), pp. 8–12.

Bishu, S.G. and Alkadry, M.G. (2017) A systematic review of the gender pay gap and factors that predict it. *Administration and Society, 49*(1), pp. 65–104.

Carlen, P. (1990) *Alternatives to women's imprisonment*. Open University Press, Milton Keynes.

Danuta Walters, S. (2018) Opinion: Why can't we hate men? *The Washington Post*, 8th June, https://www.washingtonpost.com/opinions/why-cant-we-hate-men/2018/06/08/f1a3a8e0-6451-11e8-a69c-b944de66d9e7_story.html

Doerner, J.K. and Demuth, S. (2012) Gender and sentencing in the federal courts: Are women treated more leniently?. *Criminal Justice Policy Review, 25*(2), pp. 242–269.

Dworkin, A. (1978) Pornography: The new terrorism. *NYU Review of Law and Social Change, 8*, p. 215.

Eichler, M., Reisman, A.L. and Borins, E.M. (1992) Gender bias in medical research. *Women and Therapy, 12*(4), pp. 61–70.

Flood, M. (2009) The harms of pornography exposure among children and young people. *Child Abuse Review: Journal of the British Association for the Study and Prevention of Child Abuse and Neglect, 18*(6), pp. 384–400.

Fluharty-Jaidee, J.T., DiPonio-Hilliard, T., Neidermeyer, P. and Festa, M. (2018) "Some people claim there's a woman to blame": Gender sentencing disparity in male-dominated professions: Evidence from AICPA infraction data. *Gender in Management: An International Journal, 33*(1), pp. 30–49. https://doi.org/10.1108/GM-04-2016-0085

Gillespie, L.K., Loughran, T.A., Smith, M.D., Fogel, S.J. and Bjerregaard, B. (2014) Exploring the role of victim sex, victim conduct, and victim–defendant relationship in capital punishment sentencing. *Homicide Studies, 18*(2), pp. 175–195.

Grubbs, J.B., Wilt, J.A., Exline, J.J. and Pargament, K.I. (2018) Predicting pornography use over time: Does self-reported "addiction" matter? *Addictive Behaviors, 82*, pp. 57–64.

Gullace, N.F. (1997) White feathers and wounded men: Female patriotism and the memory of the Great War. *Journal of British Studies, 36*(2), pp. 178–206.

Hamstra, M.R. (2014) 'Big' men: Male leaders' height positively relates to followers' perception of charisma. *Personality and Individual Differences, 56*, pp. 190–192.

Haylen, B.T., Ashby, D., Sutherst, J.R., Frazer, M.I. and West, C.R. (1989). Maximum and average urine flow rates in normal male and female populations—the Liverposl nomograms. *British Journal of Urology, 64*(1), 30–38.

HESA (2020) *Who is studying in HE?*, 9th February, https://www.hesa.ac.uk/data-and-analysis/students/whos-in-he (accessed 30th October 2022).

Hochschild, A.R. (1989) *The second shift*. Avon Books: New York.

Holmes, M. (2007) *What is gender?: Sociological approaches*. Sage. London.

Kooti, W., Ghasemi-boroon, M., Ghafourian, M., Asadi-Samani, M., Harizi, M., Sharafi-Ahvazi, N. and Afrisham, R. (2015) The effects of celery leave extract on male hormones in rats. *Journal of HerbMed Pharmacology*, *4*(2), pp. 56–60.

Krystal, A. and Attarian, H. (2016) Sleep medications and women: A review of issues to consider for optimizing the care of women with sleep disorders. *Current Sleep Medicine Reports*, *2*(4), pp. 218–222.

Lerner, G. (1986) *The creation of patriarchy (Vol. 1). Women and History*. Oxford University Press. Oxford.

Norman, L. (2010) Feeling second best: Elite women coaches' experiences. *Sociology of Sport Journal*, *27*(1), pp. 89–104.

Office of National Statistics (2017) *Sexual offences in England and Wales: Year ending March 2017*, https://www.ons.gov.uk/peoplepopulationandcommunity/crimeandjustice/articles/sexualoffencesinengland andwales/yearendingmarch2017 (accessed 31st October 2021).

Office of National statistics (2019) *Domestic abuse victim characteristics England and Wales: Year ending March 2019*, https://www.ons.gov.uk/peoplepopulationandcommunity/crimeandjustice/articles/domestic abusevictimcharacteristicsenglandandwales/yearendingmarch2019 (accessed 31st October 2021).

Parsons, T. and Bales, R. F. (1955). *Family: Socialization and interaction process*. London: Routledge

Pew (2018) https://www.pewresearch.org/fact-tank/2020/08/18/men-and-women-in-the-u-s-continue-to-differ-in-voter-turnout-rate-party-identification/

Pinker, S. (2011) *The better angels of our nature: The decline of violence in history and its causes*. Penguin. New York.

Regitz-Zagrosek, V. (2012) Sex and gender differences in health: Science and Society Series on Sex and Science. *EMBO Reports*, *13*(7), pp. 596–603.

Richards, T.N., Jennings, W.G., Smith, M.D., Sellers, C.S., Fogel, S.J. and Bjerregaard, B. (2016) Explaining the "female victim effect" in capital punishment: An examination of victim sex–specific models of juror sentence decision-making. *Crime and Delinquency*, *62*(7), pp. 875–898.

Risman, B.J. (2004) Gender as a social structure: Theory wrestling with activism. *Gender and society*, *18*(4), pp. 429–450.

Rubin, G. (1975) The traffic in women: Notes on the 'political economy' of sex. In Rayna R. Reiter (ed.), *Toward an Anthropology of Women*. Monthly Review Press, pp. 157–210.

Rubin, G. (1993) Misguided, dangerous, and wrong: An analysis of antipornography politics. *Bad girls and dirty pictures: The challenge to reclaim feminism*. London: Pluto, pp. 18–40.

Scaffidi, J., Mol, B.W. and Keelan, J.A. (2017) The pregnant women as a drug orphan: A global survey of registered clinical trials of pharmacological interventions in pregnancy. *BJOG: An International Journal of Obstetrics and Gynaecology*, *124*(1), pp. 132–140.

Schein, V.E., Mueller, R., Lituchy, T. and Liu, J. (1996) Think manager—think male: A global phenomenon?. *Journal of Organizational Behavior*, *17*(1), pp. 33–41.

Tam, C.C., Abrams, L.S., Freisthler, B. and Ryan, J.P. (2016) Juvenile justice sentencing: Do gender and child welfare involvement matter?. *Children and Youth Services Review*, *64*, pp. 60–65.

Walby, S. (1989) Theorising patriarchy. *Sociology*, *23*(2), pp. 213–234.

Weber, M. (1947) *The theory of social and economic organisation*, trans. A.M. Henderson and T. Parsons. William Hodge and Company Limited. Edinburgh. pp. 328–340.

World Health Organisation (2021) *Violence against women prevalence estimates, 2018*, 9th March, https://www.who.int/publications/i/item/9789240022256 (accessed 30th October 2021).

9
Atrophying Masculinity within Professional Road Cycling
Contesting 'The Male' Through a (Re)scripting of the *Anti*-Male

James J. Brittain

Introduction

Professional road cycling, long recognized as a sport that cherishes tradition and memorializes a fidelity to practice, offers a unique juxtaposition of cultural and sociopolitical significance when concerning the present. What makes this period worthy of evaluation is cycling's sociological currency in potentially challenging themes of power through its disruption of convention. With specific attention devoted to an analysis of 'the male,' and the changing conditionalities surrounding those therein, an effort is made to distinguish how cyclists inside the *peloton* (derived from the French word meaning platoon and used to describe the predominant group of cyclists within a race) may act as architects of a counter-hegemonic masculinity. Appraising the fluidity of identities in sport, the following is centred on the uniqueness of the contemporary professional male road cyclist; a noteworthy sociality that is offering provocation – coupled by contradiction – to its construction and constitution. While engaging an intellectual analysis of cycling, which focuses on a particular socioeconomic stratum of predominantly cisgender white men no-less, may appear trivial (if not verging on offensive), it is worthy to document how this distinct thematic relates to spheres of perception and power. Identifying this may then provide valuable insight into an appraisal of, and inquiry toward, social change and the politics of representation.

Since its development as an empirical technology, the bicycle has long enabled a consequential subjective identity to take shape beside its objective presence (see Vivanco, 2013). Robbins (2013, p. xvi) distinguishes how "the person on a bicycle" is both different *and* differentiates themself from others within a given society. His argument poses that "the bicycle is an identity transforming object" and thus "raises questions about … how people create and maintain social status and identity." Taking such commentary into consideration, the professional male road cyclist can be a valuable sociological figure of inquiry. Affixed to a precise activity (and object), these athletes encapsulate a distinct identity yet mutually embody complex contradictions against the backdrop of heteronormative scripts. Through analyses of autobiographical texts, related published materials, and direct fieldwork involving ethnographic research with existing and former professional male road cyclists, this work interrogates how professional male road cyclists negotiate their congruence to-and-with sport and theoretically captures a re-defining of power through modes of identification and practice. While many professional male road cyclists self-deprecate their occupation as encased in a bubble and estranged from the 'real world' (see The Secret Cyclist, 2019; Dekker, 2017; Gaimon, 2017a; Millar, 2015; Thomas, 2015; Barry, 2014; Dower, 2012; Hamilton and Coyle, 2012), it is worth highlighting that transformation, regardless of perceived magnitude, can reverberate outside the limitations of its proximal beginnings. Moving beyond a solitary vocational subculture, change(s) in this cloistered group muster the prospect to distend and inform a broader mass of how meaning and power may be re-scripted.

The 'Male' cyclist as antithetic

It is always valuable to recognize that socially-constructed conditions leave open the possibility of purposed responses and reconciled solutions. It is not simply in a vein of optimism that such a position holds merit but that alternatives have been shown to be(come) real even against the purview of being unattainable. Through a historical materialist pulse, Abdel-Shehid and Kalman-Lamb (2011) concisely point to how sport inherently facilitates this capacity for change. The authors demonstrate that sport will often enable, if not encourage, deviations to a given practice – which include challenges to conventional masculine discourses – especially if said alterations enhance gains (Abdel-Shehid and Kalman-Lamb, 2011, Chapter 8). Rooted in a political-economic pretence, this important insight can be immediately applied to the sport of cycling.

With consideration to professional male road cycling, a fundamental institutional and symbolic shift has been witnessed when the present is weighed against the past. In the pursuit of success on the road, cycling has entirely reinterpreted how strength is achieved and defined in contrast to a long-tradition heralding heteronormative stereotypes toward manliness. Revering scripts of aggression and brawn, bygone generations framed champions through conventional masculine archetypes via Eddy Merckx [professional career (*pc*), 1965–1978, Belgian] or Bernard Hinault [*pc*, 1974–1986, French], which permeated across eras from Gino Bartali [*pc*, 1935–1954, Italian] to Miguel Induráin [*pc*, 1984–1996, Spanish]. Today, however, power is determined by an inversion of such forms. Road cycling now places power-to-weight ratios as the most acute signifier of aptitude, a process that measures a racer's production of watts per kilogram. The key is to optimize the highest possible output of power while sustaining the lowest possible weight. Aside from this quantitative equation of demonstrable power is the qualitative effect of desire to replicate the ability. An obsession with power-to-weight pervades the peloton, be it existing professionals or up-and-coming amateurs seeking a contract to a top-tier team. Noted cycling commentator Carlton Kirby (2020, p. 98) signifies that in present-day cycling, a rider's size is imperative albeit characterized by diminutive proportions rather than abundance: "a good engine and aero package is vital. In motorsport, this is about light alloy power units and bodywork. In cycling, it is the rider himself who provides these elements." Capturing the mood of this shift, retired professional and recognized cycling journalist James Stout [*pc*, 2011–2013, British] even suggested the peloton experienced its own version of *heroin-chic*. When compared to a period gone by, one "can't help but notice the change in pro cyclists' bodies in the past decade. The Induráin-esque shapes of yesteryear are no longer" (Stout, 2015, p. 141). As charted by one senior rider, "when I joined the pros, everyone was lean, but they weren't skinny by today's standards" (The Secret Cyclist, 2019, p. 27). To gain some form of competitive advantage, methods to reduce weight have become institutionalized (see Marsal, 2021). Rather than exceptions, these practices are now systemic. Within pro cycling, there are cues that celebrate the "well-trained," which is predominantly underscored by leanness (Vaughters, 2019, p. 183). Former pro Jonathan Vaughters [*pc*, 1994–2003, American], currently CEO and Team Manager of a leading professional male road cycling team, has asserted that "extra bulk—is a huge penalty" (Vaughters, 2019, p. 259). Overall, the peloton has witnessed a distinct pivot from presiding interpretations of (male) power, as expressed through mass, opting rather to frame any sign of excess as lacking professionalism and individual discipline (see Thomas, 2020; The Secret Cyclist, 2019; Millar, 2015; Barry, 2014; Hincapie and Hummer, 2014; Hamilton and Coyle, 2012). Mirroring neoliberal ideology, 'leanness' is now cycling's definitive undercurrent.

Be it acclaim or apprehension, this revised model offers an important point of interpretation. A monasticism has been widely absorbed by today's professional male road cyclist. Uniform in expression, this eremitic position is clearly (and widely) adopted by all elite riders (The Secret Cyclist, 2019). The script, which frames accomplishment through a narrative of atrophy and emaciation, is now committed to memory and dutifully recited through a choreography obediently performed. Current riders are personifications of a fidelity to this script (see Kirby, 2020; Thomas, 2015; 2018; 2020; Froome, 2014). Through *this* body, one can see the preferred physicality those in the peloton (culturally, personally, and professionally) strive for – and achieve. Discerned beyond any singular individual or their garnered success, a paradigm has been structurally situated to inform (and discipline) the field. Rather than exception, the atrophied professional is the exemplified specimen, the proper fundamentalist, the most capable of adopting the peloton's current script of prosperity. Amidst all this, however, those in the peloton do more than simply replicate the exemplary cyclist; they reshape an understanding toward how 'the male' form is celebrated. From such a standpoint, one can recognize how the contemporaneous pro does not share, nor desire, in any robust demeanour, the characteristics of power through a herculean masculinity. To the contrary, those in the peloton commemorate and offer an antithetical expression of 'the male' to the heteronormative geography of sport.

The *Anti-*Male peloton

Difficult it is not to identify (the propagation of) an optimal male aesthetic. Popularly mediated, this sketch is readily projected through various communicative platforms. Not unlike the longstanding (mis)representations of the engaging female via mediums of advertisement (see Kilbourne, 1999), the sculpted ab-riddled physique is widely on display and repeated (see Rubio-Hernández, 2010; Alexander, 2003; Benwell, 2003). Beyond its overt mediation in pop-culture, various scholars have shown how this singular depiction is heavily ingrained through sport (Connell, 2005; Pope, Phillips, and Olivardia, 2000; Burstyn, 1999; Bourdieu, 1991). It takes little time for the mind's-eye to envision the branded anatomies of a David Beckham or Cristiano Ronaldo to accede the image being disseminated (see Malcolm, 2010; Rahman, 2004). One can, however, gaze critically upon such interpretations. As previously noted, a challenge can and is being constructed. Cycling provides a reversal of this presiding position. Rather than accepting sport as a homogenous totality, the peloton offers a divergence of-and-toward 'the male.' Not without contradictions, an inimitable culture is being cultivated that may hold a kernel of distinction against predominant interpretations of masculinity.

Unlike athletic counterparts in football, soccer, ice hockey, etcetera – which arguably promote certain elucidations toward the 'ideal' male body –, cycling displays a distinct sociological contest. Contrasting the promotion of the well-defined V-shaped Adonis, symbolic and structural aspirations within cycling advocate its antithesis. Power here is demarcated not through strength-as-observable but rather the absence thereof. "The peloton," as one journalist commented, "is a herd of lycra-clad skeletons on bikes" (Hanson, 2014). When surveying today's most prolific cyclists, one immediately encounters "pipe cleaner legs," "bulbous elbows," and "twig-like arms" (Stout, 2015, p. 141; see also Vaughters, 2019; GCN, 2015a; Hamilton and Coyle, 2012; Barry, 2005). These are not locutions of condemnation or ridicule, however. During various stints of ethnographic data collection, the phrase 'Tyrannosaurus' was repeatedly overheard, under the pretence of humour, harkening the absence of arm muscle in proportion to the overall power associated with the legs of the cretaceous namesake. Albeit cloaked as jest, those with bulky biceps are, in actuality, the subject of ridicule, while those with the smallest arms are subjectively praised. As has been shown, such adjectives frame the optimal form that the majority seek to replicate. The elite within professional road cycling, those who display the greatest qualitative and quantitative representations of power, far from display chiselled pectorals or biceps. To the contrary, this cohort is celebrated for their strictly sustained scarcity. As one recently retired rider suggested, those in the peloton "get paid" for the food they do not consume (Gaimon, 2017a, p. 64). Another pro replicated this praxis as the working reality of their profession: "I'm being paid to stay skinny and to make sure I'm ready to race … that is what we're being paid to do" (The Secret Cyclist, 2019, p. 15). Teetering on praise, Geraint Thomas [*pc*, 2005–*present*, Welsh], Gold Medal Olympian and winner of the 2018 *Tour de France*, nods toward those professionals who organize a sustained diet and training regimen while suggesting the less committed indulge in "all the things cyclists aren't supposed to eat" (Thomas, 2020, p. 62). In this divergence, a process of socialization – both intimately and occupationally – directly encourages the participation in a unique coding that could be theorized as *anti*-male, a script counter to the definitively endorsed interpretations of and/or aimed at men in sport. Interrogating this pragmatic form leads to a recognition of how the peloton is engaging counter-representations of what it means to be 'male,' fostered and negotiated, in part, by the riders themselves.

One of the introspective insights when (and benefits of) thinking through dominant masculinity is, no matter how intent hegemonic aspirations, its authentic existence does not equate to a totality. A room or space for alternative contingencies will always exist amid the simultaneity of the norm. It is within these gaps that a challenge to heteronormativity can develop. It is here where surrogates such as the *anti*-male can be recognized and subsist. As noted by Abdel-Shehid and Kalman-Lamb (2011, p. 71), the symbolic power of heteronormativity is only secured by a fidelity to "the repetition of codes or instructions." It is based on the weakness of the narrative's need "to be constantly asserted and reasserted in order to maintain its status," that change is plausible (Ibid, p. 71). Due to this normalization, a masculinity outside a succinctly defined and understood universality may enable existing internal circumstances and practices to challenge it. One can look to what has and continues to take place within the peloton and recognize that changes are being realized in how the riders both express and see themselves. Through a theoretical insight that conceptualizes the capitalistic manipulation of gender through hegemonic masculinity, Knuttila (2016) argues how specific codes permeate society via amalgams of culture, politics, and socioeconomics. One can apply this acumen to the world of professional road cycling to recognize how counter-hegemonic approaches can and do occur in contest to a narrowly defined androcentrism. While difficult, these new codes hold a possibility to emerge and offset patriarchal dividends that befall society through a layered discrimination that effect all (see Naiman, 2012). The following interrogates this counter-representation as an expression of power and alternative discourse that is both intrinsic and structural.

James J. Brittain

Practicing *Anti*-Male: A community of shape, shaving, and symbolism

Pierre Bourdieu (1991; 2001) long argued that sport both creates and offers the perfect grounding for specific gender cues to be mimicked. For Bourdieu, cleavages exist that distinguish the "virile" from "the effeminate" and within said confines rest rankings of what is "manly" and that which depicts its inverse (1991, p. 361; see also Bederman, 1995). Along this line of thought, sport adorns a space for hierarchal emphasis through an observable and recognized embodiment of power (Bederman, 1995). Sport can, then, be "conceived as a training in … manliness, 'forming of character' and inculcating the 'will to win' which is the mark of the true leader" – thereby prompting the scope, shape, and replication of the (scripted) masculine (Bourdieu, 1991, p. 360). From this line of thought, it could be suggested that rugby, then, salutes brute male force between opponents, while cycling promotes effeminate self-sacrificial weight loss. Through this simplistic and vulgar interpretation, Bourdieu situates one sport as personifying 'manliness' while the other cannot or does not (see also McDonald, 2014). It is from these distinctions that inconsistencies extoling sport as a heteronormative habitus arise, enabling an excavation of counter-hegemonic meanings to develop amongst each broad divergence. When revisiting that sport is not a definitive totality, one can recognize that discrepancies are always present.

The case being made is that professional road cyclists challenge the dominant symbolic locus of the athletic male body and, in so doing, dominant masculinity (see Bourdieu, 1977; 2001; Young, 1991). While not able to expel the sum of socialized baggage anchored in heterosexism, or the normative environment in which they are surrounded, the peloton does pose an alternative to a singular sport-based androcentrism. While it is certainly accurate to suggest that "the body functions as a medium through which the habitus expresses itself, as a reservoir of social experience, the body is also an essential component of the gendered habitus" (Forsey, 2012, p. 70). It is here, as shown above through the analysis of power-to-weight, where the male cyclist offers a direct contrast to deterministic approaches and/or gender-based categorizations. This revised script also witnesses the forming of further variances of unique importance to sport. For example, elite cycling engages a unique embodiment of *coercive entitlement*, which is performed against and through the self rather than directly onto another (Burstyn, 1999; see also Kalman-Lamb, 2018). In so doing, the peloton exerts an alternative masculine practice that is not executed through an immediate oppositional violence between athletic competitors. Recognition of this is noteworthy, as it broadens a demarcation of 'the male' within sport by validating a more holistic and less violent fabrication of masculinity (see Abdel-Shehid and Kalman-Lamb, 2011, p. 81).

While important to critique his binarist work on gender and sport, some of Bourdieu's ideas can prove valuable. Sport embodies distinctive shared relations that are important and intrinsic to specific fields of sociality. Providing insight in relation to the influence socio-historical formations have on contemporary identities, Bourdieu (1984, p. 209) noted:

> the universe of sporting activities … presents itself to each new entrant as a set of ready-made choices, objectively instituted possibles, traditions, rules, values, equipment, symbols, which receive their social significance from the system they constitute and which derive a proportion of their properties, at each moment, from history.

Moving from this analysis, a domain of pre-made beliefs, expectations, and practices may offer an immediate or readymade sociocultural framework on which to build alternative discourses of meaning and identity. Therefore, it is important to catechize what habits, mores, and practices are employed in road cycling so that these proxy effects of power and representation may be achieved.

Through an interrogation of the idiosyncrasies found in professional road cycling, one can recognize a series of shared constitutions amongst those in the male peloton. In *The Road Cyclist's Companion*, Drinkell (2016, p. 5) penned an entire text devoted to how "there are literally thousands of unwritten rules – from the length of your socks to the 'luft' of your cap to the nuances of behaviour when cycling in a group." Drinkell takes the hand of the inaugural enthusiast to assist their initiation into the complex world of cycling behaviours, tradition, and embraced conformity. The impact of such codes is so significant that one prominent cyclist dedicated an entire chapter in an autobiography to the subject of how one ought to behave, dress, eat, groom, and train so as to replicate how a genuine pro articulates their identity (see Thomas, 2015, pp. 285–299). Nevertheless, no better example of Bourdieu's commentary can be found outside *The Rules*. Written by a conglomerate self-described as Velominati (this is not entirely a joke), *The Rules: The way of the cycling disciple* holds a sacred-like significance to road cycling aficionados, both amateur and professional (Velominati, 2013). As inscribed on the back cover of each copy: "The Velominati embrace cycling not just as a pastime to a means of travel, but as a way of life – as obsessed with style, heritage, authenticity and wisdom as with performance. The Rules is their Bible." One can come to recognize, albeit tongue-in-cheek, how the basis of *The Rules* is to assist those who hold "the sport, its history, its culture, and its practice in a nearly religious context" (Velominati, 2013, p. 8). As a device of discursive training, the text instructs how one, to be an authentic road cyclist, must affiliate with a stringent adoption and repetition of clearly defined customs. It is from (and out of) this devotion to ritual that the peloton can and does illustrate an immaterial and material capacity to generate a culture that is substantively unique. Through their own shared internal definition and construction of the body, alongside a non-barbaric inter-relational approach of comradery over competition, a collegiality is formulated and distinguishable from sporting masculinities and a masculinity defined by heterosexism.

A pragmatic example stressing the alternative script written by those in the peloton is the universal practice of depilation. Depilation, the premeditated removal of select topographies of body hair, is a performative routine that has been shared over many generations across various groups perceived to be in antithetical relation to heteronormativity. Traditionally viewed as the physical denotation of masculinity, "male hairiness … has been regarded as a signifier of masculine virility" (Kenway and Bullen, 2010, p. 161). Even so, it must be noted that certain tenants in sport have practiced depilation for decades. Hair removal in body building, for instance, has been purposely employed to further enhance the accentuation of one's bulked physique (Klein, 2007). Buchbinder (2013, p. 144) found "the depilation of the male body has been for some time a practice in the cult of body building. It serves the purpose in competitions, together with oiling the body, of rendering the contours and musculature of the body more obvious, and more susceptible to the play of light and shadow." Bodybuilding, as a subject, is important here, as one would think that the male practitioners within the sport would represent an overt expression of dominant masculinity; yet some research has shown that not only is this group looked upon as inconsistent with heterosexuality but dually "interpreted by outsiders as feminizing" (Klein, 2008, p. 173). This echoes Kenway and Bullen's work, "in the logic of binary oppositions, then, smooth hair-free skin is considered … more 'feminine' … a state that can only be achieved through the regimes of hair removal" (2010, p. 161). Not dismissing such insights, one cannot bypass that the sculpted aesthetic in bodybuilding exudes a framing of masculinity through the blatant self-promotion and collective celebration of observable sheer mass. Albeit fluid, bodybuilding reinforces a cultural normality where muscle size, definition, and overall girth is feted, situating it in the perpetuation of dominant scripts toward the male body (see Marshall, Chamberlain, and Hodgetts, 2020). While impudent to a solitary heteronormative practice, bodybuilding is very much in compliance with the predominant performance(s) of 'the male' in sport and remains "a major feature of a hypermasculine ideal" (Berkowitz, 2020). Contrary to bodybuilding, where the calculation of prestige is directly portioned to the ever-expansive defined muscularity of the lifter, the peloton is antipode. As noted, the more emaciated the body, the greater the value. Yet, this 'less is more' mentality extends further with the professional male cyclist again proving to be a unique distinction and counterpoint.

Distinguishing itself from other forms of athleticism, cycling approaches depilation beyond norms of current heteronormative practice. Well before the rise in popularity of the hairless male aesthetic, the peloton offered a subcultural context that predates and scales the boundaries of 'manscaping' both in and out of any sport. External to the increasing acceptance of male hair removal, mainly reserved to the quadrants of the torso and genitals, the subject of leg shaving has been a long-standing custom within professional male road cycling, a practice under-addressed by those interested in the topic (see Immergut, 2010). It has been documented that "racers have done so for at least 100 years," which "likely predates the adoption of the custom by Western women" (Barry, 2011, p. 78). With precise detail, Michael Barry (2011) [*pc*, 1999–2012, Canadian], once one of the world's foremost *domestiques* (again derived from French for servant referring to riders who work to absolute exertion to reduce the workload of the leader), penned the direction, frequency, method, and timing of how a proper road cyclist is to negotiate the act of shaving one's legs. While instructional films and visual tutorials have been fashioned (see GCN, 2014a; 2014b; 2015b; 2016; Jung, 2011), few have offered a more explicit review as Barry. Exemplifying the *anti*-male, Barry underscores how leg shaving is an overt expression and statement of power in direct contention to prevailing masculine scripts. In *The Razor's Edge*, Barry (2011, p. 77) highlights the multitude of elite cyclists who – both past and present – idolized and imitated this counter-hegemonic articulation of an empowered identity: "those legs were symbolic of fitness, suffering, sacrifice, freedom, panache, and victory. And it was only because they presented themselves in the cyclist's unique and evocative aesthetic: They were shaven." Fully aware of the gender-bending entailed in the custom, the peloton continues to adopt, promote, repeat, and sustain the practice.

Every elite athlete can attest that their training began well before (and after) adolescence. In recognition of this, smoothly glistening legs in a locker room may not be the most comfortable nor inviting androcentric environment. As one current professional put it, "shaved pins don't always make you fit in with the rest of the crowd" (Juul Jensen, 2015). Here, again, Barry's (2011, pp. 78–79) work stands out:

> Having grown up immersed in a community of cyclists, and with a father who raced, I saw hair on the legs of few men. To me, it was the hirsute legs that appeared abnormal, unkempt, dirty. Not until middle school, spying the legs of my maturing classmates, did I begin to realize that the smooth-skinned cyclists were the minority. I knew I would soon face a dilemma: I wanted to be a cyclist but, like any adolescent, didn't want to be an alien. In eighth grade, the blond boy-hair on my legs began to be replaced by sprouts of the dark adolescent hair I feared. Confused, awkward, in the way of boys of that age I tried in a desperate and doomed way to erase the situation in secret. After my parents had gone to bed, I settled under the reading light in my bedroom with a pair of scissors, snipping at the pesky, dark, curly hair bristling up off my shins. Eventually, the lure of wanting to be a cyclist was stronger than wanting to be normal, and I started shaving.

Thomas, too, adds his voice to this discussion, as he reconciles the complexity of 'abnormality' in both historical and immediate contexts. Perceived as "the weird one who was into cycling …

the weird one who shaved his legs," Thomas (2018, p. 40) narrates the internal tension and eventual resolution all promising adolescent male cyclists have to face:

> When you are a twelve-year-old boy in Cardiff you do not want to be rocking up to school with shaved legs. It's a matter of choosing which *world* you belong too, the 'normal' hairy-legged world of the playground, or the smooth, clean-shaven changing rooms of the velodrome
>
> ([italics added] Thomas, 2015, p. 3).

Like most young men interested in pursuing a dream of getting paid to cycle, Christopher Juul Jensen [*pc*, 2008–*present*, Danish] is another who shares the personal experience of being forced to acknowledge his passion against the clash of governing gender conventions. He harkens how "there is always that period in a young rider's life where you have to make a choice: do I shave my legs or not?" (Juul Jensen, 2015). Again, Thomas can fondly (albeit smarting) revisit his first time. Even though over two decades have passed, Thomas (2018, pp. 40–41) faultlessly recalls the when and where of his eventual initiation to *this* world:

> The first shave came when I was at the kids' Tour of Berlin as a fourteen-year-old and been persuaded by all the other lads that there it was the thing to do. I made a terrible job of it, rushing it in a Portaloo, emerging with patches of hair and dribbles of blood interspersed down my calves.

While criticized for his juvenile tendencies and problematic sexism defaming male road cyclists as less masculine (The Secret Cyclist, 2019; Phil Gaimon, 2017b) [*pc*, 2009–2016, American] similarly recollects how difficult it was to arbitrate leg shaving as a teenage High School student. In so doing, however, he alludes that it was through this practice that a cultural embrace into the sport was felt (while in direct contention to the conventional pressure of his non-cycling peers and surroundings).

What becomes liberating in each of the above memoirs is the bridge of unity forged through unorthodoxy. It is in the negation of the norm that a collective is not only present and welcoming but encourages the ongoing countercultural behaviour of leg shaving as part of the male cyclist identity. Rather than flush and silky legs being a signifier of male embarrassment, these cyclists celebrate their limbs as appendages of power. "Perhaps," cites Barry (2011, p. 78) "it is some combination of the mystery, the difficulty, and the taboo (to men in general the act is abnormal), that has turned leg shaving into a rite of passage." Rather than seeing depilation as a secret or shame, an *anti*-male approach situates the practice as a subjective recognition of power created and echoed through its adoption (see Barry, 2011). Pragmatically loaded with symbolic meaning, sleek male legs become "a bike rider's most valuable asset" (Juul Jensen, 2015). Rather than indignity, these slender freshly shaven extremities provide a concrete example of the *anti*-male script through their cherished prestige of expressive and implicit power.

With a subculture that very much exists outside the confines of propagated gender scripts, professional male road cyclists have created a closed environment of community and symbolic security. Within the male peloton exists, then, what Simmel (2015) would refer to as a *double function*. They facilitate not simply the creation of an insulated and unified group or inner circle apart from heteronormativity but also a simultaneous context that celebrates and preserves their exclusivity. Rather than marginalized, secondary, or weak, the(ir) adoption and practice of the *anti*-male fosters a reality of power that cannot be breached by anyone unwilling to adopt these practices of shared identity. While a dominant masculine interprerion may imply these cyclists 'lack power,' it is through their elevated and redefined approach that power is created and external to those outside *their* subculture. In a fascinating turn, the *anti*-male, then, both achieves and embodies a power beyond 'the male' confined to a conventional heteronormative script.

Conclusion

As a professional male cyclist, one is occupationally incapable of accepting or subscribing to various heteronormative scripts, as having a non-existent body mass, arms of a Tyrannosaurs Rex, and smoothly shaven legs are all of necessity and structural ingredients related to performance. Those within the peloton pose a contrasting theoretical figure when compared to other forms in sport – even in comparison with other forms of cycling (see Forsey, 2012; Millar, 2011) – as they queer androcentric conventions. Research from Abdel-Shehid and Kalman-Lamb (2011, p. 91, 71) frames how heterosexism is "more than simply regulation of sexual orientation," as it "also ensures that there is a very rigid definition of who is a man and who is a woman." Their insight offers how masculinity in sport is structured and normalized to define a clearly understood binary, a function that encourages a simplistic duality that anything countering the masculine is to adopt the feminine. What is contextually significant in professional male road cycling is the blurring of such stringent codes based on the affects and effects of attention to non-descriptive narratives of man, particularly as they align with sport. As previously noted, the greater distancing from a sport-based 'male' identity (i.e., muscle mass, sculpted girth, violent aggression, etc.), the more efficient – and celebrated – the roadie becomes from an affinitive standpoint. So, too, could the application of patriarchal or even misogynist stereotypes be linked to this deduction through the fetishized practice or interest toward aesthetics, clothing, hair design, fashion, or affectual characteristics such as the negation of individual interests for that of a holistic sentimentality of collective recognition and support. All of which are absolute within the culture and pragmatism of the professional male peloton. Another way of ostensibly interpreting this is that the more a male rider adapts to and adopts the *feminine*, the better they will be(come).

The preceding chapter provides a sociological examination of the professional male road cyclist's unique location within gender and sport. Albeit one small glimpse into a more complex domain, its pursuit offers an interpretation of how alternative scripts of power are being constructed and sustained by the peloton. While a wider body of research needs to be pursued on the *anti*-male, this work hopes to begin a conversation of the fluidity of power in sport while answering how, who, and why it is articulated as such. By providing a space to recognize the peloton's re-scripting, it is hoped that barriers to understanding are dissolved so as to facilitate the construction and shaping of a better world to live and play.

REFERENCES

Abdel-Shehid, G. and Kalman-Lamb, N. (2011). *Out of left field: Social inequality and sports*. Halifax: Fernwood.

Alexander, S.M. (2003). 'Stylish Hard Bodies: Branded masculinity in Men's Health magazine', *Sociological Perspectives*, 46(4): 535–554.

Barry, M. (2005). *Inside the Postal bus: My ride with Lance Armstrong and the U.S. Postal Cycling Team*. Boulder: Velo Press.

Barry, M. (2011). 'The razor's edge', *Bicycling*, 52(6): 76–82.

Barry, M. (2014). *Shadows on the road: Life at the heart of the peloton, from U.S. Postal to Team Sky*. London: Faber & Faber.

Bederman, G. (1995). *Manliness and civilization: A cultural history of gender and race in the United States, 1880-1917*. Chicago: Chicago University Press.

Benwell, B. (2003). *Masculinity and men's lifestyle magazines*. Oxford: Blackwell.
Berkowitz, A. (2020). *Muscles and Masculinity* [Online]. Available at: https://www.psychologytoday.com/ca/blog/governing-behavior/202007/muscles-and-masculinity (Accessed 16 February 2021).
Bourdieu, P. (1977). *Outline of theory and practice*. Cambridge: Cambridge University Press.
Bourdieu, P. (1984). *Distinction: A social critique of the judgement of taste*. Cambridge: Harvard University Press.
Bourdieu, P. (1991). 'Sport and Social Class', in Mukerji, C. and Schudson, M. (eds.). *Rethinking popular culture: Contemporary perspectives in cultural studies*. Berkeley: University of California Press. pp. 357–373.
Bourdieu, P. (2001). *Masculine domination*. Cambridge: Polity.
Buchbinder, D. (2013). *Studying men and masculinities*. London: Routledge.
Burstyn, V. (1999). *The rites of men: Manhood, politics, and the culture of sport*. Toronto: University of Toronto Press.
Connell, R. (2005). *Masculinities*. Berkeley: University of California Press.
Dekker, T. (2017). *Descent*. Boulder: Velo Press.
Dower, J. (2012). *Bradley Wiggins: A year in yellow* [documentary film]. London: Sky Atlantic.
Drinkell, P. (2016). *The road cyclist's companion*. London: Cicada.
Forsey, C. (2012). *Men on the edge: Taking risks and doing gender among base jumpers*. Halifax: Fernwood.
Froome, C. (2014). *The climb*. London: Penguin.
Gaimon, P. (2017a). *Draft animals: Living the pro cycling dream (once in a while)*. New York: Penguin.
Gaimon, P. (2017b). *Ask a pro*. Boulder: Velo Press.
Global Cycling Network. (2014a). *How to Shave Your Legs Like a Pro* [Online]. Available at: https://www.youtube.com/watch?v=dzpsJQN4o-Y (Accessed 14 October 2016).
Global Cycling Network. (2014b). *Ask the Pros - Shave or Wax? 2014 Amgen Tour of California Coverage* [Online]. Available at: https://www.youtube.com/watch?v=Q8xUUWObV1Y (Accessed 14 October 2016).
Global Cycling Network. (2015a). *Guns of the Peloton – Which Pro Cyclist Has the Strongest Arms? Vuelta A España 2015* [Online]. Available at: https://www.youtube.com/watch?v=5lXJe9kX190 (Accessed 13 December 2020).
Global Cycling Network. (2015b). *GCN Does Science - Should You Shave or Wax Your Legs?* [Online]. Available at: https://www.youtube.com/watch?v=Wcr9p_MgsCE (Accessed 14 October 2016).
Global Cycling Network. (2016). *Why Do Cyclists Shave Their Legs? Abu Dhabi Tour 2016* [Online]. Available at: https://www.youtube.com/watch?v=c9DM_sSbMlo (Accessed 14 October 2016).
Hamilton, T. and Coyle, D. (2012). *The secret race: Inside the hidden world of the Tour de France: Doping, cover-ups, and winning at all costs*. New York: Bantam Books.
Hanson, A. (2014). *The Skinny on Weight Loss for Cyclists* [Online]. Available at: http://better-biking.com/archives/646 (Accessed 19 November 2016).
Hincapie, G. and Hummer, C. (2014). *The loyal lieutenant: Leading out Lance and pushing through the pain on the rocky road to Paris*. New York: HarperCollins Press.
Immergut, M. (2010). 'Manscaping: The tangle of nature, culture, and male body hair', in Moore, L.J. and Kusot, M. (eds.). *The body reader: Essential social and cultural readings*. New York: New York University Press. pp. 287–304.
Jung, N.C. (2011). *Andy Schleck's tour* [documentary film]. Copenhagen: Nordvision Fonden.
Juul Jensen, C. (2015). *The Vanity of the Pro Cyclist* [Online]. Available at: https://rouleur.cc/editorial/vanity-pro-cyclist/ (Accessed 6 January 2018).
Kalman-Lamb, N. (2018). *Game misconduct: Injury, fandom, and the business of sport*. Halifax: Fernwood.
Kenway, J. and Bullen, E. (2010). 'Consuming skin: Demographics of female subjection and abjection', in Sandlin, J.A. and McLaren, P. (eds.). *Critical pedagogies of consumption: Living and learning in the shadow of the 'shopocalypse'*. New York: Routledge. pp. 157–168.
Kilbourne, J. (1999). *Can't buy my love: How advertising changes the way we think and feel*. New York: Touchstone.
Kirby, C. (2020). *Magic spanner: The world of cycling according to Carlton Kirby*. London: Bloomsbury Sport.
Klein, A. (2007). 'Size matters: Connecting subculture to culture in bodybuilding', in Thompson, J.K and Cafri, G. (eds.). *The muscular ideal: Psychological, social, and medical perspectives*. Washington: American Psychological Association. pp. 67–83.

Klein, A. (2008). *American sports: An anthropological approach*. New York: Routledge.
Knuttila, M. (2016). *Paying for masculinity: Boys, men and the patriarchal dividend*. Halifax: Fernwood.
Malcolm, D. (2010). *Sport and sociology*. London: Routledge.
Marsal, A. (2021). *How Did Bodies of the Tour de France Riders Change Over Time* [Online]. Available at: https://www.welovecycling.com/wide/2021/01/19/how-did-bodies-of-the-tour-de-france-riders-change-over-time/ (Accessed 20 January 2021).
Marshall, K., Chamberlain, K., and Hodgetts, D. (2020). 'Male bodybuilders on Instagram: Negotiating inclusive masculinities through hegemonic masculine bodies', *Journal of Gender Studies*, 29(5): 570–589.
McDonald, I. (2014). 'Portraying sporting masculinity through film: Reflection on Jorgen Leth's *A Sunday in Hell*", in Hargreaves, J. and Anderson, E. (eds.). *Routledge Handbook of Sport, Gender and Sexuality*. New York: Routledge. pp. 480–487.
Millar, D. (2011). *Racing in the dark: The fall and rise of David Millar*. London: Orion.
Millar, D. (2015). *The racer: Life on the road as a pro cyclist*. London: Yellow Jersey Press.
Naiman, J. (2012). *How society works: Class, power, and change*. Fifth Edition. Halifax: Fernwood.
Pope, H., Phillips, K.A., and Olivardia, R. (2000). *The Adonis complex: The secret crisis of male body obsession*. New York: Free Press.
Rahman, M. (2004). 'David Beckham as a historical moment in the representation of masculinity', *Labour History Review*, 69(2): 219–233.
Robbins, R. (2013). 'Series foreword', in Vivanco, L.A. *Reconsidering the bicycle: An anthropological perspective on a new (old) thing*. New York: Routledge. pp. xv–xvi.
Rubio-Hernández, M.delM. (2010). 'The representations of men depicted in *Men's Health* magazine', *Revista Comunicación*, 8(1): 57–70.
The Secret Cyclist (2019). *The Secret Cyclist: Real life in the professional peloton*. London: Yellow Jersey Press.
Simmel, G. (2015). 'Fashion', in Kivisto, P. (ed.) *Social theory: Roots & branches*. New York: Oxford University Press. pp. 104–109.
Stout, J. (2015). 'Eating habits of (pro) cyclists: The weight debate', *Ride: Cycling Review Issue*, 68: pp. 140–145.
Thomas, G. (2015). *The world of cycling according to G*. London: Quercus.
Thomas, G. (2018). *The Tour according to G: My journey to the Yellow Jersey*. London: Quercus.
Thomas, G. (2020). *Mountains according to G*. London: Quercus.
Vaughters, J. (2019). *One-way ticket: Nine lives on two wheels*. New York: Penguin.
Velominati. (2013). *The rules: The way of the cycling disciple*. London: Sceptre.
Vivanco, L.A. (2013). *Reconsidering the bicycle: An anthropological perspective on a new (old) thing*. New York: Routledge.
Young, I.M. (1991). *Throwing Like a Girl and other essays in feminist philosophy and social theory*. Bloomington: Indiana University Press.

10
Rainbow Dancing and the Challenge of Transgender Inclusion in Finland

Anna Kavoura and Santtu Rinne

Rainbow dancing in Finland and the challenge of transgender inclusion

According to the rules and regulations of the World Dance Sport Federation (WDSF) — the world governing body for DanceSport — a dance couple 'consists of a male and a female partner' (WDSF, 2019, p. 24). This definition does not leave any space for same-sex and gender-neutral dance couples. *Transgender* and *non-binary* dancers — i.e., dancers who find that gender labels assigned to them at birth are inconsistent with their sense of self (Stryker and Whittle, 2006) — are, therefore, excluded from mainstream ballroom dancing competitions organized under these rules.

However, as a result of international lesbian, gay, bisexual, transgender, intersex, queer, asexual, allies and more (LGBTIQA+) activism, some community-organized social dancing events and competitions (e.g., the Pink Jukebox Trophy, the Rendez-Vous de Paris, the Berlin Open, the Nordic Open and the Gay Games) have made space for gender and sexual diversity. As acknowledged by the European Same-Sex Dance Association (ESSDA, 2021), the roots and base of these events are the expression of LGBTIQA+ identities and relationships. Even mainstream national dance organizations, such as USA Dance, have begun advocating for a gender-neutral policy (USA Dance, 2019). Specifically, the National Dance Council of America (NDCA) recently changed the longstanding definition of the dance couple to 'a leader and follower without regard to the sex or gender of the dancer' (NDCA, 2021, p. 5).

Progress has also been made in the representational realm of dance, since television dance shows finally started featuring same-sex couples as well as dance bodies and performances which challenge gender expectations (Butler et al., 2014; Mocarski et al., 2013; Richardson, 2018). For example, in the UK's 2020 Strictly Come Dancing, former Olympic boxer Nicola Adams entered the first ever same-sex pairing in the history of the show; yet, her entrance triggered controversial public reactions that included both supportive comments and homophobic complaints (Wallace, 2020). As dance scholars have argued (Boyd, 2015; Richardson, 2018), despite recent notable progress, these shows continue extensively depending on hetero- and cis-normative stereotypes, and the ways dance couples and their performances are coded and judged are often shaped by homophobic and transphobic discourses.

Transgender and non-binary dancers continue facing multiple barriers, such as binary and gender-specific practices which dominate competitive dance culture as well as a lack of representation and professional opportunities (Scher, 2020). However, to our knowledge, the topic of trans inclusion in dance remains absent from scholarly work, with the exception of an article by Mocarski and colleagues (2013) focusing on Chaz Bono, the first transgender contestant in the reality show Dancing With the Stars (DWTS). These authors argued that while Bono's appearance on DWTS constitutes an important positive step towards acceptance of transgender dancing bodies, the way Bono appears in this show promotes a particular and maybe privileged transgender subjectivity. The authors further argued that trans subjectivities which appear in (and are mediated by) the media might not represent all trans and non-binary subjectivities and experiences. Therefore, the aim of this chapter is to enhance understandings of transgender experiences in DanceSport and explore the potential and challenges for transgender inclusion. Particularly, we focus on the Rainbow and Same-Sex dancing scene in Finland and how this context has been experienced by the second author, a Rainbow trans dancer and instructor. Given that there is considerable lack of research on transgender issues in dance, we draw on previous studies on transgender inclusion in sport as well as studies on gender issues in dance before we outline the context of Rainbow and Same-Sex dancing.

Trans inclusion in sport and the potential of queer spaces

While progressive changes have occurred within the last decade regarding recognizing genders outside the traditional two-sex system (i.e., the gender binary), sport institutions continue normalizing the belief that all people are either male or female, reinforcing participation barriers for transgender and non-binary people in sport (Travers, 2014). Specifically, research shows that transgender people face several challenges in sport, including exclusion, discrimination, verbal and physical harassment and abuse, prejudice, a lack of inclusive and comfortable environments and a lack of understanding from others (Caudwell, 2014; Cohen and Semerjian, 2008; Hargie, Mitchell and Somerville, 2017; Jones et al., 2017; Kavoura and Kokkonen, 2020; Klein, Paule-Koba and Krane, 2019; Pérez-Samaniego et al., 2019). These challenges derive from the gendered categories, facilities and practices embedded in sport, the lack of knowledge pertaining to transgender issues and the persistent circulation of gender stereotypes about what male and female bodies can (and cannot) do (Lucas-Carr and Krane, 2012; Semerjian, 2019). Transgender bodies complicate stereotypical understandings about gender and therefore are often *abjected* (i.e., dehumanized and excluded; Butler, 1990, 1993; Pérez-Samaniego et al., 2019), as they are seen as threatening the rules of mainstream competitive sport (Semerjian, 2019).

One strategy employed by transgender sport people to cope with the hostile, exclusionary climate characterizing most mainstream competitive sport cultures is the search for (or creation of) queer alternative sporting spaces and networks (Kavoura and Kokkonen, 2020; Travers and Deri, 2011). While not totally free from gender boundaries and stereotypes, queer sporting spaces can offer a model for 'a less sex-binary-based sporting future' (Travers and Deri, 2011, p. 503). As Halberstam (2005) argued, queer spaces develop in opposition to cis- and heteronormative institutions and encompass alternative practices and methods of alliance as well as the potential to open new narratives and discourses. Same-Sex and Rainbow dancing networks and events are such spaces of resistance to binary understandings of gender in dance. Dancers who participate in Same-Sex and Rainbow dancing events are allowed to deviate from society's gender expectations and can enjoy more freedom of expression in their performances (Butler et al., 2014). Therefore, Same-Sex and Rainbow dancing contexts are interesting sites for exploring alternative, non-binary ways of organizing dance practices (and sport in general) and identifying approaches and processes contributing towards more gender-inclusive, equitable and ethical dance (and sport) cultures.

Challenging gender roles in dance: The development of Same-Sex and Rainbow dancing

Dance has been characterized as a particularly gendered (and often feminized) arena, with rigid heteronormative dichotomies of male/female and masculine/feminine (Boyd, 2015; Butler et al., 2014; Richardson, 2018). Scholars who have studied the topic argue that cis-women dancers (especially those who can perform femininity and grace in ways aligning with gender norms) are more celebrated on the dancing floor, while cis-men as well as transgender and non-binary folk are implicated in discourses of homophobia, transphobia and effeminophobia (Mocarski et al., 2013; Richardson, 2018). 'Rebellious dancing bodies' (i.e., bodies that exceed normative gender expectations, Boyd, 2015, p. 686) are heavily critiqued and regulated and are often deprived of access to events (such as mainstream competitions, reality shows and television or theatre performances). When these rebellious bodies make it to the dance floor, they are declared by the judges to be immeasurable or unjudgeable (Boyd, 2015).

Among the different forms and cultures of dance, DanceSport (i.e., competitive ballroom dancing) is a context characterized by disciplined gender performance and rigid definitions of masculinity/ femininity (Butler et al., 2014). Traditionally, a dance couple in DanceSport consists of a man and a woman, with men dancing the leader's role and women the follower's role. People not identifying as cis-gender and/or heterosexual might feel alienated by these heteronormative rules of DanceSport. For dancers transgressing the gender binary rules, Rainbow and Same-Sex dancing organizations and events offer a more inclusive and safe space where they are allowed to be themselves.

Rainbow and Same-Sex dancing organizations and events worldwide have been developed with the aim of providing opportunities for LGBTIQA+ people to dance (including participating in competition) and of challenging the heteronormative culture and rules of DanceSport. Having roots in LGBTIQA+ activism, these organizations work towards a dancing climate where people can feel safe to express themselves, their LGBTIQA+ identities and their intersections (see, for example, ESSDA, 2021). In Finland, competitive Same-Sex and Rainbow dancing started growing in about 2007, with the second author among the founding members of this movement. In this chapter, we explore the challenges and opportunities for transgender inclusion in the contexts of Rainbow and Same-Sex dancing in Finland as these have been experienced by the second author. The aim is to provide new insights into the experiences of trans people in dance (and in sport in general) and to provide recommendations for enhancing access and positive experiences of trans people in dance (and sport) contexts.

Method and procedures

This chapter is part of the first author's ethnographic and participatory action research (PAR) study on trans-inclusive sport spaces, as approved by the Social Science Cross-School Research Ethics Committee at the University of Brighton. Following the principles and ethics of PAR research with trans participants (Singh, Richmond and Burnes, 2013; Vincent, 2018), this larger study engages members of the trans sporting community as co-researchers and respects their wishes on how much (and in what ways) they want to contribute and whether they want to be anonymized or be credited for their contribution in this research.

Santtu (second author) was invited to contribute to this research, as he is the co-founder of a Rainbow dancing school in Finland with a visible trans-inclusive policy, and he also defines himself as a pansexual, transgender, transmasculine person. After reading the participant information letter, Santtu agreed to participate and signed an informed consent. Together, we had multiple, extensive discussions on how we could best explore issues of trans inclusion/exclusion in the Rainbow and Same-Sex dancing scene, and we decided to place Santtu's narrative at the centre of this chapter.

To facilitate the co-construction of Santtu's narrative, we conducted two individual interviews during which the first author took the role of the interviewer and the second author the role of the interviewee. The interviews occurred on 6 October 2020 and 10 January 2021 and were conducted virtually via Microsoft Teams (due to COVID-19 restrictions on face-to-face meetings). The interviews lasted 3 hours and 13 minutes, were recorded and transcribed. The transcripts were sent to Santtu to read, comment on and approve. During the first interview, a semi-structured interview guide was used to ensure that certain topics related to gender expression and experiences of inclusion/exclusion in dance would be addressed. The second interview was an open discussion stimulated by the questions, thoughts and comments that the first transcript generated to both the interviewer and interviewee.

Data analysis and interpretation was a collaborative effort between the two authors, following the principles of narrative analysis (Smith and Sparkes, 2009) and inspired by queer theoretical perspectives (Butler, 1990, 1993, 2004; Halberstam, 1998, 2005, 2011). The first author offered her interpretations first, and the second author commented, offering more layers to the analysis. In what follows, we provide Santtu's narrative with a focus on the opportunities and challenges met in the context of Rainbow and Same-Sex dancing. In concluding this chapter, we provide recommendations for enhancing access and positive experiences for trans people in dance, DanceSport and sport in general.

Santtu's story

Santtu was born in Finland 39 years ago and took his first dance lessons at age five. He remembers that while he enjoyed dancing as a kid, he felt alienated by the cis- and heteronormative culture of dance:

Santtu: Actually, I did start dancing when I was five. I wanted to go to this wrestling training, but I wasn't allowed to, since my parents thought that it's too rough. Then suddenly I found myself with my cousin at a DanceSport club, and I bet it was not my choice (laughter), but luckily I did like it. So, the training was fun. My cousin dropped out at some point, and then I could dance with the teachers. We had, like, three of them, and I enjoyed dancing with them very much. Then I got a dance partner. Some, let's say I assume a guy, and then we had this, like, playful first competition and it was cis- and heteronormative in that way also that, you know, you have to wear a dress and so on, and I didn't quite like it. So, I quit.
Anna: This was the reason that you quit?
Santtu: This combination, yeah, I didn't really want to dance with that guy, and I didn't feel comfortable wearing a dress.

As a young person, Santtu tried and enjoyed various sports (e.g., basketball, football, swimming and martial arts), until he rediscovered social dancing in 2003 when studying psychology in Berlin. The reintroduction to dancing happened in a queer-friendly space, a context in which Santtu felt much more comfortable compared to the alienating experience as a child in the mainstream and cis-/heteronormative DanceSport club. Santtu started practising dance seriously, and before long, he found himself in the competitive arena of DanceSport. By 2007,

Santtu started competing in same-sex dancing events with his ex-partner, with whom he formed a couple in life and in dance for over ten years. Santtu and his partner trained hard, Santtu dancing the leader's role and his partner (who identified as a cis woman) dancing the follower's role. They travelled extensively to participate in competitions and dancing camps or train with highly esteemed dance teachers. Over the years, Santtu and his partner won several A-Class medals in international same-sex dancing competitions (e.g., the Gay Games, Eurogames and World Championships of Same-Sex Dancing). At the same time, they started offering shows, workshops and lessons in Finland. They decided to use the term 'rainbow couple dancing lessons' for the offered classes, as they found this term more gender-inclusive and neutral than 'same-sex dancing'.

During his dance career, Santtu was quite open about his gender and sexuality to some of his close circle of friends. However, similar to what previous research has shown (e.g., Klein, Paule-Koba and Krane, 2019; Ravel and Rail, 2008), in Santtu's case, coming out as trans has also been a never-ending, difficult process he had to repeat several times in dance events or every time he found himself in a new context:

> I was quite open back then [about my gender and sexuality], and then it is always … you have to do it so many times. So, it took a while before I openly spoke about it [when I moved] in Helsinki, actually. Because people make assumptions, and then there are so many things one has to consider, like work, studies and being public in many ways. So, it was a new situation to be in. To be a student and to be in the work life. As a student it is perhaps easier to be out, while in the work life there are more risks. So. there were a lot of things that I hadn't spoken about.

Finally, Santtu decided to come out publicly on his personal Facebook profile as a transgender and pansexual human being, as he felt empowered to share the ways in which he defined himself in terms of gender and sexuality with a larger audience, and he was growing tired of constantly having to repeat the coming out process in dance (and other) events:

> I came out as transgender on Facebook in 2019, which wasn't the first time I came out as trans. When we were still at the [name of dance organization], there was this one class where they sort of assumed that there were either mixed [gender] couples or same-sex couples. And then it was like, OK now mixed [gender] couples come to the dance floor and then same-sex couples. So, there are, like, two rounds, and first there were mixed [gender] couples on the dance floor, gemischtgeschlechtlich in German, and then gleichgeschlechtlich, like same-sex. So then, I was like … I took my partner's hand, and then we walked to the dance floor when it was mixed [gender] couples' turn, and then there was … the coach was like, 'What are you doing there?', sort of assuming that we should wait for the same-sex couples' turn, and then I was, like, well, 'Ich bin gemischtgeschlechtlich' … meaning 'I'm mixed; therefore we are a mixed couple'. And OK, then we danced. Maybe it wasn't our best dance performance, but anyway, so we danced there and then.

As previous research has shown (e.g., Klein, Paule-Koba and Krane, 2019), Santtu felt that coming out publicly was a difficult but fulfilling experience, as it allowed him more freedom to express his genders in dance and elsewhere. After coming out, he also felt supported by colleagues and friends on a broad scale.

In 2019, Santtu and his partner broke up their marriage and competitive dance partnership but kept teaching (both together and separately). Their students are now actively competing in both same-sex and mixed-gender dance competitions, and some have been involved in the development of Rainbow Dancers Finland, an organization which aims to promote Rainbow and Same-Sex dancing. Santtu is still considering competition possibilities but frequently faces challenges when trying to enter a DanceSport competition dancing the leader's role (and according to his gender expressions) in Finland and abroad.

Opportunities for transgender inclusion in Rainbow and Same-Sex dancing

As previously stated, Rainbow and Same-Sex dancing developed in opposition to the cis- and heteronormative culture of mainstream ballroom dancing, therefore allowing LGBTIQA+ people more freedom to express a diversity of genders and sexualities. Santtu has experienced this context as empowering and as a space where he can express himself and connect with others in meaningful ways: '[Dance] has been for me an important way to express myself and my genders'. In (and through) dance, he has also felt accepted and supported by the dancing community(ies) and others:

> The first coach I had, for example, was accepting of my genders. So that was a quite special coaching relationship in that way. […] He also encouraged us to become professional dance teachers.

Therefore, Santtu's narrative is in line with findings from previous studies advocating trans and non-binary people's participation in sports as a potential source of individual empowerment (Greey and Barker-Ruchti, 2019; Klein, Paule-Koba and Krane, 2019).

In addition to the climate of acceptance, the Same-Sex and Rainbow dancing movement has helped make dancing more accessible and inclusive for the members of the trans community through challenging traditional cis- and heteronormative dance roles and the men-lead/women-follow paradigm. As Santtu explained:

> We have chosen to speak about leaders and followers, while in mainstream clubs there is … or used to be … probably in many clubs it is still so, that it's like men lead and women follow. […] In our lessons, everybody can choose themselves whether they want to lead or follow or do both, maybe leading in Latin and following in ballroom, for example, or the other way around.

This is congruent with scholarly work pointing to the potential of queer (sport) spaces to challenge normative gender binary and formal gender rules and expectations (Halberstam 2005; Travers and Deri, 2011). As Halberstam (2005) argued, queer spaces produce alternative meanings and allow their participants to imagine their futures in ways that are not available to them in mainstream discourses (e.g., of traditional binary sport). In sport, we can begin to imagine these new, 'alternative and more-livable futures' (Linghede and Larsson, 2017, p. 292), by beginning to see those that already exist in the lives of queer athletes (e.g., Anderson, Magrath and Bullingham, 2016; Klein, Paule-Koba and Krane, 2019) or are presently under construction in local queer and trans-inclusive sport contexts and subcultures (e.g., Travers and Deri, 2011). The Rainbow and Same-Sex dance scenes are such contexts of resistance to the cis- and heteronormative patterns and meanings of mainstream dance (and sport in general), and it is therefore important to explore (and learn from) the possibilities and challenges encountered in these spaces.

Persisting challenges to transgender inclusion

Despite sharing positive experiences of empowerment and inclusion, Santtu also described several challenges related to being a trans dancer. As previous studies in other sports contexts have shown (e.g., Cohen and Semerjian, 2008; Jones et al., 2017), major challenges derive from the gendered nature of facilities, categories and practices. For example, Santtu finds particularly frustrating the gendered rules of organizations (including same-sex dancing organizations), the gender categories in dance competitions and the lack of clear policies related to trans inclusion:

> I think that some people in the Finnish Dance Sport Association are positive about trans inclusion, but there are big international influences and rules coming from international [dance] organizations that one needs to consider and make the issue challenging. I think we are moving towards a positive direction internationally. There have been discussions and working groups to make dance more trans-inclusive. However, in the rules … it could be made clearer that people can define themselves and choose in which competition category they want to sign up. So that one wouldn't have to think whether it is possible or not, or if it's really possible, you know. For example, I think that ESSDA has published this booklet where it is formulated somehow that trans and non-binary people are included. But that was, like, in the booklet and not in the rules or in the general practice. I remember there was this annual dance competition [name of the competition] where I went with my ex-partner, and we signed up for the same-sex class, but then there were not enough couples and there was also a mixed [gender] class, so they decided to put us there, but only for the show. And I thought, 'OK, now we are mixed, now we are in the class where I want to be'. But it was just for the show for us, and they wouldn't judge us against the other couple. So, we went, like … I don't know, five minutes before the final began, we went to ask the judges, 'Can you judge us? Can you put us in the real competition?' And they decided there that yes, they agreed that they would do it, and then that was, like, the first time we were in a mixed competition, and it was in the Rainbow dancing culture.

As Boyd (2015) has argued, dancing bodies which exceed normative gender expectations are often deprived of access to competitions, and when they finally make it to the competition dance floor, they are declared by the judges to be immeasurable or unjudgeable. The Rainbow and Same-Sex dancing culture make positive steps towards trans inclusion (and one could say that trans inclusion appears to be the norm in their everyday practices), but unequal treatment during competition events and unequal access to safe and gender-inclusive facilities continue posing a problem for trans dancers. As Santtu explains, in the absence of trans-inclusive policies and structures, one would have to go through very rigid, inhumane, medicalized and bureaucratic procedures controlling gender (see also Cohen and Semerjian, 2008) to compete according to their gender expression:

Santtu: In Finland, you know, you have in your ID and passport, the so-called official gender marker, and you can only change it through the trans process, and that includes for example enforced sterilization. So, in Finland, still, if one would like to take that route … If, for example, I would like to go as a lead to a mainstream DanceSport competition, so that would be only possible through going through the trans process and then changing the gender marker, and then I could enter a dance competition.
Anna: How long would that process take?
Santtu: At least two years.

Another major challenge reported by Santtu is the lack of visibility and often misrepresentation of trans dancers (see also Mocarski et al., 2013). For example, Santtu found very frustrating and disappointing that his and his partner's dance performances were often coded by judges and the media as 'two women dancing':

> When we were there at the [name of television dancing show], that was of course, very positive and empowering experience the whole day. I think we could give our best, or very close to that in jive at that moment, and it was important also that we did express ourselves as we were there. I also expressed my genders, but it's always of course also a matter of interpretation, or how people see it. So, it was also a quite negative experience for me, that there was this line like 'two girls dancing' ... which was a little bit ... not a little bit, but quite disappointing then in the end. So, on the one side, it was very positive that 3.4 million people were watching, and this was of course very special for the whole Rainbow dancing and Same-Sex dancing community. But then there was this comment ... why did they put it there?

As Mocarski and colleagues (2013) argued, on rare occasions when trans dancers appear in television shows, they are mediated in ways which reinforce binary understandings of gender, which are particularly rigid in dance (and sporting) activities.

Finally, a persistent challenge found in previous research (e.g., Hargie, Mitchell and Somerville, 2017) and experienced by Santtu is the gendered nature of locker rooms. As Halberstam (1998) has argued, public toilets and locker rooms are important sites for social policing of the gender binary. Hargie and colleagues (2017) further revealed that the gendered nature of the locker room is the number one barrier to sport participation for transgender people, and Santtu has fought to remove this barrier in his training facilities:

> I managed to speak to the people who lead the building where we are teaching, in which there are a lot of different sports clubs and all different kinds of sports. I asked them whether they could provide a unisex or gender-neutral, gender-inclusive dressing room. I think it took, like, one or two months and several emails and phone calls, but now there is a [gender-neutral] dressing room and private shower and toilet.

As the above illustrates, in the face of a visible lack of gender-neutral facilities and protective policies, transgender people themselves play a key role in mobilizing change and advocating for the rights of those living outside the gender binary (Stryker, 2008).

Concluding thoughts

Our findings reveal that the Same-Sex and Rainbow dancing movement has helped make dancing more accessible and inclusive for members of the trans community by offering empowering experiences (including possibilities of belonging and competing) and challenging traditional cis- and heteronormative dance roles and the men-lead/women-follow paradigm. Yet, certain challenges for trans-inclusion persist, such as the gendered politics and rules of national and international dance associations, the lack of clear policies related to trans inclusion, the lack of visibility and misrepresentation of trans dancers and the lack of gender-inclusive locker rooms.

Of course, these study results cannot be generalized, as transgender experiences in dance are heterogeneous, individually unique and contextually different. However, we believe our findings have important implications for those interested in enhancing access and positive experiences of trans people in dance, DanceSport and sport in general. An important step, suggested by many scholars before us (e.g., Cunningham, Buzuvis and Mosier, 2018), is creating gender-neutral bathrooms and locker rooms in all dance (and sport) facilities. In addition, our findings are congruent with previous studies (e.g., Mocarski et al., 2013; Semerjian, 2019) advocating the need to raise the visibility of trans dancers (and sports people in general) and the awareness of trans issues, so trans people need not be alone in advocating for their basic human rights. Finally, clear, protective and gender-inclusive policies must be written by governing bodies of dance. Given that many Same-Sex and Rainbow dancing activities are at least partially organized in non-binary ways already, and proposals for trans-inclusion have been outlined by several dance organizations (see, for example, NDCA, 2021), it might not be too difficult to make gender-inclusive dance competitions a future reality. In fact, following the thoughts of queer and critical scholars (e.g., Halberstam, 2005; Linghede and Larsson, 2017), in this chapter, we have argued that this alternative (more livable) future is already constructed by the risks trans dancers are willing to take in the supportive context of Same-Sex and Rainbow dancing.

Acknowledgements

The preparation of this chapter was supported by a grant from the Finnish Cultural Foundation (SKR/00201235).

REFERENCES

Anderson, E., Magrath, R., and Bullingham, R. (2016) *Out in sport: The experiences of openly gay and lesbian athletes in competitive sport*. London and New York: Routledge.

Boyd, J. (2015) '"You bring great masculinity and truth": Sexuality, whiteness, and the regulation of the male body in motion', *Feminist Media Studies*, 15(4), pp. 675–690.

Butler, J. (1990) *Gender trouble: Feminism and the subversion of identity*. New York: Routledge, Chapman & Hall.

Butler, J. (1993) *Bodies that matter: On the discursive limits of 'sex'*. London and New York: Routledge.

Butler, J. (2004) *Undoing gender*. New York and London: Routledge.

Butler, S., Mocarski, R., Emmons, B., and Smallwood, R. (2014) 'Leaving it on the pitch: Hope Solo's negotiation of conflicting gender roles on Dancing with the Stars', *Journal of Gender Studies*, 23(4), pp. 362–375.

Caudwell, J. (2014) '[Transgender] young men: Gendered subjectivities and the physically active body', *Sport, Education & Society*, 19(4), pp. 398–414.

Cohen, J.H., and Semerjian, T.Z. (2008) 'The collision of trans-experience and the politics of women's ice hockey', *International Journal of Transgenderism*, 10(3–4), pp. 133–145.

Cunningham, G.B., Buzuvis, E., and Mosier, C. (2018) 'Inclusive spaces and locker rooms for transgender athletes', *Kinesiology Review*, 7(4), pp. 365–374.

ESSDA (2021) *ESSDA mission statement*. Available at: http://essda.eu/essda-organisation/essda-mission-statement/ (Accessed: 8 February 2021).

Greey, A., and Barker-Ruchti, N. (2019) 'An auto-ethnographic account of one athlete's journey to reconciling gender diversity through elite boxing: A case of a gender nonbinary boxer' in Barker-Ruchti, N. (ed.) *Athlete learning in sport: A cultural framework*. London and New York: Routledge, pp. 153–164.

Halberstam, J.J. (1998) *Female masculinity*. Durham: Duke University Press.

Halberstam, J.J. (2005) *In a queer time and place: Transgender bodies, subcultural lives*. New York and London: New York University Press.

Halberstam, J.J. (2011) *The queer art of failure*. Durham and London: Duke University Press.

Hargie, O.D.W., Mitchell, D.H., and Somerville, I.J.A. (2017) '"People have a knack of making you feel excluded if they catch on to your difference": Transgender experiences of exclusion in sport', *International Review for the Sociology of Sport*, 52(2), pp. 223–239.

Jones, B.A., Arcelus, J., Bouman, W.P., and Haycraft, E. (2017) 'Sport and transgender people: A systematic review of the literature relating to sport participation and competitive sport policies', *Sports Medicine*, 47(4), pp. 701–716.

Kavoura, A., and Kokkonen, M. (2020) 'What do we know about the sporting experiences of gender and sexual minority athletes and coaches? A scoping review', *International Review of Sport and Exercise Psychology*, 14(1), pp. 1–27. doi: 10.1080/1750984X.2020.1723123

Klein, A., Paule-Koba, A.L., and Krane, V. (2019) 'The journey of transitioning: Being a trans male athlete in college sport', *Sport Management Review*, 22(5), pp. 626–639.

Linghede, E., and Larsson, H. (2017) 'Figuring more livable elsewheres: Queering acts, moments, and spaces in sport (studies)', *Journal of Sport and Social Issues*, 41(4), pp. 290–306.

Lucas-Carr, C.B., and Krane, V. (2012) 'Troubling sport or troubled by sport', *Journal for the Study of Sports and Athletes in Education*, 6(1), pp. 21–44.

Mocarski, R., Butler, S., Emmons, B., and Smallwood, R. (2013) '"A different kind of man": Mediated transgendered subjectivity, Chaz Bono on Dancing With the Stars', *Journal of Communication Inquiry*, 37(3), pp. 249–264.

NDCA (2021) *NDCA rules and regulations*. Available at: https://www.ndca.org/pdf/2021%20January%20-%20Compiled%20Rule%20Book%20Master%20v1.pdf (Accessed: 8 February 2021).

Pérez-Samaniego, V., Fuentes-Miguel, J., Pereira-García, S., López-Cañada, E., and Devís-Devís, J. (2019) 'Experiences of trans persons in physical activity and sport: A qualitative meta-synthesis', *Sport Management Review*, 22(4), pp. 439–451.

Ravel, B., and Rail, G. (2008) 'From straight to gaie?: Quebec sportswomen's discursive constructions of sexuality and destabilization of the linear coming out process', *Journal of Sport & Social Issues*, 32(1), pp. 4–23.

Richardson, N. (2018) '"Whether you are gay or straight, I don't like to see effeminate dancing": Effeminophobia in performance-level ballroom dance', *Journal of Gender Studies*, 27(2), pp. 207–219.

Scher, A. (2020) 'For transgender dancers, progress can't come fast enough', *NBC News*, 8 March. Available at: https://www.nbcnews.com/feature/nbc-out/transgender-dancers-progress-can-t-come-fast-enough-n1147911 (Accessed: 8 February 2021).

Semerjian, T.Z. (2019) 'Making space: Transgender athletes' in Krane, V. (ed.) *Sex, gender, and sexuality in sport: Queer inquiries*. London and New York: Routledge, pp. 145–162.

Singh, A.A., Richmond, K., and Burnes, T.R. (2013) 'Feminist participatory action research with transgender communities: Fostering the practice of ethical and empowering research designs', *International Journal of Transgenderism*, 14(3), pp. 93–104.

Smith, B., and Sparkes, A.C. (2009) 'Narrative analysis and sport and exercise psychology: Understanding lives in diverse ways', *Psychology of Sport and Exercise*, 10(2), pp. 279–288.

Stryker, S. (2008) *Transgender history: The roots of today's revolution*. New York: Seal Press.

Stryker, S., and Whittle, S. (2006) *The transgender studies reader*. New York and London: Routledge.

Travers, A. (2014) 'Sport', *TSQ: Transgender Studies Quarterly*, 1(1–2), pp. 194–196.

Travers, A., and Deri, J. (2011) 'Transgender inclusion and the changing face of lesbian softball leagues', *International Review for the Sociology of Sport*, 46(4), pp. 488–507.

USA Dance (2019) *Gender neutral announcement*. Available at: https://usadance.org/news/470072/Gender-Neutral-Announcement.htm#:~:text=USA%20Dance%20plans%20to%20make,compete%20on%20the%20floor%20together (Accessed: 8 February 2021).

Vincent, B.W. (2018) 'Studying trans: Recommendations for ethical recruitment and collaboration with transgender participants in academic research', *Psychology & Sexuality*, 9(2), pp. 102–116.

Wallace, E. (2020) 'Nicola Adams and the importance of LGBTQ+ representation on television', *Redbrick*, 17 November. Available at: https://www.redbrick.me/nicola-adams-and-the-importance-of-lgbtq-representation-on-television/ (Accessed: 19 April 2021).

WDSF (2019) *WDSF competition rules*. Available at: https://www.worlddancesport.org/rule/all (Accessed: 18 January 2020).

11

The Politics of Minority Ethnic Women's Leisure Time and Physical Activity in Denmark

Adam B. Evans, Sine Agergaard and Verena Lenneis

Introduction

In the 'Global North,' sport and leisure time physical activity (LTPA) has long been a field uncritically associated with the promotion of 'apolitical' values such as democracy, equity, inclusion and social integration (e.g., Donnelly, 2008; Kidd and Donnelly, 2000; Thiel et al., 2016). Of course, it is a myth that LTPA is apolitical, and the provision of LTPA programmes is interdependent with political goals and policy decisions (Thiel et al., 2016). Such goals might include, for example, support for gender equity or the integration of migrants into a host society (e.g., Walseth, 2016). In the face of multiple moral panics and the polarisation of attitudes towards ethnic minorities across much of Europe, however, LTPA has become more overtly politicised. Sports events provide an outlet for protest movements such as Black Lives Matter and #MeToo, whilst counter-protest movements have also contested such movements at both competitive and grass-roots levels (e.g., Evans et al., 2020; Abrams and Bartlett, 2019).

In relation to policies about social integration of ethnic minorities, particularly regarding gender equality and women's emancipation (Lenneis and Agergaard, 2018), policy debates are often subsumed within wider social issues such as migration, citizenship, cultural legitimacy and democratic processes. What's more, there is a need to locate the lived experiences of being physically active amongst gendered and racialised groups within the policy environments and social contexts that shape them. For example, such processes in Denmark have problematised the feminine Muslim body such that it has become a political pawn in relation to specific LTPA settings and spaces (Agergaard, 2016, 2019; Lenneis and Agergaard, 2018). Here, we outline how Danish political debates have politicised the spaces of LTPA in relation to race/ethnicity and gender. Specifically, we situate the experiences of Muslim women in LTPA within political debates that objectify and problematise their bodies, and seek to govern them in specific ways. First, however, we summarise evidence to suggest how the Muslim community has been problematised.

Islam in Europe and the politics of exclusion

The rise of illiberal democratic policies, exclusionary politics (often more recently referred to as 'populist' movements) has driven a propagation and re-invigoration of nationalist politics in parts of the Global North. In the drive towards monism and moralism in the definition of 'the people,' such politics have served to problematise the bodies, culture and experiences of those considered 'other' from the perceived majority (Mudde, 2004; Mudde and Kaltwasser, 2012). In such cases, the majority is defined according to notions of monoculturalism, and of conferred rights in defining culture. The 'will of the people' may be a contested term, but to many populists, the right of the majority to be 'the people' is incontrovertible. Such actions can often constitute a challenge to the foundations of liberal democracy, including provision for the protection of minorities, pluralism and the separation of powers, due to their tendency to re-state primordial ideologies, essentialist notions of national identity and, in some cases, explicit xenophobia (Evans et al., 2020; Bairner 2009; Brubaker, 2017; Elgenius and Rydgren, 2019).

Consequently, several racialised groups continue to be problematised, surveyed, censured and discriminated against in many 'Western' societies. For example, the Muslim community has seen a resurgence in the number of Orientalist and nationalist discourses directed at them, which often characterise them as morally problematic or even threatening to the notion of a monadic 'majority' European culture. Such discourses tend to caricature Islamic culture as homogenous, despotic, patriarchal, ideologically backward and illiberal, and (apparently without irony) as a threat to Western Liberal Democracy (Curtis, 2009; Agergaard, 2016, 2019). Such views have led to a rise in anti-Islamic, nationalist and anti-immigrant sentiment across much of Europe, even amongst nominally liberal or social democratic political parties (e.g., Agergaard, 2018, 2019; Williamson, 2020). Subsequently, increasingly stringent, critical and restrictive immigration and integration policies can be observed, often combined with public anti-Muslim debates, moral panics and affected 'concerns' with aspects of Islamic culture (Thangaraj et al., 2018; Lenneis and Agergaard, 2018).

Despite evidence to the contrary, such sentiments are often implicitly based upon the assumption that Muslims are 'migrants' who require acculturation and integration into the majority culture, despite many Muslims being European citizens of various countries. Often, such sentiments intersect with gendered discourses, such as an assumed 'failure' to educate younger people about majority liberal values (Agergaard et al., 2016). That many in the Muslim community reside in relatively deprived areas and often identify with both their ancestral and host cultures is taken as evidence that these communities remain unintegrated, or that parallel societies exist (Lenneis and Agergaard, 2018). The result can be the 'racialisation of space' (Cohen, 2008), in which (often-negative) stereotypes can be propagated, leading to the ghettoisation and 'color-coding' of neighbourhoods (Cohen, 1996). Such policies can turn relative population densities into absolute markers of racial division, often articulated through images of confrontation such as defining deprived areas as 'no go areas' for the majority. The racialisation of space can also underpin moral panics focusing upon 'invasions' (Burdsey, 2006), where minorities or migrants can be positioned as a threat to an imagined national community in which nation and race fuse (Cohen, 2008; Bairner, 2009, Anderson 1983). Yet, despite these tendencies, more general public discourses about ethnic minority groups often overlook or even deny the existence of systemic racism (Gudrun Jensen et al., 2017; Evans et al., 2020).

Moreover, debates continue concerning the extent to which Islamic culture is compatible with Western culture, including in relation to gendered ideals (Agergaard, 2016; Korteweg and Yurdakul, 2014). For example, Muslim women are often discursively constructed as oppressed (Meret and Siim, 2013), and this oppression is symbolically represented by the veil (e.g., the *Hijab, Niqab* or *Burqa*). This article of clothing is considered by some to be evidence of the patriarchal nature of Muslim society (e.g., Meret and Siim, 2013). Both the *Niqab* or *Burqa*, for example, are now banned in Denmark. Conversely, in Scandinavia, an assumed achievement of gender equality is a relatively well-established narrative. Although the extent of gender equality has often been over-stated here (e.g., Borchorst, 2008; Evans and Pfister 2021), it remains an often-considered moral imperative that has become both nationalised and instrumentalised as populist (and, increasingly, other) parties seek to highlight difference between indigenous 'Western' populations and immigrant communities. Such exceptionalism has had far-reaching impacts on Danish policy concerning the Muslim community, many of whom are, ironically, Danish citizens.

Nevertheless, the Muslim community in Denmark has increased significantly. The number of immigrants from Islamic countries to Denmark has quadrupled within the last 30 years (Statistics Denmark, 2019), and immigrants comprise 13% of Denmark's population. Moreover, an additional 4% are classified as 'descendants' [of migrants], or *efterkommers* (Kristensen, 2020; Bergmann, 2017; Statistics Denmark, 2019; Gudrun Jensen et al., 2017). The official use of the term *efterkommer* is illustrative of wider attitudes towards migration. Literally translated as the 'after-comers,' the descendants of migrants remain differentiated from the host population, irrespective of whether they have Danish citizenship or share cultural identity with 'ethnic Danes.' Although *efterkommers* might be legally Danish, they are often not considered 'true' Danes due to their religious beliefs, cultural practices and, in some cases, their appearance or 'race' (Gudrun Jensen et al., 2017). Conversely, those described as 'Ethnic Danes,' typically people of white-Northern European ancestry, are rarely qualified in this way, being equated with a 'race-less,' normalised identity intertwined with powerful notions of nationality (Agergaard, 2019; Hylton and Lawrence, 2016). So powerful have these rather primordial notions become that some argue that nationalist sentiments and opposition to multiculturalism have become a major pillars of Danish politics (Bergmann, 2017).

Recent times have seen the inexorable rise of nationalist, right-wing populism in the form of the anti-immigrant 'Danish People's Party.' This group has gained political influence by citing the 'problems' caused by immigration and the non-integration of migrants, particularly Muslims. Such a strategy has proved so effective that such views now dominate across all party-political agendas, including liberal and social-democratic parties (Mouritsen and Olsen, 2013; Rydgren, 2010). Hence, many public and political debates and policies specifically target 'non-Western' (Muslim) immigrants and their descendants. In part, this is due to the (self-perpetuated) association of Danish values and Denmark "as a progressive welfare state that advocates social justice, humanitarianism and tolerance" (Gudrun Jensen et al., 2017, p. 66), whilst Islamic culture is described as a threat to the Danish welfare state, identity and culture. The Muslim community is also often presented as homogenous, just as Danish culture is presented as a monoculture, creating a 'binary analytic' between Western ('us') and Islamic ('them') cultures (Mohanty, 1988), despite the continuation of extensive debates about which cultural values and artifacts constitute 'Danishness' (Gudrun Jensen et al., 2017).

The results are an increasingly discriminatory and oppressive policy environment, including a legal bill to confiscate asylum seekers' valuables (now reversed), and since 2018, an 'anti-ghetto plan' aimed at combatting a perceived threat to indigenous culture in areas with high 'non-Western' populations. The latter policy focuses upon predominantly socio-economically deprived neighbourhoods in Danish cities within which many Muslims reside. Moreover, it permits mass housing evictions if the proportion of 'non-Western' residents is over 50% (soon to be reduced to 30%), and enforces mandatory day-care for children aged over one year (often in a day-care outside their local neighbourhood) to ensure children are raised with more 'Danish' values. Non-compliance results in withdrawal of child welfare benefits. Whilst historically, such policies are more readily associated with the far right, they are now also proposed by centre-left politicians such as Prime Minister Mette Frederiksen. Frederiksen, for example, has explicitly stated that the Danish government has a target of accepting zero asylum seekers due to the existential threat that migrants pose to 'Danish' society (TV2, 2021), to the extent that Damascus is now considered safe enough to deny Syrian refugees residency permits (McKernan, 2021). For other residents, the notion that those with mixed heritage can simultaneously hold mixed or multiple identities and allegiances appears to be absent, and there is a strong suspicion that 'integration' is really a synonym for 'assimilation' in such policies (Agergaard, 2019). Furthermore, the lack of assimilation of the Muslim population has been used to justify such repressive policies, and the pre-eminence of such assumptions can also be seen in relation to the way in which participation in LTPA has been politicised.

Muslim participation in LTPA: Experiencing the politics of exclusion

Previous literature has investigated the integrative potential LTPA holds for ethnic minority groups. Studies consistently outline how sport and LTPA are assumed to support social integration in multi-ethnic settings (Janssens and Verweel, 2014; Theeboom et al., 2012), yet participation can still be problematic. For example, inclusion can be relatively limited for ethnic-minority club members, and voluntary exclusion can occur (Evans and Piggott, 2016; Spaaij, 2012). Conversely, minority-ethnic LTPA settings can enable the development of networks across ethnic divisions, facilitate minority-ethnic participants' access to high-status positions, and create supportive environments away from everyday racism and institutionalised 'white privilege' (Walseth, 2016; Bradbury, 2011; Fletcher and Walle, 2015; Evans et al., 2020).

Furthermore, gender also shapes discursive construction of LTPA among minority-ethnic communities. For example, Muslim women's mode of dress and activity choices have become a topic of political discussion and regulation, including a headscarf-ban in sports associations (an act now reversed) (Benn et al., 2011) and ban on the *burkini* (a form of swimming attire providing full-body coverage) in public spaces in several European countries (Sommier, 2019). This can be problematic for Muslim women, for whom the importance of embodied faith is significant. That is, "outward manifestations [of Muslim identity are] inseparably connected to internalised belief and the interconnectedness of faith, body and identity" (Benn et al., 2011, p. 24). Contrary to the narratives outlined above in which Western and Islamic values are held in a binary distinction, studies have instead described how the "mismatch between Western and Islamic cultural requirements for sport-related environments" (Miles and Benn, 2016, p. 724) can be complex and exacerbated by a lack of practical solutions.

Such solutions include provision of gender-segregated spaces where Muslim women can maintain privacy and a sense of refuge (Miles and Benn, 2016; Rana, 2017; Thorpe et al., 2020). Hence, the importance of gender-segregated swimming spaces to Muslim women is consistent across multiple studies, including amongst participants who otherwise do not object to mixed-gender spaces (Walseth, 2016; Miles and Benn, 2016; Kuppinger, 2015). Nevertheless, whilst gender-segregated LTPA has featured extensively in several political debates (e.g., Lenneis and Agergaard, 2018; Rana, 2017; Almila, 2020), the voices of Muslim women themselves are rarely heard. Instead, a predominantly instrumentalist focus on LTPA as a means of promoting health or social integration has often neglected Muslim women's everyday lived experiences of LTPA (Walseth, 2016; Spaaij et al., 2019). Consequently, there is a need to shift focus beyond simply describing barriers to engagement with sport and physical activity and that avoids the "production of knowledge about Muslim women that starts from a position of deficit" (Toffoletti and Palmer, 2017, p. 158).

Therefore, the final section of this chapter focuses on how political and personal experiences intertwine in the Danish context. Here, the legitimacy of gender-segregated swimming was debated between May 2016 and February 2017 (Lenneis and Agergaard, 2018) and resulted in gender-segregated swimming being banned during public opening hours in municipal swimming facilities in Denmark's second largest city, Aarhus (Lenneis and Agergaard, 2018). We will now examine this debate and its consequences.

Gender-segregated swimming and 'Danishness' in Aarhus

Although considered by many of those involved more a 'point of principle' than a significant social issue, debates concerning gender-segregated swimming in Aarhus again highlighted a perceptually oppositional relationship between 'Danishness' and Islamic culture (Lenneis and Agergaard, 2018). The notion that one could be simultaneously Danish and a Muslim was absent. Hence, participants in gender-segregated swimming were assumed to be all Muslims and migrants (they weren't) who resided in the same socio-economically deprived area (they didn't). This space was considered a ghetto where 'Muslim' rather than 'Danish' culture was dominant, and within which a so-called 'parallel society' was assumed to exist that spatially and culturally segregated Denmark and reduced social integration. Gender-segregated swimming was considered an extension of this 'parallel,' subverted space. Both were discursively constructed as threats to the culture of the majority.

Consequently, although it was admitted part-way through the debates that gender-segregated LTPA could help citizens remain healthy and active, many politicians highlighted how the 'threat' of alternative values to 'Danish' society was more significant than any such benefits. Moreover, although completely absent from these debates, the Muslim women who participated in gender-segregated swimming were presented as oppressed by their husbands, from whom they needed to be 'liberated' along with the 'un-Danish environments they [came] from [in their local area]' (Peter Udengaard of the Social Democratic party, cited by Lenneis and Agergaard, 2018, p. 713). Notably, a gender-segregated swimming programme in a wealthier area of the city dedicated to nude winter swimming was not criticised, presumably because many participants were white Danish women, and nude swimming (along with sexual liberation) is associated with Danish liberal values (*frisind*). Ironically, several politicians in the debate argued that all citizens should have equal access to public space (irrespective of their gender), as anything else was 'un-Danish.' And yet such a judgement was only applied to those circumstances where being of Muslim faith was a motivation to participate. In such circumstances, it was assumed LTPA must be structured along religious grounds, and the swimming pool became a 'Muslim' space. Having a religious motivation to participate was, therefore, considered unacceptable, irrespective of whether other motivations were also evident.

It is hard to see such caricatures imposed upon the Muslim community as anything other than racist. Similarly, the problematisation of gender-segregated swimming in the case of a socially deprived area in which a Muslim diaspora was present, but not in relation to gender-segregated nude swimming in a wealthier area, is also hard to justify beyond culturally racist arguments. Here we again see the racialisation of space writ large on two scales: in descriptions of the Muslim community and the 'ghettoes' in which its members apparently resided, and also in terms of the swimming spaces in which Muslim women participants (particularly from a low socio-economic class) might constitute a majority. Such a possibility was apparently intolerable in a 'public' (i.e., 'ethnically Danish') space. It seemed that the implicit assumption was that the majority of participants were Muslim; this was therefore a Muslim space, which made it antagonistic to other (secular) public spaces in which the majority were assumed to be ethnic Danes (i.e., white). Where Muslim women were not present or were in the minority, such a qualification was simply not applied. In other words, the women-only nude swimming programme was not labelled 'secular,' 'Christian' nor 'Danish,' and its legitimacy was not questioned. Such white privilege rarely demands qualification; it is both normative and culturally hegemonic. Hence, the public (or 'the people') in such spaces were not problematised.

The result of these debates was a ban on women-only swimming in municipal swimming pools during public opening hours, although not outside of these times. Presumably, Muslim women could still swim, therefore, even if it was in the middle of the night. Moreover, the implications of these arguments were not lost on participants, who were aware how the debate and its consequences interfered with their freedom of choice and was considered oppressive (Lenneis and Agergaard, 2018). Nevertheless, there were signs of resistance. For example, an activist group consisting of mainly non-Muslim women resisted the ban, calling out the characterisation of Muslim women as oppressed. Yet, Muslim women remained largely absent from both the debates *and* the protest movements. Similar observations can be made about the broader national context, where protest movements such as Black Lives Matter have resulted in the Danish mass media beginning to take a critical stance about everyday racism in Denmark (Cramon, 2020). Here too, though, the voices of members of minority communities remain largely absent. Nevertheless, we did speak to participants in the women-only swimming programmes in Aarhus, and it is to their experiences that our discussion now turns.

The lived experience of politicised Muslim women

Following the debates outlined above, we conducted an ethnographic study (Lenneis et al., 2020) into the lived experience of the participants in women-only swimming at two separate sites with the pseudonyms '*Vestskolen*' (at a state school swimming pool at weekends, organised by a multi-ethnic sport club) and at '*Byensbad*' (a public swimming pool in a socially deprived area of Aarhus organised by a large swimming club from a wealthier area of the city). In brief, the study took a transnational feminist approach to investigate the relationship between gender relations and the nationalist projects relating to citizenship, origin and culture apparent in the study context. In this sense, following Yuval-Davis (2011), we drew upon Benedict Anderson's (1983) concept of nations as 'imagined communities' to analyse how symbols, language, cultural codes of behaviour and style of dress played a crucial role in determining whether participants felt belonging to the Danish 'nation.' After Yuval-Davis (2006, 2011), we distinguished between 'belonging,' or people's emotional attachment to and identification with the national collective, and the 'politics of belonging' relating to ethic and political value systems. Such aspects of belonging also have a spatial aspect (Antonsich, 2010).

The study consisted of participant observations conducted by two of the present authors for twice a week for two hours each for a period of two months, together with interviews with regular participants. Key foci included participants' (migration) biographies, motivations for participating and their experiences of the activity, and their attitudes and perceptions of the political debate outlined above. Semi-structured interviews were shaped by observations and field notes pertaining to informal conversations, behaviours and practices in the groups. Following thematic analysis (Terry et al., 2017), several themes were constructed, of which we now reprise relating to the intersection of politics, gendered body and space. Pseudonyms are used throughout.

Consistently, participants contrasted their experiences of racializing processes between the swimming space and broader public spaces by reflecting on their perceptions of (non)belonging (Yuval-Davis, 1993, 2006, 2011), particularly in relation to how belonging was contested in the political pressure to adopt 'normative' (i.e., 'white') Danish identities and values. Initially, the prevalence of expectations that one should swim in mixed-gender spaces had proved problematic, and most stated that they were uncomfortable in such environments. Such feelings were exacerbated by the necessity of wearing a burkini in mixed-gender spaces (including at the beach), which participants felt highlighted their alterity, to the extent that it prevented participation. Participants considered the burkini to be both physically uncomfortable and heavy, and felt unease due to fears about the potentially negative attention such a swimsuit would attract in public in Denmark. Amira explained:

> I want to avoid the risk of running into people who will throw some negative comments at me. […] Let's assume I'd dress in a burkini, which I would not do, because… let me try to put that in a nice way, I don't think that I'd be able to cope with those kind of people that will stop and tell me that I shouldn't be there or that I should take the burkini off.

Here the consequences of the heightened attention paid to feminine-Muslim swimming attire by the Danish mass media and politicians can be observed, because of the construction of the burkini as a visible sign of 'otherness' and a signifier of non-belonging. Indeed, experiences of being 'othered' based on their attire, including the headscarf, were also commonly experienced throughout participants' lives.

When reflecting on the political debates, participants described feeling "tired, disappointed, angry, sad and hurt" (Meher) about the preoccupation with Muslim dress-code, beliefs and culture, which they often felt relied upon sweeping generalisations. They also described feeling how these debates and the decision to ban women-only swimming had violated their freedom of choice, and their rights to express their identity and religious beliefs, both considered fundamental human rights. Moreover, most rejected assimilation and maintained a sense of their own cultural heritage, whilst simultaneously emphasizing that they felt 'Danish,' despite the public stigma and hostility often directed towards them. Several held Danish passports, with several born in Denmark. Therefore, as Danish-Muslims, many of the women expressed how their identities were multiple, and whilst they might exist locally, their identity was an amalgamation of local and transnational cultural awareness. Yet, most were resigned to never being accepted as 'Danes.' As Nabila explained:

> Forget that somebody will come to you and tell you that you're Danish. No, no… maybe they tell *you* [referring to Verena, a 'white', non-Danish researcher], but not *me*. I will always be a foreigner.

Hence, participants were keenly aware of the monadic and mono-racial presentation of a narrow definition of 'Danishness' (Simonsen 2018). Within this definition, biological descent ('whiteness') and 'non-religiousness' were two criteria of belonging in Denmark to which participants felt they could never adhere, irrespective of their choices and personal feelings (Yuval-Davis, 2006).

Such feelings of alterity and otherness outside the gender-segregated swimming space contrasted with feelings of belonging and inclusion within it. Participants emphasised how such sessions provided comfort, a sense of well-being and familiarity with others around them in a way which emphasised a lack of surveillance and judgement. The combination of religious sensitivity and tolerance and feelings of socially acceptable maintenance of modesty were assigned great value, and most participants described how being a Muslim guided their conduct in everyday life, irrespective of whether they chose to embody their faith by wearing a headscarf or burkini. Indeed, although Islamic values had shaped their decision to participate in gender-segregated swimming, the women were at pains to emphasise how abiding by these precepts was a matter of choice, and strongly resisted the suggestion their decisions were enforced by their husbands or other men. Instead, women-only swimming, as with being a Muslim, was considered an amalgamation of religious duty and personal choice, and in enacting this agency, women demonstrated a "capacity for action that historically specific relations of subordination enable and create" (Mahmood, 2011, p. 203). Here, the women felt safer and "could be more open and be themselves" (Farzaneh). Not being subjected to the male or 'white' gaze for a time was considered liberating (Rana, 2017). As Jazmin outlined:

> I'd say, for Muslim women, it's mostly about religion. Because they don't want to, they cannot swim among men, they just can't. […] But if you remove the religious aspect, I'd say it's for many women pleasant to swim without men staring at you. It's very pleasant, in a way liberating, that you don't have to worry about your booty or bosom dangling […]

Indeed, it was striking how little the women focused upon one another's ethnicity in this setting, despite their heterogeneous cultural backgrounds (including Somalis, Arabs, Syrians and Turks), and several expressed a wish that more ethnic Danish women join them. Thus, a sense of 'shared sisterhood' was emphasised in which a sense of community was present, despite few of the women socialising regularly outside the pool space. In short, the notion that gender-segregated swimming fostered the development of a parallel society was simply untrue; women-only swimming, as experienced by participants, was rarely more than an interlude in their wider lives. The disjuncture between wider political debates and the individual experience of LTPA could therefore hardly be clearer.

Conclusion

Our discussion has highlighted how the politics of exclusion have long resulted in the racialisation of space. That is, the demographic characteristics of an area into absolute markers of the 'ethnicity' of spaces and neighbourhoods, leading to their ghettoisation and 'color-coding' such that they are considered divided from other spaces. Such processes have once more gained pace due to the resurgence of populist and nationalist politics, within which common narratives are often reproduced, focusing on 'threats' to the cultural majority and the existence of 'parallel societies.' In the Danish context, for example, Muslim culture is often positioned as antagonistic to an idealised, monadic majority culture, in which values such as liberalism, gender equality and democracy are assumed to reside. In contrast, many Islamic values are negatively portrayed as oppressive, illiberal and patriarchal.

The spaces and places of LTPA have been similarly racialised, albeit more ephemerally. In the Danish context, LTPA is often discursively constructed as a site for the reproduction of 'Danish' majority cultural values such as inclusion and democracy – and gender equality. This assumption is based upon a long history of 'Danish Associationalism,' including the strengthening of social cohesion and Danish values through LTPA (Ibsen and Ottesen, 2003). Hence, the existence of programmes and activities in which ethnic minorities – and their apparently 'anti-Danish' values – comprise a majority of participants has been problematised. Such programmes have been characterised in Danish political debates as an invasion of 'public' space by those holding alien values, contra the legitimate 'public' which is conceived of as a monocultural, ethnically (white) Danish one. The fact that some of the activities are gender-segregated is considered further evidence of difference. Hence, the racialisation of LTPA space is conceptualised as an extension of the 'anti-ghetto plan': that is, the ghettoisation of LTPA only exists for as long as activities associated with the presence of ethnic minorities are delivered.

Such racializing political constructions of the gender-segregated swimming space are, however, at odds with the lived experience of participants in the Danish city of Aarhus. For them, the gender-segregated swimming space was considered a safe-haven, where a shared sense of sisterhood could be developed in a supportive environment, and within which participants could express their cultural identity without the judgmental gaze perceived elsewhere. Far from being oppressed by their male relations, participants emphasised the voluntary nature of participation, and the group had a casual membership who rarely socialised with one another outside the sessions themselves. What's more, most participants considered themselves *both* Danish and Muslim. Contrary to the extension of a parallel society into the public spaces of LTPA in Denmark, therefore, in this case, women-only swimming appeared to be ephemeral, and a brief respite for participants from the political discourses that characterised (and often stigmatised) them. Our observations, therefore, highlight the importance of understanding the politicisation of gender in terms of the complex intersections between gender, ethnicity, religion and other social inequalities.

REFERENCES

Abrams, M. and Bartlett, M. L. (2019) 'SportToo: Implications of and best practice for the #MeToo movement in sport.' *Journal of Clinical Sport Psychology*, 13(2), pp. 243–258.

Agergaard, S. (2016) 'Religious culture as a barrier? A counter-narrative of Danish Muslim girls' participation in sports.' *Qualitative Research in Sport, Exercise and Health*, 8(2), pp. 213–224.

Agergaard, S. (2018) *Rethinking sports and integration: Developing a transnational perspective on migrants and descendants in sports*. London: Routledge.

Agergaard, S. (2019) 'Nationalising minority ethnic athletes: Danish media representations of Nadia Nadim around the UEFA women's Euro 2017.' *Sport in History*, 39(2), pp. 130–146.

Agergaard, S., Michelsen La Cour, A. and Gregersen, M. T. (2016) 'Politicisation of migrant leisure: A public and civil intervention involving organised sports.' *Leisure Studies*, 35(2), pp. 200–214.

Almila, A.-M. (2020) 'Hijab, sport and schooling in Finland: From principles to practice.' *Youth and Globalization,* 2(1), pp. 38–64.

Anderson, B. (1983). *Imagined communities: Reflections on the origins and spread of nationalism*. London: Verso.

Antonsich, M. (2010) 'Searching for belonging: An analytical framework.' *Geography Compass*, 4(6), pp. 644–659.

Bairner, A. (2009) 'National sports and national landscapes: In defence of primordialism.' *National Identities*, 11(3), pp. 223–239.

Benn, T., Dagkas, S. and Jawad, H. (2011) 'Embodied faith: Islam, religious freedom and educational practices in physical education.' *Sport, Education and Society*, 16(1), pp. 17–34.

Bergmann, E. (2017) 'Denmark: From multi-ethnic and supra-national empire to little Denmark.' *Nordic nationalism and right-wing populist politics*. London: Springer.

Borchorst, A. (2008) 'Woman-friendly policy paradoxes? Childcare policies and gender equality visions in Scandinavia', in Melby, K., Carlsson Wetterberg, C. and Ravn, A. B. (eds.) *Gender equality and welfare politics in Scandinavia: The limits of political ambition*. Bristol: Policy Press, pp. 27–42.

Bradbury, S. (2011) 'From racial exclusions to new inclusions: Black and minority ethnic participation in football clubs in the East Midlands of England.' *International Review for the Sociology of Sport*, 46(1), pp. 23–44.

Brubaker, R. (2017) 'Between nationalism and civilizationism: The European populist moment in comparative perspective.' *Ethnic and Racial Studies,* 40(8): pp. 1191–1226.

Burdsey, D. (2006) *British Asians and football: Culture, identity, exclusion*. London: Routledge.

Cohen, R. (2008) *Global diasporas: An introduction*. London: Routledge.

Cohen, R. (1996). Homing devices. In Amit-Talai, V. and Knowles, C. (Eds). *Re-situating identities: The politics of race, ethnicity, and culture*, pp. 68–82. Toronto: University of Toronto Press.

Cramon, L. (2020) '30 fortællinger slår fast, at vi er for ringe til at sige fra over for Racisme i Danmark (30 accounts emphasize that we fail to say no to racism in Denmark).' Available at: www.Information.dk (Accessed 13th March 2021).

Curtis, M. (2009) *Orientalism and Islam: European thinkers on oriental despotism in the Middle East and India*. Cambridge: Cambridge University Press.

Donnelly, P. (2008) 'Sport and human rights.' *Sport in Society*, 11(4), pp. 381–394.

Elgenius, G. and Rydgren, J. (2019) 'Frames of nostalgia and belonging: The resurgence of ethno-nationalism in Sweden.' *European Societies*, 21(4), pp. 583–602.

Evans, A. B., Agergaard, S., Campbell, P. I., Hylton, K. and Lenneis, V. (2020) "Black lives matter:' Sport, race and ethnicity in challenging times.' *European Journal for Sport and Society*, 17(4), pp. 289–300.

Evans, A. B. and Pfister, G. U. (2021) 'Women in sports leadership: A systematic narrative review.' *International Review for the Sociology of Sport*, 56(3), pp. 317–342.

Evans, A. B. and Piggott, D. (2016) 'Shooting for Lithuania: Migration, national identity and men's basketball in the East of England.' *Sociology of Sport Journal*, 33(1), pp. 26–38.

Fletcher, T. and Walle, T. (2015) 'Negotiating their right to play: Asian-specific cricket teams and leagues in the UK and Norway.' *Identities*, 22(2), pp. 230–246.

Gudrun Jensen, T., Weibel, K. and Vitus, K. (2017) "There is no racism here': Public discourses on racism, immigrants and integration in Denmark.' *Patterns of Prejudice*, 51(1), pp. 51–68.

Hylton, K. and Lawrence, S. (2016) "'For your ears only!" Donald Sterling and backstage racism in sport.' *Ethnic and Racial Studies*, 39(15), pp. 2740–2757.

Ibsen, B. and Ottesen, L. (2003) 'Sport and welfare policy in Denmark: The development of sport between state, market and community.' *Sport and Welfare Policies*. Reading (PA): Hofmann.

Janssens, J. and Verweel, P. (2014) 'The significance of sports clubs within multicultural society. On the accumulation of social capital by migrants in culturally "mixed" and "separate" sports clubs.' *European Journal for Sport and Society*, 11(1), pp. 35–58.

Kidd, B. and Donnelly, P. (2000) 'Human rights in sports.' *International Review for the Sociology of Sport*, 35(2), pp. 131–148.

Korteweg, A. C. and Yurdakul, G. (2014) *The headscarf debates: Conflicts of national belonging*. Redwood city (CA): Stanford University Press.

Kristensen, R. N. (2020) 'Hvor Mange Muslimer Er Der i Danmark? [How Many Muslims Are There in Denmark?]' [Online]. Available at: https://www.mm.dk/tjekdet/artikel/hvor-mange-muslimer-er-der-i-danmark (Accessed 14th April 2020).

Kuppinger, P. (2015) 'Pools, piety, and participation: A Muslim women's sports club and urban citizenship in Germany.' *Journal of Muslim Minority Affairs*, 35(2), pp. 264–279.

Lenneis, V. and Agergaard, S. (2018) 'Enacting and resisting the politics of belonging through leisure. The debate about gender-segregated swimming sessions targeting Muslim women in Denmark.' *Leisure Studies*, 37(6), pp. 706–720.

Lenneis, V., Agergaard, S. and Evans, A. B. (2020) 'Women-only swimming as a space of belonging.' *Qualitative Research in Sport, Exercise and Health*, 14(1), pp. 37–52. https://doi.org/10.1080/2159676X.2020.1844790

Mahmood, S. (2011) *Politics of piety: The Islamic revival and the feminist subject*. Princeton NJ: Princeton University Press.

McKernan, B. (2021) 'Denmark strips Syrian refugees of residency permits and says it is safe to go home.' *The Guardian online*. Available at: https://www.theguardian.com/world/2021/apr/14/denmark-revokes-syrian-refugee-permits-under-new-policy (Accessed 6th May 2021).

Meret, S. and Siim, B. (2013) 'Gender, populism and politics of belonging: Discourses of right-wing populist parties in Denmark, Norway and Austria', in *Negotiating gender and diversity in an emergent European public sphere*. London: Springer.

Miles, C. and Benn, T. (2016) 'A case study on the experiences of university-based Muslim women in physical activity during their studies at one UK higher education institution.' *Sport, Education and Society*, 21(5), pp. 723–740.

Mohanty, C. (1988) 'Under Western eyes: Feminist scholarship and colonial discourses.' *Feminist review*, 30(1), pp. 61–88.

Mouritsen, P. and Olsen, T.V. (2013) 'Denmark between liberalism and nationalism.' *Ethnic and Racial Studies*, 36(4), pp. 691–710.

Mudde, C. (2004) 'The populist zeitgeist.' *Government and Opposition*, 39(4), pp. 541–563.

Mudde, C. and Kaltwasser, C. R. (2012) *Populism in Europe and the Americas: Threat or corrective for democracy?*. Cambridge: Cambridge University Press.

Rana, J. (2017) 'Ladies-only!', in Ratna, A and Samie, S. F. (eds.) *Race, gender and sport: The politics of ethnic 'other' girls and women*. London: Routledge, pp. 148–167.

Rydgren, J. (2010) 'Radical right-wing populism in Denmark and Sweden: Explaining party system change and stability.' *SAIS Review of International Affairs*, 30(1), pp. 57–71.

Sommier, M. (2019) 'Insights into the construction of cultural realities: Foreign newspaper discourses about the burkini ban in France.' *Ethnicities,* 19(2), pp. 251–270.

Spaaij, R. (2012) 'Beyond the playing field: Experiences of sport, social capital, and integration among Somalis in Australia.' *Ethnic and Racial Studies*, 35(9), pp. 1519–1538.

Spaaij, R., Broerse, J., Oxford, S., Luguetti, C., Mclachlan, F., Mcdonald, B., Klepac, B., Lymbery, L., Bishara, J. and Pankowiak, A. (2019) 'Sport, refugees, and forced migration: A critical review of the literature.' *Frontiers in Sports and Active Living,* pp. 1, 47. https://doi.org/10.3389/fspor.2019.00047

Statistics Denmark. (2019) 'Indvandrere i Danmark [Immigrants in Denmark].' Available at: https://www.dst.dk/Site/Dst/Udgivelser/GetPubFile.aspx?id=29446&sid=indv2019 (Accessed 2nd March 2020).

Terry, G., Hayfield, N., Clarke, V. and Braun, V. (2017) 'Thematic analysis,' in Willig, C. and Rogers, W. S. (eds.) *The Sage handbook of qualitative research in psychology*. London: Sage, pp. 17–37.

Thangaraj, S., Ratna, A., Burdsey, D. and Rand, E. (2018) 'Leisure and the racing of national populism.' *Leisure Studies*, 37(6), pp. 648–661.

Theeboom, M., Schaillée, H. and Nols, Z. (2012) 'Social capital development among ethnic minorities in mixed and separate sport clubs.' *International Journal of Sport Policy and Politics*, 4(1), pp. 1–21.

Thiel, A., Villanova, A., Toms, M., Friis Thing, L. and Dolan, P. (2016) 'Can sport be "un-political"?' *European Journal for Sport and Society*, 13(4), pp. 253–255.

Thorpe, H., Ahmad, N., Marfell, A. and Richards, J. (2020) Muslim women's sporting spatialities: Navigating culture, religion and moving bodies in Aotearoa New Zealand. *Gender, Place & Culture*, 29(1), pp. 52–79. https://doi.org/10.1080/0966369X.2020.1855123

Thylin, J. (2017) *'The Burkini as a symbolic threat: Anthropological perspectives on the ban of the burkini on French beaches 2016.'* Thesis published by the Lund University Department of Social Anthropology.

Toffoletti, K. and Palmer, C. (2017) 'New approaches for studies of Muslim women and sport.' *International Review for the Sociology of Sport*, 52(2), pp. 146–163.

TV2 (2021). 'Mette Frederiksen: Målet er nul asylansøgere til Danmark.' Available athttps://nyheder.tv2.dk/politik/2021-01-22-mette-frederiksen-malet-er-nul-asylansogere-til-danmark (accessed 24th February 2021)

Walseth, K. (2016) 'Sport within Muslim organizations in Norway: Ethnic segregated activities as arena for integration.' *Leisure Studies*, 35(1), pp. 78–99.

Williamson, L. (2020.) 'France Islam: Muslims under pressure to sign French values charter.' *BBC*. Available at: https://www.bbc.com/news/world-europe-55132098 (Accessed 24th February 2021).

Yuval-Davis, N. (1993) 'Gender and nation.' *Ethnic and Racial Studies*, 16(4), pp. 621–632.

Yuval-Davis, N. (2006) 'Belonging and the politics of belonging.' *Patterns of Prejudice*, 40(3), pp. 197–214.

Yuval-Davis, N. (2011) *The politics of belonging: Intersectional contestations*. London: Sage.

12

Patriarchal Politics of Women Footballers in Australia

Changing the Narrative from Welfare to Women Saving Men's Football

Michael Burke, Matthew Klugman and Kate O'Halloran

Introduction

In 2016, the Australian Football League (AFL) announced that its inaugural A F L Women's (AFLW) would begin in 2017. The news that the most watched sport in Australia would now have an elite national competition for women was widely celebrated as a significant step towards gender equality (O'Halloran, 2018a). Yet, the development of the AFLW – and the associated narratives of progress – was still shaped by assumptions and practices of sexist oppression that have worked to undermine and constrain the new league. Even before the league began, the telling of its pre-history was problematic and indicative of a discourse that was yet to fully grapple with the layers of sexism that mould sports in Australia.

One important and telling example concerned the accounts of the earlier formation of a junior women's competition in Victoria, the Australian state in which the sport was initially developed, and from which it is still largely run. Penny Cula-Reid, in particular, was frequently credited for her contribution to the progress of the AFLW by forcing the existing adult leagues to create a junior women's competition. As Paul Amy (2016), a Melbourne journalist, told his readers:

> She'll be a trailblazer in 2017 just as she was almost 15 years ago when, as a schoolgirl, she went to the Victorian Civil and Administrative Tribunal and effectively forced AFL Victoria to create a youth girls competition.

In 2004, Cula-Reid, Emily Stayner and Helen Taylor had courageously taken on both the state governing body (Football Victoria) and their local Melbourne suburban junior league (the Moorabbin Saints Junior Football League). At issue was the 2003 decision by Football Victoria disallowing girls from competing against boys after the age of 12. Despite the narrative of Amy and others, this was not a case about creating an alternative 'youth girls competition'. It was a case about the continued participation with the clubs that Cula-Reid, Stayner and Taylor had already been playing with (Cula-Reid had been playing with her club since the age of 6).

The Moorabbin Saints Junior Football League (MSJFL) argued that the exclusion of girls over 12 was necessary both to protect the safety of girls and to avoid the possibility that boys would change their playing behaviours if girls were allowed to continue playing past the age of 12. The first justification suggested that young women, unlike young men, are incapable of making rational decisions regarding their safety in playing contact sports. As the presiding judge, Justice Stuart Morris, noted scathingly, this rationale 'belongs in another age. Put simply, such an approach is sexist, even when well-intentioned' (Taylor v Moorabbin Saints Junior Football League and Football Victoria, 2008, s. 53). It is an example of what Wood and Garn (2016, p. 242) classify as 'benevolent sexism', a crucial support for more hostile forms of sexism because it presents the women footballer as requiring protection and control. The second justification suggested that the desires and interests of males are more important than the desires, interests and participation of female players (Burke, 2014). Justice Morris noted that the lived experiences of the players suggested that adolescent men did not alter their playing behaviour when adolescent women were present on the field. But even if the young men had altered the way they played football, that would not justify the exclusion of young women from these games.

Cula-Reid, Stayner and Taylor did not win the case. While Justice Morris ruled that girls could now play against boys until the age of 14, he gave the football competitions the right to decide whether the girls played against boys up to the age of 16:

> Whether the three complainants can play in the coming season rests with the football associations. It is lawful for the football associations to exclude them from the under 15 and under 16 competitions. It is equally lawful for the associations to allow them to play (s. 91).

The MSJFL responded by deregistering Cula-Reid and Stayner (who were 14 by this time), while Taylor was only allowed to play until she was 14. A worthwhile by-product of this case was the recognition of the need for the development of junior leagues for women footballers in Victoria. Such junior leagues were soon created. However, their creation rested on the exclusion of girls from the previously established under 15 and 16 junior Australian Rules football competitions in Victoria. An exclusion that continues at the time of writing.

The orientation that we take in this chapter is a radical feminist one, particularly informed by Nancy Fraser's (2009, 2017) explanation that feminist justice requires both cultural recognition and economic redistribution, and that neither of these goals should be sacrificed to a de-radicalised narrative of individual or identity-group empowerment. While we cannot challenge all of the historical, organisational and cultural structures that a feminist football league hoping to achieve cultural recognition would need to address and dismantle, we will suggest a counter-narrative of women's football that may commence this process. Elizabeth Grosz denotes three interweaving levels of misogynistic oppression in philosophical discourse: sexism, patriarchy and phallocentrism. Sexism is understood as 'the *unwarranted* differential treatment of the two sexes, to the benefit of one at the expense of the other' (Grosz, 1988, p. 93, italics in original). Sexism refers to explicit acts, such as openly hostile remarks or practices towards women, which force women to practice a discourse in the same way as men (Thompson, 1994). Overt sexism could be largely eradicated in philosophy without interrupting the underlying structures of gender oppression (Grosz, 1988). Patriarchy is a hierarchical system that places men's issues, actions, knowledge and values as superior to those of women (Code, 2014; Grosz, 1988). Phallocentric discursive systems operate to collapse the two sexes into a single, universal subject, and, in doing so, the subject is made 'congruent only with the masculine' (Grosz, 1988, p. 94). There is no conceptual space within phallocentric discourse for women to develop an autonomous set of issues, actions, values or strategies for opposing sexism and patriarchy from their subjective set of experiences. Each possibility for women confirms the primacy of the male standard; they may become identical to, the inferior opposite of, or the complement to the standard (Grosz, 1988; Thompson, 1994).

The exclusion of Cula-Reid, Stayner and Taylor (and many other young women) from playing Australian Rules football against young men in under 15 (or under 16) competitions is emblematic of the ongoing sexism, patriarchy and phallocentrism of the existing football competition bureaucracy. The young women were positioned as in need of protection, the playing behaviour of the young men was deemed more important than the participation of the women and there was no space to consider the subjective experiences of the young women (the pleasures, for example, of competing against the young men). The continued exclusion upholds the problematic rationales used to justify this discrimination.

Moreover, the women who ran the Women's Victorian Football League were not placed in charge of the new junior competitions for girls and young women. Up until this point, women had relatively autonomous control over (adult) women's football, partly because (as with other football codes) the men's football organisations generally ignored women's football leagues (Lenkic and Hess, 2016; Cox and Pringle, 2011). The shift in discursive control to the men who already ran the junior competitions for boys was a sign of what would come with the advent of the AFLW as men took control of the growing market for female participants (Woodhouse, Fielding-Lloyd and Sequerra, 2019). The expanded discursive control of men over football discourse would undermine the resistant and transformative potential of both girls' and women's football.

It could be argued that the creation of the junior competitions for young women – and especially the creation of the AFLW – is testament to how the AFL (and the broader football industry) is working to eliminate sexism. However, while these developments are important, this chapter will show that not only do some overt forms of sexism remain, but that patriarchy and phallocentrism continue to structure the discourse around women playing Australian Rules football. Drawing on the feminist theories of Grosz and others, we consider the enduring sexist narratives around female footballers, the AFL's struggle to respond to the sexist targeting of players – particularly in relation to online abuse, the patriarchal development of rules for the AFLW competition and the broader phallocentrism that continues to constrain what an elite national competition for women could look like and become. We conclude by exploring how these existing discourses might be deconstructed and replaced with more affirmative alternatives. In particular, we outline a more powerful narrative around football participation rates that suggests that it was the men's football competitions of the early 2000s, at least at the community level, that were saved by the growth in the women's game.

Forms of football sexism

'Professional Australian Rules football is a man's game', observed Beverley Poynton and John Hartley in 1990; 'Men play, coach, promote, officiate, administrate, commentate and follow footy' (Poynton and Hartley, 1990, p. 144). The 'incursions' into this purportedly male space have frequently met with misogynistic hostility and backlash (Klugman, 2016; Faludi, 1992). In 1947, the then captain-coach of the Richmond Victorian Football League team, Jack Dyer, responded to the debate about women playing football with claims that women were physically and mentally unsuited to the game, that 'their minds would be bewildered by the rules', and that participation in football would imperil their 'chance to become mothers', 'harden their muscles' and 'coarsen their whole appearance' (Lenkic and Hess, 2016, pp. 117–118). Such heteronormative and homophobic allusions remain typical of many comments about women playing football. More recently, Patrick McCauley, poet and writer, revealingly wrote that:

> Although …the AFL sponsors and supports girls' football in schools, the true spectacle and essential attraction of the game requires thirty-six exquisitely fit testosterone-pumped men attempting to subdue each other with speed and skill. Football is men's business - it is quite possibly sacred men's business - and the attempts to feminise it are *ideologically driven, nasty and envious attempts at a weird kind of retribution* which could prove absolutely counter-productive.
>
> (2008, p. 1, our emphasis)

Since the inception of the AFLW competition, the female players have been frequently vilified with sexist abuse on various forms of social media (O'Halloran, 2019b). Instead of investing in additional moderation and proactive responses, the AFL, its media partners and social media companies have largely ignored the issue. Things came to a head in 2019 when the AFL's primary television partner, Channel 7, published a picture of Carlton AFLW player Tayla Harris kicking for goal. Though Harris' classic kicking action in the striking image was similar to celebrated photos of male players like E.J. Whitten and Nicky Winmar, the abuse the photo received was 'degrading, sexist, transphobic' and 'homophobic' (Symons, 2019a). Yet, rather than call out the trolling, and/or block them and delete their comments, Channel 7 deleted the picture. It was a fundamentally defensive reaction which suggested the photo itself was the cause of the problem, rather than the misogynist insults (O'Halloran, 2019b).

AFLW fans responded with an impressive show of force from a fan group that is frequently demeaned. They took pride in the image, and their stinging critique of the complicity of the football industry led both Channel 7 and the AFL to apologise (Symons, 2019a). It was a unifying show of resistant group agency (Dworkin and Messner, 1999), which arose from the shared consciousness of subjection to sexist abuse and athletic trivialisation. The AFLW subsequently created badges with that image of Harris, and a corporate sponsor of the game commissioned a statue (Symons, 2019b). Yet, neither the AFL nor its subsidiary AFLW organisation have made eliminating sexist abuse (and sexism in general) a priority.

Perhaps the passivity of the AFL is shaped by the broader discourse that female players should be 'grateful' that they have an elite national competition at all, and that the AFLW is 'lucky' to receive widespread commercial media coverage (Riley, 2019). As an example, the chief football journalist for the Melbourne's *Herald-Sun* tabloid newspaper, Mark Robinson (2018), expressed this position when women players argued that the AFLW season should be extended to an 11-week season. Robinson wrote:

> the lashing by the [AFLW] players of the AFL is over the top…The AFLW standard is only average. It's played in slow motion… Skills are poor. Fitness is improving, scoring is low… and most of half of the population won't give it a second thought… I watch it. I like the contest… But the product is out of whack in regards to performance and its coverage. The players like to call themselves elite, professional part-timers - and, yes, they sacrifice plenty to play - but with that has come a *sense of entitlement*…
>
> (2018, our emphasis)

The responses to Robinson's article in the online comments section revealed significant contempt towards the AFLW game in 182 of the 226 comments. The sporting spectacle was labelled as 'a joke', 'junk', 'crap', 'comical' and 'not REAL football' [capitalisation occurred in many comments]. Guarded 'support' for the players and competition came from 20 comments, but all 20 followed the theme of 'improvement in the spectacle will occur over time'. Patriarchal 'truth' making in football can also be found coming from the supporters of women's football. In one such example, a comment claimed that: 'We have actually become so aware of being sexist that we are out of whack with reality and we expect women to be as good as the men'.

As those calling out this backlash noted, among other things, such analyses did not challenge the current male standard of 'good' football (O'Halloran, 2018b). The longstanding patriarchal and phallocentric spaces, traditions and practices in football view both the male footballer and the organisation of men's football as the standards for excellence in this sport, with patriarchal metrics like speed, power and range of kicks driving negative comparisons (Jeanes et al., 2021). In traditional football discourse, the part-time woman footballer is an inferior version of the full-time male footballer. But, paraphrasing Code (2014, p. 149), the existence of the woman footballer [and other Others], both in history and now, is the contradiction that the phallocentric view of the 'white male centre' can no longer sustain.

Sexism also exists at the community sport level, where women's participation is fitted around the 'requirements' of men's leagues, clubs and players, as if historical sexism provides justification for ongoing access inequities around such things as grounds, training slots, sponsorship and gym equipment (Jeanes et al., 2021). Historical ownership is used to view any justice-based change to ground usage as an *unfair intrusion* (Pelak, 2002). The discursive force of patriarchy is solidified when the history of inequity, exclusion, trivialisation and disdain is forgotten in the celebration of contemporary 'equality'. In an important corrective, Pavlidis cautions 'against an orientation towards gratitude, for opportunities women have been "given" and for inequitable pay and conditions' (2020, p. 6; see also O'Halloran, 2018b).

Patriarchal rules and phallocentric constraints

The new AFLW league was celebrated by many as a chance for women to finally be able to play Australian Rules football at an elite, national level that mirrored that of the AFL(M) competition for men. Yet, the AFL decided that it was necessary to amend the rules under which the women would play in order to 'ensure this is a great game to play and exciting to watch' (AFL News, 2016). Key changes include making the ball smaller, making the game significantly shorter and reducing the number of players on the field (for a summary, see Table 1 in Pavlidis, Toffoletti and Sanders, 2020, p. 7). As Hibberd notes, the smaller ball was harder to kick accurately and did not travel as far, making it harder for women to demonstrate the skills valued by so many men (Hibberd, 2021). Further, Sanders (2020, p. 686) explains that the uniforms that were chosen by the AFL represented a patriarchal necessity that the female footballer was 'a legitimately feminine footballing body', a discursive response by male football organisations towards the historical normalisation and acceptance of all forms of sexuality in women's football.

The AFL justified these changes on the basis that these would 'ensure' that AFLW was 'exciting to watch' (AFL News, 2016). Not only did this imply that if women played with the same ball and rules as the men that the games would be unexciting, it also denied women the chance to play exactly the same game as the men, and for many, departed from the game they had played at junior levels. As one veteran women's footballer noted: 'I'm happy there is an AFL[W] just disappointed the game I've played for 21 year has to be changed for an audience that largely didn't know it existed prior to this year' (Pavlidis, Toffoletti and Sanders, 2020, p. 10).

In a process emblematic of the patriarchal practices of the current Australian Rules football bureaucracy, these rule changes were imposed on women by a group largely made up of men with no transparency for the purported good of the game (Lane, 2018). As Pavlidis, Toffoletti and Sanders (2020) show, this process has also been resisted and critiqued by AFLW fans. However, a broader phallocentrism also constrains the development of the AFLW competition. The AFL runs both the AFL(M) and AFLW competitions as if the interests of these competitions always align. The effect of this is that whenever there is a potential conflict between these two leagues, the interests of the men's competition prevail. Not only does the AFLW season currently go for less than half the duration of the AFL(M) season in order to avoid a clash, but at the onset of the second and third AFLW seasons, the AFL even spent more money paying men to play in a newly created experimental AFL(M) pre-season competition – named AFLX – than most women received to play the entire AFLW season (Hinds, 2019). The AFLX experiment failed, but it was a sign of a football bureaucracy that continues to prioritise the development of men's football rather than to invest resources in enabling the AFLW to become the best league it can be, independent of what that means for men's football (O'Halloran, 2019a).

Three steps to political discourse change

Nancy Fraser (2009, p. 99) argues that the second wave feminist cultural transformation of society 'legitimated the transition to a new form of capitalism: post-Fordist, transnational, neoliberal'. Unfortunately, this occurred at precisely the time that second wave feminists and women footballers both needed a 'larger, holistic vision of a just society' (Fraser, 2009, p. 99), one that 'redoubled attention to the critique of political economy' (Fraser, 2009, p. 109). Fraser concludes by suggesting that for feminism to achieve the broader emancipatory goal of gender justice, its proponents must 'become more historically aware as we [feminists] operate on a terrain that is also populated by our uncanny double [of neoliberalism]' (2009, p. 114; also see Fraser, 2017). Far more powerful justice narratives can be developed in football, where a recognition of past sexist, patriarchal and phallocentric injustice becomes the starting point for contemporary redress. Funding of women's football, whether by public government or by the men's football organisations and clubs that have benefitted from exclusive access to at least partially publicly funded infrastructure, is not an issue of welfare, but rather an issue of reparation for the systemic discrimination throughout history that still significantly impacts public and corporate investment decisions. But driving this idea into the public discourse will be difficult. We propose three introductory steps that would help to produce a more politically affirmative narrative for women footballers that resists sexist, patriarchal and phallocentric underpinnings. In so doing, we are answering the call by Toffoletti, Francombe-Webb and Thorpe to develop 'new critical vocabularies' to challenge 'the new framing of old modalities of sexism and inequality, in a period characterised by neoliberalism and postfeminism' (2018, p. 8).

Step one - Deconstructing benign sexism

This is the easiest step to enact. Men's leagues in Australian Rules football began in the latter half of the nineteenth century in Victoria, and then in the other colonies (Wedgewood, 2005). For around 100 years, men's football clubs and leagues at all levels benefitted from public resourcing of grounds, facilities and club rooms, which produced historical ownership of football discourse and infrastructure (Jeanes et al., 2021). This ownership thrived through a period of 'state-organized capitalism' (Fraser, 2009, p. 97) where governments and councils saw the provision of funds for men's sporting clubs as a useful subsidisation in the social life of communities with a return of the promotion of 'inclusion, social equality and cross-class solidarity' (Fraser, 2009, p. 101). Women were apparent in various supportive and spectating roles in producing this solidarity, but the game was considered a men's game (Lenkic and Hess, 2016). Men, and a very specific form of masculinity, had a proprietary role over the game (Pavlidis, 2020).

Over recent years, a number of reports have lamented the death of country and community football sides (e.g., Boyle, 2018; Flanagan, 2016). These reports utilise the very same discourses that supported generous investment by councils in sporting grounds, rooms and maintenance for men's football; that the leisure activities of men deserve public subsidy for the good of the community (Frost, Lightbody and Halabi, 2013; Riley, 2019; Spaaj, 2009). Yet, a quantitative analysis of sub-elite participation in Australian Rules football reveals a sport only partly in decline at the community level.

An investigation of AFL Annual Reports (2000–2019) reveals the following trends in domestic participation:

- Large increase in overall participation numbers, but substantially in Auskick (introductory program), junior (age 8–12) and youth (age 13–17) at community club level;
- No increase in men's community club numbers beyond the Under 17s level, and a decrease at the senior men's level;
- Enormous increase in women's participation numbers in all categories, including junior, youth and senior community club football, such that the increase in overall female participants almost offsets a larger decrease in overall senior male participants.

In community club football, the growth in women participants between 2016 and 2018 was almost 6,000 more than the growth in overall participation. Given that youth and junior men's participation was also growing, the ongoing decline in men's participation has been substantial, but the growth in women's participation has frequently helped to offset this.

Step two - Publicising women's football history

The massive growth in women playing the game has been driven by the passionate advocacy of the volunteer workforce of female players and administrators that grew the game organically. Yet, this history has received much less focus than that afforded to the development of the men's game (Lenkic and Hess, 2016; Race and Chiera, 2019). 2021 is the 40th anniversary of the inception of the first women's competitive Australian Rules football league – the Victorian Women's Football League – however, there appear to be no plans by the AFL to commemorate this anniversary. This is one of a number of indications the AFL is not interested in promoting the history of women's football prior to the AFLW. For example, each season the player adjudged to have had the best AFLM season is awarded the Brownlow Medal in honour of former great male footballer Charles Brownlow. However, the best AFLW player each season is simply awarded the Most Valuable Player, despite there being plenty of great women players from the years preceding the AFLW (for more on this erasure of earlier history, see O'Halloran, 2018b).

It is important to remember that the legal-taxation status of the AFL is as a 'not-for-profit' organisation that frequently ends each year with a surplus in the tens of millions (O'Halloran, 2019c). It has two responsibilities: the management of the elite, commercialised and mediatised leagues for men and women and the development and sustenance of the game in the broader community for *all* participants. Only the second responsibility justifies its not-for-profit status, and it is a responsibility that the AFL has historically ignored. It took until 2009 for the AFL to include a photograph of a women footballer in its Annual Report. And it only began to specifically mention growth in women's football in its annual development reports from 2011 onwards. It was not until 2016 that there appeared a separate section in either the CEO's or

Chairman's reports on these potential growth opportunities in women's football, after two of its clubs – Melbourne and the Western Bulldogs – had taken it on themselves to initiate exhibition matches for the best women players in Australia.

Step three - Changing the discourse from 'gratitude for welfare' to 'women saving the game'

This will be the hardest shift to make as it comes up against the sexist, patriarchal and phallocentric nature of the current Australian Rules football bureaucracy and governance. The implication in our opening quote by journalist Paul Amy – that the VCAT case 'effectively forced AFL Victoria to create a youth girls competition' – suggests that some sort of welfare-based decision has been made by the ruling body for football towards women participants. The women's professional football league and community-based women's teams and leagues are often suggested as the beneficiary of welfare from the men's clubs and leagues in the popular football media. This produces what Orloff and Shiff (2016, p. 111) call 'perverse alliances', where individual narratives of empowerment and opportunity from women participants are selectively used 'by neoliberal and conservative elites in ways that undermine further movement toward gender equality' (Orloff and Shiff, 2016, p. 113), and reinforces the primacy of the men's game.

The effects of the contraction of the football economy post-COVID creates a need for an affirmative political discourse. Funding of women's football by public government and by existing football organisations is both an issue of redress for the systemic discrimination throughout history *and of reward for expanding the participatory market of football*. We would agree with Rowe that:

> The virus did not cause… sporting inequalities, but it exacerbated them, starkly revealing elite sport's reckless dependency on a small number of entities requiring a constant injection of capital, *the inadequacy of the 'trickle down' to women's… and community sport, and the inadequate public funding of grassroots sport.*
>
> (2020, pp. 707–708, our emphasis)

And further from Rowe (2020, pp. 710), the post-COVID sporting world should avoid 'repeating the mistakes… [which] reward the already well-remunerated', and rather develop 'more accessible and less discriminatory' policies and practices.

Conclusion

Margaret Thornton, the Australian feminist legal scholar, has noted 'That a demonstrably hostile entity was expected to transmute itself miraculously into a beneficent one has been a central paradox perennially besetting feminist reformism' (2006, p. 151). Increasing participation rates in women's football in Australia is something that should be celebrated, but 'with reserve' (Adams and Leavitt, 2018, p. 153). The development of a professional women's football league, and the support for new women's leagues and teams, have both frequently been presented as benevolently extending the opportunities for women in this sport. This chapter has explored various ways that the development of this league has been shaped and constrained by overt sexism, patriarchal logic and broader phallocentrism.

We have also outlined the way the emergence of women playing Australian Rules football can become a site for resistance to phallocentric discourses in football. The resistant response involves 're-telling' the story of women's football from a precarious welfare narrative of new opportunities being provided by male sport organisations to a politically empowering narrative of women's sports leagues saving male sport organisations from the consequences of their historical sexism, patriarchy and phallocentrism. We believe that this feminist standpoint position could also be useful in other traditionally male sport contexts where participation by women is exploding, such as with other football codes (Cox and Pringle, 2011; Kanemasu, Johnson and Molnar, 2018) and with ice-hockey (Adams and Leavitt, 2018).

The three-step process for producing this more politically empowering narrative is a necessary, but by no means sufficient, condition for women gaining epistemic authority over their sport. Androcentric control of the football discourse has a long and durable history, and is supported by men occupying most of the powerful positions in football organisations and in the mainstream football media. Without greater representation by women in these spaces of discursive control, it is possible that the new narrative could be drowned out in a chorus of self-congratulatory gender equity branding.

REFERENCES

Adams, C. and Leavitt, S. (2018) '"It's just girls' hockey": Troubling progress narratives in girls' and women's sport', *International Review for the Sociology of Sport*, 53(2), pp. 152–172. doi: 10.1177/1012690216649207.

AFL Annual Reports. 2005—2019. Available at: www.afl.com.au/annual-reports (Accessed: 12 January, 2021).

AFL News (2016) 'Rules for AFL Women's Announced.' Available at: www.afl.com.au/news/2016-10-19/rules-for-afl-womens-announced (Accessed: 19 October, 2016).

Amy, P. (2016) 'Penny Cula-Reid Picked Up in AFL Women's Draft, 13 years after Helping get Girls League Set Up', *Herald Sun*, 13 October. Available at: www.heraldsun.com.au/leader/localfooty/penny-culareid-picked-up-in-afl-womens-draft-13-years-after-helping-get-girls-league-set-up/news-story/9e692e5cca813aa74a53b86cc6079014 (Accessed: 2 February, 2017).

Boyle, T. (2018) 'Country Football: Australian Folklore's Dying Giant', *The Age*, 19 May. www.theage.com.au/sport/afl/country-footy-australian-folklore-s-dying-giant-20180519-p4zgac.html (Accessed: 20 May, 2018).

Burke, M. (2014) 'Women's standpoints and internalism in sport', *Journal of the Philosophy of Sport*, 41(1), pp. 39–52. doi: 10.1080/00948705.2013.858399.

Code, L. (2014) 'Ignorance, injustice and the politics of knowledge: Feminist epistemology now', *Australian Feminist Studies*, 29(80), pp. 148–160. doi: 10.1080/08164649.2014.928186.

Cox, B. and Pringle, R. (2011) 'Gaining a foothold in football: A genealogical analysis of the emergence of the female footballer in New Zealand', *International Review for the Sociology of Sport*, 47(2), pp. 217–234. doi: 10.1177/1012690211403203.

Dworkin, S. and Messner, M. (1999) 'Just do … what? Sport, bodies, gender', in Ferree, M.M., Lorber, J. and Hess, B. (eds.), *Revisioning Gender*. Thousand Oaks, CA: Sage Publications, pp. 341–361.

Faludi, S. (1992) *Backlash: The Undeclared War Against Women*. London: Chatto & Windus.

Flanagan, M. (2016) 'Fish Creek Part of Football's Shrinking Eco-System', *The Age*, 9 December. Available at: www.theage.com.au/sport/afl/fish-creek-part-of-footballs-shrinking-ecosystem-20161208-gt6x5h.html (Accessed: 14 January, 2019).

Fraser, N. (2009) 'Feminism, capitalism and the cunning of history', *New Left Review*, 56, pp. 97–117.

Fraser, N. (2017) 'The end of progressive neoliberalism', *Dissent*, Spring, pp. 130–134. Available at: www.dissentmagazine.org/online_articles/progressive-neoliberalism-reactionary-populism-nancy-fraser.

Frost, L., Lightbody, M. and Halabi, A. (2013) 'Expanding social inclusion in community sports organizations: Evidence from rural Australian football clubs', *Journal of Sport Management*, 27(6), pp. 453–466. doi: 10.1123/jsm.27.6.453.

Grosz, E. (1988) 'The in(ter)vention of feminist knowledges', in Caine, B., Grosz, E.A. and de Lepervanche, M. (eds.) *Crossing Boundaries: Feminisms and the Critique of Knowledges*. Sydney: Allen & Unwin, pp. 92–104.

Hibberd, G. (2021) *Never Surrender: The Inside Story of the Giants AFLW 2020 Season*. Melbourne: Hutch Industries.

Hinds, R. (2019) 'AFLW Wise to Follow Taylor Swift's Advice and Ignore the Social Media Haters in Season Three', *ABC*, 8 February. Available at: www.abc.net.au/news/2019-02-08/aflw-needs-to-ignore-social-media-and-twitter-haters/10790890 (Accessed: 8 February, 2019).

Kanemasu, Y., Johnson, J. and Molnar, G. (2018) 'Fiji's women rugby players: Finding motivation in a 'hostile' environment', in Molnar, G., Amin, S. and Kanemasu, Y. (eds.) *Women, Sport and Exercise in the Asia-Pacific Region: Domination-Resistance-Accommodation*. London: Routledge, pp. 141–158.

Klugman, M. (2016) 'Female spectators, agency, and the politics of pleasure: An historical case study from Australian rules football', *The International Journal of the History of Sport*, 33(17), pp. 2086–2104. doi: 10.1080/09523367.2017.1332047.

Lane, S. (2018) *Roar: The Stories Behind AFLW: A Movement Bigger Than Sport*. Melbourne: Random House.

Lenkic, B. and Hess, R. (2016) *Play On! The Hidden History of Women's Australian Rules Football*. Richmond, Victoria: Echo Publishing.

McCauley, P. (2008) 'Australian Rules Football as Secret Men's Business', *Quadrant Online*. Available at: https://quadrant.org.au/magazine/2008/09/australian-rules-football-as-secret-men-s-business/ (Accessed: 14 January, 2019).

Mike-Jeanes, R., Spaaj, R., Farquharson, K., McGrath, G., Magee, J., Lusher, D. and Gorman, S (2021) 'Gender Relations, Gender Equity, and Community Sports Spaces', *Journal of Sport and Social Issues*, 45(6), pp. 545–567. doi: 10.1177/0193723520962955.

O'Halloran, K. (2018a) 'Bracing for the Backlash to Women's Sport', *Crikey Inq.*, 3 October. Available at: www.crikey.com.au/2018/10/03/aflw-mo-hope-backlash/ (Accessed: 11 December, 2020).

O'Halloran, K. (2018b) 'AFLW Expansion can be a Double-edged Sword for VFL Community Clubs', *Guardian Australia*, 16 May. Available at: www.theguardian.com/sport/2017/may/16/aflw-expansion-can-be-a-double-edged-sword-for-vfl-community-clubs (Accessed: 11 December, 2020).

O'Halloran, K. (2019a) 'The AFL's Hypocrisy is On Show, and the Gimmicky AFLX Adds Salt to the Wound', *ABC*, 25 February. Available at: www.abc.net.au/news/2019-02-25/aflw-still-fighting-aflx-for-the-limelight/10841882 (Accessed: 11 December, 2020).

O'Halloran, K. (2019b) 'AFLW's Tayla Harris is Not First Female Athlete Targeted By Trolls, and Even Some Male Players', *ABC*, 21 March. Available at: www.abc.net.au/news/2019-03-21/tayla-harris-trolls-arent-only-problem/10921784 (Accessed: 11 December, 2020).

O'Halloran, K. (2019c) 'Pay Equity for Elite Athletes', *Saturday Paper*, 23–29 November. Available at: www.thesaturdaypaper.com.au/sport/afl/2019/11/23/pay-equity-elite-athletes/15744276009107#hrd (Accessed: 30 November, 2019).

Orloff, A.S. and Shiff, T. (2016) 'Feminism/s in power: Rethinking gender equality after the second wave', in Orloff, A.S., Ray, R. and Savci, E. (eds.) *Perverse Politics? Feminism, Anti-Imperialism Multiplicity*. Bingley, UK: Emerald Group Publishing Limited, pp. 109–134. doi: 10.1108/SO198-871920160000030003.

Pavlidis, A. (2020) 'Being grateful: Materialising "success" in women's contact sport', *Emotion, Space and Society*, 35, pp. 1–7. doi: 10.1016/j.emospa.2020.100673.

Pavlidis, A., Toffoletti, K. and Sanders, K. (2020) '"Pretty disgusted honestly": Exploring fans' affective responses on Facebook to the modified rules of Australian Football League, Women's', *Journal of Sport and Social Issues*, 46(1), pp. 103–123. doi: 10.1177/0193723520964969.

Pelak, C.F. (2002) 'Women's collective identity formation in sports: A case study from women's ice-hockey', *Gender & Society*, 16(1), pp. 93–114. doi: 10.1177/0891243202016001006.

Poynton, B. and Hartley, J. (1990) 'Male-gazing: Australian rules football, gender and television', in Brown, M.E. (ed.) *Television and Women's Culture: The Politics of the Popular*. Sydney: Currency, pp. 144–182.

Race, E. and Chiera, J. (2019) 'The Importance of Queer Players in the Survival of Women's Australian Football', *The Guardian Australia*, 24 August. Available at: www.theguardian.com/sport/2019/aug/24/the-importance-of-queer-players-in-the-survival-of-womens-australian-football (Accessed: 24 August, 2019).

Riley, E. (2019) 'The myth of the leg-up for women's sports', *Eureka Street*, 29(1). Available at: www.eurekastreet.com.au/article/the-myth-of-the-leg-up-for-women-s-sports (Accessed: 25 January, 2020).

Robinson, M. (2018) 'Over-promoting the AFLW Has Created the Problems We See Now', *Herald Sun*, 13 August. Available at: www.heraldsun.com.au/sport/afl/expert-opinion/mark-robinson/over-promoting-the-aflw-has-created-the-problems-we-see-now/news-story/8a5653becd75b204f9487d70e5a9e1f3 (Accessed: 13 August, 2018).

Rowe, D. (2020) 'Subjecting pandemic sport to a sociological perspective', *Journal of Sociology*, 56(4), pp. 704–713. doi: 10.1177/1440783320941284.

Sanders, K. (2020) 'Sportscapes: Contested bodies, gender and desire within a female Australian rules football team', *International Review for the Sociology of Sport*, 55(6), pp. 685–702. doi: 10.1177/1012690219837898.

Spaaj, R. (2009) 'The glue that holds the community together? Sport and sustainability in rural Australia', *Sport in Society*, 12(9), pp. 1132–1146. doi: 10.1080/17430430903137787.

Symons, K. (2019a) 'Photo of AFLW Player Tayla Harris is Not the Problem, the Vile Trolls Are', *The Guardian Australia*, 20 March. Available at: www.theguardian.com/sport/2019/mar/20/photo-of-aflw-player-tayla-harris-is-not-the-problem-the-vile-trolls-are (Accessed: 11 December, 2020).

Symons, K. (2019b) 'Tayla Harris Has Been Immortalised in Bronze. It is a Win for Women's Sport', *Guardian Australia*, 11 September. Available at: www.theguardian.com/sport/2019/sep/11/tayla-harris-has-been-immortalised-in-bronze-it-is-a-win-for-womens-sport (Accessed: 11 December, 2020).

Taylor v Moorabbin Saints Junior Football League and Football Victoria (2008) *Victorian Civil and Administrative Tribunal*, 158. Available at: https://jade.io/article/739945.

Thompson, D. (1994) 'Defining feminism', *Australian Feminist Studies*, 20, pp. 171–192.

Thornton, M. (2006) 'Feminism and the changing state: The case of sex discrimination', *Australian Feminist Studies*, 21(50), pp. 151–172. doi: 10.1080/08164640600731747.

Toffoletti, K., Francombe-Webb, J. and Thorpe, H. (2018) *New Sporting Femininities: Embodied Politics in Postfeminist Times*. Cham, Switzerland: Palgrave. doi: 10.1007/978-3-319-72481-2.

Wedgewood, N. (2005) '"Doin' it for themselves!" A case study of the development of a women's Australian rules football competition', *The International Journal of the History of Sport*, 22(3), pp. 396–414. doi: 10.1080/09523360500048696.

Wood, Z.C. and Garn, A.C. (2016) 'Levelling the playing field? Perspectives and observations of coed intramural flag football modifications', *Sociology of Sport Journal*, 33(3), pp. 199–207. doi: 10.1123/ssj.2015-0095.

Woodhouse, D, Fielding-Lloyd, B. and Sequerra, R. (2019) 'Big brother's little sister: The ideological construction of Women's Super League', *Sport in Society*, 22(12), pp. 2006–2023. doi: 10.1080/17430437.2018.1548612.

13
A Gendered Focused Review of Sports Diplomacy

Verity Postlethwaite, Claire Jenkin and Emma Sherry

Introduction: Origins of the term sports diplomacy

The definition and function of sport in international politics is interpreted and operationalised in many ways. At a global level, organisations such as the International Olympic Committee (IOC), the Commonwealth Games Federation (CGF), and the United Nations (UN) engage with political entities to further their mission and purpose. A crucial point of difference is the recognition of members of these organisations. In 2020, the IOC recognised 206 National Olympic Committees whilst the UN recognised 193 states. The difference in numerical recognition and the definition of recognised political actors varies between the UN and the IOC. Further to this, there are differences between nations' and territories' political and sporting footprint. For example, the United Kingdom (UK) is recognised in the IOC and the UN as a unified state and National Olympic Committee. Yet, in the CGF, the home-nations compete as England, Northern Ireland, Scotland, and Wales, and each have a lead body for Commonwealth sport (such as the Commonwealth Games Wales). This evidence around recognition illustrates that a political entity's sporting and political footprint may not be globally unified or consistent.

In academic literature, this is furthered by scholars of diplomacy who see classifications of territories, and their participation in international community activities, as potent to both the international (sport/non-sport) organisation and the territory. At a national level, the link to diplomacy extends to how different sport and political entities represent, negotiate, and communicate with each other (Beacom 2012; Dichter and Johns 2014; Murray 2017; Dichter 2020). Brentin and Tregoures (2016) illustrate this explicitly in Kosovo's case and their use of representation at sporting organisations, such as the IOC, to gain international community recognition and a pathway into the UN state membership. Although not members of the UN, the function of sport for Kosovo has served the purpose of growing the nation in terms of recognition and identity. Hassan (2018) develops the debate about sport being used as a 'Trojan horse', as many state-based activities interlock with sport to further political agendas such as strategic influence, economic performance, and international image. As discussed by Brentin and Tregoures (2016) and Hassan (2018), sport and politics in a complex age involve a range of actors, outcomes, and activities.

A growing phrase and area of exploration is that of sports diplomacy. Murray (2017) argues that academics have not engaged fully with the connection between sport and diplomacy until recently. In the early to mid-2010s, a raft of Special Issues in peer-reviewed journals, such as Diplomacy & Statecraft and a Special Issue commissioned to focus on 'Diplomacy and Sport' (Rofe and Dichter 2016), peppered sport and diplomacy-based academic fields with the connection between the two concepts. Further to this, edited book collections and monographs emerged on specific sport organisations, such as Dichter and Johns' (2014) collection on *Sport, Statecraft, and International Relations since 1945*. In the past decade, the growth in literature demonstrates a heightened and coordinated academic effort to conceptualise and empirically analyse sports diplomacy activities.

A disputed element of the origin of the phrase, sports diplomacy, is how it is positioned against other diplomatic concepts, such as public diplomacy, nation branding, and soft power (Zintz and Parrish 2019; Dichter 2020). While a thorough debate of definition and position is beyond the scope of this chapter, the phrase's tenants involve international relations between nations and territories, non-state actors, and individuals across the broad spectrum of global sporting activities. In a recent European Union (EU) commissioned report, the importance of harnessing the 'unconventional' and 'soft power' tools of sports diplomacy was a key aim for the body to 'amplify key EU diplomatic messages' with traditional and an expanded understanding of 'agents of this diplomacy' (Zintz and Parrish 2019, p. 3). The EU's knowledge emphasises the focus on the means and processes of exchanges, not necessarily the message or the outcome. Sport, in this sense, becomes the vehicle for a message or agenda. This idea is well versed in historical examples of Ping-Pong diplomacy between the United States and China (Hong and Sun 2000), ice hockey during the Cold War (Soares 2007, Leichtová and Zákravský 2021) or global relations and boycotts of sporting events in isolating Apartheid South Africa (Cornelissen 2008).

At a cursory glance, academic scholarship, thought and practice are seldom considered with a sustained gendered lens. In this chapter, such a lens is used to view how particular spaces are informed by bias or dominance towards men's or women's perspectives and/or experiences. A trope connected to sport and politics is that it is male-dominated, and that women and girls are often excluded or face challenges in accessing organised sport (Adams 2016; Sherry and Rowe 2020). Black and Peacock (2013, p. 711) make the precise point that up until the recent decades, the IOC have been (and remains, to a considerable extent) 'an "old boys club" with membership heavily drawn from aristocratic circles and prone to brokering backroom deals through elitist power networks'. Although the IOC has made efforts around gender equity and equality since 2013, there has still not been a female President out of the nine to date. Sherry and Rowe (2020, p. 1) agree with this sentiment around gender and international sport, stating that the recent increased attention and growth has been due to the historically bad and poor opportunities in women's sport. Desjardins (2021) argues further that recent strategies from international sports organisations and event bid committees often fail to acknowledge the policies and practices that disenfranchised women's sport in the first place. This lack of accountability raises doubts on the authenticity of actions by multiple stakeholders who have historically not supported women's sport. Building on the points raised in this section about diplomacy and using a gendered lens in understanding sports spaces, this chapter now turns to studies on academia and industry to consider whether sports diplomacy fits the male-dominated trope and if there are shifts towards gender equity.

Gendered review of sports diplomacy literature

So far, this chapter has consciously included and highlighted sports diplomacy scholarship by prominent female academics, such as Heather Dichter and Scarlett Cornelissen. However, beyond highlighting female authored scholarship, this chapter includes a thorough gendered review of sports diplomacy literature. As previously mentioned, this chapter includes data from two studies. This section is based on an integrative review of sports diplomacy peer-reviewed journal articles. Conducting integrated or systematic studies of existing literature allows for patterns and trends to empirically emerge and support or challenge anecdotal thoughts about a field of research (Schulenkorf, Sherry and Rowe 2016; Jenkin et al. 2017; Walzel, Robertson and Anagnostopoulos 2018; Hanlon, Jenkin and Craike 2019). An integrated academic literature review of the phrase 'sports diplomacy' was conducted, which collected 224 peer-reviewed journal articles between 2000 and 2020, and analysed through varying quantitative and qualitative points using NVivo software. One aspect of the review was to consider gendered elements involved in sports diplomacy-focused academic research as well as exploring the authorship and governance of sports diplomacy in academia.

Firstly, each peer-reviewed journal article was catalogued against the lead researcher's gender (male or female). The findings demonstrated that lead researchers' gender extended the previously recognised trope of a male-dominated sport and political space into the sports diplomacy academic space. Of the 224 peer-reviewed journal articles reviewed, 22% had a female lead author, and 78% had a male lead author. This is a grim statistic at face value and shows a male-dominated academic field in the past two decades. Moreover, the proportion of female to male lead authors is consistent and not improving in terms of balance (see Figure 13.1). As discussed elsewhere, the gender imbalance in wider academic publishing is being considered (for example, Taylor and Francis Editor Resources and Author Services n.d.; Martínez-Rosales et al. 2021) and is prevalent in other academic spaces too, as discussed by the Taylor and Francis case study on 'The Clinical Neuropsychologist' (n.d.). Concerning sports diplomacy, based on the statistics and trends in this integrated review, male lead authors' dominance continues to prevail.

A further finding of the integrated review was to catalogue the most frequently published journals. From the 224 peer-reviewed journal articles reviewed, the most frequent journals were: The International Journal of the History of Sport (43), Sport in Society (20), Diplomacy & Statecraft (13), and Journal of Sport History (11). Of these four journals (as of January 2021), out of the four lead editors, one was female, and out of 20 listed executive editorial committee (or equivalent) members, four were female (and two represent the same person on two different journal committees). Two of the four journals had 100% male lead editors and executive editorial committees. Again, as highlighted above, these are grim statistics about the gender balance on the four editorial boards; moreover, this continues to the trope of the male dominance in the governance of academic publishing (Taylor and Francis Resources and Authors Services n.d.; Martínez-Rosales et al. 2021). This gender-focused aspect of the review of the articles' authorship and journals' governance is vital for many reasons. This chapter holds academic practices as accountable as diplomatic practices and looks at the academic space through a gendered lens. It further reinforces the ever-present male-dominated tropes in sport into areas within academia, such as publishing. Specifically, it empirically demonstrates the male-dominated outputs and governance connected to sports diplomacy peer-reviewed journal articles and journals.

Beyond the administrative and authorship aspects of the integrated review, a number of the articles featured females in the research focus. As discussed here, the role of females in sports diplomacy activities in this scholarship varies. Notably, there are trends of female-dominated sporting spaces, such as diplomatic envoys or athlete tours. Many of the pieces look at historical cases and bring to life experiences of women in sports diplomacy, mainly focusing on female athletes during the Cold War. Brown (2015), Cervin (2015) and Dyreson (2019) discuss the importance of sporting females in the era of the Cold War, in particular, their role and value in cultural diplomacy programs and contexts. Brown (2015) challenges the

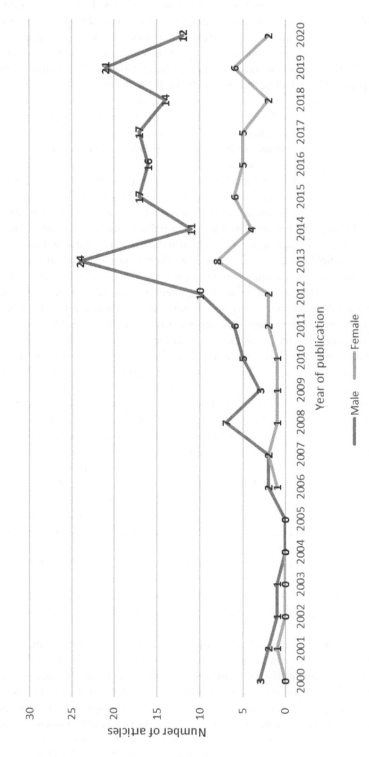

Figure 13.1 Lead Researcher Gender (articles from 2000 to 2020)

limited presentation by Cold War scholarship to how women participated in the American State Department goodwill tours in the 1950s. The tennis players Brown discusses moved beyond domestic images of wives and mothers into highly skilled and accomplished women amateurs on global tours. In a similar vein, Cervin (2015) focuses on the Soviet Union and Romanian gymnastic teams' tours of America and Australia in the 1970s as a form of Cold War cultural diplomacy. The gendered nature of the athletes and sport in media representation, such as being demure and non-threatening guests, contributed to the diplomatic role and gymnasts' popularity. Again, media representation features heavily in the Dyreson (2019) piece, as the author documents a Cold War romance between American athlete Harold Connolly and Czech athlete Olga Fikotova, after the 1956 Olympics. The American State Department tracked and leveraged the romance and 'in the Connollys, American cold warriors discovered the perfect couple for promoting this ideological concept [of personal liberty]' (Dyreson 2019, p. 44). The three pieces here demonstrate the use of females as athletes, guests and promoting ideological concepts. However, there is little engagement in the literature with females as leaders or political actors.

Beyond the East-West dichotomy, other historical pieces focus on China (before the 1970s and the Ping-Pong diplomacy episode) and the 'Two Chinas', where female athletes represented the 'strong body-mind heroine image' (Kuo 2019, p. 375). Shuman (2013) uses media images to demonstrate types of representation of, and communication about, female athletes. In the context of the Games of the New Emerging Forces in the early 1960s, the representation of friendship and honour between Asian, African, and Latin American nations is depicted by a cartoon image of three female athletes with different skin tones: a 'China shirt represents the Chinese athlete' and symbolically she is the central Table and the winning athlete (Shuman 2013, p. 270). The role of female sports and athletes is valued in promoting friendship and communicating images of strength. Although there are contrasts between how the different athletes convey feminine or national ideals, based on the different diplomatic and ideological aims of the varying nations, there are commonalities to female athletes' visual and media use in sporting competition and tours in the historical scholarship presented here.

There are notable omissions, too, as few articles reference females as political or sport leaders, and most articles focus on female athletes or female bodies, which reflect stereotypical female ideologies (Shuman 2013). This chapter does not suggest that there are no studies on females in governance or leadership roles, as this is a burgeoning area of published research (e.g., Pfister 2019; Piggott and Pike 2020; Banu-Lawrence, Frawley and Hoeber 2020). However, the contemporary sports diplomacy literature included in the integrated review used as the basis for this chapter was mainly limited to national sports organisations or comparisons between national sports organisations or regions. In the contemporary sports diplomacy literature included in this review, women's sports are featured as part of the empirical or conceptual framework, i.e., a component, not the central focus. For example, in Abdi et al. (2018, p. 370; 2019), women's sport is positioned as a form of soft power and a 'form of Sports Human Capital'. In their data collection methods, the authors collected expert responses through a survey about sports diplomacy, of which 36.77% were female. Further to this, in a monitoring and evaluation study of a USA Government and University-based SportsUnited 'Sports Visitors Program', the researchers differentiated the participants by gender to compare results (Baker et al. 2015; Dixon et al. 2019). The articles here demonstrate the rise of including demographics of people involved in their research. While neither of these studies went beyond a male/female gender reporting or focused centrally on gender elements, both highlighted the relevance of gender in terms of forms of sport and people's experiences in sports diplomacy activities.

Other contemporary pieces cited female athletes' participation at elite sport mega-events or large single sport events (e.g., tennis Dumitriu 2018). Beacom and Brittain (2016) and Postlethwaite and Grix (2016) use the London 2012 Olympic and Paralympic Games as markers of symbolic female participation and agendas by the IOC and International Paralympic Committee (IPC). Notably, at the London Games, female athletes from Iran, Saudi Arabia, Brunei, and Qatar participated and promoted this through mass media and sporting organisation communication channels. The connection made by both pieces here is to the extent to which international sports organisations can influence competing states' social and moral policies, i.e., female and disability empowerment. The different moral missions set out clearly by the IOC (in its Charter and codified through Olympism) and the IPC (in its mission and vision) include elements of inclusion and equality, therefore a prime point of discussion for the dynamics between sport and diplomacy. For example, it is significant that a state, such as Saudi Arabia, which has limited rights for women in their domestic policy landscape, has acquiesced through sport to engage with gender participation and equality (Chatziefstathiou and Henry 2012; Postlethwaite and Grix 2016). To understand further, the contemporary practices of organisations and states must be considered; thus, the following section will turn from a gender-focused review of academic work to that of sport diplomacy practice.

Gendered review of sports diplomacy activities (Australia and UK)

This section will review and compare a selection of gender-based sports diplomacy activities from Australia and the UK. Sport and diplomatic activities are synonymous with these nations both historically and in the contemporary era (Murray 2017; Woodward 2020). Yet, few academic studies have attempted to compare the how, what, who, and why of sports diplomacy in Australia and the UK. With sports diplomacy more broadly, the Australian Government recently launched the second iteration of their *Sports Diplomacy 2030* (DFAT 2019, p. vi), a national sports diplomacy policy document projecting an 'even more successful' national sports sector and continued source of national pride. A year later, the British Council (2020, p. 42) - a UK Government grant in aid receiving organisation - commented that 'surprisingly', the concept of 'sports diplomacy' has not, to date, attracted as much attention in the UK as it has in other countries.

Pertinent to this chapter is the similarity in ideologies around female empowerment, gender equality and equity between Australia and the UK. Our analysis of responses to an online survey and interviews with Australian or British-based individuals connected to the field found that in relation to both Australian and UK practitioners, the viewpoint on gender and sports diplomacy was a conscious objective to explore and emerged as a theme of discussion. Firstly, of the 33 survey respondents, 13 were female and 20 were male (a mixture of UK and Australia public sector, private sector, and third sector middle or senior managers). In the interview study, five were female and eight were male. How many male or female voices the project wanted to collect was not predetermined, as the focus related to expertise. However, it is notable that the gender balance was reasonable here and can be attributed to the sports diplomacy, as opposed to a pure diplomacy, focus of our project. With this in mind, the tracking the gender balance of participants has been a conscious feature throughout. Secondly, based on the survey responses and integrated literature review, a question was included in the interview guide to directly ask interviewees about the male-dominated trope associated with sports diplomacy and whether this is particularly true in activities directed towards female empowerment. The following discussion represents a triangulation of the integrated literature review, publicly accessible document analysis, survey responses and interview responses. In the empirical data presented below, if publicly accessible, then the sources are referenced. Where survey or interview data is used, the voices are presented through pseudonyms. This has been pre-agreed with the research participants to protect their anonymity whilst acknowledging their role in practice.

Based on rich sporting histories on the international stage, Australia and the UK have cultural and political similarities and connections, in particular, as to how they approach elite and grassroot sporting activities (Beacom 2008; Maynard 2009). For example, there is a connection between them and the Commonwealth, particularly leadership, participation, and hosting the Commonwealth Games (Australia in the Gold Coast in 2018 and the UK in Birmingham in 2022). Further to the historical Commonwealth connections, the two nations both share popularity for sports, especially rugby union, cricket, and netball. This popularity domestically has galvanized a zeal from both nations to host international sporting events, such as the Olympic and Paralympic Games (most recently Sydney 2000 and London 2012) or women's sport World Championships such as the Netball World Cup (most recently Liverpool 2019) or the Women's FIFA (Federation Internationale de Football Association) Football World Cup™ (awarded to a joint bid between Australia and New Zealand for 2023).

Given these cultural and political similarities in sport, plus a growth in investment in women's sport in the past decade, it seemed prudent and valuable to explore these two countries. Firstly, through an exploration of the role of Australian and UK women in international sport governance, particularly in the leadership of international sports organisations. Notably, in the UK, there are explicit sports diplomacy activities connected to the UK Sport strategy and investment around international relations, where an *International Leadership Programme* fosters talented individuals to 'attain leadership positions in international sporting organisations' as a mechanism to support 'the UK to have a strong, respected and supportive voice in international sport' (UK Sport, Online). In both the survey and interviews, this investment in people was raised, in particular, concerning promoting gender-specific agendas. One interviewee described:

> And we, as a global citizen in the UK, and while I say this broadly, our moving into the new strategy, we want to see more women around the table of leadership in international sport… And that's [just] not British woman, that is women, women around the world.
>
> (Public Sector, UK)

Further to this comment, despite the investment mentioned above, other interviewees noted the effort and expertise needed for an individual to negotiate and bid for such roles, especially a female. As noted here:

> I think it is really good to see somebody … like Laura McAllister trying to gain election for the FIFA [Federation Internationale de Football Association] Council. I mean, anybody that even runs for election is quite impressive to get to that point; but if she manages to pull that off, I mean that is going to be a tough gig … in what I would say probably a largely male culture.
>
> (Non-Governmental Organisation/Private Sector, UK)

The example cited by the interviewee is the 2020/1 bid by Professor Laura McAllister to become a member Union of European Football Association's representative for women on FIFA's ruling council, and thus 'the first woman to have played the game to be elected to such a position' (British Council Wales 2020; Wales Online 2020). The narrative in these examples showcases the diplomacy it takes in getting any person, more so a female, elected to the leadership spheres of international sport.

The UK national federations and state bodies are working in a more synchronised manner to help UK females obtain such roles. To date, the UK currently has four women who lead international federations (Zena Wooldridge, World Squash Federation President 2020 to present; Liz Nicholl, International Netball Federation President 2019 to present; Dame Louise Martin, Commonwealth Games Federation President 2015 to present; Kate Cathiness, World Curling Federation President 2010 to present). In the biographies and press releases for these roles, the women are credited as the 'first female president of an Olympic Winter Sports Federation' or the 'first female to hold this office in the history of the Commonwealth Sports Movement' (World Curling, Online; Commonwealth Sport, Online). The efforts and diplomatic activities of enabling women to bid for and gain these roles demonstrate a direct, gendered sports diplomacy effort from the UK. Moreover, given that the feats are associated with 'firsts', they also demonstrate the effort a woman must invest for these positions, which appear far more significant than their male counterparts who seemingly benefit (and have been benefitting) from the historical male culture in international sports federations.

Australian counterparts, both male and female, acknowledged other efforts and diplomatic activities in non-international federation settings, particularly around Australian support for sport-for-development activities in the Pacific Islands. A direct strategic priority for Australia is to 'strengthen communities in the Indo-Pacific' region, and it is delivered through many initiatives, including promoting 'gender equality', whilst also creating 'leadership pathways and increasing participation of women and girls in sport', such as the *Pacific Sport Partnerships* (DFAT 2019, p. 11). In an interview with an Australian stakeholder who directly engages in these activities, there was a substantive acknowledgement of cultural differences and authentic partnership building, the fundamentals of diplomacy to develop the gender initiatives from policy into practice. The interviewee reflected:

> And then you are adding the cultural complexities and dimensions as well and, how do you respectfully and thoughtfully approach these issues in different countries where concepts around gender and gender roles are still, are different to ours. And I guess approaching it in non-judgmental ways, otherwise there will just be breakdowns of relationships and the inability to form partnerships that are actual partnerships.
> (Non-Governmental Organisation/Private Sector, Australia)

Here, similar to the integrated review pieces, there are sensitivities to the role and interpretation of gender between countries, plus how this can genuinely contribute to 'actual' partnerships, rather than merely being symbolic. An important question that warrants further research is how indigenous populations view the 'west-knows-best' approach in relation to sport diplomacy? As in addition to resisting gender-based transformations, there could be anti-colonial resistance and, thus, objection to Western support and guidance. Given the rich and diverse communities and cultures in the regions targeted by Australia and the UK, more must be done to understand indigenous women's perspectives and gender-related challenges. For example, the approach outlined by the interviewee above may empower indigenous women to lead the change, but more needs to be done to account for indigenous voices and how they view and engage with external, Western-based sports diplomacy activity. A limitation of the study presented here is that we did not contact or interview people in countries where Australia and the UK have sport programmes; therefore, we suggest future studies consider this and include more diverse voices.

The Australian strategies around sport and diplomacy alongside extracts about practice show an increase in bringing sports diplomacy activities as a way and means to reflect on differences and opportunities to further particular strategies and ideologies around gender. An Australian interviewee shared an example of success in this area around female participation in non-athlete roles in the Pacific Games, stating:

> Yes, it [sports diplomacy] is dominated by male voices. Although we believe we are having success in changing that, for example that the last Pacific Games, the… programme in its entirety was completely run by females… it was 100% females involved, in terms of the administration of the event.
>
> (Third Sector, Australia)

The success measurement here is not about there simply being female participation in the Pacific Games. It is reframed around female involvement in the administration and organisation of the event. Similar to the framing of administrators and leaders by UK Sport in international sport governance, the interviewee here sees it as part of their organisation's role to change the male voice domination and promote female involvement in organisation and leadership roles at more local level, i.e., the Pacific Games and in the Pacific nations. Again, it is beyond the scope of this chapter to explore the culture of the Pacific region; however, elsewhere scholars have noted how many Pacific Nations have not traditionally embraced the female involvement in sport or societal administration and governance (Khoo, Schulenkorf and Adair 2014; Kanemasu and Molnar 2017). This type of gendered agenda and activity between Australia and the Pacific Islands is reflected on further by one interviewee, who, similar to Hassan (2018), uses a 'Trojan horse' analogy:

> It [sport] is also, I use that term again, a Trojan horse for gender equality. It is a space where people are much more open to that sort of gender participation… sport has some unique advantages in that regard.
>
> (Private Sector, Australia)

The points and activities raised by both UK and Australian interviewees speak to using sport to promote and influence international sport and particular strategic regions. A distinct difference between the diplomatic practices and the diplomatic academic literature is the operational and strategic use of gender and women in leadership or administration by industry, as opposed to literature, which centres on depicting and using female athletes for diplomatic means. What needs to be unpacked further are the similarities and differences between UK and Australian practices, plus to hear views from indigenous populations who engage with sports diplomatic activities delivered by Australia and the UK.

Conclusion

The snapshot of academic literature from the field of sports diplomacy showed some problematic trends around continued male-dominated authorship, studies and gatekeepers in the area. However, we also highlighted excellent examples of female-authored pieces and work that focused on females in the sphere of sports diplomacy. Nevertheless, far more can be done to acknowledge, consult, and develop academic infrastructure and voices to promote more research on women and sports diplomacy and increase the number of female authors and editors. In the latter section of this chapter, a snapshot of practice from Australia and the UK supports the trope that sports diplomacy remains male-dominated. However, the strategies and activities by the two nations are using sport to challenge such tradition. The UK has explicit strategy and practices for promoting and enabling females to attain positions of power in international sport. In Australia, the focus is on strategic partnership with the Pacific region and using different initiatives to promote gender equality. Diplomacy (explicit or implicit) is needed across the activities of these two nations to navigate some of the challenges and complexities of global sport or regional relations. Here, the evidence and analysis demonstrate how Australia and UK-based practices are attempting to counter the tropes that sport and politics are male-dominated, especially around leadership and decision making. Beyond Australia and the UK, there is a trend across international sports to increase balanced gender representation in leadership and decision making tangibly. For example, the Association of Summer Olympic International Federations governance review now includes a measure of gender representation (ASOIF 2018). Such efforts and actions indicate an emerging challenge to male domination, and sports diplomacy offers a way to consider this, especially between nations and cultures. Based on the above, this chapter argues that there is a clear need for future studies and practice to use a gendered lens to inform their thoughts and actions. This type of approach would allow for more nuanced thinking in how sport is studied and led, and how sport diplomacy is practiced in local, national, regional, and global settings.

REFERENCES

Abdi, K., Talebpour, M., Fullerton, J., Ranjkesh, M.J. and Jabbari Nooghabi, H. (2018) 'Converting sports diplomacy to diplomatic outcomes: Introducing a sports diplomacy model', *International Area Studies Review*, 21(4), pp. 365–381. doi:10.1177/2233865918808058

Abdi, K., Talebpour, M., Fullerton, J., Ranjkesh, M.J. and Nooghabi, H.J. (2019) 'Identifying sports diplomacy resources as soft power tools', *Place Branding and Public Diplomacy*, 15(3), pp. 147–155. https://doi.org/10.1057/s41254-019-00115-9

Adams, M. (2016) 'Feminist politics and sport', in Bairner, A., Kelly, J. and Lee, J. (eds.) *Routledge Handbook of Sport and Politics*. Routledge: London, pp. 143–154.

Association of Summer Olympic International Federations (2018) *Second Review of International Federation Governance*. Available at: https://www.asoif.com/governance (Accessed: 07/11/2020).

Baker, R.E., Baker, P.H., Atwater, C. and Andrews, H. (2015) 'Sport for development and peace: A program evaluation of a sport diplomacy initiative', *International Journal of Sport Management and Marketing*, 16(1-2), pp. 52–70. https://doi.org/10.1504/IJSMM.2015.074932

Banu-Lawrence, M., Frawley, S. and Hoeber, L. (2020) 'Women and leadership development in Australian sport organisations', *Journal of Sport Management*, 34(6), pp. 568–578. https://doi.org/10.1123/jsm.2020-0039

Beacom, A. (2008) 'A question of motives: Reciprocity, sport and development assistance', *European Sport Management Quarterly*, 7(1), pp. 81–107. https://doi.org/10.1080/16184740701270386

Beacom, A. (2012) *International Diplomacy and the Olympic Movement*. London: Palgrave Macmillan.

Beacom, A. and Brittain, I. (2016) 'Public diplomacy and the International Paralympic Committee: Reconciling the roles of disability advocate and sports regulator', *Diplomacy & Statecraft*, 27(2), pp. 273–294. https://doi.org/10.1080/09592296.2016.1169795

Black, D. and Peacock, B. (2013) 'Sport and diplomacy', in Cooper, A., Heine, J. and Thakur, R. (eds.) *The Oxford Handbook of Modern Diplomacy*. Oxford: Oxford University Press, pp. 708–714.

Brentin, D. and Tregoures, L. (2016) 'Entering through the sport's door? Kosovo's sport diplomatic endeavours towards international recognition', *Diplomacy & Statecraft*, 27(2), pp. 360–378. https://doi.org/10.1080/09592296.2016.1169799

British Council (2020) *The sources of soft power*. Available at: https://www.britishcouncil.org/research-policy-insight/policy-reports/sources-soft-power (Accessed: 07/11/2020).

British Council Wales (2020) *Creating a sports diplomacy strategy for Wales*. Available at: https://wales.britishcouncil.org/en/creating-sports-diplomacy-strategy-wales (Accessed: 07/11/2020).

Brown, A. (2015) 'Swinging for the State Department: American women tennis players in diplomatic goodwill tours, 1941-59', *Journal of Sport History*, 42(3), pp. 289–309. https://doi.org/10.5406/jsporthistory.42.3.0289

Cervin, G. (2015) 'Gymnasts are not merely circus phenomena: Influences on the development of women's artistic gymnastics during the 1970s', *The International Journal of the History of Sport*, 32(16), pp. 1929–1946. https://doi.org/10.1080/09523367.2015.1124859

Chatziefstathiou, D. and Henry, I. (2012) *Discourses of Olympism: From the Sorbonne 1894 to London 2012*. Basingstoke: Palgrave Macmillan.

Commonwealth Sport (Online) *Dame Louise Martin re-elected as CGF President*. Available at: https://thecgf.com/news/dame-louise-martin-re-elected-cgf-president (Accessed: 07/11/2020).

Cornelissen, S. (2008) 'Scripting the nation: Sport, mega-events, foreign policy and state-building in post-apartheid South Africa', *Sport in Society*, 11(4), pp. 481–493. https://doi.org/10.1080/17430430802019458

Department of Foreign Affairs (DAFT) Australian Government (2019) *Sports Diplomacy 2030*. Available at: https://www.dfat.gov.au/people-to-people/sport/Pages/sports-diplomacy-2030 (Accessed: 07/11/2020).

Desjardins, B.M. (2021) 'Mobilising gender equality: A discourse analysis of bids to host the FIFA Women's World Cup 2023™', *International Review for the Sociology of Sport*, 56(8), pp. 1189–1205. https://doi.org/10.1177/1012690221998131

Dichter, H.L. and Johns, A.L. (eds.) (2014) *Diplomatic Games: Sport, Statecraft, and International Relations since 1945*. Kentucky: University Press of Kentucky.

Dichter, H.L. (ed.) (2020) *Soccer Diplomacy: International Relations and Football since 1914*. Kentucky: University of Kentucky Press.

Dixon, M.A., Anderson, A.J., Baker, R.E., Baker, P.H. and Esherick, C. (2019) 'Management in sport for development: Examining the structure and processes of a sport diplomacy initiative', *International Journal of Sport Management and Marketing*, 19(3-4), pp. 268–292. https://doi.org/10.1504/IJSMM.2019.099787

Dumitriu, D.L. (2018) 'Media construction of sport celebrities as national heroes', *Revista Română de Comunicare și Relații Publice*, 20(2), pp. 21–33.

Dyreson, M. (2019) 'The Californization of Olympian love: Olga Fikotová and Harold Connolly's Cold War romance', *Journal of Sport History*, 46(1), pp. 36–61. https://doi.org/10.5406/jsporthistory.46.1.0036

Hanlon, C., Jenkin, C. and Craike, M. (2019) 'Associations between environmental attributes of facilities and female participation in sport: A systematic review', *Managing Sport and Leisure*, 24(5), pp. 294–306. https://doi.org/10.1080/23750472.2019.1641138

Hassan, D. (2018) 'Sport and politics in a complex age', *Sport in Society*, 21(5), pp. 735–744. https://doi.org/10.1080/17430437.2018.1400782

Hong, Z. and Sun, Y. (2000) 'The butterfly effect and the making of "ping-pong diplomacy"', *Journal of Contemporary China*, 9(25), pp. 429–448. https://doi.org/10.1080/713675951

Jenkin, C.R., Eime, R.M., Westerbeek, H., O'Sullivan, G. and Van Uffelen, J.G. (2017) 'Sport and ageing: A systematic review of the determinants and trends of participation in sport for older adults', *BMC Public Health*, 17(976). https://doi.org/10.1186/s12889-017-4970-8

Kanemasu, Y. and Molnar, G. (2017) 'Double-trouble: Negotiating gender and sexuality in post-colonial women's rugby in Fiji', *International Review for the Sociology of Sport*, 52(4), pp. 430–446. https://doi.org/10.1177%2F1012690215602680

Khoo, C., Schulenkorf, N. and Adair, D. (2014) 'The benefits and limitations of using cricket as a sport for development tool in Samoa', *Cosmopolitan Civil Societies: An Interdisciplinary Journal*, 6(1), pp. 76–102. https://doi.org/10.5130/ccs.v6i1.3737

Kuo, C. (2019) 'The heroine of free China: A new image of diplomatic envoys and the female body of the Liangyou Women's National Basketball Team in the 1950s', *The International Journal of the History of Sport*, 36(4-5), pp. 375–387. https://doi.org/10.1080/09523367.2019.1622524

Leichtová, M.B. and Zákravský, J. (2021) 'Cold War on ice? Soviet ice-hockey dominance and foreign policy', *Sport in Society*, 24(6), pp. 1033–1054. https://doi.org/10.1080/17430437.2020.1723550

Martínez-Rosales, E., Hernández-Martínez, A., Sola-Rodríguez, S., Esteban-Cornejo, I. and Soriano-Maldonado, A. (2021) 'Representation of women in sport sciences research, publications, and editorial leadership positions: Are we moving forward?', *Journal of Science and Medicine in Sport*, 24(11), pp. 1093–1097. https://doi.org/10.1016/j.jsams.2021.04.010

Maynard, J. (2009) 'Transnational understandings of Australian aboriginal sporting migration: Sporting walkabout', *The International Journal of the History of Sport*, 26(16), pp. 2376–2396. https://doi.org/10.1080/09523360903457031

Murray, S. (2017) 'Sports diplomacy in the Australian context: Theory into strategy', *Politics & Policy*, 45(5), pp. 841–861. https://doi.org/10.1111/polp.12218

Pfister, G. (2019) 'Women's roles and positions in European sport organisations: Historical development and current tendencies', in Lough, N. and Geurin, A.N. (eds.) *Routledge Handbook of the Business of Women's Sport*. Abingdon: Routledge, pp. 269–279.

Piggott, L.V. and Pike, E.C. (2020) '"CEO equals man": Gender and informal organisational practices in English sport governance', *International Review for the Sociology of Sport*, 55(7), pp. 1009–1025. https://doi.org/10.1177%2F1012690219865980

Postlethwaite, V. and Grix, J. (2016) 'Beyond the acronyms: Sport diplomacy and the classification of the International Olympic Committee', *Diplomacy & Statecraft*, 27(2), pp. 295–313. https://doi.org/10.1080/09592296.2016.1169796

Rofe, J.S. and Dichter, H.L. (2016) 'Prologue: Diplomacy and sport', *Diplomacy & Statecraft*, 27(2), pp. 207–201. https://doi.org/10.1080/09592296.2016.1169780

Schulenkorf, N., Sherry, E. and Rowe, K. (2016) 'Sport for development: An integrated literature review', *Journal of Sport Management*, 30(1), pp. 22–39. https://doi.org/10.1123/jsm.2014-0263

Sherry, E. and Rowe, K. (2020) *Developing Sport for Women and Girls*. Abingdon: Routledge.

Shuman, A. (2013) 'Elite competitive sport in the People's Republic of China 1958-1966: The Games of the New Emerging Forces (GANEFO)', *Journal of Sport History*, 40(2), pp. 258–283.

Soares, J. (2007) 'Cold war, hot ice: International ice hockey, 1947-1980', *Journal of Sport History*, 34(2), pp. 207–230.

Taylor and Francis Author Services (Online) *Gender and publishing: A PhD student's perspective*. Available at: https://authorservices.taylorandfrancis.com/gender-and-publishing-a-phd-students-perspective/ (Accessed: 07/11/2020).

Taylor and Francis Editor Resources (Online) *Increasing diversity on your editorial board*. Available at: https://editorresources.taylorandfrancis.com/the-editors-role/managing-editorial-boards/598-2/# (Accessed: 07/11/2020).

UK Sport (Online) *International relations*. Available at: https://www.uksport.gov.uk/our-work/international-relations/people-development (Accessed: 07/11/2020).

Wales Online (2020) *Being Laura McAllister, the formidable Welsh woman who overcame huge barriers and is fighting for a top spot on FIFA*, 30th December. Available at: https://www.walesonline.co.uk/sport/football/football-news/being-laura-mcallister-formidable-welsh-19494185 (Accessed: 07/11/2020).

Walzel, S., Robertson, J. and Anagnostopoulos, C. (2018) 'Corporate social responsibility in professional team sports organisations: An integrative review', *Journal of Sport Management*, 32(6), pp. 511–530. https://doi.org/10.1123/jsm.2017-0227

Woodward, R. (2020) 'Sport and UK soft power: The case of Mount Everest', *The British Journal of Politics and International Relations*, 22(2), pp. 274–292. https://doi.org/10.1177%2F1369148120908502

World Curling (Online) *President*. Available at: https://worldcurling.org/about/president/ (Accessed: 07/11/2020).

Zintz, T.Z. and Parrish, R. (2019) *Promoting a strategic approach to EU sports diplomacy. Background paper*. Available at: https://www.edgehill.ac.uk/law/files/2019/05/Sports-Diplomacy-Background-Paper-v2.pdf (Accessed: 07/09/2020).

14
Gender Politics in British University Sport
Exploring Contemporary Perceptions of Femininity and Masculinity

Amelia Laffey and Stuart Whigham

Introduction

To say women and sport have had a tumultuous history would be an understatement; however, opportunities for women have significantly increased, with prospects to play and compete in most sports (Reeser 2005; Senne 2016). Nonetheless, women still have significantly lower participation rates, there is gender pay disparity in most sports, and women's sport is largely underrepresented in the media (Connell 2002, 2012; Trolan 2013; Fink 2015; Mullins 2015). It is necessary to understand what obstacles remain in place and to what extent those include institutional sexism or lingering attitudes regarding an aversion to women in sport (Messner 1992; Senne 2016). Therefore, this chapter explores these factors within a British university setting, as universities and education systems can be viewed as gendered institutions (Connell 2008). Drawing upon original empirical research, the chapter unfolds the current impact of contemporary perceptions of 'masculinity' and 'femininity' on female athletes in British university sport by investigating their experiences in relation to how gender roles and relations are negotiated in that context.

In contrast to the comparatively well-resourced nature of university sport in the North American context, where the impact of Title IX legislation has partially redressed the relative underfunding of female sport (Brake 2010; Yiamouyiannis and Osborne 2012; Belanger 2017), British university sport is significantly less professionalised, is predominantly focused on sub-elite participation, and therefore possesses a relatively lower status (Brunton and Mackintosh 2017; Phipps 2020, 2021). Nonetheless, as Phipps (2021, p.82) argues: 'sport is often perceived as an integral and significant part of student life in the UK, with universities a space where students often try new sports for the first time, playing an important role in making students feel part of their new environment'. As gendered inequalities in terms of status, funding, and provision for female university sport in Britain remain evident (Brunton and St Quinton 2020; Ogilvie and McCormack 2020), the gendered politics of this important facet of the British sporting system deserves attention. To this end, we scrutinise the discourse of traditional gender roles in sport (Markula 2001; Connell 2008) and the historical context of women in sport that shows how women have been seen as the 'other' (Messner 1992; Hargreaves 1994; Connell 2002; Connell and Messerschmidt 2005). Structures that influence these beliefs and perceptions are explored, specifically looking at the notions of 'hegemony' and 'hegemonic masculinity' derived from the work of Antonio Gramsci and R.W. Connell (Gramsci, Hoare and Nowell-Smith 1998; Connell 2002, 2012; Carrington and McDonald 2009).

Hegemony, gender politics, and sport

Gramsci and Connell - hegemony and the subordination of femininity

Antonio Gramsci explains the structures within society and how they can be countered by using the concepts of hegemony. Hegemony is what Gramsci uses to describe the system of alliance and power relations of society's ruling groups and the ways in which this position of power is sustained. For the chapter, the development and adaptation of this theory to the way men exercise authority over women will be considered; this is referred to as *hegemonic masculinity* (Gramsci, Hoare and Nowell-Smith 1998; Connell 2005). The concept of hegemony is used to describe the cultural dynamic by which cultural power in society is asserted and maintained by a group (Connell 2005).

Derived from this border conceptualisation of hegemony, hegemonic masculinity refers to the pattern of gender relations that enables men to gain dominance over women, and the continuation of dominance (Connell and Messerschmidt 2005). Hegemonic masculinity is not necessarily a specific set of characteristics, but the form of masculinity that inhabits the hegemonic position (Connell 2005). Therefore, hegemonic masculinity is differentiated from other forms of masculinity, specifically subordinated forms, such as those from working classes and gay men (Connell and Messerschmidt 2005). The dominant form of masculinity, hegemonic masculinity, is constructed and portrayed as distinct from working class, gay, black, and, importantly, feminine cultural practices (Kimmel, Hearn and Connell 2005). However, those who hold institutional power or wealth might be, in their personal lives, far from the hegemonic pattern, and those who most visibly display hegemonic masculinity may just be exemplars, such as sports stars (Connell 2005, 2011).

Acknowledging this diversity in masculinity is not adequate. Hegemonic masculinity sought to recognise the relations between various masculinities such as dominance, alliance, and subordination (Connell 2005). Connell (2009) states that gender is not a fixed system but instead always open to change due to its complex structure that is full of tension and historically changing. Within masculinity, gender politics is present, and through practices of exclusion, exploitation, and intimidation, these relations are constructed (Connell 2005). Connell (2008) reiterates that the various patterns of masculinity are not equally available or respected. Most present in American and European societies is the dominance of heterosexual men, with oppression positioning gay men at the bottom of the gender hierarchy among masculinities (Connell 2005). This is a result of 'gayness', from the perspective of hegemonic masculinity, being easily associated with femininity, which may explain the ferocity of homophobic attacks (Connell 2005).

Similar to normative definitions of masculinity, hegemonic masculinity faces the same problem that not a great deal of men actually meet hegemonic standards of masculinity (Connell 2005; Connell and Messerschmidt 2005). However, hegemonic masculinity can also be seen as normative in the sense that it embodies what is the most esteemed way of being a man, and all other men must position themselves around it (Connell and Messerschmidt 2005). Hegemonic masculinity 'ideologically legitimated the global subordination of women to men' (Connell and Messerschmidt 2005, p.832). Men in general gain from the subordination of women; therefore, another key aspect of masculinity is that of complicit hegemonic masculinity. Connell (2005) suggests that masculinities that are constructed so that they can receive the benefits of the patriarchy, without running the risks of being viewed as on the front lines of the patriarchy, are complicit.

As demonstrated above, hegemonic masculinity is constructed in relation to subordinate masculinities, but also to what Connell (1987) describes as 'emphasised femininity'. Emphasised femininity is grounded in heterosexuality and associated with white, middle class, traditionally feminine women (Mattsson 2015; Domeneghetti 2019). Cockburn and Clarke (2002) suggest that to show emphasised femininity is to appear conventionally pretty and fashionable, paying a significant amount of attention to one's appearance. Connell (1987) suggests that emphasised femininity is constructed as a subordinated counterpart to hegemonic masculinity and is often performed specifically to men. Although it is based on subordination, emphasised femininity represents a femininity that is very strong and, therefore, Connell (1987) states that it can cultivate legitimacy and acceptance for women.

Women who represent a femininity close to emphasised femininity do so based on heterosexuality, which in turn creates specific ideas about how women should present themselves (Mattsson 2015). Connell (1987) argues that emphasised femininity is not a position that has the potential to challenge gender structures as it is still based on their subordination and a response to men's preferences. Women may be able to gain a small amount of power through occupying this position, but it will never be enough to oppose male dominance (Mattsson 2015). For example, those who fit the pattern of emphasised femininity could be less marginalised than other femininities such as lesbianism, but are still subordinated by men as they are obliging to the desires of masculinity (Connell 1987; Domeneghetti 2019). Therefore, the term 'emphasised' was specifically used instead of 'hegemonic' as this form of femininity is grounded in current gender relations, existing in a patriarchal society where all femininities must be constructed in the context of female subordination (Connell 1987; Domeneghetti 2019).

As illustrated above, the work of Connell is heavily influenced by Gramsci's concept of hegemony and the relations of dominance and subordination between groups. Gramsci explains in more detail the dynamics of these relations and, thus, how power is gained and maintained. Gramsci states that, instead of coercion, hegemony is obtained through consent by the ruled groups positively receiving the values and attitudes disseminated by the ruling class (Gramsci, Hoare and Nowell-Smith 1998). Traditional social relations are often supported in these attitudes and values, therefore making the ruling class ideologies become common sense. Gramsci outlines the different structures in society within which these ideologies and values are disseminated, naming them 'civil society' (Gramsci, Hoare and Nowell-Smith 1998). Examples of civil society include religion, education, the media - and, in the current day, social media and sport (Carrington and McDonald 2009).

The above theories are relevant to the current discussion of gender politics as they offer an insight into the wider workings of power relations between the ruling and subordinated groups in society. As universities are an important aspect of the education system, they constitute part of the structures which Gramsci refers to as 'civil society' (Gramsci, Hoare and Nowell-Smith 1998; Carrington and McDonald 2009). These concepts can therefore be used to examine how universities perpetuate hegemonic norms regarding femininity and masculinity, and are therefore highly relevant when examining gender politics in university sport.

Gramsci, Connell, and gender in sport and university sport

Sport is a critical location for patriarchal values and structures and masculine hegemony to be constructed and reconstructed. It is seen as a significant part of the exclusivist self-sustaining male culture (Connell 2012). In a sporting context, the limitations of male and female bodies are put on display and their capacities debated (Messner 2002). Women's sporting performances are pitted against men's with their times, distances, and skills compared and discussed.

Connell (2012) states that sport has become a key apparatus of gender hegemony in wealthy countries and a crucial feature of masculine imagery.

Within society and sport, hegemonic masculinity endorses an idealised version of masculinity that focuses on competitiveness, aggression, and force, marginalising women and men that do not adhere to this form of masculinity (McKay 1997; Connell 2012). Consequently, an idealised form of femininity, being delicate and fragile, is also encouraged through hegemonic masculinity, and, as Messner (1992) suggests, the aggressive characteristics of sport have sought to counter feminisation. Consequently, the arguably sexist, aggressive, and violent culture that sport historically possessed meant that the introduction of women was not widely accepted (Senne 2016).

Hegemonic masculinity works to maintain these ideologies of femininity and masculinity most effectively through civil society, particularly the media and sporting governing bodies where females are largely underrepresented and male interests dominate (Connell 2002; Trolan 2013; Fink 2015; Mullins 2015). It is men who own teams, earn significantly higher salaries, and, in both women's and men's sports, dominate coaching positions (Connell 2012). The amount of coverage of women's sport in traditional media outlets is also significantly lower than that of their male counterparts (Cooky, Messner and Hextrum 2013). In addition to this, sport remains male dominated through pitting women's performance against a hegemonic masculine standard (Connell 2012). Furthermore, and pertinently for our analysis, gendered inequalities such as this are evident in the gender politics of sport within the domain of educational institutions.

Connell (2008) shows how gender and masculinity are constructed in physical education and school sports. These areas of the curricula have a large capacity to promote hegemonic forms of masculinity and therefore can be viewed as 'masculine vortices' (Connell 2008; Mooney and Hickey 2012). Connell (2008) states that due to the strongly-ingrained histories and working patterns of the education system, these organisations are gendered. It has long been acknowledged that there is a connection between the construction of masculinity and sports in childhood, and schools provide the foundations for this process (Messner 1990; Connell 2008). Physical education and sport are prone to benefit those who most embody, and comply with, hegemonic masculinity (Pringle 2008; Mooney and Hickey 2012). Certain sports which involve violence and physical confrontation are seen as a test of manhood; they therefore become intertwined with the definition of hegemonic masculinity in schools (Connell 2008).

This chapter explores whether universities continue to promote hegemonic masculinity through sport in this same fashion in the British context. In contrast to the abundance of literature on the North American context, to date there has been a relative lack of consideration of the British context (Brunton and Mackintosh 2017). For example, Phipps' recent (2020, 2021) work has scrutinised the extent to which British universities have successfully tackled gendered and homophobic discrimination in university sport, emphasising the ongoing challenges faced in achieving such goals. Furthermore, Ogilvie and McCormack's (2020) study of the impact of 'gender-collaborative' training opportunities in British university sport highlighted similarly entrenched gender hierarchies and segregation, whilst illustrating the potential for challenging gender dichotomies through mixed-gender sports participation. However, notwithstanding these recent contributions, the gendered nature of British university sport, and the extent to which gender politics continues to blight the experiences of female participants, remains under-explored.

Methods

This chapter aims to explore women's experiences in sport and exercise in a university setting, with a specific focus on gender politics within the university sport context. The current research employed a feminist methodology and collected all the data from women's perspectives. As Walters (2005) states, the most trustworthy information about these topics is women's lived experiences. This challenges traditional gendered science, which has previously cast women in passive roles and prohibited them from scientific practices due to being 'emotional' and 'incapable of reason' (Somekh and Lewin 2006). Weiner (2004) gives three main principles as a guide to feminist research, with the first stating that it should include a critique of the assumptions about women and the unexamined forms of knowledge that are dominant. The other principles state that feminist research should be committed to improving opportunities for females, and that research should develop professional and personal practices that are fair for women (Weiner, 2004). In this light, feminist research should have a feminist perspective, not just methodology, and should include an ongoing criticism of non-feminist scholarship to bring about social change; this is called emancipatory feminist work (Somekh and Lewin 2006). This approach is in keeping with the aim of this chapter, so that interventions can be put in place to allow women a more gender balanced experience in university sports.

Interviews were used to obtain an in-depth understanding of not just what can be inferred from the experiences women talk about, but also their own point of view and the impact of these experiences on their behaviour. Participants were recruited through promotional material at a university in England. The sample size was 12, allowing for interviews of an in-depth nature for each participant (ranging from 19 to 57 minutes in length). The age range of the participants was 19–23 years. All participants were current students who were or had been a member of a sports team at the university. The interviews consisted of questions centring on: (a) what the words 'feminine' and 'masculine' mean to them, (b) how they believe their peers perceive female athletes, (c) their experiences in sport as a female throughout their life and at university, and (d) how these experiences have influenced participants' current behaviour. Pseudonyms were used in the discussion for the participants' names for anonymity.

The interview-data was analysed through coding and thematic analysis, with themes being determined in a cyclical process between data and theory, i.e., the work of Gramsci and Connell. The thematic analysis approach followed a process of open and axial coding, with the themes subsequently allocated to subcategories aligned with the aforementioned theoretical frameworks. This process allowed for an abductive practice which oscillated between inductive analysis and theoretical categorisation (Macdonald and Armour 2012; Atkinson 2017; Veal 2018). In the following sections, we present the findings of the study in conjunction with relevant theory and existing research.

Discussion

Hegemonic masculinity, male superiority, and female inferiority in university sport

One of the principal themes that emerged from the interviews regarding gender politics was that of the double standards the university's female athletes face. Simone (cheerleader) explains how some of the university staff judge female and male athletes differently:

> …they [staff] literally just focus on what they're wearing all the time… 'they're [cheerleaders] not wearing anything'… like, 'they're showing too much skin, they look like baby prostitutes'. … they don't focus on that when [male] rowers are walking around with… no shirts on.

Similar criticisms are not offered to men for the same actions, suggesting how hegemonic masculinity operates within sport to legitimate the subordination of women (Connell and Messerschmidt 2005). The problem for those who criticise is not with the actions, but with the gender. The examples Simone gives shows how athletes are sexualised and infantilised, by comparing them to 'baby prostitutes'. This is another tactic used by male members of the university staff to undermine and marginalise their athletic ability, thereby maintaining male superiority. A similar experience was shared by Nina (gymnast):

> ...spectators would be like 'why do they wear stuff like that?'... 'why do they dress like little prostitutes?'... actually, it's not us that chooses to look like that - that's actually the sport that puts us on it.

The hegemony of gymnastics and various other sports set these uniforms that are revealing and draw sexualised attention to the female athletes' bodies. The over-sexualisation of female athletes' bodies is then used against them to criticise them and diminish their athletic ability (Connell 2002; Trolan 2013; Mullins 2015).

It is not only uniforms that female athletes are subject to criticism for, but also their athletic physiques due to looking too 'manly'. Most participants have received criticism for looking 'too muscular', or, at least, are aware of other female athletes having or fearing this form of criticism. Katherine (rower) explained:

> ...no one wants an athletic [masculine] body and it takes away their [female athletes] femininity, and stuff like that... everyone goes: 'but don't do that because then you'll get bulky and then you'll look like a man'.

Instead of being accepted as a by-product of their sport and celebrated for their athletic achievement, women's muscular bodies are attacked. This is a result of a strong muscular body being counter to hegemonic ideas of femininity, being delicate (Messner 1992). As Connell (1987) states, those who represent femininities contrasting to emphasised femininity are marginalised to an even greater extent; in the British university sport context, such marginalisation has also led to homophobic labelling of female participants (Phipps 2020). Women who are not conventionally pretty or who have an image that is assumed to be associated with masculinity do not align with emphasised femininity and, therefore, are lower in the gender hierarchy (Cockburn and Clarke 2002). This is due to emphasised femininity being based on heterosexuality and heterosexual men's desires, therefore anything outside of this spectrum is further subordinated by masculinities (Connell 1987).

With sport being an arena where female and male bodies, and their proficiencies, are put on display, it is commonly used as an institution to affirm the male body's superiority (Messner 2002). Kerri (volleyball) observed the following:

> ... female sports are kind of looked down as being, like, weaker... it's like Carly Lloyd... she's on a US women's team for soccer... kicked a 50-yard field goal and... everyone's like 'well, girls like still can't do that'... it's like, 'we can', even though... we're looked down on as being like less athletic...

It is widely known that females and males have biological differences, meaning that women and men compete separately in sports, as is the case for the majority of sports in the British university sport system (Ogilvie and McCormack 2020). However, as Ayeisha (hockey) explains, this is often used as an argument against the participation of women in sport:

> …oh, you know, if men and women are equal, why don't they compete against each other? It's not that they shouldn't do it because they aren't equal - it's because their biology is completely different.

Ayeisha gives an example of how people attempt to use biological determinism to subordinate women in sport. This is extremely damaging as it suggests that the only purpose of sport is to compete at an elite level, yet British university sport has a much more complex place in society as a cultural and social activity (Brunton and Mackintosh 2017). Echoing Phipps' (2021) arguments, this aspect of British university sport reinforces a binary view of the female and male bodies, erroneously presuming all men to have a genetic predisposition to be a good athlete and the opposite for women (Connell 2002). Katherine (rower) informs us how these views manifest themselves across sports and at the university: '…I feel like it's especially at uni. It's really male orientated and people don't see like some female sports as a sport'. It is not just through structural aspects, but, as Katherine states, there is an attitude towards women's sports that views them as lesser and, in some cases, not even as 'real sports'. This supports the notion that sport is used to promote masculine imagery and cultivate male hegemony (Connell 2012). This provides further evidence of the potential benefits for challenging this gender essentialism through the 'gender-collaborative training' opportunities recommended in Ogilvie and McCormack's (2020) recent work on the British university sport context.

Furthermore, the underfunding of female sports results in sport not being a viable career option for women. Therefore, there are lower participation rates at university level, with only 49% of female students taking part in physical activity once a week compared to 65% of males (Women in Sport 2017). As Maya (basketball) states:

> …females have no career out of sport. Basically, they don't really get the chance… So, there's less opportunity and less chance for them to succeed usually in sport, so I think the discouragement comes from there [lack of financial support]…

Through the vast disparity between women's and men's sports in relation to pay and funding, attitudes supporting male dominance and female subordination filter down to the amateur and novice levels (Connell and Messerschmidt 2005). Universities are not immune to such gender binary attitudes dominant in wider society. In fact, many of these gender binary-informed issues, such as funding differentials, are present across British university sport due to the lack of legislative instruments in the British context, which would have yielded the same effects as Title IX has in the American system (Ogilvie and McCormack 2020; Phipps 2021).

Gender politics in university sport

This section further examines the gender politics within British university sport, especially how male dominance remains at universities and is connected to the wider society. These attitudes are made apparent in the form of microaggressions, everyday brief communications that become normalised and insult women's sporting abilities (Allen and Frisby 2017). Allen and Frisby (2017) identify many instances of microaggressions in sports media based on female athletes' attractiveness and race, whilst sexually objectifying them. Nina (gymnast) describes an example in a university sport context:

> …[a senior member of staff] at my university… described our female rowing team as 'a social rowing team'. It was in the context of why the novice rowers often train with the female team, and he was like 'that's because it's more of our social rowing team'… Both male and female are, like, international, like, elite athletes, and therefore to describe international GB rowers as 'social rowers' is like the most patronising thing I've ever heard.

Here we see how female athletes can participate in sport, reaching elite level, yet are still not taken seriously. It is to be expected that there is a culture within the university that sees female athletes as second class to men when this is the attitude held by senior staff members at the university, echoing the arguments of Yiamouyiannis and Osborne (2012) on the American university sport context. Many of the participants expressed the belief that the university's male sports teams were significantly prioritised in various ways. For instance, Ellen (hockey) noted:

> …men get the training times they want for the gym… The girls, we get like 7am in the morning, and they [men] get midday and times they'd rather, and I think that's really unfair… we're like in the same league as them [men] and doing better in the league than them [men]…

Putting more emphasis on male sports suggests that traditional 'masculine' attributes such as strength and athletic ability are only valued for the male students to possess, thus legitimising the 'lad culture' of British university sport (Phipps and Young 2015; Phipps 2020). This highlights how education systems are gendered organisations and construct gender through their practices (Connell 2008). Whilst Students' Unions can go some way to challenge such practices, their diminishing political status within British university life means that power has been centralised by university staff and management (Brooks, Byford and Sela 2015). This lack of interest in the female sports teams and the prioritisation of the men's teams will deter many people from taking part in sport, which again reinforces sport as a predominantly male domain.

This attitude towards women's sport manifests itself structurally as well, meaning that women are not given the opportunities or resources needed to succeed. As Caitlin (netballer) explained:

> I think females, across whatever level, have to be pushed. They have to push themselves a bit more to be seen, to be noticed and to be recognised. I think the [female] elite have to work a lot harder to be female elite athletes than males.

This traditional and normalised prioritisation of male athletes displays male hegemony within the university, an aspect of civil society, favouring the men's teams and requiring the women's teams to prove themselves 'worthy' of the same treatment. This highlights sports' tendency to advantage those who habitually embody hegemonic masculinity and marginalise femininity (Mooney and Hickey 2012).

As well as stereotypes surrounding the more masculine sports, female-dominated sports and those perceived as more feminine are also subject to stigmatisation. Ellen (hockey) explains: 'as in cheerleaders, they're all like really pretty, and skinny, and airheads, is probably like a stereotype. Caitlin (netball) adds that:

> Netball, for sure, is known as… you're like blonde, like tanned, quite tall girls, quite bitchy… cheerleaders have a different kind of stereotype as well just 'cause you're… like, I don't know… like quite, I don't know if it's bad to say, like more like catty, like quite glammed-up girls.

It is not only women who display masculine traits are the subject of negative stereotypes; even those who perform femininity or 'emphasised femininity' - what society expects from women - can receive negative labels. Due to the gender hierarchy and hegemony, femininity is subordinated through these stereotypes and language (Connell and Messerschmidt 2005). Hegemonic power is at play here through the women adhering more closely to traditional ideologies of femininity. Some of these stereotypes are maintained by women to allow them to be viewed as more feminine and therefore more acceptable to others in society, showing how consent for these ideologies has been ascertained.

Emphasised femininity is grounded in the acceptance of existing gender relations (Mattsson 2015); females may, therefore, try to gain some form of power through embracing what they perceive as more feminine activities. However, as Connell (1987) states, all forms of femininity are constructed in the context of male domination and therefore cannot challenge the current gender relations. Instead, those women at universities who participate in sports more closely aligned with emphasised femininity may achieve a slightly elevated stage of the gender hierarchy than women performing other forms of femininity, but all female athletes remain within the constraints of hegemonic masculinity and related stereotypes. It is then ironic that women are so heavily judged by their appearance and there is so much pressure for them to focus on the way they look, yet when they do, especially in the field of sport, they are condemned for it. Many people wish to uphold sport with hegemonic ideologies of masculinity pivotal to its character, and consequently anything that threatens this value system is fought against through criticism and tactics of ostracisation (Messner 1992; Connell 2012).

Conclusions

Many of the participants in this study expressed how women are objectified and judged on their appearance above all else both in wider society and university sport. The current research confirmed criticisms of female athletes that are particularly pertinent in relation to their appearance such as muscularity. Comments are frequently made about female athletes looking 'like a man' and losing their femininity as a result of hegemonic ideologies, and the performances of femininity and masculinity, society has become accustomed to (Messner 1992; Connell 2002).

Some of the participants also identified stereotypes such as 'bitchy' and 'airheads' relating to those in sports such as netball and cheerleading, the more 'feminine' sports within universities. These sports were found to be devalued by males due to hegemonic masculinity rejecting femininity and social domains displaying femininity. Therefore, sport founded on ideologies of masculinity that celebrates aggression and competitiveness (Messner 1992) is a challenging arena for women to negotiate successfully. For instance, many of the participants expressed that women's sports were devalued by others and female athletes were seen as inferior to men and assumed to be recreational rather than competitive and serious contenders. This provides further evidence for the existence of gendered hierarchies found in recent analyses of university sport context (Ogilvie and McCormack 2020; Phipps 2020, 2021). Participants also expressed and had evidence from their experiences that male teams were prioritised by their university, even when male athletes were the same or lower level than their female counterparts. Therefore, all the evidence points towards the enduring perpetuation of a gender binary discourse that reinforces female inferiority and subordination in sports (Connell 2008).

Given that the findings presented and discussed in this chapter derived from a specific culture of gender politics at one university, it is important for future research to extend the scope of investigation to encompass sporting cultures found across universities in the UK. Such research will allow for further insight into the opportunities available to female athletes within university settings, as well as the comparative degrees of funding and status available across women's and men's sports. Such knowledge will be crucial to ensuring a truly equitable experience for women and men in this sporting context going forward.

REFERENCES

Allen, K. and Frisby, C.M. (2017) 'A content analysis of microaggressions in news stories about female athletes participating in the 2012 and 2016 Summer Olympics', *Journal of Mass Communication Journalism*, 7(3), p. 334. doi: 10.4172/2165-7192.1000334.

Atkinson, J., (2017) *Journey into social activism: qualitative approaches*. New York: Fordham University Press.

Belanger, K. (2017) *Invisible seasons: Title IX and the fight for equity in college sports*. Syracuse, NY: Syracuse University Press.

Brake, D.L. (2010) *Getting in the game: Title IX and the women's sports revolution*. New York, NY: NYU Press.

Brooks, R., Byford, K. and Sela, K. (2015) 'The changing role of students' unions within contemporary higher education', *Journal of Education Policy*, 30(2), pp. 165–181.

Brunton, J. and Mackintosh, C. (2017) 'Interpreting university sport policy in England: Seeking a purpose in turbulent times?', *International Journal of Sport Policy and Politics*, 9(3), pp. 377–395.

Brunton, J.A. and St Quinton, T. (2020) 'Applying Stage-Based Theory to engage female students in university sport', *Journal of Human Sport and Exercise*, 16(1), pp. 11-25. doi: 10.14198/jhse.2021.161.02.

Carrington, B. and McDonald, I. (2009) *Marxism, cultural studies and sport*. London: Routledge.

Cockburn, C. and Clarke, G. (2002) '"Everybody's looking at you!": Girls negotiating the "femininity deficit" they incur in physical education', *Women's Studies International Forum*, 25(6), pp. 651–665.

Connell, R.W. (1987) *Gender and power*. Stanford, CA: Stanford University Press.

Connell, R.W. (2002) *Gender*. Cambridge: Polity Press.

Connell, R.W. (2005) *Masculinities*. 2nd edition. Cambridge: Polity Press.

Connell, R.W. (2008) 'Masculinity construction and sports in boys' education: A framework for thinking about the issue', *Sport, Education and Society*, 13(2), pp. 131–145.

Connell, R.W. (2009) *Gender: In world perspective*. Cambridge: Polity Press.

Connell, R.W. (2011) *Confronting equality: Gender, knowledge and global change*. Cambridge: Polity.

Connell, R.W. (2012) 'Supremacy and subversion – Gender struggles in sport', *Asia-Pacific Journal of Health, Sport and Physical Education*, 3(3), pp. 177–179.

Connell, R.W. and Messerschmidt, J. (2005) 'Hegemonic masculinity', *Gender and Society*, 19(6), pp. 829–859.

Cooky, C., Messner, M. and Hextrum, R. (2013) 'Women play sport, but not on TV: A longitudinal study of televised sport media', *Communication and Sport*, 1(3), pp. 203–230.

Domeneghetti, R. (2019) "On me bed, son': The (Re)presentation of (emphasised) femininity in English 'tabloid' newspaper coverage of Euro 2016', *International Review for the Sociology of Sport*, 54(7), pp. 873–887.

Fink, J.S. (2015) 'Female athletes, women's sport, and the sport media commercial complex: Have we really "come a long way, baby?"', *Sport Management Review*, 18(3), pp. 331–342.

Gramsci, A., Hoare, Q. and Nowell-Smith, G. (1998) *Selections from the prison notebooks of Antonio Gramsci*. London: Lawrence and Wishart.

Hargreaves, J. (1994) *Sporting females: Critical issues in the history and sociology of women's sports*. London: Routledge.

Kimmel, M., Hearn, J. and Connell, R. (2005) *Handbook of studies on men and masculinities*. Thousand Oaks: Sage.

Macdonald, D. and Armour, K., (2012) *Research methods in physical education and youth sport*. London: Routledge.

Markula, P. (2001) 'Beyond the perfect body: Women's body image distortion in fitness magazine discourse', *Journal of Sport and Social Issues*, 25(2), pp. 158–179.

Mattsson, T. (2015) "Good girls': emphasised femininity as cloning culture in academia', *Gender and Education*, 27(6), pp. 685–699.

McKay, J. (1997) *Managing gender*. New York: SUNY Press.

Messner, M. (1990) 'Boyhood, organized sports, and the construction of masculinities', *Journal of Contemporary Ethnography*, 18(4), pp. 416–444.

Messner, M. (1992) *Power at play: Sports and the problem of masculinity*. Boston: Beacon.

Messner, M. (2002) *Taking the field: Women, men, and sports*. Minneapolis: University of Minnesota Press.

Mooney, A. and Hickey, C. (2012) 'Negotiating masculine hegemony: Female physical educators in an all-boys' school', *Asia-Pacific Journal of Health, Sport and Physical Education*, 3(3), pp. 199–212.

Mullins, N.M. (2015) 'Insidious influence of gender socialization on females' physical activity: Rethink pink', *Physical Educator*, 72(1), pp. 20–43.

Ogilvie, M.F. and McCormack, M. (2020). 'Gender-collaborative training in elite university sport: Challenging gender essentialism through integrated training in gender-segregated sports', *International Review for the Sociology of Sport*, 56(8), pp. 1172–1188. doi: 1012690220980149.

Phipps, A. and Young, I. (2015) 'Neoliberalisation and "lad cultures" in higher education', *Sociology*, 49(2), pp. 305–322.

Phipps, C. (2020) '"We already do enough around equality and diversity": Action taken by student union officers to promote LGBT+ inclusion in university sport', *Sociology of Sport Journal*, 37(4), pp. 310–318.

Phipps, C. (2021) 'Thinking beyond the binary: Barriers to trans* participation in university sport', *International Review for the Sociology of Sport*, 56(1), pp. 81–96.

Pringle, R. (2008) "No rugby - no fear': Collective stories, masculinities and transformative possibilities in schools', *Sport, Education and Society*, 13(2), pp. 215–237.

Reeser, J.C. (2005) 'Gender identity and sport: Is the playing field level?', *British Journal of Sports Medicine*, 39(10), pp. 695–699.

Senne, J.A. (2016) 'Examination of gender equity and female participation in sport', *Sport Journal*, 22, pp. 1–10.

Somekh, B. and Lewin, C. (2006) *Research methods in the social sciences*. London: Sage.

Trolan, E.J. (2013) 'The impact of the media on gender inequality within sport'. *Procedia - Social and Behavioral Sciences, International Conference on Humanities and Social Sciences*, 91, pp. 215–227.

Veal, A., (2018) *Research methods for leisure and tourism* (5th ed.). London: Pearson Education Limited.

Walters, M. (2005). *Feminism: A very short introduction*. Oxford: Oxford University Press.

Weiner, G., (2004) 'Critical action research and third wave feminism: a meeting of paradigms', *Educational Action Research*, 12(4), pp. 631–644.

Women In Sport (2017) 'Case Study: This BUCS Girl Can - Getting Female Students Active', *Women In Sport* [online]. Available at: https://www.womeninsport.org/research-and-advice/our-publications/bucs-girl-can-getting-female-students-active/ (Accessed 12 May 2021).

Yiamouyiannis, A. and Osborne, B. (2012) 'Addressing gender inequities in collegiate sport: Examining female leadership representation within NCAA sport governance', *Sage Open*, 2(2), pp. 1–13.

15
The Gender Politics of Sex Integrated Sport
The Case of Professional Golf

Ali Bowes

Introduction

On 13th February 2021, the Australian edition of the Daily Telegraph posted an article about two professional golfers, and siblings, Min Woo Lee and his sister Minjee Lee. The clickbait headline, 'The new Aussie golf star who couldn't beat his own sister' (Linden 2021; see also Porter 2021), is indicative about the status of women within golf cultures. At the time, Minjee was ranked the 8th best in the world on the Women's World Golf Rankings, compared to Min Woo's 198th ranking on the men's Official World Golf Ranking. But the implication was that Min Woo should be beating his sister, and that is because she is a woman. Whilst this sentiment about men and women, or boys and girls, in sport is not a new phenomenon, the sport they play makes it an interesting point of discussion. The unusual aspect of this sporting sibling rivalry is that golf is a sport where men and women *can* compete against each other.

As Hargreaves and Anderson (2016) explain, modern, organised sport is a distinctly gendered activity. They recognise gender as a 'very complex and changing social category of analysis in relation to the "opposite" sex and within one's sexual category', thereby understanding gender as a cultural category and sex as a biological one (Hargreaves and Anderson 2016, p. 4). However, the two terms are often used interchangeably in common-sense discourse, with the gender binary socially constructed in line with interpretations of biological sex differences. The gendering of men and women produces the gendered social order in which men benefit (Lorber 2010). In simple terms, boys and girls have expectations placed on them based on the socially constructed perception of their biological sex. These are then played out in the world of sport, and because socially constructed biology-informed beliefs about gender differences in sport appear natural, they become taken for granted (Willis 1982, cited in Hargreaves and Anderson 2016). At this juncture, it is important to highlight how the terms 'sex' and 'gender' are going to be used throughout this chapter. The notion of sex is used when considering the parameters placed onto sporting competition determined by biological factors, as such, competitions that feature both men and women defined as 'mixed-sex' competition, an industry-accepted term used within golf. On the other hand, the term 'gender' is used when referring to characteristics that refer to socially constructed norms of men and women.

Feminist politics has contributed to the increasing access and opportunity women have in sporting environments. However, sport predominately operates in sex-segregated spaces. The historical development of modern sport, as we know it, is one that has been imbued with gendered ideologies of female frailty and male superiority (Hargreaves 1994), which has served to position women as the 'weaker sex'. Subsequently, men and women typically operate in separate spaces in the professional sporting world, which Anderson (2008) describes as naturalised through this notion of physical difference between the sexes. Western cultural sport norms dictate that male and female athletes need distinct spaces to compete (Pieper 2016), and with that separation comes a hierarchy. Competitive men's sport - often simply termed 'sport' - symbolically validates male privilege, and women's sport – clearly gender-marked as 'women's sport' – is then considered secondary to men's sport.

This distinction is evident in the organisation of professional golf – with professional tours for women carrying the descriptor 'Ladies'. In Europe, the premier tour for men is known as the European Tour, whilst women compete in the Ladies European Tour (LET). The most prestigious professional tours in the world, located primarily in the United States of America, also feature similar gender-marking for the women's version: The Ladies Professional Golf Association (LPGA) Tour and the Professional Golf Association (PGA) Tour. We can also see the impact of gender marking in the phrasing of the aforementioned world golf rankings: one is the 'official' ranking, whilst the other is the 'women's' ranking. In considering the gendered nature of sport, this 'purposeful division of the sexes becomes an important topic for scholars interested in the (re)production of inequality' (Channon et al. 2016, p. 1111). In other words, the doing of gender in a sport context can (re)produce difference in the lives of men and women, making sex differences seem persistent and natural.

The history and culture of golf as a sex-segregated sport has resulted in women's position seen as subordinate. Typically, women's participation was not particularly welcomed nor taken seriously, and golf cultures have normalised exclusionary and discriminatory practices towards women to this day (Reis and Correia 2013). Year-on-year, the growth of male participation in the sport outnumbers women, with world golf's ruling body, the Royal & Ancient (R&A), noting an increasing 'gender gap' (Fry and Hall 2018). However, in recent years, there have been increasing examples of women competing against men in professional golf tournaments at the highest level. There has also been the growth of innovative developmental golf tours, advertised as 'gender-equal' and 'inclusive', providing golf tournaments open to both male and female golfers. These tournaments make adjustments to tee boxes, with women teeing off closer to the hole than men, to equalise any expected biological sex-differences in performance (Bowes and Kitching 2020b).

For example, in the UK, the Clutch Pro Tour runs 18, 36 and 54 hole tournaments, with male and female professionals playing for the same trophy, same prize fund and same season-long order of merit (Clutch Pro Tour 2021). Similarly, the 2020 Pro Tour runs 18 hole tournaments for men and women golfers, with competitors playing for the same trophy, prize fund, and season-long order of merit. On the Clutch Pro Tour, women play a minimum of 11% less yardage than men (Clutch Pro Tour 2021), and on the 2020 Pro Tour, women play a course that is a minimum of 15% shorter than men under 50 (2020 Pro Tour 2021). Given the increasing opportunities for men and women to compete against each other in the sport, especially at a professional level, this chapter will present a critical discussion on the gender politics at play during sex-integrated professional golf tournaments. It will examine the complexities of sex integration in a sporting domain by interrogating notions of the 'naturalness' of sex differences, the use of 'gendered' tee boxes, and the unusualness of men and women competing in the same event, for the same trophy.

Men versus women in golf

Golf has consistently been a site of gender discrimination (Tofilon 2005) with the history of the sport – even to the current day - rife with exclusionary practices against women. This is despite golf lending itself, more than other male-dominated sports, to equitable practices. The handicap system enables any golfer to compete against better (or even the best) golfers, irrespective of gender. Equally, the length of the course can be adjusted via the use of different tee boxes, making a course longer or shorter (and thus harder or easier). In this way, the challenge in the sport is about ability, and not sex. Because of this, as McGinnis, Gentry and McQuillan (2008, p. 20) explain, golf would seem an ideal sport for the embodiment of gender equity: 'nothing is inherent in the sport, except for the rituals, that should advantage men or require segregated play'. Different handicaps, staggered tees, as well as variably sized equipment means the sport is set up to enable anyone to play against each other. Despite this, golf is gendered at all levels.

Regardless of the structure and organisation of elite-level professional golf tours being sex-segregated, there have been examples of women competing against men throughout history. The LPGA Tour and the PGA Tour played a combined mixed-team event for 30 years, the JCPenney Classic, but this has not featured since 1999 (Romine 2018). As of 2020, six women have been involved in PGA Tour stroke-play events. The first was Babe Didrickson Zaharias in 1938 and 1945, followed by Shirley Spork in 1952 - both women were founders of the LPGA Tour in 1950. Arguably the most famous involvement was Annika Sorenstam in 2003, at the Bank of America Colonial Professional Golf Association (PGA) Tournament (Billings et al. 2006), as well as Suzy Whaley's involvement in the same year at the Greater Hartford Open (Hundley 2004). A young Michelle Wie made her name initially participating in men's events between 2004 and 2008, competing 13 times including eight times in the PGA Tour. Brittany Lincicome became the sixth woman when she competed at the Barbasol Championship in 2018. Yet, only Zaharias has played a full PGA tournament – 'making the cut' twice in 1945. Most tournaments feature a half-way cut after two rounds of 18 holes, with the bottom half of the field 'missing the cut', and the top half playing out the remaining 36 holes of the tournament. Although Wie made the cut in one of her 13 appearances, it was in a minor tour event and not on the premier PGA Tour. There are likely to be more women competing against men as golf tours look to continually innovate their events in the future.

In Europe, there has been an increase in non-traditional tournaments that have seen men and women competing against each other, rather than one-off invites. The European Tour launched the GolfSixes in 2017, inviting women competitors for the first time in the 2018 version (Bowes and Kitching 2019; 2020a). In 2019, the LET combined with the European Senior Tour (then known as the Staysure Tour, for professional male golfers aged 50 and over) and the Challenge Tour (the European Tour feeder tour) to host the Jordan Mixed Open. This event featured 40 players from each tour competing for the same trophy and prize fund, playing to the same pins but from different tees: over the 18 holes, the Challenge Tour played 7100 yards, the Senior Tour played 6601 yards and the LET played 6139 yards (Cooper 2019). The event was won by Challenge Tour player Daan Huizing, beating LET player Meghan MacLaren by two strokes, with the leading Senior Tour player – Jose Coceres – finishing tied fourth. The announcement of the Scandinavian Mixed Open would be the first time the European Tour was combining with the LET to co-sanction an event. Players would be competing for the same trophy and same prize fund, with the women playing off closer tees. The inaugural 2020 tournament was postponed due to COVID-19, but the competition is scheduled to feature in the 2021 season.

This integration of women into men's professional events has received both general and academic attention, particularly around media coverage (Billings et al. 2006; Billings, Angelini and Eastman 2008; Bowes and Kitching 2019; 2020a) and more recently the women players' experiences (Bowes and Kitching 2020b). When women compete against men, they become the primary focus of the media coverage – emphasising the unusualness of this practice in elite sport settings (Billings et al. 2006; Bowes and Kitching 2020a; 2020b). Women's involvement within men's professional golf has been found to bring increased visibility of women in the sport (Bowes and Kitching 2020a). However, there are gendered angles to women's involvement. Sorenstam, at the aforementioned PGA Colonial in 2003, was four times more likely to be compared to a male golfer than her male counterparts in the same competition (Billings et al. 2006). In other research into the media coverage of the 2019 Solheim Cup, women competitors were often benchmarked against male players of a similar style or personality (Bowes et al. 2020; Bowes and Kitching 2021). On the whole, this body of research emphasised the complex, gendered nature of women's involvement in competitive golf against men, in relation to media coverage.

The gender politics of sex-integrated golf

In considering the possibility of sex-integrated sport more generally, the examples of both Sorenstam and Wie can be seen to act as fuel for the myth of women's incapability to compete with men at the highest level (Sailors 2016); both women failed to make the cut in PGA Tour events, and in fact only Zaharias has made the cut in a men's strokeplay event (Beall 2020). Sailors (2016) cautioned that although most elite male athletes can beat most elite female athletes in sports that privilege men (and specifically white, Western men, such as golf), it should not be a presumption that every elite male will outperform every elite female. The GolfSixes events have provided further evidence to this from the world of golf, where four of the female players, playing in two teams of two, beat men's teams for places in the quarterfinals of the competition (Bowes and Kitching 2019; 2020a; 2020b). Despite this, the belief is that men should, or will, beat women, because it is one of the fundamental cornerstones of the socially constructed binary found in sport, as well as broader Western societies (Kane 1995). These ideas will need to be unpicked and developed to understand the gender politics of sex-integrated golf.

Often, the gender politics of golf are rooted in basic biological assumptions that women's physiology makes them less capable of playing the sport. In golf, females are widely perceived as physically inferior to their male counterparts – simply measured by driving distance - which is frequently used to frame women as less able golfers (McGinnis, McQuillan and Chapple 2005). This contributes to the socially constructed gendering of women golfers, stereotyped as slower, less able, less competitive, and less powerful players (McGinnis and Gentry 2002; McGinnis, McQuillan and Chapple 2005). This can be considered via the nuances of the statistics from the 2020 PGA Tour and the 2020 LPGA Tour (PGA Tour 2020; LPGA Tour 2020).

Table 15.1 highlights some key performance indicators from the PGA and LPGA Tours (LPGA Tour average is not available, which is arguably due to the lack of performance data available in women's sports). The 2020 PGA Tour driving statistics have the average driving distance as 296.4 yards off the tee, with Bryson DeChambeau, the season leader, at 322.1 yards. The leading player on the LPGA tour in driving distance, Bianca Pagdanganan, finished the 2020 season with an average of 283.1 yards. Of course, though, there are women on the LPGA Tour that will outdrive some of the men on the PGA Tour, and Pagdanganan would be sitting 186th on the PGA Tour ranking, above eight players that includes six PGA Tour champions and multiple winners such as Matt Kuchar and Jim Furyk.

Despite the difference in length, there are driving metrics where women golfers come out on top. Marina Alex of the LPGA Tour led the way in 2020 with 83.4% driving accuracy, compared

Table 15.1 Performance Indicators

	PGA tour leader	PGA tour average	LPGA tour leader	LPGA tour average
Driving Distance (Yards)	322.1	296.4	283.1	N/A
Driving Accuracy (% of tee shots on fairway)	74.5	60.22	83.4	73.08
Greens in regulation (%)	74.22	66.3	77.6	66.02
Putts per round	27.88	29.03	28.69	N/A

to Jim Furyk on the PGA Tour with 74.5%, and a tour average of 60.22%. Other common metrics used to distinguish golf performance - greens in regulation and putting averages, are decidedly similar. Greens in regulation is a statistic that tracks the number of greens a golfer reaches within the expected number of strokes in relation to par, which always includes two putts. For example, a par four would require reaching the green on the second shot. Sei Young Kim on the LPGA Tour led the way with 77.6%, with Jim Furyk recording a PGA Tour best of 74.22%. The PGA Tour average for putts per round was 29.03; Ian Poulter top of the rankings with a tour average of 27.88, and Leona Maguire recording an LPGA Tour best of 28.69. The difference in driving distance is often used as a marker of inferiority, yet women are more accurate off the tee, and there is little difference in other key aspects of the game. However, the superiority of male players is often emphasised when women step into 'their' arena and men prevail – the aforementioned examples are cases in point.

To counter the relative physical dominance of men in terms of power and strength (evidenced via driving distance), there are strategies in place that are seen to 'level the playing field' in golf: specifically, the 'ladies tee' (McGinnis and Gentry 2006). As Channon et al. (2016, p. 114) explain, different rules which seemingly 'handicap' men and provide women an apparently necessary competitive advantage – such as the shortening of the length of the golf course via gendered tee boxes – actually and symbolically emphasise biological differences. It has been found that women only play approximately 86% of the men's golf course (Arthur et al. 2009). However, this may challenge the notion that women can compete on a 'level playing field' with men as some will question whether the competition was fair in the first place (Bowes and Kitching 2020b). After all – playing devil's advocate – if women have less distance to play across the golf course, this might be problematic should, for example, the longest women off the tee match up against the shortest men. The notion that all women should play off the front tee when competing against men is based on assumptions around both gender and sex, and not golfing ability.

The reality is that tee boxes have become infused with gendered politics. Golf courses typically offer between three and five tee boxes from which male golfers may elect to play their tee shot, whilst women are (culturally) restricted to playing the front tees, on average 46 yards closer to the hole (Hundley 2004; Arthur et al. 2009). The freedom of choice over tee boxes that men have imply that men are always stronger, more skilled and more qualified than women, regardless of their golfing ability. The unintended consequence of differing tee boxes marks and highlights women as different or 'other' (McGinnis, Gentry and McQuillan 2008). The global ruling body of golf, the R&A (2016), admit in their pace of play manual that the closest tee is often gendered and is referred to as the 'ladies tee', and found that this gendering of tee boxes hinders the ability of players to appropriately select the tee boxes suitable for their ability. In short, men do not want to play off the front 'ladies' tee (R&A 2016). Channon et al. (2016) note that the use of alternative playing conditions, such as forward tees for women, reduces the ability to see women's performances as justifiably equal to men's performances. Furthermore, the legitimacy of adjusting tee length by biological sex (and not by ability, as the alternative tee boxes are designed for) in sex-integrated golf have been questioned (Bowes and Kitching 2020b). This biological rationale perpetuates the assumption that all men are equal, and all women are equal, and all men are superior to all women, and all men and all women have the same physical characteristics and/or abilities.

Sex-integrated golf competitions are complex in their organisation. There is a recognition that those who cannot drive the ball as far (women) require a closer tee box than those who can (men). Clearly, this practical solution to make the game more equitable is not one that is based purely on ability but based on gender assumptions. Research examining women golfers' experiences of competing against men highlighted the centrality and complexity of gender politics, again in relation to tee boxes and their performance (Bowes and Kitching 2020b). The women golfers were honest in concluding that the men did not expect to lose to them, demonstrating the significance of gender within understanding success in sport. Despite playing off forward tees, which would in principle nullify any (perceived) biological sex differences and make the competition purely about who could get the ball in the hole in the least amount of shots, it was still a space where men were seen as superior (Bowes and Kitching 2020b).

To add further nuance, when the women were successful, they often used the tee box location to dismiss the significance of their success. Their 'narratives of competing against men centre on, and are restricted by, a strong biological argument' (Bowes and Kitching 2020b, p. 13). This was used in two ways, to justify a diminished performance (for example, a 'we didn't win because we're women and men are stronger and better' sentiment), or to diminish their performance (for example, 'we won, but we were playing off forward tees so we had an advantage'). In this way, 'the notion is presented that the women obviously were never going to win, simply because (all) men are inherently, biologically, better than them' (Bowes and Kitching 2020b, p. 13). Perhaps then, women can never win – symbolically at least; they might *actually* win and lift the trophy, but the 'levelled playing field' is something that *could* always be contested. Interestingly, women golfers that compete against men position themselves as empowered agents of change who, by their very involvement, challenge the perceptions of women as second-rate athletes (Bowes and Kitching 2020b). The notion of women competing against, and beating men, could therefore have transformative potential, challenging sexual hierarchies and gendered assumptions about men and women's sporting capabilities (Channon et al. 2016). Politically, this can be understood as resistance to the gendered social order (Lorber 2010).

Concluding thoughts: Understanding sex-integrated golf

This chapter aimed to present a discussion on the complexities of sex integration in golf by critically considering the role that tee boxes play in 'gendering' the ability of professional golfers in mixed-sex competition. The R&A (2016) are encouraging a de-gendering of tee boxes, highlighting how men are reluctant to play from the closest tees due to their association with women golfers. In golf, the notion of ability is inextricably tied with gender, which results in the length of the hole being adjusted on gendered terms, and justified with biological arguments (Hundley 2004; Bowes and Kitching 2020b). However, golf is a sport where sex-integrated competition is becoming increasingly common. Golf organisations can see the commercial value in the interest of the 'battle of the sexes' (Bowes and Kitching 2019b). This brings these complex sex/gender/ability questions to the fore. This includes considering the appropriateness of standardised tees for men and women competitors, when the tee box location should be decided on the ability of the golfer. Obviously, there is no simple solution to this for mixed-sex tournament organisers, given the vast differences in length of drive on both the men's and women's professional (and amateur) tours. The aim here is to merely highlight the complex nature of tee box location and its entanglement with gendered ideologies.

The gender politics at play in mixed-sex golf positions women's inclusion as both empowering and problematic. As De Haan, Sotiriadou and Henry (2016, p. 1250) note: mixed-sex participation can be viewed as a 'currency of equality', yet can simultaneously 'be seen as a violation of social gender expectations concerning the normative gender behaviour of athletes'. In this way, women can compete against men, but it challenges gendered stereotypes and the everyday assumptions about women's bodies and capabilities. With differing tee boxes, the notion of physical difference, and, on the part of women, inability, is emphasised, in some way negating narratives of equality.

Sailors (2016) questioned: should women compete against men? She responded to this question by challenging the notion that a 'yes' or 'no' will suffice, concluding with four possible answers (whilst also suggesting that none of these are entirely adequate): (1) No, so there's no point in talking about it; (2) No, but they should make the attempt anyway; (3) Yes, so mix all the competition and get on with it; and (4) Yes, but there are good reasons not to allow it. The answer is clearly much more complex and context dependent. The arguments about men and women competing in professional sport versus amateur sport, or contact sport versus non-contact sport, where the stakes are different in all settings, highlight the need for a much more nuanced discussion of sex-integrated sport practices. We can look to the successes of Fallon Sherrock competing against men in darts as another example.

Women competing against men in the sport of golf presents an interesting case study for thinking about the impact of gender on sport. For McLachlan (2016), to this day, gender is still a 'complex question' in sport, and this discussion of sex-integrated golf and different tee boxes further confirms that. However, McLachlan (2016) also notes that, related to the complexity of gender, sexism is an 'urgent problem' in sport. Although writing about cycling, McLachlan (2016) highlights how there are layers of institutional and cultural sexism that exist within sport, and whose effects are felt especially hard in the women's professional arena. Arguably, the same can be said about women in golf. Outside of these innovative events where men 'allow', or 'invite' women into their competitions, the inherent sexism in golf at a professional level is evident in relation to the number of events available and the prize funds received.

REFERENCES

2020 Pro Tour (2021) *Rules and Regulations*. Available at: https://2020protour.co.uk/tc/ (Accessed: 13 February 2021).

Anderson, E. (2008) '"I used to think women were weak": Orthodox masculinity, gender segregation, and sport', *Sociological Forum*, 23 (2), pp. 257–280.

Arthur, M.M., Van Buren III, H.J. and Del Campo, R.G. (2009) 'The impact of American politics on perceptions of women's golfing abilities', *American Journal of Economics and Sociology*, 68 (2), pp. 517–539.

Beall, J. (2020) 'Did you know: Only one woman has made a cut in PGA Tour history', *Golf Digest*, 15 April. Available at: https://www.golfdigest.com/story/did-you-know-only-one-woman-has-made-a-cut-in-pga-tour-history (Accessed: 13 February 2021).

Billings, A.C., Angelini, J. and Eastman, S (2008) 'Wie shock: Television commentary about playing on the PGA and LPGA tours', *The Howard Journal of Communications*, 19 (1), pp. 64–84.

Billings, A.C., Craig, C.C., Croce, R., Cross, K.M., Moore, K.M., Vigodsky, W. and Watson, V.G. (2006) '"Just one of the guys?" Network depictions of Annika Sorenstam in the 2003 PGA Colonial Tournament', *Journal of Sport and Social Issues*, 30 (1), pp. 107–114.

Bowes, A. and Kitching, N. (2019) '"Here come the girls": Examining professional golf organisations' online media representations of female professional golfers in a mixed-gender event', *Ethical Space*, 16 (2/3), pp. 12–20.

Bowes, A. and Kitching, N. (2020a) '"Battle of the sixes": Investigating print media representations of female professional golfers competing in a men's tour event', *International Review for the Sociology of Sport*, 55 (6), pp. 664–684.

Bowes, A. and Kitching, N. (2020b) '"Wow these girls can play": Sex integration in professional golf', *Qualitative Research in Sport, Exercise and Health*, 13 (2), pp. 217–234.

Bowes, A. and Kitching, N. (Forthcoming 2021) 'The Solheim Cup: Media representations of golf, gender and national identity'. In Dashper, K. (ed.) *Sport, Gender and Mega-Events*. Bingley: Emerald Publishing Limited.

Bowes, A., Bairner, A., Whigham, S. and Kitching, N. (2020) 'Women, war and sport: The battle of the 2019 Solheim Cup', *Journal of War & Culture Studies*, 13 (4), pp. 424–443.

Channon, A., Dashper, K., Fletcher, T. and Lake, R.J. (2016) 'The promises and pitfalls of sex integration in sport and physical culture', *Sport in Society*, 19 (8-9), pp. 1111–1124.

Clutch Pro Tour (2021) *Clutch Golf Policy and Conditions 2021*. Available at: https://www.clutchprotour.co.uk/ (Accessed: 13 February 2021).

Cooper, M. (2019) 'Jordan Mixed Open involves world-first male, female and senior golfers', *Forbes*, 3 April. Available at: https://www.forbes.com/sites/matthewjcooper/2019/04/03/jordan-mixed-open-involves-world-first-male-female-and-senior-golfers/?sh=2acaf69c43bb (Accessed: 14 February 2020).

De Haan, D., Sotiriadou, P. and Henry, I. (2016) 'The lived experience of sex-integrated sport and the construction of athlete identity within the Olympic and Paralympic equestrian disciplines', *Sport in Society*, 19 (8-9), pp. 1249–1266.

Fry, J. and Hall, P. (2018) 'Women's, girls' and family participation in golf: An overview of existing research', *The R&A*. https://www.randa.org/~/media/files/downloadsandpublications/workingforgolf/raresearchdocfull.ashx

Hargreaves, J. (1994) *Sporting Females*. London: Routledge

Hargreaves, J. and Anderson, E. (2016) 'Sport, gender and sexuality: Surveying the field'. In Hargreaves, J. and Anderson, E. (eds.) *The Routledge Handbook of Sport, Gender and Sexuality*. London: Routledge, pp. 3–18.

Hundley, H.L. (2004) 'Keeping the score: The hegemonic everyday practices in golf', *Communication Reports*, 17 (1), pp. 39–48.

Kane, M.J. (1995) 'Resistance/transformation of the oppositional binary: Exposing sport as a continuum', *Journal of Sport and Social Issues*, 19, pp. 191–218.

Linden, J. (2021) 'The new Aussie star who couldn't beat his own sister', *The Daily Telegraph, Australia*, 12 February.

Lorber, J. (2010) *Gender Inequality: Feminist Theories and Politics*. Oxford: University Press.

LPGA Tour (2020) *Statistics*. Available at: https://www.lpga.com/statistics (Accessed: 13 February 2021).

McGinnis, L. and Gentry, J.W. (2002) 'The masculine hegemony in sports: Is golf for "ladies"?', *Advances in Consumer Research*, 29, pp. 19–24.

McGinnis, L.P. and Gentry, J.W. (2006) 'Getting past the red tees: Constraints women face in golf and strategies to help them stay', *Journal of Sport Management*, 20, pp. 218–247.

McGinnis, L., McQuillan, J. and Chapple, C.L. (2005) 'I just want to play: Women, sexism, and persistence in golf', *Journal of Sport and Social Issues*, 29 (3), pp. 313–337.

McGinnis, L.P., Gentry, J.W. and McQuillan, J. (2008) 'Ritual-based behavior that reinforces hegemonic masculinity in golf: Variations in women golfers' responses', *Leisure Sciences*, 31 (1), pp. 19–36.

McLachlan, F. (2016) 'Gender politics, the Olympic Games, and road cycling: A case for critical history', *The International Journal of the History of Sport*, 33 (4), pp. 469–483.

PGA Tour (2020) *Statistics*. Available at: https://www.pgatour.com/stats.html (Accessed: 13 February 2021).

Pieper, L.P. (2016) '"Preserving la difference": The elusiveness of sex-segregated sport', *Sport in Society*, 19 (8-9), pp. 1138–1155.

Porter, E. [@ewanports] (2021, Feb 12). Seriously, @dailytelegraph, this is a disgraceful headline. Especially in this day and age. Min Woo and Min Jee are great young people. Bring back @EvinPriest!. Twitter. https://twitter.com/ewanports/status/1360374762824994823.

R&A (2016) *Pace of Play Manual*. Available at: https://www.randa.org/pace-of-play-manual/rules/3-the-golf-course/subrules/2-tees (Accessed: 14 February 2021).

Reis, H. and Correia, A. (2013) 'Gender inequalities in golf: A consented exclusion?', *International Journal of Culture, Tourism and Hospitality Research*, 7 (4), pp. 324–339.

Romine, B. (2018) 'Monahan: Mixed-team event with PGA Tour, LPGA players in works'. Available at: https://golfweek.usatoday.com/2018/04/30/monahan-mixed-team-event-with-pga-tour-lpga-players-in-works/ (Accessed: 25 May 2021).

Sailors, P.R. (2016) 'Off the beaten path: Should women compete against men?', *Sport in Society*, 19 (8-9), pp. 1125–1137.

Tofilon, J.L. (2005) 'Masters of discrimination: Augusta National Golf Club, freedom of association, and gender equality in golf', *Journal of Gender, Race & Justice*, 9 (1), pp. 189–210.

16
Reclaiming Women's Voice in Masculine Competitive Sports Cultures
Playing to Win?

Adi Mohel

Introduction

In 2019, after finishing their race hand-in-hand, British triathletes Jess Learmonth and Georgia Taylor-Brown had their first/second places taken away and were disqualified from the Tokyo 2020 triathlon trial by the International Triathlon Union (ITU). This disqualification was based on competition rule 2:11, which states that triathletes must not 'finish in a contrived tie situation where no effort to separate the finish times has been made' (Ingle 2019). This incident represents two different and conflicting models of sport: The *Power and Performance Model*, which defines sports as a competition based on strict universal rules and hierarchy, proving excellence through competitive success and striving for victory over others at all costs; and the *Pleasure and Participation Model*, which emphasizes competing *with* rather than *against* and values personal empowerment, self-expression and pleasure (Coakley 2017). The *Power and Performance Model* is around which modern sports have been organized as illustrated by the above-mentioned triathletes' case (Coakley 2017).

When articles about the above example were published in Israel (Aharoni 2019; Haarets Sports 2019), debates arose around whose actions (the athletes' or ITU's) represent the 'real' spirit of sports. However, this debate quickly became a discussion about gender norms and behaviours. The readers' reactions that supported the ITU's decision referred to the athletes' act as feminine, childish, unsportsmanlike and unprofessional (Aharoni 2019, Haarets Sports 2019). This implies that 'real' sports is associated with masculine values of striving for victory at all costs: '…If they were men it would never have happened, because we compete till the end, and we do not give hands like little girls' (online comment on: Aharoni 2019). Those who sided with the athletes argued against the masculine values emphasizing winning at all costs as the most important in sports. 'This is a new message that excellence is also brotherhood and cooperation. Well done to British women. This is an important message in a competitive and cruel world like ours' (online comment on: Haarets Sports 2019). This discussion raises three important points, around which this chapter revolves, regarding modern sports culture and the roles that masculine and feminine values play in it:

1 The assumption that masculine values of winning at all costs are 'real' sports values (Messner 1990, 1988);
2 The assumption that if women aspire to be 'real' athletes, they should conform to the Performance Model;
3 The potential and challenges for women to introduce a feminine discourse to modern sports systems (Lenskyj 1994; Hargreaves 2004).

Organized performance sport politics and hegemonic masculinity

Following the rise of industrial capitalism, traditional masculinity was challenged by economic and social changes (Messner 1990). In this context, modern sport has come to serve as primary institutional means to validate and perpetuate male superiority (Messner 1988; Theberge 2000). Organized team sports began to flourish in Britain and North America at the end of 19th century (Messner 1988; Theberge 2000), creating a homosocial setting, with the majority of rewards and opportunities being available only to men (Lever 1978; Theberge 2000). According to Messner (1988), organized sports have been a crucial arena in the struggle over social conceptions of masculinity and femininity. Therefore, sports became a fundamental arena of ideological contest in terms of power relations between men and women (Messner 1990). Originally, sport was deployed to be a space for courage and masculinity where the 'male character' can be developed and the win-at-all-cost ideology instilled (Bourdieu 2005; Messner 1990). However, as femininity were/are associated with a different set of values and behaviour patterns (Stevenson 2006), women wishing to partake and be successful at sport were branded unfeminine (Whitehead and Biddle 2008; Messner 1990).

The divide between Performance and Participation Models relates to gender as well as to the politics of who rules and dominates sports. As international and national sports organizations are responsible for setting rules and norms around which modern sports is organized, men have been in charge (Bourdieu 1992). Furthermore, high-performance sports are widely promoted by people with wealth and power because those are based on a capitalist ideology that celebrates competitiveness and defines competition as the only fair and natural way to distribute rewards (Coakley 2017). People in leadership positions also have the tendency to promote athletes who share similar values, ideology and social status (Anderson 2009; Sartore and Cunningham 2007). By emphasizing strength, power and speed as well as the need to outperform others, sports reaffirm gender disparities and support a form of gender ideology that favours men. Thus, as long as men are in control, there will be an emphasis on power and performance sports (Coakley 2017), which explains why alternative sports not bound by zero-sum ideology receive little attention.

In Israel, we can see a similar example of how sports budget policies are organized around the Power and Performance model in a way that benefits male athletes. For example, the most significant criteria for government support in competitive sport clubs are numerical indices such as the number of athletes, top teams and leagues, and level of public interest. Assigning the greatest weight to these parameters reflects and preserves the existing gap between male and female sports. This helps to maintain the status quo, i.e., more boys and men are engaged in publicly funded sports activities, and promotes the perception that sports are a male preserve. This statistics-based gender bias is reflected in the division of budgets. In 2018, only 23% of all registered competitive athletes in Israel (aged 13 and above) were women and, thus, men enjoyed 76.7% of the sport budgets (Seigelshifer 2018). Another example of hegemonic masculinity is that the sports with the largest number of women (like Netball and 'Mamanet' – see Chapter 31 in this volume) were not recognized as competitive leagues according to government criteria, and, thus, not entitled to government support. An analysis of sports budget policy in Israel revealed three major barriers to women's participation in organized sports:

1 The criteria for government support do not take into account the different needs of men and women in sports;
2 Lack of female representation in management and influential positions in sports organizations;
3 The prevailing perception that sport is more suitable to men than women (Seigelshifer 2012).

Hence, there is a need to understand the experiences and needs of female athletes, and then reimagine existing criteria in a way to reflect those needs (Seigelshifer 2012).

The role discourses, especially masculine hegemonic discourse, play in constructions of gender in sport organizations indicates how deeply gender is embedded (Claringbould and Knoppers 2012). To address such gender-based barriers for participation and leadership in sports organizations, we must consider not only structural barriers and policy change (Claringbould and Knoppers 2012; Shaw and Frisby 2006), but also the voices of those who are in the margins of the sports arena, e.g., those who drop out or choose not to participate in sports. Without their voice, we receive a skewed image of sports participation and miss the experiences of those who are not, or do not consider themselves, athletes (or coaches or managers). In this context, the values and experiences brought to sport by women has the potential to reimagine traditional power and performance sports and support the growth of the more inclusive Pleasure and Participation model (Shaw and Frisby 2006). In doing so, new questions can be asked (Hargreaves 2004), and new sport meanings and practices developed, based on which new policies can be implemented (Shaw and Frisby 2006).

The lost voices of female athletes: Ethics of care and gendered sports experiences

Gilligan's theory of *Ethics of Care* exposes the marginalized voices and narratives of female athletes, and the forces that marginalized them from mainstream sports. Prior to Gilligan's (1995) research, studies on human moral development had been based almost exclusively on male experiences. As a result, male experiences were taken as the norm, whereas women's experiences and moral values were considered deviant or flawed. Similar approaches could be found in sports socialization research (Messner and Musto 2016; Lenskyj 1994), where gender thinking resulted in the assumption that if females were socialized to be more like men, they would be better equipped to succeed in sport (Lenskyj 1994) as well as in other social milieus as adult women (Lenskyj 1994; Lever 1978).

When exploring the unique moral perspectives of girls and women, Gilligan (1995) also found that boys and girls speak in different voices because they go through different socialization processes from a young age. Girls learn to define themselves primarily through their relationships and connections with others, while boys define themselves through construction of positional identities and develop a sense of self based on separation from others. Gilligan (1995) criticizes the assumption that different means inferior and describes its implication on both women and men. Women's emphasis on relationships was considered a shortfall, preventing them from developing a rational and objective sense of judgment. As a result, adolescent girls in her research went through a process of psychological dissociation, in which they learn to disconnect themselves from their inner feelings and perspectives and adapt their view to what is considered to be the norm-meaning male perspectives (Gilligan 1995).

In the same way, we can see evidence of women in sport organizations who have internalized masculine behaviours and leadership styles as the norm, and try to adapt themselves to these norms in order to be accepted and promoted to influential positions (Claringbould and Knoppers 2012; Shaw and Frisby 2006). For example, women testify how they try to use a more objective approach and take things 'less personally' at work meetings (Claringbould and Knoppers 2012). These approaches trickle down all the way to young athletes. Lough (2001) found that young athletes, who were exposed to feminine leadership styles emphasizing dialogue, interaction and connectedness, were more inspired to take leadership roles themselves. However, they had limited opportunities to experience this kind of mentoring in the world of sports, as most coaches emphasized winning-at-all-cost at the expense of personal development.

Gilligan (1995) provides a relevant example from Lever's (1978) research on sex differences in children's games in relation to the hierarchy between boys' and girls' attitudes towards play and competition. Lever (1978) notes how girls put personal relationships in the centre of their play activity even at the expense of the game itself. In the face of disagreement, they would stop the game until they have solved their personal conflict. Boys, on the other hand, created universal rules which they applied and negotiated in the case of a conflict (Lever 1978). Studies conducted in recent years on girls in competitive sports have further validated the importance of relationships among young female athletes (Partridge and Knapp 2016; Whitehead and Biddle 2008, Zarrett et all 2020; Cooky 2016; women sports and fitness foundation 2012)). One conclusion is that coaches and sports teams should be aware of how social relationships and conflicts among team members directly affect team performance and cohesion (Partridge and Knapp 2016). In addition, friendships provide comfort at times of insecurity and hardships and make the activities more enjoyable for young female athletes (Whitehead and Biddle 2008). On the other hand, personal-social conflicts are more common in women's teams, and when they are not addressed, they significantly impair the team's performance and motivational climate (Holt, Knight and Zukiwski 2012). However, since coaches are usually trained to identify girls' interest and potential in sport according to the dominant Performance Model (Cooky 2016), they often, as demonstrated later, dismiss these aspects of young female athletes as childish and unsuitable for professional sports. Furthermore, Ramati Dvir (2017) observes how the hierarchy between the values of the Performance Model are emphasized not only in competitive sports, but also through agents like physical education (PE) teachers. A study focusing on PE teachers in Israel showed that they see more value in instruction that emphasizes measurable achievements, referring to this as teaching 'sports', while describing the games they teach in elementary school as 'nonsense' (Ramati Dvir 2017). Ironically, this attitude contradicts the goals of PE as stated by the very same teachers - to enable students to enjoy physical activity, persevere over time and adopt a healthy lifestyle.

Gilligan (1995) criticizes that Lever (1978) underestimated the skills that girls develop in their games which boys do not, such as empathy and sensitivity to others. Messner (1990) also refers to this example, focusing on the lost experience of male athletes caused by their early socialization as male athletes. Former athletes described how they were initially drawn to sports for the same reasons often related to girls - being with friends, belonging to a community or family and developing close bonds (Cooky 2016; Holt, Knight and Zukiwski 2012). However, at a very early stage, sport structures and athletic careers undermine the possibility of boys learning to transcend their fears of intimacy, thus becoming able to develop close and intimate relationships. The competitive sports environment teaches boys that it is not enough just to be with other athletes, but that the key to acceptance is being better than them (Coakley 2017; Messner and Musto 2016, Adams et al. 2010). As a result, boys have the tendency to develop a narrow definition of success in which performance and winning become central (Adams et al. 2010, Messner 1990; Coakley 2012, 2017). On the other hand, girls who are used to defining themselves through their relationship with others often find success, winning and competitive aspects of sport threatening (Gilligan 1995). Consequently, girls' and women's experiences in sports can help us ask new questions about the willingness of boys and men to embrace such a limited model of success based only on competitive values. Their different perspectives can be key for challenging and transforming masculine-centred sport cultures (Gilligan 2016; Hargreaves 2004).

Methods

A way female athletes can act as social agents for changing hegemonic sports discourses is by disrupting the gendered hierarchies and assumptions that appear normal (Claringbould and Knoppers 2012; Shaw and Frisby 2006). Finding contradictions in hegemonic discourses can help undo gender norms in sports organizations and offer new meanings and practices that create room for more diversity (Claringbould and Knoppers 2012). This study explores these disruptors by analyzing the narratives of female Israeli athletes who chose to drop out of sports despite their love for it, but re-joined on their own terms as adults. This study retrospectively explores the conflicts they experienced (and still do) as young competitive athletes, with specific focus on conflicts between their own perspectives, needs and feelings, and the way they were socialized into acting and thinking as competitive athletes in performance sports.

The data in this chapter is based on semi-structured interviews carried out in 2021 with eight former high-performance athletes between the ages of 29–42, who dropped out of competitive sports at a young age (14–17) and returned to sports in their 30s. Participants play today in organized or semi-organized, informal leagues. Each interview lasted around 60 minutes, and participants were assigned a pseudonym. Post-data collection, qualitative data were put to thematic analysis and the key themes are presented below.

Separating what happens 'on' and 'off' the field

All the athletes in the study expressed motivations towards sports which were aligned with the Pleasure and Participation Model. In other words, even though competition was involved, it was not the primary objective. Thus, the focus was on connection between people, self-expression, support for others and the notion that the body is to be nurtured and enjoyed in a quest for challenging experiences as well as belonging to a community (Coakley 2017). The social aspect was especially dominant in both their current experiences as adult athletes and their memories as young athlete. Ella (42, swimming, basketball) said:

> I really liked the team, but less the competitiveness aspect of swimming. There you are alone. Alone in the water. The only thing that held me there was that we were a very united team, but at some point that was not enough either. In basketball, I had a lot of fun because of the team and the fact we were together in it… It obviously suited me.

Similarly, Shelly (35, basketball) noted: 'I really like the idea of cooperation, that many different entities, many individuals, unite for a common goal and succeed in it'. However, these values and needs soon collided with the hegemonic masculine values to which athletes are expected to adhere. Both male and female coaches in this study demanded from their athletes to detach personal relationships from what was happening 'on the field'. From their perspective, this was an important skill for a professional athlete. Even coaches who did see the value of emphasizing pleasure and connection as part of the training process at younger ages perceived it as a barrier to succeed at a competitive level. This approach was internalized by the female athletes in this study, who often perceived 'girl issues' as something they needed to eradicate to become 'real' professional athletes.

However, when intra-team conflicts and relationships are managed well, those can significantly impair the team's performance, cohesion and motivation (Holt, Knight and Zukiwski 2012). Although the athletes interviewed in this study initially related their decision to quit sports at a young age to feeling of overload and burnout, they retrospectively pinpointed a connection between these feelings and the change in social dynamics that had occurred in their team at the time. Miri (30, basketball) said:

> The dynamics in the team became less pleasant, which was one of the main reasons [to drop out] … It was more of a political struggle - who's playing, who's not playing. This girl takes the ball from that girl. That was a real turnoff. I didn't want that struggle so much…

Furthermore, Lia (40, basketball) said:

> At first, I played with those who were a year younger, they were actually really nice and I had a lot of fun playing with them. When they put me in a team of older girls… I was pretty much ignored. So, I didn't enjoy it. As if the fun I had previously had in basketball was no longer there… If I had felt better socially, then surely, I would have stayed.

Hills and Croston (2012) presented similar findings in their research on girls in PE classes. They demonstrate how girls with high social status received more passes and were treated more leniently for their mistakes. However, these opportunities to prove ability and improve professional status were not available to girls with low social status. Accordingly, the change in social status reduced opportunities for Miri, Lia and other participants to prove themselves and feel meaningful in the team, until they eventually lost their passion for the game.

The gap between narratives of dropping out due to feelings of social exclusion, and overload and lack of interest in the game, can be explained by the tendency of sports organizations to attribute the burnout of young athletes to their personal failure in dealing with pressures involved in high-performance sports, rather than a symptom of a lack of social support in their sporting environment (Coakley 2016). In the above cases, athletes reported that they did not receive appropriate emotional guidance and support from their coaches, team managers or parents to cope with the emerging challenges in their relationship with the team.

The assumption that focusing on relationships is a disadvantage for athletes ignores the significance of social connections and their contribution to professional or amateur success (Fisher 2016; Gilligan 2016). In fact, previous research found that coaches' interventions and investment in activities off the field improved the relationships and the team's performance (Partridge and Knapp 2016). This is an example where the Performance and Participation Models can work in harmony to enhance performance.

'This is a competitive team, not a play group': Ethics of care vs. excellence

The prevailing perceptions among coaches, as expressed by participants, was that girls are less competitive and do not have the same drive to win as boys. This perception is reinforced in studies showing that due to their different socialization process, boys respond more positively to incentives than girls, and that their achievements improve as the task becomes competitive (Gneezy et al. 2009; Lever 1978). As noted before, girls, who are used to defining themselves through their relationship with others, often find success associated with winning and competitive aspects of sport threatening (Gilligan 1995, Zarett et al.). Other studies have also found that girls did not like some aspects of competition such as being aggressive or fighting (Women Sports and Fitness Foundation 2012). Female athletes, including the ones in this study, were motivated to participate in sports because they liked competition and viewed it as an opportunity to prove themselves (Dwyer et al. 2006, Women Sports and Fitness Foundation (2012). Participants described how being good, being valued and feeling strong were aspects they enjoyed. Also, they enjoyed challenging themselves and competing against their own best achievements and not necessarily against others. Especially during their first years as athletes, they were empowered by learning new skills, growth opportunities and personal expression (Coakley 2017) and being meaningful for the success of the team. Shelly (35, basketball) said:

> Everyone knew that I was a basketball player and that I had potential, and it was cool that I was a basketball player, and I didn't want to lose that. And when it came time for Wingate [the Israeli national institute for sport excellence, where national team practice takes place], it was a major source of pride, wow, she's on her way to the Israeli national team.

Similarly, Anat (40, Volleyball) said:

> It was like; Wow! I fell in love. I am part of the school team. I am part of a group. It is no longer [just] a playgroup… There is some kind of team spirit. The team's outfit arrives and each one chooses her number, and the name is written on the back … it gives a lot of strength, a lot of power.

However, these aspects of competitiveness were not in line with the approach their coaches tried to instil. Coaches appeared to perceive winning as the main goal and the way to get there was by being aggressive and better than others, and not by cooperation (Coakley 2017; Messner 1990). These perceptions were also internalized by athletes in this study who were, in Gilligan's (2016, p. 83) words, caught 'between their empathy and desire for connection and society [here the sports environment] that places a premium on separateness and independence, between an impulse to work cooperatively and the rewards to be gained by working competitively'. In a similar vein, Rachel (basketball, 30) noted:

> As a young girl, I didn't question it [competition]. I was told that winning was the goal, so winning was the goal. At some point, for a year or two I had less fun, felt less connected to this goal, and when I started thinking about it, I said to myself I just want to play for the fun of it.

Yaara (30, Judo, Volleyball) also expressed: 'It [competitiveness] felt cruel. It reminded me of the girls who wanted to beat me at Judo. It is not that I can't give you a fight, but I don't won't that energy. I don't want it to be a part of me'.

The fact that their initiation process into competitive sports did not leave room for developing connections, cooperation and caring affected not only their relations with competing athletes, but also with their own teammates. Anat (40, Volleyball) explains that as a young high-performance athlete, she was taught that losing was not an option: 'There is no such thing [as losing]. You have to win! You want to be first. You want to be the best'. When asked what the response was when they did lose, she remembered a situation which reflects the conflict between her sports organization's norms and her own values:

> Wow, we were depressed for a week. I even remember a situation where one girl actually lashed out at another, [making an accusation] that we lost because of her because she made a lot of mistakes... I remember on the bus back home. I felt uncomfortable. I wasn't part of this situation personally. I kind of reverted into myself.

Although Anat said she decided to drop out of volleyball at 16 as she felt burnout, she implied it was the team's climate that had a major effect on her decision. When describing her decision to return after more than 25 years, she emphasized how it had to be a team with a different climate than what she had experienced as an adolescent athlete: 'That's why I don't go to all those competitive leagues. I'm looking for a place where I can play for fun. .... And they all come with the same vibe. Now whoever has a slightly more extreme vibe, finds herself outside...'

Anat chose to resolve her conflict with the dominant sport model by finding an alternative semi organized team in which the dominant norms emphasize the importance of participants' pleasure and relationship. However, other athletes, as adults in organized amateur teams, found themselves negotiating the legitimacy of their will to be competitive while having fun with friends, with their sports environment prioritizing winning. Shelly noted: 'I don't know if we can say that basketball should be less aggressive. I would like it to be a less aggressive game, but that's not legitimate... [but] purpose is. This is a competitive league, not a playgroup. The coach tells me that a lot'. Rachel further explained:

> I contradict myself. Because I say I want a real league, but I don't mind losing ... A league is competitive, and if you don't want to be competitive, go play basketball in the neighbourhood... In my view, a league can be non-competitive, but still taken seriously. Maybe this requirement doesn't really make sense.

These quotes indicate a sense of confusion and, perhaps, conflict created by the gap between Performance and Pleasure Models. The hierarchical differentiation between competitive sports (emphasising winning as an end per se) and leisure playgroups (emphasising participant satisfaction) (Coakley 2012) prevents athletes from finding the balance they seek. Even as adults and being more aware of their feelings and goals, participants in this study still doubt and question their own logic and perspective as female athletes and their desires for a more equal balance between Performance and Pleasure Models.

Fisher (2016) argues that caring and performance excellence are intertwined. Some of the athletes demonstrate this point by finding their own way to be competitive and assertive, while still prioritizing social relationship. For instance, Lia (40, Basketball) chose to come back to play in an amateur league after a two-decade break and she claims that she is now more aggressive on the field, and no longer 'drifting like a leaf in the wind' as she did as a child:

> ...ever since I went back to basketball ... I try to unite [players] around me, to make it a social aspect as well. It isn't really mandatory, but that's the way it happened. And it adds a lot. Because when you have the social aspect - you sweat, you do sports, you compete and you do it with friends. So, it's the full package.

Anat describes how she now has a meaningful relationship with her teammates that strengthens cohesion:

> I don't push anyone, I don't stress. On the contrary, I teach. I teach anyone who's interested… It feels like a family. Very pleasant and very accepting and very accommodating, containing, and kind of embracing, enveloping… The moment you arrive there you already think about the next time.

The personal experience presented here indicates that whilst the participants struggled with the balance between Performance and Pleasure Models of sport in their youth as they felt that they had to comply with dominant standard, they gained more control over their sport experience as adults. In other words, participants' narratives demonstrate how they are more able and comfortable connecting with ways that empower themselves as well as their teammates (Miller 1991; Surrey 1991).

Conclusion

This study sought to explore female athletes' marginalized discourse and their struggle to balance the Performance and Pleasure Models during different stages of their sport involvement. By asking questions that separate 'ideal' morality and women's personal experiences, Gilligan (1995) exposes the gaps between women's voices and hegemonic male discourse. In the same way, it was evident that although athletes in this study accepted and internalized the male hegemony-informed Performance Model, they spoke of different needs and motivations when describing their own experiences as competitive athletes.

Trying to balance the two Models created contradictions and conflicts in the athletes' experiences. These contradictions in the women's narratives represent challenges to the hegemonic sports discourse, leading to athletes' values clashing with sports organizations' agenda. Therefore, listening to female athletes' narratives provide us a foundation for imagining alternative more inclusive models for competitive sports organizational structures. Structures which value solidarity, attachment, self-expression and mutual support, and are not exclusively driven by a win-at-all-cost ideology. The transformation participants demonstrated in this chapter in relation to their engagement in/with sports can help deviate from the established sporting binaries such as professional vs. empowering, competitiveness vs. relationships and masculine vs. feminine and generate a more balanced, inclusive discourse. Developing and implementing this new discourse can help sports organizations design new policies, money allocation criteria and strategies for promoting female athletes as well as other marginalized groups. It can change the values coaches are expected to instil in young children, and the way sports organizations, sports fans, athletes and their parents perceive success as a result of cooperation and mutual support rather than a single model of superiority over others. Without a change in the overarching discourse around sport and placing more emphasis on the Pleasure Model, it will be near impossible to create and implement new policies and practices to achieve a more equal footing for performance and pleasure and thereby increase women's participation in and enjoyment of sports.

REFERENCES

Adams, A., Anderson, E. and McCormack, M. (2010) 'Establishing and challenging masculinity: The influence of gendered discourses in organized sport', *Journal of Language and Social Psychology*, 29(3), pp. 278–300.

Aharoni, O. (2019) 'The winners were disqualified for crossing the finish line hand in hand', *Ynet Sports*. Available at: https://www.ynet.co.il/articles/0,7340,L-5569675,00.html (Accessed on 15 August 2019).

Anderson, E.D. (2009) 'The maintenance of masculinity among the stakeholders of sport', *Sport Management Review*, 12(1), pp. 3–14.

Bourdieu, P. (2005) *Questions de Sociologie (Sociology in Question)*. Tel Aviv: Resling Publishing.

Claringbould, I. and Knoppers, A. (2012) 'Paradoxical practices of gender in sport-related organizations', *Journal of Sport Management*, 26(1), pp. 404–416.

Coakley, J. (2012) 'Play group versus organized competitive team: A comparison', in Eitzen S. (ed.), *Sports Contemporary Society*, ninth edition. Oxford: Oxford University Press, pp. 25–33.

Coakley, J. (2016) 'Burnout among adolescent athletes: A personal failure or social problem?', *Sociology of Sport Journal*, 9(3), pp. 271–285.

Coakley, J. (2017) *Sport in Society: Issues and Controversies*, twelfth edition. NY: McGraw-Hill Education.

Cooky, C. (2016) '"Girls just aren't interested": The social construction of interest in girls' sport', in Cooky, C. and Messner, M. (eds.), *No Slam Dunk: Gender, Sports and the Unevenness of Social Change*. New Jersey: Rutgers University Press, pp. 113–138.

Dwyer, J.J.M., Allison, K.R., Goldenberg, E.R. and Fein, A.J. (2006) 'Adolescent girl's perceived barriers to participation in physical activity', *Adolescence*, 41(161), p. 75.

Fisher, L.A. (2016) '"Where are your women?" The challenge to care in the future of sport', *Sex Roles*, 74(7-8), pp. 377–387.

Gilligan C. (1995) *In a Different Voice: Psychological Theory and Women's Development*. Tel-Aviv: Sifriat Poalim Publishing.

Gilligan, C. (2016) *Joining the Resistance*. Tel Aviv: Hakibuts Hameuchad Publishing.

Gneezy, U., Leonard, K.L. and List, J.A. (2009) 'Gender differences in competition: Evidence from a matrilineal and a patriarchal society', *Econometrica*, 77(5), pp. 1637–1664.

Haarets Sports (2019) 'Instead of competing for first place, they decided to cross the finish line together. The judges did not like it', *Haarets Sports* (online). Available at: https://www.haaretz.co.il/sport/other/1.7687634 (Accessed on 15 August 2019).

Hargreaves, J. (2004). 'Querying sport feminism: Personal or political?', in Giulianotti, R. (ed.), *Sport and Modern Social Theorists*. New York: Palgrave Macmillan, pp. 187–205.

Hills, L.A. and Croston, A. (2012). '"It should be better altogether": Exploring strategies for "undoing" gender in coeducational physical education', *Sport, Education and Society*, 17(5), pp. 591–605.

Holt, N.L., Knight, C.J. and Zukiwski, P. (2012) 'Female athletes' perceptions of teammate conflict in sport: Implications for sport psychology consultants', *Sport Psychologist*, 26(1), pp. 135–154.

Ingle, S. (2019) 'Winning British triathletes disqualified after crossing line hand-in-hand', *The Guardian*, 12 August. Available at: https://www.theguardian.com/sport/2019/aug/15/winning-triathletes-jess-learmonth-georgia-taylor-brown-disqualified-tokyo-hand-in-hand-triathlon

Lenskyj, H.J. (1994) 'Girl-friendly sport and female values', *Women in Sport and Physical Activity Journal*, 3(1), pp. 35–36.

Lever, J. (1978) 'Sex differences in the complexity of children's play and games', *American Sociological Review*, 43(4), pp. 471–483.

Lough, N.L. (2001). 'Mentoring connections between coaches and female athletes', *Journal of Physical Education, Recreation & Dance*, 72(5), pp. 30–33.

Messner, M.A. (1988) 'Sports and male domination: The female athlete as contested ideological terrain', *Sociology of Sport Journal*, 5(3), pp. 197–211.

Messner, M. (1990) 'Boyhood, organized sports, and the construction of masculinities', *Journal of Contemporary Ethnography*, 18(4), pp. 416–444.

Messner, M.A. and Musto, M. (2016) 'Introduction: Kids and sports', in Messner, M.A. and Musto, M. (eds.), *Child's Play Sports in Kids' Worlds*. New Jersey: Rutgers University Press, pp. 1–19.

Miller, J.B. (1991) 'Women and power', in Jordan, J.V., Kaplan, A.G., Stiver, I.P., Surrey, J.L. and Miller, J.B. (eds.), *Women's Growth in Connection: Writings from the Stone Center*. London: Guilford Press, pp. 197–205.

Partridge, J.A. and Knapp, B.A. (2016) 'Mean girls: Adolescent female athletes and peer conflict in sport', *Journal of Applied Sport Psychology*, 28(1), pp. 113–127.

Ramati Dvir, A. (2017) 'Hegemonic discourse and the missing discourse among P.E. teachers', in Lachover, E., Peled, E. and Komem, M. (eds.), *Girls and Their Bodies: Voice, Presence, Absence*. Jerusalem: Magness Publication, pp. 113–129.

Sartore, M.L. and Cunningham, G.B. (2007) 'Explaining the under-representation of women in leadership positions of sport organizations: A symbolic interactionist perspective', *Quest*, 59(2), pp. 244–265.

Seigelshifer, V. (2012). *Changing the rules of the game: A gender perspective on sports allocation in Israel*, Adva Center. Available at: https://adva.org/wp-content/uploads/2015/02/sport-eng2PDF1.pdf

Seigelshifer, V. (2018). *In sport too women are left behind*, Adva Center, 28 March 2018. Available at: https://adva.org/he/gender-inequality-sport/

Shaw, S. and Frisby, W. (2006) 'Can gender equity be more equitable?: Promoting an alternative frame for sport management research, education, and practice', *Journal of Sport Management*, 20(4), pp. 483–509.

Stevenson, B. (2006) 'Title IX and the evolution of high school sports', *Contemporary Economic Policy*, 25(4), pp. 486–505.

Surrey, J.L. (1991) 'Relationship and empowerment', in Jordan, J.V., Kaplan, A.G., Stiver, I.P., Surrey, J.L. and Miller, J.B. (eds.), *Women's Growth in Connection: Writings from the Stone Center*. London: Guilford Press, pp. 162–180.

Theberge, N. (2000) 'Gender and sport', in Coakley, J. and Dunning, E. (eds.), *Handbook of Sports Studies*, London: SAGE publication, pp. 322–333.

Whitehead, S. and Biddle, S. (2008) 'Adolescent girls' perceptions of physical activity: A focus group study', *European Physical Education Review*, 14(2), pp. 243–262.

Women Sports and Fitness Foundation (2012) *Changing the game for girls*. Available at: https://www.womeninsport.org/wp-content/uploads/2015/04/Changing-the-Game-for-Girls- Policy-Report.pdf

Zarrett, N., Veliz, P.T. and Sabo, D. (2020) *Keeping Girls in the Game: Factors that Influence Sport Participation*. New York, NY: Women's Sports Foundation.

17
Towards Equality in Women's Sport, Exercise and Physical Activity
Complexities and Contradictions

Claire-Marie Roberts

Introduction

Women have been fighting for equality throughout history, and although gains have been made in specific areas, sport still belongs to and is predominantly governed by men (Osborne and Skillen 2020). Generally, the participation of boys and men in physical activity (PA), exercise and sport outnumbers girls and women in almost every age group. Despite large-scale changes in leisure patterns in the twentieth century, women's consumption of, and participation in, sport has significantly lagged behind men's. This originates in part from the sociocultural norms emanating from the Victorian era which established women as the physically weaker and inferior sex (Fauvel 2014). The widespread belief at this time placed childbearing at the centre of women's destiny and, therefore, social norms developed to protect their reproductive ability. Part of these norms involved the avoidance of energetic activities to remain healthy (Fauvel 2014). Notably, any foray into sport or exercise was frowned upon and even thought to lead to dementia in women (Morantz-Sanchez 1996). Although historically rooted, these sociocultural beliefs have prevailed as societal norms. Such norms are greatly responsible for a variety of complexities and contradictions that have led to inequalities in women's sport, exercise and PA. The weaker/inferior sex narrative endures, yet research demonstrates women live longer, have a survival advantage and are beginning to outperform men in ultra-endurance events (e.g., see https://runrepeat.com/state-of-ultra-running). These outdated societal beliefs and norms generate a gendered inequality of opportunities. Males' efforts in sport, exercise and PA are actively encouraged and celebrated, while the dominant PA-related driver for females is appearance-related. Furthermore, whilst there is pressure on females to conform to the Western feminine ideal, society expects them to achieve this through sport, exercise and PA labelled as "feminine".

The mass media routinely ascribes low cultural value to women's sport through unequal coverage. Indeed, when women's sports do attract coverage, sportswomen are often sexualised, marginalised and objectified. However, there are additional complexities and contradictions in sport, exercise and PA for pregnant women. Dated and unscientific societal beliefs that pregnancy should be inactive can hamper women's ability to experience a healthy pregnancy and birth and cause conflict and confusion regarding engagement with PA during this time. Specifically, in elite sport, motherhood for women athletes has the potential to generate a complex range of challenges including a potential gamble with their career, and a lack of organisational support structures around maternity and postpartum, which magnify the inequalities already present in sport. This chapter will examine these complexities and contradictions in greater depth and suggest remedial action to reduce existing inequalities in sport, exercise and PA spheres.

Sex and gender

Defining sex and gender is complex. Terminology in this area is intricate and controversial (Hyde et al. 2019). The dominant approach currently suggests that 'sex' is the term used to describe distinct biological differences between males and females that involve X and Y chromosomes which help determine sex at birth (Hyde et al. 2019). 'Gender' on the other hand is considered to be differences between men and women that are socially and culturally constructed and involve norms and expectations (e.g., Muehlenhard and Peterson 2011). There are counter positions to this approach. Yoder (2003) has argued that biological and sociocultural factors are so entwined that the differentiation between sex and gender should be abandoned. Additionally, some people are intersex or sex diverse, and they may self-identify as transgender, cisgender, non-binary, genderfluid, bigender or agender. Although the debate surrounding the use of sex and gender to identify individuals is outside of the scope of this chapter, the terms will be used within the chapter as follows: where the terms 'men' and 'women' are used, sex is referred to. Conversely, where 'male' and 'female' are referred to, gender is the topic of discussion.

Sex differences

Contrary to the Victorian characterisation of women as the inferior sex (that endures in today's society), recent research has revealed the opposite. It is well-publicised that the life expectancy of women exceeds that of men by around 4.2 years, with a projected increase to 4.8 years by 2050 (Eskes and Haanen 2007). Women, in fact, have a survival advantage over men – across all ages and phases of their lifespan. Women's biological immunoresponse, driven by the presence of higher levels of oestrogen, brings about anti-inflammatory and vasoprotective characteristics (Zarulli et al. 2018), meaning females enjoy more life longevity and robustness in the face of environmental challenge than men. In sport, exercise and PA, however, research and practice continually demonstrate sex differences in performance, with men generally outperforming women in most sports. This performance disparity ranges from 0 to 17% (Tiller et al. 2021). Endocrinologically, biologically and physiologically, this may be accounted for through the combination of a more than 15-fold increase of circulating testosterone after puberty in men (Handelsman, Hirschberg and Bermon 2018), coupled with their greater maximal aerobic capacity (Péronnet and Thibault 1989), women's higher percentage of body fat, lower red cell mass for a given body weight and typically smaller lungs (Joyner 2017). The differences between the sexes are not only biological. There are also sociocultural differences in the development of men and women in sport. In childhood, boys participate in a greater range and duration of motor activities than girls (Hines 2004), and there is reportedly more motivation amongst male children to participate in sport and PA (Chen and Darst 2002; Knisel et al. 2009) due to parental and social influences.

However, even with these biological and sociocultural constraints, sex differences in sport and exercise performance continue to diminish over time as female participation and engagement increases (Altavilla et al. 2017). Specifically, Tiller et al. (2021, p. 908) have recently noted that female athletes may have an advantage over male athletes in ultra-endurance events due to a "combination of greater relative distribution of type-I (oxidative) fibres, greater fatigue-resistance owing to neuromuscular, contractile, and metabolic factors, better substrate efficiency (higher rates of lipid oxidation), lower energetic requirements, and higher subcutaneous body fat". Many studies have additionally noted that female athletes in general have the psychological advantage when it comes to pacing for longer distance events. Researchers suggest that female athletes are better at executing an even pacing strategy, thereby placing them at a competitive advantage over male competitors across long distance events (e.g., March et al. 2011; Nikolaidis, Ćuk and Knechtle 2019; Renfree, Crivoi do Carmo and Martin 2016). Despite the blend of biological differences between the sexes and their relative impact on sport and exercise performance, women competitors are continuing to close the gap.

Parental and social influences

To close the gap between women and men in sport, exercise and PA contexts is continually hampered by socially perpetuated gender norms and expectations (Strandbu, Bakken and Stefansen 2020). For example, gender norms support male participation in sport over female's as it provides an environment to build and reinforce masculinity (Messner 2011). In addition, males achieve greater status through the development of athletic ability, and this does not currently apply to females (Heinze et al. 2017, p. 636). Parents, as socialising agencies, may unwittingly reinforce these gender norms through their gendered beliefs and practices by dedicating more time and resources to boys' sporting endeavours than for girls'.

Furthermore, certain types of activities have historically been characterised as "masculine" (e.g., football, rugby and combat sports) or "feminine" (e.g., gymnastics, dancing and ice-skating), which can impact negatively on the equality of sport and athlete development and internalise harmful gender stereotypes at an early age (Chalabaev et al. 2013). Such gender stereotypes can result in parents and society questioning women's sexuality, a devaluation of their athletic accomplishments and an unhealthy obsession with their appearance. This unjustified focus on women athletes' bodies can lead to a vast array of negative consequences, including high dropout rates, an inability to meet athletic performance goals, sport devaluation and, more concerningly, complex sub-clinical behaviours such as disordered eating and clinical psychological concerns such as depression.

The role of the media

In sport, exercise and PA, it could be argued that the media is discriminatory. For example, numerous studies have demonstrated that the sport media dedicate more space and greater significance to men and men's sport regardless of type, level, competitor age, nationality, etc. (Bernstein 2020). More concerningly, even when there are efforts to increase the coverage of women's sport, studies have identified the emergence of more subtle ways of undermining female athleticism (Bernstein 2020). The general message that women's sport competitions are less important is continually reinforced because it consistently receives less media exposure. However, before the COVID-19 pandemic and related national lockdowns, women's participation in sport and the media coverage of women's elite sport competitions had been on a "widely acknowledged, hard-won yet still fragile upward trajectory" (Osborne and Skillen 2020, p. 412).

Yet, the default position was to continue to ensure men's elite sport competitions could continue to operate, behind closed doors during the pandemic, with little or no similar focus on women's sport. It has been argued that this approach was reflective of the low cultural value assigned to women's sport – both in terms of participation and competition today (Osborne and Skillen 2020). A combination of a media defined by hegemonic masculinity and homogenous male-led cultural and organisational structures in sporting bodies may perpetuate these complex inequalities for women in sport, exercise and PA.

Pregnancy – A quintessentially indisputable sex difference

It is widely accepted that regular, moderate to vigorous PA, exercise and sport are fundamental to human physical and mental health throughout the lifespan. However, the contradictions for women are rarely more evident than in pregnancy or in the postpartum phase. In the context of sport, where sex equality is premised on the similarities between males and females (Brake 2008; 2010), pregnancy and motherhood offer a quintessentially indisputable sex difference (Roberts and Kenttä 2019). Interestingly, the reproductive abilities and concerns about preserving those has historically been cited as an excuse to exclude women from sport (Jette 2011; Kardel 2005; Vertinsky 1994). Certainly, the myth that pregnancy and sport/exercise are incompatible centre around conflict between the physical demands of athleticism and a dated perception of the passive, inactive state of pregnancy (e.g., Brake 2009). Competitive sport is about the non-pregnant body. This perception is at odds with the science which demonstrates that sedentary behaviour during pregnancy results in a shorter gestation and inhibited foetal growth (Jones et al. 2021), plus the increased risks of type 2 diabetes, cardiovascular disease, metabolic syndrome and an adverse effect on mental wellbeing (Fazzi et al. 2017). To overturn this common perception, the physical and psychological health benefits of exercising in pregnancy have been promoted internationally. In the UK, for example, the Royal College of Obstetricians and Gynaecologists recommend 150 minutes per week of moderate intensity exercise or activity. To help facilitate this, recently, major sportswear brands such as Nike and Adidas have launched specific maternity clothing lines because of 'consumer demand'. If consumer demand is driving the launch of the maternity sportswear market, then it appears that the work to overturn the passive, inactive narrative around pregnancy is beginning to have an impact. However, there is a wider societal consideration around exercising and playing sport while pregnant. Despite the clear messaging that exercise and PA have fundamental health benefits for pregnant women and their unborn children, many women have faced a public backlash when openly exercising or training. It appears that the Victorian narrative around pregnant bodies is still ingrained within societal norms. Women then are in a conundrum – exercise to protect their own and their unborn child's health and face public criticism for it or exercise privately, away from critical public view.

Motherhood

In elite sport, women amid their athletic career with a desire to start a family often face a difficult decision – end their involvement in competitive sport or gamble with their livelihood or fertility by delaying attempts to conceive (Palmer and Leberman 2009; Pedersen 2001). Athletes citing pregnancy and motherhood as the reasons for athletic career termination often attract additional criticism centred on a failure to reach their full potential in their sport (Nash 2011; Palmer and Leberman 2009; Spowart, Burrows and Shaw 2010). In many sports, optimal fertility often corresponds with peak performance and therefore the decision to have children is delayed. Those who choose to wait to have children until their athletic career has concluded face the unenviable gamble with their own fertility. Gigi Fernández, a 17 Grand slam doubles champion tennis player, has spoken openly about her struggles with infertility as a result of delaying motherhood to focus on her athletic career. Having eventually conceived through in-vitro fertilisation (IVF), she now encourages younger athletes to consider freezing their eggs. However, this option is not open to all athletes, as cost remains a great barrier to this service (Johnston et al. 2022). Additionally, there are medical risks associated with ovarian stimulation and delaying pregnancy when over 35 years of age. There may also be ethical and/or religious incompatibilities and a likely unhealthy reinforcement of the 'value' of having genetically related children by opting for this service (Petropanagos et al. 2015). Finally, IVF does not always result in pregnancy. Goold (2017) describes IVF as a lottery rather than an insurance policy for those with concerns about fertility. For those not willing to give up their career prematurely, or to wait until they retire, the decision to have a baby mid-athletic career is fraught with danger. As having a baby has been anecdotally described as a significant physiological event (Roberts and Kenttä 2019), whether an athlete can return to the same levels of training and competition postpartum is always unpredictable. Despite this gamble, a growing number of women have achieved both personal and high-performance sport goals (e.g., Darroch, Giles and McGettigan-Dumas 2016). High profile athletes such as Laura Kenny, Sarah Storey, Serena Williams, Alex Morgan and Allyson Felix have all spoken openly about their experiences as athlete mothers and the challenges faced in returning to their sport.

To increase the likelihood of being able to return to training and competition, conception is often a meticulously planned event (Cunnama 2017; Roberts and Kenttä 2019). Olympic and Paralympic athletes often plan conception carefully within the 4-year cycle, and other athletes use league dates and international competitions as benchmarks to work around. In a study by Roberts and Kenttä (in press), Olympian athlete mother participants reported combining a period of injury rehabilitation with pregnancy to minimise the layoff from their sport training and competition. For active women, whether recreational or elite, returning to exercise, training or competition postpartum provides a number of challenges. For white Western women (body ideals can vary by cultural factors), the pressure to regain their pre-pregnancy bodies quickly in line with the dictates of normative femininity (Nash 2015) can cause body-related distress and dissatisfaction (Raspovic et al. 2020). In reality though, for the majority of the population, the transition to motherhood is characterised by declines in PA (Limbers et al. 2020), despite the fact that PA moderates stress (Limbers, McCollum and Greenwood 2020), is beneficial for postnatal depression (Downs et al. 2008), postpartum weight reduction (Davenport et al. 2011), fatigue (Yang and Chen 2018), pelvic floor strength (Mørkved and Bø 2014), and role modelling for children (Edwardson and Gorely 2010). For those women who do experience a decrease in PA postpartum, there are several negative outcomes that result from this inactivity trend. These include poorer physical and mental health, disordered eating and higher body weight (e.g., Walker et al. 2016). The barriers to engaging in PA, exercise or sport postpartum are multifaceted. For many women, these include the amount of time taken up with childcare, issues with time management, perceptions of their health in the context of competition responsibilities, lack of support from family members, friends and/or co-workers (Carter-Edwards et al. 2009) and lack of guidance and support from medics and midwives. Although the benefits of exercise postpartum for the physical and mental health of women are clear, there are multiple barriers and women have the tendency to engage with PA to "normalise" physical appearance against Western feminine body ideals, rather than for health reasons (Dworkin and Wachs 2004).

The ethic of care and gendered separate spheres

Traditional gender ideologies are defined as "individuals' levels of support for a division of paid work and family responsibilities that is based on the belief in gendered separate spheres" (Davis and Greenstein 2009, p. 87). Those "gendered separate spheres" (Davis and Greenstein 2009, p. 87) in heteronormative settings predominantly relate to females defaulting to childcare and homemaking while men are seen as the primary providers for the family (Dixon and Wetherell 2004). To extend traditional gender ideology, the expectation that women's moral development specifically centres on notions of care and responsibility for others (O'Brien, Lloyd and Ringuet-Riot 2014) produces an expectation that they routinely self-sacrifice for the sake of others. Although the social norms governing women's behaviour are often rooted in a gender hierarchy and legislation, they are often internalised (Miller and Brown 2005). This stereotype can lead to a perception of the roles and responsibilities of mothers that are incongruent with self-care and healthy behaviour focused on PA, exercise and sport (Roberts and Kenttä 2019).

Certainly, for elite athletes, this gendered ideology and the expectations associated with an ethic of care are often considered incongruent with the pursuit of a career in elite sport, which involves intense training and extensive travelling (Freeman 2008), leaving limited time for the care of others. Moreover, it is noteworthy that athletes must primarily focus on their own needs to align to cultural norms in elite sports, making it difficult to engage in caring roles. Once athlete mothers negotiate the immediate barriers on return to sport, such is the weight of societal expectations and cultural norms that they often report a distinct sense of guilt when they spend time away from their children while training and competing (Appleby and Fisher 2009). Indeed, a lack of support for the athletes' roles as mothers has been attributed to a high level of psychological discomfort (Freeman 2008). Furthermore, the additional pressure of high-performance standards in sport, combined with performing the role of the 'perfect' mother – striving for the myth that women can 'have it all' – causes a high degree of psychological distress when athlete mothers realise they are unable to meet all expectations (Choi et al. 2005).

The logistical challenges of training for high-performance competition whilst caring for children can divide athlete mothers. While athletes from individual sports may be able to create their own schedules on their return to sport postpartum, others may be more constrained – especially if they are re-joining team training. For athletes who have more autonomy over their training time, sessions can be scheduled around breastfeeding (if applicable) and childcare. This issue has been discussed anecdotally by both Jessica Ennis-Hill – Olympic, World and European Heptathlon champion who gave birth to her son mid-athletic career – and Helen Glover – Olympic, World and European rowing champion who gave birth to three children before returning to international competition. Both women have spoken of having to adapt their training to align with their children's schedules, rather than following an evidence-based approach to training scheduling like most elite athletes. For those returning to sport and having to follow team training schedules, athletes' new role as a mother may change the dynamic within the team as competing demands emerge (Roberts and Kenttä 2019). For some athlete mothers, the guilt of leaving their child with someone else for prolonged periods during training and competition may generate high levels of psychological discomfort.

Sport governance

For athlete mothers, the consequences of gender ideology, and its interplay with sport culture and structures, present further challenges. We celebrate the emergence of athlete mothers, and they often prevail despite the sporting culture and associated policies which lag far behind.

For example, until recently, athlete awards, sponsorship and sport science and medical support could be withdrawn if the athlete became pregnant (Roberts and Kenttä in press). Many sports remain unequipped to support pregnant or postpartum athletes. From a lack of maternity policies to an absence of expertise on training and competing during and after pregnancy, governing bodies of sport and international sporting organisations and federations remain ill-equipped. Whilst record numbers of Olympic and Paralympic mothers were the subject of increased media attention and glorification at the Tokyo 2020 Games, the absence of relevant policies of the International Olympic Committee (IOC), the home nation Olympic Committees (e.g., the British Olympic Association) and the governing bodies of sport remain a barrier to many women athletes.

It is well-publicised that some sponsorship deals had pregnancy clauses in them, which financially penalised sponsored women athletes for having children mid-athletic career. For example, Allyson Felix, the six-time Olympic Gold Medallist representing the USA in athletics, had her sponsorship with Nike reduced by 70% when she was pregnant, and in postpartum. In addition, Alysia Montaño and Kara Goucher – two of Felix's teammates – broke their non-disclosure agreements with Nike to reveal similar stories. Sponsorship is the tip of the proverbial iceberg for athlete mothers. Serena Williams' tennis ranking was reduced from No.1 to No.451 on her comeback to the sport, which prompted a debate about the Women's Tennis Association's (WTA) lack of maternity policies. In Spain, anecdotal reports suggest that anti-pregnancy clauses are used widely in professional sporting contracts where athletes can have their contracts terminated if they become pregnant. In the UK, for sports that fall under the jurisdiction of UK Sport (the nation's high-performance sports agency investing in Olympics and Paralympics), Athlete Performance Awards continue through pregnancy and post-birth, and encourage the sport and individual athlete to mutually agree a time frame and training plan for their return. This is not necessarily the case for professional sports that sit outside of the UK Sport framework and is certainly not the norm internationally.

For athlete mothers competing at major, multi-sport events such as the Olympics and the Paralympics, further challenges are presented. At the Olympics and Paralympics, for example, children are not allowed in the Olympic Village. Although athletes can reside outside the Olympic Village with their families, recent policies enacted by the IOC for the Tokyo Olympics prevented athlete mothers from bringing young babies and nursing infants with them to the Games. After a U-turn by the IOC and the Japanese government, the policy was changed at the last minute to allow children and caregivers to accompany athlete mothers. The revised policies were, however, restrictive due to the COVID-19 pandemic and unworkable for many. The presence of pregnancy clauses in sponsorship contracts, ranking reductions for layoffs, outdated and unworkable sport policies and procedures are additional and unnecessary stressors for elite athletes. The lack of understanding of the needs of athlete mothers reflects the deep-rooted heteropatriarchal system that still dominates sporting culture and structures.

The future

Despite a great deal of growth in women's sport, and a more universal acceptance of women's engagement in exercise and PA, there remains work to be done to achieve full equality in these areas. Despite the dominant narrative, women are in no way the weaker sex. The greater longevity and survival advantage mean that they are continually able to challenge the sex gap in sport and exercise despite the significant advantage of high levels of testosterone afforded to men.

Traditional gender norms and expectations still place women at a distinct disadvantage to men in the sport, exercise and PA spheres. In many cases, such norms are reinforced by parents and other socialising agencies. As a society, valuing the breadth and equality of PA opportunities for both genders from an early age is vital. Additionally, we should recognise the risks of labelling sports as "masculine" and "feminine" and the damaging consequences of reinforcing gender stereotypes in children's early years. As parents, family members, teachers, coaches and sport administrators, we need to recognise how we might actively disrupt these troubling social norms and challenge the status quo. Young women have as much right to participate and excel in, for example, boxing than they do in ballet (e.g., Gentile, Boca and Giammusso 2018). However, the contradiction of females' involvement in sport, exercise and PA generally remains to perpetuate the white Western feminine ideal and disapproves "masculine sports".

This recommendation extends to the media. Although media representations of women's sport and female athletes have empirically demonstrated male bias and the maintenance of hegemonic values in sport (Bruce 2015), since 2018–19, coverage of women's sport has demonstrated a 'fragile upward trajectory' (Osborne and Skillen 2020, p. 412). Yet, there is more work to be done to continually redress the balance to transform society's views on gender equality as well as in normalising women's sport.

Normalising sport, exercise and PA participation in healthy pregnancies is critical in overturning archaic perceptions that pregnancy should be a passive and inactive state. Specifically, it is important to provide credible and trustworthy practical advice to women (Nobles et al. 2020) and celebrating and supporting pregnant women in their active endeavours. It is imperative that policymakers, maternity services and PA stakeholders are aligned in their guidance to women on this matter and can disseminate it with 'clarity and consistency' (Macrae 2019, p. 1).

For women athletes who choose to have children in combination with their athletic career, the best professional guidance should be available to help negotiate difficult, life- and potentially career-changing decisions. Yet, when athletic career with motherhood is combined, the woefully unprepared sporting system means that the odds are already against athlete mothers. For active women who become mothers in heteronormative relationships, strong role modelling from men in the form of equally shared childcare responsibilities is likely to help erode the outdated view that women should be children's' main carer. This will allow women the time and the space to be able to engage in sport, exercise or PA for the benefit of their own mental and physical health and wellbeing, whilst providing opportunities for role-modelling gender-specific behaviours to their children.

Finally, governing bodies of sport should introduce robust and workable maternity policies for their athletes which are in line with other Western industries. This recommendation includes the requirement for individualised support in the pre-natal, pregnancy and postpartum phase in the form of sport science and medicine and coaching, but also from an employment law perspective, to include pay (where possible), contracts, sponsorship, rankings and the like. A suitable and sufficient period of remunerated maternity leave with full coaching, sport science and medicine support should be available to ensure equality with men in sport is achieved. In fact, every reasonable step should be taken not to penalise women for having children during their athletic career. Sport governing bodies should be able to acknowledge that women have significantly different biology to men, and therefore if they make a choice to have children during their athletic career, that sport has an absolute duty to accommodate them (e.g., Brake 2008). When it comes to federations, leagues and competitions – a wholescale review of policies and structures with a view to considering how best to support the needs of female athletes at various stages of their lifecycle, including in pregnancy or as a nursing mother, is an urgent and long overdue requirement.

REFERENCES

Altavilla, G., Di Tore, P.A., Riela, L. and D'Isanto, T. (2017) Anthropometric, Physiological and Performance Aspects that Differentiate Male Athletes from Females and Practical Consequences. *Journal of Physical Education and Sport*, *17*, pp. 2183–2187.

Appleby, K.M. and Fisher, L.A. (2009) "Running in and out of Motherhood": Elite Distance Runners' Experiences of Returning to Competition after Pregnancy. *Women in Sport and PA Journal*, *18*(1), pp. 3–17.

Bernstein, A. (2020) Women, Media, and Sport. *The International Encyclopedia of Gender, Media, and Communication*. pp. 1–9. Wiley-Blackwell. Doi: 10.1002/9781119429128.iegmc240.

Brake, D.L. (2008). The Invisible Pregnant Athlete and the Promise of Title IX. *Legal StudiesResearch Paper Series*, *32*, 324–359.

Brake, D. L. (2010). *Getting in the game: Title IX and the women's sports revolution*. NYU Press: New York.

Bruce, T. (2015). Assessing the Sociology of Sport: On Media and Representations of Sportswomen. *International Review for the Sociology of Sport*, *50*(4–5), 380–384.

Carter-Edwards, L., Østbye, T., Bastian, L.A., Yarnall, K.S., Krause, K.M. and Simmons, T.-J. (2009) Barriers to Adopting a Healthy Lifestyle: Insight from Postpartum Women. *BMC Research Notes*, *2*(1), p. 161.

Chalabaev, A., Sarrazin, P., Fontayne, P., Boiché, J. and Clément-Guillotin, C. (2013). The Influence of Sex Stereotypes and Gender Roles on Participation and Performance in Sport and Exercise: Review and Future Directions. *Psychology of Sport and Exercise*, *14*(2), pp. 136–144.

Chen, A. and Darst, P.W. (2002) Individual and Situational Interest: The Role of Gender and Skill. *Contemporary Educational Psychology*, *27*(2), pp. 250–269.

Choi, P., Henshaw, C., Baker, S. and Tree, J. (2005) Supermum, Superwife, Supereverything: Performing Femininity in the Transition to Motherhood. *Journal of Reproductive and Infant Psychology*, *23*(2), pp. 167–180.

Cunnama, J. (2017) 'Chronicles of a pregnancy athlete' [vlog]. Available at https://en794gb.facebook.com/jodieann.swallow/posts/1283077375146152 (Accessed 19th May 2021).

Darroch, F., Giles, A.R. and McGettigan-Dumas, R. (2016) Elite Female Distance Runners and Advice during Pregnancy: Sources, Content, and Trust. *Women in Sport and PA Journal*, *24*(2), pp. 170–176.

Davenport, M., Giroux, I., Sopper, M., & Mottola, M. (2011). Postpartum Exercise Regardless of Intensity Improves Chronic Disease Risk Factors. *Medicine & Science in Sports & Exercise*, 43(6), 951–958.

Davis, S.N. and Greenstein, T.N. (2009) Gender Ideology: Components, Predictors, and Consequences. *Annual Review of Sociology*, *35*(1), pp. 87–105.

Dixon, J. and Wetherell, M. (2004) On Discourse and Dirty Nappies. *Theory and Psychology*, *14*(2), pp. 167–189.

Downs, D. S., DiNallo, J. M, Kirner, T. L. (2008) Determinants of Pregnancy and Postpartum Depression: Prospective Influences of Depressive Symptoms, Body Image Satisfaction, and Exercise Behavior. *Annals of Behavioral Medicine*, 36(1), pp. 54–63.

Dworkin, S.L. and Wachs, F.L. (2004) Getting your Body Back. *Gender and Society*, *18*(5), pp. 610–624.

Edwardson, C. L. & Gorely, T. (2010). Parental influences on different types and intensities of physical activity in youth: A systematic review. *Psychology of Sport and Exercise*, 11(6), pp. 522–535

Eskes, T. and Haanen, C. (2007). Do Women Live Longer than Men? *European Journal of Obstetrics and Gynecology and Reproductive Biology*, *133*(2), pp. 126–133.

Fauvel, A. (2014) Crazy Brains and the Weaker Sex: The British Case (1860-1900). *Clio*, 37 | 2013, online since 15 April 2014, connection on 19 April 2019. http://journals.openedition.org/cliowgh/352

Fazzi, C., Saunders, D.H., Linton, K., Norman, J.E. and Reynolds, R.M. (2017) Sedentary Behaviours during Pregnancy: A Systematic Review. *International Journal of Behavioral Nutrition and Physical Activity*, *14*(1), p. 1–13.

Freeman, H.V. (2008) *A qualitative exploration of the experiences of mother-athletes training for and competing in the Olympic Games* (Doctoral dissertation). Philadelphia: Temple University.

Gentile, A., Boca, S. and Giammusso, I. (2018) "You Play Like a Woman!" Effects of Gender Stereotype Threat on Women's Performance in Physical and Sport Activities: A Meta-Analysis. *Psychology of Sport and Exercise*, *39*, pp. 95–103.

Goold, I. (2017) Trust Women to Choose: A Response to John a Robertson's 'Egg Freezing and Egg Banking: Empowerment and Alienation in Assisted Reproduction'. *Journal of Law and the Biosciences*, *4*(3), pp. 507–541.

Handelsman, D.J., Hirschberg, A.L. and Bermon, S. (2018) Circulating Testosterone as the Hormonal Basis of Sex Differences in Athletic Performance. *Endocrine Reviews*, *39*(5), pp. 803–829.

Heinze, J.E., Heinze, K.L., Davis, M.M., Butchart, A.T., Singer, D.C. and Clark, S.J. (2017) Gender Role Beliefs and Parents' Support for Athletic Participation. *Youth and Society*, *49*(5), 634–657.

Hines, M. (2004). Androgen, estrogen, and gender: Contributions of the early hormone environment to gender-related behaviour. In Eagly, A.H., Beall, A.E. and Sternberg, R.J. (Eds.), *The Psychology of Gender* (2nd ed.). New York: Guilford Press, pp. 9–37.

Hyde, J.S., Bigler, R.S., Joel, D., Tate, C.C. and van Anders, S.M. (2019) The Future of Sex and Gender in Psychology: Five Challenges to the Gender Binary. *The American Psychologist*, *74*(2), pp. 171–193.

Jette, S. (2011). Exercising caution: the production of medical knowledge about physical exertion during pregnancy. *Canadian Bulletin of Medical History*, *28*, 293–313.

Johnston, M., Fuscaldo, G., Gwini, S.M., Catt, S. and Richings, N.M. (2022) Financing Future Fertility: Women's Views on Funding Egg Freezing. *Reproductive Biomedicine and Society Online*, *14*, pp. 32–41.

Jones, M.A., Catov, J.M., Jeyabalan, A., Whitaker, K.M. and Gibbs, B. (2021) Sedentary Behaviour and PA across Pregnancy and Birth Outcomes. *Paediatric and Perinatal Epidemiology*, *35*(3), pp. 341–349.

Joyner, M.J. (2017) Physiological Limits to Endurance Exercise Performance: Influence of Sex. *The Journal of Physiology*, *595*(9), pp. 2949–2954.

Kardel, K.R. (2005) Effects of Intense Training during and after Pregnancy in Top-Level Athletes. *Scandinavian Journal of Medicine and Science in Sports*, *15*(2), pp. 79–86.

Knisel, E., Opitz, S., Wossmann, M. and Keteihuf, K. (2009) Sport Motivation and PA of Students in Three European Schools. *International Journal of Physical Education*, *46*, pp. 40–53.

Limbers, C.A., McCollum, C., Ylitalo, K.R. and Hebl, M. (2020) PA in Working Mothers: Running Low Impacts Quality of Life. *Women's Health (London, England)*, *16*. Doi: 10.1177/1745506520929165.

Limbers, C.A., McCollum, C. and Greenwood, E. (2020) PA Moderates the Association Between Parenting Stress and Quality of Life in Working Mothers during the COVID-19 Pandemic. *Mental Health and Physical Activity*, *19*, p. 100358. Doi: 10.1016/j.mhpa.2020.100358.

Macrae, E.H.R. (2019) "Provide Clarity and Consistency": The Practicalities of Following UK National Policies and Advice for Exercise and Sport during Pregnancy and Early Motherhood. *International Journal of Sport Policy and Politics*, *12*(1), pp. 147–161.

March, D.S., Vanderburgh, P.M., Titlebaum, P.J. and Hoops, M.L. (2011) Age, Sex, and Finish Time as Determinants of Pacing in the Marathon. *Journal of Strength and Conditioning Research*, *25*(2), pp. 386–391.

Messner, M. (2011) Gender Ideologies, Youth Sports, and the Production of Soft Essentialism. *Sociology of Sport Journal*, *28*, pp. 151–170.

Miller, Y.D. and Brown, W.J. (2005) Determinants of Active Leisure for Women with Young Children-an "Ethic of Care" Prevails. *Leisure Sciences*, *27*(5), pp. 405–420.

Morantz-Sanchez, R. (1996) *The Eternally Wounded Woman: Women, Doctors, and Exercise in the Late Nineteenth Century*. Baltimore: The Johns Hopkins University Press.

Mørkved, S., Bø, K. (2014). Effect of Pelvic Floor muscle Training During Pregnancy and After Childbirth on Prevention and Treatment of Urinary Incontinence: A Systematic Review. *British Journal of Sports Medicine*, 48, s.299–310.

Muehlenhard, C.L. and Peterson, Z.D. (2011) Distinguishing Between Sex and Gender: History, Current Conceptualizations, and Implications. *Sex Roles*, *64*, 791–803.

Nash, M. (2011) 'You Don't Train for a Marathon Sitting on the Couch': Performances of Pregnancy 'Fitness' and 'Good' Motherhood in Melbourne, Australia. *Women's Studies International Forum*, *34*, pp. 50–65.

Nash, M. (2015) Shapes of Motherhood: Exploring Postnatal Body Image Through Photographs. *Journal of Gender Studies*, *24*(1), pp. 18–37.

Nikolaidis, P., Ćuk, I. and Knechtle, B. (2019) Pacing of Women and Men in Half-Marathon and Marathon Races. *Medicina*, *55*(1), p. 14.

Nobles, J., Thomas, C., Banks Gross, Z., Hamilton, M., Trinder-Widdess, Z., Speed, C., Gibson, A., Davies, R., Farr, M., Jago, R., Foster, C. and Redwood, S. (2020) "Let's Talk about Physical Activity": Understanding the Preferences of Under-Served Communities when Messaging PA Guidelines to the Public. *International Journal of Environmental Research and Public Health*, *17*(8), p. 2782.

O'Brien, W., Lloyd, K. and Ringuet-Riot, C. (2014) Mothers Governing Family Health: From an "Ethic of Care" to a "Burden of Care." *Women's Studies International Forum*, *47*, pp. 317–325.

Osborne, C.A. and Skillen, F. (2020) Women in Sports History: The More Things Change, the More They Stay the Same? *Sport in History*, *40*(4), pp. 411–433.

Palmer, F.R. and Leberman, S.I. (2009) Elite Athletes as Mothers: Managing Multiple Identities. *Sport Management Review*, *12*(4), pp. 241–254.

Pedersen, I. K. (2001). Athletic career: 'Elite sports mothers' *as a social phenomenon*. *International Review for the Sociology of Sport*, *36*, 259–274.

Péronnet, F. and Thibault, G. (1989) Mathematical Analysis of Running Performance and World Running Records. *Journal of Applied Physiology*, *67*(1), pp. 453–465.

Petropanagos, A., Cattapan, A., Baylis, F. and Leader, A. (2015) Social Egg Freezing: Risk, Benefits and Other Considerations. *Canadian Medical Association Journal*, *187*(9), pp. 666–669.

Raspovic, A.M., Prichard, I., Yager, Z. and Hart, L.M. (2020) Mothers' Experiences of the Relationship Between Body Image and Exercise, 0–5 Years Postpartum: A Qualitative Study. *Body Image*, *35*, pp. 41–52.

Renfree, A., Crivoi do Carmo, E. and Martin, L. (2016) The Influence of Performance Level, Age and Gender on Pacing Strategy during a 100-km Ultramarathon. *European Journal of Sport Science*, *16*(4), pp. 409–415.

Roberts, C.-M. and Kenttä, G. (2019) Motherhood in the exercising female. In Forsyth, J. and Roberts, C.-M. (Eds.), *The Exercising Female: Science and its Application*. Oxford: Routledge, pp. 224–235.

Roberts, C.-M. and Kenttä, G. (in progress). Motherhood as an athletic career transition.

Spowart, L., Burrows, L. and Shaw, S. (2010) "I Just Eat, Sleep and Dream of Surfing": When Surfing Meets Motherhood. *Sport in Society*, *13*(7-8), pp. 1186–1203.

Strandbu, Å., Bakken, A. and Stefansen, K. (2020) The Continued Importance of Family Sport Culture for Sport Participation during the Teenage Years. *Sport, Education and Society*, *25*(8), pp. 931–945.

Tiller, N.B., Elliott-Sale, K.J., Knechtle, B., Wilson, P.B., Roberts, J.D. and Millet, G.Y. (2021) Do Sex Differences in Physiology Confer a Female Advantage in Ultra-Endurance Sport? *Sports Medicine*, *51*(5), pp. 895–915.

Vertinsky, P.A. (1994) *The Eternally Wounded Woman: Women, Doctors and Exercise in the Late Nineteenth Century*. Manchester: Manchester University Press.

Walker, L.O., Xie, B., Hendrickson, S.G. and Sterling, B.S. (2016) Behavioral and Psychosocial Health of New Mothers and Associations with Contextual Factors and Perceived Health. *Journal of Obstetric, Gynecologic and Neonatal Nursing*, *45*(1), pp. 3–16.

Yang, C. L., & Chen, C. H. (2018). Effectiveness of Aerobic Gymnastic Exercise on Stress, Fatigue, and Sleep quality During Postpartum: A Pilot Randomized Controlled Trial. *International Journal of Nursing Studies*, *77*, 1–7.

Yoder, J. (2003) *Women and Gender: Transforming Psychology* (2nd ed.). Upper Saddle River, NJ: Pearson/Prentice Hall.

Zarulli, V., Barthold Jones, J.A., Oksuzyan, A., Lindahl-Jacobsen, R., Christensen, K. and Vaupel, J.W. (2018) Women Live Longer Than Men Even during Severe Famines and Epidemics. *Proceedings of the National Academy of Sciences - PNAS*, *115*(4), pp. E832–E840.

Part III
Intersecting Gender

18
Postcoloniality, Gender and Sport
A Snapshot of the Literature and Insights from Fiji

Yoko Kanemasu and Atele Dutt

Introduction

Recent years have seen a rise of intersectional approaches in feminist sport studies, as well as repeated calls for greater attention to the experiences of athletes who have thus far received marginal research attention (e.g., Hargreaves, 2000; Scraton and Flintoff, 2013). Accordingly, there is today a growing body of research literature that engages with the interface between sport, gender, sexuality, 'race'/ethnicity and other axes of oppression, informed by multiracial/transnational feminisms and related critical theories. This chapter provides a brief, critical overview of a specific section of this literature with a particular focus on postcoloniality and highlights a persisting paucity of research undertaken in the Global South. The chapter subsequently outlines some key, existing contributions in understanding the diversity and complexity of the postcolonial condition mediating and mediated by women's relationship with sport, followed by a consideration of the case of Fiji.

Feminist sport scholars have recently been asking 'whether it is any longer appropriate to centralise gender relations or whether we need far more complex engagement with the intersections of difference' (Scraton and Flintoff, 2013, p. 96). The growing literature in this field, however, tends to be Global-North-oriented. It centres on the sporting experiences of 'diasporic and racial Others' (Ratna, 2018, p. 198), or women of colour, immigrant women and Muslim women in North America, Europe and the broader Global North. This is evident in Ratna's (2018) review of gender, 'race' and sport literature, which found that a third of relevant publications concerned African American women, another third South Asian and/or Muslim women in diasporic and other locations and a final third women of colour from across the Global North and South. This points to a relative dearth of research in and about the postcolonial Global South. Even in a recent special issue of the *Sociology of Sport Journal* dedicated to sport, feminism and the Global South (Toffoletti et al., 2018), the focus is predominantly the North's engagement with the South, i.e., its marginalisation of, power over, and epistemological and ontological imposition on the South, especially through sport-for-development programmes. As the special issue editors acknowledge, the contributions dealt largely with 'the problems that arise when

Northern theory produced in the urban metropole predominates in feminist and sport debates' (Toffoletti et al., 2018, p. 194). While such work is clearly of immense value, we also need to know more about Southern women's lived experiences of sport not necessarily directly facilitated by the North.

In addition, existing studies of gender and sport in postcolonial contexts are often undertaken by researchers located in the metropole. This is likely attributed to markedly less resources (e.g., research grants, library databases and resources, technical support, conference opportunities) available to researchers in the South, as well as the privileged status of English-language research employing Northern paradigms, theories, methods and researcher/institutional networks. In other words, global disparity in the availability of, and access to, institutional and material resources and academic cultural and social capital may significantly constrain 'who speaks, whose voices are heard, which perspectives are validated, and on whose terms' (Toffoletti et al., 2018, p. 193).

Consequently, research inquiry into postcoloniality, gender and sport has been noted as relatively underdeveloped and often textual-based (Scraton and Flintoff, 2013). Dewar's (1993, p. 214) observation nearly three decades ago that feminist sport scholarship may be 'speaking from the centre' remains pertinent in some respects, although much has been done to address this. In particular, feminist sport research can benefit further from empirical, local analyses of the diversity, complexity and specificity of the socio-historical configurations of postcoloniality and how these multifariously intersect women's relationship with sport across the Global South. This can complement the existing interest in 'what the North does to the South' in international development contexts. There are several significant contributions to this end, which are briefly explored below.

Emerging insights from the postcolonial Global South

It is important to acknowledge the burgeoning body of work that interrogates the imposition of neo-liberal sport discourse and/or Western feminism on the Global South. One of the central arguments emanating from this work is that Western, neoliberal feminist discourse of empowerment, mobilised in Southern contexts, renders sport participation, physical activity and gender justice a matter of individual agency, divorcing them from structural inequalities embedded in the processes and effects of colonialism and neo-colonialism. Researchers have demonstrated this in media representations of women athletes (e.g., Stevenson, 2018), sport governance (e.g., Henne and Pape, 2018; Pike and Matthews, 2014), and, especially, Northern-designed/funded sport-for-development programmes (e.g., Hayhurst, 2013, 2014; Hayhurst et al., 2016; Hayhurst et al., 2018; Henne and Pape, 2018; Nicholls et al., 2010; Saavedra, 2009). This literature critically exposes, among other things, the continuing colonialism of and through sport in the Global South, with a donor-centred logic of 'development' serving as a key medium.

Beyond this literature, there are notable examples of in-depth engagement with women's sporting experiences under varied postcolonial conditions. First, there is a diverse body of work about indigenous peoples, gender and sport in settler colonies in North/South America, Australia and New Zealand (e.g., Ferreira et al., 2016; Hall, 2014; Hargreaves, 2000; Hokowhitu, 2004; Leseth, 2014; McGuire-Adams and Giles, 2018; Norman et al., 2019; Olive et al., 2019; Paraschak and Forsyth, 2010; Parry et al., 2020; Stronach et al., 2016; Thorpe et al., 2020). The contributions of these studies are too diverse to summarise here, yet they collectively show that indigenous peoples' relationship with sport needs to be examined against the dynamics of settler-colonial power and indigenous decolonisation struggle, especially the politics of cultural assimilation and the production of gendered and racialised (neo)colonial subjects. Second, and particularly important from the point of view of this chapter, is research from across the postcolonial Global South (e.g., Allen, 2014; Hargreaves, 1997, 2000; Jones, 2003; Molnar et al., 2019; Nauright, 2014; Pelak, 2005, 2010; Ruffié et al., 2011; Saavedra, 2003; Shehu, 2010; Sikes and Bale, 2020). Again, this body of work is too broad and rich to summarise here; hence, we briefly consider two contributions below, as they are directly relevant to this chapter.

James H. Mills (2005, 2006) examines women's football in Manipur, a region merged with India in 1949 following the end of British rule. Mills shows how Manipuri women's dominance in contemporary Indian football is intricately linked with the region's history, indigenous cultural practices and postcolonial ethnic politics. He outlines the long history of female autonomy in the region's Meitei ethnic community, where women historically played key roles in religious rituals, to which indigenous dance, games and sporting activities were central. They also engaged in collective economic work and political actions, such as against the British colonial administration and the Indian state, albeit within the existing patriarchal system. In this context, modern Manipuri women footballers' prominence at the national level has become a medium of the negotiation of Meitei identity to emphasise its difference from other ethnic groups in competition for regional resources as well as to challenge Indian cultural/political hegemony. The indigenous tradition of women's team games and collective action thus underlies the modern sport, which has taken on renewed significance and meanings in its postcolonial socio-political milieu. It is 'a complex story that combines long-established patterns of female autonomy with the emergence of modern identities and agendas in which powerful female agents cooperate in a variety of acts of definition and resistance' (Mills, 2006, p. 74).

Simon Creak (2014, 2015) presents an in-depth historical study of the symbolic link between physicality, masculinity and authoritarian state power in Laos. Creak carefully traces how diverse ideologies of Laos's successive colonial, royalist, revolutionary and post-socialist regimes shared an enduring concern with masculine physicality, which became central to the fostering of postcolonial Lao national identity, 'with the ultimate objective of constituting, performing, and reinforcing state power' (Creak, 2015, p. 240). One of the insights emerging from his analysis is that the associations between physical culture, masculinity and state power became increasingly militarised in parallel with the country's military expansion. Under these conditions, sporting events like the Lao National Games and the hosting of the 2009 Southeast Asian Games came to serve as a powerful state spectacle that 'encapsulated the military and masculine cultures of the new Lao state, demonstrating the extent to which the disciplined male body became a motif of independent Laos' (Creak, 2014, p. 116).

These studies, along with others, illuminate some of the ways in which varied sociopolitical trajectories of postcolonial nations shape and are shaped by gendered relations of power in the sporting arena. While the historical and ongoing power of metropolitan capital and states indelibly structures the conditions of postcolonial peoples' sporting practices, these are configured in the context of differential histories and cultures with their own dynamics of power that need to be accounted for. Mills's study shows how Manipuri women's football success is bound up with the (re)construction of Meitei identity vis-à-vis not only British colonialism but Indian rule and postcolonial regional ethnic politics. In Creak's study, aggressive masculine physicality, variously fashioned by a succession of colonial and postcolonial regimes, has become essential to Laos' modern statehood in the context of dependence on foreign aid and investment from not only Northern but especially neighbouring Asian countries. These and other existing studies help us begin to unpack the multifarious and historically-specific articulations between gender and sport under postcolonial conditions. To explore such articulations, in the remainder of the chapter, we examine the case of Fiji, an island nation in a geographical region seldom studied by feminist sport researchers.

Fiji's 'violent' postcolonial heteropatriarchy, nationalism and women's physical pursuits

Physicality and postcolonial social order

Fiji is a former British colony (1874–1970) located in the Pacific Islands region. Its population of 885,000 consists mainly of indigenous Fijians (57%) and Indo-Fijians (34%) who are largely the descendants of colonial indentured labourers (Fiji Bureau of Statistics, 2020). The developing economy depends mainly on tourism and sugar exports. Although it is classified as an upper-middle income country by the World Bank, 28% of the population according to official statistics (Fiji Bureau of Statistics, 2020), and 45% according to a Fijian economist (Narsey, 2014), live in poverty. The post-independence period has seen recurrent political instabilities, most significantly coups d'état in 1987, 2000 and 2006 with severe political and economic consequences. After the 2006 coup, democratic rule was not restored until 2014.

In postcolonial Fiji, constructions of a precolonial history of tribal warfare, indigenous masculinity, spirituality and chiefly authority engendered a highly militarised culture (Halapua, 2003; Teaiwa, 2005). Militarised, indigenous masculinity rests on physical power, which is embodied in the military forces dominated overwhelmingly by indigenous men (Teaiwa, 2005). The physical and political might of the military was not only spectacularly asserted in three coups d'état, but is also evident in the country's long history of military labour trade, originating from its involvement in the World Wars. Since 1978, Fiji has sent approximately 30,000 soldiers on international peacekeeping operations (Kumar, 2020) – indeed, more UN peacekeeping troops than any other nation on a per-capita basis (Siegel and Feast, 2014). Thousands of indigenous men (and some women) have also been recruited into the British Army since the early 1960s and as private military and security personnel in high-conflict areas since the early 2000s (Kanemasu and Molnar, 2017). The small island country has thus developed an international reputation for soldiery and related physical might.

Such primacy of indigenous masculine physical power is integral to the country's ethno-racial and gender relations, both of which have rested essentially on the exercise/threat of physical force. Ethnic politics, rooted in the colonial government's ethnically divisive development policy, escalated in the postcolonial era despite intra-ethnic, class-based and regional disparities/conflicts, culminating in three ethno-nationalist coups (two military takeovers in 1987 and one civilian putsch in 2000). These coups entailed violence targeting Indo-Fijians, their homes, businesses and properties (most visibly in 2000) as well as their long-term socio-political marginalisation (Naidu, 2007; Trnka, 2008). Masses of Indo-Fijians subsequently emigrated, whose proportion of the population dropped from 51% in 1986 to 37% in 2007 (Pangerl, 2007). In the most recent coup of 2006, the military dramatically shifted its position from championing ethno-nationalism to advocating multi-ethnic nationhood. However, ethno-nationalism, coupled with cultural and religious conservatism, never receded from the country's socio-political landscape and retains considerable indigenous Fijian followings today (see MacWilliam, 2019).

Similarly, the marginalisation of women and gender-/sexually-nonconforming Fijians has taken physical as well as socio-political forms. In Fiji and the broader Pacific, gender equality has historically been defined as contradictory to both biblical teachings and cultural 'tradition'. Feminist and non-heteronormative activism has been perceived as a Western imposition and affront to indigenous heritage (Slatter, 2011). Tradition, as in many other postcolonial locations, has been 'reified and essentialised ... not only to preserve the value of local practices, but to de-legitimate other possible claims to recognition, giving rise to an ideological rendering of traditional*ism*' (Lawson and Hagan Lawson, 2015, pp. 1–2, emphasis in original). This traditionalism assumes great potency when articulated with discourse of anti-imperialist nationalism. As a prominent Fijian feminist, Patricia Imrana Jalal (2002, p. 13), once commented: 'it is relatively easy for anti-feminist forces to derail a feminist campaign in Fiji by saying it is anti-Fijian'.

Out of this convergence of militarism, masculinism, physicality, traditionalism and nationalism emerged a particular variant of postcolonial heteropatriarchy, whose legitimacy rests not only on its perceived cultural and biblical sanction, but often on undisguised violence. That is, 'violent expressions of masculine authority have become normalised with devastating effects' (George, 2016, p. 102). Civil society activism has been curtailed repeatedly by the coups and breakdowns of democratic rule (Mishra, 2012). Despite a number of legislative and policy breakthroughs achieved via women's advocacy (see Fiji Women's Rights Movement, 2020), gender relations on the ground for the majority of grassroots women remain decidedly unequal and have direct and far-reaching impact on their wellbeing and life chances. In particular, women and non-heteronormative Fijians encounter pervasive threats of violence. Sixty-four percent of ever-partnered Fijian women have experienced physical and/or sexual violence by a male partner [Fiji Women's Crisis Centre (FWCC), 2013] as against the global prevalence of 30% partner violence (World Health Organisation, 2013). Additionally, 71% have been physically and/or sexually abused by a male partner or non-partner (FWCC, 2013). Non-heteronormative Fijians face risks of systematic bullying, physical assaults and rape in their daily life, despite constitutional ban on discrimination on the basis of sexual orientation or gender identity/expression [Fiji National Civil Society Joint Submission, 2014; Diverse Voices and Action (DIVA) for Equality, 2019].

Women, sport and violent postcolonial heteropatriarchy

It is such a violent form of postcolonial heteropatriarchy that underlies the scope for sport participation and resistance by women. Militarised, indigenous masculine physical power manifests not only in state apparatuses, but also in everyday cultural practices including sports, most conspicuously rugby, which is seen as a modern expression of the indigenous warrior ethos and valorised for its historical links with chiefly authority and Christian faith (Kanemasu and Molnar, 2013a). In Teaiwa's (2005, p. 217) words: '[m]ilitarism disarticulated from indigenous warfare rearticulates itself with modern sports'. This articulation exercises immense symbolic power, for the men's seven-a-side national team's international fame is widely celebrated as a symbol of national pride in the face of the island nation's geopolitical marginality (Kanemasu and Molnar, 2013b). Indeed, rugby serves as a 'unifying' tool of postcolonial nation-building, which was most vividly demonstrated in 2016, when the men's rugby sevens side won the country's first-ever Olympic Gold medal, with thousands of Fijians (of all ethnicities and genders) singing and shouting in frenzied celebrations across the country. Such genuine pride the game invokes in most, if not all, Fijians also serves to endorse its underlying traditionalist, masculinist and ethno-racial discourses.

Accordingly, women who transgress the culturally sanctioned masculine practice of rugby incur severe retributions, exacerbated by many of them being, or suspected of being, transmasculine and lesbian (Kanemasu and Johnson, 2019). The small community of predominantly indigenous Fijian women rugby players have long struggled against heteropatriarchal marginalisation at family, community and institutional levels. Kanemasu and Molnar (2013a, 2017) have documented instances of women prevented from playing rugby by their family and beaten or turned out of their homes for non-compliance. A great many of them experience violence (largely but not exclusively) from men in their families and communities, ranging from verbal abuse to punching and kicking. Spectator violence in the form of misogynistic/lesbophobic jeering and ridicule has also been noted as commonplace, although somewhat decreasing (Kanemasu and Johnson, 2019). In short, women rugby players bear the brunt of the coercive power of the violent postcolonial heteropatriarchy.

Non-indigenous women, especially Indo-Fijians, experience this postcolonial heteropatriarchy somewhat differently. The dominant discourse of indigenous, masculine physical superiority locates them in a position of double marginalisation, whereby their pursuit of sport or physical activity is negated in racialised as well as gendered terms. Notably, Indo-Fijian men, whose masculine physicality has been consistently eclipsed in the nation's postcolonial ethnic politics, have cultivated their own sporting spaces, primarily association football, which is multi-ethnic in terms of player population and Indo-Fijian-dominated in administration. They have also developed sporting enclaves like car racing, practiced, organised and supported almost exclusively by Indo-Fijian men, countering the hegemonic indigenous masculine physicality. By contrast, Indo-Fijian women are largely absent in organised sports and exercise (Kanemasu, 2019; Sugden et al., 2020). Those who overcome parental disapproval and other family- and community-level barriers to entering the sporting arena must confront entrenched stereotypes of Indo-Fijian physical inferiority. Unless they opt to play recreationally in Indo-Fijian-only environments (which some do for a sense of security), they must negotiate the racialised discourse of physicality that can shape the attitudes of (largely indigenous) athletes, coaches and officials around them. It is not surprising, then, that netball, the most popular women's sport in Fiji, is dominated by indigenous women athletes and officials, mirroring men's rugby (Sugden et al., 2020): the two most prestigious sports of the nation each serve to consecrate indigenous physical supremacy in a deeply gendered manner.

Resisting postcolonial heteropatriarchy in/through sport

The postcolonial heteropatriarchy and its constitutive discourses, thus, condition and are conditioned by gendered sporting practices. It is also within this terrain that women resist their marginalisation. As Kandiyoti (1988) highlighted with her concept of 'patriarchal bargain', women's responses to gender injustice vary widely according to opportunities available under each variant of (hetero)patriarchy. In Fiji, where equal rights discourse does not enjoy cultural legitimacy and legislative protection for gender parity in sport/education (like Title IX in the United States) does not exist, a formal recourse is not an option, which shapes an absence of public and formally-articulated resistance by sporting women. Up against a violent form of postcolonial heteropatriarchy, Fijian women's resistance has to date been mostly covert and infrapolitical, as well as relentless and persistent.

While Fiji has a long history of women's activism dating back to the early 1900s, it was initiated and, to some degree, continues to be led by educated professional women [in civil society organisations (CSOs)] and indigenous chiefly women (in indigenous women's organisations) (Mishra, 2012). Sports like rugby, played by largely grassroots, working-class/unemployed women, remained mostly outside of formal advocacy for many years. In the past decade, feminist/lesbian CSOs began to work closely with some women's rugby clubs, and most recently, regional/international bodies like Oceania Rugby and UN Women have partnered with the Fiji Rugby Union in promoting gender equality in/through the sport. But women rugby players' primary response over the years has been to keep playing the game, i.e., collective and persistent refusal to give in to heteropatriarchal sanctions, with their closely-knit community serving as a critical mutual support mechanism (Kanemasu and Johnson, 2019). Women rugby players have also found transformative possibility in the appropriation of rugby nationalism. Given rugby's immense symbolic power, they have sought to claim cultural legitimacy by attaining international success, or, as Fijians commonly say, by 'putting Fiji on the world map'. The national team has recently qualified for the 2021 World Cup, a prestigious feat with which the women hope to begin to uncouple the game from heteropatriarchal traditionalism (Kanemasu and Molnar, 2019).

Indo-Fijian women, who are differently located in the postcolonial hierarchies of ethnicity, gender and physicality, have differently responded to their marginalisation. Faced with multiple layers of domination, few Indo-Fijian women are found in competitive, team sports. But a small number of women have staked their claim to athleticism by employing options and strategies and occupying spaces immediately available to them. These are found in individual and/or recreational athletic pursuits such as jogging, gym workout and martial arts. This sporting resistance tends to be solitary in that in most cases it is not facilitated/supported by athletic communities, networks or camaraderie (Kanemasu, 2019). In this respect, their 'patriarchal bargain' is distinct from that of indigenous women rugby players: it is a doubly covert, unobtrusive strategy that nevertheless maximises their options for physical autonomy within the limits of the existing arrangements of gender and ethnic politics.

Conclusion

Our central argument in this chapter was that, despite the growth of feminist sport studies over the past decades and increasing research attention to the multidimensionality of gender politics in sporting contexts, there remains significant scope for extending this inquiry to the postcolonial Global South. Emerging studies of sport and gender in postcolonial locations illustrate how gendered relations of power take heterogenous forms and effects as a result of vastly differential trajectories of postcolonial communities and nations, within which women experience sport and physical activity. Our view is that greater empirical, local analysis is needed to account for such complexity and diversity of women's sporting experiences under postcolonial conditions. To contribute to this project, we presented a brief examination of the case of Fiji. In postcolonial Fiji, heteropatriarchy has become deeply fused with militarism, traditionalism, (anti-imperial and ethno-) nationalism and the primacy of physicality, often assuming violent manifestations. We intended to show that, where physicality takes a central place in postcolonial nationhood and relations of power underpinning it, sport participation is not just about exercising one's right but about direct engagement with such relations of power. This by no means presents an exhaustive analysis of the realities lived by Fijian women in pursuit of sport. Our limited purpose here was to show that feminist sport studies can gain meaningfully from mapping the 'varieties of patriarchy' (Hunnicutt, 2009) under diverse historical, socio-cultural and politico-economic conditions and how these are interwoven with women's varied experiences of, and responses to, gender injustice in sporting contexts. Such a project, in our view, can contribute usefully to feminist sport scholarship in the face of continuing epistemic violence (Spivak, 1988) against women in many geographical and structural locations.

REFERENCES

Allen, D. (2014) '"Games for the boys": Sport, empire and the creation of the masculine ideal' in Hargreaves, J. and Anderson, E. (eds.), *Routledge Handbook of Sport, Gender and Sexuality*, London: Routledge, pp. 21–29.

Creak, S. (2014) 'Rituals of the masculine state: Sports festivals, gender and power in Laos and Southeast Asia' in Hargreaves, J. and Anderson, E. (eds.), *Routledge Handbook of Sport, Gender and Sexuality*, London: Routledge, pp. 112–120.

Creak, S. (2015) *Embodied Nation: Sport, Masculinity, and the Making of Modern Laos*, Hawaii: University of Hawaii Press.

Dewar, A. (1993) 'Would All the Generic Women in Sport Please Stand Up? Challenges Facing Feminist Sport Sociology', *Quest*, 45, pp. 211–229.

Diverse Voices and Action (DIVA) for Equality. (2019) *Unjust, Unequal, Unstoppable: Fiji Lesbians, Bisexual Women, Transmen and Gender Non Conforming People Tipping the Scales toward Justice*. Suva, Fiji.

Ferreira, M.B.R., Mizrahi, E., and Capettini, S.M.F. (2016) 'Indigenous women, games and ethno-sport in Latin America' in López de D'Amico, R., Benn, T., and Pfister, G. (eds.), *Women and Sport in Latin America*, Abingdon: Routledge, pp. 186–198.

Fiji Bureau of Statistics. (2020) *Bula and Welcome*, available at: https://www.statsfiji.gov.fj/index.php (Accessed: 10 October 2020).

Fiji National Civil Society Joint Submission. (2014) *United Nations Universal Periodic Review Fiji*, available at: https://ilga.org/wp-content/uploads/2016/02/Shadow-report-12.pdf (Accessed: 1 October 2020).

Fiji Women's Crisis Centre. (2013) *Somebody's Life, Everybody's Business! National Research on Women's Health and Life Experiences in Fiji (2010/2011)*, Suva: Fiji Women's Crisis Centre.

Fiji Women's Rights Movement. (2020) *Mapping of Recommendations from Convention on the Elimination of All forms of Discrimination against Women (CEDAW)*, available at: http://www.fwrm.org.fj/images/FWRM_CEDAW_Recommendations_Mapping.pdf (Accessed: 1 November 2020).

George, N. (2016) '"Lost in translation": Gender violence, human rights and women's capabilities in Fiji' in Biersack, A., Jolly, M., and Macintyre, M. (eds.), *Gender Violence and Human Rights: Seeking Justice in Fiji, Papua New Guinea and Vanuatu*, Canberra: ANU Press, pp. 81–125.

Halapua, W. (2003) *Tradition, Lotu and Militarism in Fiji*. Lautoka: Fiji Institute of Applied Studies.

Hall, M.A. (2014) 'Toward a history of aboriginal women in Canadian sport' in Forsyth, J. and Giles, A.R. (eds.), *Aboriginal Peoples and Sport in Canada: Historical Foundations and Contemporary Issues*, Vancouver: UBC Press, pp. 64–94.

Hargreaves, J. (1997) 'Women's Sport, Development, and Cultural Diversity: The South African Experience', *Women's Studies International Forum*, 20(2), pp. 191–209.

Hargreaves, J. (2000) *Heroines of Sport: The Politics of Difference and Identity*, Abingdon: Routledge.

Hayhurst, L.M.C. (2013) 'Girls as the "New" Agents of Social Change? Exploring the 'Girl Effect' Through Sport, Gender and Development Programs in Uganda', *Sociological Research Online (Special issue: Modern Girlhoods)*, 18(2), pp. 192–203.

Hayhurst, L.M.C. (2014) 'Using postcolonial feminism to investigate cultural difference and neoliberalism in sport, gender and development in Uganda' in Okada, C. and Young, K. (eds.), *Sport, Social Development and Peace*, London: Emerald, pp. 45–65.

Hayhurst, L.M.C., Giles, A.R., and Wright, J. (2016) 'Biopedagogies and Indigenous Knowledge: Examining Sport for Development and Peace for Urban Indigenous Young Women in Canada and Australia', *Sport, Education & Society*, 21(4), pp. 549–569.

Hayhurst, L.M.C., Sundstrom, L.M., and Arksey, E. (2018) 'Navigating Norms: Charting Gender-Based Violence Prevention and Sexual Health Rights Through Global-Local Sport for Development and Peace Relations in Nicaragua', *Sociology of Sport Journal*, 35, pp. 277–288.

Henne, K. and Pape, M. (2018) 'Dilemmas of Gender and Global Sports Governance: An Invitation to Southern Theory', *Sociology of Sport Journal*, 35, pp. 216–225.

Hokowhitu, B. (2004) 'Tackling Māori Masculinity: A Colonial Genealogy of Savagery and Sport', *The Contemporary Pacific*, 16(2), pp. 259–284.

Hunnicutt, G. (2009) 'Varieties of Patriarchy and Violence Against Women: Resurrecting 'Patriarchy' as a Theoretical Tool', *Violence Against Women*, 15(5), pp. 553–573.

Jalal, P.I. (2002) 'Gender and Race in Post Coup D'etat Fiji: Snapshots from the Fiji Islands', *Development Bulletin*, 59, pp. 28–30.

Jones, D.E.M. (2003) 'Women and sport in South Africa: Shaped by history and shaping sporting history' in Hartmann-Tews, I. and Pfister, G. (eds.), *Sport and Women: Social Issues on International Perspective*, London: Routledge, pp. 130–144.

Kandiyoti, D. (1988) 'Bargaining with Patriarchy', *Gender and Society*, 2(3), pp. 274–290.

Kanemasu, Y. (2019) 'Going it alone *and* strong: Athletic Indo-Fijian women and everyday resistance' in Molnar, G., Amin, S., and Kanemasu, Y. (eds.), *Women, Sport and Exercise in the Asia-Pacific Region: Domination-Resistance-Accommodation*, London: Routledge, pp. 92–110.

Kanemasu, Y. and Molnar, G. (2013a) 'Problematising the Dominant: The Emergence of Alternative Cultural Voices in Fiji Rugby', *Asia Pacific Journal of Sport and Social Science*, 2(1), pp. 14–30.

Kanemasu, Y. and Molnar, G. (2013b) 'Pride of the People: Fijian Rugby Labour Migration and Collective Identity', *International Review for the Sociology of Sport*, 48(6) pp. 720–735.

Kanemasu, Y. and Molnar, G. (2017) 'Private Military and Security Labour Migration: The Case of Fiji', *International Migration*, 55(4), pp. 154–170.

Kanemasu, Y. and Molnar, G. (2019) 'Against All Odds: Fijiana's Flight from Zero to Hero in the Rugby World Cup', in: Harris, J. and Wise, N. (eds.), *Rugby in Global Perspective: Playing on the Periphery*. London: Routledge, pp. 24–36.

Kanemasu, Y. and Johnson, J. (2019) 'Exploring the Complexities of Community Attitudes towards Women's Rugby: Multiplicity, Continuity and Change in Fiji's Hegemonic Rugby Discourse', *International Review for the Sociology of Sport*, 54(1), pp. 86–103.

Kumar, V. (2020) 'Peacekeeping duties – 67 servicemen lost in the past 42 years, says Konrote', *Fiji Times*, 13 November 2020, available at: https://www.fijitimes.com/peacekeeping-duties-67-servicemen-lost-in-the-past-42-years-says-konrote/ (Accessed: 20 November 2020).

Lawson, S. and Hagan Lawson, E. (2015) *Chiefly Leadership in Fiji: Past, Present, and Future*, SSGM Discussion Paper 2015/5, Canberra: Australia National University.

Leseth, A.B. (2014) 'Experiences of Moving: A History of Women and Sport in Tanzania', *Sport in Society*, 17(3), pp. 479–491. doi:10.1080/17430437.2013.815514.

MacWilliam, S. (2019) *Modernising Tradition: Elections, Parties and Land in Fiji*. Department of Pacific Affairs Discussion Paper 2019/2, Canberra: Australian National University, available at: https://openresearchrepository.anu.edu.au/bitstream/1885/158164/1/dpa_dp2019_2_macwilliam_final.pdf (Accessed: 10 October 2020).

McGuire-Adams, T.D. and Giles, A.R. (2018) 'Anishinaabekweg Dibaajimowinan (Stories) of Decolonization Through Running', *Sociology of Sport Journal*, 35(3), pp. 207–215.

Mills, J.H. (2005) '"Nupilal": Women's war, football and the history of modern Manipur' in Mills, H.H. (ed.), *Subaltern Sports: Politics and Sport in South Asia*, London: Anthem Press, pp. 173–190.

Mills, J.H. (2006) '"Manipur Rules Here": Gender, Politics, and Sport in an Asian Border Zone', *Journal of Sport & Social Issues*, 30(1), pp. 62–78.

Mishra, M.C. (2012) 'A History of Fijian Women's Activism (1900-2010)', *Journal of Women's History*, 24(2), pp. 115–143.

Molnar, G., Amin, S., and Kanemasu, Y. (eds.) (2019) *Women, Sport and Exercise in the Asia-Pacific Region: Domination-Resistance-Accommodation*, London: Routledge.

Naidu, V. (2007) 'Coups in Fiji: Seesawing Democratic Multiracialism and Ethno-nationalist Extremism', *Devforum*, 26, pp. 24–33.

Narsey, W. (2014) 'The Facts on Poverty and Social Justice', *The Fiji Times*, 26 July, available at: https://narseyonfiji.wordpress.com/2014/07/27/the-facts-on-poverty-and-social-justice-the-fiji-times-26-july-2014/ (Accessed: 5 May 2021).

Nauright, N. (2014) 'African Women and Sport: The State of Play', *Sport in Society*, 17(4), pp. 563–574.

Nicholls, S., Giles, A.R., and Sethna, C. (2010) 'Perpetuating the "Lack of Evidence" Discourse in Sport for Development: Privileged Voices, Unheard Stories and Subjugated Knowledge', *International Review for the Sociology of Sport*, 46, pp. 249–264.

Norman, M.E., Hart, M., and Petherick, L. (2019) 'Indigenous Gender Reformations: Physical Culture, Settler Colonialism and the Politics of Containment', *Sociology of Sport Journal*, 36, pp. 113–123.

Olive, R., Osmond, G., and Phillips, M.G. (2019) 'Sisterhood, Pleasure and Marching: Indigenous Women and Leisure', Annals of Leisure Research, 24(1), pp. 13–28. doi: 10.1080/11745398.2019.1624181.

Pangerl, M. (2007) 'Notions of Insecurity among Contemporary Indo-Fijian Communities', *Asia Pacific Journal of Anthropology*, 8(3), pp. 251–264.

Paraschak, V. and Forsyth, J. (2010) 'Aboriginal Women "Working" at Play: Canadian Insights', *Ethnologies*, 32(1), pp. 157–173.

Parry, K.D., Cleland, J., and Kavanagh, E. (2020) 'Racial Folklore, Black Masculinities and the Reproduction of Dominant Racial Ideologies: The Case of Israel Folau', *International Review for the Sociology of Sport*, 55(7), pp. 850–867.

Pelak, C.F. (2005) 'Negotiating Gender/Race/Class Constraints in the New South Africa: A Case Study of Women's Soccer', *International Review for the Sociology of Sport*, 40(1), pp. 53–70.

Pelak, C.F. (2010) 'Women and Gender in South African Soccer: A Brief History', *Soccer & Society*, 11(1-2), pp. 63–78.

Pike, E.C.J. and Matthews, J.J.K. (2014) 'A post-colonial critique of the international "movements" for women and sexuality in sport' in Hargreaves, J. and Anderson, E. (eds.), *Routledge Handbook of Sport, Gender and Sexuality*, London: Routledge, pp. 75–83.

Ratna, A. (2018) 'Not Just Merely Different: Travelling Theories, Post-Feminism and the Racialized Politics of Women of Colour, *Sociology of Sport Journal*, 35, pp. 197–206.

Ruffié, S., Ferez, S., Lauzanne, M., and Dumont, J. (2011) 'Sport and Gender Construction in the Postcolonial Context: Between East and West – The Paradoxical Effects of Globalization', *Current Sociology*, 59(3), pp. 328–346.

Saavedra, M. (2003) 'Football Feminine - Development of the African Game: Senegal, Nigeria and South Africa', *Soccer and Society*, 4(2/3), pp. 225–253.

Saavedra, M. (2009) 'Dilemmas and opportunities in gender and sport-in-development' in Levermore, R. and Beacom, A. (eds.), *Sport and International Development: Global Culture and Sport*, London: Palgrave Macmillan, pp. 124–155, available at https://doi.org/10.1057/9780230584402_6 (Accessed: 5 October 2020).

Scraton, S. and Flintoff, A. (2013) 'Gender, feminist theory, and sport' in Andrees, D.L. and Carrington, B. (eds.), *A Companion to Sport*, London: Blackwell, pp. 96–111.

Shehu, J. (ed.) (2010) *Gender, Sport and Development in Africa: Cross-cultural Perspectives on Patterns of Representations and Marginalisation*, Dakar: Council for the Development of Social Science Research in Africa.

Siegel, M. and Feast, L. (2014) 'For Fiji's military rulers, U.N. peacekeeping a useful mask', *Reuters*, 4 September, available at: http://www.reuters.com/article/us-fiji-un-crisis-idUSKBN0GZ0GV20140904 (Accessed: 20 September 2020).

Sikes, M. and Bale, J. (2020) *Women's Sport in Africa*, Abingdon: Routledge.

Slatter, C. (2011) 'Gender and custom in the South Pacific', *New Zealand Yearbook of New Zealand Jurisprudence*, available at http://www.nzlii.org/nz/journals/NZYbkNZJur/2011/11.html (Accessed: 15 September 2020).

Spivak, G.C. (1988) 'Can the subaltern speak?' in Nelson, C. and Grossberg, L. (eds.), *Marxism and the Interpretation of Culture*, Illinois: University of Illinois Press, pp. 21–78.

Stevenson, P. (2018) 'Empowerment Discourses in Transnational Sporting Contexts: The Case of Sarah Attar, The First Female Saudi Olympian', *Sociology of Sport Journal*, 35, pp. 238–246.

Stronach, M., Maxwell, H., and Taylor, T. (2016) '"Sistas" and Aunties: Sport, Physical Activity, and Indigenous Australian Women', *Annals of Leisure Research*, 19(1), pp. 7–26.

Sugden, J., Kanemasu, Y., and Adair, D. (2020) 'Indo-Fijian Women and Sportive Activity: A Critical Race Feminism Approach', *International Review for the Sociology of Sport*, 55(6), pp. 767–787.

Teaiwa, T. (2005) 'Articulated Cultures: Militarism and Masculinities in Fiji during the Mid 1990s', *Fijian Studies*, 3(2), pp. 201–222.

Thorpe, H., Brice, J., and Rolleston, A. (2020) 'Decolonizing Sport Science: High Performance Sport, Indigenous Cultures, and Women's Rugby', *Sociology of Sport Journal*, 37(2), pp. 73–84.

Toffoletti, K., Palmer, C., and Samie, S. (2018) 'Introduction: Sport, Feminism and the Global South', *Sociology of Sport Journal*, 35, pp. 193–196.

Trnka, S. (2008) *The State of Suffering: Political Violence and Community Survival in Fiji*, New York: Cornell University Press.

World Health Organisation. (2013) *Global and Regional Estimates of Violence Against Women: Prevalence and Health Effects of Intimate Partner Violence and Nonpartner Sexual Violence*, Geneva: WHO.

19
From Disability to "Adaptivity"
Bethany Hamilton in Sean McNamara's *Soul Surfer* (2011)

Tatiana Prorokova-Konrad

Introduction

In 2003, at the age of 13, American surfer Bethany Hamilton lost her left arm to a shark. Despite that tragic event, Bethany continued to surf and she has become one of the most famous athletes globally. Bethany has also become an inspirational role model for people who experience disabilities, women, and athletes in general, challenging and breaking disability and gender stereotypes in sport and empowering individuals worldwide. Bethany has written several memoirs (e.g., Hamilton 2018) and shares her own experiences and lessons from her life (see Hamilton 2021). In doing so, she has been helping people believe in themselves, as well as proving that experiencing disability and being a woman are not medical diagnoses, but rather cultural labels that have been (ab)used to discriminate in the sporting world and beyond.

Sean McNamara's *Soul Surfer* (2011) tells Bethany's story: from her childhood to the life after the attack. This essay examines the film's portrayal of Bethany's story, which is about accepting and ultimately *overcoming* her disability. Bethany, in real life, once commented on disability in sport as follows:

> I think disabled is a very degrading title for athletes. I feel like I'm an incredibly abled person… If anything, I encourage ESPYs [Excellence in Sports Performance Yearly Awards] to… change the category to Best Adaptive Athlete, so athletes that have adapted to unique situations in their life. I would have been stoked to be in the category if that was what it was called
>
> (n.d., quoted in Barney 2016, n.p.)

This view on disability in sport is precisely what the film zeroes in. This chapter focuses on Bethany's strategy and ability to adapt to the new reality after the shark attack, as portrayed in *Soul Surfer*. The film does not depict disability as a drawback, but rather considers it as a way of *being*. Therefore, this chapter examines the intersection of disability and gender, and suggests that in the film, adaptivity not only foregrounds disability as a legitimate, *normal* condition, but also communicates gender as an important aspect in Bethany's professional career. That Bethany "surfs like a girl" is celebrated through her ability to adapt. In my discussion of adaptivity, I also provide an ecocritical reading of Bethany's disability and gender, arguing that the film *naturalizes* Bethany's body through the images of the 2004 Indian Ocean tsunami that caused death and devastation in Thailand – the county where Bethany goes to help affected individuals.

The body of a woman: Gender and disability in *Soul Surfer*

Bethany Hamilton is an outstanding athlete. Yet, except for her achievements in sport, the woman (teenage girl at the time of the attack) drew the attention of audiences worldwide with her rare story of survival, struggle, and overcoming. Bethany's story tells us more than just about the life of an athlete; it tells us about the life of a woman experiencing disability who participates in sport. It, thus, tells us about gender, disability, the body, and the politics through which these terms are negotiated and understood in various sociocultural environments. I emphasize that while Bethany herself strongly opposes references to herself as a disabled athlete, insisting that she is physically much stronger and fitter than many other (able-bodied) people, I use the term "disabled" in my analysis to examine the portrayal of Bethany's differently shaped body in *Soul Surfer* and how such a depiction transforms her as a woman and athlete. The concept of "disability" is complex; it is interpreted differently and used to communicate different ideas. In the medicalized world, for example, the concept of "disabled" may be used in a discriminatory fashion, thereby reinforcing the dichotomy between "able" and "disabled" (Cohen, Shachar, Silvers, and Stein 2020). Floris Tomasini (2019, p. 1) shares that disability as a notion and the way its meaning has been constructed might be constrictive on various levels:

> I found that impairment and disability to be normatively restrictive labels. Either, there was a danger of fixating too much on restoration from physiological abnormality. Or, there was this creeping sense of entitlement, where as a disabled person I could expect some form of special treatment or positive discrimination.

While I may not consider the term "disabled" offensive, I posit that the exclusion of and discrimination against people who experience disabilities is the result of societal rejection and unwillingness to accept and accommodate diversity, and not the outcome of specific impairments and forms of disability (Cohen, Shachar, Silvers, and Stein 2020). Bethany's story narrated in *Soul Surfer* vividly illustrates that a person with disabilities cannot only adapt and feel comfortable in society, when society welcomes them, but also be much more successful in sport than an able-bodied individual. Considering "disability" a restrictive term, Bethany re-envisions her own body as a body of an athlete that simply needs to identify her strengths and train hard in order to perform well.

In her seminal exploration of the body, *Volatile Bodies: Toward a Corporeal Feminism*, Elizabeth Grosz (1994, p. x) argues:

> bodies, cannot be adequately understood as ahistorical, precultural, or natural objects in any simple way; they are not only inscribed, marked, engraved, by social pressures external to them but are the products, the direct effects, of the very social constitution of nature itself.

Thus, the body is a complex bio-social phenomenon that functions on different levels and is marked by different signifiers that determine its social, cultural, political, economic, and other roles. That the body is redefined through gender, and vice versa, and how this process is carried out, have been discussed by gender studies scholars in detail (Butler 1990; 1993; Conboy, Medina, and Stanbury 1997). The body of a cis-gender woman, for example, has been (mis)interpreted by patriarchy to facilitate its abuse and exploitation. Similar to other cultural spheres, in sport, women have been oppressed multi-fold: first, by not being allowed to take part in or excluded from competitions (for examples, please see Hargreaves 1994 and McLeod 2011). This historic discrimination has been considerably based on the presumption that a woman's body is a weak body, a body that differs from a man's body in a variety of ways; such differences enable an exclusion of women from the sporting world. For example, in the nineteenth and early twentieth centuries, scientists largely argued that women's bodies were not made for sports and that sport activities can even ruin a woman's health, thus foregrounding bio-medical rationale for exclusion (Heggie 2020). This was a way to promote gender inequality across the cultural spectrum, including the sporting world, by using science as a logical basis yet employing false scientific data (Heggie 2020).

Cooky and Messner (2018) foreground the fact that more women athletes take part in various kinds of sport today, which has led to a transformation of a cultural understanding of women in sport. Girls, according to Cooky and Messner (2018), are no longer exclusively part of the audience but are also active participants. Crucially, such a transformation of women's role in the sporting world has been widely – and positively – depicted in popular culture, which is the sign of a cultural transformation (Cooky and Messner 2018). This observation, however, is most relatable to Western societies, for in some non-Western countries, women often have more challenging barriers (Molnar, Amin, and Kanemasu 2019). The cultural transformation of perceiving gender in sports is intrinsically the message that *Soul Surfer* attempts to convey, too, focusing on a teenage girl who is obsessed with surfing: surfing is her life, it is the air she breathes, the hobby that she enjoys the most, the career that she sees for herself in the future. Along with her brothers and other teenage boys who surf, Bethany is viewed as a successful and devoted athlete. The opening scenes in the film depict Bethany at the beginning of her career, when teenagers train for and participate in local competitions, and there is no explicit gender discrimination among the characters. The audience realizes that the relationships among some of the characters are tight, but this is rather the result of select characters (including Bethany) being more successful athletes than others, which makes some other teenagers envious. This, however, has a gender resonance, as from a young age, Bethany has to fight for her place in the sporting world.

Despite their quite positive observation regarding inclusion of women in sport, Cooky and Messner (2018, p. 5) emphasize that discrimination against women is still part of life in the sporting world:

> The continuing barriers to full and equal participation for young people, the far lower pay for most elite-level women athletes, and the continuing dearth of fair and equal media coverage all underline how much still has yet to change before we see gender equality in sports.

A woman's body is continuously oppressed in the sporting world, largely so because of its gendered categorization formulated via the gender binary that classifies a woman's body as unfitting for sports. It is worth noting, however, that in sport, especially in elite sport, bodies are generally exploited, medicalized, and regimented (McNamee 2014). Women experience a higher degree of that, but men are also not immune. *Soul Surfer* explores Bethany's body not so much as a gendered body but as a disabled body and a white, Western athletic body. The film depicts the attack in detail, supplying the audience with the heart-breaking images of injured

Bethany, her friends trying to deliver her safely first to the shore and then to the hospital, her mother driving to the hospital and realizing that inside the ambulance that she spots on the road is her daughter, her father whose knee operation is postponed because a teenager attacked by a shark would be delivered to the hospital soon, and the medical personal desperately trying to save the life of the teenage girl. *Soul Surfer* thus emphasizes the symbolic meaning of the shark attack, dividing Bethany's life in two parts: before and after the attack. This is a common narrative in disability, for athletes with acquired disability are often used as inspirational stories. However, this narrative is problematic for several reasons. First, paradoxically, it contributes to the stigmatization of disability emphasizing that *even* being disabled, an athlete can achieve success. Second, it completely disregards numerous other athletes who are disabled from birth and whose stories might be not so dramatic, but who nonetheless experience discrimination and overcome personal, societal, economic, political, and other boundaries as they fight for their place in the sporting world. While stories like Bethany's are important and they shape the meanings of gender and disability in sport, they should not be foregrounded and perceived as general experiences of athletes with disabilities.

That Bethany survives and grows even further as a professional surfer is clear from the outset of the film. The film's focus on the tragedy of the attack, however, makes the viewer sympathize with the injured girl because she will become *disabled* at a young age, having such a strong interest in surfing. *Soul Surfer*, thus, in these scenes, suggests that disability is a diminishing characteristic that, first, will not allow the teenage girl to lead the same life as her able-bodied friends do and, second, poses a serious threat to her professional career as a surfer. When Bethany wakes up after a long and complex surgery, the focus of her family, herself, and, inevitably, the audience is on the girl's body, and specifically, the missing arm. Disability is expected to prevent the girl's dreams to become a great surfer from coming true because, as the scenes after the attack (specifically, in the hospital and shortly after Bethany arrives home) demonstrate, the general belief is that a disabled person cannot be an athlete. Indeed, surfing is considered unattainable, for even making a sandwich is now a difficult task for the girl. Through the scene in the kitchen, when Bethany is trying to make a sandwich, however, the film ponders the meaning of Bethany's new bodily condition, foregrounding the issues of impairment and disability. To specify, through the scene, the film suggests that Bethany has an impairment that might lead to disability but does not have to. The film thus juxtaposes "impairment" and "disability" to emphasize that the two are not the same: a minor impairment in some cases might lead to occupational disability, but there are also examples when individuals with major impairments fully perform all tasks that their profession requires (Brigham 2019).

The film does not discriminate against women athletes, but, quite the contrary, celebrates the presence of girls and women in surfing. Yet, the inclusion of disability as a derogative and limiting characteristic of one's body (as portrayed in the scenes shortly after the surgery) reclassifies the body of Bethany and inevitably relocates it to a precarious, discriminatory territory. Shortly after the attack, Bethany is depicted as a vulnerable individual, and disability emphasizes the vulnerability of her gender, too, as Bethany is now portrayed as a helpless girl. Bethany appears in the scenes after the surgery as dependent, weak, and desperate. Lamenting on how much "biology and medicine" play a role in formulating the meaning of body, Grosz (1994, p. x) notes:

> It [the body] has generally remained mired in presumptions regarding its naturalness, its fundamentally biological and precultural status, its immunity to cultural, social, and historical factors, its brute status as given, unchangeable, inert, and passive, manipulable under scientifically regulated conditions.

Depriving the body of agency allows one to impose specific views on the body and thus construct it culturally, politically, and economically. In the film, Bethany is reduced to a mere agency-less body that is interpreted by those who surround her as a *different* body that is unfitting for surfing. Through the disabled character, *Soul Surfer* throws into relief how deeply rooted the perception of disability as an abject category is and demonstrates how such a discriminating view affects the lives and perception of, in this case, a woman athlete.

Gender and sport studies scholars remind us that in history, sport was viewed as a "spectacle for the public," and this remains true even today (Appleby and Foster 2013, p. 1). Sport is a space to foreground the body as physically strong, if not supreme, compared to the bodies of individuals outside the sporting world. It is not only the performance of an athlete that matters and draws attention of viewers, but also their body as an instrument through which certain activities are performed and results achieved. The body of an athlete thus largely contributes to formulating sport as a platform for not only competition, but also contemplation. This is particularly pertinent to aesthetic sports. There the body's role is even more central given that emphasis is placed on corporeal presentation. Surfing is one such sport, with one sub-category for judging being "flow." The inclusion of people with disabilities in sport, including surfing, is an important step to re-envision the competing body and the body of an athlete more generally. A disability and sport studies scholar, Jill M. Le Clair (2012), emphasizes that some of the oppressed groups, and specifically women and disabled individuals, have gained recognition and radically transformed their status from the oppressed to the equal individuals through sports, in particular *during* their performances. What happens when an athlete is a *disabled woman*? Elisabet Apelmo (2017, p. 2) argues that the body of a disabled woman athlete is perceived as both "deviant" (i.e., different from a certain norm) and "accomplished" (i.e., normalized) – because it is "disabled" and "sporting." In *Soul Surfer*, shortly after the surgery, Bethany's disabled body is portrayed as a deviant body that does not belong to surfing. In order to surf, one, as the film seems to insist for a long time, needs two arms: to hold the board, swim, rise out of the water, and keep one's balance. Having lost an arm, Bethany is depicted as having been deprived of a specific instrument – a bodily instrument – through which her sporting performance can be carried out. After several unsuccessful attempts to surf, Bethany seems to give up thus – for a moment – accepting her body as unfit for surfing. At that point in the film, the body as a gendered and disabled object is reclassified as "useless" and hence un-sporty. The film thus displays a perspective that discriminates against both women and disabled individuals in sport.

Unable to perform well (and sometimes at all) for some time after the attack, Bethany is excluded from the surfing world as an athlete: it is the moment when her gender and disability become particularly noticed as she is relocated into a vulnerable group of disabled women. Her body as a body of a woman *and* a disabled body is viewed as now lacking capacity to compete with other surfers. The body is thus reclassified as unfitting for *able-bodied* sport. Here, I would like to refer to Rosemarie Garland-Thomson's important claim about the necessity to establish "feminist disability theory." Garland-Thomson (2002), among other scholars, recognizes the oppression that certain individuals have been able to exercise towards others by manipulating and misinterpreting gender and disability. Garland-Thomson (2002, p. 3) writes:

> the goal of feminist disability studies … is to augment the terms and confront the limits of the ways we understand human diversity, the materiality of the body, multiculturalism, and the social formations that interpret bodily differences.

Both feminism and disability studies are important prisms through which to understand the place and perception of women in sports in general and of disabled women, in particular.

According to Garland-Thomson (2002, p. 3): "integrating disability as a category of analysis and a system of representation deepens, expands, and challenges feminist theory." And vice versa: being sensitive to gender inequality in discussions about disabled athletes is potentially a richer and more productive approach to discrimination and inequality in sport more broadly. Cooky and Messner (2018, p. 4, italics in original) emphasize that sport itself has contributed considerably to reinforce gender inequality, for example, by legitimizing "beliefs in *categorical* differences" such as that men are in multiple ways physically superior to women. Certainly, individuals should compete with those who, according to a number of parameters, have similar circumstances and can perform on the same level. In disability sport, for instance, as DePauw and Gavron (2005, p. 246) argue: "classification" of individuals is conducted "to enable each competitor, regardless of severity of impairment, to compete in a fair manner with others of similar ability/disability." Reclassifying women as weak, disabled, and incapable to compete are criminal ways to promote inequality in sport in general and in disability sport, in particular. Scholars emphasize that how able-bodied individuals view people with disabilities plays a crucial role in constructing the meanings of gender and disability in sport and argue that these views often shape the perceptions of people with disabilities about themselves (e.g., Haegele, Yessick, and Zhu 2018; Cottingham et al. 2018; Pullen and Silk 2020). When Bethany, after the attack, is literally out of surfing, she is out not because she cannot do that activity, but because there is no one at first who can prove her the opposite.

Adaptivity as a political statement

The only person who, according to *Soul Surfer*, does not give up hope for Bethany to become a successful surfer if she continues training is her father. The father understands the challenge for both him, as Bethany's father and trainer, and Bethany who is just beginning to learn her new body condition and discover ways in which she has to transform to reclaim her surfer life. While initially Bethany rejects this idea, finding it simply unrealistic, she soon decides to continue with surfing with the help of her father. From that moment on, the audience witnesses Bethany training hard, transforming her body to find ways through which she can surf again.

In this part of *Soul Surfer*, Bethany refuses to see disability as a mere diagnosis that sets a limit on her individuality, on her dreams, and on the ways she wishes to live her life. She is offered a prosthesis, however, as soon as she realizes that it will not help her surf (because it will not be able to bear the weight of a surfboard), she rejects it. This decision suggests that it is not the visual appearance of the post-shark-attack body that bothers Bethany, but rather the supposedly limited functionality of her transformed body. Bethany considers a prosthesis as an instrument with the help of which her body can be reconstructed and returned to its previous shape and function. She doubts the physical potential of her changed body, viewing it as, indeed, a *disabled* body. Having been training only for a short while, Bethany enters a competition and loses against another – able-bodied – girl. Upset with her performance, Bethany decides that she will never compete again, thereby giving in to the dominant narrative of disability.

To find distraction from her athletic career, Bethany decides to join a group of volunteers and travels with them to Phuket, Thailand, to help individuals affected by the Indian Ocean tsunami. One of her tasks there is to help children to stop being afraid of the ocean. Bethany herself had to overcome a similar fear earlier: a fear of going into the water where dangers hide, a fear of surfing in the waters where her arm had been taken. The children in Phuket also see the ocean as a dangerous place, as a power that destroyed their homes, killed their friends and relatives, and harmed them in multiple other ways.

Bethany's visit to Thailand is a crucial event in the film for several reasons. First, it helps Bethan to reimagine her own tragedy and see her disability in a different light. Second, the images in Thailand naturalize Bethany's body. Bethany realizes that the loss that she observes in Phuket is incomparable to her own loss. The film by no means undermines Bethany's tragedy, yet it suggests that unlike is the case with the victims of the tsunami, Bethany's life can and does go on. The limits that are now set on her by herself and society are artificial and one can overcome them. It is at that moment that Bethany finally realizes that she should understand her body not as a dis-abled body but rather as a body that can adapt. Instead of thinking about disability, Bethany realizes that adaptivity is the key to her success. When Bethany is back from Thailand, her father mounts a small holder on the board – which is not against the rules – and advises Bethany that it will help her to get on her surf easier. This adaptation to the surfboard, indeed, is the solution, as Bethany soon realizes that she is now able to catch even strong waves. Her body is no longer an unknown, alien body to her; Bethany's post-attack body becomes *natural* to her.

Surfing is a kind of sport that involves a direct interaction of the human – an athlete – with the nonhuman world, i.e., the ocean, the wind, and the sun. Bethany has to learn to feel the ocean to be able to surf successfully, with a minor adaptation to the board. Most of her life she spends in the ocean, training, swimming, surfing. Such closeness to water makes her relationship with the nonhuman world much tighter than other humans might have. However, she loses her arm while being in this environment, as a result of another nonhuman (a shark) attacking her. While trying to master part of the nonhuman world, the girl is being attacked by this very world. Certainly, the actions of other individuals, and especially Bethany's father, after the attack, aimed at catching and killing the shark, thus punishing it for what it naturally does and did to Bethany are serious ethical issues and deserve detailed consideration on their own. But such a tight connection between the human (Bethany) and the nonhuman world (the natural environment in which she trains and competes) provides an important perspective on Bethany's body and (dis)ability. The inclusion of the natural catastrophe in Thailand in the film, the effects of which Bethany experiences as well, is crucial, too. Through the tsunami in Thailand, the audience is reminded again how much more powerful nature is compared to humans. But the film also emphasizes that humans are a part of the natural world, that human and nonhuman worlds coexist with each other. The film thus foregrounds what Stacy Alaimo (2010, p. 2) terms as "the material interconnections of human corporeality with the more-than-human world," for the human is part of the environment and the environment cannot be viewed without the human. Alaimo refers to Garland-Thomson's crucial observation regarding disability and the environment:

> Disability studies reminds us that all bodies are shaped by their environments from the moment of conception. We transform constantly in response to our surroundings and register history on our bodies. The changes that occur when body encounters world are what we call disability.
>
> (n.d., quoted in Alaimo 2010, p. 12)

When I claim that the human is part of the environment, I, therefore, consider the human as a direct agent that influences and transforms the environment, but I also view the human as a *natural* body that is a natural part of the environment. Bethany's disability is hence not exactly dis-ability of her body but rather a transformation that she experiences as a result of an interaction with the environment while still remaining part of the natural world. This transformation does not necessarily disempower her body. Rather, it calls for Bethany's recognition of her body as a material object that can adapt. DePauw and Gavron (2005, p. 246, my italics) emphasize how important it is to classify athletes according to certain parameters "to provide for meaningful athletic competition based upon *ability*, not disability" (although such a classification system can be and has been critiqued [see Peers 2012]). Similarly, once Bethany realizes that she should focus not on what she cannot do but rather what she can do, on her ability rather than dis-ability, she is able to train her body and achieve results. The words of Bethany Hamilton quoted in the opening section of this chapter underline Bethany's unwillingness to view herself as an individual and an athlete who is incapable of doing something, for she calls herself "an *incredibly abled* person" (n.d., quoted in Barney 2016, n.p., my italics). This, in turn, emphasizes the crucial role of adaptivity for people with disabilities. Viewing oneself as a person who is *able* to do something rather than someone who is incapable of performing the same task in a way that for various reasons might be considered more popular and natural is key to understanding disability sport and tackling the problem of inequality in sport more generally, including gender inequality and discrimination against individuals with disabilities.

Conclusion

Bethany Hamilton's narrative is a story of courage, survival, and fight. She has learnt to accept her body, discovered ways to adapt it, (re)made her body fit for surfing and proved that "surfing like a girl" is an activity that an athlete should be proud of. In *Soul Surfer*, Bethany's love for surfing and inability to imagine her life without this sport is the key factor that makes her successfully adapt to her new reality. Bethany learns not to view her body as a body that lacks something compared to other, able-bodied humans; she learns not to view her post-amputation body as a body that cannot surf in the way that it used to. For Bethany, her body is a material object that can adapt to a new reality: one simply needs to train it in a proper way. It is worth pointing out that should the injury be more severe, Bethany's story might have been a different story. Therefore, while adapting and training are essential, those too, like the body, both able and disabled, have limitations.

Scholars emphasize that through disability, one can see how discriminating some aspects of sport are. Recognizing sport's marginalizing tendencies has a potential to change the existing systems of oppression and inequality in the field (DePauw 1997, cited in Fitzgerald 2009, p. 2). *Soul Surfer* celebrates Bethany's will to re-join the surfing world, stamina, and ability to adapt while learning more about her own body. The film not only supports women in sports and shows them positively but also emphasizes their *ability* in sport, whether it is a competition among able-bodied or disabled athletes. It is through the recognition of the gender-disability intersection that *Soul Surfer* foregrounds socio-political and cultural intricacies that surround sport and athletes in particular, calling to acknowledge athletes' will and ability to compete and their incredible power to reimagine, readjust, and readapt their bodies.

REFERENCES

Alaimo, S. (2010) *Bodily natures: science, environment, and the material self.* Bloomington: Indiana University Press.
Apelmo, E. (2017) *Sport and the female body.* London: Routledge.
Appleby, K.M., and Foster, E. (2013) 'Gender and sport participation', in Roper, E.A. (ed.) *Gender relations in sport.* Rotterdam: Sense Publishers, pp. 1–20.
Barney, L. (2016) 'Bethany Hamilton: surfing with only one arm isn't as hard as beating the stigma', *The Guardian*, 25 August, n.p. Available at: https://www.theguardian.com/sport/2016/aug/25/bethany-hamilton-surfing-espy-award (Accessed: 5 November 2020).

Brigham, C.R. (2019) 'Common metrics for impairment ratings', in Martinez, S.F., Rondinelli, R.D., and Eskay-Auerbach, M. (eds.) *Medical impairment, disability evaluation and associated medicolegal issues*. Philadelphia: Elsevier, pp. 533–540.

Butler, J. (1990) *Gender trouble: feminism and the subversion of identity*. New York: Routledge.

Butler, J. (1993) *Bodies that matter: on the discursive limits of "sex"*. New York: Routledge.

Cohen, I.G., Shachar, C., Silvers, A., and Stein, M.A. (eds.) (2020) *Disability, health, law, and bioethics*. Cambridge: Cambridge University Press.

Conboy, K., Medina, N., and Stanbury, S. (eds.) (1997) *Writing on the body: female embodiment and feminist theory*. New York: Columbia University Press.

Cooky, C., and Messner, M.A. (2018) 'Introduction', in Cooky, C. and Messner, M.A. (eds.) *No slam dunk: gender, sport and the unevenness of social change*. New Brunswick: Rutgers University Press, pp. 1–11.

Cottingham, M., Hums, M., Jeffress, M., Lee, D., and Richard, H. (2018) 'Women of power soccer: exploring disability and gender in the first competitive team sport for powerchair users', *Sport in Society: Cultures, Commerce, Media, Politics* 21(11), pp. 1817–1830.

DePauw, K.P., and Gavron, S.J. (2005) *Disability sport*. Champaign: Human Kinetics.

Fitzgerald, H. (2009) 'Bringing disability into youth sport', in Fitzgerald, H. (ed.) *Disability and youth sport*. London: Routledge, pp. 1–8.

Garland-Thomson, R. (2002) 'Integrating disability, transforming feminist theory', *NWSA Journal* 14(3), pp. 1–32. Available at: https://www.jstor.org/stable/4316922 (Accessed: 22 October 2020).

Grosz, E. (1994) *Volatile bodies: toward a corporeal feminism*. Bloomington: Indiana University Press.

Haegele, J.A., Yessick, A., and Zhu, X. (2018) 'Females with visual impairments in physical education: exploring the intersection between disability and gender identities', *Research Quarterly for Exercise and Sport* 89(3), pp. 298–308.

Hamilton, B. (2018) *Be unstoppable: the art of never giving up*. California: Zondervan.

Hamilton, B. (2021) Personal website. Available at: bethanyhamilton.com (Accessed: 22 October 2020).

Hargreaves, J. (1994) *Sporting females: critical issues in the history and sociology of women's sport*. London: Routledge.

Heggie, V. (2020) 'Health, gender and inequality in sport: a historical perspective', in Günter, S. (ed.) *EveryBody tells a story: zur Geschichte von Sport-, Körper- und Bewegungskulturen*. Wiesbaden: Springer, pp. 31–52.

Le Clair, J.M. (2012) 'Introduction: global organizational change in sport and the shifting meaning of disability', in Le Clair, J.M. (ed.) *Disability in the global sport arena: a sporting chance*. London: Routledge, pp. 4–25.

McLeod, K. (2011) *We are the champions: the politics of sports and popular music*. Abingdon: Ashgate Publishing.

McNamee, M. (2014) *Sport, medicine, ethics*. London: Routledge.

Molnar, G., Amin, S.N., and Kanemasu, Y. (2019) *Women, sport and exercise in the Asia-Pacific region: domination, resistance, accommodation*. London: Routledge.

Peers, D. (2012) 'Patients, athletes, freaks: Paralympism and the reproduction of disability', *Journal of Sport and Social Issues* 36(3), pp. 295–316.

Pullen, E., and Silk, M. (2020) 'Gender, technology and the able national Paralympic body politic', *Cultural Studies* 34(3), pp. 466–488.

Soul Surfer. (2011) Directed by Sean McNamara. Culver City: Sony Pictures Releasing.

Tomasini, F. (2019) *Vulnerable bodies: new directions in disability studies*. London: Palgrave Macmillan.

20
Women's Parasport Experiences of Sacrifice, Conflict, and Control
Always Tilting

Nancy Spencer, Eri Yamamoto and Bobbi-Jo Atchison

Introduction

Tilting is a skill in the sport of wheelchair basketball. It involves an athlete rising up onto one wheel to increase their reach at tip-off, and when shooting, blocking, and rebounding, to outmatch an opponent. Tilting is being "always on the edge of your tread… that point in time where you are about to go over" (Peers, personal communication 26 March 2021). Tilting is "to cause something to move into a sloping or uneven position, or to be in this position" (Cambridge Dictionary 2021).

Always tilting, within the research presented here, refers to the waysin which athletes found themselves in precarious positions within the context of making personal sacrifices, experiencing conflict, and lacking control in women's parasport. Pseudonyms are used with the exception of one athlete, Danielle Peers, who asked to be identified. In this chapter, we prioritise the stories of 12 Canadian athletes, shared through interviews in an interpretive description study (Thorne 2016) about their parasport journeys. Athletes identified as women or non-binary, with varied impairment diagnoses (i.e., visual impairment, muscular dystrophy, spinal cord injury, minimal disability, and cerebral palsy) and competed at the highest level of parasport competition, the Paralympics, in a variety of sports (i.e., goal ball, wheelchair basketball, skiing, swimming, cycling, athletics, and curling). Our use of disability language and terminology reflects several disability models (i.e., rights-based, social, and experiential) in keeping with athletes' self-identification, citations and how these models and languages resonate for us, the authors (see Peers, Spencer-Cavaliere and Eales 2014). Using a feminist disability studies lens, we draw attention to the ways in which the stories presented here run counter to the empowerment narrative that often accompanies research about and with athletes who experience disability (see Peers 2009; Pullen and Silk 2020; Purdue and Howe 2012a). As a result of the intersection of gender and disability, athletes endured even more intense and compounded discrimination than if either of these axes were considered separately (Hargreaves 2000; Kim 2013). Consequently, here we examine "the dynamics of difference and sameness" in consideration of gender and disability (Cho, Crenshaw and McCall 2013, p. 787) acknowledging that personal stories are essential to a critical understanding of the lived experience of disability and gender (Bush et al. 2013; Garland-Thomson 2005) in parasport. We foreground the stories.

Personal sacrifice

> A few days ago, I was revaluating my whole life and the whole thing about why did I even go down this path [elite parasport], I should have just gone to law school and I'd be so much better off for so many reasons. I'm 38 years old and I don't have a boyfriend or a husband, and, oh yeah, I guess I should start thinking about if I wanna have kids, start thinking about it. So, this is my own experience that I'm going through now. So, if I had to speak to a younger version of myself or whatever, I don't know where I bought that myth of the you must, or just showing the organizations…the coaches, that I'm totally committed. That's fine, but it shouldn't have been at the expense of my entire life, and in a way on paper, if you look at me on paper it doesn't look like it was 'cause I've got two degrees in the meantime, and I have a job. But truly, in terms of personal life, in terms of starting my own family and that sort of thing, it [elite parasport] definitely came at that expense. And at the expense of my professional, my career outside of my sports (Stacy).

To compete at the elite level, athletes dedicated significant amounts of time and energy to training, play, and travel. Prioritising sport over relationships and health were well-recognised sacrifices of elite competition. It is an "unbalanced way of living" – shared Amanda.

Family and relationships

To compete at the elite level, athletes made sacrifices regarding family life (e.g., having children and significant others/partners). Karen explained:

> The negative side is when you are going away from your family and you're missing things that you wish you'd been home for, so that's a little sad. Times in your kids' lives when you wish you would have been home.

Personal relationships were often described as supportive of making an athletic career possible, but were also characterised as something sacrificed. Prioritising her athletic career came at the cost of Tracy's relationship:

> I was married at the time and so my marriage went down the tube 'cause I was never around, one of the major reasons, lots of reasons, but that's one of the major reasons was that I just wasn't around.

In anticipation that family and relationships would be difficult to maintain, some athletes made deliberate decisions to forgo relationships while competing. These decisions were often met with questions, criticism, and social pressure to fulfil "women's role[s]." Arissa explained:

> I think they're [others] always like, 'well, you're older, playing a sport, why aren't you having a family? Why don't you settle down? Why are you still single? … Why are you still so focused on this game, right, why are you doing what you're doing?'…I think part of it too is people didn't realize…I was focused as an athlete to play parasport at the highest level.

In addition to the criticisms Arissa experienced, also apparent in the above quote was a lack of understanding others had about the nature of commitment to elite parasport. When asked to elaborate about the pressures she experienced in the context of women's versus men's parasport, Arissa explained:

> At the time, there was a lot of people on the men's side that were getting married and that were involved in relationships and things like that, so yeah, I think they would have a different perspective on it. Because maybe if I was to get into a relationship at that time, and decided to have a family, I wouldn't actually be able to be playing at that high level, or if I did, there would be big sacrifices…

Christina described the support she needed to continue playing on the national team because she was a mother:

> So, I was the only person on our team that had a child during my career right…I was able to do that 'cause I was in a relationship at the time and had a lot of support but to me it becomes a choice for people. They choose either or. They don't feel like they can do both so I think that's for just women in sport and if you have a disability and have a child obviously the demands and trying to balance that can be even greater.

Emphasised in Christina's quote was how athletes often choose between having children or competing and how being a woman athlete with an impairment provided greater challenges to having children and remaining competitive. In support, Jessica, who was not a parent at the time of competing, but was at the interview, hypothesised how difficult it would have been to maintain these dual roles.

> I made the choice to be a stay-at-home mom and so I couldn't imagine having to leave and travel as I did if I had a child…a partner might be different 'cause they could probably travel with you but a kid it's a little bit harder… I finished everything before I decided to settle down and have a kid and that would be a very hard decision for me even now and he's 5…

Danielle explained how "decisions" made about family life and relationships were not really choices.

> Everything else moved because of sport…You don't get to decide what tournaments to go to or not. You don't get to decide when to train. So yeah, I missed funerals and weddings and important partner moments and had to reschedule vacations 40 times or not have them.

The sacrifices related to family and maintaining relationships occurred during the athletes' careers, but had lasting impact on their lives.

Health and injury

Although being physically active is closely associated with health, sport and being an elite athlete were often characterised as having detrimental consequences for the athletes' health and wellbeing, both physically and mentally. The gravity of these consequences was captured by Danielle:

> I was lucky enough to be a strong enough athlete that I had some negotiation room, but like I had agreements with my coach…I would not, for example, train without a physio there in case I had a respiratory failure, that I would not train twice a day 'cause it's

particularly hard on my body…I certainly had them [coaches] trump that on numerous occasions because 'we really wanna win this game'….as soon as you have [sport] goals, ethics and wellbeing and health and actually pretty much everything you find important goes out the window.

Karen shared her concerns about her health that were specific to her experiences as a woman with an impairment. She said:

…bladder infections, when you're traveling and you can't really get into bathrooms very well and I don't think guys have as much trouble with that. Less women have indwelling catheters and more guys do, so you know if [you are a man and] you can't get into a bathroom, you can just empty your leg bag someplace else, where women [with] internal catheters [have] to make sure you can get into a bathroom. And our game [wheelchair basketball] is 2 1/2 hours long and so you are dealing with making sure you get to the bathroom and I don't know why the guys don't seem to have as big a concern…for us, female athletes, always the biggest concern is 'oh my gosh how are we all going to manage with few available bathrooms.'

Injuries were a critical concern for athletes and invoked issues associated with disability and gender. Amanda had experienced many injuries in her sports career. She brought an x-ray displayed in her house, as an artifact to her interview:

Essentially, the art on my walls dictates my Paralympic journey more than anything…I've had a lot of surgeries, injured myself a lot, and gotten a lot of metal put in my body. So, my Paralympic journey is very tied to all the injuries that I've sustained…those [x-rays] are on the wall are a constant reminder of my ability to persevere…

Amanda further recounted a story of sustaining a severe injury at an international competition. After some time in a foreign hospital, she was medically evacuated to Canada.

It [the injury] had me definitely contemplating retirement…And it was an injury that was outside of my realm of maintaining my composure over because obviously losing the use of both of your arms as a wheelchair athlete or wheelchair user is a massive problem, and I was like, how long? If I have surgery on both of my shoulders, 'so what, am I going to a rehab hospital again?' 'cause I don't know how I'm gonna transfer without either of my arms. So, we ended up opting to only do surgery on one of them, not the other. So, after about 1 week there [hospital] and 2 weeks at home, I was able to start transferring a bit, so was able to go home straight from the hospital in Vancouver, which was good, 'cause I wasn't really looking forward to a rehab hospital and was hoping my boyfriend wouldn't leave me over this [injury]…

Physical injury was addressed by many athletes; however, mental wellbeing was also a prominent feature. Several participants spoke about the "burn out" they experienced. For Wendy, feeling burnt out led to her decision to retire. She talked about her experience at a Paralympic Games. Despite winning several medals, she was relieved the competition ended:

I was getting pretty burnt out, so even though London [Paralympics] was like very successful…I definitely was feeling the stress and the burnt out part of it…I was just more excited that I was finally through it 'cause it was a really, really long meet. It's just I could feel the mental stress of it…

Danielle further supported the challenges of burnout and leaving sport. They said: "Both times that I stopped sport I went through depression.…I don't think it was…like the whole world ended.…But there was definitely like a shift…there was grieving. There was very real grieving. There were very real losses."

Maintaining physical and mental health was pivotal to athletic success. However, participation in elite sport also resulted in coerced decisions (e.g., playing injured) that were not in the athletes' best interest. Several extreme examples were shared (e.g., respiratory failure, lack of future mobility) highlighting how performance and winning were prioritised over health and had relationship consequences. Athletes also experienced burnout and difficulties in retirement.

Control and conflict

Other challenges emerged for athletes around issues of control (i.e., who does and does not have it) and conflicts that developed as a result. Athletes talked about lacking control over their bodies and training, the sport decisions that affected them, which often led to conflict. When discussing these challenges, athletes also described how control and conflict were tied to gender and disability. Coaches, trainers, and parasport administrators, who were almost exclusively male, were implicated in exerting and maintaining this control and adhering to an ethos of high-performance sport in keeping with traditional understandings of masculinity.

Lack of voice

One prominent form of control experienced by athletes was associated with silencing of their voices. Danielle described an equipment change in wheelchair basketball: "not a single athlete was consulted. Not a single female athlete was on the board." They further articulated this was also a gender issue as "female athletes had no control over their own sport" and the decisions makers, the ones with power, where "a couple male refs, the head of [national federation] who's never played the [sport]…." Danielle further explained:

> … it upsets me that a man is deciding the history of our sport. This isn't a bunch of 10-year-olds. These are fully grown women, women who are legal experts. We're perfectly capable of making decisions for the future of our own sport, but we have no capacity to do so or we're undermined any time we attempt to do so.

Stacy also highlighted this power differential as it related to gender and disability:

> …So, then you're doubly denying them…the insult happens and then they speak up about it and people are like in disbelief about it. So, I still think that voice for…women with a disability… there's still so much to do and it has to be louder and stronger and more cohesive somehow.

Issues related to gender, power, and lack of voice in parasport were common themes when athletes spoke about challenges. When asked about the differences between women's and men's parasport, Stacy said: "…I think there was probably a desire to control the female athletes more than the male athletes, but I think that's because…we were speaking up."

Coach control and conflicts

Although players acknowledged the value of coaches and positive impact they had, coaches were frequently discussed in the context of control and conflict. Wendy viewed these conflicts as inherent to elite sport. According to her: "with any national sport you're gonna get the politics of coaching and conflict, the butting heads, different things like that." In fact, several athletes described how coaching was "male dominated" (Stacy) and that most coaches had no experience with disability, which had particular consequences. Stacy explained that as an experienced female athlete, she was confident in speaking her mind, but that doing so led her coaches to think she was undermining them. She shared:

> If things weren't fair, I would say 'that's not fair.' I feel that on my team, at that time, if a guy were to say those things, it would be OK, but because I was a woman and also the same age as the coaches essentially, I was seen as undermining their authority and they were used to coaching [able-bodied] 12-year-olds prior to coaching our national team 'cause this is par for the course [less experienced coaches] in parasport.

Stacy's comment highlighted the need for coaches to be knowledgeable about athletes with impairment and this current lack of expertise. In the following quote, she expanded and also identified how negative assumptions about disability were prevalent among some of the coaches.

> They [coaches] came from the able-bodied world so those of us who could move and function in an able-bodied way were those that they could understand…I'm articulate, and I'm bilingual, and I tried in every language and in every which way, it didn't matter, I explained everything. I'm very intelligent, I sent them articles, it didn't matter what I did, I had the physios and the doctors try to explain it to them too, they never understood how my disability works, how it works in [my sport], how…fatigue, temperature, different things could affect it. And they just didn't wanna hear it, they didn't care…I think in some way they wanted us all to be able-bodied. In fact, one of our coaches said to us, to his athletes, his world cup, world champion Paralympic athletes [about performance]… 'real' world cup racers do it. We were all so shocked we were speechless…. none of us said anything 'cause we were blown away.

In summing up the current state of coaching in her sport, Stacy shared:

> …the vast majority, the bulk of the team of the coaches that we had going into 2010 [Winter Paralympics] for instance, they came straight from able-bodied, [men's sport] and were wonderful [athletes], and wonderful [sport] coaches [but]… they don't know how to coach people with a disability, and they don't know how to coach women…. And I also don't think there's anything wrong in saying that you coach a disabled person slightly differently.

Considering stories

The stories recounted here are not the stories we often read about women's parasport in popular and scholarly literature. These are not stories of empowerment and inspiration that commonly take the Paralympic centre stage (Braye, Dixon and Gibbons 2013; Howe 2011;

Peers 2009; Pullen and Silk 2020; Purdue and Howe 2012a). To clarify, athletes also shared affirming experiences with coaches, opportunities to exert independence and to develop a meaningful sense of community, as positive aspects of their parasport journeys. Other narratives associated with disability (e.g., supercrip, impairment, stigma) were also present. These too are critical and complicated themes, which need further exploration. Here, we consider the stories of sacrifice, control, and conflict, drawing on the concept of empowerment through an intersectional lens of gender and disability.

Empowerment is a multilevel construct and commonly applied framework across a range of disciplines that can be understood as a process whereby people who are marginalised assume social and political power over their own lives (Joseph 2020; Zimmerman 1995). Within the context of parasport, empowerment is part of a dominant narrative used to demonstrate the possibilities of sport in the lives of athletes who experience disability (Purdue and Howe 2012a). Simultaneously, parasport and Paralympism are critiqued for furthering the marginalisation, oppression, and disempowerment of athletes who are storied as overcoming the tragedy of disability, passive and anonymous, among other negative portrayals (Braye, Dixon and Gibbons 2013; Peers 2009; Pullen and Silk 2020). Empowerment is woven within feminist theories that centralise "the importance of the social, political and economic structures that shape human societies and stress gender must be considered when examining the effects of oppression and domination and power and powerlessness in our society" (Turner and Maschi 2015 p. 151). Mainstream feminist work has been critiqued for its lack of attendance to the relationship between the female body and disabled body leading to the emergence of feminist disability studies (Garland-Thomson 2005; Hardin 2007). In 2007, Hardin (2007, p. 39) critiqued the scarcity of research focused on "the understanding of gender and sport in light of disability," despite a call from DePauw (1997) and others a decade earlier to attend to these intersections. Subsequently, Hardin's (2007) study with elite female wheelchair basketball players through a feminist disability studies lens revealed the complexity of these intersections, as athletes' narratives simultaneously exposed their empowerment and marginalisation through parasport. We too engage with feminist disability studies in our analysis of parasport athletes' stories to go beyond "research and scholarship about women with disabilities" to reveal systems of exclusion, discriminatory practices and power relations in women's parasport (Garland-Thomson 2005, p. 1557).

It became apparent, as we conducted interviews, that differences and sameness associated with gender and disability in sport were connected to various forms of marginalisation. Acknowledged disparities and discrimination in women's parasport span a range of topics including (a)sexualisation, lack of representation, less media coverage, fewer resources, negative attitudes, cultural, religious and social beliefs, embodiment, and identity, among others (see Bush et al. 2013; Buysse and Borcherding 2010; Ferguson and Spencer 2021; Hardin 2007; Hargreaves and Hardin 2009; Harmon 2020).

Stories of sameness and difference

The sacrifices described by the athletes had impact on all aspects of their lives. On the surface, these sacrifices can be viewed as athletes' "uncritical acceptance of and commitment to…a value system framed by…the sport ethic," which in essence captures "what it means to be a real athlete" and is demonstrated by persevering through adversity, extreme dedication, and sacrificing all other life experiences for the goals and norms of sport (Hughes and Coakley 1991, p. 308). Though athletes were critical of these sacrifices, this sport ethic was apparent in their commitment to parasport, resulting in the loss of professional and personal opportunities and relationships, and risking quality of life (threatening) injuries. These themes also resonated with previous research focusing on the sacrifices of elite sport in general (Shogan 1999). Critically, these losses, risks, and consequences were intimately woven and compounded within gender and disability discourses of marginalisation, reflecting the oppression of women and individuals with non-binary gender identities and physiologies (Harmon 2020) and who experience disability (Clark and Mesch 2018).

Highlighted in the athletes' stories was a deep commitment to training and competition and the need to prioritise sport over all else, which for athletes in women's parasport appeared to be even more compounded. In reflection, several athletes questioned their decisions and expressed that others around them also challenged these decisions. Simultaneously, their male counterparts did not appear to experience the same criticisms and challenges. A number of critiques are invoked here. First, there is failure on the part of others to afford women's parasport the same legitimacy as men's parasport, as men did not appear to struggle or have to choose between multiple roles that came with being an elite athlete, such as being in relationship and/or having a family (Hargreaves 2000). This reinforces previous findings that athletes in women's parasport are not considered to be serious athletes (Buysse and Borcherding 2010) and their accomplishments matter less than those of parasport men (Hargreaves and Hardin 2009; Richard, Joncheray and Dugas 2017). Second, these findings reflect gender norms and inequities that have and continue to privilege men's sport and devalue women's sport (see Hargreaves and Anderson 2014). Third, also implicated are gender norms and ideals as athletes go against prescribed gender roles and stereotypes in their decisions to choose sport over heteronormative expectations of motherhood and being in romantic relationships. Interestingly, expectations by parasport outsiders that athletes prioritise relationships and having a family appear to challenge athletes' disabled stereotyping as both asexual and unfit parents (Garland-Thomson 2005; Zitzelsberger 2005). However, it could be that athletes' association with their role as an athlete, given the socially constructed juxtaposition of disability and ability, was more difficult for outsiders to reconcile than with the gender constructed roles of partner and parent. At least in the current context, this runs counter to the idea that "femininity is pushed to the background and sometimes even completely erased behind the stigma of disability (Richard, Joncheray and Dugas 2017, p. 70).

In navigating issues of health, which had both quality of life and life-threatening consequences, some athletes appeared to reproduce a form of hegemonic masculinity to be strong and endeavour, as they pushed their bodies to the limit (Hargreaves 2000). Masculinity narratives are often discussed within the context of men's parasport, as men seek acceptance as athletes, distancing themselves from disability in challenging the ableist culture that places ability and disability in opposition (Garland-Thomson 2005; Pullen and Silk 2020). Within women's parasport, we observed some similar responses (e.g., x-rays as sources of pride, pushing through injury). Critical to examinations of empowerment in parasport is an understanding and dismantling of ableist practices (Silva and Howe 2018). Ableism is:

> A network of beliefs, processes and practices that produces a particular kind of self and body (the corporeal standard) that is projected as the perfect, species-typical and therefore essential and fully human. Disability then is cast as a diminished state of being human.
>
> (Campbell 2001, p. 44)

Ableist coaching attitudes and practices appeared when one coach degraded "his world cup, world champion Paralympic athletes" stating they were not "real" athletes compared to non-disabled competitors. This reflects Townsend et al.'s (2020, p. 358) critique that parasport is often "conceptualised as a site of domination whereby coaches and coaching position disability in opposition to high-performance sport." This was further compounded as coaches and those with power over the sport were primarily men. This undermining and devaluing of parasport athletes, and specifically women's parasport athletes, reflects the privileging of both mainstream sport and men (Pullen and Silk 2020).

Coaches' controlling and oppressive behaviours put athletes' bodies at risk, undermined their private lives, and determined their competitive possibilities. Unlike Ashton-Shaeffer et al.'s (2001) study of women Paralympians' experiences of resistance and empowerment in wheelchair basketball, where participants expressed regaining control over their bodies as a function of their engagement in elite sport, athletes in our study often expressed the opposite. Athletes felt powerless when in conflict with coaches and endured various consequences (e.g., playing injured, being cut, being silenced, foregoing personal events and relationships), as previously reported in the literature (see Wachsmuth, Jowett and Harwood 2017). While one athlete did express a record of achievement through injury (i.e., displaying x-rays as art) which could be interpreted as a form of corporeal resistance (Purdue and Howe 2012b) often associated with masculinity, being subjected to these various disciplinary technologies left athletes disempowered (Peers 2009), further reinforcing disabled women's status as subordinate (Garland-Thomson 2005). Previous research also supports the existence of disabling coaching practices in parasport (Bush et al. 2013; Ferguson and Spencer 2021; Townsend, Smith and Cushion 2015). Furthermore, due to male/female power dynamics, women parasport athletes are unlikely to report when their coaches mistreat them (Alexander, Bloom and Taylor 2020).

Peers (2009, p. 661) noted: "as athletes move towards more elite levels of participation one might expect their increased "empowerment" would lead to increased autonomy over their bodies and their sports." According to the athletes, this was often not the case. As numerous athletes articulated, individual health was deprioritised and placed in peril, and decisions were made by coaches and others in positions of power who were not representative of the athletes, their needs, and desires. It has been long recognised that both men's and women's parasport is controlled by nondisabled men (Hargreaves 2000; Purdue and Howe 2012a) and women parasport athletes have identified this as highly problematic to their wellbeing (Alexander, Bloom and Taylor 2020).

Other stories and more stories

Within the context of women's parasport, power differentials were magnified by gendered and ableist sport practices and systems that discriminated heavily against athletes in women's parasport (Pullen and Silk 2020; Richard, Joncheray and Dugas 2017). As noted by Silva and Howe (2018, p. 17), empowerment within parasport demands that the athletes become "the active creators of parasport cultures, rather than as mere recipients of services 'for' them...with particular emphasis on decision making processes and structures." For empowerment to occur, individuals' who experience disability must "speak and act for themselves rather than being subordinated and dominated by able-bodied oppressors" (Purdue and Howe 2012a, p. 912), in the case of women's parasport, able-bodied oppressors who are also men.

Within the context of sport, where exists a substantive history of mistreatment, exclusion, and discrimination of athletes through sexism, classism, homophobia, ableism, and racism, there remains a pervasive need for intersectional approaches (Harmon 2020; Townsend, Smith and Cushion 2015). While we did not examine race or class, these and other axes of power need to be centralised in parasport research as highly relevant to our understanding of athlete experiences and to critically evaluating and valuing difference (Silva and Howe 2018). Elite sport has been identified as a site of significant inequality where dominant norms and understandings are rarely questioned (Harmon 2020), and this is true of parasport (Pullen and Silk 2020). While some critical and intersectional work in the area of parasport exists, the need for research that addresses the disparities and discrimination resulting from the intersection of social divisions in order to generate new understanding leading to a more socially just world is needed (Bush et al. 2013). Central to this work must be the stories of parasport athletes, the "other stories", the stories that challenge, resist, and have the potential to disrupt structures of power, creating opportunities for change and perhaps, even, empowerment (Peers 2009; Silva and Howe 2018).

We acknowledge the experiences of all athletes in this study. Our focus here, on issues in women's parasport, most of which are associated with being a women, is not to exclude the athletes who do not identify as women. We value different identities and recognise other forms of oppression and discrimination occurring in women's parasport beyond what is discussed here. We used the terms, "women's parasport", "athletes in women's parasport" and "women's parasport athletes" to be as inclusive as possible. Despite not addressing all individual identities in our critiques, we support the significance of such work. In closing, we also acknowledge Dr. Danielle Peers for their generous questioning of ideas.

REFERENCES

Alexander, D., Bloom, G.A. and Taylor, S.L. (2020) 'Female Paralympic athlete views of effective and ineffective coaching practices', *Journal of Applied Sport Psychology*, 32(1), pp. 48–63. doi: 10.1080/10413200.2018.1543735.

Ashton-Shaeffer, C. et al. (2001) 'Women's resistance and empowerment through wheelchair sport', *World Leisure Journal*, 43(4), pp. 11–21. doi: 10.1080/04419057.2001.9674245.

Braye, S., Dixon, K. and Gibbons, T. (2013) '"A mockery of equality": An exploratory investigation into disabled activists' views of the Paralympic Games', *Disability and Society*, 28(7), pp. 984–996. doi: 10.1080/09687599.2012.748648.

Bush, A. et al. (2013) 'Disability [sport] and discourse: Stories within the Paralympic legacy', *Reflective Practice*, 14(5), pp. 632–647. doi: 10.1080/14623943.2013.835721.

Buysse, J-A.M. and Borcherding, B. (2010) 'Framing gender and disability: A cross-cultural analysis of photographs from the 2008 Paralympic Games', *International Journal of Sport Communication*, 3(3), pp. 308–321. doi: 10.1123/ijsc.3.3.308.

Cambridge Dictionary (2021) *Tilt*. Available at: https://dictionary.cambridge.org/dictionary/english/tilt?q=tilting (Accessed: 24 January 2021).

Campbell, F.K. (2001) 'Inciting legal fictions: Disability's date with ontology and the ableist body of the law', *Griffith Law Review*, 10(1), pp. 42–62.

Cho, S., Crenshaw, K.W. and McCall, L. (2013) 'Toward a field of intersectionality studies: Theory, applications, and praxis', *Journal of Women in Culture and Society*, 38(4), pp. 785–810. doi: 10.1086/669608.

Clark, B. and Mesch, J. (2018) 'A global perspective on disparity of gender and disability for deaf female athletes', *Sport in Society*, 21(1), pp. 64–75. doi: 10.1080/17430437.2016.1225808.

DePauw, K.P. (1997) 'The (in)visibility of disability: Cultural contexts and "sporting bodies"', *Quest*, 49(4), pp. 416–430. doi: 10.1080/00336297.1997.10484258.

Ferguson, J.J. and Spencer, N.L.I. (2021) '"A really strong bond": Coaches in women athletes' experiences of inclusion in parasport', *International Sport Coaching Journal*, 8(3), pp. 283–292. doi: 10.1123/iscj.2020-0052.

Garland-Thomson, R. (2005) 'Feminist disability studies', *Signs Journal of Women in Culture and Society*, 30(2), pp. 1557–1587. doi: 10.1086/423352.

Hardin, M. (2007) '"I consider myself an empowered woman": The interaction of sport, gender and disability in the lives of wheelchair basketball players', *Women in Sport and Physical Activity Journal*, 16(1), pp. 39–52. doi: 10.1123/wspaj.16.1.39.

Hargreaves, J. (2000) *Heroines of sport: The politics of difference and identity*. Abingdon, Oxon: Routledge. doi: 10.4324/9780203466063.

Hargreaves, J. and Anderson, E. (2014) *Routledge handbook of sport, gender and sexuality*. Hoboken: Routledge.

Hargreaves, J. and Hardin, B. (2009) 'Women wheelchair athletes: Competing against media stereotypes', *Disability Studies Quarterly*, 29(2), p. 7. doi: 10.18061/dsq.v29i2.920.

Harmon, S.H.E. (2020) 'Gender inclusivity in sport? From value, to values, to actions, to equality for Canadian athletes', *International Journal of Sport Policy and Politics*, 12(2), pp. 255–268. doi: 10.1080/19406940.2019.1680415.

Howe, P.D. (2011) 'Cyborg and supercrip: The Paralympics technology and the (dis)empowerment of disabled athletes', *Sociology*, 45(5), pp. 868–882. doi: 10.1177/0038038511413421.

Hughes, R. and Coakley, J. (1991) 'Positive deviance among athletes: The implications of overconformity to the sport ethic', *Sociology of Sport Journal*, 8(4), 307–325. doi: 10.1123/ssj.8.4.307.

Joseph, R. (2020) 'The theory of empowerment: A critical analysis with the theory evaluation scale', *Journal of Human Behavior in the Social Environment*, 30(2), pp. 138–157. doi: 10.1080/10911359.2019.1660294.

Kim, M.Y. (2013) 'Women with Disabilities: The Convention through the Prism of Gender', in Sabatello, M. and Schulze, M. (eds.) *Human rights and disability advocacy*. Philadelphia, PA: University of Pennsylvania, pp. 113–130.

Peers, D. (2021) Telephone conversation with Nancy Spencer, 26 March.

Peers, D. (2009) '(Dis)empowering Paralympic histories: Absent athletes and disabling discourses', *Disability and Society*, 24(5), pp. 653–665. doi: 10.1080/09687590903011113.

Peers, D., Spencer-Cavaliere, N. and Eales, L. (2014) 'Say what you mean: Rethinking disability language in Adapted Physical Activity Quarterly', *Adapted Physical Activity Quarterly*, 31(3), pp. 265–282. doi: 10.1123/apaq.2013-0091.

Pullen, E. and Silk, M. (2020) 'Gender, technology and the ablenational Paralympic body politic', *Cultural Studies*, 34(3), pp. 466–488. doi: 10.1080/09502386.2019.1621917.

Purdue, D.E.J. and Howe, P.D. (2012a) 'Empower, inspire, achieve: (Dis)empowerment and the Paralympic games', *Disability and Society*, 27(7), pp. 903–916. doi: 10.1080/09687599.2012.695576.

Purdue, D.E.J. and Howe, P.D. (2012b) 'See the sport, not the disability: Exploring the Paralympic paradox', *Qualitative Research in Sport, Exercise and Health*, 4(2), pp. 189–205. doi: 10.1080/2159676X.2012.685102.

Richard, R., Joncheray, H. and Dugas, E. (2017) 'Disabled sportswomen and gender construction in powerchair football', *International Review for the Sociology of Sport*, 52(1), pp. 61–81. doi: 10.1177/1012690215577398.

Shogan, D. (1999) *The making of high performance athletes: Discipline, diversity, and ethics*. Toronto: University of Toronto Press. doi: 10.3138/9781442657236.

Silva, C.F. and Howe, P.D. (2018) 'The social empowerment of difference: The potential influence of Para sport', *Physical Medicine and Rehabilitation Clinics of North America*, 29(2), pp. 397–408. doi: 10.1016/j.pmr.2018.01.009.

Thorne, S. (2016) *Interpretive description: Qualitative research for applied practice*. 2nd ed. New York: Routledge. doi: 10.4324/9781315426259.

Townsend, R.C. et al. (2020) '"It's not about disability, I want to win as many medals as possible": The social construction of disability in high-performance coaching', *International Review for the Sociology of Sport*, 55(3), pp. 344–360. doi: 10.1177/1012690218797526.

Townsend, R.C., Smith, B. and Cushion, C.J. (2015) 'Disability sports coaching: Towards a critical understanding', *Sports Coaching Review*, 4(2), pp. 80–98. doi: 10.1080/21640629.2016.1157324.

Turner, S.G. and Maschi, T.M. (2015) 'Feminist and empowerment theory and social work practice', *Journal of Social Work Practice*, 29(2), pp. 151–162. doi: 10.1080/02650533.2014.941282.

Wachsmuth, S., Jowett, S. and Harwood, C.G. (2017) 'Conflict among athletes and their coaches: What is the theory and research so far?', *International Review of Sport and Exercise Psychology*, 10(1), pp. 84–107. doi: 10.1080/1750984X.2016.1184698.

Zimmerman, M.A. (1995) 'Psychological empowerment: Issues and illustrations', *American Journal of Community Psychology*, 23(5), pp. 581–599. doi: 10.1007/BF02506983.

Zitzelsberger, H. (2005) '(In)visibility: Accounts of embodiment of women with physical disabilities and differences', *Disability and Society*, 20(4), pp. 389–403. doi: 10.1080/09687590500086492.

21

Muslim Women and Sport

Obstacles and Perspectives in Socio-Political Contexts

Fabrizio Ciocca

Introduction

The concept of modern sport, as we know it, was born in England during the second half of the nineteenth century (Holt 1990), conceived while taking predominantly into account White, male, Western bodies. Similarly, when the public-school system emerged, it was predominantly reserved for males belonging to higher social classes to practice sport with the aim to reinforce masculine traits: aggressiveness, strength, self-denial, comradeship, etc. (Teja 2011). This cultural formation was also connected in some ways with the Muscular Christianity movement founded in 1850, aiming at promoting physical strength and health as well as an active pursuit of Christian ideals associated with masculinity both in personal life and politics (Schwer 1998). Sport-related male hegemony, including consequent values and practices, extensively underscored national and international sporting events. For instance, in the first modern Olympic Games (1896), women were completely excluded. While in the next Olympics (1900), of the over 1000 participants, 11 were women, they could still not compete officially. Women's participation at the Olympics was only allowed at the 1920 Games, held in Antwerp, Belgium (Borzì 2018).

Despite the gradual increase in women's right and the number of female athletes, it has taken a whole century to have almost as many women as men at the Olympic Games. At the Rio 2016 Olympics, the number of female athletes reached 4,700, equating to 45% of all participants (Rio Olympic Games Committee, 2016). The ten most represented nations had a relatively balanced gender split such as: United States with 554 athletes (262 males/292 females), Brazil 448 (238 males/210 females), Germany 423 (227 males/196 females), China 412 (157 males/255 females), France 401 (232 males/169 females), Great Britain 366 (202 males/164 females), Japan 338 (174 males/164 females), Italy 314 (170 males/144 females), Canada 314 (128 males/186 females) and Spain 305 (162 males/143 females). On the other hand, in Muslim-majority countries, out of 1,100 participants, only 200 were females. This number, however, was still the highest ever reached, both in total participants and female ones (Olympian Database 2018). Considering the total number of female athletes at the Rio Games reveals that only 1.8% (!) of them were Muslim and only 20% of all the Muslim athletes were female. Therefore, it is safe to note that the number of Muslim women at the Olympics is still low, and they are underrepresented. There may be many reasons for the lack of participation, but it is pertinent to note that the richest countries are also those with the highest number of athletes at the Olympic Games (World Population Review 2021). Furthermore, most of the richest nations also have predominantly Western cultures and, thus, long-term cultural connection with modern sports traditions, which is an additional element that has a bearing on a county's capability to field athletes.

In Muslim countries, sport and its development have often had a different trajectory. In many instances, it was only after World War Two that, with the process of decolonisation, sport participation increased in the now independent Muslim countries. Some Muslim nations were particularly keen on embracing sport to reach political goals. Tunisia, for example, organised and hosted many international sporting events, furthering both its reputation as a stable nation and president Bourgiba's secular ideology (Amara 2016). Also, in Iraq, sport was used to endorse the Ba'ath party's socialist politics, thus helping the increase in women participation in sport (Al-Watter et al. 2011). According to Sfeir (1985), nationalism, experienced in many Islamic countries, produced a more liberated attitude towards women and their involvement in sport because it broke with old traditions and offered women more opportunities in all social sectors than in the past. Women's inclusion in the public sphere also represented an essential part of the making of the modern nation (Pepicelli 2017), and sport was considered a tool to internationally showcase this change. However, the relationship between sport and Islam is not without controversy. In fact, it may be argued that Islam itself is averse to women's sport participation due to its strict regulations, while others believe that the tension lies in the conservative and patriarchal interpretations of religious texts. In this context, the following section offers an exploration of how scholars and the Muslim world view relate between Islam and sport.

Islam and sport: A theoretical framework

With the spread of sport in Islamic societies, Muslim scholars started to question themselves, analysing sporting participation on the basis of Islamic laws (*fiqh*) to understand if it is to be considered *halal* or *haram* (legitimate or forbidden). Many sport activities are characterised by physical contact and include the possibility for men and women to share the same public spaces (as it can happen in swimming pools, gyms, physical education (PE) lessons or in a martial arts training). Those characteristics of sport can become challenging for Islamic theology.

As of now, Muslim jurists reached a general consensus about declaring sport as a perfectly legitimate physical and recreational activity (Fasting and Walseth 2003), and this position is supported by many different *hadith* - the records of stories about the Prophet. For example, some *hadith* refer specifically to Muhammad's physical activities: he liked running, riding horses and camels, archery, swimming and wrestling (Manaz 2005). He not only practiced many sports of his period, but he even encouraged men and women to undertake physical activities and teach those to their children: "the right due to the child from his parent is to teach him writing, swimming, archery" (Sobirin, 2017) hadith nr. 5477). Furthermore, the fact that Muslims face many challenges during their life (e.g., Ramadan fasting, pilgrimage to Mecca and various movements as part of ritual prayer), it could be suggested that some kind of physical activity is useful to strengthen their body (Kizar 2018). Therefore, given that physical activity can be considered consistent with the Islamic faith, another question arises: what is the right context in which physical activity can be practiced by men and women?

According to Al-Fadel (2002), for Islam, acceptable recreational and physical activities are those which are performed during free time, and only with the goal of satisfying one's inner needs, without the desire of some material or symbolic profit. Hamiche (2013) argues that every Muslim should practice some sport, because Islam asks to be strong morally, mentally and physically, to give glory to God. Similarly, Das and Haldar (2010) believe that the limited participation of Muslim women in sport is ascribed to a wrong religious interpretation or traditional cultural factors, while a careful reading of texts demonstrates how Islam promotes physical activity and a healthy lifestyle for both men and women. However, like every human activity in Islam, sport must be subjected to one's self obligations to God, and should not distract from respecting religious prescriptions. Therefore, sport should be practiced in respect of dress code of modesty, keeping separate spaces for genders, and avoiding causing harm (Fedele 2017).

Al-Khalidi and Awamreh (2014) highlight how Islam specifically forbids every recreational or physical activity with leisure as its ultimate goal and showing parts of the body that are not supposed to be exposed to others according to Islamic law. According to Jani et al. (2019), a core issue is that many Muslims have been brainwashed by a Western narrative stating that sport performances will improve if less and purpose-designed clothing is used according to a competition-based vision, following a set of rules designed by Western men, contrasting with the Islamic principles of modesty. Shavit and Winter (2011) analysed a hundred fatwas (a non-binding formal ruling given by a legal scholar of Islam) on questions about sport, issued between 2001 and 2009 by Sunni jurists, belonging to two different currents: *Wasatiyya* and *Salafiyya*. They show a consensus on the legitimacy of sport activity, respecting both Islamic dress code and gender-based separation of spaces, but there are some notable differences.

Scholars adhering to the *Wasatiyya* current, the *moderate* approach, are more interested in finding practical solutions that can coexist with modernist views (in particular for Muslims living in non-Muslim countries), while the *Salafiyya* movement, the *conservative* approach, is more interested in a strict following of religious prescriptions in order to prevent contamination with Western values (Cesari 2014; Ranstorp 2020). One illustrative example of this dichotomy is the burkini, a swimsuit for women. Most Wasati jurists approve it (as long as it does not show body shape too much), while Salafi ones issued bans on sport practice outside of domestic space. Therefore, an "Islamic vision" of sport can arise, and its fundamental elements are: practicing physical activity with the goal of improving psychophysical well-being and respecting a dress code and gender separation of spaces. Currently, in the wide and varied Islamic world, there is a heated theological debate between a position that can be considered either orthodox or liberal. Since the 1990s, this debate was joined by Muslim scholars, like Fatima Mernissi, Amina Wadud and Asma Barlas, proponents of the so called Islamic Feminism, endorsing different readings of Islamic scriptures, often as an alternative to the traditional ones (Pepicelli 2010). This branch of Islamic feminists demands equal access and opportunities and do not accept the argument for gender segregation, nor the necessity of wearing hijab. Their view maintains that there are no religious rules which prohibit or regulate dress codes in order for Muslim women to participate in sport (Benn, Jaward and Pfister 2011).

It must also be taken into account that the Islamic Ummah, the whole community of believers, is composed of approximately 1.8 billion people, and is fractured by many significant cultural, social and historical differences. All those differences influence the degree of women participation in sport in their respective countries. There are nations that opt for an inclusive attitude towards the matter, investing in the sport sector, while other nations do not give sport much attention, and consider it an activity out of the boundaries of their political and social agendas. Nevertheless, since the Rio Olympics, there has been a continuous increase in Muslim women's sport participation. Still, women often face some form of exploitation, both in Islamic and non-Islamic contexts. In the last thirty years, a revival of Islamic movements has happened in different Muslim countries, endorsing a strict adherence to traditional religious prescriptions, with effects on women's possibility to participate in sports. Simultaneously, there has been a general increase in xenophobic and Islamophobic movements across Western countries, seeing Muslims as unfriendly or threatening. This has resulted in requests from Muslim women to modify certain practices (e.g., wearing a headdress when practicing in sport, or participating in separated spaces), which are seen as indicators of an - alleged - Islamisation process of modern society, and fiercely fought by populist and far right political groups (Bairner 2015; Judis 2016; Salmela and Von Schave 2017).

"Athletic woman" - A clash between political visions in Turkey

Turkey was the first Islamic nation to take part at the Olympic Games in Berlin in 1936. At Rio 2016, Turkey had the largest female delegation and won the most medals (eight, equally divided between male and female athletes) ahead of other Muslim countries participating in the event. Geographically, 97% of its territory is situated in Asia; Turkey is nonetheless a European nation as far as sport is involved, with all of its teams taking part in European championships and competitions. Since Kemal Ataturk, the general that founded the Turkish Republic in 1923, sport has rapidly become a way to show the world the metamorphosis of a nation that was ready to embrace modernity, leaving behind many of its traditions. In order to give credit to this narrative and prove how Turkey was modernised, women's participation in sport was of utmost importance: women were presented as equal citizens, freed by the Republic from the Oppressive Ottoman rule and Islamic way of life (Cosar and Yegenoglu 2011). However, these privileges were reserved to women related to families with the highest socio-economic status in the nation.

With the turn of the millennium, the AKP (Adalet ve Kalkınma Partisi – Justice and Development Party) - party of Recep Tayyip Erdogan, current president of Turkey - joined the political scene and a renewed emphasis was given to the importance of faith, tradition, family and to the role of women as "mother and bride" (Ayata and Tutuncu 2008, p.378). Erdogan, during a televised speech on 30 May 2016 (BBC, 2016), said: "a family must have at least three children and no Muslim family should consider birth control or family planning". Sehlikoglu (2016) affirms that the role of women athletes in Muslim countries is a matter that is often not just confined to sport, but becomes a clash between two visions: a more "modernist" and a more "Islamist", both of which are still within a patriarchal system, as shown by the recent Turkish experience. This contrast materialised in 2008, when volleyball player and captain of the Turkish women's national team Aysum Ozbek chose to leave competitive sport and adopt the Islamic headdress (the use of a headdress in official sport competitions is forbidden by law since 1980). Ozbek had represented a symbol of a modern and progressive Turkey, but after her retirement, she became an example of the country's Islamisation. Whether Ozbek is criticised for sport participation by saying that she did not initially respect Islam or, later, made to be a model for the perfect Muslim woman, according to Sehlikoglu (2016), both visions ignore the athlete's personal choices.

Hacisoftaoglu and Koca (2011) highlight a contrast between the secular Turkish nation and the Muslim identity of pious women who often feel forced to choose between their career and their adherence to Islamic prescriptions. The consequence, cited by Erhart (2016), was a polarisation in the political debate, with one group affirming that the presence of Muslim women in stadiums reduced violence and another saying that aggressiveness is not exclusive to males, and similar segregationist measures were pointless. The presupposition by the government was that the presence of women with their children at football events, enforced by the intrinsic sobriety of Muslim women, would prevent the typical male aggressiveness, thus reducing hooliganism. Interestingly, over time, evidence emerged that several women in the stadia began to insult opposing fans, leading to the shattering of the government's narrative. Erhart points out that the political debate was again polarised between two visions: those who argued that due to the presence of good Muslim women the stadium violence had been reduced and those who argued that aggression is not exclusive to men alone and, thus, similar "segregationist" measures were useless.

Despite Erdogan and his party trying to emphasise and instil a set of values that Muslim women should embody, even when involved in physical activities, in the last twenty years, women participation in sport increased as never before. From 1997 to 2012, according to the Turkish Ministry of Youth and Sports, the number of female athletes tripled, reaching almost 60 thousand (most practiced sports were volleyball, taekwondo, basketball and karate). Nevertheless, Turkey is still facing a difficult relationship between Turkish Islam and the secular state (Yavuz and Öztürk 2019), which seems to be extended even to sport, and, as a consequence, female athletes are often positioned between traditional and progressive political groups, without leaving them sufficient freedom to choose how and when to practice sports.

Arab countries: Through setbacks and successes

In the last thirty years, Arab countries, consisting of 22 nations for a total of circa 320 million people (Hanafi 2009), have seen a steady increase in women's sport participation and sport competition-related performance. Since Moroccan hurdler Nawal Al-Mutawaki won a gold medal at Los Angeles Olympics in 1984 (first medal for an Arab Muslim woman at the Olympic games), thirteen females earned medals until Rio 2016 Games. However, some conservative and radical groups have been trying to restrict women's participation in sports, arguing that women need to respect their Islamic social roles. In some extreme cases, female athletes received death threats. For example, Algerian Hassiba Boulmerka, who was the first woman from an Arab country to win an Athletic World Championship (Tokyo 1991), was subsequently subjected to death threats by fundamentalist groups because she showed parts of her body during competitions. Nevertheless, those threats were not sufficient to stop Boulmerka from taking part at the Barcelona Games in 1992, winning a gold medal. Habiba Ghribi, the first Tunisian woman winning a gold medal in athletics (during London 2012), also received threatening messages on social media for inappropriate clothing and anti-Islam behaviour from Salafi groups, and some ultra-conservative voices demanded the withdrawal of her nationality.

According to scholars (Koca et al. 2009; Gieb-Stuber et al. 2011; Harkness 2012; Abdelkader et al. 2017), women participation in sports is still strongly influenced by cultural and social acceptance of some behaviours in Arab societies. Al-Ansari (2011) mentions runner Ruqaya Al-Ghasara and long-distance runner Mariam Jamal, both athletes from Bahrain who took part in the Beijing 2008 Games. Al-Ghasara competed wearing a veil and became a role model for Islamic devotion, while Jamal (Ethiopian naturalised Bahraini citizen) received extensive criticism for her lack of respect towards the Islamic dress code (Al-Ansari 2011). Abdelkader et al. (2017) state that women have faced many barriers and discrimination in the Arab world because they were perceived too weak for sport (and sport to be harmful to women's health) and it was believed that sport deprived women of tenderness and femininity. According to Abdelkader et al. (2017), there are many challenges that female athletes are forced to face: the conservative stance of religious elites, the issuing of fatwas against female sport participation and rigid rules of modern sport which do not allow them to wear hijabs or burkinis in competitions. It is also problematic that sport federations may not always be unified in their approaches to the inclusion of Muslim women. For instance, FIFA (Federation Internationale de Football Association) permitted the use of veil in official women football matches in 2014 while FIBA (Fédération Internationale de Basketball) in basketball tournaments only in 2017.

Harkness and Hongsermeir (2015) believe that approaches to the issue of women in sport by MENA (Middle East and North Africa) countries should be seen as a form of resistance against a patriarchal society, where male power, cultural and religious constraints create a barrier limiting women potential to take part in sport competitions. Consequently, Harkness and Hongsermeir (2015) note that there are different behaviour patterns taken on by women hoping to become athletes: (1) *Merge athletics and Islam*; (2) *Play sports in gender-segregated settings*; (3) *Adhere to sartorial customs*; (4) *Get the family aboard*; (5) *Play sports at school*. For instance, devoted Muslim athletes, who seek high adherence to religious practices and values, usually adopt the first strategy and assess each sport on a case-by-case basis. The second strategy, competing in gender-segregated settings, can arise from the wish for a gender-autonomous space that restrict access to family. The respect of a dress code is a consequence of the need to maintain some sort of continuity between the athletic and social life, trying to escape the forms of ostracism reserved to those women who choose not to wear hijab. Some women seek family endorsement, affirming that physical activity can increase performance when carrying out filial duties. The fifth approach is to practice sport in school, often the only public space where girls are allowed to do so. As schools are a public institution, they may be the only place where female sports can obtain some sort of legitimisation.

Individual strategies aside, it is pertinent to highlight that whenever an Islamic government was/is in power, taking into consideration a generic movement towards an increased respect for Islamic traditions, or those countries which imposed harsher Sharia laws (e.g., Iran in 1979), there has never been an effective prohibition of or limitation to the participation of women in sports. However, it has been essential to organise sport activities within the context of socially acceptable behaviours underpinned by Islamic believes (Jahromi 2011). The approach to sport seems to have been the foremost issue posed on conservative regimes. However, even countries which traditionally were hardly encouraging towards women's participation in sport, like Gulf monarchies, have recently seen an increase in initiatives to promote dedicated athletic activities. For example, Saudi Arabia allowed a female athlete to take part in the 2012 Olympic Games for the first time, agreed to let women enter stadiums (in gender-reserved spaces) in 2018 and kick-started the first women's football league in November 2020 (BBC, 2021). This emancipation of women in sport is subsequent to the desire, for many Arab countries, to organise international sport events and to give an image of heightened sensibility to these matters, even if there are still many political and social barriers to overcome.

Diasporic contexts

Muslims in the West are under pressure to demonstrate loyalty to their religion and their nationality, and sport is another field to reconcile their multiple identities. For conservative-nationalistic movements and national authorities in Europe, sport is another public and secular space needing protection from the over-visibility of Islamic identity (Amara 2013). Academic literature (Benn, Dagkas and Jawad 2011; Burrmann and Mutz 2016; Pfister 2011; Charrier and Parmantier 2014; Didierjean 2015) shows how the degree of participation of Muslim women in sport is limited both in schools and in private structures like gyms and clubs. Where school PE or sport environment challenge the right of Muslim women that contrast with their embodied faith, the results is inevitably non-participation, negotiation or coercion (Hardman and McGee 2012). To contextualise this challenge to Muslim women's embodied identity in sport, the rising levels of racism and Islamophobia in Western societies during the last decades, especially against veiled women (easy to identify in social contexts) must be taken into account. Many Muslims are perceived as incapable of fitting in Western societies, or seen as a threat to national values of those societies. Many populist and nationalist European political groups tried to increase their popular consensus using those themes (e.g., Lega in Italy, Front National in France and Alternative für Deutschland in Germany). Notable political leaders have also reinforced this hostile attitude. For example, in 2016, Donald Trump, then president of the United States of America, declared to CNN: "Islam hates us and there is a little distinction between the religion and radical Islamic terrorism". Similarly, British Prime Minister Boris Johnson has compared women wearing burkas to "letter boxes" in 2018 in an article for the Telegraph. In October 2020, French President Emmanuel Macron said that "Islam is a religion that is in crisis all over the world" (Lester 2020), while announcing new measures to stop religious (i.e., Islamic) influence in the public and educational sectors (reinforcing pre-existing ones, like the ban on wearing hijab in public schools).

In this political context, episodes of discrimination towards Muslim girls and women who want to wear hijab while practicing sport are always increasing. Between 2019 and 2020, two Muslim teenagers aroused public views in the United States: the sixteen-year-old Noor Abukaram and fourteen-year-old Najah Aqeel. Both were disqualified from competitions they took part in (a 5 km long foot race in Ohio and a volleyball tournament in Tennessee) because they were wearing hijabs (Wray 2019, Elassar, 2020). In both cases, the reason given was that wearing a veil is not permitted by regulations of the different sport federations. Similar cases have also taken place in the northern regions of Italy. For instance, a thirteen-year-old girl of Egyptian origin living in Milan was rejected by a gym with the justification that the veil could get stuck in the machinery (Lalucenews, 2019). Khadija Tajeddine, a twenty-eight-year-old of Moroccan origin could not access a gym because, as the owner said: "I do not accept Batman or nuns here" (ImolaOggi, 2019). In France, after a law in 2004 banned the use of religious symbols in schools, with the consequence that wearing Islamic veil was banned too, leading to preventing many Muslim girls from taking part in PE lessons and/or going to swimming pools. Consequently, an intense debate arose, which is ongoing at the time of writing. The controversy stirred up when Decathlon (a chain store selling sport and outdoor gear) started offering in its stores a veil created specifically for Muslim runners in February 2019. This decision was opposed by many citizens and politicians, with the Minister of Health, Agnès Buzyn, going as far as saying that running hijab did not correspond to the French values and Aurore Bergè, Macron's spokesperson, even suggested boycotting the company. Decathlon responded that their goal was to increase democratisation in sport by offering a product to Muslim women, without expressing any kind of judgement. However, after threats to its workers, the company withdrew the product from the market (Robinson, 2019). It may not be possible to prove a direct connection between Islamophobia in public opinion and the particular episodes mentioned above; however, one thing can be clearly observed: in Western societies, requests of recognition of Islamic values and practices, even in sport contexts, are perceived as a form of Islamisation. There is a general non-acceptance of requests coming from Islamic minority groups with cultural and religious values extremely different to those in the majority. Such multi-ethnic and multi-cultural tensions have been taking place with increased frequency and testing the threshold of many sport organisations as well as Westerns societies.

Conclusion

Analysis of existing research and information presents a complex picture around women, sport and Islam. As an increasing number of women taking part in sports both at a professional and amateur level, their emancipation in this context seems to have become a fertile ground for growing political conflicts. Depending on the cultural and geographical context, a large swath of populist movements, whether they originate from religious, xenophobic or identity reasons, have risen to curb the freedom of choice of Muslim women who wish to practice sport. In this context, since the spring of 2020, after the COVID-19 pandemic began, many governments adopted extreme measures of lockdown and, thus, sport/physical activity became arguably the only outlet for people who were limited in their daily activities. Consequently, new questions are being asked about the future of sport and what will need to be done to keep it alive. In this emerging debate, the problem of gender empowerment for Muslim women must be of primary relevance. The global sport system will need to rethink itself and play a key role in reconsidering the matter of empowerment for Muslim women from manipulations, especially considering that sport has been a primary male domain for an extensive time. Some possible solutions that can be adopted are asking Islamic nations to increase their endorsement of women participation in sport, in exchange for the possibility to organise international events. Another approach could be to rethink regulations in various sports (concerning dress codes and the use of spaces in sports facilities) which could have a positive effect in contexts where Muslims are a minority, helping them take part in sports events, competitions or school lessons.

REFERENCES

Abdelkader, H., Harbi S., Kesri, N. and Latreche, N. (2017) 'Arab women's right to practice sport between criminalization and prohibition', *International Journal of Multidisciplinary Thought*, 6, pp. 63–72.

Al-Ansari, M. (2011) 'Women in sport leadership in Bahrain', in Benn, T., Pfister, G. and Jawad, H. (eds.), *Muslim Women and Sport*. Abingdon: Routledge, pp. 79–91.

Al-Fadel, A. (2002) 'No leaders for recreational programs', *Journal of Knowledge*, 87, Riyad Ministry of Knowledge.

Al-Khalidi, J. and Awamreh, M. (2014) 'Recreational education in Islam', *British Journal of Education*, 2, pp. 70–80.

Al-Watter N.S.Y, Hussein F., Hussein A.A (2011) *Women's narrative of sport and war in Iraq*, in *Muslim women and Sport*, Routledge, 2011

Amara, M. (2013) 'Sport and Muslim in Europe: In between or on the margin?', *Religions*, 4, pp. 644–656.

Amara, M. (2016) 'Sport and political transition in Tunisia: Another terrain of competition between Islamists and seculars', in Testa, A. and Amara, M. (eds.), *Sport in Islam and in Muslim Communities*. Abingdon: Routledge, pp. 103–112.

Ayata, A. and Tutuncu, F. (2008) 'Party politics of the AKP (2002-2007) and the predicaments of women at the intersection of the Westernist, Islamist and feminist discourses in Turkey', *British Journal of Middle Eastern Studies*, 35(3), pp. 363–384.

Bairner, A. (2015) 'Assessing the sociology of sport: On national identity and nationalism', *International Review for the Sociology of Sport*, 50, pp. 375–379.

BBC (2016) *Turkey's Erdogan warns Muslims against birth control*. Available at: https://www.bbc.com/news/world-europe-36413097 (Accessed: 15 March 2021).

BBC (2021) *Saudi Arabia first women's football league kicks off*. Available at: https://www.bbc.com/news/world-middle-east-54988746 (Accessed: 20 March 2021).

Benn, T., Dagkas, S. and Jawad, H. (2011) 'Embodied faith: Islam, religious freedom and educational practices in physical education', *Sport, Education and Society*, 16, pp.17–34.

Benn, T., Jaward, H. and Pfister, G. (eds.) (2011) *Muslim Women and Sport*. London: Routledge.

Borzì, I. (2018) *13 luglio 1908 le prime Olimpiadi al femminile*. Available at: http://www.globusmagazine.it/144012-2/#.X4qrNtAzZPY (Accessed: 14 April 2021).

Burrmann, U. and Mutz, M. (2016) 'Sport participation of Muslim youths in Germany', in Testa, A. and Amara, M. (eds.), *Sport in Islam and in Muslim Communities*. Abingdon: Routledge, pp. 33–49.

Cesari, J. (ed.) (2014) *The Oxford Handbook of European Islam*. Oxford: Oxford University Press.

Charrier, D. and Parmantier, C. (2014) 'Pratiques sportives des jeunes filles musulmanes d'origine maghrébine: Quand les politiques sportives locales se mêlent de l'intime familial', *Revue Européenne du Management du Sport*, 43, pp. 33–48.

Coşar, S. and Yegenoglu, M. (2011) 'New grounds for patriarchy in Turkey? Gender policy in the age of AKP', *South European Society and Politics*, 16, pp. 555–573.

Das, S. and Haldar, D. (2010) 'Modern physical education and sports and involvement of Muslim girls. A crucial problem', in Final Seminar, Department of Physical Education, Jadavpur University.

Didierjean, R. (2015) 'La pratique sportive des immigrées à l'épreuve de la comparaison: l'exemple des filles d'origine turque en France et en Allemagne', *Sciences sociales et sport*, 8, pp. 103–124.

Elassar, A. (2020) *A Muslim athlete was disqualified from her high school volleyball match for wearing a hijab*. Available at: https://edition.cnn.com/2020/09/27/us/hijab-volleyball-disqualified-nashville-trnd/index.html (Accessed: 15 March 2021).

Erhart, I. (2016) 'Women, Islamic feminism and children-only soccer in Erdogan's Turkey: Empowerment or discrimination', in Testa, A. and Amara, M. (eds.), *Sport in Islam and in Muslim Communities*. Abingdon: Routledge, pp. 66–80.

Fasting, K. and Walseth, K. (2003) 'Islam's view on physical activity and sport', *International Review for the Sociology of Sport*, 38, pp. 45–60.

Fedele, V. (2017) 'Religione, sport e mascolinità: l'islam diasporico e le storie dei pugili musulmani', *Funes Journal of Narratives and Social Sciences*, 1, pp. 46–61.

Gieb-Stuber, P., Kremers, S., Luft, S. and Schaller. J. (2011) 'Palestinian women's national football team aims high: A case study to explore the interaction of religion, culture, politics', in Benn, T., Pfister, G. and Jawad, H. (eds.), *Muslim Women and Sport*. Abingdon: Routledge, pp. 169–184.

Hacisoftaoglu, I. and Koca, C. (2011) 'Religion and the state: The story of a Turkish elite athlete', in Benn, T., Pfister, G. and Jawad, H. (eds.), *Muslim Women and Sport*. Abingdon: Routledge, pp. 198–210.

Hamiche, A. (2013) 'Sports in Islamic perspectives', *The Peninsula Magazine*, 17, pp. 1–3.

Hanafi, H. (2009) 'The limits of integration processes in the Arab world', *The Federalist Debate*, 1(22). Available at: www.federalist-debate.org/index.php/component/k2/item/176-the-limits-of-integration-processes-in-the-arab-world (Accessed: 5 May 2021).

Hardman, K. and McGee, J. (2012) 'Muslim schoolgirl's identity and participation in school-based physical education in England', *Sportlogia*, 8, pp. 29–41. doi: 10.5550/sgia.120801.en.029M.

Harkness, G. (2012) 'Spring forward: Female Muslim soccer players in Iraqi Kurdistan', *Soccer and Society*, 13, pp. 720–738.

Harkness, G. and Hongsermeir, N. (2015) 'Female sports as non-movement resistance in the Middle East and North Africa', *Sociology Compass*, 9(12), pp. 1082–1093.

Holt, R. (1990) *Sport and The British: A Modern History*. Oxford: Oxford University Press.

Imolaoggi (2019) *Musulmana velata esclusa da palestra privata, è bufera*. Available at: https://www.imolaoggi.it/2019/05/03/musulmana-velata-esclusa-da-palestra-privata-e-bufera/ (Accessed: 15 March 2021).

Jani, M., Ahmad, S., Diah, N. and Rahim, A. (2019) 'Integrating the principle of Maqasid Al-Shari ah and sport in the context of Muslim participation: A critical appraisal', *International Seminar on Islamic Studies*, 25th–26th September 2019, Koley Universiti Pahang.

Jahromi M.K. (2011) *Physical activities and sport for women in Iran*, in *Muslim Women and Sport*, Routledge

Judis, J.B. (2016) *The populist explosion: How the Great Recession transformed American and European politics*. Columbia Global Reports, New York.

Kizar, O. (2018) 'The place of sports in the light of Quran, Hadiths and the opinions of the Muslim scholar in Islam', *Universal Journal of Educational Research*, 6, pp. 2663–2668.

Koca, C., Bulgu, N., Henderson, F. and Hulya, A. (2009) 'Constraints to leisure-time physical activity and negotiation strategies in Turkish women', *Journal of Leisure Research*, 41, pp. 225–251.

Lalucenews (2019) *Hai il velo, non entri nella mia palestra, la storia di Rawan e la New Energy di Busnago*. Available at: https://www.laluce.news/2019/10/15/hai-il-velo-non-entri-nella-mia-palestra/ (Accessed: 30 March 2021).

Lester, D. (2020) 'President Macron says Islam "in crisis all over the world", prompting backlash'. *The Independent*, 2 October. Available at: https://www.independent.co.uk/news/world/europe/macron-france-islam-speech-seperatism-religion-b746835.html (Accessed: 10 April 2021).

Manaz, A. (2005) 'Islam and sport', *Conference: Interfaith Committee for the XX Olympic Winter Games*, Italy.

Olympian Database (2018) *List of countries in the Olympics, facts about medallists and sports for all Olympic countries*. Available at: https://www.olympiandatabase.com/index.php?id=11837&L=1 (Accessed: 18 April 2021).

Pepicelli, R. (2010) *Femminismo islamico: Corano, diritti, riforme*. Roma: Carocci Editore.

Pepicelli, R. (2017) 'Rethinking gender in Arab nationalism: Women and the politics of modernity in the making of nation-states. Cases from Egypt, Tunisia and Algeria', *Oriente Moderno*, 97, pp. 201–219.

Pfister, G. (2011) 'Muslim women and sport in diasporas: Theories, discourses and practices - Analysing the case of Denmark', in Benn, T., Pfister, G. and Jawad, H. (eds.), *Muslim Women and Sport*. Abingdon: Routledge, pp. 41–76.

Ranstorp, M. (2020) *Contextualising Salafism and Salafi Jihadism*. Danish Centre for Prevention of Extremism.

Rio Olympic Games Committee (2016) *More than 11,000 athletes will compete in the first edition of the Olympic Games in South America*. Available at: https://web.archive.org/web/20160821031645/https://www.rio2016.com/en/athletes (Accessed: 14 April 2021).

Robinson, M. (2019) *Retailer Decathlon abandons sports hijab launch in France following backlash*. Available at: https://edition.cnn.com/2019/02/27/europe/decathlon-sports-hijab-sale-halted-france-intl-scli/index.html (Accessed: 30 March 2021).

Salmela, M. and Von Schave, C. (2017) 'Emotional roots of right-wing political populism', *Social Science Information*, 56, pp. 567–595.

Schwer, M.A. (1998) 'Imperial muscular Christianity: Thomas Hughes's biography of David Livingstone', in Day, G. (ed.), *Varieties of Victorianism*. London: Palgrave Macmillan, pp. 25–39. doi: 10.1007/978-1-349-26742-2_2.

Sehlikoglu, S. (2016) 'Contestations and dichotomies concerning women's bodies and sport in contemporary Turkey. From Aysum Özebk to Neslihan Darnel', in Testa, A. and Amara, M. (eds.), *Sport in Islam and in Muslim Communities*. Abingdon: Routledge, pp. 113–123.

Sfeir, L. (1985) 'The status of Muslim women in sport: Conflict between cultural tradition and modernization', *International Review for the Sociology of Sport*, 20, pp. 283–306.

Shavit, U. and Winter, O. (2011) 'Sports in contemporary Islamic law', *Islamic Law and Society*, 18, pp. 250–280.

Sobirin M. (2017) '*Reviving Prophet's sport tradition in modern day Indonesia: does "follow the Prophet" mean radical?*', in Proceedings of the International Conference on Qur'an and Hadith Studies (ICQHS 2017), Atlantis Press

Teja, A. (2011) 'Le origini dello sport moderno', in *Conference "Uno sport per l'uomo aperto all'assoluto"*, Roma.

World Population Review (2021) *Richest Countries in The World 2021*. Available at: https://worldpopulationreview.com/country-rankings/richest-countries-in-the-world (Accessed: 20 April 2021).

Wray, M. (2019) *Muslim teen 'humiliated' after being disqualified from Ohio race for wearing hijab*. Available at: httpsglobalnews.ca/news/6078058/muslim-teen-hijab-disqualified/ (Accessed: 14 April 2021).

Yavuz, H. and Öztürk, A. (2019) Turkish secularism and Islam under the reign of Erdoğan, *Southeast European and Black Sea Studies*, 19, pp. 1–9.

22

The Politics of Passing for Trans and Non-Binary People in Physical Activity in the UK

"Yeah, Congratulations! You Look like a Cis Person, Well Done!"

Abby Barras

Introduction

Encouraging the general population to participate in regular physical activity (PA) has been 'a key part of UK public health initiatives since the end of the Second World War' (Barras et al. 2021, p. 57), but the ability to do so easily is not necessarily a given for everyone. Many transgender and non-binary people face more barriers to participation in PA than cisgender people, due to their gender identity (Jones et al. 2017a, 2017b). The purpose of this chapter is to explore what part passing plays in creating barriers, and how cisgenderism underpins a systemic challenge to the inclusion of transgender and non-binary people in PA and related areas.

For transgender people, including non-binary people (shortened to "trans" hereafter), whose bodies are frequently policed and politicised in sporting contexts, there is often fear and hesitation about participating in PA. Recent research (Jones et al. 2017b; Pérez-Samaniego et al. 2019) notes how the participatory experiences of trans-people in PA can often be less inclusive compared to cisgender people (shortened to "cis" hereafter). Reasons for these experiences vary, but can include transphobia and discrimination (Barras 2019; Barras et al. 2021), use of language (Phipps 2019), design of space and facilities (Caudwell 2020; Lewis and Johnson 2011; Oakleaf and Richmond 2017) and what is known by the trans community as passing, which this chapter will go on to discuss.

The spaces where PA takes place, such as changing rooms, often involve intense social interactions between people. For example, needing to undress in front of others and the wearing of form-fitting garments, such as swimwear. Often, these spaces become sites of gendered meaning for individuals to perform and confirm their gender, and they may find themselves 'drawing upon dominant social understandings to define themselves and others as legitimate and intelligible (or not)' (Carrera-Fernández and DePalma 2020, p. 749). This legitimacy and intelligibility are frequently measured by cisgenderism, the term used to denote the assumption or belief that cisgender identities or expressions are more legitimate than their transgender counterparts (Serano 2007).

Passing warrants further discussion regarding PA, because as Barker and Scheele (2020 p. 143) note: 'trans people are unsafe in many public and domestic spaces, risking discrimination, ridicule and even violent attack if their transness is read. At the same time, they're often seen as a danger in places like public toilets or changing rooms.' Trans people have reported that sporting spaces are not always a welcoming environment (Caudwell 2020), and the binary nature of PA can sometimes cause significant barriers to participation for trans people (Barras 2019). PA – and sport more generally – is frequently segregated by gender, including women-only and men-only teams, single-sex changing facilities and gender-specific clothing. These binary lines, and consequently the many activities which often only accommodate those individuals who visibly conform to the gender binary, can in turn 'enforce social constructions of gender, effectively excluding many transgender participants from sport' (Phipps 2019, p. 4). This can be due to a lack of gender-neutral spaces, available changing cubicles and unnecessary gendered language from staff (Phipps 2019). This can result in trans people experiencing harassment, stigmatisation, isolation and body dissatisfaction (Jones et al. 2017a), leading to trans people 'choosing not to participate in these activities or choosing to participate in individual sports that avoid body exposure and are less demanding in terms of social recognition' (Piggott 2020, p. 7).

According to research carried out by Pride Sports for Sport England (2016), 64% of LGBT people who identified as something other than male or female (e.g., genderfluid or genderqueer) were not active enough to maintain good health. As there is an established link between PA, self-esteem and reduced levels of stress (Jewett, Kerr and Tamminen 2019), this is an important consideration for those whose mental health would benefit from PA inclusion. *The Trans Mental Health Study* (McNeil, Bailey and Ellis 2012) reported that rates of current and previously diagnosed mental ill health were high amongst many participants. This study also revealed the difficulty of engaging with PA for people who identify as trans, leading to being excluded from the substantial positive change participation may bring to mental and physical health.

The rationale for the focus on the politics of passing in PA for trans people in this chapter is due to it being an area with little existing research. This carries with it the potential for creating new knowledge about trans people's lived experiences of their participation in PA. Whilst the term 'sport' can offer a kind of catch-all for the inclusion of more 'traditional' types of activities such as running, cycling, swimming or playing tennis, using instead the term 'PA' allows the inclusion of more diverse activities such as yoga, roller derby or circus gymnastics, which, in turn, allows for a more authentic collection of trans people's experiences.

PA, as defined by the World Health Organisation (2020), can be understood as 'any bodily movement produced by skeletal muscles that requires energy expenditure [and] refers to all movement including during leisure time, for transport… or as part of a person's work' (World Health Organisation 2020, n.p.). This means that PA is something many people engage in as both a way to stay fit and healthy and as a way to establish and maintain connections to friends, family and community, which instils a sense of belonging (Centre for Social Justice 2020, n.p.; Public Health England 2020 n.p.; Sherry 2010). This is of particular importance for some marginalised groups, such as trans people, where there is evidence they are more likely to have poor mental health or experience mental distress and can find it hard to ask for or access the necessary help they need (Jewett, Kerr and Tamminen 2019). In contrast to PA, sport can be defined as being 'a usually competitive physical activity which aims to use, maintain or improve physical ability and skills while providing entertainment to participants, and in some cases, spectators' (Allender, Cowburn and Foster 2006, p. 827). PA therefore differs from sport in the way in which it can include both informal activities such as walking the dog or cycling to work and active recreation such as playing football in the park.

Defining gender identity

"Transgender' (oft abbreviated as 'trans') is an umbrella term for people whose gender identity or presentation does not match the sex they were assigned at birth. It can refer to people who identify as trans men, trans women or those who identify as non-binary, though it is important to recognise that non-binary is a valid gender identity in its own right (Twist et al. 2020). The term trans covers a variety of experiences, expressions and identities including gender queer, gender fluid and gender non-conforming, though it is not limited to these descriptions and an individual may use terms inter-changeably over the life-course. For example, a person may identity as gender-queer but not necessarily as trans (Richards, Pierre-Bouman and Barker 2018).

Non-binary identities can be described as people who are not fully boys or girls (Fisher and Fisher 2018). The term can be understood as accommodating people who identify as having a gender which is in-between the usual fixed binaries of masculine and feminine, or as fluctuating between these two. It also includes people who feel that they have no gender, either permanently or some of the time (Richards, Pierre-Bouman and Barker 2018). This study uses the term 'trans' as an umbrella term but acknowledges these are identities in their own right and respects the position that sex/gender must always be self-defined (Anderson and Travers, 2017). "Cisgender" is the term for someone whose gender identity corresponds with their birth sex.

On passing

> "Passing" is the commonly used term for when a trans person is correctly gendered by strangers. Goffman (1963, p. 73) described passing 'as a practice by which a social identity that is deemed socially abnormal is nicely invisible and known only to the person who possesses it.' As Nicolazzo (2016) explains, passing occurs within various communities and includes racial passing (Butler 1990, 2004), disability passing (Brune and Wilson 2013) and gender-based passing. Bernstein-Sycamore (2006) offers a critical analysis of what passing means across a variety of identities, including race and disability, and not just for those who are trans. Rather, Bernstein-Sycamore (2006, p. 1) explores and critiques passing through 'the various systems of power seen (or not seen) in the act of passing,' concluding that 'in a pass/fail situation, standards may vary, but somebody always gets trampled.' Therefore, passing comes at a price, both personally and politically, due to what the trans community call "passing privilege."

Passing privilege is the advantage which comes from passing as cisgender. However, within the trans community, passing is sometimes a contested term because it implies there is something false or surreptitious about a person being seen as their authentic self, or "looking trans." Thus, passing is not always a desirable or wanted practice, and a trans person who passes as cisgender, or non-trans, may feel a loss due to not being seen by others as trans (Nicolazzo 2016). Butler's (1990) work on gender performativity draws parallels between how the impossible socio-cultural standards by which individuals are expected to pass can have negative effects on a person's life and livelihood. As will be revealed later, this can have a real-life impact on some of the people in this study in relation to participating in PA.

Like Bernstein-Sycamore (2006), trans author and activist Julia Serano's theory on passing is that it is perpetuated by the cisgender population and their 'incessant need to gender every person they see as either female or male' (Serano 2007, p. 177). This in turn, argues Serano, stems from the necessity to change one's appearance to conform to a (Western) gender normative representation. As Butler (1990) argued, sex, gender and sexuality are performative acts which individuals constantly display through their clothing choices, mannerisms and behaviours, all of which are culturally situated. This means our gender presentations may be fluid and ever changing but are still measured and legitimised by cisgenderism. This is because passing requires the constant repetition of gendered behaviours considered normative by others, further essentialising gender differences. In turn, these gender differences 'support gender inequality through mechanisms of exclusion and violence toward those who transgress these norms' (Carrera-Fernández and DePalma 2020, p. 748). Passing becomes a tool for both perpetuating cisgender privilege and avoiding the power of cisgenderism. Whilst at times passing might not be a desired or permanent status for some participants, it was frequently unavoidable in the context of PA. Passing was an essential and necessary aspect of PA participation, where not passing could have severe consequences for inclusion.

Methods

The focus of this chapter is concerned with how passing and passing privilege impacts on the participatory experiences of trans people in PA. In order to do this, the author has drawn on a qualitative data set gathered as part of a larger study, which explored the lived experiences of transgender and non-binary people who take part in PA in the UK. The aim of this study was to identify any barriers which could be reduced to improve inclusion for members of this community. The author conducted a total of 18 semi-structured interviews with UK-based adults aged between 23 and 70. All the participants self-identified as trans and/or non-binary.

Six interviews were conducted in person and 12 over the telephone. Participants were recruited via emails to local LGBTQI+ sports groups detailing the study and requesting gatekeepers to circulate to members, as well as posters displayed at the UK-based 2018 Trans, Non-Binary and Intersex Conference. Interviews were an average of 90 minutes long, and all participants were asked about their experiences in PA and how their gender identity had impacted on such experiences. Individuals were also asked if they had faced any barriers to participation and if they had any suggestions to improve inclusivity for trans people in PA. All of the participants were, as adults, actively engaged in some form of PA, including circus-skills, water polo and climbing, with some playing competitively. The participants in this chapter were involved in PA openly in their preferred gender identity. Participants' names have been anonymised and pseudonyms used.

Discussion

The rapidly evolving resistance to trans human rights, in conjunction with persistent antagonism towards trans people and their inclusion in public life, positions many trans people at intersecting axes of inequality. Further issues such as access to single-sex spaces and sport being questioned by those in the gender-critical feminist movement can have a direct impact on mental-health and well-being (Pearce, Erikainen and Vincent 2020). These can contribute to trans identities and lived experiences being overlooked and side-lined under the guise of concerns about cis women's safety in single-sex spaces and fairness in sport.

There are some occasional positive conversations about trans people and their visibility in the media both in the UK and the USA, which reflect a slow shift towards improvement and understanding of trans issues and representation. On his first day in office on 20th January 2021, US President Joe Biden signed an executive order expanding protections for transgender students, and later that month he appointed Dr Rachel Levine as assistant health secretary, the first openly trans woman to hold this post. In the UK on 6th May 2020, Vic Parsons in *PinkNews* reported that the judicial review sought by LGB Alliance co-founder, Ann Sinnott, to exclude trans women from single-sex spaces like prisons or refuges, was refused on the grounds that it was "unarguable" and its interpretation of the Equality Act 2010 is "wrong in law" (Parsons 2021). In other words, trans people are as entitled to use these spaces as cis people. However, as Hines (2019, p. 145) writes, 'these matters are not purely didactic…the protection of gender and sexual norms that fuel the panic of "gender fraud," can, literally, be a matter of life and death.'

Trans people's right to participate in PA and sport, especially at elite level, continues to generate debate and controversy (Piggott 2020). These debates frequently centre on the notion that embracing trans rights threatens women's sports. In a speech to the Conservative Political Action Conference on 28th February 2021, former US President Donald Trump told the audience that "Joe Biden and the Democrats are pushing policies that would even destroy women's sports" (Ennis 2021, n.p.). The discriminatory language employed by Trump reflects similar flashpoints in the UK regarding the inclusion of trans people in sport, most frequently concerning trans women. These discussions have become particularly fraught with considerable opposition from the gender-critical feminist movement (Phipps 2019), for example, the staging of public protests by campaigners such as *Fair Play for Women* about the inclusion of trans women to swim in Hampstead Heath's women-only pond in London (Richards 2019).

Missing from these discussions are the lived experiences of trans people themselves, and their inclusion in PA. Trans people often experience greater barriers to participation in PA compared to cis participants, and the spaces and facilities where PA takes place are frequently cited as problematic (Caudwell 2020). Changing rooms are often organised along gender binary lines, and they can feel disorientating for some trans people unless they pass as cisgender (Warner 2000; Yeadon-Lee 2016). For anyone who transgresses gender norms (no matter if they are trans or not), they may well be subject to the authority of cisgenderism (Nicolazzo 2016; Serano 2007).

Negotiating changing rooms

Public spaces can pose unique systemic challenges for some trans people (Doan 2010; Fiani and Han 2019), and changing rooms can be particularly so, in that they are quintessentially panoptic (Doan 2010). Bodies are often in varying stages of undress, and whilst there is no requirement to be naked, there is often an expectation of some nudity. Changing rooms are often difficult spaces for trans people to negotiate due to concerns about safety and fear of confrontation unless they pass (Barker and Scheele 2020), and the lived experiences of participants in this chapter confirmed that this fear was brought sharply into focus due to a person's gender identity being policed by other users of that space. When talking about how it feels to use gendered changing rooms to get changed before swimming, Miles (25, trans man) said:

> A lot of the men's changing rooms don't have cubicles to change in…when you get changed it's quite scary, you don't know who else is changing there, and you don't know what their views are. In terms of safety, I do get worried…when I was more androgynous, and I was changing in the women's spaces I would still get asked to leave sometimes.

Miles had not undergone top surgery (the common term for chest reconstruction surgery), and did not fully pass as male, which meant he had to continue using the women's changing rooms at the pool. The appearance of breasts on a person are often the strongest visual clue used to signify a person's gender (Fisher and Fisher 2018), and the removal of breasts through top surgery often has a significant impact on how a person's gender is read. Yet, Miles did not quite pass as female either, and on one occasion, he was confronted by two teenage girls in the changing rooms. One of the girls asked Miles why he was in the women's changing rooms. Miles said that he "never liked saying, well I am [female], 'cos I never felt that way, it made me feel weird saying that I was a woman. They wouldn't believe me… so I'd have to flatten my jumper back to show them, show them I had a chest."

Miles's experience demonstrates the power of cisgenderism, the 'structuring of social norms around the assumption that everyone has cis bodies and experiences' (Pearce 2018, p. 220). The girls in the changing room, a single-sex space, whose own bodies and experiences we can assume to be cisgender, bestowed on them the authority to challenge Miles. In turn, this leads to a delegitimisation of Miles's own transgender identity, and his own designation of his gender and his body (Bartholomaeus and Riggs 2017). In contrast, James (28, trans masculine, non-binary) reflects on how he found it "difficult to participate [in sport] …as a trans person [before top surgery]. It's got easier, just because, you know, I pass."

Both Miles and James were subjected to the authority of cisgenderism, which both policed and authorised their presence in gender-segregated spaces because their presence there was deemed to be at odds with other (cisgender) users. Being confronted in the changing room resulted in Miles having to submit to a non-consensual biographical disclosure, which resulted in the disruption of his gender identity and concerns for safety. When this happened, Miles had to say, "I'm not a boy and then I'd feel really awful. I felt like I had to pretend to be female to use it [the changing rooms]."

Having to disclose an intimate aspect of a person's body in order to satisfy the authority of cisgenderism was also experienced by Alix (27, trans masculine, non-binary). Alix was questioned by a person at a personal training session about their top surgery scars in the changing rooms. Alix said:

Alix: It's telling someone that their body is less valid I think…there was the whole "we couldn't tell" going on as well.
Abby: You pass, so that means that everybody's happy!
Alix: Yeah, congratulations! You look like a cis person, well done! (laughs).

Alix's experience here is significant in the ways in which the recognition of a person's gender identity is authenticated by another person – a cisgender person – and that the power of this authority qualifies them to confer this authenticity. In Alix and Mile's cases, this authentication was conferred by strangers, which in both cases was neither sought out nor welcomed. Participating in PA required them to unwillingly disclose their gender identity and risk destroying their own passing privilege to satisfy the cisgender environment (Serano 2007).

Trans people navigating PA

Passing was not only negotiated in changing rooms. Some participants acknowledged that their passing privilege allowed for a more stress-free experience when participating in PA. For example, Persia (trans woman, 70) did not worry about being confronted when she went swimming at a public pool because she has "small hips and a wider top, like swimmers, women swimmers are like that." Persia explained, when she goes swimming "nobody notices." Persia passes as cisgender and is not subject to the same questions as Miles and Alix.

Persia passes not only as female when she goes swimming, she also passes as a female swimmer, because her "small hips and a wider top" are physical attributes commonly associated with a swimmer's physique. There is a meaningful intersection at play in Persia's experience here, the connection between a person's gender identity and their sporting identity, which become aligned through their ability to pass: Persia's body is not just a woman's body; it is a woman swimmer's body. This forms what Fiani and Han (2019, p. 188) call 'a foundation of resilience' upon which Persia is able to validate her gender identity when she goes swimming. As Bartholomaeus and Riggs (2017, p. 16) note when talking about cisgenderism in education, the benefits of not having one's gender brought into question can mean 'there are no battles regarding the use toilets/bathrooms and changing rooms.' However, cisgenderism also negatively impacts on cisgender people, 'in that the gender binary creates narrow and restrictive expectations, such as in the form of what people do, like, wear and feel based on gender' (Bartholomaeus and Riggs 2017, p. 16).

After all, many people wrestle with body confidence in settings where PA takes place, and swimming in particular can trigger anxieties (Caudwell 2020). Considering how exposed bodies can be in swimming pools, it is easy to understand how the passing privilege Persia and James allude to facilitates a less stressful participatory experience because their gender is read as cis. When Persia's experience of swimming is contrasted to that of Miles's, who was not always read as his preferred gender identity, it highlights how inclusion in PA is compromised by cisgenderism, and the impact this can have on trans people.

Creating spaces for trans people in PA

The existence of spaces and sessions designed only for trans people to participate in PA may advocate for inclusivity but may still present challenges. Like passing privilege, there are both benefits and limitations for these spaces and sessions. As Miles said: "it's nice that there are trans specific places and clubs, like swimming, that's really important, 'cos it's intimidating. You feel very self-conscious." These spaces (and the trans inclusive organisations operating them) enable users to feel safe, accepted and without the need to negotiate the authority of cisgenderism. Miles said: "that's what brings it [doing sport] all together. 'Cos there's a space where you can support each other during a game." Alix also noted: "people know they can go to those spaces [and feel ok], which gyms in general just aren't doing." Alix would only swim "at a trans specific swim group." James found going to a trans-only swimming session meant he was still able to do the activity he enjoyed. However, James knew:

> some people won't go [or who] wouldn't feel comfortable going alone…they go with another, usually trans person, so they feel safe, or they'll go to a trans only space like the swimming… people really rave about that, it's really given people an opportunity to do something they otherwise wouldn't have done.

The existence of these spaces, arguably much like the spaces aimed at new parents or LGBT communities, certainly provide an important and necessary service. This is clearly of great benefit to those participants who feel self-conscious about being involved in PA, but trans-only spaces and sessions are limited and not always available. Therefore, some participants, such as Alix, would still use, as they called them, "straight" sporting spaces, which are more frequently available. The lack of trans-only spaces and sessions make it challenging for individuals to establish a regular exercise routine. In addition, trans-only sessions often run much less frequently than cisgender sessions, at inconvenient times, such as late in the evening, and were often subject to cancellation at short notice (Brighton and Hove Trans Needs Assessment 2015).

Whilst Joe (26, trans masculine, non-binary) was transitioning, they stopped playing water polo and instead joined a women's (LGBT) rugby team. They described how passing as male caused confusion for the opposite team, because:

> My breasts were really small to start with, I'm tall… my voice got deep…I was quite hairy, and they were like, what are you doing here (laughs)? I'd play at the back and yell and everyone would turn around and say there's a man on the team!

Joe's experience shows gender identity is often signalled by the body and its physical characteristics. These physical characteristics are frequently binary-framed, that men are hairy, and women are not, or that breasts are only acceptable on women, as was Miles's experience. It is not that Joe's body is *not* passing as male, it is that it *is* passing as male, and is viewed as being in the wrong place/wrong team. The allowances for this confusion are rarely given in favour of inclusion for the trans participant – rather, the space a person occupies when they do not pass is often challenged by others (who are cisgender) and without consent. Rather, the impact a trans person's presence has on a cis person's experience in PA is privileged. This is in part due to the cisgenderism prevalent in PA and the value placed on passing.

The impact of not passing

The anxiety Miles felt about being in a "male space" and the concern about safety and violence (having experienced trans/homophobic bullying in the past) was shared by Alix. Alix spoke of how when they use the changing room at the gym, they move between the communal area and the shower area wearing a towel around their lower body (Alix had not had 'bottom surgery'). They said:

> There were two guys having a conversation behind me, one of the men had gone out on a date with a woman and found out she was trans, and it was one of the most horrific things that had happened to him…I was frozen by my locker, I had a towel around me…if I'd turned around, they would have seen that I was trans…it could get violent, so I stood there for ages in my locker, waiting for them to leave.

These experiences can have an impact on future visits. Alix said that even though a person may have had surgery to help them pass better, "you're worried that if there's a space you want to use, you worry you're going to get assaulted, or verbally assaulted. And all you want to do is get changed."

Passing can be understood as belonging both to the tyranny of assimilation (Bernstein-Sycamore 2006), and, as Butler (2004) understands it, a protective force. As this chapter has revealed, trans people often have to strive to 'embody the norm' (Butler 2004, p. 217) as a survival method in the context of binary PA inclusion. Alix must assimilate in the changing rooms to ensure survival, which in turn means denying their own gender identity, at least by cisgender standards. Trans embodiment is then neither fixed nor concrete, because certain spaces require a person to pass by cisgender expectations. As participants' lived experiences have shown, a person needs to occupy a presentation considered 'normal' by cisgender people if they are to be able to use the same gendered spaces, or risk confrontation and possible harm.

This was also reflected in Abelson's (2014) research examining how trans men construct their masculinities in public spaces such as on public transport or in the gym. Abelson found that respondents' masculine practices changed depending on who they interacted with and the level of safety (or potential violence) they perceived. Respondents' concerns for safety, and their masculine practices, changed according to variation in transition, physical location, audience and their physical stature. Trans men, argued Abelson (2014), do not become immune to the threat or reality of violence (from other men) by virtue of now being seen as men. Whilst they enjoyed increased access to public spaces or found that their body afforded them a new sense of safety, their 'geography of fear shifted' (Abelson 2014, p. 558). That is, these trans men now experienced a new set of fears, brought on by 'the privilege of male violence' (Abelson 2014, p. 558). This meant that the trans men in Abelson's research felt that their change of position relative to women was not always a positive change, because it involved the possibility of being subjected to other men's violence in a new way. Like the participants in this chapter, their perceptions of safety changed based on their own body, the space they were in and the people they engaged with. Abelson's research highlights similarities with the participants in this research, because of these perceptions of safety, such as in changing rooms or showers, and the ways in which cisgender people often control the spaces where PA takes place. Passing did not resolve this, because cisgendered expectations still demanded trans men not only present as cis male, but act like cis men, too.

Concluding thoughts

This chapter highlighted that experiences of passing for trans people are varied and can have an impact on their PA inclusion due to the gender-segregated nature of the PA environment. More importantly, passing is often only required by cisgendered expectations regarding who should be occupying a particular space. However, passing is not always desired or welcomed by some individuals, and passing privilege sometimes brought with it its own set of issues.

Being read as your preferred gender requires the constant repetition of considered normative behaviours (Carrera-Fernández and DePalma 2020). This is labour-intensive for some trans people, but not engaging in this performativity, or failing at it, can have consequences. These consequences included being confronted in spaces or having to disclose one's transgender identity non-consensually. Therefore, for many trans people undergoing transition (and even once they pass), negotiating PA is anxiety inducing. A person's gender presentation, thus, becomes intrinsic to their PA participation. This raises questions about safety in PA, not just for those who are trans, but also those who may not conform to cisgender expectations of masculine and feminine stereotypes.

Within changing rooms, the binary gender norms, stereotypes and presumptions, which characterise many sporting communities, can be a barrier not only for trans people, but for cis men and women too. Navigating gendered spaces was challenging for many participants who had experienced both direct hostility and a sense of threat in these spaces. As this chapter argued, barriers to PA participation are often due to existing gender binaries in and how activities are organised. Even so, trans people in this study still found a way to negotiate their participation. Sporting spaces, like bodies, are gendered, where intense social interactions between people often take place, becoming sites of meaning for individuals to perform and confirm their gender. In these spaces, people often draw upon dominant social understandings of gender to define themselves and others as legitimate users of that space (Abelson 2014; Kauer and Rauscher 2019). The body exposure these spaces require can be a significant barrier to people unwilling or unable to conform to cisgendered corporeal expectations.

Some of these issues could be addressed, for example, by additional cubicles which would afford more privacy for users, not necessarily just for people who identify as trans. The ways in which spaces such as changing rooms and gyms are laid out could be reconfigured to accommodate not just gender-diverse people, but those who may have cultural/religious needs. Gendered clothing and pronouns are easily adapted, and bodies of all shapes, sizes and ages might feel more welcome in these spaces (Spandler et al. 2020). However, the onus of making PA more inclusive for trans people should be on the managers of those spaces and not subject to the authority of cisgenderism.

A common reason for participating in PA is that it maintains (or improves) physical health and well-being but can also improve mental health and quality of life (Sherry 2008). Being read as their correct gender helped some participants to affirm their gender identity and align in with their sporting identity. Through everyday repetition, gender norms are entrenched in PA and associated areas 'to the point that they appear commonsensical, factual, and natural' (McBride 2021, p. 105). Against this backdrop, it becomes imperative to foreground the lived experiences of trans people in PA, and the barriers which need to be challenged.

REFERENCES

Abelson, M.J. (2014) 'Dangerous privilege: Trans men, masculinities, and changing perceptions of safety', *Sociological Forum*, 29(3), pp. 549–570.

Allender, S., Cowburn, G. and Foster, C. (2006) 'Understanding participation in sport and PA among children and adults: A review of qualitative studies', *Health Education Research*, 21(6), pp. 826–835.

Anderson, E. and Travers, A. (2017) *Transgender athletes in competitive sport*. London: Routledge.

Barker, M.J. and Scheele, J. (2020) *Gender: A graphic history*. London: Icon.

Barras, A. (2019) 'Hostility to elite trans athletes is having a negative impact on participation in everyday sport', *The Conversation*, 22 March. Available at: https://theconversation.com/hostility-to-elite-trans-athletes-is-having-a-negative-impact-on-participation-in-everyday-sport-113296 (Accessed 1 July 2021).

Barras, A., Frith, H., Jarvis, N. and Lucena de Mello, R. (2021) 'Timelines and transitions: Understanding transgender and non-binary people's participation in everyday sport and physical exercise through a temporal lens', in Clift, B., Gore, J., Gustafsson, S., Bekker, S., Costas Battle, I. and Hatchard, J. (eds.), *Temporality in qualitative inquiry: Theories, methods and practices*. Oxon: Routledge, pp. 57–71.

Bartholomaeus, C. and Riggs, D.W. (2017) *Transgender people and education*. 1st edn. New York: Palgrave Macmillan.

Bernstein-Sycamore, M. (2006) *NOBODY PASSES: Rejecting the rules of gender and conformity*. 1st edn. New York: Seal Press.

Brighton and Hove Trans Needs Assessment (2015) *Trans community research*. Available at: https://www.brighton.ac.uk/_pdf/research/sec/brighton-hove-trans-community-research-project-2015.pdf (Accessed 4 April 2021).

Brune, J.A. and Wilson, D.J. (2013) *Disability and passing: Blurring the lines of identity*. 1st edn. USA, Philadelphia: Temple University Press.

Butler, J. (1990) *Gender trouble*. 1st edn. London: Routledge.

Butler, J. (2004) *Undoing gender*. 1st edn. London: Routledge.

Carrera-Fernández, M. and DePalma, R. (2020) 'Feminism will be trans-inclusive or it will not be: Why do two cis-hetero woman educators support transfeminism?', *The Sociological Review*, 68(4), pp. 745–762.

Caudwell, J. (2020) 'Transgender and non-binary swimming in the UK: Indoor public pool spaces and un/safety', *Frontiers in Sociology*, 5(64), pp. 1–12.

Centre for Social Justice (2020) *A level playing field: Equalising access to sport and access for young people after Covid-19*. Available at: https://www.centreforsocialjustice.org.uk/wp-content/uploads/2020/12/CSJ-Sports_Policy_Paper-FINAL.pdf (Accessed 26 February 2021).

Doan, P. (2010) 'The tyranny of gendered spaces', *Gender, Place and Culture*, 17(5), pp. 635–654.

Ennis, D. (2021) 'What Donald Trump's transphobia really means for women's sports', *Forbes*, 28 February. Available at: https://www.forbes.com/sites/dawnstaceyennis/2021/02/28/what-donald-trumps-transphobia-really-means-for-womens-sports/?sh=333087925e66 (Accessed 10 April 2021).

Fiani, C.N. and Han, H.J. (2019) 'Navigating identity: Experiences of binary and non-binary transgender and gender non-conforming (TGNC) adults', *International Journal of Transgenderism*, 20(2-3), pp. 181–194.

Fisher, F. and Fisher, O. (2018) *The trans teen survival guide*. London: Jessica Kingsley Publishers.

Goffman, E. (1963) *The presentation of self in everyday life*. 2nd edn. London: Penguin.

Hines, S. (2019) 'The feminist frontier: On trans and feminism', *Journal of Gender Studies*, 28(2), pp. 145–157.

Jewett, R., Kerr, G. and Tamminen, K. (2019) 'University sport retirement and athlete mental health: A narrative analysis', *Qualitative Research in Sport, Exercise and Health*, 11(3), pp. 416–433.

Jones, B.A., Arcelus, J., Bouman, W.P. and Haycraft, E. (2017a) 'Sport and transgender people: A systematic review of the literature relating to sport participation and competitive sport policies', *Sports Medicine*, 47(4), pp. 701–716.

Jones, B.A., Arcelus, J., Bouman, W.P. and Haycraft, E. (2017b) 'Barriers and facilitators of physical activity and sport participation among young transgender adults who are medically transitioning', *International Journal of Transgenderism*, 18(2).

Kauer, K.J & Rauscher, L. (2019). Negotiating gender among LGBTIQ athletes: sport as a space for disruption and reproduction. In: K. Krane. (Ed.) *Sex, gender, and sexuality in sport: Queer inquiries* (49–66). London, UK: Routledge.

Lewis, S. and Johnson, C. (2011) 'But it's not *that* easy: Negotiating (trans)gender expressions in leisure spaces', *Leisure/Loisir*, 35(2), pp. 115–132.

McBride, R.S. (2021) 'A literature review of the secondary school experiences of trans youth', *Journal of LGBT Youth*, 18(2), pp. 103–134.

McNeil, J., Bailey, L. and Ellis, S. (2012) *The trans mental health study*. Available at: http://acthe.fr/upload/1445680190-trans-mental-health-study-2012.pdf/ (Accessed 8 May 2021).

Nicolazzo, Z. (2016) 'It's a hard line to walk: Black non-binary trans* collegians' perspectives on passing, realness, and trans*-normativity', *International Journal of Qualitative Studies in Education*, 29(9), pp. 1173–1188.

Oakleaf, L. and Richmond, L.P. (2017) 'Dreaming about access: The experiences of transgender individuals in public recreation', *Journal of Park and Recreation Administration*, 35(2), pp. 108–119.

Parsons, V. (2021) 'Judge throws out LGB alliance founder's fight to ban trans women from single-sex spaces', *Pink News*, 6 May. Available at: https://www.pinknews.co.uk/2021/05/06/lgb-alliance-ann-sinnott-judicial-review-fails-london-high-court-equality-act/ (Accessed 1 June 2021).

Pearce, R. (2018) *Understanding trans health: Discourse, power and possibility*. UK, Bristol: Policy Press.

Pearce, R., Erikainen, S. and Vincent, B. (2020) 'TERF wars: An introduction', *The Sociological Review Monograph*, 68(4), pp. 677–698.

Pérez-Samaniego, V., Fuentes-Miguel, J., Pereira-García, S., López-Cañada, E. and Devís-Devís, J. (2019) 'Experiences of trans persons in physical activity and sport: A qualitative meta-synthesis', *Sport Management Review*, 22(4), pp. 439–451.

Phipps, C. (2019) 'Thinking beyond the binary: Barriers to trans* participation in university sport', *International Review for the Sociology of Sport*, 56(1), pp. 81–96.

Piggott, L. (2020) 'Transgender, intersex and non-binary people in sport and PA: A review of research and policy'. Available at: https://sramedia.s3.amazonaws.com/media/documents/f0a71dc4-c08b-43f9-a4c2-0968ecb8e331.pdf.

Pride Sports for Sport England (2016) *Sport, PA & LGBT*. Available at: https://www.sportengland.org/media/11116/pride-sport-sport-physical-activity-and-lgbt-report-2016.pdf (Accessed 7 July 2019).

Public Health England (2020) *Health matters: PA - prevention and management of long-term conditions*. Available at: https://www.gov.uk/government/publications/health-matters-physical-activity/health-matters-physical-activity-prevention-and-management-of-long-term-conditions#wider-role-and-benefits-of-physical-activity (Accessed 5 February 2021).

Richards, A. (2019) 'Row erupts after Hampstead Heath's women's pool allows transgender bathers', 31 December. Available at: https://www.standard.co.uk/news/london/row-erupts-after-hampstead-heath-women-s-pool-allows-transgender-bathers-a3729056.html (Accessed: 7 March 2022)

Richards, C., Pierre-Bouman, W.P. and Barker, M-J. (2018) *Genderqueer and non-binary genders*. 1st edn. London: Palgrave Macmillan.

Serano, J. (2007) *Whipping girl: A transsexual woman on sexism and the scapegoating of femininity*. 1st edn. USA, New York: Seal.

Sherry, E. (2008) '(Re)engaging marginalized groups through sport: The Homeless World Cup', *International Review for the Sociology of Sport*, 45(1), pp. 59–71.

Spandler, H., Erikainen, S., Hopkins, A., Caudwell, J., Newman, H. & Whitehouse, L. (2020). *Non-binary inclusion in sport*. Leap Sports. Available from: https://leapsports.org/files/4225-Non-Binary%20Inclusion%20in%20sport%20Booklet.pdf. (Accessed 3 March 2022).

Twist, J., Vincent, B., Barker, M.J. and Gupta, K. (2020) *Non-binary lives*. 1st edn. London: Jessica Kingsley Publishers.

Warner, M. (2000) *The trouble with normal: Sex, politics, and the ethics of queer life*. 1st edn. Cambridge, Mass: Harvard University Press.

World Health Organisation (2020) 'Physical activity'. Available at: https://www.who.int/news-room/fact-sheets/detail/physical-activity (Accessed 8 February 2021).

Yeadon-Lee, T. (2016) *Trans bodies, trans selves: A resource for the transgender community*. 1st edn. Oxford: Oxford University Press.

Part IV
Gender, Politics, Sport and Physical Activity Case Studies

Part IV

23
Gender Politics of Social Media
A Case Study of Megan Rapinoe

Connor MacDonald and Jamie Cleland

Introduction

Sport has been used as a site for political and social activism for decades (see Bairner, Kelly and Lee, 2016), but over the last decade, a number of high-profile sportsmen and women have increasingly started to advocate their personal views on various topics via their social media platforms, such as Facebook, Twitter, and Instagram. One of the most pertinent reason behind this is that these platforms provide opportunities for sportsmen and women to control the message they want to convey to their followers and the wider media that breaks away from a reliance on the traditional sports media that had previously dominated the narrative of activism in sport throughout the twentieth century.

To understand how social media platforms have been utilized for political and social activism, this chapter is split into two main sections. As we explain in the first part of this chapter, before the introduction of social media in the twenty-first century, most political and social activism (that which was widely recognized) was often undertaken by black sportsmen who used their status, via the traditional sports media, to predominantly challenge racial injustice. However, in the twenty-first century, high-profile sportswomen have increasingly become an influential component of more multifaceted and intersectional activism that has moved away from purely racial matters (although they continue to remain prominent). Thus, in the second part of this chapter, we focus on one of the most prominent examples of this multifaceted gendered activism: American soccer player Megan Rapinoe, who has often used her social media platforms to advocate her personal views on a range of social and political issues, including sexual orientation and gender equality, racial injustice, military conflict, and human rights. Here, we examine elements of Rapinoe's activism, and how her identity as a cisgender, white, openly lesbian, successful professional sportswoman gives added substance to her personal views presented via her social media platforms.

Gendered political and social activism in sport

Cooper, Macaulay and Rodriguez (2019, pp. 154–155) define activism as 'engagement in intentional actions that disrupt oppressive hegemonic systems by challenging a clearly defined opposition while simultaneously empowering individuals and groups disadvantaged by

DOI: 10.4324/9781003093862-27

inequitable arrangements.' Throughout history, sports have always contained athletes engaging in some form of political or social activism. Much of the focus of the mainstream media has often concentrated on the activism of black sportsmen and how they have used their high-profile status to fight for racial justice and social change. For example, in his 2016 keynote address at the North American Society for the Sociology of Sport conference, prominent sociologist Harry Edwards proposed a framework consisting of four waves to explain athlete activism in the United States (US) and how black sportsmen had utilized the traditional platforms available to them, notably the sports media, to try and influence some form of change in sport and wider society (see Edwards, 2017).

The first wave occurred from the turn of the twentieth century until the end of World War II and consisted of black athlete activists such as Joe Louis and Jack Johnson fighting for greater racial recognition for the black community. Jesse Owens was also an important figure during this wave, particularly through his sporting accomplishments at the 1936 Olympic Games in Berlin that challenged Hitler's Aryan race ideology (Milford, 2012). According to Edwards, the second wave (from 1946 to the 1960s) was led by black sportsmen such as Jackie Robinson and comprised calls for desegregation and better access to US society as well as the sports industry for black Americans. The third wave (from the 1960s to the 1970s) consisted of the emergence of the Civil Rights Movement and Black Power Movement and was led by black sportsmen including Muhammad Ali, Tommie Smith, and John Carlos, who demanded greater respect and racial justice for the black community.

Following the third wave, Edwards referred to the period from the 1970s until the beginning of the twenty-first century as one of stagnation, with a lack of black athlete activism taking place during this time. Some of the reasons for this was the success of high-profile black sportsmen such as basketballer Michael Jordan and golfer Tiger Woods, with the growing commercial value of their individual image resulting in a form of economic protection surrounding their endorsement deals and not wanting to be viewed as portraying what could be perceived as a controversial image to their sponsors or millions of fans following their career (Agyemang, 2012; Cunningham and Regan, 2012; McDonald, 1996).

From 2005 onwards, Edwards refers to a fourth wave, largely in response to the treatment of black Americans by police officers and the racial bias experienced in the US justice system. This has led to a broader activist movement seeking greater social and legal justice and includes support from male and female athletes across a range of sports, including high-profile black American sportsmen and women such as tennis players Venus and Serena Williams and basketballer LeBron James. However, other non-American athletes are also prominent activists, such as British tennis player Andy Murray, who regularly speaks out about gender equality in tennis.

While sportsmen have often been viewed as the arbiters of protest and activism, sportswomen have also played an important role, but with much less publicity. Possibly stemming from the patriarchal history of sport (see Messner and Sabo, 1990), the activist endeavors of sportswomen have not received the same public exposure, yet they have been a prominent force against social and political inequity (Cooky and Antunovic, 2020). Borders (2018), for example, highlights the long history of women's basketball players in the US being extremely vocal activists for the Black Lives Matter (BLM) movement that has seen them regularly raise awareness on racial injustice within the US justice system. In fact, it may have been in women's college basketball in the US where one of the first BLM protests was championed by an individual athlete. Ariyana Smith took a knee, raised a fist, and raised her other hand to mimic putting her hands up – a common order given by police and a symbol used in racial justice activism – during the playing of the national anthem, then laid down in defiance for the 2014 killing of Mike Brown by police in the US (Cooky and Antunovic, 2020; Zirin, 2014). Although Smith's actions put her basketball career in jeopardy, she did not receive the widespread attention that some of her male sporting counterparts have received for similar actions – as we discuss later in the chapter. Indeed, Smith is not alone as even as far back as the 1970s, athletes like tennis player Billie-Jean King were not gaining the same attention as their male counterparts. It took a 'Battle of the Sexes' tennis match between King and Bobby Riggs to be seen as a watershed moment in girls and women's sport (particularly in advancing the professionalization of women's tennis), yet King did not recognize her activist identity until much later in the twentieth century (Spencer, 2000).

Even though athlete activism may have been a rare occurrence given the number of sportsmen and women who have participated in different sports across the world throughout history, since the turn of the twenty-first century, there is a more vocal number of high-profile athletes willing to share their personal opinions on a broad range of social and political issues on their own terms rather than through a third party such as the traditional sports media (Schmittel and Sanderson, 2015), which has a history of framing the narratives and discourses surrounding the identity and actions of athletes that reaffirm dominant ideologies and hegemonies (Cooky and Antunovic, 2020; McClearen, 2015; Milford, 2012; Spencer, 2000). One of the factors helping a resurgence of activism that Edwards (2017) referred to is the introduction of social media platforms such as Twitter, Facebook, and Instagram. Given their widespread consumption, they help connect high-profile athletes with millions of fans or followers where opinions and information can be immediately disseminated, shared, debated, supported, or contested without any framing from the mainstream media. They also subsequently appeal to the wider mass media who are constantly searching for news stories to drive traffic to their own stories and platforms.

As suggested by Boykoff and Carrington (2020, p. 830): 'Celebrities exude mediatized individuality and personify social value through their accomplishments, skills, status, and outward appearance.' Whether elite athletes will become activists, according to Kaufman (2008), depends on the context as well as their social relations. However, the list of public-facing sporting activists is not exhaustive, which is why those athletes willing to publicly state their personal views on political and social issues receive significant attention from fans, followers, and the media. One of the most high-profile athlete activists in the twenty-first century is former San Francisco 49ers National Football League (NFL) quarterback Colin Kaepernick. In protesting against racial injustices taking place across the US (such as the killing of unarmed black men and women by the police), Kaepernick initially sat on the bench during the playing of the American national anthem at a pre-season NFL game against Green Bay Packers in August 2016, but then changed his protest to kneeling for the remainder of the season.

Although widely acclaimed for using his on-field and off-field platforms to raise awareness of racial injustice and giving added momentum to protests taking place under the banner of BLM, Kaepernick's much publicized stance negatively impacted his career as he was blacklisted and subsequently no NFL team decided to sign him from the 2017–18 season. However, his actions did encourage collective action amongst other players in the NFL and subsequently across other sports who also used on-field kneeling at the start of their matches to highlight racial injustice taking place in the US and other parts of the world (Cooper, Macaulay and Rodriguez, 2019). Despite receiving support for his stance, Kaepernick was also labelled anti-American in other quarters, including some NFL and wider sport fans and by sections of the media and politicians including the then US President Donald Trump, who argued that he was being disrespectful to the American flag and the military who serve the country by protesting during the playing of the national anthem (Martin and McHendry, 2016).

It is not just racial injustice that athletes actively look to highlight, however, but also other issues surrounding social justice and inequalities, lesbian, gay, bisexual, and transgender (LGBT+) rights, human rights, politics, and military conflict. As suggested by Schmidt (2018, p. 2): 'While sports might once have been "just a game", today the sporting world intersects with nearly every other part of social life.' The traditionally held belief that politics and sport should be kept separate simply does not hold anymore. While on-field protests remain in place in some quarters before the start of matches, it is the exposure provided by social media platforms like Facebook, Instagram, and Twitter that really brings the views of elite athletes into the lives of millions of people across the world.

Megan Rapinoe

One prominent social and political activist is US soccer player Megan Rapinoe. Reflecting the growth of women's sport from the late twentieth century and subsequent interest in high-profile sportswomen, Rapinoe has a global audience interested in her general profile, including her image, the sport she plays, and her views on social and political matters. This is helped by her presence on various social media platforms which has amassed, at the time of writing, 2.2+ million Instagram followers, 748,000+ Facebook followers, and 916,000+ Twitter followers. Although there are other high-profile sportswomen who engage in social and political debate via a variety of social media platforms, Rapinoe's presence as a white, openly lesbian woman (she came out in 2012), and the various debates in which she engages outside of racial injustice add a different dimension to contemporary athlete activism. For example, as well as highlighting matters of racial injustice, Rapinoe has also become an outspoken campaigner for social change on a range of issues, including gender and sexual orientation equality, domestic violence, military conflict, a higher minimum wage, as well as campaigning for better prisoner rights given her brother has served time in prison.

To give a sense of the profile of Rapinoe, at the 2019 Women's World Cup, not only did she contribute to the US team's success by winning the Golden Boot by being the highest goal scorer across all of the players competing in the tournament, but she also received the Golden Ball for being voted the most valuable player across all the competing teams. Moreover, outside of the success of the World Cup, she also received the Ballon d'Or award in 2019 after being voted as the best female soccer player in the world.

Rapinoe came into the activism spotlight in September 2016, when she knelt during the national anthem ahead of her game for Seattle Reign in the National Women's Soccer League in the US. When probed for the reasons why she did this, Rapinoe explained how she wanted to show solidarity with Colin Kaepernick in protesting racial inequality and police brutality, but to also raise the inequalities she had faced as a lesbian woman (Frederick, Pegoraro and Schmidt, 2020). Later in 2016, Rapinoe also knelt during a national team game, forcing US Soccer to change their policy in 2017 that required players to stand during the national anthem. While the traditional media framed their coverage on the method of her protest (i.e., kneeling and the inspiration gained from Kaepernick), Rapinoe was able to convey her own reasons behind the protest on her social media platforms by locating it within the racial injustice Black Americans face every day in the US (Coombs *et al.*, 2020).

Despite finding support for her on-field stance, Schmidt and colleagues (2019) examined the comments left on the public Facebook pages in the immediate aftermath of the national anthem protests of Colin Kaepernick and Megan Rapinoe in 2016 and found dominant themes of nationalism, patriotism, and militarism amongst the many dissenters willing to publicly disapprove of their actions. Indeed, dissent levied towards activist sportsmen and women is not new. Athletes who have previously decided to take a social or political stance have often faced an intense and loud backlash (Kaufman, 2008; Sanderson, Frederick and Stocz, 2016), and some of this backlash could even be potentially damaging to their career (Darnell, 2012). Rapinoe, for instance, is someone who consistently vocalizes her opinions and standpoint on various social and political issues across her social media platforms and has consequently suffered some repercussions from within the US national team as well as reputational damage, yet this pales in comparison to what Colin Kaepernick has faced.

From a political standpoint, Rapinoe was often critical of the previous US president, Donald Trump. In the build up to the 2016 US presidential election, for example, Rapinoe attended campaigns supporting Trump's opponent, Hillary Clinton. Stemming from her open political position, Rapinoe retained an active presence on Twitter during the 2020 US presidential and senate elections. She is an open and staunch democratic supporter and has used her social media platforms to endorse prominent congressional democrats like Alexandria Ocasio-Cortez, Bernie Sanders, and Elizabeth Warren. On her social media platforms in the build up to the 2020 elections, she highlighted important election information, encouraged her followers to get out and vote, and celebrated the nomination of Joe Biden as the next US president to replace Trump. This is evidenced by her posts on Instagram where many were explicitly political, such as her discussions with political figures and supportive posts towards BLM (e.g., a post on Instagram advertising The Movement for Black Lives with a picture that read 'Defund the Police!') and an accompanying post that listed out demands. Posts like these led to a significant number of comments, some of which levied dissent and abuse towards Rapinoe, as well as social justice and the liberal/left-wing political ideology more generally (we discuss the various layers of resistance towards Rapinoe's activism later in the chapter).

While Trump was in office, further spotlight was paid to Rapinoe when a video recorded before the 2019 Women's World Cup was released of her responding to a journalist's question of whether she would attend the White House to meet with the then president should the team win the tournament with: 'I'm not going to the fucking White House' (Frederick, Pegoraro and Schmidt, 2020, p. 2). The publication of this view led to Donald Trump replying via Twitter that Rapinoe should 'never disrespect our Country, the White House, or our Flag, especially since so much has been done for her & the team' (Frederick, Pegoraro and Schmidt, 2020, p. 2). Not surprisingly, much media fanfare followed, and Rapinoe was quickly forced to clarify her comments, which she did alongside the coach of the US women's national team, Jill Ellis, where she took the opportunity to publicly implore the support from her teammates as well as highlight the platform she has to debate issues of inequality and injustice as such a high-profile sportswoman:

> …considering how much time and effort and pride we take in the platform that we have, and using it for good, and for leaving the game in a better place and hopefully the world in a better place – I don't think that I would want to go and I would encourage my teammates to think hard about lending that platform or having that co-opted by an administration that doesn't feel the same way and fight for the same things we fight for.
>
> (Das, 2019, para. 3)

Indeed, the fallout with Trump during the 2019 Women's World Cup did not deter Rapinoe who used the spotlight of winning the tournament to lead calls for an equal pay structure and conditions for women playing soccer for the US national team given the significant pay disparity between the men and women's national teams. At the heart of this campaign was that since the inaugural Women's World Cup in 1991, the US women's team has won the tournament four times, while the US men's team has not won one (the first men's World Cup was in 1930). Viewed as a more liberal approach taken by Rapinoe and her fellow activists – a demand for change that includes an oppressed group (i.e., women playing for the national team) in an oppressing power structure (i.e., that which is controlled by men) – it was argued that this afforded their stance, and eventual lawsuit, more positive media coverage and greater pressure being applied to the need for pay equality for the national women's team (Cooky and Antunovic, 2020).

While previous analysis of Rapinoe's activism (see, for example, Bullingham and Postlethwaite, 2018; Schmidt et al., 2019) points to widespread support in the mainstream media, other research has found that Rapinoe can be seen as a polarizing character due to her unmitigated approach for justice and her demand for attention while she has the platform and the spotlight to do so (Frederick, Pegoraro and Schmidt, 2020). For example, Cavalier and Newhall (2018) refer to the negative response by fans to US Soccer publicly showing support for same-sex marriage (of which Rapinoe was a prominent advocate), with fans stating that sport and politics should remain separate (however unlikely that continues to be).

Similar responses were found to posts Rapinoe made on Instagram and Facebook during the 2020 US election. Some of this dissent took the form of support for Donald Trump and/or viciously denigrating his opponent, Joe Biden, as demonstrated in response to an Instagram post featuring a video discussion between Rapinoe and Joe and Jill Biden (May 1, 2020). Other posts, like Rapinoe advertising an upcoming discussion with Democratic Congresswoman Alexandria Ocasio-Cortez regarding the passing of a stimulus package bill for COVID-19 relief (March 30, 2020), questioned their intelligence. However, it was in this post where we began to find a larger amount of explicit misogynistic rhetoric and insults (through the use of words like 'bitch' and 'cunt'). While these are not uncommon responses towards public figures, especially a high-profile sportswoman like Rapinoe, the abuse she received in the comment sections on posts were sexist *and* homophobic. By way of illustration, some of the comments responding to a Facebook post of a childhood photo of Rapinoe with the text stating 'most likely to be an activist' (May 12, 2020) referred to her as looking like 'a little boy' and 'a dude' and calling her a 'freak,' while comments from another post featuring a quote from her new book (November 10, 2020) labeled her 'disgusting,' with another lambasting her for supporting transgender rights. Another comment went even further in their dislike of Rapinoe's activism: 'Disrespectful cunt. Kneel with Kaepernick. we [sic] will find a way to deal with shit like you. one [sic] way or the other [sic].'

As we have already presented, some of the reasons behind comments like those discussed above are because her activism challenges dominant and privileged systems and identity groups, particularly surrounding gender, sexuality, and race, and this leads to various forms of resistance and backlash from general dissenters through to homophobes and misogynists. While the mainstream media have largely been supportive of Rapinoe's stances on various issues, their platforms do not often allow for the public's direct responses (such as by leaving comments at the end of articles) to those athletes actively speaking out about social and political issues. Conversely, social media offers a public opportunity for all internet-users, whether you are a fan or follower or not, to immediately respond; thus, dissent and sometimes vitriolic attacks can be found on these platforms. Yet, the level of dissent found in the responses does not deter Rapinoe in championing the social and political activism she believes in publicly conveying.

Indeed, she is not alone in this. The vilification of athletes who take a political and social activist stance is, once again, nothing new (Frederick, Sanderson and Schlereth, 2017; Kaufman, 2008), especially if the message is seen by dissenters as more radical or challenging to traditional norms such as the dominance of male patriarchy, whiteness, and heterosexuality. For instance, when the BLM movement was championed by black sportsmen LeBron James, Chris Paul, Dwayne Wade, and Carmelo Anthony at the 2016 ESPYS, the dialogue taking place on social media turned quite toxic and racist (Frederick, Pegoraro and Sanderson, 2019). Unfortunately, this sort of reaction to racial and gendered activism on social media has become worse. At the time of writing, added pressure is being placed on social media companies by various governments across the world to rid their platforms of opportunities to engage in hate speech.

Despite this, it is also important to recognize how Rapinoe's social media presence also exists within a liberal-capitalist framework. Amongst the tweets, Facebook, and Instagram posts of the great feats of her teammates, her excitement in watching basketball games, celebrating her engagement with WNBA star Sue Bird, and her activist and political posts is the subsequent exposure to many advertisements. More specifically, this is in reference to her commercial partnerships with companies, such as Visa, but this is often located within a wider message of, for instance, empowerment of girls and women.

The privileges that come with a successful sporting career allows Rapinoe the platform to speak out and stand in solidarity with political and social justice movements, some very radical in nature, yet still attract various endorsement contracts that she publicizes to her wider audience. It is also important to recognize the privilege of whiteness (see Long and Hylton, 2002; Cleland, Adair and Parry, 2022) that Rapinoe captures within the realm of sports activism and how she can avoid having her 'race' define and impact her career like it has some prominent black athletes such as Colin Kaepernick. For example, despite protesting on similar issues by using the same method, Kaepernick has not received nearly as many endorsement contracts as Rapinoe and has still not been hired to play in the NFL. The racism found in corporate America, specifically advertising and marketing (Boulton, 2020), outlines that athlete activism that diverts from the status quo can negatively impact the consumption of products associated with that individual athlete (Mudrick, Sauder and Davies, 2019). Moreover, the stereotypes associated with black activists (e.g., abrasive, aggressive, violent, anti-American – see, for example, Banks, 2018) seem to play an important role in why someone as outspoken as Rapinoe still manages to gain endorsement contracts with various organizations and continue to work as a professionally paid athlete yet remain so openly political.

Capitalism, and the companies that exist in this global economic model, have been known to co-opt radical movements, and activism in sport is one frontier that has not remained untouched. For instance, Nike's commercials that starred Kaepernick were making a statement by having the advert cinematically center on him, yet did not say much about the racial injustices he was fighting against. Banet-Weiser (2018), Cooky and Antunovic (2020), and Darnell (2012) have all argued that different forms of activism are more acceptable and visible (i.e., corporate feminism and activism that do not challenge power structures), while more radical activism that challenges traditional, orthodox power structures are rendered less visible and are often denigrated. However, there seems to be more of a blend, or at least less of a discrete dichotomy or binary, in play when viewing Rapinoe's posts on her social media platforms. Here, Rapinoe's activism, and the platforms she uses to display such activism, are paradoxical. On the one hand, while some of the activism she has been associated with could be seen as being more liberal, some of her posts and standpoints certainly challenge various power structures and the traditional structure of society. And what better set of globally popular platforms like Twitter, Instagram, and Facebook to project a liberal, socially progressive standpoint than by a high-profile, successful white sportswoman like Rapinoe.

Conclusion

This chapter has examined gendered political activism by focusing on Megan Rapinoe, who provides an important case study given her presence as a white, openly lesbian woman, who has a successful sporting career. Her on-field success has provided her with off-field capital that is actively played out to millions of people via her social media platforms. Although social media offers an autonomy for athletes to publicly share their views – which differs from the traditional reliance on the newsprint media to interpret and share their opinions and thoughts – Rapinoe's presence on Twitter, Instagram, and Facebook exists within a capitalist and Western-liberal context, juxtaposing the more radical elements of her posts. In some ways, given the profile of Rapinoe, she has become a leader of white sportswomen that transcends the boundaries of the soccer pitch. And while this may lead to dissent and various forms of discriminatory abuse from people posting comments in response to her messages, her large following are also supportive of her role-model status, and her activism, particularly in relation to her openness about her sexuality and her campaign for greater gender equality.

As we have illustrated in this chapter, Rapinoe has effectively used social media platforms to support her stance on challenging authority and campaigning for positive social and political change. However, it must be recognized that this resistance takes place within the context of her privileged position as a successful, white sportswoman, located within the paradox of online activism – a space that can promote radical ideas, while simultaneously kowtowing to neoliberal discourse and institutions. Social media, and the way Megan Rapinoe and other activist athletes are using it, offers a new story-telling means of communication that breaks away from the traditional sports media who have dominated sport activism narratives for decades (Cooky and Antunovic, 2020). Indeed, a consequence of this action is that there is a willingness for the mainstream media to report on the issues Rapinoe raises to the wider public via their own channels of communication, thus expanding the calls, as well as resistance, for some form of social and political change to take place. Subsequently, sport as a realm for activism is becoming more prominent, and socially recognized and accepted, where personal narratives expressed on social media are increasingly finding a way into the wider public discourse.

REFERENCES

Agyemang, K. (2012) 'Black male athlete activism and the link to Michael Jordan: A transformational leadership and social cognitive theory analysis', *International Review for the Sociology of Sport*, 47(4), pp. 433–445, DOI: 10.1177/1012690211399509.

Bairner, A., Kelly, J. and Lee, J.W. (2016) *Routledge handbook of sport and politics*. London: Routledge.

Banet-Weiser, S. (2018) *Empowered: Popular feminism and popular misogyny*. Durham, NC: Duke University Press.

Banks, C. (2018) 'Disciplining Black activism: Post-racial rhetoric, public memory and decorum in news media framing of the Black Lives Matter movement', *Continuum*, 32(6), pp. 709–720, DOI: 10.1080/10304312.2018.1525920.

Borders, L. (2018) 'Inspiring and empowering women: The WNBA leading the way into the 21st century', *Journal of Legal Aspects of Sport*, 28(2), pp. 121–125, DOI: 10.18060/22566.

Boulton, C. (2020) 'Corporate ads said Black Lives Matter. But the industry creating them is nearly all white', *NBC News*, 18 July. Available at: https://www.nbcnews.com/think/opinion/corporate-ads-said-black-lives-matter-industry-creating-them-nearly-ncna1231540 (Accessed: 3 May 2021).

Boykoff, J. and Carrington, B. (2020) 'Sporting dissent: Colin Kaepernick, NFL activism, and media framing contests', *International Review for the Sociology of Sport*, 55(7), pp. 829–849, DOI: 10.1177/1012690219861594.

Bullingham, R. and Postlethwaite, V. (2018) 'Lesbian athletes in the sports media: Ambivalence, scrutiny and invisibility', in Magrath, R. (ed.) *LGBT athletes in the sport media*. London: Routledge, pp. 51–74.

Cavalier, E. and Newhall, K. (2018) '"Stick to soccer": Fan reaction and inclusion rhetoric on social media', *Sport in Society*, 21(7), pp. 1078–1095, DOI: 10.1080/17430437.2017.1329824.

Cleland, J., Adair, D. and Parry, K. (2022) 'Fair go? Indigenous rugby league players and the racial exclusion of the Australian national anthem'. *Communication & Sport*, 10 (1): 74-96. DOI: 10.1177/2167479520935598

Cooky, C. and Antunovic, D. (2020) '"This isn't just about us": Articulations of feminism in media narratives of athlete activism', *Communication & Sport*, 8(4-5), pp. 692–711, DOI: 10.1177/2167479519896360.

Coombs, D., Lambert, C., Cassilo, D. and Humphries, Z. (2020) 'Flag on the play: Colin Kaepernick and the protest paradigm', *Howard Journal of Communications*, 31(4), pp. 317–336, DOI: 10.1080/10646175.2019.1567408.

Cooper, J., Macaulay, C. and Rodriguez, S. (2019) 'Race and resistance: A typology of African American sport activism', *International Review for the Sociology of Sport*, 54(2), pp. 151–181, DOI: 10.1177/1012690217718170.

Cunningham, G. and Regan, M. (2012) 'Political activism, racial identity and the commercial endorsement of athletes', *International Review for the Sociology of Sport*, 47(6), pp. 657–669, DOI: 10.1177/1012690211416358.

Darnell, S. (2012) 'Paying the price for speaking out: Athletes, politics and social change', *International Council of Sport Science and Physical Education special bulletin*, 63, pp. 1–6.

Das, A. (2019) 'Megan Rapinoe digs in after Trump criticism: "I stand by the remarks"', *New York Times*, 27 June. Available at: https://www.nytimes.com/2019/06/27/sports/soccer/megan-rapinoe-trump-white-house.html (Accessed: 2 January 2021).

Edwards, H. (2017) 'Framing a century of black athlete activism', 3 April. Available at: https://www.isenberg.umass.edu/news/harry-edwards-framing-century-black-athlete-activism (Accessed: 13 March 2021).

Frederick, E., Pegoraro, A. and Sanderson, J. (2019) 'Divided and united: Perceptions of athlete activism at the ESPYS', *Sport in Society*, 22(12), pp. 1919–1936, DOI: 10.1080/17430437.2018.1530220.

Frederick, E., Pegoraro, A. and Schmidt, S. (2020) '"I'm not going to the f*** ing White House": Twitter users react to Donald Trump and Megan Rapinoe', *Communication & Sport*. Available at: https://journals.sagepub.com/doi/abs/10.1177/2167479520950778?journalCode=coma

Frederick, E., Sanderson, J. and Schlereth, N. (2017) 'Kick these kids off the team and take away their scholarships: Facebook and perceptions of athlete activism at the University of Missouri', *Journal of Issues in Intercollegiate Athletics*, 10, pp. 17–34.

Kaufman, P. (2008) 'Boos, bans, and other backlash: The consequences of being an activist athlete', *Humanity & Society*, 32(3), pp. 215–237, DOI: 10.1177/016059760803200302.

Long, J. and Hylton, K. (2002) 'Shades of white: An examination of whiteness in sport', *Leisure Studies*, 21(2), pp. 87–103, DOI: 10.1080/02614360210152575.

Martin, S. and McHendry Jr, G. (2016) 'Kaepernick's stand: Patriotism, protest, and professional sports', *Journal of Contemporary Rhetoric*, 6(3-4), pp. 88–98.

McClearen, J. (2015) 'The paradox of Fallon's fight: Interlocking discourses of sexism and cissexism in mixed martial arts fighting', *New Formations*, 86, pp. 74–88, DOI: 10.3898/NEWF.86.04.2015.

McDonald, M. (1996) 'Michael Jordan's family values: Marketing, meaning, and post-Reagan America', *Sociology of Sport Journal*, 13(4), pp. 344–365, DOI: 10.1123/ssj.13.4.344.

Messner, M. and Sabo, D. (1990) *Sport, men and the gender order: Critical feminist perspectives*. Champaign, IL: Human Kinetics.

Milford, M. (2012) 'The Olympics, Jesse Owens, Burke, and the implications of media framing in symbolic boasting', *Mass Communication and Society*, 15(4), pp. 485–505, DOI: 10.1080/15205436.2012.665119.

Mudrick, M., Sauder, M.H. and Davies, M. (2019) 'When athletes don't "stick to sports": The relationship between athlete political activism and sport consumer behavior', *Journal of Sport Behavior*, 42(2), pp. 177–199.

Sanderson, J., Frederick, E. and Stocz, M. (2016) 'When athlete activism clashes with group values: Social identity threat management via social media', *Mass Communication and Society*, 19(3), pp. 301–322, DOI: 10.1080/15205436.2015.1128549.

Schmidt, H.C. (2018) 'Sport reporting in an era of activism: Examining the intersection of sport media and social activism', *International Journal of Sport Communication*, *11*(1), pp. 2–17, DOI: 10.1123/ijsc.2017-0121.

Schmidt, S., Frederick, E., Pegoraro, A. and Spencer, T. (2019) 'An analysis of Colin Kaepernick, Megan Rapinoe, and the national anthem protests', *Communication & Sport*, 7(5), pp. 653–677, DOI: 10.1177/2167479518793625.

Schmittel, A. and Sanderson, J. (2015) 'Talking about Trayvon in 140 characters: Exploring NFL players' tweets about the George Zimmerman verdict', *Journal of Sport and Social Issues*, *39*(4), pp. 332–345, DOI: 10.1177/0193723514557821.

Spencer, N.E. (2000) 'Reading between the lines: A discursive analysis of the Billie Jean King vs. Bobby Riggs "Battle of the Sexes"', *Sociology of Sport Journal*, *17*(4), pp. 386–402, DOI: 10.1123/ssj.17.4.386.

Zirin, D. (2014) 'Interview with Ariyana Smith: The first athlete activist of #BlackLivesMatter', *The Nation*, 19 December. Available at: https://www.thenation.com/article/interview-ariyanasmith-first-athlete-activist-blacklivesmatter/ (Accessed: 2 January 2021).

24

Gender and the Politics of Patriarchy in Zimbabwean Football Administration

Tafadzwa B Choto and Manase Kudzai Chiweshe

Introduction

Football is a popular sport in Zimbabwe. Though no official statistics exist, Chiweshe (2013) attests that football is arguably the most popular sport in the country. The administration of football in Zimbabwe has been often described negatively as being characterized by maladministration, lack of transparency and corruption (Ncube 2014; Chiweshe 2014). Literature focusing on football administration in Zimbabwe is scant, and most of what has been written focuses on apparent failures and challenges confronted by football administrative bodies like the Zimbabwe Football Association (ZIFA). Ncube (2014) and Choto (2016) focus predominantly on the politicisation of football administration in Zimbabwe and how that has negatively impacted the operations of administrative bodies like ZIFA, who are forced to prioritize the interests of the political elite over administrative best practices like meritocracy. Chiweshe (2019) focuses on the "Asiagate Scandal", a match fixing corruption scandal that engulfed football administration in Zimbabwe. This chapter offers a connected but nuanced analysis of the experiences of Henrietta Rushwaya, who was the first and only female chief executive of ZIFA. The chapter situates the experiences of Henrietta Rushwaya as a female football administrator within the wider patriarchal and political discourses in Zimbabwe.

The inclusion of women in football administration has largely been tokenistic and can be defined as negative integration (Williams and Hess 2015). Negative integration is when the inclusion of women in mainstream football administration has exacerbated their situation and led to entrenchment of further gender inequalities. The negative integration, according to Williams and Hess (2015), is expressed firstly in the delayed incorporation of female football by international and national football federations as long as they could without threatening the continuation of the monopoly of what is termed "legitimate football". This situation is aptly illustrated by Hofmann and Sinning (2016) using the illustrative case of how the German Football Federation deliberately stifled the development of women's football in the 1970s and 1980s. This highlights that there is a somewhat accepted distinction between male football, which is assumed to be the genuine and legitimate football, and female football, which is generally viewed as being a counterfeit. This constructed legitimacy of male football draws its strongest justification in the historical lateness of the professionalisation and organisation of female football. The negative integration, according to Williams and Hess (2015), is also demonstrated in the peripheral treatment of female football when compared to male football. For instance, the vast technological support and specialisation around male football compared to the closed and unappealing organisational treatment that is given to the female game by male-dominated football associations.

Engh (2011) argues that administrative integration of women's football into the male-dominated South African Football Association (SAFA) in 2000 meant that female football administrators lost power and the women's subcommittee did not have a representative in the SAFA national executive committee, which is the highest decision-making body in South African Football. This is also true in the context of Sweden, where, according to Hjelm and Olofsson (2003), the integration of women's football into the Swedish Football Federation (SFF) resulted in men exerting total dominance over women's football. This is reflected by the fact that for the first decades following the integration of women's football into the SFF, there was no female on the SFF board or any woman within central management and no woman participated in the annual meetings or elected in the representative assembly. These statistics speak to the fact that the late administrative integration had negative reconfigurations on both the female game and on the female football administrators who lost their previous autonomy and the capital to navigate and strategically position themselves in a hostile andronormative context.

An overview of gender and patriarchy in Zimbabwe

Traditional, pre-colonial societies in Zimbabwe were male dominated, with women, even if economically active, mostly excluded from control over the means of production such as land comparable to the proletariat in industrial societies, who had very little control over their productive output (Cheater 1985). Generally, women were also excluded from formal political and jural authority, which was possessed and inherited by males (Cheater 1985). The influence of women politically and judicially was therefore limited to informal spaces (Bourdillon 1976). Males not only controlled the economic, political and judicial spaces, but also asserted their control over the reproductive capacities of women, an essential part in establishing their masculine identity (Kesby 1999). Women's authority and visibility in traditional Zimbabwean societies such as the Shona and the Ndebele, like in other pre-colonial African societies (e.g., Swazi), was generally more pronounced in the domestic spaces where they could exert control over their daughters and those of her patrilineal kin (Marwick 1966; Cheater 1985).

The coming of colonialism in the 1890s, to some extent, worsened the marginalisation of women through establishment of the gendered migrant labour system, whereby men went to work in the urban areas, farms and mines whilst women and old men were left in native communal areas (Cheater 1985). The gendered migrant labour practices entrenched the "ideology of domestication", that is, the ideological basis foregrounding women's restriction to domestic spaces and exclusion from economic and political public spaces (Cheater 1990). Colonialism also resulted in the enactment of legislation that strengthened male hegemony of females; for instance, the Land Husbandry act articulated that only male heads of households could own land. Whilst the Native Adultery Punishment Ordinance acknowledged married women as being properties of their husbands, outlawing all forms of infidelity and adultery (Barnes 1992). Indigenous women were at this point confronted by an alliance between indigenous and European structures of patriarchal control, which reinforced and transformed each other, evolving into new structures of domination (Schmidt 1990).

The attainment of political independence in 1980, to a limited extent, transformed the constellation of powers governing gender relations and to a certain extent helped roll back some of the structural and legislative oppressive arrangements that undermined women during the colonial period (Kesby 1999). The ideological basis behind this transformation can be attributed to the discursive legacy of Marxist feminism which was articulated in post-independent socialist policies such as growth with equity as well as in legislative instruments like the Legal Age of Majority Act and the Sex Disqualification Removal Act, which gave women equal access to social services like education, as well as full legislative authority, none of which had existed during the pre-colonial and colonial period (Kesby 1999). The significance of these developments need not be over emphasized, but must be understood as only one element of the complex, post-independence political dynamics in which the ruling nationalist regime sought to balance the competing interests of its heterogeneous base. The practical reality is that the legislative edicts of the state have remained very much limited by patriarchal discourses and practices which considerably affect gender relations on the ground (Kesby 1999).

Football politics and gender in Zimbabwe

Darby (2002) documents that the advent of colonialism in the last half of the nineteenth century radically transformed African societies. Part of this transformation included the erosion of its traditional sports and cultural forms and replacing them with western sport traditions. The history of football in Africa thus begins with Europe and is an indelible legacy of colonialism (Akindes 2010). In colonial Zimbabwe, football was introduced by the members of the Pioneer Column that arrived in Salisbury (modern-day Harare) in 1890, who played football as part of their recreational activities (Guillianotti 2004). Football was subsequently introduced to the indigenous Africans by the missionaries and political authorities for their hegemonic and ideological reasons (Zenenga 2012). For the colonial authorities, sport, and football in particular, was a cost-effective means of socially controlling the indigenous urban populace. It was believed to be an activity that would consume their energies and time which would have been normally devoted to congregating and expressing their dissatisfaction with the new colonial political order (Novak 2006; Stuart 1995). On the part of the missionaries, the motivation for introducing football among the Africans in colonial Zimbabwe and other African countries such as Nigeria was to spread Christian moralities rooted in Victorian androcentric ideologies that emphasized sobriety, obedience, discipline and cooperation among young African males (Darby 2002). Football became, therefore, an important social site where political and religious discourses intersected and a tool in the construction of new moral discourses among the native Africans which aligned with the expectations of the colonial political elites. From the perspective of political authorities, football was, thus, simply a tool to control the hostile and aggressive militarized masculinities that characterized the pre-colonial socio-political order (Darby 2002).

Whilst the European colonialists saw football as a useful tool in entrenching their social and political hegemony, they unwittingly created an important frontier for resistance and political confrontation (Darby 2002). For instance, the political space in Rhodesia was repressive with trade unions and political organisations banned, but football clubs were one of the few spaces where Africans had some degree of autonomy and control (Stuart 1995). The football crowd in the stadia provided cover to the nationalistic and political leaders constantly fearful of Government spies and arrest (Stuart 1995). Football stadia, thus, became an integral element in the political struggle against colonialism, a kind of safe space for political meetings and political orientation of the populace. The role of certain African football teams in the resistance against colonialism has also been highlighted. Stuart (1995) argues that the formation of Dynamos football club in 1963 not only coincided with the heightening of black nationalistic efforts but was a direct challenge to the colonial administration and the imposition of proto-apartheid policies. Dynamos football club was formed in 1963 in the Harare African Township, the oldest African suburb in Salisbury. From its formation, Dynamos identified with the African working class. The team's success on the playing field was demonstrated by it winning the Rhodesian Premier League by outwitting the predominantly white Salisbury Callies in the year it was formed. This quickly transformed it into a medium by which urban Africans could demonstrate their strength and resilience against the governing white minority (Choto, Chiweshe and Muparamoto 2017).

The attainment of independence in 1980 brought the Zimbabwe African National Union (ZANU) into power, which was very much conscious of the double-edged role of football in promoting both hegemonic and counter-hegemonic discourses (Zenenga 2012). The nationalist regime, therefore, harnessed the popularity of football to promote its nationalistic vision. Part of this strategy involved infiltrating the administration of football. From 1980, almost every member of the ZIFA's executive had some links with ZANU and its political successor the Zimbabwe African National Union Patriotic Front (ZANU PF), which was formed as a result of a merger between the two nationalistic political parties ZANU and the Zimbabwe African People's Union (ZAPU) in 1987. ZIFA has, thus, been argued to be a mere extension of ZANU PF (Muponde and Muchemwa 2011; Ncube 2014). Football administration in Zimbabwe is an important constituency that the political establishment strategically invades and controls in order to avert political resistance and accumulate political capital (Choto 2016). Ncube (2014) argues that, since independence, despite efforts by the ruling ZANU PF party to gain the support of the masses through football by putting football as part of the major political events like the independence day celebrations, ZANU PF has found itself being challenged through the football discourse. The main political challenger to ZANU PF, the Movement for Democratic Change (MDC), appropriated football symbols such as whistles and red cards as part of their political strategy to oppose ZANU PF (Chiweshe 2018). Through utilizing football symbolism in their political struggle against the opposition, MDC revived the role that football had played during the colonial period, as an instrument in the struggle against a repressive, colonial political order.

Despite its long-term political significance, historically, football in Zimbabwe was mostly consumed in football stadia. However, football stadia have been a well-recognised space associated with masculinity and, thus, these venues are often considered inappropriate spaces for "upright" women (Chiweshe 2014). Football stadia in Zimbabwe are spaces where orthodox forms of hegemonic masculinity are reproduced and affirmed, which promote a sexist and misogynistic attitude towards females. Phallic symbols punctuate everything about football fandom in Zimbabwe. Football fandom is traditionally a patriarchal institution that effectively serves the reproduction of hegemonic masculinity and allows little room for women, because femininity is constructed as an object of sexual conquest and physical inferiority and, thus, clashes with values associated with football. Stadium language reinforces this masculinity and makes meaning only in that context, which is why the same language is not spoken at home. Football stadia are places where hegemonic masculine traits, practiced in society perversely through patriarchy, are openly celebrated and reinforced. For instance, male superiority may be expressed via singing within the context of stadiums to reinforce beliefs about women's inferiority as part of everyday life in Zimbabwe (Chiweshe 2018; Ncube and Chawana 2018). Consequently, for Chiweshe (2018), football stadia are environments where men use language as a powerful tool to entrench women's subordination. Through this language, stereotypes about women are passed across generations of men. Football songs are a form of language expression that conveys meaning not only about the game but society's gender values in

Gender and the Politics of Patriarchy

general. Therefore, the songs sung in Zimbabwean football stadia align with the hegemonic hetero-normative discourse which normalizes heterosexuality and reinforces male sexual dominance

Document analysis

This chapter is based on document analysis which seeks to analyse emergent themes from a variety of written sources including journals, newspaper reports, books and working papers. Document analysis is a form of qualitative research in which documents are interpreted by the researcher to give voice and meaning to a selected topic (Bowen 2009). The focus of the analysis should be a critical examination, rather than a mere description, of the documents. Document analysis works best when the purpose is to recognise patterns. Document analysis, like other analytical methods in qualitative research, requires that data be examined and interpreted in order to elicit meaning, gain understanding and develop empirical knowledge (Corbin and Strauss 2008). Specifically, the researchers adopted a grounded theory approach that involved the simultaneous collection and analysis of data (Thornberg and Charmez 2014). Data was collected from newspaper articles, academic publications and Facebook posts concerning Henrietta Rushwaya and football in Zimbabwe. The data analysis involved focus and theoretical coding where emerging themes from the data were captured, synthesised and then related to broader perspectives on the narratives and experiences of women in Zimbabwe.

The politics of ZIFA and the rise of Henrietta Rushwaya

The administration and structuring of Zimbabwean football is similar to that of England and South Africa with two main bodies being mandated with football administration in Zimbabwe, namely the ZIFA and the Zimbabwe Premier Soccer League (ZPSL) (Ncube 2014). The ZIFA constitution article 1.1 states that ZIFA is a private organisation responsible for the governance of Zimbabwean football. ZIFA is in charge of all the national teams and is also responsible for all organized football in the country from the lower divisions to the ZPSL. The supreme legislative body of ZIFA is the congress or assembly, which is composed of ZIFA councillors drawn from the five ZIFA affiliates, namely the Premier Soccer league, Women's football, National Association of Secondary School heads, Futsal representatives and beach football representatives. The executive functions of ZIFA are conducted by the ZIFA Executive or the ZIFA board, which is composed of seven elected officers including the President and the Vice President. The third body is the ZIFA secretariat, which is composed of employed ZIFA officials headed by the Chief Executive Officer and responsible for the day-to-day running of the association.

The origins of ZIFA date back to May 1963, when two racially segregated football associations united to form a non-racial football body, the National Football Association of Rhodesia (NFAR), which was renamed the Zimbabwe Football Association at independence in 1980 (Ncube 2014; Novak 2020). The history of ZIFA from 1980 has been characterized by power struggles between individuals and rival camps, which have intersected with ethnic identities and political affiliations, as well as corruption and maladministration (Ncube 2014; Choto 2016). Particularly evident is the relationship between ZIFA administrators and the ruling ZANU PF where the party sees football administration as an important constituency in its quest to maintain political hegemony. As a result, many ZIFA administrators like Leo Mugabe, Philip Chiyangwa, Rafiq Khan and even Henrietta Rushwaya are members of ZANU PF (Ncube 2014; Choto 2016). In addition to being dominated by people with political links to the ruling

ZANU PF, ZIFA has also been male dominated, with all the principal officers at ZIFA from 1980 being male and Henrietta Rushwaya being the first woman to be appointed the ZIFA Chief Executive Officer in May 2007 (Ncube 2014).

Henrietta Rushwaya was born in 1968; a trained teacher by profession, she joined the Sports and Recreation Commission (SRC) around 1998. In 2000, she earned a scholarship to study Sports Management in Norway. On returning from Norway in 2004, she was appointed to be the director of Sports in the office of the Vice-President of Zimbabwe Joseph Musika (Dzamara 2007). She was subsequently appointed to be the Chief Executive Officer of ZIFA in March 2007, a post she held until October 2010 when she was dismissed on allegations of mismanagement of funds, corruption and insubordination (Ncube 2014). To a certain extent, Rushwaya's appointment was perceived positively as an important step in liberating a traditionally inaccessible domain for women, but her appointment and conduct were also very much controversial (Ncube 2014), which will be analysed below.

Narratives around Henrietta Rushwaya as a football administrator

Henrietta Rushwaya as a moral misfit

Henrietta Rushwaya, like most women involved in football in Zimbabwe, has often been labelled especially by football fans both in the stadia and digital platforms as being of questionable moral standing. Damion (2009) notes that one dominant narrative among male football fans is that Henrietta Rushwaya was appointed to the apex of football administration because of the sexual favours she offered to powerful politicians. This narrative negates the fact that she had a recognized qualification in sports management and solely interprets her appointment as being purely nepotistic. This narrative is also emphasised on Facebook and comments on online newspaper stories. One notable example is a comment on a story in the Newsday of October 25, 2012 where Rushwaya had apparently hired a new legal team to represent her in a legal case against ZIFA. The comment noted: "This is embarrassing ZIFA should learn to employ people of integrity and good repute rather than hiring people of dubious character, look she is prostituting even in football; our beloved game has gone to the dogs". In this post, Rushwaya is represented as being morally unfit to be a football administrator, with this moral unfitness being connected to assumed sexual promiscuity.

It is interesting to note that the newspaper article had not mentioned Rushwaya's sexual conduct but some of the commentators somehow managed to link Rushwaya's appointment as ZIFA CEO with her being sexually immoral. This narrative was also reflected in the football stadia itself. For instance, a post on May 26, 2012 by Soccer 24 Zimbabwe (a Facebook page dedicated to reporting news about football in Zimbabwe) noted that: "When Henrietta Rushwaya made her way into the football stadia, a section of football fans started chanting, prostitute". Other Facebook users who commented on this post agreed with this narrative that had been articulated in the stadia and even went on to label her as a prostitute and an immoral woman. This association of women occupying public roles in traditionally male-dominated spaces with prostitution is not unique to football; it can also be observed in politics where female politicians like Thokozani Khupe and Joyce Mujuru, who become leaders of the Movement for Democratic Change – Tsvangirai (MDC-T) and the Zimbabwe People's First (ZPF), have also been labelled as prostitutes by rival supporters (Hove 2019). Historically, Jeater (1990) has argued that in colonial Rhodesia, the morality discourse was effectively a tool utilized by colonial and African patriarchal systems to socially sanction and control women who were perceived to be "independent". That is, women who, for instance, migrated to urban centres, mines and abandoned rural areas did not conform to the expectations of submissive and passive emphasized femininity and, consequently, were at the receiving end of social sanctions meted out by the patriarchy. This social sanctioning was an ideological weapon utilized by the African patriarchy with the primary intent of discouraging other women from following the example of these rogue females, thereby maintaining male control of their productive and reproductive capacities (Jeater 1990; Kesby 1999).

In relation to football that has been defined as the last bastion of hegemonic masculinity (Welford 2008), the very presence of a woman in a position of administrative authority and power over males possesses a significant threat to male privilege and prestige. The labelling of female administrators as "prostitutes" can, thus, be interpreted as a means through which threatened males communicate to both women in leadership positions as well as to women aspiring to be in such positions that they are not welcome and not suited for holding positions of power. Patriarchy, therefore, sustains its hegemony in football through the construction of negative portrayal of and narratives around women by attacking those who directly challenge its dominance. In this sense, the rise of Henrietta Rushwaya can be understood as a major threat to the androcentricity of Zimbabwean football as well as to stereotyped notions of passive emphasised femininity. Therefore, the misogynistic attacks directed at her are reflective of the attempts by football patriarchy to reassert its threatened dominance and hegemony.

Henrietta Rushwaya as a political pawn

The appointment of Henrietta Rushwaya as ZIFA CEO was argued to be a confirmation of the mainstream political interference with Zimbabwean football administration (Ncube 2014). Particularly, the rise of Henrietta Rushwaya to become ZIFA CEO was attributed to her relationship with the then Vice President Joseph Musika. Ncube (2014) quotes another ZIFA administrator, Mwandibhuya Kennedy Mutepfa, who noted that because Rushwaya was a political appointee, some members of the ZIFA board feared to question her decisions as they were afraid to offend the powerful politicians that supported her. From this perspective, football administrators such as Rushwaya are seen as mere opportunists who have been propelled to represent the interests of powerful male political figures. This argument is also articulated by Pannenborg (2010), who argues that African football administration is characterized by patronage, whereby politically connected individuals take up positions in football administrative organisations for political or prestigious purposes. The implications of this being that many employees in football administration organisations are hired not based on merit or capability, but on the bidding of the patron. From this perspective, one can argue that female football administrators, like Rushwaya, in a politicised patriarchal context such as Zimbabwe find themselves enmeshed in a highly politicized male-dominant environment. An environment where women are used merely for political expediency. However, it is also important to note that at the very core of this argument is the refusal to recognize the independent agency of women and the ability of Rushwaya to navigate her way to power within a male-dominated social system. Rushwaya is depicted as a political pawn whose placement served the interests of the male political elite.

Rushwaya's rise can also be understood as reflecting a shift in political ideologies on gender. Nyambi (2018) argues that there was a radical shift in the political ideology of the ruling ZANU PF from being a male-dominated institution to a more gender accommodative entity where the role of women was now epitomized and valorised in preparing for the elevation of Joyce Mujuru to the Vice Presidency in 2004. This shift in ideology had an impact beyond politics. It can plausibly be argued that the appointment of Rushwaya to be the ZIFA CEO in 2007 coincided with this ideological shift. For Hove (2019), the appointment of Joyce Mujuru in 2004 was not simply a reflection of gender sensitivity based on political principles; rather it was part of a political strategy to contain rival male-dominated political factions within the ruling political elite. Patriarchy, embedded in the political establishment in Zimbabwe, often uses women as part of the greater ploy to maintain its political hegemony (Bhatasara and Chiweshe 2021). The appointment of Mujuru, similar to Rushwaya, though marketed as a positive step towards the empowerment of women, can be understood as being part of the wider struggle between male political elites.

The end of the Rushwaya era, corruption scandals and scapegoating

Henrietta Rushwaya was dismissed as the Chief Executive officer of ZIFA on 26 October 2010 after a disciplinary trial appointed by ZIFA ruled her dismissal for mismanagement and insubordination (Newsday 2010). Prior to her dismissal, she had been implicated in the Asiagate match fixing scandal, a match fixing football scandal that involved the Zimbabwe senior men's football team between 2007 and 2009 where Zimbabwe deliberately lost to low ranking Asian teams (Ncube 2017). Rushwaya was also implicated in the "Limpopogate", another match fixing scandal involving the Zimbabwe and Swaziland football Match in 2016. The narratives on the Asiagate and Limpopogate scandals hugely revolve around the central role of Rushwaya in the scandals; for instance, the Newsday(2010) constructs Rushwaya as being the "core central point" in the match fixing scandals, whilst Macdonald (2020) describes Rushwaya as "the Asiagate Queen mother". Collectively, these narratives give the impression that Henrietta Rushwaya was the chief instigator and main beneficiary of these corruption scandals. It is, however, important to appreciate that the roots of corruption and match fixing in Zimbabwean football can be dated back to as early as 1997 when Wilson Raj Perumal, the convicted football match fixer, claimed to have first contacted Zimbabwean football officials, about a decade before Rushwaya was appointed as the ZIFA CEO (Chiweshe 2019). Secondly, many other individuals were allegedly involved in these scandals, from ZANU PF politicians like Walter Mzembi to other football administrators such as Godfrey Japajapa and sports journalists like Robson Sharuko and Hope Chizuzu (Ncube 2017; Chiweshe 2019). The implication of this is that the football corruption scandals cannot be exclusively blamed upon one individual, but these scandals, as Chiweshe (2019) argues, reflect more of institutionalised and systematic operations involving all sectors of the Zimbabwean football community. It is therefore plausible to argue that narratives that emphasise and centralise the role of Rushwaya in football corruption and ultimately the decline of football in Zimbabwe reflect, to a certain extent, an element of scapegoating through which dominant patriarchal narratives achieve the paradoxical feat of ascribing power to women whilst simultaneously taking it away (Kent 2021).

It is also interesting to note that similarities do exist between the dismissal and scapegoating of Henrietta Rushwaya and that of Joyce Mujuru, the former Vice-President of Zimbabwe, in December 2014. Mujuru was dismissed, among other things, on allegations of corruption, insubordination and of plotting to usurp power, which allegedly could be traced from the time of her appointment in 2004 (Machivenyika 2015). Wholly blaming Joyce Mujuru and her allies for the emergence and prevalence of corruption in Zimbabwe is extreme, as corruption in Zimbabwe is more systemic and embedded in the wider political and economic system that sustains it and can be traced back to the 1980s (Moyo 2014). The scapegoating of Mujuru can be understood as reflecting the tendency of Zimbabwean political patriarchy to reassert itself through constructing women as destabilising agents in public spaces, thus justifying their exclusion (Bhatasara and Chiweshe 2021). This argument is strengthened by the fact that both Rushwaya and Mujuru were succeeded by males, in the process reinforcing the androcentricity of both football and political spaces in Zimbabwe.

Conclusion

Zimbabwean football administration is characterised by the intertwining of political and patriarchal ideologies, which construct narratives that sustain and reassert the androcentricity of Zimbabwean football. The operation of these ideologies is demonstrated in the experiences of Henrietta Rushwaya as the ZIFA CEO in 2007 and the narratives that have been constructed concerning her as expressed in traditional and social media. Rushwaya's rise to become the first female ZIFA CEO represented a direct challenge to the historical male dominance in Zimbabwean football. Football patriarchy responded to this threat through the construction and promulgation of narratives that sought to undermine the individual capabilities and agency of Rushwaya and that of women in general. Henrietta Rushwaya's rise to the apex of Zimbabwean football administration was constructed as being the result of the benevolence of powerful men as opposed to her individual agency and merit. Henrietta Rushwaya has also been ascribed negative social identities such as being labelled as a prostitute and being scapegoated for ruining Zimbabwean football. These identities are constructed with the intent of discouraging other women who might aspire to be sport leaders, thus preserving the existing patriarchal hegemony. The experiences of Henrietta Rushwaya are, to a certain extent, mirrored by the experiences and narratives constructed of female politicians like former Vice President Joyce Mujuru, who like Rushwaya has been constructed as being a moral misfit and scapegoated as being corrupt, leading to her eventual removal from office. Zimbabwean football administration is, therefore, closely and intricately intertwined with Zimbabwean politics, with both being androcentric spaces, where patriarchy seeks to maintain and reassert its hegemony at all costs.

REFERENCES

Akindes, G.A. (2010) *Transnational Television and Football in Francophone Africa: The Path to Electronic Colonization?* PhD Thesis. Ohio: Ohio University.

Barnes T. (1992) "The Fight for Control of African Women's Mobility in Colonial Zimbabwe, 1990-1939," *Signs: Journal of Women in Culture and Society*, 17(3)

Bhatasara, S. and Chiweshe, M.K. (2021) 'Women in Zimbabwean politics post November 2017.' *Journal of Asian and African Studies*, 56(2), pp. 218–233.

Bourdillon, M. (1976) *The Shona peoples: An ethnography of the contemporary Shona, with special reference to their religion.* Gwelo: Mambo Press.

Bowen, G.A. (2009) 'Document analysis as a qualitative research method.' *Qualitative Research Journal*, 9(2), pp. 27–40.

Cheater, A.P. (1985) *The Role and Position of Women in Pre-colonial and Colonial Zimbabwe.* Paper Presented at the Workshop on The Role of Women in National Rehabilitation and Development. UNESCO, Harare.

Cheater, A.P. (1990) 'The ideology of "communal" land tenure in Zimbabwe; mytholensis enacted?' *Africa*, 60, pp. 188–206.

Chiweshe, M.K. (2013) Online Football Fan Identities and Cyber-Fandoms in Zimbabwe, in Chuka Onwumechili and Gerard Akindes (eds.), *Identity and Nation in African Football: Fans, Community and Clubs.* New York: Palgrave Macmillan.

Chiweshe, M.K. (2014) 'One of the boys: Female fans' responses to the masculine and phallocentric nature of football stadiums in Zimbabwe.' *Critical African Studies*, 6(2-3), pp. 211–222.

Chiweshe, M.K. (2018) Zimbabwe, in De Waele, J.-M., Gibril, S., Gloriozova, E. and Spaaij, R. (eds.), *Palgrave International Handbook of Football and Politics*. London: Palgrave McMillan, pp. 447–468.

Chiweshe, M.K. (2019) 'Money, football and politics: Asiagate and the scourge of match fixing in Zimbabwe.' *Review of Nationalities*, 9(1), pp. 111–121.

Choto, T.B. (2016) *The Zimbabwe Football Association and the politics of football administration in Zimbabwe: A sociological analysis*. Unpublished Master's Thesis. Zimbabwe: University of Zimbabwe.

Choto, T.B., Chiweshe, M.K. and Muparamoto, N. (2017) 'Football fandom, ethno-regionalism and rivalry in post-colonial Zimbabwe: Case study of Highlanders and Dynamos Football clubs.' *Soccer & Society*, 20(1), pp. 153–167.

Corbin, J. and Strauss, A. (2008) *Basics of Qualitative Research: Techniques and Procedures for Developing Grounded Theory*. London: Sage Publications Ltd.

Darby, P. (2002) *Africa, Football, and FIFA: Politics, Colonialism, and Resistance*. 2nd edition. London: F. Cass.

Damion, E. (2009) *Gender, Sport and Development in Africa: Cross Cultural Perspectives of Representation and Marginalization*. Dar es Salaam: African Books Collective, University of Zimbabwe.

Dzamara, I. (2007) 'Iron Lady, Rushwaya – how the ZANU PF patronage system works', *The Zimbabwean*, 24 August. Available at: www.thezimbabwean,co/2007/08/iron-lady-rushwaya-how-the-zanu-pf-patronage-system-works-2408-07/ (accessed 07 August 2021).

Engh, M. (2011) 'Tackling femininity: The heterosexual paradigm and women's soccer in South Africa.' *The International Journal of the History of Sport*, 28(1), pp. 137–152.

Glaser, B. and Strauss, A. (2008) *The Discovery of Grounded Theory: Strategies for Qualitative Research*. London: Aldine Transaction.

Guillianotti, R. (2004) Between Colonialism, Independence and Globalization: Football in Zimbabwe, in Armstrong, G. and Guillianotti, R. (eds.), *Football in Africa*. New York: Palgrave Macmillan, pp. 80–99.

Hjelm, J. and Olofsson, E. (2003) 'A breakthrough: Women's football in Sweden.' *Soccer & Society*, 4(2-3), pp. 182–204.

Hofmann, A.R. and Sinning, S. (2016) 'From being excluded to becoming world champions: Female football coaches in Germany.' *The International Journal of the History of Sport*, 33(14), pp. 1652–1668.

Hove, M. (2019) 'When a political party turns against its cadres: ZANU PF factional infightings 2004-2017.' *African Security*, 12(2), pp. 200–233.

Jeater, D. (1990) *Marriage, Perversion and Power: The Construction of Moral Discourse in Southern Rhodesia 1890–1930*. Unpublished PhD Thesis. Oxford: University of Oxford.

Kent, J. (2021) 'Scapegoating and the "angry black woman."' *Group Analysis*, 54(3), pp. 354–371.

Kesby, M. (1999) 'Locating and dislocating gender in rural Zimbabwe: The making of space and the texturing of bodies, gender, place and culture.' *Journal of Feminist Geography*, 6(1), pp. 27–47.

Macdonald, R. (2020) 'Asiagate Queen mother Henrietta Rushwaya to spend weekend behind bars?', *News of the South*, 30 October. Available at: www.newsofthesouth.com/asiagate-queen-mother-henrieta-rushwaya-tospend-weekend-behind-bars/ (accessed 07 August 2021).

Machivenyika, F. (2015) 'ZANU PF expels Joyce Mujuru slew of allegations cited plots traced as far back as 2004', *The Herald*, 03 April. Available at: https://www.herald.co.zw/zanu-pf-expels-joice-mujuru-slew-of-allegations-cited-plots-traced-as-far-back-as-2004/ (accessed 07 August 2021).

Marwick, B.A. (1966) *The Swazi: An Ethnographic Account of the Natives of the Swaziland Protectorate*. 2nd edition. London: Frank Cass.

Moyo, S. (2014) *Corruption in Zimbabwe: An Examination of the Roles of the State and Civil Society in Combating Corruption*. PhD Thesis. University of Central Lancashire.

Muponde, R. and Muchemwa, K. (2011) 'Dictatorships, disasters, and African soccer: Reflections on a moment in Zimbabwean soccer.' *African Identities*, 9(3), pp. 279–290.

Newsday (2010) 'Rushwaya fired', *Newsday*, 10 October. Available at: https://www.newsday.co.zw/2010/10/2010-10-26-rushwaya-fired/ (accessed 09 August 2021).

Ncube, L. (2014) *The Beautiful Game? Football, Power, Identities, and Development in Zimbabwe*. PhD Thesis. Durban: University of Kwazulu-Natal.

Ncube, L. (2017) 'Sports journalists and corruption in Zimbabwean football: Reflections on the Asiagate scandal.' *Communicatio*, 43(3-4), pp. 19–35.

Ncube, L. and Chawana, F. (2018) 'What is in a song? Constructions of hegemonic masculinity by Zimbabwean football fans.' *Muziki*, 15(1), pp. 68–88.

Novak, A. (2006) Rhodesia's 'rebel and racist' Olympic team: Athletic glory, national legitimacy and the clash of politics and sport, *The International Journal of the History of Sport*, 23:8, 1369-1388, DOI: 10.1080/09523360600922287

Novak, A. (2020) 'Rhodesia and FIFA: Racial discrimination, political legitimacy and football 1960 to 1980.' *Soccer and Society*, 22(3), pp. 266–279.

Nyambi, O. (2018) '"Warriors" and "Mighty Warriors": National football team nicknames and the politics and politicization of national identity in Zimbabwe.' *National Identities*, 20(3), pp. 259–276.

Pannenborg, A. (2010) *Football in Africa: Observations about Political, Financial, Cultural and Religious Influences*. Amsterdam: NCDO Publications Series Sport and Development.

Schmidt, E. (1990) 'Negotiated spaces and contested terrain; men, women and the law in colonial Zimbabwe, 1890–1939.' *Journal of Southern African Studies*, 16, pp. 622–648.

Stuart, O. (1995) The Lions Stir: Football in African Society, in Wagg, S. (ed.), *Giving the Game Away: Football, Politics and Culture on Five Continents*. London: Leicester University Press, pp. 24–51.

Thornberg, R. and Charmez, K. (2014) Grounded Theory and Theoretical Coding, in Flick, U. (ed.), *The Sage Handbook of Qualitative Data Analysis*. London: Sage Publications, pp. 153–169.

Welford, J. (2008) *What's the score? Women in football in England*. PhD Thesis. Loughborough: Loughborough University.

Williams, J. and Hess, R. (2015) 'Women, football and history: International perspectives.' *The International Journal of the History of Sport*, 32(18), pp. 2115–2122.

Zenenga, P. (2012) 'Visualizing politics in an African sport: Political and cultural constructions in Zimbabwean soccer.' *Soccer and Society*, 13(2), pp. 250–263.

25
Women in Golf
Policy and Progress

Niamh Kitching

Introduction

Even though the status of women in sport has improved on many levels, women athletes, participants and fans are still marginalised in some environments (e.g., see Alsarve and Johansson 2021). While golf has attempted to shake its exclusionary, dated image, it does so in the face of falling participation rates globally and the golfer participant profile remaining – ordinarily – a white, middle aged and middle-class man. The total registered golfers in Europe fell by 7% or over 300,000 between 2010 and 2019 while women comprise just 27% of adult golfers (Sports Marketing Surveys 2019). In America, golf participant numbers also fell by over 5 million between 2003 and 2019 (McGinnis, Gentry and Haltom 2021). While the Covid-19 pandemic brought about an unprecedented increase in golf participation, new golfers in Great Britain and Ireland who identified as female, ethnic minority, gay or lesbian expressed a sense that their presence was unusual or attracted attention (The R&A 2021a). With the overall picture indicating a decline in golf, this could be counterbalanced with effective implementation of inclusive approaches. Therefore, this chapter examines the Royal and Ancient (R&A) – a global golf governing body – and its contribution to promoting women in golf (see also Kitching, 2017).

Given the role of the British monarchy in the pursuit from the mid-fifteenth century, golf became known as 'the royal and ancient game' (Green 1994; Stirk 1995). One of the most celebrated golf clubs of the time was formed in 1754 as the Royal and Ancient Golf Club of St. Andrews, Scotland. From this period onwards, the Royal and Ancient club began to gain a profile globally for its authority around the rules of golf, and the town of St. Andrews became known as the 'home of golf'. From 1897 to 2003, the Royal and Ancient Golf Club – references to the R&A prior to 2004 refer to the Royal and Ancient Golf Club, while post 2004 references denote the 'new' R&A – of St. Andrews was responsible for overseeing the rules of golf (excluding USA and Mexico), hosting a number of male golf tournaments (including the Open championship) and developing the game in existing and emerging golfing nations (The R&A d). In 2004, the club devolved responsibility for these operations to a newly formed group of companies called the R&A, which was formed 'separate and distinct from The Royal and Ancient Golf Club of St. Andrews' (The R&A b). The current role of the

R&A includes running championships, golf rules and governance, and the development of golf worldwide, and it is one of the few global governing bodies of sport remaining in the UK.

Since its inception in Scotland, golf has always been delineated by gender. Therefore, this chapter analyses evidence of women's historically subordinate role in golf. The evidence used in this chapter is initially drawn from literature around women's recreational participation and experiences in golf, followed by an array of newspaper articles, press conference quotes and golf governing body literature. As this chapter revolves around the Scotland-based R&A, much of the evidence recounted is UK centred. Before examining the R&A's direct efforts in women's golf, the next section summarises the historical and contemporary literature on the visibility and experiences of women in golf and the barriers to their participation. This is followed by an appraisal of the R&A's stance on male membership clubs, its 2017 merger with the Ladies Golf Union (LGU) and the launch of the R&A women in golf charter.

Women's golf – from inception to the current day

Until the mid-1800s in Britain, women were rarely tolerated in golf settings, and, thus, it was seldom that a female golfer would be seen on the course. For years women were far removed from the 'real golf' played by men (George 2009) and were restricted to secret games that involved little more than putting (Concannon 1995). Writing on the acceptance of women in British golf clubs prior to 1914, Vamplew (2010) states that golf clubs were homosocial spaces for males of similar social backgrounds, where they could dine, drink and play cards, away from women. Golf settings were controlled social spaces for women, who were often perceived as inferior, emotionally unstable and organisationally incompetent in sport and as a result occupied a secondary role in the golf setting (Haig-Muir 1998; Vamplew 2010). While male members were afforded the privileges of full membership, giving them uncontested weekend playing rights (justified by the male working week), women formed 'ladies' sections through which, in many clubs, they became known as associate members (Cousins 1975). Discrimination of women in golf was permissible, and many women appeared to accept their marginal position (George, Kay and Vamplew 2007). George (2010) reports that tension existed not only between women and men but also between different groups of women. As a result, women's golf developed independently from the men's game (George, Kay and Vamplew 2007; Vamplew 2010). Separate from the R&A, the LGU formed in 1893 as the governing body for female golf in Great Britain and Ireland.

The effects of women's subordinate positions in early golf are visible to this day, particularly so in both the participation trends and the evidence around women's experiences. In Europe, women comprise 27% of total golfers; in Austria, this figure is 40%, 37% in Germany, 36% in Switzerland and 28% in Sweden, while more established golfing nations have figures as low as 13% (Scotland and Wales) and 14% (England) (Sports Marketing Surveys 2019). In their interactions with male players and coaches, female players have reported feeling ignored, overlooked, singled out in relation to slow play and have described themselves as being 'objectified', 'othered' and highly visible as women (McGinnis and Gentry 2002; McGinnis, McQuillan and Chapple 2005; McGinnis and Gentry 2006; Mitchell, Allen-Collinson and Evans 2016). From the evidence presented here, gender discrimination does not end once a woman gains access to a golf club.

Further to the visibility of women in golf environments, research contends that golf is ordinarily male. There is evidence of a patriarchal effect of fathers, brothers and partners as key influencers, gatekeepers and socialising agents for women who take up golf (Shin and

Nam 2004; Reis and Correia 2013). While male-only golf clubs garner much attention, 'associate' memberships mentioned earlier are still in existence, upheld by contentious legislations providing for the 'needs' of women in some countries (McCann 2019; Song 2007). From gendered scorecards, tee boxes, inadequate facilities and the lack of gender-specific merchandise, equipment and products, the presentation of golf is regarded as normatively male (Hundley 2004; Arthur, Del Campo and Van Buren 2011). Women professionals face access and rights discrimination, fewer opportunities for career progression and are more likely to leave the industry (Kitching, Grix and Phillpotts 2017; MacKinnon 2013). All in all, this evidence demonstrates how males are likely to have more access to the privileges associated with power and decision making in golf environments. This male valorisation will mean that female golfers are often positioned as the 'other', whereby their involvement is deemed different, unexpected or less important. The ensuing sections take a closer examination of the R&A: (1) its stance on male-only golf clubs and (2) its merger with the LGU and its introduction of the women in golf charter.

Male-only golf clubs and the R&A Open championship

Since their initiation, the R&A and LGU regularly hosted their golf championships at male-only membership venues in the UK. Countless anecdotes exist – including personal ones – outlining the exclusion of female golf participants, athletes and employees from and within these types of settings (see Kitching 2011; Kitching, Grix and Phillpotts 2017). Professional golfer Leona Maguire spoke about how after performing well in one particular tournament, she and her family went to the clubhouse of an all-male member venue to get food, where her Dad was told 'they can't come up here' (Farrell 2020). Green (1994) recounted the tale from the 1965 LGU Ladies' British Amateur Open at a stormy St. Andrews, where a group of competitors sheltered in front of the R&A clubhouse. A club official approached, requesting them to lower their umbrellas because they were spoiling the view of the Old Course enjoyed by the male members in the lounge. These examples not only illustrate the male-only venue choices made for tournaments (all here by the LGU), but the resultant privilege of male power and positioning, thereby legitimising women's exclusion from and marginalisation in these settings.

In 2012, Augusta National, the host venue for the annual Masters tournament (male professional golf major) admitted female members for the first time, and this appeared to initiate debate around male-only clubs in the UK. Another male professional golf major tournament – the oldest and most internationally renowned of the four male majors – is the Open championship, which is hosted by the R&A. The 2019 Open tournament in Royal Portrush became the largest sporting event ever held in Northern Ireland, generating over £100 million economic benefit to the region (The Open 2019). Just 14 golf club venues (all links courses) have hosted the Open championship in its 160-year history; currently there are nine venues in the UK and Ireland that share this role. The last time the championship was held in a male-only members club was in 2013 at Muirfield, Scotland, a tournament which the Scottish First Minister and avid golfer Alex Salmond chose to boycott (BBC Scotland 2013). Concurrently, two UK government ministers said hosting the tournament at Muirfield sends out the 'wrong message' and was 'very, very out of touch' (Channel 4 News 2013). During a press conference ahead of the tournament, the CEO of the R&A, Peter Dawson, faced a barrage of questions about staging such a world-renowned event at a male-only membership club. He commented:

> We've got, as you mentioned, politicians posturing, we've got interest groups attacking the R&A, attacking the Open and attacking Muirfield…to be honest, our natural

reaction is to resist these pressures, because we actually don't think they have very much substance… I think in the last ten years we've put…about 30 million pounds into women's golf. And that's what the Open championship's success brings with it. So it's not all bad.

(PGA Tour 2013, para 7).

Dawson and the R&A remained steadfast in their defence of male-only member clubs hosting the Open championship. He also commented:

Obviously, the whole issue of gender and single-sex clubs has been pretty much beaten to death recently… Single-sex clubs are in a very small minority in the UK… they are perfectly legal. In our view they don't do anyone any harm. And we think the right of freedom of association is important. And we've explained our view that we think they have no material adverse effect on participation…

(PGA Tour 2013, para 7).

Dawson's position in defending gender-segregated clubs is worthy of discussion. Given the enormity of the Open championship event, it is likely that the members of Open venue courses such as Muirfield have access to resources, networking opportunities and decision making and all the associated social, economic and cultural capital. When these tournaments are held at male-only member clubs, this access is likely limited to these members. Further, as mentioned heretofore, the message perpetuated through Dawson's words and the actions of the R&A is that male-only clubs are valid. The political and media criticism surrounding the 2013 Open championship at Muirfield became a turning point for the R&A. In 2014, it emerged that a key sponsor of the Open Championship (HSBC bank) had spoken out against the all-male policy of some of the nine venues on the Open rotation. Giles Morgan from the bank commented:

…it would be much more palatable if it was played where there was not a sense of segregation. We would like to see it solved so we don't keep talking about it. I don't want to be in a position where we have to justify our sponsorship. The R&A are very clear that we are uneasy…they are acutely aware that things need to change and move on. I think they will end up with the right answer.

(Dunsmuir 2014).

In response to these comments, an R&A spokesperson said that the organisation was undergoing a 'period of reflection' which they had promised after the 2013 Open. A journalist for the Scottish Herald commented:

…that it has taken the concerns of a significant sponsor to initiate action on the issue says little for their [R&A] self-awareness. The trophy presentation party at Muirfield last year consisted of half-a-dozen white middle aged (or older) men in blazers, epitomising almost every denunciation of the association. It was beyond parody. The parochialism of the R&A is, at times, quite astonishing. The governing body appear reluctant to show any sign of capitulation in the face of public pressure, neglecting to acknowledge the fact that they have a responsibility to promote the game for both sexes.

(Egelstaff 2014).

Though Peter Dawson of the R&A appeared not to bow to political pressure in 2013, later in 2014, it emerged that the R&A was seriously considering the removal of venues like Muirfield from the Open championship schedule should they remain as male-only clubs. It is thought that the potential return of golf to the 2016 Olympic Games further increased this pressure, given the International Olympic Committee's commitments to equality (Gibson 2014). Towards the end of 2014 (and on the same date as the Scottish independence referendum), the worldwide all-male membership of around 2500 at the Royal and Ancient Golf Club of St. Andrews voted to end its 260-year-old male-only policy. Announcing the vote result at the front of the R&A clubhouse, and in a complete turnabout from his 2013 comments, club secretary Peter Dawson (R&A CEO) called this 'right for golf' (Gibson 2014). In 2015, Dawson retired and was succeeded by Martin Slumbers as CEO, while in the same year, another club on the Open rotation, Royal St. George's, voted to admit female members. In May 2016, a similar vote was held at Muirfield Golf Club, but following a campaign by 'no' voter members, the club failed to reach the two-third majority needed to enact a rule change to admit women members. In a letter to members, the no voters cited slow play worries and fears about making women feel uncomfortable, and in alluding to the potential development of a new course and clubhouse at the venue which could cater for women members, the letter mentioned that the clubhouse 'design would no doubt benefit from female input' (The Scotsman 2016). In an unprecedented move, the R&A immediately stripped Muirfield of its Open Championship status, and the following year, the members reversed their vote and balloted to allow women to join the club. In 2016, the members of another Open rotation course, Royal Troon, voted overwhelmingly in favour of admitting women members. Thus, by 2017, all clubs on the Open championship rotation admitted female members.

This section outlined the key events influencing the R&A's decision to remove male-only member clubs from the Open championship. It appears from this evidence that it was the threat of losing sponsors that called the R&A to action, more so, perhaps, than principles of equity, diversity and inclusion. In effect, while women applicants can now apply to these clubs, simply permitting women applicants does nothing for women's access to power in these settings, and it is likely that women's voices will remain in the minority for a time to come. Nonetheless, while legislation in many countries still upholds the right to male member clubs and associate member categories and while these changes in membership status may be more about optics and money, the R&A have begun to gradually deviate from their previously unwavering positions.

The R&A and women's golf – the merger and the charter

In line with other mergers in gender-segregated golf governing bodies in the UK and Ireland, in 2017, the R&A merged with the LGU. Interestingly, through this amalgamation, the R&A took on governance responsibility for women's golf in Britain and Ireland along with overseeing a number of women's golf tournaments (The R&A 2016). At the announcement in 2016, CEO Martin Slumbers commented in relation to the R&A's role in increasing participation in women's golf:

> We're convinced, that one of the most important elements for the game to grow is family golf, and by merging here, the R&A will not only learn about [the] women's and girls' game, but will be able to encourage, enhance, and bring more family golf together, and develop the game right across the board [video].
>
> (The R&A 2016).

Through the merger, the R&A acquired the Women's British Open (rebranded in 2020 as the American International Group [AIG] Women's Open), one of the five majors in professional women's golf. The R&A saw this tournament as part of its strategy to grow women's golf, and at the time, its CEO Martin Slumbers commented: 'We are determined to accelerate the progress we have made in women's golf and inspire more girls and women to take up golf' (BBC Sport 2020).

Shortly after the merger with the LGU, the R&A commissioned a study on women's and girls' participation in golf. The study identified numerous barriers affecting women and girls' participation and like other reports and previous R&A statements (e.g., Lunn and Kelly 2017) positioned 'family golf' to attract more women to the sport. In the foreword written for the report, Martin Slumbers was forthright in identifying the importance of women, girls and family golf:

> More and more women are seeking an active lifestyle which includes fun and friendship, both for themselves and their families, and have been identified as the key decision-makers in how families spend their leisure time. That has to mean there is a tremendous opportunity for growth if golf can find the right way of appealing to women and more generally to families.
>
> (Fry and Hall 2018, p. 2).

These events and statements are more encouraging from the R&A in terms of beginning to acknowledge and recognise women golfers. However, the language used, at times, shows how women and girls are often welcomed in golf for economic reasons and not necessarily for equity or inclusion purposes. In the above comments, women are identified as the 'key decision makers' for leisure time, while there is mention of the growth of golf. These commercial oriented lines are tied up with one of the justifications the golf industry uses for growing women's golf, with one golf report suggesting that there are 36.9 million 'latent' women golfers globally (Syngenta 2016), and family golf has become more regularly referenced in golf development literature and policy (e.g., McGinnis, Gentry and Haltom 2021). Through the merger and Slumber's mention of bringing 'family golf together', traditional family structures are implied, perhaps alongside the sharing of access, networking and social, economic and cultural capital that might only be acquired from grandfathers, fathers and brothers. This is perhaps further evidence of patriarchy previously mentioned where men act as gatekeepers and socialising agents in distributing power and resources and reproducing traditional golf club culture.

Following the release of the 2018 report, the R&A launched the Women in Golf Charter. The Charter was launched at an event hosted by BBC broadcaster Hazel Irvine at the View in the Chard, London in May 2018 (The R&A 2018). The charter has five stated goals (The R&A c):

1 Strengthen the focus on gender balance and provide a united position for the golf industry;
2 Commit national federations and organisations to support measures targeted at increasing the participation of women, girls and families in golf;
3 Call upon signatories to take positive action to support the recruitment, retention and progression of women working at all levels of the sport;
4 Set individual targets for national associations for participation and membership and reporting progress annually;
5 Develop an inclusive environment for women and girls within golf.

At the launch, which was attended by the UK Minister for Sport, Martin Slumbers announced an increase in investment in women's, girls' and mixed golf by £80 million over 10 years and stated:

> The Charter is a strong statement of intent from the golf industry that it has to change and a commitment on behalf of all of us to take measures designed to achieve positive change

for women, girls and families. This is crucial to growing participation in the sport in the years ahead. We ask our affiliates and partners around the world to pledge their support and commitment to achieving this vision and to help us ensure that we have a thriving sport in 50 years' time…

(The R&A 2018).

As detailed on the R&A website (randa.org), many golf organisations and sponsors globally have become charter signatories, where in signing up they must detail their commitments to women's and girls' golf. Since the Charter launch, the R&A have developed several initiatives, including the #FOREeveryone toolkit and resources, the women in golf leadership development programme, and held a week of activity around the 2021 International Women's Day (see randa.org). All of these developments illustrate the change in direction in the R&A's rhetoric since the 2013 Open at Muirfield. While the governing body is now apparently committed to change, there remain questions around if and how the strategies that are being pursued will have any impact on the visibility and women's participation in golf.

Introducing women to golf – the evidence

There is some – though limited – evidence around the recruitment and retention of women into golf. Some women golfers place more value on the social and group culture rather than competitive elements of golf, but research has also found that the emphasis on mixed, social events indicated to female golfers that the serious play was left for the men (Shotton, Armour and Potrac 1998; Wood and Danylchuk 2011; Danylchuk, Snelgrove and Wood 2015; McGinnis, McQuillan and Chapple 2005; McGinnis and Gentry 2002). Golf coaches can play an important role as gatekeepers for novice golfers, but evidence also exists that coaches show more interest in and report more of a growth mindset about men golfers rather than women golfers (Shapcott and Carr 2020). While many golf governing bodies have committed to well marketed campaigns with heteronormative images, or one-off/short-term coaching programmes for women - thereby suggesting a magic wand approach to increasing women's participation in golf -some organisations are focusing on embedded practices of gender segregation and male domination at a local level. For example, R&A women in golf charter signatory, the Swedish Golf Federation (SGF) launched Vision 50/50 in 2013 to respond to what they considered a threat to the future of golf. While women typically comprise over a quarter of golf participants in Sweden, the industry is overwhelmingly male dominated, with 90% of club managers and close to 100% of course managers male (Step Up Equality 2020). The programme has a key focus on leadership and education at club level, and one of its key aims is to create a better atmosphere at golf clubs. The Federation states:

> It is only when we challenge prevailing norms and structures that we can make a change that becomes sustainable over time… cultural practices are a strong barrier with many on the "inside" acting in opposition under the belief that the environment is already inclusive and functioning well.
>
> (Step Up Equality 2020).

Here, the SGF identifies the practices and culture at the interface of interactions on the course, in the meeting rooms and in the clubhouse as central in attempting to bring about equity of access and opportunity in golf. The Federation also states that 'vision 50/50 is a long-term change work, where it can take years for effects to be measured in actual numbers'

(Swedish Golf Federation 2021). Vision 50/50 is dedicated to confronting gender inequality in a narrow-focused way and at a local level, whereby clubs undergo a dedicated programme of education and reflection on their commitment to equal opportunities for women. In their annual report for 2020, SGF reported that female board members of golf clubs have increased from 26% in 2014 to 33% in 2019, and though pandemic-related, in 2020, the number of women participants increased by 10,068, an increase of 8% on 2019, making golf one of the most popular sports for women in Sweden (Swedish Golf Federation 2020).

Conclusion

The focus of this chapter was a critical analysis of the R&A's approach to women's golf from the year 2013. It could be deemed that up until the R&A's 2017 merger with the LGU, the organisation had no official obligation to work for women's golf. However, as the body responsible for the rules, governance and development of golf, the R&A has a responsibility to embrace openness and diversity. At that Open championship press conference at Muirfield in 2013, Peter Dawson commented that the R&A has 'been through 250 years of existence without getting into political comment' (PGA Tour 2013, para 7). From 2014 onwards, the organisation went from publishing little beyond the rules of golf to more regular communication of reports and policy, such as, for example, 'the truth about golf' (The R&A and International Golf Federation 2018) and the international consensus on golf and health (The R&A 2020). However, while organisations, like the SGF, are promoting an increase in women on boards at club level, at the time of writing, just one of the R&A's nine strong executive leadership team is female. While superficially it may appear that some progress has been made at the highest administrative levels, locally it is likely that the same people, in the same clubs and organisations are making the same decisions on access, the allocation of resources and the distribution of power in golf.

One of the aims of this chapter was to assess if a historically male-dominated sport such as golf is ready for change. Be it pressure from political circles, the International Olympic Committee or sponsors, or even perhaps a change of CEO, the R&A has initiated changes in a relatively short period of time. However, these turns are miniscule when compared with the pervasive patriarchal power relations that still exist in many golf clubs, and it appears that the R&A are playing catch up with some golf governing bodies. The SGF example highlights how first there is a need to recognise the need for change at local (club) level, and only when this occurs can there be real progress made. Other countries have been shown to be similarly ambitious in their change rhetoric, with Golf Australia calling for 'a whole of sport approach; change management capability and an innovative and transformational mindset' (Golf Australia 2018). Furthermore, while focused education over a long period in Swedish golf clubs appears to be fruitful, there are many complexities in embarking on change at a sports club level, particularly where private clubs are concerned. In summary, golf has a long road to travel towards equity, diversity and inclusion.

REFERENCES

Alsarve, D. and Johansson, E. (2021) 'A gang of ironworkers with the scent of blood: a participation observation of male dominance and its historical trajectories at Swedish semi-professional ice hockey events', *International Review for the Sociology of Sport*, 57(1), pp. 54–72. https://doi.org/10.1177%2F1012690221998576.

Arthur, M., Del Campo, R. and Van Buren III, H. (2011) 'The impact of gender-differentiated golf course features on women's networking', *Gender in Management: An International Journal*, 26, pp. 37–56.

BBC Scotland (2013) *Salmond avoids Open Championship at men-only Muirfield*. Available at: https://www.bbc.com/news/uk-scotland-edinburgh-east-fife-23097851 (Accessed 12 May 2021).

BBC Sport (2020) *Women's Open drops 'British' from title in sponsorship rebrand*. Available at: https://www.bbc.com/sport/golf/53497474 (Accessed 27 September 2021).

Channel 4 News (2013) *It's a man's world at Muirfield, home to the 2013 Open*. Available at: https://www.channel4.com/news/the-mans-world-of-muirfield-home-to-the-2013-open (Accessed 12 May 2021).

Concannon, D. (1995) *Golf: the early days*, London: Salamander.

Cousins, G. (1975) *Golf in Britain: a social history from the beginnings to the present day*, London: Routledge and Kegan Paul.

Danylchuk, K., Snelgrove, R. and Wood, L. (2015) 'Managing women's participation in golf: a case study of organizational change', *Leisure/Loisir*, 39, pp. 61–80.

Dunsmuir, A. (2014) 'The R&A "likely to end men-only award"', *The Golf Business*, 12 March. Available at: https://www.thegolfbusiness.co.uk/2014/03/the-ra-likely-to-end-men-only-award/ (Accessed 12 May 2021).

Egelstaff, S. (2014) 'Money talks, and it is telling the R&A they should not support male-only golf clubs', *The Herald Scotland*, 24 January. Available at: https://www.heraldscotland.com/sport/13142070.money-talks-telling-r-not-support-male-only-golf-clubs/ (Accessed 12 May 2021).

Farrell, S. (2020) 'We went to the clubhouse to eat and the guy shook his head and said "they can't come up here"', *The42.ie*, 9 September. Available at: https://www.the42.ie/leona-maguire-lpga-5199950-Sep2020/ (Accessed 12 May 2021).

Fry, J. and Hall, P. (2018) *Women's, girls' and family participation in golf: an overview of existing research*. St. Andrews, Scotland: The Royal and Ancient Golf Club.

George, J. (2009) '"An excellent means of combining fresh air, exercise and society": females on the fairways, 1890-1914', *Sport in History*, 29, pp. 333–352.

George, J. (2010) 'Ladies First'?: Establishing a Place for Women Golfers in British Golf Clubs, 1867–1914, Sport in History, 30:2, 288–308, DOI: 10.1080/17460263.2010.481211

George, J., Kay, J. and Vamplew, W. (2007) 'Women to the fore: gender accommodation and resistance at the British Golf Club before 1914', *Sporting Traditions*, 23, pp. 79–98.

Gibson, O. (2014) 'R&A decision to admit women is hailed as symbolic moment for sport', *The Guardian*, 18 September. Available at: https://www.theguardian.com/sport/2014/sep/18/royal-ancient-women-golf (Accessed 12 May 2021).

Golf Australia (2018) *Vision 2025 - the future of women and girls in golf*, Melbourne, Australia: Golf Australia.

Green, R. (1994) *The illustrated encyclopedia of golf*. Hampton-upon-Thames, UK: Ted Smart.

Haig-Muir, M. (1998) 'Qualified success? Gender, sexuality and women's golf', *Sporting Traditions*, 14, pp. 37–52.

Hundley, H. (2004) 'Keeping the score: the hegemonic everyday practices in golf', *Communication Reports*, 17, pp. 39–48.

Kitching, N. (2011) *Practice' makes perfect: locating young people in golf club culture*. Doctor of Philosophy (Research), University of Limerick.

Kitching, N. (2017) 'Women in golf: a critical reflection', in Toms, M. R. (ed.) *Routledge international handbook of golf science*. London: Routledge, pp. 404–413.

Kitching, N., Grix, J. and Phillpotts, L. (2017) 'Shifting hegemony in "a man's world": incremental change for female golf professional employment', *Sport in Society*, 20, pp. 1530–1547.

Lunn, P. and Kelly, E. (2017) *Golf in Ireland: a statistical analysis of participation*. Dublin: Economic and Social Research Institute/Confederation of Golf in Ireland.

Mackinnon, V. (2013) 'Golf industry attrition: challenges to retaining qualified golf professionals, particularly women', *Sport & EU Review*, 5, pp. 9–29.

McCann, M. (2019) 'Why private golf clubs are legally still able to discriminate against women', *Sport Illustrated*, 1 July. Available at: https://www.si.com/golf/2019/07/01/private-golf-clubs-muirfield-augusta-women-discrimination (Accessed 24 February 2021).

McGinnis, L. and Gentry, J. (2002) 'The masculine hegemony in sports: is golf for "ladies"?', *Advances in Consumer Research*, 29, pp. 19–24.

McGinnis, L., McQuillan, J. and Chapple, C. (2005) 'I JUST WANT TO PLAY: Women, sexism, and persistence in golf', *Journal of Sport & Social Issues*, 29, pp. 313–337.

McGinnis, L. and Gentry, J. (2006) 'Getting past the red tees: constraints women face in golf and strategies to help them stay', *Journal of Sport Management*, 20, pp. 218–247.

McGinnis, L., Gentry, J. and Haltom, T. (2021) 'Gender, millennials, and leisure constraints: exploring golf's participation decline', *Journal of Policy Research in Tourism, Leisure and Events*, 13, pp. 59–76.

Mitchell, S., Allen-Collinson, J. and Evans, A. (2016) '"Ladies present!": an auto/ethnographic study of women amateur golfers at an English provincial golf club', *Qualitative Research in Sport, Exercise & Health*, 8, pp. 273–286.

PGA Tour (2013) *The Open Championship interview: Peter Dawson and Jim McArthur*. Available at: https://www.pgatour.com/what-they-said/2013/07/17/the-open-championship-interview-peter-dawson-and-jim-mcarthur-.html (Accessed 25 February 2021).

Reis, H. and Correia, A. (2013) 'Gender inequalities in golf: a consented exclusion?', *International Journal of Culture, Tourism and Hospitality Research*, 7, pp. 324–339.

Shapcott, S. and Carr, S. (2020) 'Golf coaches' mindsets about recreational golfers: gendered golf experiences start on the practice tee', *Motivation Science*, 6, pp. 275–284.

Shin, E. and Nam, E. (2004) 'Culture, gender roles and sport: the case of Korean players on the LPGA Tour', *Journal of Sport & Social Issues*, 28, 223–244.

Shotton, P., Armour, K. and Potrac, P. (1998) 'An ethnographic study of gender influences on social behaviour of members at a private golf club', *SOSOL: Sociology of Sport Online*, 1(2).

Song, E. (2007) 'No women (and dogs) allowed: a comparative analysis of discriminating private golf clubs in the United States, Ireland and England', *Washington University Global Studies Law Review*, 6, pp. 181–203.

Sports Marketing Surveys (2019) *European golf participation report 2019*. The R&A/European Golf Association.

Step Up Equality (2020) *Women's leadership and decision making within sport: a handbook of best practice*. Step Up Equality - co-funded by the Erasmus+ programme of the EU.

Stirk, D. (1995) *Golf: the history of an obsession*. London: Past Times.

Swedish Golf Federation (2020) *Swedish case studies*. Stockholm: Swedish Golf Federation.

Swedish Golf Federation (2021) *Statistics*. Available at: https://golf.se/om-golfsverige/analyser-och-statistik/statistik/ (Accessed 26 February 2021).

Syngenta (2016) *Unlocking golf's true potential: global customer insights*. Cambridge: Syngenta.

The Open (2019) *The 148th Open delivers £100 million of economic benefit to Northern Ireland*. Available at: https://www.theopen.com/latest/economic-benefit-royal-portrush (Accessed 12 May 2021).

The R&A (2016) *Ladies Golf Union and The R&A complete merger*. Available at: https://www.randa.org/News/2016/12/Ladies-Golf-Union-and-The-RandA-complete-merger (Accessed 13 May 2021).

The R&A (2018) *The R&A unveil new women in golf charter*. Available at: https://www.randa.org/News/2018/05/The-RandA-unveil-Women-in-Golf-Charter-at-The-Shard-in-London (Accessed 13 May 2021).

The R&A (2020) *Golf and health*. St. Andrews, Scotland: The Royal and Ancient.

The R&A (2021a) *2020 GB&I golf participation report*. Available at: https://www.randa.org/en/news/2021/05/gbandi-golf-participation-report (Accessed 10 March 2022).

The R&A (2021b) *About the R&A*. Available at: https://www.randa.org/en/about-us (Accessed 25 February 2021).

The R&A (2021c) *Women in golf charter*. Available at: https://www.randa.org/TheRandA/Initiatives/WomenAndGolfCharter (Accessed 25 February 2021).

The R&A (2021d) *The Royal and Ancient Golf Club*. Available at: https://www.randa.org/en/heritage/the-royal-ancient/the-royal-ancient-golf-club (Accessed 12 May 2021).

The R&A and International Golf Federation (2018) *The truth about golf*. St. Andrews, Scotland: The Royal and Ancient/International Golf Federation.

The Scotsman (2016) *Muirfield 'no' bid cites slow play, foursomes fear and lunch*. Available at: https://www.scotsman.com/sport/muirfield-no-bid-cites-slow-play-foursomes-fearand-lunch-619905 (Accessed 12 May 2021).

Vamplew, W. (2010) 'Sharing space: inclusion, exclusion, and accommodation at the British golf club before 1914', *Journal of Sport & Social Issues*, 34, pp. 359–375.

Wood, L. and Danylchuk, K. (2011) 'Playing our way: contributions of social groups to women's continued participation in golf', *Leisure Sciences*, 33, pp. 366–381.

26
Narratives of Women Surfers
Rethinking Pre-constructed Gender Bias

Aimee Vlachos and Nuria Alonso Garcia

Introduction

Creating and sharing stories is an integral part of the human experience; stories inspire, heal and elevate the voices of the disfranchised and challenge hegemonic discourses. Storytelling invites us to reflect on our personal trajectories, honor cultural legacies and develop an awareness of the multiple voices involved in crafting authentic narratives (Cragoe 2019; De Sousa Santos 2014; Mignolo 2000). The act of storytelling should be respectful and dignifying and can also be a form of empowerment, a way to reclaim one's sense of identity, voice and agency (Lim 2020). There is empirical evidence of women's empowerment through sports as they challenge restrictive norms of femininity typically linked to the female physique (Dowling 2000). This chapter centers around the narratives of women surfers who felt empowered and liberated by telling their stories.

The chapter examines gender equality in sports - specifically surfing, which has predominantly been viewed as a masculine endeavor - through the stories of Californian women surfers first collected in 2008 and revisited a decade later. Narratives of women surfers provide insight into the social construction of gender and the socially accepted performance of gender stereotypes (Butler 2010) associated with competitive sports. The subculture of surfing is influenced by mainstream culture and has the tendency to replicate the gender norms. Gender is often pertinent to subcultural status, and full inclusion is difficult for female participants (Wheaton and Beal 2003), particularly since the institution of competitive sports has contributed to normalize male privilege and perpetuate inequity in sports access and participation (Channon, Dashper, Fletcher, and Lake 2015). The assumptions that women are less capable to engage in sports, highly emotional and in need of protection from men's inevitably superior strength and power have been historically permeating women's identity (Anderson 2008).

To unpack the complex interconnection between power, privilege and identity in relation to women surfers, a postmodern feminism framework was used. Olsen (1996, cited in Pasque 2013, p. 101) states that "postmodern feminists see the female as being cast into the role of 'other' and there is a rejection of the concept that there is only one-way to be a woman." This represents a reaction to first and second waves of feminism that sought to challenge male hegemony and achieve legal and political equality with men by integrating women across society (Lotz 2003) and unify diverse women by appealing to a universal sisterhood. However, women have not a single voice or vision of reality, they belong to groups based on their shared backgrounds, identities and struggles, and are not a cohesive unit (Mann and Huffman 2005). In the early 1990s, the third wave of feminism helped underpin wider social constructions of male-controlled power structures. Most third-wavers refuse to think in terms of us vs. them, stay away from the term "feminist" as they find the word limiting and exclusionary (Rampton 2015). The third wave of feminism had a global, multicultural and multilingual scope, and it avoided simplistic answers or artificial categories of identity, gender and sexuality (Archer 2013). Its transversal politics means that differences such as those of ethnicity, class, sexual orientation, etc. are celebrated and recognized as dynamic, situational and provisional. Third-wave feminist epistemologies include many voices in the construction of a social reality that is not conceived in terms of fixed structures and power relations, but in terms of performance within contingencies (Budgeon 2011).

In the early 2000s, fourth wave feminism has been impacted by social media activism and characterized by the #MeToo and the #TimesUp movements (Langone 2018). This movement has grown rapidly, and numerous accusations against men in powerful public positions have catalyzed feminists in efforts that differ from previous iterations and aim to promote inclusion and more systematically dismantle gender and sexual binaries that have fragmented the movement. As Rampton (2015, 19) states: "feminism is part of a larger consciousness of oppression along with racism, ageism, classism, ableism, and sexual orientation (no "ism" to go with that)." The unprecedented number of women who were elected to office in the US in 2018 and 2020 is a powerful manifestation of the fourth wave of feminism's success. The main feature of the fourth wave of feminism is its reliance on social media (Shiva and Zohreh 2019). This movement taking place on the Internet has been active around issues such as the gender pay gap and cultural sexism, which aligns with our results. The ability to control content in online spaces may offer a way for female athletes not only to exert some control over their media representations, but to boost their athletic endeavours to a level of prominence that would not have been attainable through traditional media (Pavlidis and Fullagar 2014).

Gender politics is undergoing a new permutation. Feminism has become more mainstreamed, leading to the resurgence of mass feminist mobilization (Rottenberg 2019), driven by a deep resentment towards entitled and privileged men. This new type of feminist is incited to accept full responsibility for her own well-being and self-care regardless of the current socio-economic and cultural structure in place (Rottenberg 2019). Placing the focus on the individual level provides a unique opportunity for the woman surfer to enact change in the water.

Surfing through feminist lenses

Though women have participated only on the fringes of surfing, they have been sexualized and represented in surf culture and the media as a symbolic trophy, as portrayed in the series of 1960s Beach Party films starring Frankie Avalon and Annette Funicello. Ormrod (2002, p. 9) describes the role women played in these films: "strong women are either 'tamed' or punished". In Beach Party and other surf exploitation films, "real" women do not surf; they ride on male surfers' shoulders, adore the daredevil exploits of their surfer boyfriends or wait for their men on the beach. Gender performance in sports is analyzed through the lens of social perceptions in historic contexts, and male surfers in the sixties represent the masculine ideal, associated with heterosexuality and the white, middle-class dream (Ormrod 2002). Pavlidis and Fullagar (2014) noted that depictions of female athletes in traditional media (e.g., magazines and television) were filtered through masculine values, often resulting in marginalized and/or sexualized portrayals that did not accurately reflect women's athletic achievements.

Male surfers still today perceive women surfers to be occupying a marginalized position within the space of surfing (Cromley 2016). Within male-dominated physical cultures, the marginalization or exclusion of women occurs through cultural understandings and expectations of how the activities should be performed, or through assumptions about male and female appropriate performances (Olive, McCuaig and Phillips 2015, cited in Cromley 2016). The popularity of surfing in Western culture became male dominated due to gender conformity as males were in both the social and cultural position to be able to participate in the sport (Cromley 2016). According to Olive, McCuaig, and Phillips (2015, cited in Cromley 2016), the greatest barrier for women surfers is the role men play in continuing to differentiate women within male-dominated surfing cultures. The sexualization of female surfers is a compromise that allows women to be represented in surfing media without alienating participants in the dominant, hyper-masculine aspect of the sub-culture (Roy and Caudwell 2014). Sexualization of female surfers has therefore been a lucrative strategy for advertisers to reconcile the otherwise contradictory demands of two indispensable market segments (Roy and Caudwell 2014). Roy and Caudwell (2014) suggested that publishers of surfing magazines may be deeply invested in sexualizing their representations of female surfers because these sexualized portrayals constitute a means of bridging the masculine culture of the sport with the growing market segment of female surfers.

Methodology

To address the key research objectives, this study used qualitative methods that allowed an in-depth exploration and understanding of women surfers' experiences. A phenomenological study (Creswell 2013; Maxwell 2013) was designed to explore how inequality is still experienced by female surfers in southern California and centred on the following questions: (1) *How have women's surf experiences in regard to inequality changed over the past decade?* and (2) *What social and/or institutional practices still exist to perpetuate inequality in surfing?*

Interviewees were invited to share their personal narratives, the *story of self* (Ganz 2010), as a way to convey their sense of identity and to recount the *choice points* in their lives. Participants also reflect on their collective consciousness, the *story of us* (Ganz 2010), and discuss the shared values and experiences of the women surfing community. In an initial 2008 research study conducted by the authors, the same participants were interviewed, and they had all identified their challenges participating in the masculine sport of surfing. Considering the dramatic increase of women surfers in Orange County, California, this study set out to determine whether the women surfers interviewed in 2008 have been able to change their perceptions of the men they surf with. This longitudinal approach has proved impactful to assess if the surfing culture has become more inclusive.

Participants

The participants in the study were ten female surfers residing in Orange County, California with different levels of surfing expertise (from advanced beginner to intermediate) and experience (average years of surfing experience: 13). The same participants were part of an initial 2008 research study conducted by the author (Vlachos, 2008). The participants interviewed were all still active members of Wahine Kai Surf Club. The goal of Wahine Kai Surf Club is to create a community of women surfers who will support each other to grow physically and spiritually in the sport of surfing, and this organization is relevant to the qualitative research collected, which is why it is named (www.wahinekai.org). All of the participants still surf in Orange County, California, and surf on a weekly basis. It is important to note that the participants included their cumulative experience due to time off from the sport due to work commitments, moves and child raising. This is relevant because it allows comparisons to be drawn based on participants' surfing experiences in 2008 as compared to 2018.

Data collection

This study consisted of a series of semi-structured interviews composed by open-ended questions and designed to allow participants to offer their opinions and to share their views freely. The data from the interviews was collected in November of 2018 in Huntington Beach, California. Each participant was only interviewed once, and participants were asked to verify the accuracy of information during the thematic analysis and interpretation stage by reviewing the transcript of the interviews. Pseudonyms were used to protect participants' identity.

This study replicated the interview questions posed originally to the same participants in 2008, and they were designed to focus on women surfers' experiences while surfing in Southern California with respect to gender inequality, surfing ability, surfing frequency, surfing locations and surfing companions (Vlachos, 2019). The interview questions were crafted to examine to what extent gender inequality still exists in the surfing sub-culture and how such inequality is perpetuated by media or societal perceptions of femininity and masculinity.

Results

In the study, it became evident that the most significant constraints for women seeking to participate in male-dominated sports are socio-culturally ingrained, and women's societal perceptions as risk-avoidant caregivers have inhibited them and caused them to experience self-doubt when engaging in action sports. Thorpe, Toffoletti, and Bruce (2017) believe that societal shifts have led to feminism being viewed as no longer necessary and to creating "new modes" of the empowered woman. To what extent such observation is applicable when it comes to surfing is an aspect this chapter revolves around.

In-depth interviews demonstrated that women surfer participants have achieved a sense of empowerment, self-esteem and camaraderie with other female surfers that have shaped their lives and identities. The stories collected from women surfers unveiled the importance of overcoming the danger of the single narrative and recognizing the multiple stories that make up communities at both the local and international levels. The data analysis was performed in relation to the two main research questions that guided this study. Results are organized by themes, and evidence from the data is given for each theme in the form of direct quotations. Two main themes emerged in response to the first research question: *the growing and supportive culture of women surfers* and *the perceived ongoing gendered inequality in surfing*.

The growing and supportive culture of women surfers

Participants reported that during the past decade, women surfers have become more common in Orange County, and that female surfers have their own distinctive surfing style and culture. Specifically, participants expressed that women surfers' style tended to emphasize grace and endurance more than strength, although participants added that women surfers could be as strong as men. Additionally, women surfers' culture, when women surfed together, emphasized socialization and supportiveness, in contrast to the culture of male surfers, which emphasized solitary activity and competitiveness.

Krystle, for example, stated that although surfing sites were "never dominated by women," "I'm seeing a lot of women out there … There's certainly more now than before." Kim also observed that there are more women surfers at a beach that tended to be less crowded: "at Bolsa [beach in Orange County], it's where I go out with a bigger group of women and there are less people there. Sometimes the women to men ratio is bigger, which is kind of refreshing." Ruth stated: "In the water I see more and more women, but from the very beginning it definitely felt like it's gone up." While these insights indicate a growing presence of female surfers in Orange County, still women reside on the margins of surfing. Samantha expressed the perception that the increasing gender equality in surfing had encouraged more women to participate:

> Nowadays, because surfing has become a more open sport, more equal sport… it's making all the women like me to start surfing. I started surfing when I was in my 30s, but I have friends that started surfing when they were 50 and that's great. That's amazing.

Eight out of ten participants expressed the perception that women surfers' surfing technique differed in visible ways from men surfers. They described women surfers' style as an alternative form of strength and endurance, rather than a weaker manifestation of male surfing. In other words, as opposed to rating men as superior to women, participants noted different but equally valuable styles of surfing. In addition to perceiving the increasing number of women surfers as having a distinctive surfing style from men, nine out of ten participants perceived female surfers as having a way of interacting with one another that differed from the ways in which they interacted with men and the ways in which men interacted with other men. Sara noted: "The women are supportive. It's definitely community in practice where I'm learning from them about everything from gear to where to go, so I'd say that's the most supportive experience I've had." In sum, participants described the interactions of female surfers as emphasizing supportiveness and sociability, while interactions with or between men surfers were perceived as emphasizing solitary activity and competition.

Perceived ongoing gendered inequality in surfing

Male surfers still perceive women surfers to be occupying a marginalized position within the space of surfing (Cromley 2016). Within male-dominated physical cultures, the marginalization or exclusion of women occurs through cultural understandings and expectations of how the activities should be performed as per gender expectations (Olive, McCuaig and Phillips 2015, cited in Cromley 2016). While participants perceived women surfers as increasing in numbers and as defining their own culture and surfing style, they also perceived gender inequality as ongoing in the activity. They noted that women surfers experienced pressure to prove their competence and that they occasionally experienced a level of aggression from men surfers. Kristin stated that women surfers needed to prove themselves so men surfers would not see them as weak and take opportunities from them. Heidi believed that men surfers tended to perceive women surfers as incompetent and to take advantage of this perceived incompetence. Women also reported that men have aggressively cut them off when they were paddling toward a wave, used inappropriate language toward them, and that behaviour coming from men had impacted their self-perceptions of surfing competence. Sofia explained:

> I could hear high school kids [boys] yelling at me, saying stupid names. ... I just felt mortified. I was just; 'Oh my god! What am I doing here?' I felt super embarrassed. I don't know. Yeah, and then I was done with that... It took like a year to go back [to surf at Huntington Beach].

These quotes correlate with Rottenberg's (2019) observation that feminism is being driven by a deep resentment towards entitled and privileged men. In this context, women surfers may be perceived as feminists who are taking over and trespassing on a male domain. As a consequence, as participants noted, men surfers had the tendency to perceive women surfers as out of place and may even display aggressive surfing behaviour around them (e.g., cutting them off when paddling towards a wave; although, it is to be noted that beginner surfers, regardless of their gender, may also experience similar attitudes from advanced male surfers). Seven out of ten participants suggested that the ongoing inequality to cause women surfers to feel intimidated around men surfers may be a reason why more women do not enter or remain in surfing. One example of the ongoing inequality in surfing stems from the way that men and women surfers are depicted in the media.

Perceived differences in media depictions and sponsorship of women surfers

All ten participants reported the perception that social and institutional practices that maintained inequality in women's surfing included inaccurate media depictions of women surfers, such as sexualization, and a lack of sponsors and promotion for women surfers. Regarding media depictions of women surfers, participants reported that women surfers were often portrayed as engaging in a leisurely lifestyle choice, lying on the beach in a bikini or watching men surfers from the beach. This portrayal supports the ongoing sexualization of women surfers. Though women have participated only on the fringes of surfing, they have been sexualized and represented in surf culture and the media as a symbolic trophy, as far back as the 1960s. The Beach Party film series, starring Frankie Avalon and Annette Funicello, is an illustrative example of such gendered depiction. Ormrod (2002) noted that in these films, strong women are either "tamed" or punished.

While men surfers tended to be depicted as actively surfing in the mass media, women surfers were portrayed as more sexualized and objectified to such an extent that women surfers who did not match traditional gender standards in their appearance were perceived as having difficulty obtaining sponsorship, regardless of their skill level. These depictions have long historical roots in the Beach Party film series and other 1960s surf films, all of which reinforced that "real" women do not surf; they ride on surfers' shoulders, adore the daredevil exploits of their surfer boyfriends or wait for their men on the beach (Ormrod 2002). The mass media's use of the surfer girl image directly connects with women's ability to enter the sport (Reed 2010). The media attention of female surfers illustrates what it means to be feminine and a surfer. Rather than focusing on their surfing accomplishments, mass media tend to focus on how they look in a bikini. According to Reed (2010), very few women surfers are blond-haired, blue-eyed and sitting on a beach. They are in the water surfing, wearing a wetsuit and riding the waves just like the men. Sarah described this media obsession with female surfers' bodies:

I think women, the focus is not quite as much on their athleticism but more about a bunch of other stuff, you know. If they're too masculine, or not too masculine, but if they appear more what the culture thinks is masculine or if they're really hot.

Other participants reported that women surfers were not given the same prominence in competition as men and that gender differences in media depictions of surfers accounted for some of the gender inequality in the sport as a whole. Ruth lamented on women surfers' media presence as follows: "we are of course influenced by what we see in the media, and if we're seeing constantly guys ripping and performing in the water and women watching the horizon from the sand, what do you expect?" The most recent documentary *Girls Can't Surf* (2020) corroborates the participants' perceptions and details how historically women have faced sexism and social backlash as they advocate for agency, equality and visibility.

Gendered behavioural expectations for male and female surfers

Participants reported the perception that social practices that maintained inequality in women's surfing included the pressure for men and women to adhere to traditional gender roles, with behavioural manifestations including masculine objectification of women and belittlement. The expectation towards women is to be submissive and attractive. Lisa commented that "women surfers are expected to be cute and pretty." A man who taught Samantha how to surf had attempted to keep her in a traditionally feminine position of subordination and dependence in her practice of the sport. Samantha recalled: "While he taught me how to surf, he didn't really allow me to succeed on my own." Participants emphasized that women surfers were just as qualified to surf as men, and that gendered expectations that classified women surfers as inferior to men surfers in skill and/or ability were inaccurate. For instance, Ruth explained that:

> There are women who can hold their own with the guys, absolutely. I don't think inherent ability [differs between men and women surfers] at all. I think women are strong enough for all kinds of waves. You're seeing women now doing big wave surfing, competing with big waves, cutting, whipping the lip just like any other guy.

The way in which participants described men and women surfers as tending to differ was in their performance of gendered behavioural expectations, with men surfers tending to be more aggressive and competitive, and women surfers tending to be more cooperative. Kim explained:

> I think the men are more aggressive. I think they have more confidence and I think they have less fear in terms of injury, and I think the confidence is that they are just going to be better at it because I think they are less fearful and more confident of their ability.

If men surfers outperformed women, this was because men surfers aggressively pursued opportunities to practice and improve, occasionally at the expense of less aggressive women. Sofia explained this as follows:

> I think [men surfers] get more opportunity than women, so environment is important. So, if you get an environment where women aren't welcome, they won't get as many waves. They may not get out as often. They may wait for buddies. So, they may have an opportunity to become better surfers because they're getting more opportunities. That's in anything in any field. If you're given more opportunities, you can get better.

Notable in this quotation is the perception that men and women surfers do not differ in their innate ability, but that society-wide gendered behavioural expectations give men an advantage in skill-building that might eventually result in gendered performance disparities. Within male-dominated physical cultures, the marginalization or exclusion of women occurs through cultural understandings and expectations of how the activities should be performed, or the assumptions about male and female performances (Olive, McCuaig and Phillips 2015, cited in Cromley 2016). The popularity of surfing in Western culture became male dominated because, due to gender conformity, men were in both the social and cultural position to be able to participate in the sport (Cromley 2016). According to Olive, McCuaig, and Phillips (2015, cited in Cromley 2016), the greatest barrier for women surfers is the role men play in continuing to marginalize women within male-dominated surfing cultures. Usher and Gomez (2018) found that women surfers are subject to greater feelings of constraint than their male counterparts. Previous researchers have found that constraints for women in action sports included family obligations, safety concerns and societal norms. While noting that surfing had increased in popularity among women in recent decades, the authors acknowledged that "women are often told they do not belong in high-risk, physically demanding adventure activities" (Usher and Gomez 2018, p. 149), and that this expression of a societal norm might in part account for the ongoing underrepresentation of women in surfing.

Conclusion

Findings indicated that the number of women surfers had increased over the past ten years and that women surfers were defining their own style of surfing (based on grace and endurance, as opposed to strength) and their own culture of sociability and supportiveness (in contrast to the masculine culture of solitary activity and competitiveness). Perceived inequality in women's surfing was ongoing as well as decreasing, with the caveat that women surfers felt pressured to demonstrate their competence to men in order to establish their right to surf. Their perseverance nonetheless correlates with the current fourth wave of feminism where women are incited to accept full responsibility for their own well-being and self-care regardless of the current socio-economic and cultural structure in place (Rottenberg 2019).

Institutional practices that perpetuate inequality in women's surfing included depictions and sponsorship of men and women surfers in the media, with men surfers being depicted as active, powerful athletes, and with women surfers appearing as sexualized bodies through portrayal as passive lifestyle participants, rather than actively engaged in the sport. Social practices included gendered behavioural expectations for both men and women surfers, resulting in expressions of gender binarism. For men, this involved masculinity such as aggression and objectification of women, and for women femininity that culminated in sexualization, objectification and pressurization to assume a passive role.

To overcome such gender binarism, Bush (2016) argued that the establishment of women on an equal basis with men in surfing might involve female surfers' achievement of their own separate identity and subculture. Findings in the present study indicated that female surfers are indeed establishing such an identity and subculture. Bush (2016) found that female surfers were creating social spaces in which their feminine identities could manifest independently of hegemonic masculinity and could develop and sustain relationships with other female surfers that were supportive, thereby reinforcing their surfing identities. Participants in this study voiced the pertinence of the supportive role of such women driven and focused surfing community.

The fourth wave of feminism has been moulded by (amongst other things) the Occupy Movement, The Women's March of 2017 (a worldwide protest of President Trump) and the unprecedented number of women who were elected to US Congress in 2018. The fourth wave activists found themselves being politicized as they were trying to address structural and systemic problems. Raised in an environment where women are taught that they are equal to men, they are now demanding that society treat them as such. The women interviewed for this study confirmed this belief when participants emphasized that women surfers were just as qualified as men surfers, and that gendered expectations and perceptions that characterized women surfers as inferior to men surfers in skill or ability were inaccurate. The participants also pointed to the fact that given the same support and opportunities, women surfers can perform as well as male surfers, but as long as the broader culture of surfing is driven by traditional gender binarism and related belief systems, women will continue to remain on the margins of this awe-inspiring activity.

REFERENCES

Anderson, E. (2008) 'I used to think women were weak: Orthodox masculinity, gender segregation, and sport', *Sociological Forum*, 23(2), pp. 257–280.

Archer, M. (2013) 'Third wave feminism's unhappy marriage of poststructuralism and intersectionality theory', *Journal of Feminism Scholarship*, 28(4), pp. 54–73.

Budgeon, S. (2011) *Third Wave Feminism and the Politics of Gender in Late Modernity*. New York, NY: Palgrave MacMillan.

Bush, L. (2016) 'Creating our own lineup: Identities and shared cultural norms of surfing women in a U.S. East Coast community', *Journal of Contemporary Ethnography*, 45(3), pp. 290–318.

Butler, J. (2010) *Gender Trouble*, 2nd edn. New York, NY: Routledge.

Channon, A., Dashper, K., Fletcher, K. and Lake, R. (2015) 'The promises and pitfalls of sex integration in sport and physical culture', *Sport in Society*, 19(8), pp. 1–15.

Cragoe, N. (2019) 'Oversight: Community vulnerabilities in the blind spot of research ethics', *Research Ethics*, 15(3), pp. 1–15.

Creswell, J.W. (2013) *Qualitative Inquiry & Research Design: Choosing among the Five Approaches*. Thousand Oaks, CA: Sage Publications.

Cromley, C. (2016) '"We have to establish our territory": How women surfers "carve out" gendered spaces within surfing', *Sport in Society*, 19(8-9), pp. 1289–1298.

De Sousa Santos, B. (2014) *Epistemologies of the South: Justice against Epistemicide*. New York, NY: Routledge.

Dowling, C. (2000) *The Frailty Myth: Redefining the Physical Potential of Women and Girls*. New York, NY: Random House.

Ganz, M. (2010) 'Leading change. Leadership, organization and social movements', in Ni. Nohria, N. and Khurana, R. (eds.) *Handbook of Leadership Theory and Practice: A Harvard Business School Centennial Colloquium* (Chapter 19). Cambridge, MA: Harvard Business School Publishing Corporation.

Langone, A. (2018) '#MeToo and Time's Up founders explain the difference between the 2 movements — And how they're alike', *Time Magazine*. Available at: https://time.com/5189945/whats-the-difference-between-the-metoo-and-times-up-movements/ (Accessed: 25 September 2021).

Lim, N. (2020) *Liberation is Here: Women Uncovering Hope in a Broken World*. Downers Grove, Illinois: Intervarsity Press.

Lotz, A. (2003) 'Communicating third-wave feminism and new social movements: Challenges for the next century of feminist endeavor', *Women and Language*, 26(1), pp. 2–9.

Mann, S. and Huffman, D. (2005) 'The decentering of second wave feminism and the rise of the third wave', *Science and Society*, 69(1), pp. 56–91.

Maxwell, J.A. (2013) *Qualitative Research Design: An Interactive Approach*. Thousand Oaks, CA: SAGE Publications.

Mignolo, W. (2000) *Local Histories/Global Designs: Coloniality, Subaltern Knowledge's, and Border Thinking*. Princeton, NJ: Princeton University Press.

Ormrod, J. (2002) 'Issues of gender in Muscle Beach Party' (1964) [Motion picture series]', *Scope: An Online Journal of Film Studies*, 3, pp. 1–19.

Pasque, P. (2013) '(Re)membering and (re)living: A methodological exploration of postmodern and constructivist feminists approaches to interviewing women leaders in higher education', *Journal about Women in Higher Education*, 6(1), pp. 99–126.

Pavlidis, A. and Fullagar, S. (2014) 'Women, sport and new media technologies: Derby Grrrls online', in Bennett, A. and Robards, B. (eds.) *Mediated Youth Cultures*. London, England: Palgrave.

Rampton, M. (2015) 'Four waves of feminism', *Pacific University Oregon Magazine*, October 2015. Available at: https://www.pacificu.edu/about/media/four-waves-feminism (Accessed: 25 October 2020).

Reed, R. (2010) '*Women on waves, surfing toward gender equality*' (Master's thesis). Long Beach CA: California State University.

Rottenberg, C. (2019) '#MeToo and the prospects of political change', *Soundings: A Journal of Politics and Culture*, 71, pp. 40–49.

Roy, G. and Caudwell, J.C. (2014) Women and Surfing Spaces in Newquay, UK. *Routledge Handbook of Sport, Gender and Sexuality*. Oxen, UK: Routledge.

Shiva, N. and Zohreh, N. (2019) 'The fourth wave of feminism and the lack of social realism in cyberspace', *Cyberspace Studies*, 3(2), pp. 129–146.

Thorpe, H., Toffoletti, K. and Bruce, K. (2017) 'Sportswomen and social media: Bringing third-wave feminism, postfeminism, and neoliberal feminism into conversation', *Journal of Sport and Social Issues*, 41(5), pp. 3–13.

Usher, L. and Gomez, E. (2018) 'Female surfers' perceptions of regulatory constraints and negotiation strategies', *Journal of Park and Recreation Administration*, 36(1), pp. 149–165.

Vlachos, A. (2008) '*Girls don't surf: The gender inequality of women surfers*' (Master's thesis). Long Beach, CA: California State University.

Vlachos, A. (2019) '*Understanding the relationship between gender and women surfers in Southern California*' (Doctorate dissertation). Daphne, AL: United State Sports Academy.

Wheaton, B. and Beal, B. (2003) 'Keeping it real', *International Review for the Sociology of Sport*, 38, pp. 155–176.

27
Fitness Practitioners' Overcoming of Self-objectification
The Problem with 'Legs, Bums and Tums'

Hannah Kate Lewis

Introduction

Aetiological explanations of women's body dissatisfaction and disordered eating have been rooted in some branches of political science – namely feminist and objectification theories.

Since the mid-20th century, feminist scholars, such as de Beauvoir (1949), have been highlighting how damaging representations of the body cause women to internalise patriarchal messages about themselves. Morris (2019, p. 41) also highlighted that 'women fully absorb cultural objectification until they become alienated from their own bodies'.

The explanation of the phenomenon of internalising patriarchal surveillance or objectification can be argued to originate from Foucauldian thought and the metaphor of the patriarchal panopticon (Foucault 1979). The Panopticon of the Patriarchy metaphor takes Jeremy Bentham's, a utilitarian philosopher, 'perfect prison' idea and interprets it through a gendered lens, acknowledging that it can be a useful tool in understanding how body dissatisfaction develops among those identifying as women (Foucault 1979).

Body dissatisfaction, defined as negative feelings about one's own body, has been said to be a critical component of the majority of eating disorders (Watson and Vaughn 2006). Eating disorders are severe psychiatric disorders characterised by a difficult relationship with food alongside body image disturbance. An estimated 1.25 million people in the UK experience an eating disorder, 90% of whom identify as female (Beat 2021). Given that eating disorders have the highest mortality rate of any psychiatric disorder (Beat 2021), identifying potential risk factors of body dissatisfaction is of importance.

The role of the diet and exercise industry has previously been analysed by Bordo (1999, p. 192) as a critical factor in the development of eating disorders, stating that they arise out of 'reproducing normative feminine practices of our culture [i.e. male dominance and female subordination]… which train the female body in docility and obedience to cultural demands while at the same time being experienced in terms of 'power' and 'control'. The diet industry is a lucrative trade – valued at approximately £2 billion per year (British Heart Foundation 2021) – which promotes weight-loss through altered food regimens, increased physical activity, and/or supplement use which promise to suppress appetite and/or 'burn fat'.

The term 'False Hope Syndrome' is commonly used to describe the mechanism by which people continue to engage with the diet and fitness industry: 'unrealistic expectations about dieting set dieters up for failure and then promote renewed efforts at weight loss' (Trottier, Polivy and Herman 2005, p. 142). This encapsulates how the diet and fitness industry predominantly lures those identifying as women in with false promises of renewed self-confidence and happiness once a smaller body – a body conforming to societal standards – has been achieved (Trottier, Polivy and Herman 2005). As evidence demonstrates, physical changes to the body which occur due to dieting are often short-lived, which can act as a catalyst for repeated attempts to lose weight, often resulting in bulimic or purging eating disorders which include behaviours such as excessive and compulsive exercise (American Psychiatric Association 2013). Yet, in a study by Bratland-Sanda and Sundgot-Borgen (2015), it was estimated that only 29% of fitness practitioners had an appropriate knowledge of such disorders. Therefore, this chapter seeks to explore the relationship between body politics, body dissatisfaction with disordered eating, and the diet and fitness industry. Crucially, this chapter will introduce potential solutions with case studies of fitness practitioners wishing to overturn this innate objectification through the use of non-diet, body functionality approaches.

Self-objectification: A risk factor for body dissatisfaction in exercise and fitness

Despite the evidence demonstrating the positive effects of exercise on individual well-being, research has shown that these psychological effects are not universal as they are not experienced equally across genders (Strelan, Mehaffey and Tiggemann 2003). Feminist approaches, such as objectification theory (Fredrickson and Roberts 1997), have proved useful in understanding this phenomenon. Objectification theory also attempts to explain the negative psychological effects including body dissatisfaction and disordered eating experienced by some of the women who exercise and utilise fitness and leisure centres (Prichard and Tiggeman 2005).

Objectification theory can be defined as 'societal norms [which] influence women to internalise cultural standards of beauty and thinness as their own' (Hauff 2016, p. 99) and demonstrates negative psychological consequences such as: 'body shame, anxiety, body surveillance, and internalisation of the thin ideal' (Hauff 2016, p. 99). This theory argues that women come to see themselves as an object to be under surveillance, mainly by the patriarchal gaze and evaluated on the basis of their appearance. The origins of this theory can be identified in Foucault's interpretation of Bentham's panopticon idea, which has since received feminist critique on its application to the role of internalising the patriarchal gaze of surveillance on women's appearance and the idea of them having 'docile bodies' (Bordo 1999; Duncan 2007; Bartky 1997, pp. 93–111).

To bring this theory into practice, a study conducted in Australia (Strelan, Mehaffey and Tiggemann 2003) demonstrated that self-objectification and appearance-related motivations for exercise and physical activity were shown to have a significantly negative impact on body satisfaction and self-esteem. However, functional motivations for exercise were demonstrative of an increased body satisfaction and self-esteem (Strelan, Mehaffey and Tiggemann 2003). This empirical evidence offers encouragement that objectification theory can be utilised to understand the potential risks of body dissatisfaction in the fitness realm, and that body functionality approaches could be a potential practical solution to manage levels of self-objectification (Strelan, Mehaffey and Tiggemann 2003).

A practical solution to self-objectification: Non-aesthetic, body functionality approaches

Resisting traditional body politics, some exercise and fitness practitioners have demonstrated a shift towards body functionality approaches ('function over form') to reduce the focus on aesthetics and self-objectification. The notion of 'body functionality' was highlighted a decade ago in Cash and Smolak's (2011) seminal piece as a potential future direction of body image research which required further investigation. Since then, body functionality has been used in both physical and psychological intervention studies in an attempt to help those identifying as women to overcome the negative psychological effects of self-objectification and alienation from their bodies. By definition, body functionality:

> comprises everything that the body can do or is capable of doing, including functions related to internal processes (e.g., healing from a cold, digestion), physical capacities (e.g. walking, stretching), bodily senses and sensations (e.g., sight, experiencing pleasure), creative endeavours (e.g., drawing, singing), communication with others (e.g., via body language, eye contact), and self-care (e.g., sleeping, showering).
>
> (Alleva et al. 2015, p. 82).

Psychological interventions such as *Expand Your Horizon* – which is a creative writing-based body functionality programme – has positively demonstrated that by shifting their focus from their body's aesthetic to its functional ability with a concerted cognitive effort, levels of self-objectification among women can decrease and levels of body satisfaction can increase (Alleva et al. 2015). In addition, physical interventions exploring the role of body functionality have largely been based around yoga practice, due to this being considered as an embodying activity (Halliwell, Dawson and Burkey 2019). For example, one study found that a four-week yoga-based intervention increased body connectedness and satisfaction and decreased self-objectifying body surveillance. The yoga intervention was based on Anusara, Iyengar, and Vinyasa styles and focused on body connection, appreciation of function, acceptance, and self-respect (Halliwell, Dawson and Burkey 2019).

It is also promising to see body functionality used in national campaigns to promote physical activity. The *This Girl Can* campaign ran by Sport England (2015) in the UK and the *#jointhemovement* campaign, hosted by the Queensland government in Australia, are two initiatives which promote diversity of appearance in women by offering realistic depictions of exercise in a non-objectified manner (Mulgrew et al. 2018). Women featured in these two campaigns are shown to have a range of body sizes, shapes, and abilities, and are shown to be engaging in exercise where they are visibly sweating with body fat 'jiggling' (Mulgrew et al. 2018). The hope with these campaigns was to encourage women to view their bodies in functionality terms as well as normalising the body's appearance during exercise (Mulgrew et al. 2018).

Instead of conforming to patriarchal standards of appearance which are perhaps maintained by self-objectification, and by rejecting the surveillance of the patriarchy, women may be able to renegotiate their motivations for exercising and moving their bodies. In sum, shifting women's focus to the functionality of their bodies through psychological and physiological interventions – or perhaps a combination of both – can decrease self-objectification, thus decreasing the risk of body dissatisfaction and therefore eating disorders. This is achieved by encouraging women to think of their body as 'active, dynamic, and instrumental' as opposed to 'passive, static, and aesthetic' (Alleva et al. 2015, p. 82). The following two case studies will explore how UK-based fitness practitioners are promoting this approach in their practice.

Case study methodology

To explore how body functionality approaches were being adopted in practice, two physical activity organisations in the UK who advertised themselves as using non-aesthetic approaches to exercise were approached by the author. A case study design – as described by Bryman (2012) – was adopted. Semi-structured interviews were then used to explore how case study participants felt their practice helped people to maintain or improve their body image. Interviews also focused on the ways in which participants observed self-objectification and disordered eating that had been experienced by people in their industry. All in all, two participants were invited to partake in the personal and in-depth data collection process. Interviews were recorded, transcribed verbatim, and analysed. Interview transcripts were put to thematic decomposition analysis following Stenner (1993). Based on the outcome of the analysis, what follows below are two case studies to illuminate the key findings of the data collection process.

Case Study 1: *Hannah Lewin Fitness Ltd* – One-to-one personal training for women in recovery from disordered eating

Hannah Lewin is a London-based personal trainer. She works in a firmly 'non-diet approach' to health and fitness, closely aligned with pre-existing non-aesthetic frameworks such as body functionality and Health at Every Size® (HAES®).

Hannah describes her practise as a 'hybrid of physical training as well as confidence building'. Importantly, Hannah states that creating 'a safe space to fail' (i.e., resist the patriarchy) is more important when working with women who are at risk of or recovering from disordered eating, and challenging rules of perfectionism and control which can be traced back to the internalisation of the patriarchal gaze. In collaboration with her clients, she supports tangible, long-term and non-aesthetic goals and believes it is 'quite reductionist to reduce someone's efforts or progression to a number on a scale or other fat-loss measurements'.

Whilst Hannah's approach emerged quite organically and was inspired by her own lived experiences, it was also a response to the pre-existing practises harmful to women's wellbeing in the fitness industry. Hannah anticipated that her approach would be welcomed due to the rise of clean eating [while the term 'clean eating' has been defined in numerous ways, often dependent on diet paradigms, here it refers to the practice of including more whole foods and omitting/ reducing highly processed foods (British Heart Foundation 2021)] in the media and promoted by social media influencers and was passionate about creating that safe space for women who wanted to engage in physical activity without the pressure of the diet industry influencing their motivations. Consequently, Hannah began offering one-to-one sessions inside a gym but recognised that this environment was not conducive to what she was trying to achieve, acknowledging that her individual practice contributes to a wider ideology, which we have witnessed become more mainstream over recent years.

The novelty of the approach has led to much misunderstanding: 'people think anti-diet means anti-health, which is not the case'. When describing how her peers reacted, Hannah states that there was a lack of understanding and lack of awareness: 'people just naturally expected that if you were supporting someone to move or exercise, that you, of course, had to input on their diet'. This misunderstanding from her peers speaks to the wider, systemic issues of healthism across the fitness industry – which Hannah is attempting to separate from the diet industry – as mentioned by Bordo (1999).

Hannah has observed that over the years, the role of and association with femininity in exercise has altered. Whilst the fitness industry at one time associated women with more 'delicate' physical activity such as Pilates, yoga, and 'legs, bums, and tums', there has been a shift 'over the last decade where it has become more acceptable for women to do exercises like strength training and CrossFit'. Examining this phenomenon, it could be argued that this is an active resistance to the gaze of the patriarchy, and an attempt to claim high intensity and strength-based physical activity and exercise, which are areas traditionally associated with men and masculinity.

Regardless of the type of physical activity or exercise, Hannah emphasises that the type of language used by fitness practitioners can have an influence on the behaviour, motivation, and wellbeing of their clients. 'I think there is a lot of toxic language. I think when we hear things like 'Crush it! You're killing it! Feel the burn!' It is very aggressive terminology. I've found the more aggressive the language is, the more restricted their diet is – there is definitely a massive correlation between aggressive language and restrictive dieting'. Hannah also noted that: 'I think the more we objectify what we're eating and how we're moving the more that goes into objectifying ourselves.... 'Legs, bums and tums' classes are *literally looking at your body parts as objects*'. [italics added for emphasis]

In terms of adapting her practise to support those in recovery from body image disturbance and eating disorders, Hannah suggests being mindful of the impact that the different eating disorders can have on the body: 'I see it as rehab – with people in recovery from bulimia. For example, [there has been] a lot of cardiac pressure and pressure on the lungs, the neck... the whole chest area. With anorexia, we're looking at things like bone density being reduced or being compromised... the heart again – lots of cardiac and circulation issues'.

In sum, Hannah's case exemplifies how practitioners working in a one-to-one setting can successfully navigate the body politics and pressures faced by women when engaging in physical activity. Whilst offering an alternative way of working, Hannah's practice also speaks to wider activist movements such as body image activism and feminism, which are rooted in overcoming self-objectification.

Case Study 2: *School of Strut* – An inclusive and empowering dance school

Zoe McNulty is a London-based fitness instructor and teaches dance class for the *School Strut*. Zoe describes her practise as 'helping those who identify as women to feel better about their bodies irrespective of their shape or size, through the medium of dance'. She states that a 'key element is modelling [positive] body image and how I feel about my body in in a slightly larger than what society says a dancer and a fitness instructor should be', as well as "modelling the environment and making it safe, friendly, warm and inviting, so that my attendees feel really relaxed and able to move without judgement'. A central focus of Zoe's practise is 'tapping into the feminine power', as her marketing is aimed towards those who identify as women.

Zoe recounts how her practice emerged 'by accident', as a result of 'the perfect storm'. She was asked to teach a dance class in heels to emulate the emerging trend coming from America, where women would perform movements such as squats, lunges, and some elements of dance in their heels, which aimed to progress their balance and stability. This inspired her to create a dance class where women would gain functional benefits of training in heels, yet the benefits stretched far beyond what she had imagined. After the first class, the emotional and psychological benefits of dancing in heels became clear – women were sharing how the class had improved their body confidence and body image and felt a sense of liberation from their appearance anxiety.

When discussing the impact of the fitness industry on women's wellbeing, Zoe stated that: 'when a woman walks into a leisure centre or a gym, the assumption is that they are there to lose weight or burn calories or to get smaller… I think that in itself is a hurdle and a barrier'. Zoe shared how she had felt first-hand the negative effects of the messaging from the fitness industry: 'the only way that I've ever felt good about my body is getting smaller'. When describing how her peers reacted to her approach, Zoe remembers it being 'quite difficult… it was literally like I was going against the grain, swimming uphill…people couldn't get their head around the fact that you don't have to lose weight'. She shared how because of her own appearance, and the approach she advocates for, others in the fitness industry have aggressively disagreed with and 'rejected her message', as well as treated her unfavourably because she 'didn't fit their ethos'.

In terms of adapting the traditional approach to fitness to focus on self-acceptance rather than self-objectification, Zoe strongly recommends being mindful of the language used, and avoiding any mention of changing one's body shape or burning calories, including objectifying language such as 'bingo wings' and 'thunder thighs'. Furthermore, Zoe advises that: 'If you focus on your body parts, you're trying to fix something for the future – for that mythical time when one day you will be happy, and [your body parts] will look how you want them to look'.

When talking about her clients who may have had experience of body dissatisfaction and disordered eating, Zoe recognises the importance of being compassionate and empathetic whilst acknowledging her professional boundaries: '[People] do confide in me… and they're not, necessarily looking for an answer from me… they just know that I'll listen and understand, and just be a shoulder to cry on. I'm not a psychologist, I'm not a nutritionist. Those are deep beyond my remit. I would just try and refer people to [more appropriate] services'.

To conclude, Zoe's practice demonstrates how group-based movement classes cannot only reject the patriarchal, but in fact attempt to reclaim it. She demonstrates how her practice meets people when they are experiencing body dissatisfaction and highlights how, although specialist, multi-agency working is required for severe cases. The solidarity of a group class can also speak to wider body image activism and feminist movements which seek to overcome gender-based self-objectification.

Reflections on the two case studies

From comparing the above two case studies, we can see that Hannah Lewin's approach to her practise is rooted in overcoming the self-objectification that was once intrinsic to the fitness industry. Whilst some of her clients have already felt the repercussions of that objectification and are in recovery from body dissatisfaction and disordered eating, we can also identify how a non-aesthetic, functionality approach can be a positive solution to preventing body image and eating disturbance in the first place. The golden-thread that appears to run throughout Hannah's one-to-one personal training practice is that an awareness of potential risk factors – such as the use of language – makes for a personalised approach with the client's wellbeing at the fore.

From reflecting on Zoe McNulty's practice, we can conclude that her size-inclusive, non-diet approach to dance-based fitness classes – which prioritises women embracing their (emphasised) femininity – can have profound effects on both a client's physical and mental health. By opening the discourse on the legacy of self-objectification in the fitness industry, Zoe is able to create a safe environment for her clients to process feelings of body dissatisfaction and move towards body acceptance, whilst recognising when her clients may require specialist help and support.

Interestingly, both approaches differ due to how they approach femininity. Whilst Hannah Lewin's personal training focuses of functional strength training and rejects the traditionally feminine approaches to movement, Zoe McNulty's dance training tries to encourage clients to embrace and reclaim the femininity that society has forced upon them by wearing heels, thereby overturning the expectation for women to have 'docile bodies' (Bartky 1997, pp. 93–111). Perhaps, the common denominator is the *freedom* of movement inherent in functional training or the *freedom* of choice in dance to be (or not) 'heeled up' for exercise. In both cases, it seems that a non-prescriptive, person-centred approach gives women the autonomy to engage in the movement which is most suitable to their individual needs. In this sense, the approaches are similar in that they both emerged from the practitioner's own lived experience of self-objectification, body dissatisfaction and 'False Hope Syndrome' that they felt from years of working in the fitness industry. This lived experience can be seen as the catalyst for encouraging both practitioners to shift gears in how they approach their practice.

However, practitioners should not have to experience first-hand the detrimental effects of the fitness industry's objectifying language before altering their approaches.

In fact, in Australia, there has been a concerted effort between two Australian organisations (*InsideOut Institute for Eating Disorders* and *Fitness Australia*) to raise awareness and overcome the risk factors of body dissatisfaction and eating disorders in the fitness industry at a national level. This collaboration led to the publication of '*Eating disorders: Recommendations for the fitness industry*', which proposed five recommendations for the fitness industry to adhere to in order to improve awareness and mitigate the risk factors for body dissatisfaction and eating disorders. The five recommendations are introduced and elaborated on below with the view to recommend them as a template to follow globally.

International good practice example

Eating disorders: Recommendations for the fitness industry in Australia

In February 2020, two Australian organisations (*InsideOut Institute for Eating Disorders* and *Fitness Australia*) collaboratively published a set of five recommendations to address key issues in the fitness industry and to offer guidance around the complex interface of eating disorders and excessive exercise. Whilst the five recommendations were not intended to be a replacement for wider industry training and targeted policy development, they were established in order to 'assist fitness businesses and exercise professionals to work effectively with clients who present with symptoms of an eating disorder, or have an eating disorder, exercise disorder or muscle dysmorphia, and to sensitively and appropriately address issues of health and safety within a fitness facility or setting' (InsideOut Institute and Fitness Australia 2020). The five recommendations are as follows:

- **Recommendation 1: Support a Healthy, Inclusive Environment**
  The first recommendation identifies some of the risks associated with fitness and leisure centre environments, and advocates for all promotional material to focus on health benefits as opposed to body shaming, weight-loss approaches, as well as recognising that weight is not a modifiable behaviour, therefore not a target for behaviour change.

- **Recommendation 2: Recognise Warning Signs and Refer Appropriately**
  The second recommendation recognises the broad range of physiological, behavioural and social warning signs associated with eating and/or exercise disorders and provides examples of these to aid identification. This recommendation also reiterates the importance of a pre-exercise screening tool to provide an opportunity to discuss any potential risks and concerns.
- **Recommendation 3: Identify Suitable Referral Processes for Higher Risk Clients**
  Whilst upskilling fitness practitioners by raising awareness of eating disorders is paramount, this recommendation emphasises the profound physical and mental health implications of eating disorders and consequently the need for fitness practitioners to recognise and remain in their Scope of Practice and refer appropriately to medical professionals when necessary.
- **Recommendation 4: Identify clients with extreme forms of dieting, binge eating, self-inducing vomiting and misuse of laxatives, diuretics, diet pills or performance and image enhancing drugs (PIEDs) and implement appropriate actions**
  This recommendation encourages a compassionate approach to clients who may be engaging with inappropriate eating behaviours such as restrictive, bingeing and purging, and encourages close collaboration between fitness professionals, senior management, and health professionals.
- **Recommendation 5: Support Recovery in Collaboration and Maintain Best Practice**
  The final recommendation stresses the importance of a collaborative, multi-disciplinary approach when supporting the treatment and recovery maintenance of people with an eating disorder. This point also refers to the importance of advising clients to reduce or cease exercise when they fail to adhere to the guidance offered to them by healthcare professionals.

By producing these recommendations, the organisations involved have acknowledged the intersection between physical activity and disordered eating, with the first recommendation demonstrating the impact of non-inclusive, objectifying environments on people's mental wellbeing. This international example of good practice should encourage other nations to commit to overcoming the potential damage caused to people's body image by the fitness and diet industries.

From both case studies, we can see that when the interviewed practitioners first introduced their novel approaches to client care, the fitness industry was perhaps not as receptive as it is in today's culture. However, there seems to be a growing commitment from the fitness industry to overcome risk factors to body dissatisfaction. For example, a campaign which launched in 2020 – Fitness Professionals Against Weight Stigma (FPAWS) – demonstrates that there may be a shift on the horizon from weight-centric, body objectifying models of fitness to more liberating, non-aesthetic, and functionality-based models. This emerging trend will hopefully have an impact on the UK fitness industry to replicate the collaboration and proposed recommendations from the example in Australia, in order to support fitness practitioners to become more aware of risk factors, symptoms, and appropriate referrals for clients with eating disorders.

Conclusion

Whilst the aetiology of body dissatisfaction and eating disorders is multifactorial and inclusive of biological, psychological, and social factors, we now recognise the extent to which self-objectifying language from the fitness industry, which targets women (and to some extent men as well), can act as a sociocultural risk factor, and, thus, approaches to remedy this are important to explore and implement. This chapter has introduced the body functionality theory as an approach to implement in the fitness industry and explored how it has translated practically to be used by fitness practitioners in the two case studies provided. The impact of self-objectification on women's mental health and wellbeing can be detrimental, and both practitioners have actively structured their practice to intentionally set themselves apart from the traditional body-shaming approaches still embedded in the fitness industry. In this sense, the legacy of body-shaming and self-objectifying messages from the fitness industry is in dire need of reform via collaborative, multidisciplinary efforts from appropriate agencies to create a similar set of recommendations and guidance such as the international good practice example from Australia. By making this a mainstream issue led by public health agencies – instead of fringe campaigns from individuals – we can ensure that functionality focused approaches are embedded and prioritised in fitness practices with the view to potentially prevent the disproportionate body dissatisfaction that we see among many fitness industry clients today.

REFERENCES

Alleva, J.M., Martijn C, Van Breukelen GJ, Jansen A, Karos K. (2015) 'Expand Your Horizon: A programme that improves body image and reduces self-objectification by training women to focus on body functionality'. *Body Image*, 15, pp. 81–89.

American Psychiatric Association (2013) *Diagnostic and statistical manual of mental disorders* (5th ed.). Washington, D.C.: American Psychiatric Publishing.

Bartky, S.L. (1997) 'Foucault, femininity and the modernization of patriarchal power'. In Conboy, K., Medina, N. and Stanbury, S. (eds), *Writing on the body: Female embodiment and feminist theory*. New York: Columbia University Press, pp. 129–154.

Beat (2021) *Statistics for journalists*. Available at: www.beat.co.uk [accessed: January 2021]

de Beauvoir, S. (1949) *The second sex*. Paris: Gallimard.

Bordo, S. (1999) 'Feminism, Foucault and the politics of the body'. In Price, J. and Shildrick, M. (eds), *Feminist theory and the body*. New York: Routledge, pp. 179–202.

Bratland-Sanda, S. and Sundgot-Borgen, J. (2015) 'I'm concerned – What do I do? Recognition and management of disordered eating in fitness center settings'. *International Journal of Eating Disorders*, 48, pp. 415–423.

British Heart Foundation (2021) *4 reasons why you shouldn't follow the latest diet*. Available at: https://www.bhf.org.uk/informationsupport/heart-matters-magazine/nutrition/ask-the-expert/clean-eating [accessed: October 2021]

Bryman, A. (2012) *Social research methods* (4th ed.). Oxford: Oxford University Press.

Cash, T.F. and Smolak, L. (2011) 'Future challenges for body image science, practice, and prevention'. In Cash, T.F. et al. (eds), *Body image: A handbook of science, practice, and prevention* (2nd ed.). New York: Guilford Press, pp. 471–478.

Duncan, M.C. (2007) 'Bodies in motion: The sociology of physical activity'. *Quest*, 59(1), pp. 55–66.

Foucault, M. (1979) *Discipline and punish*. New York: Vintage.

Fredrickson B.L. and Roberts T-A. (1997). Objectification Theory: Toward Understanding Women's Lived Experiences and Mental Health Risks. *Psychology of Women Quarterly*, 21(2):173–206. doi:10.1111/j.1471-6402.1997.tb00108.x

Halliwell, E., Dawson, K. and Burkey, S. (2019) 'A randomized experimental evaluation of a yoga-based body image intervention'. *Body Image*, 28, pp. 119–127.

Hauff, C.R. (2016) 'Dress to impress or dress to sweat? Examining the perceptions of exercise apparel through the eyes of active women'. *Women in Sport and Physical Activity Journal*, 24(2), pp. 99–109.

InsideOut Institute and Fitness Australia (2020) *Eating disorders: Recommendations for the fitness industry*. Available at: https://bp-fitnessaustralia-production.s3.amazonaws.com/uploads/uploaded_file/file/452587/ED_Fitness_Recommendations_FINAL.pdf [accessed: October 2021]

Morris, A.G. (2019) *The politics of weight: Feminist dichotomies of power in dieting*. London: Palgrave Macmillan.

Mulgrew, K.E., McCulloch K., Farren E., Prichard I., Lim M.S.C. (2018) 'This girl can #jointhemovement: Effectiveness of physical functionality-focused campaigns for women's body satisfaction and exercise intent'. *Body Image*, 24, pp. 26–35.

Prichard, I. and Tiggemann, M. (2005) 'Objectification in fitness centers: Self-objectification, body dissatisfaction, and disordered eating in aerobic instructors and aerobic participants'. *Sex Roles*, 53, pp. 19–28.

Sport England (2015) *This girl can*. Available at: http://www.sportengland.org/our-work/national-work/this-girl-can [accessed: January 2021]

Stenner, P. (1993) 'Discoursing jealousy'. In Burman, E. and Parker, I. (eds), *Discourse analytic research: Repertoires and readings of texts in action*. London: Routledge, pp. 94–132.

Strelan, P., Mehaffey, S.J. and Tiggemann, M. (2003) 'Brief report: Self-objectification and esteem in young women: The mediating role of reasons for exercise'. *Sex Roles*, 48(1), pp. 89–95.

Trottier, K., Polivy, J. and Herman, C.P. (2005) 'Effects of exposure to unrealistic promises about dieting: Are unrealistic expectations about dieting inspirational?' *International Journal of Eating Disorders*, 37, pp. 142–149.

Watson, R. and Vaughn, L.M. (2006) 'Limiting the effects of the media on body image: Does the length of a media literacy intervention make a difference?' *Eating Disorders*, 14(5), pp. 385–400.

28
Sex Integration and the Potential of Track-and-Field

A New Norm

Anna Posbergh

Introduction

In 2017, World Athletics introduced the mixed 4x400-metres relay event for the World Relays competition in Nassau, Bahamas, which consisted of two men and two women, and no set running order. This was the first time that this event, or any combined event with men and women, was held at a World Athletics-sponsored or major international track-and-field (throughout this chapter, the term 'track-and-field' is used to refer to the sport of 'athletics') competition. In its inaugural running, the team from the Bahamas led from start to finish, blazing to victory nearly three seconds ahead of the United States team. With several commentators remarking that 'they'd never heard support quite as vociferous as [on the] home straight' (Olympics 2017, para. 11), the International Olympic Committee voted to add the mixed relay event to its 2021 Tokyo Summer Games programme.

Including a mixed sporting event in which men and women literally compete side-by-side on the global stage is a rarely seen phenomenon, especially in long-established sports such as track-and-field. Outside of the mixed 4x400-metre relay, men and women compete individually in almost identical track-and-field events, but often train and travel together. The (potential for) closeness between male and female track-and-field athletes is particularly visible in United States-based universities where a substantial number of men's and women's track-and-field programmes combine athletic staff, funding and resources. Although this is predominantly attributable to the passage of Title IX (Suggs 2006), it is a particularly notable trend given the historical inequities between men and women athletes. While sport as an institution purportedly upholds a hegemonic system that ranks men and women on the basis of '[their] own merit and through [their] own efforts' (Brohm 1978, p. 55), the essentialization of performance-related traits to male bodies – and simultaneous construction of these characteristics as unnatural or unacceptable in female bodies – continues to re-establish a power hierarchy between men and women (Anderson 2008; Cahn 2015; Erikainen 2020). Maintaining the idea of the *naturally* athletic male body, men are thus generally more enthusiastically welcomed than women into competitive sporting environments (Cahn 2015; Lenskyj 2013; Messner 1988).

Despite sport's identity as 'clearly a gendered activity' (Birrell 2000, p. 61), there are several sports, in addition to track-and-field, that utilize sex-integrated training and competition environments.

The close proximity between men and women in such settings subsequently presents the possibility to disrupt normative gender divisions, as athletes' lived experiences directly contradict sport's traditional sex-based hierarchy, separation and power structures (Priyadharshini and Pressland 2016). Though permanently erasing sex segregation in sport remains uncertain (and probably unlikely), the popularity of combining the sexes in training environments and competition events continues to grow (Price 2019), especially in track-and-field. While previous research has examined the impacts of gender ideologies and power structures on male or female track-and-field athletes (see Ashbolt, O'Flynn and Wright 2018; Posbergh and Jette 2021), there is limited understanding as to how male *and* female track-and-field athletes perceive gender(ed) performance, abilities and bodies.

This chapter addresses this gap by utilizing a post-structuralist framework to explore how ten university track-and-field athletes (four women, six men) who are part of a sex-integrated programme navigate gendered norms and hierarchies. As an extension of structuralism, post-structuralism focuses on the constitution of meaning, reality and subjectivity within a set or sets of structures, especially those constituted in discourse (Andrews 2000; Weedon 1997). More specifically, post-structuralists suggest the impossibility of a fixed and stable relationship between individuals (i.e., subjects) and structures, institutions and languages (Cole 1993; Rail 2002; Weedon 1997). With the importance of agency, individuals form their own unique experiences between and within power structures (Foucault 1977, 1978). Consequently, the process of developing the subject is 'never complete, always in process, and always constituted within, not outside, representation' (Hall 1994, p. 222). In other words, individuals are constantly shaped by (new) cultural practices, which emerge from particular contexts, places and times.

In this chapter, a post-structuralist perspective allows examination of how male and female track-and-field athletes 'negotiate the ways in which [they] challenge broader socio-cultural gender discourses and stereotypes as well as their own relationships with and understandings of themselves' (Pavlidis and Olive 2014, p. 220). Through this focus, this chapter explores how combined training and competition environments, under the backdrop of sport's gender norms, ideologies and politics, shape the embodied experiences of male and female track-and-field athletes. As sex-segregation is premised on the superiority of male bodies and the inferiority of female bodies, this chapter problematizes this binary logic to investigate the possibility of reimagining sport into a more equitable playing field despite the deeply engrained gender politics and ideologies that persist within it. Notably, while there remains variation around how the terms *sex* and *gender* are defined and understood (see Butler 2004; Chambers 2007; Erikainen 2020), throughout this chapter, the term *sex*, particularly as it appears in 'sex-integrated' and 'sex-segregated', refers to physical, biological, chromosomal and hormonal characteristics of bodies (Krane and Barak 2013). For this reason, this chapter uses 'sex-integrated' and 'sex-segregated' to denote the biocentric nature of these two competition categories in sport.

In what follows, this chapter first gives a brief substantive literature review on feminist scholarship in sex integration and track-and-field before outlining the project methods. Next, the three major themes (insiders and outsiders; normalizing sex integration; reinforcing and reframing gender norms) that emerged from qualitative interviews with ten university track-and-field athletes are discussed before considering the implications of these findings. The chapter concludes with suggestions on reimagining sport into a more inclusive space, especially for women athletes.

Gender politics, sport and sex integration

Initially used as a tool to (re)produce dominant forms of masculinity and heterosexuality in boys (Adams, Anderson and McCormack 2010; Anderson 2009), sport maintains a masculine identity that emphasizes the biological and social differences between conventional male and female bodies (Cole 1993; Kane 1995). Consequently, the creation of bio-centric binary categories reifies the idea that male bodies are *naturally* suited for the demands of sport (e.g., strength, power, aggression) while female bodies lack similar physical and social suitability (Cahn 2015; Erikainen 2020; Hargreaves 2002). The resulting gendered power relations and alignment of male bodies with sport often result in the unacceptance or disbelief around successful women athletes. Such women are subsequently described as 'unfeminine' and sometimes subjected to gender questioning, in addition to widespread struggles to receive the same recognition, resources and credibility as male athletes (LaVoi, Baeth and Calhoun 2019; Musto, Cooky and Messner 2017).

Part of sport's characterization as a 'male preserve' (Dunning 1986) is influenced by the separation of women's sports from men's sports (McDonagh and Pappano 2008). While ostensibly a strategy to permit female participation, a growing number of scholars have questioned the reasons behind sex segregation practices in sport (see Anderson 2008; Channon et al. 2018; Kerr and Obel 2018; Tännsjö 2000). For example, McDonagh and Pappano (2008) summarize these rationales as three 'I's: (1) female *inferiority* compared to males; (2) the need to protect females from *injury* in competition with males; and (3) the *immorality* of females competing directly with males. At the centre of each argument is the assumption of the 'frail' female body, influenced by historical and contemporary medical concerns around the impacts of strenuous activity on women (Erikainen 2020; Hargreaves 2002; Vertinsky 1990), and thereby requiring protection, separation or demotion of female athletes. As such, women's sports frequently feature standards and regulations predicated on social and biological differences between male and female bodies that imply women are 'lesser than', 'different from' or 'derivative of' men's sports (Cahn 2015, p. 222). These disparities are particularly illustrated in track-and-field when considering implement height (i.e., hurdles), implement weight (i.e., shot put, discus throw, hammer throw), event distance (i.e., 100-metre/110-metre hurdles), and number of events in multi-event competitions (i.e., pentathlon/heptathlon and heptathlon/decathlon). Though physiological traits are given as justifications for some of these event differences, ultimately, women still throw lighter implements, jump over shorter obstacles and run fewer metres.

Scholars have also investigated the ways in which the distinct characteristics of women's and men's sports become embodied in the (gendered) experiences of athletes (see van Amsterdam, Claringbould and Knoppers 2017; Wellard 2015). For women, they often find themselves in a double bind, navigating traditional ideals of femininity while maintaining necessary strength and size (Burrow 2016; Cahn 2015; Hardy 2015). Especially in high-level sport where successful athletes, regardless of sex, require *masculine* virtues – which are celebrated in male athletes – female athletes are often met with stigmatization and ridicule. Women of colour, especially Black women, are particularly impacted by such double standards and racial stereotypes of hyper-sexuality and the natural/superior black athlete (Cahn 2015; Lansbury 2014). To typify these unique overarching struggles of female athletes, scholars have coined the phrase the 'female apologetic': a process by which women over-emphasize their femininity in an attempt to *apologize* for their necessarily strong bodies (Davis-Delano, Pollock and Ellsworth 2009; Hardy 2015). On the other hand, male athletes are encouraged to embrace forms of masculinity, even to the point of potentially developing long-term physical, emotional, psychological and relational damage (Zhang et al. 2011; Pringle 2003).

Given the reinforcement of gender stereotypes through the implementation of sex segregation, and when considering the potential detriments to athletes' health, scholars have suggested moving towards sex-integrated sport to create a safer, fairer and more equal playing field. In this vein, Channon et al. (2018, p. 2) write: 'the fundamental "promise" of sex integration lies in the fact that it challenges us to reject a priori assumptions of male superiority and to entertain a very different vision of sex difference and gender relations'. Such sex-integrated sports *do* exist in the current sporting milieu, as previous research has outlined (see Bowes and Kitching 2021; Channon 2013, 2014; Channon et al. 2018; Dashper 2012), though these usually involve a third party such as horses, dogs, cars, boats or, in the case of track-and-field, a baton.

Yet, track-and-field incorporates characteristics of both sex segregation and sex integration. While maintaining separate men's and women's categories, (university) track-and-field teams often train and even compete together (e.g., the mixed 4x400-metre relay), have identical physiological needs and participate in similar competition events. This hybrid structure offers an opportunity for track-and-field athletes to negotiate gender stereotypes and expectations that undergird sport and, more broadly, society. Creating successful sex-integrated spaces, as university and professional-level track-and-field organizations have done, offers the potential to reimagine the traditional gender binary and corresponding exclusionist political climates that understand sex/gender through reductive and biocentric definitions. As such, there is need to investigate how and if men and women in a sex-integrated environment challenge, accommodate or reinforce sport's traditional gender politics, and how their experiences might help reimagine the sporting landscape.

Navigating gender, training together

This chapter is part of a larger project that examines how current male and female university track-and-field athletes perceive an ideal athlete (see Posbergh and Jette 2021). The purpose of specifically interviewing track-and-field athletes was to explore how male and female athletes negotiate gendered ideologies, structures and politics that underpin sport as they train and compete in a sex-integrated environment.

Data was collected through semi-structured interviews with ten current track-and-field athletes at a United States Division I university. Interviews were recorded with an audio-recording device and transcribed verbatim. Given the comparative nature of the project, female participants' transcripts were kept as a separate dataset from male participants' transcripts; however, the same analytic process was used for both datasets. Specifically, data was analysed using thematic analysis, a recursive method that draws on the idea of a 'central organising concept' to generate themes which are thought of as 'key characters In the story we are telling about the data' (Clarke and Braun 2018, p. 108; Braun and Clarke 2006, 2019). Following familiarization with the data, the two datasets were coded separately with codes given for sentences or sections of data that focused on how participants understood or experienced training with members of the opposite sex, how they viewed sex segregation and sex integration more generally and/or their interpretations of gender norms and stereotypes. After examining and collating the codes, significant broader patterns of 'meaning' were developed into themes, which were later reviewed, defined and named (Braun and Clarke 2013). Upon analysing both sets of data, the themes were then compared between the two datasets. In total, three themes were generated:

1 Insiders and outsiders;
2 Normalizing sex integration; and
3 Reinforcing and reframing gender norms.

This chapter engages in this comparative analysis of how men and women navigate (sporting) gender norms. The following section presents extracts from these interview transcripts that illustrate patterns across participant responses, with pseudonyms given to participants to protect anonymity.

Insiders and outsiders

Participants were expressly aware of track-and-field's sex-integrated structure and often established an insider-outsider distinction between those who were in track-and-field versus those who were not. In particular, participants drew from their own experiences in other sports or previous interactions with non-track-and-field athletes to underscore this unique characteristic. As Matt pointed out: 'I never played any other sports that had women on the team, so it's kind of different – it's actually very different'. In a similar manner, Paul commented on the reactions of non-track-and-field athletes 'looking in' on track-and-field's sex-integrated environment as he remarked: 'For a lot of people looking at it [they think], "you work out with girls", but it's not…we're all running'. While Paul's observation indicated his awareness of the peculiarity of sex integration in track-and-field, he problematized these outsider reactions by focusing on the shared activities of male and female track-and-field athletes: running. Through redirecting attention to 'running', he subtly reframed the narrative to emphasize similitude rather than (sex) difference. While both Matt and Paul later recognized these sex differences and corresponding gender stereotypes – a point to which this chapter will return later – their reiteration of sameness between them and their female teammates subtly challenged sport's fundamental gender politics, especially those which undergird sex segregation.

Adding a gendered layer to the insider-outsider distinction, Jenny drew attention to how women athletes were perceived by outsiders. She noted:

> If you look on the outside, [people] look for the guy because he runs…so much faster. So, they'll just focus more on the fastest and the best, instead of focusing on just the events. But it makes sense because if you're just looking at something from the outside, you wouldn't really understand that much unless you're actually in the sport.

Jenny pointed out how non-track-and-field athletes lacked 'insider' knowledge into whether an athlete was considered 'good' at their event. Consequently, outsiders exclusively watched the 'fastest and the best' (e.g., male athletes). While Jenny understood why this was the case, she criticized the reliance on these 'objective' standards as it often diminished female success, especially in situations where a woman was comparatively better at her event after accounting for different male/female times and standards. In contrast, track-and-field athletes had an insider perspective and were thus able to discern a truly 'good' athlete, regardless of sex. Jenny later explained that the result of this divergence, inside and outside of the university level, contributed to the lower recognition, pay and respect that women receive for their performances, even if they were of proportionate calibre to their male counterparts. However, for track-and-field athletes, the combination of insider knowledge for track-and-field athletes and commonness of sex-integrated training created more opportunities to contradict traditional sporting gender stereotypes and norms, such as the biologically superior male athlete/inferior female athlete.

Normalizing sex integration

After establishing a clear distinction between insiders and outsiders, male participants categorically normalized track-and-field's sex-integrated organization. For example, when asked how men and women practicing together influences the training environment, Tyler stated: 'But like, I've always done that'. Through this brief comment, Tyler suggested the typicality of boys/men and girls/women training together in track-and-field across all ages. Later, when addressing the physiological differences between men and women, specifically women's generally slower running times as compared to men, Tyler commented: 'there is a difference in time management throughout a workout… but I think [the women] find a way to overcome that and I feel like it's pretty consistent now'. Though Tyler was cognizant of the 'time management' challenges associated with sex integration – endocrinological research generally points to a 10–12% performative difference between men and women (Betancurt et al. 2018) – he no longer perceived these obstacles as significant. Likewise, Matt remarked, 'I'm so used to being around girls, it's just so normal to me now…I like pushing the girls to work harder and there's obviously guys who are bigger and faster than me…it's not like having women is holding me back'. While recognizing the differences in speed and times between men and women, Matt perceived these differences as intrinsic to track-and-field's training environment and, for Matt, actually serving as a beneficial characteristic. Tyler and Matt's experiences were also shared by several other male participants to establish a 'new norm' (see Posbergh and Jette 2021).

Despite concerted efforts to normalize sex integration, male participants did not express a widespread proclivity for this 'new norm' and, instead, offered mixed opinions. Even those who indicated their general support frequently qualified their responses with the aspects that they did not like as much. Sean, for example, initially stated: 'I personally do enjoy [training with men and women]' but later said, 'sometimes I do wish that it was a little more separate…if the men only train with men, it's more of a team environment'. While supporting sex integration, Sean quickly explained that it was not always his preference as he believed that sex segregation was more suitable for developing a 'team environment', thus reflecting the reality that men and women, even though they train together, compete as separate teams. James seconded these reservations and was 'not really the biggest fan of the men and women training together' as 'it kind of makes it less intense sometimes', which stemmed from his perception that women were less competitive than men and, thus, dampened the training atmosphere. Thus, James' reasoning behind his disregard for sex-integrated training reinforced stereotypes of 'weaker' and 'emotional' female athletes (Cahn 2015; McClearen 2017). Regardless of their personal feelings, all male participants recognized sex-integration as track-and-field's dominant structure, which was best summarized with James' comment: 'that's just how it is'.

Conversely, female athletes enthusiastically endorsed sex integration. Although they did not directly comment on its typicality – as their male teammates had – their enjoyment indirectly normalized the structure. Much of their support manifested in feeling as though their training was improved and their workouts were of higher quality, as exemplified by Sarah's response: 'I definitely like [training together], way better. I feel like it makes you want to run way faster'. Her response was echoed by Jenny, who similarly noted: 'I've always done a lot of workouts with the guys… it's good just to have someone that's so much faster who's just going to pull you along through the workout'. In both of their remarks, Sarah and Jenny acknowledged the training discrepancies between men and women and welcomed the difference, perceiving it as a means of improving their training. Through appreciating the challenge and, at times, compatibility of training with men, female participants notably contradicted historical and contemporary reasons for maintaining sex segregation, specifically, that women would find it discouraging to train (and compete) against men (Tännsjö 2000). Of additional importance is that both sexes agreed – albeit through different means – that it was possible for men and women to train together despite physiological differences. Either through characterizing it as an obstacle of the past or an asset in the present, male and female participants enjoyed or at least accepted being part of a sex-integrated environment.

Reframing and reinforcing gender norms

Despite negotiating dominant ideas of sex-based differences, participants continued to reinforce gender stereotypes, especially when discussing emotions and appearances. While nearly all participants recognized that athletes required the same physical, mental and emotional capacities to succeed, upon further reflection, they often contradicted or qualified this assertion. In particular, male participants focused on the purportedly different emotional states between men and women, which sharply contrasted from their previous acceptance of sex-based physiological differences for training purposes. As Sean commented: 'I think it could be more difficult [for women] to be emotionally stable, I don't know, but I think it might be more difficult. But I think [the ideal female athlete] is definitely the same [as the ideal male athlete]'. While Sean reiterated that the ideal athlete was not sex-specific, he also hesitantly posited that women emotionally struggled more than men. Charles contextualized this observation within the dynamics of the team, explaining that: 'with the ladies on the team, oftentimes if they're really having a bad day… you have to do your best to get the rest of the group to push them aside…otherwise it really does bring down the morale'. By describing the diasporic influence of women's negative emotions, Charles broadly characterized women as more emotionally expressive, to the detriment of others. In doing so, he subtly reified the historical medical stereotype of the 'hysterical woman' and corresponding concepts of female inferiority – mentally, emotionally and physically – and male superiority (Cahn 2015; Erikainen 2020; Vertinsky 1990).

Similarly, some male participants suggested that sex-based biological differences were somehow linked to attitude and competitive differences. While describing the competitive nature of women athletes, Tyler commented: 'Female…I mean, they have everything similar to a guy, but I think…their levels, I feel, aren't at the same level as a guy's level. [It's] more of a biological thing…there's something out there, but I don't know exactly what'. While initially maintaining the similarity between men and women, the remainder of Tyler's halting response contradicted this assertion. Rather, he remarked that there was an unknown biological discrepancy between men and women that rendered women less competitive and invested in the outcome of performance as compared to men.

However, female participants did not share the opinion that women were not as competitive or emotionally stable as men. Rather, they commented on the egoism of their male teammates, despite having previously framed a sex-integrated environment as a training benefit. In particular, Lisa spoke to her strong distaste towards this demeanour, commenting that: 'I feel like a lot of male athletes are really cocky and I don't like that. I don't like that at all'. Soon after this assertion, Lisa indicated her preference for her female teammates' company: 'it's more of a supportive environment when there are more girls training with me'. In contrast to Charles' negative perception of women's emotionality, Lisa welcomed this expressivity. Although she maintained the stereotype of the more 'emotional' female athlete, Lisa reframed the negative connotation as supportive and preferable, thereby demonstrating an agentic negotiation of dominant discourse.

In addition to their opinions and experiences on emotionality, participants also addressed bodily stereotypes and sexualization. Specifically, all participants recognized the double appearance standard for men and women, as illustrated in Katie's comment: 'male athletes, they're in shape and stuff, but it's not like the end-all-be-all like it is for women'. Her remark echoed Charles' comment on gendered bodily standards, as he soberly noted: '[men] are just not as sexualized in the same way [as women]'. Recognizing the double standards and unjust cultural meanings ascribed to female athletes, both male and female participants endeavoured to point out the prevalence of institutional sexism.

However, in contrast to their male teammates, female participants sometimes embodied these gendered expectations in their personal reflections, values and beliefs. For example, when responding to a question about the appearance of an ideal athlete, Sarah explained: 'Personally, I like to stay thin and be thin because everyone has like a six-pack and everything and I need to stay on top of things…it's definitely not good to just eat whatever you want though and look however what you want'. Later, when asked to describe the ideal female athlete,

Sarah responded: 'I would say strong, well-rounded...optimistic, motivation, determined...fast or jumps far, whatever. I'd say most of them are pretty, I guess. All the Oregon girls, all of them, so pretty'. Through maintaining the importance of feminine characteristics for the ideal female athlete, Sarah reinforced a heteronormative sex/gender binary, which is central to sport's gendered status quo (Travers 2006).

However, of greater concern was that female participants, such as Sarah, internalized this established binary. In Sarah's case, she expressed a *need* to maintain a thin figure for the purpose of 'staying on top of things'. Her ensuing example of the University of Oregon's female track-and-field athletes further reflected Sarah's belief in the necessity of physical beauty for female athletes. The relationship between aesthetics and female athletes is well-documented in terms of media objectification (Bruce 2016; Fink 2015) and social media (Toffoletti and Thorpe 2018), with the sexualization of (female) athletes portraying them as 'less capable, determined, strong, intelligent, and possessing less self-respect than the non-sexualized athletes' (Daniels et al. 2021, p. 114). Centred on her bodily appearance, the objectifying gaze is often male, further cementing the heteronormative sex/gender binary within sport (Kane, LaVoi and Fink 2013). As demonstrated in Sarah's responses, the diffusive influence of these gendered politics extends to both institutional and internalized levels, thus demonstrating its deep entrenchment in sport.

Conclusion

While post-structuralism recognizes that 'individuals actively produce multiple meanings that are, through language, products of society and culture' (Markula 2018, p. 394), these meanings are also influenced by existing power structures and relations (King 2015). The findings from this study indicate that male and female track-and-field athletes construct unique experiences through blending sport's traditional gender hierarchy *and* sex integration's potential for gender equality. Though negotiating and even challenging rationales behind sex segregation, such as the significance of sex-based physiological differences, participants continued to circulate gender stereotypes. Specifically, male participants questioned the emotional stability of their female teammates and described them as less competitive, while female participants indicated their female teammates' emotional availability and expressivity contributed to their preference for being around with women. Equally, although all participants recognized the double appearance standards that befall female athletes, some female participants disclosed their own bodily struggles or indicated a greater need/desire to uphold conventional and gendered beauty norms. These discursive negotiations occurred under the backdrop of a broad acknowledgement of the multiple sociocultural challenges that predominantly impact women and privilege men, suggesting a struggle to connect institutional awareness to internalized or personal experiences.

To reimagine sport into a more equitable playing field for (female) athletes, changes must be implemented from the top-down *and* the bottom-up. First, sport as an institution must normalize sex integration to provide opportunities to challenge longstanding stereotypes surrounding male and female athletes, as is done in track-and-field. Legal action such as Title IX has endeavoured to move towards fair and equal treatment for girls and women (Messner 2007; Suggs 2006); however, this alone cannot upend the deeply ingrained politics and ideologies that govern sport as illustrated by participants' simultaneous challenges to and retention of gender norms and stereotypes. Moreover, there often lacks requisite accountability or compliance with formal guidelines and policies (such is the case with Title IX as few United States colleges and universities are in compliance with the policy; see Jenkins 2019). As such, it is necessary to also 'conscientize' (Freire 1970) athletes, or increase critical consciousness of their own biases, to connect the recognition of structural oppressions to individual discourses and interactions. Through addressing both institutional and individual politics and beliefs, sports and athletes can thus begin dismantling sport's masculine identity and, by extension, its binary, heteronormative logic.

REFERENCES

Adams, A., Anderson, E. and McCormack, M. (2010) 'Establishing and challenging masculinity: the influence of gendered discourses in organized sport', *Journal of Language and Social Psychology*, 29(3), pp. 278–300.

Anderson, E. (2008) '"I used to think women were weak": orthodox masculinity, gender segregation, and sport', *Sociological Forum*, 23(2), pp. 257–280.

Anderson, E. (2009) 'The maintenance of masculinity among the stakeholders of sport', *Sport Management Review*, 12(1), pp. 3–14.

Andrews, D.L. (2000) 'Posting up: French post-structuralism and the critical analysis of contemporary sporting culture', in Coakley, J. and Dunning, E. (eds.) *Handbook of sports studies*. London: SAGE, pp. 106–137.

Ashbolt, K., O'Flynn, G. and Wright, J. (2018) 'Runners, jumpers and throwers: embodied gender hierarchies in track and field', *Sport, Education and Society*, 23(7), pp. 707–719.

Betancurt, J.O., Zakynthinaki, M.S., Martínes-Patiño, M.J., Cordente, M.C. and Fernández, C.R. (2018) 'Sex-differences in elite-performance track and field competition from 1983 to 2015', *Journal of Sports Sciences*, 36(11), pp. 1262–1268.

Birrell, S. (2000) 'Feminist theories for sport', in Coakley, J. and Dunning, E. (eds.) *Handbook of Sport Studies*. London: SAGE, pp. 61–76.

Bowes, A. and Kitching, N. (2021) '"Wow these girls can play": sex integration in professional golf', *Qualitative Research in Sport, Exercise and Health*, 13(2), pp. 217–234.

Braun, V. and Clarke, V. (2006) 'Using thematic analysis in psychology', *Qualitative Research in Psychology*, 3(2), pp. 77–101.

Braun, V. and Clarke, V. (2013) *Successful qualitative research: a practical guide for beginners*. London: SAGE.

Braun, V. and Clarke, V. (2019) 'Reflecting on reflexive thematic analysis', *Qualitative Research in Sport, Exercise and Health*, 11(4), pp. 589–597.

Brohm, J.M. (1978) 'Sport, an ideological state apparatus: the neutrality of the sport field', in Brohm, J.M. (ed.) *Sport-- A prison of measured time*. London: Pluto Press, pp. 53–64.

Bruce, T. (2016) *Terra Ludus: a novel about media, gender and sport*. Rotterdam: Sense Publishers.

Burrow, S. (2016) 'Trampled autonomy: women, athleticism, and health', *International Journal of Feminist Approaches to Bioethics*, 9(2), pp. 67–91.

Butler, J. (2004) *Undoing gender*. New York: Routledge.

Cahn, S. (2015) *Coming on strong: gender and sexuality in women's sport*. Champaign: University of Illinois Press.

Chambers, S.A. (2007) '"Sex" and the problem of the body: reconstructing Judith Butler's theory of sex/gender', *Body and Society*, 13(4), pp. 47–75.

Channon, A. (2013) 'Enter the discourse: exploring the discursive roots of inclusivity in mixed-sex martial arts', *Sport in Society*, 16(1), pp. 1293–1308.

Channon, A. (2014) 'Towards the "undoing" of gender in mixed-sex martial arts and combat sports', *Societies*, 4(4), pp. 587–605.

Channon, A., Dashper, K., Fletcher, T. and Lake, R.J. (2018) *Sex integration in sport and physical culture: promises and pitfalls*. New York: Routledge.

Clarke, V. and Braun, V. (2018) 'Using thematic analysis in counselling and psychotherapy research: a critical reflection', *Counselling and Psychotherapy Research*, 18(2), pp. 107–110.

Cole, C.L. (1993) 'Resisting the canon: feminist cultural studies, sport and technologies of the body', *Journal of Sport and Social Issues*, 17(2), pp. 77–97.

Daniels, E.A., Hood, A., LaVoi, N.M. and Cooky, C. (2021) 'Sexualized and athletic: viewers' attitudes towards sexualized performance images of female athletes', *Sex Roles*, 84(1-2), 112–124.

Dashper, K. (2012) 'Together, yet still not equal? Sex integration in equestrian sport', *Asia-Pacific Journal of Health, Sport and Physical Education*, 3(3), pp. 213–225.

Davis-Delano, L.R., Pollock, A. and Ellsworth, V. (2009). 'Apologetic behavior among female athletes: a new questionnaire and initial results', *International Review for the Sociology of Sport*, 44(2-3), 131–150.

Dunning, E. (1986) 'Sport as a male preserve: notes on the social sources of masculine identity and its transformations', *Theory, Culture & Society*, 3(1), 79–90.

Erikainen, S. (2020) *Gender verification and the making of the female body in sport: a history of the present*. Abingdon: Routledge.

Fink, J.S. (2015) 'Female athletes, women's sport, and the sport media commercial complex: have we really "come a long way, baby"?', *Sport Management Review*, 18(3), pp. 331–342.

Foucault, M. (1977) *Discipline and punish: the birth of the prison*. New York: Pantheon Books.

Foucault, M. (1978) *The history of sexuality: volume 1*. London: Pantheon Books.

Freire, P. (1970) 'Cultural action and conscientization', *Harvard Educational Review*, 40(3), pp. 452–477.

Hall, S. (1994) 'Cultural identity and diaspora', in Williams, P. and Chrisman, L. (eds.) *Colonial discourse and post-colonial theory: a reader*. London: Harvester Wheatsheaf, pp. 222–237.

Hardy, E. (2015) 'The female "apologetic" behaviour within Canadian women's rugby: athlete perceptions and media influences', *Sport in Society*, 18, pp. 155–167.

Hargreaves, J. (2002) *Sporting females: critical issues in the history and sociology of women's sport*. New York: Routledge.

Jenkins, W. (2019, October 23) *Hundreds of colleges may be out of compliance with Title IX. Here's why*. Available at: https://www.chronicle.com/article/hundreds-of-colleges-may-be-out-of-compliance-with-title-ix-heres-why/.

Kane, M.J. (1995) 'Resistance/transformation of the oppositional binary: exposing sport as a continuum', *Journal of Sport and Social Issues*, 19(2), pp. 191–218.

Kane, M.J., LaVoi, N.M. and Fink, J.S. (2013) 'Exploring elite female athletes' interpretations of sport media images: a window into the construction of social identity and "selling sex" in women's sports', *Communication and Sport*, 1(3), pp. 269–298.

Kerr, R. and Obel, C. (2018) 'Reassembling sex: reconsidering sex segregation policies in sport', *International Journal of Sport Policy and Politics*, 10(2), pp. 305–320.

King, S. (2015) 'Poststructuralism and sociology of sport', in Giulianotti, R. (ed.) *Routledge handbook of the sociology of sport*. London: Routledge, pp. 93–104.

Krane, V. and Barak, K.S. (2013) 'Current events and teachable moments: creating dialog about transgender and intersex athletes', *Journal of Physical Education, Recreation and Dance*, 83(4), pp. 38–43.

Lansbury, J. (2014) *A spectacular leap: black women athletes in twentieth-century America*. Fayetteville: University of Arkansas Press.

LaVoi, N.M., Baeth, A. and Calhoun, A.S. (2019) 'Sociological perspectives of women in sport', in Lough, N. and Geurin, A. (eds.) *Routledge handbook of the business of women's sport*. New York: Routledge, pp. 36–46.

Lenskyj. H. (2013) *Gender politics and the Olympic industry*. London: Palgrave Macmillan.

Markula, P. (2018) 'Poststructuralist feminism in sport and leisure studies', in Mansfield, L., Caudwell, J., Wheaton, B. and Watson, B. (eds.) *Palgrave handbook of feminism and sport, leisure and physical education*. London: Palgrave Macmillan, pp. 393–408.

McClearen, J. (2017) *Converging media and divergent bodies: articulations of powerful women in the Ultimate Fighting Championship*. Doctoral Thesis. University of Washington. Available at: https://digital.lib.washington.edu/researchworks/handle/1773/40006 (Accessed: 12 May 2021).

McDonagh, E. and Pappano, L. (2008) *Playing with the boys: why separate is not equal in sports*. Oxford: Oxford University Press.

Messner, M.A. (1988) 'Sports and male domination: the female athlete as contested ideological terrain', *Sociology of Sport Journal*, 5(3), pp. 197–211.

Messner, M.A. (2007) *Out of play: critical essays on gender and sport*. Albany: State University of New York Press.

Musto, M., Cooky, C. and Messner, M.A. (2017) '"From fizzle to sizzle!" Televised sports news and the production of gender-bland sexism', *Gender and Society*, 31(5), pp. 573–596.

Olympics (2017, June 30) *Intrigue, passion and unpredictability make mixed 4x400m relay a crowd favourite.* Available at: https://www.olympic.org/news/intrigue-passion-and-unpredictability-make-mixed-4x400m-relay-a-crowd-favourite.

Pavlidis, A. and Olive, R. (2014) 'On the track/in the bleachers: authenticity and feminist ethnographic research in sport and physical cultural studies', *Sport in Society*, 17(2), pp. 218–232.

Posbergh, A. and Jette, S.L. (2021) '"Track's coed, I never thought of it as separate": exploring collegiate male athletes' experiences in track and field', *Sociology of Sport Journal*, 39(1), pp. 47–55 (published online ahead of print 22 July). Available at: https://doi.org/10.1123/ssj.2020-0117 (Accessed: 15 September 2021).

Price, K. (2019) *9 new mixed-gender events in Tokyo represent more Olympic medal opportunities for Team USA.* Available at: https://www.teamusa.org/News/2019/July/23/9-New-Mixed-Gender-Events-In-Tokyo-Represent-More-Olympic-Medal-Opportunities-For-Team-USA (Accessed: 26 April 2021).

Pringle, R. (2003) *Doing the damage? An examination of masculinities and men's rugby experiences of pain, fear and pleasure.* Doctoral thesis. University of Waikato. Available at: https://hdl.handle.net/10289/13244 (Accessed: 14 May 2021).

Priyadharshini, E. and Pressland, A. (2016) 'Doing femininities and masculinities in a "feminized" sporting arena: the case of mixed-sex cheerleading', *Sport in Society*, 19(8-9), pp. 1234–1248.

Rail, G. (2002) 'Postmodernism and sport studies', in Maguire, J. and Young, K. (eds.) *Theory, sport and society.* Amsterdam: JAI, pp. 179–207.

Suggs, W. (2006) *A place on the team: the triumph and tragedy of Title IX.* Princeton: Princeton University Press.

Tännsjö, T. (2000) 'Against sexual discrimination in sports', in Tännsjö, T. and Tamburrini, C. (eds.) *Values in sport: elitism, nationalism, gender equality and the scientific manufacture of winners.* London: E and FN Spon, pp. 101–115.

Toffoletti, K. and Thorpe, H. (2018) 'Female athletes' self-representation on social media: a feminist analysis of neoliberal marketing strategies in "economies of visibility"', *Feminism and Psychology*, 28(1), pp. 11–31.

Travers, A. (2006) 'Queering sport: lesbian softball leagues and the transgender challenge', *International Review for the Sociology of Sport*, 41, 431–446.

Van Amsterdam, N., Claringbould, I. and Knoppers, A. (2017) 'Bodies matter: professional bodies and embodiment in institutional sport contexts', *Journal of Sport and Social Issues*, 41(4), pp. 335–353.

Vertinsky, P. (1990) *The eternally wounded woman: women, doctors, and exercise in the late nineteenth century.* Manchester: Manchester University Press.

Weedon, C. (1997) *Feminist practice and poststructuralist theory.* Cambridge: Blackwell.

Wellard, I. (2015) *Researching embodied sport: exploring movement cultures.* New York: Routledge.

Zhang, Z., Chen, G., Jiang, Y. and Zhang J. (2011) 'Sports and masculinity', *Journal of Physical Education*, 18(3), pp. 72–77.

29
Gender Justice and Women's Football
A Macro and Micro Analysis of the Game in England

Hanya Pielichaty

Introduction

Significant gains in women's football have been made since 2010 in connection with increased professionalisation, as documented by the International Federation of Professional Footballers (FIFPro 2020a), commercial buy-in (Vitality 2020) and media coverage (Petty and Pope 2019). While football remains the most popular sport for girls and women to play in England [Football Association (FA) 2021], there continues to be problems. Increases in participation rates and growing popularity in girls' and women's sport does not necessarily equate to cultural change in gender relations (Jeanes et al. 2020; Pielichaty 2020). Perpetual issues and complexities regarding the stability and resourcing of professional women's football [Fédération Internationale de Football Association (FIFA) 2018; Woodhouse, Fielding-Lloyd and Sequerra 2019] arguably consolidate its marginalised status as 'other' (Dunn and Welford 2015). The gender politics imbued in the game is such that meaningful transformation and equity could be unreachable if nothing changes.

The world in which we live is gendered and that includes the political environment and how our everyday lives feed into it (Celis et al. 2013). Risman (2004) argues that gender should be understood as a social structure situated on the same level as the economy and polity. Another way to look at gender politics is through the study of gender regimes and gendered social patterning as contributory to the way in which the world is perceived (see Celis et al. 2013). Politics can be understood as the relationship between power and authority and how this permeates social, political and economic dimensions (see Waylen et al. 2013). This concerns the distribution of power and how the social patterning of gender influences women's participation in both politics and society (Moghadam 2010). These social patterns can be mapped against cultural valuations of gender. The conventional and rigid binary system of gender, prevalent in Western discourses, causes cultural conflict and disadvantage to those whose identities are not compatible with normative perceptions of gender and sexuality (see Monro 2005; Butler 2004). The participation of women in the traditionally masculine sport of football could be viewed as a challenge to this rigid binary system. By enhancing our understanding of those who challenge these binary systems, we will be able to create a more strategic approach to promoting transformation.

The purpose of this chapter is to examine the gender politics in and around women's football with a focus on social patterning in connection with gender. As well as considering macro-level valuations of society, Parry (2014) also calls for an emphasis on micro-level experiences to inform our social justice practices. This chapter will analyse women's football at both the macro (holistic) and micro (everyday) level to make sense of society. The presence of gender politics as mediated through gender patterning will then be examined across experiences linked to positive change and cultural stagnation to highlight the variety of gendered football practice. In doing so, a gender justice lens will be applied to understand where problematic gendered social patterns exist and how they can be disturbed and remodelled to instigate social change.

Gender justice and everyday experiences

Gender justice is part of a wider movement for social justice and is concerned with the fight for equality and equity. It is significant in understanding how our society is built and maintained and can be defined as 'a process that hopes to eradicate the socially constructed differences between men and women. It means elimination, exclusion, oppression and exploitation against women' (Nawaz 2013, p. 290). The extent to which equality, as positioned through gender justice, is a direct comparison between men and women does vary, and as such the pursuit for gender justice is complex (see Watson and Scraton 2017). The way gender affects the everyday lives of women and the institutions and spaces which they occupy is of importance to the field of sport and leisure. The inextricable link between society and sport has long been recognised (see Jarvie 2018). The struggles that take place in society more broadly often manifest in our sporting spaces. Although, sport and leisure do not only reveal injustices but can also be 'sites for the negotiation of individual and collective power struggles' (Long, Fletcher and Watson 2017, p. 3).

Everyday practices and their connection with social movements are significant as to how we express ourselves (see Yates 2015). The importance of everyday patterns should not be underestimated, and people can confront (or consolidate) inequalities in their daily lives. Individuals can act as agents to defy socio-typical rules and informally challenge injustices in everyday activism (Mansbridge and Flaster 2007). Feminist social justice scholarship places value on the everyday experiences to inform wider social change, 'creating a society that is outside the bounds of patriarchy' (Parry 2014, p. 350). Everyday challenges, therefore, can potentially be used to tackle discriminatory gender patterning, which too will be considered in relation to women's football and gender justice.

Previous academic inquiry into gender politics in sports and leisure has focussed on the complexity of identities (Hassan and Acton 2018; Pielichaty 2019), sexualities (Caudwell 2003, 2007), ethnic 'other' females (Ratna and Samie 2018) and international events (Hoffmann et al. 2006). Gender politics is particularly nuanced when applied to athletes participating in sports who do not follow 'gender logic' (Caudwell 2003, p. 379). For example, men in cheerleading or women playing football, with both instances being regarded as having image issues (Grindstaff and West 2006; Harris 2005). The traditional, gendered patterning associated with football considers it a sport for boys and men to enjoy and a space to develop and consolidate masculine identities (see Jeanes and Magee 2011; Harding 2021). It is this conventional representation of football and the social patterns that feed into it that will be explored in this chapter.

For the purposes of this chapter, patterns will be understood as commonalities or themes that contribute to an understanding of gender politics in football. Braun and Clarke's (2019) account of reflexive thematic analysis will be used to guide this interpretation of patterning.

They describe themes as 'patterns of shared meaning underpinned or united by a core concept' (Braun and Clarke 2019, p. 593). It is the core concept of gender (in)justice which guides this chapter, and it is noted that my own research position and reflections will be instrumental in generating 'stories about the data' (Braun and Clarke 2019, p. 594). The gendered patterns that are negotiated by women in and around this patriarchal sport will be examined in connection with macro-level occurrences (policy, governance and leadership) and micro-level experiences of participation (identity, appearance and bodies).

Women's football: A macro examination

Positive patterns have emerged over the last decade promoting and furthering the structural stability of women's football. In 2021 the Women's Super League (WSL) celebrated its 10th anniversary, marking a decade of sustained professionalisation of women's football in England. In a multimillion-pound broadcasting deal, Sky Sports and the BBC have agreed a three-year contract with the FA to air the WSL games from the 2021/22 season (Wrack 2021). Furthermore, women fans of women's football are active spectators seeking to make a political point in supporting equality and the advancement of the sport (Dunn 2016), and just over a third of British adults are reportedly interested in women's football (Barclays 2019). The FA's (2020a) four-year strategy, *Time for Change*, provides a vision to unite football with a mission to change the sport and to rid it of discrimination. The specific women's football strategy, *Inspiring Positive Change* (FA 2020b), provides an inclusive account of the sport's aspirations.

The England women's and men's teams now get paid the same for their international duties in connection with match fees and bonuses (Taylor 2020). There has been an increased visibility of women head coaches (Clarkson 2019) and their successes (Hofman et al. 2014). As of 2021, women footballers will have player rights in connection with: maternity leave, pregnancy, contractual obligations and dismissal as outlined in FIFA's (2020) *Minimum Labour Conditions for Players* framework. Other changes have been made to the gendered language in football, such as the renaming of 'linesman' to 'assistant referee' several years ago (McElwee 2021), and in Finland, players compete in the Kansallinen Liiga, a gender-neutral name to avoid reference to a *women's league* (Glass 2020).

Upon deeper investigation, however, patterns of inequality continue to constrain women's football. There is a lack of attention paid to social challenges, such as stereotypes, tokenism and stigmatism in the FA's (2020b) women's football strategy. Despite the WSL's professional status, the *professionalism* of women's football still causes some concerns. Women athletes are caught between competing discourses of being resentful of their challenging working conditions, but also being grateful for being 'allowed' to play (Pavlidis 2020). Women's elite clubs continue to report structural and economic barriers linked to pay, facilities and resources (see Dale 2021; Pfister 2015). For instance, Culvin's (2021, p. 8) examination of women's football as 'work' provides welcomed insight into these areas of inequality describing football as, 'an employment field which is characterised by its gendered precariousness'. Professional footballers in this chapter demonstrate the sensitive balance, to which Culvin (2021, p. 4) refers as 'the tightrope', between *feeling* and *being* a professional footballer. *Feeling* can be thought of as the extent to which women footballers perceive their treatment to be 'professional', regarding appropriate resourcing, funding and environments available to them. Whereas the *being* relates to the reality of professional life which Culvin (2021, p. 9) notes is rife with uncertainty, surveillance and vulnerability, verbalised by one senior England international as: '[w]e do more for less'.

The fragility of professional footballers due to the COVID-19 pandemic (FIFPro 2020b) with regard to contracts and wellbeing (Clarkson et al. 2020a) and general issues reported with the ownership and management of the WSL (see Woodhouse, Fielding-Lloyd and Sequerra 2019) means that elite women's football still maintains a precarious cultural and economic position. These structural issues go some way in explaining why the WSL was ended early by the pandemic in 2020 whereas the men's Premier League continued (Wrack 2020a). Although FIFA did announce that plans to invest £800 million in women's football would remain in place (Wrack 2020b). The pandemic presented differing concerns for men's football, which involved the need to maintain fitness to be physically prepared for a return to competitive football (Mohr et al. 2020). On the other hand, the repercussions of the pandemic for women's football could be significant, the financial strain on resources in men's football may lead to issues for connecting women's clubs (Clarkson et al. 2020b). This example platforms the difficult journey to gender justice in women's football as teams continue to be heavily reliant on men's football clubs to exist and excel. The way gender justice principles are presented is also of concern to the examination of officiating, coaching and leadership, which will now be discussed.

Officiating, coaching and leadership in women's football

The FA (2020c) has reported a 72% increase in women referees since 2016, four of whom are now listed with FIFA as match officials. Although proportionally women only make up 1,718 of the total number of referees which reportedly stands at 27,451 (FA 2020a). Globally, it is French official Stephanie Frappart who has been pushing boundaries by refereeing the men's Champions League match between Juventus and Dynamo Kyiv in December 2020 (BBC 2020). Sian Massey-Ellis has also been officiating at the elite level for over a decade (Women in Football 2021); however, she still represents a minority (see Sajad 2018). This highlights that the social patterning surrounding officiating continues to be male dominant, but both Frappart and Massey-Ellis have made significant strides in advancing the opportunities for women in sport and making women visible in and around football spaces.

Challenges do continue to exist, and women coaches are under pressure to negotiate sexism, career mobility and discriminatory practices on a regular basis (Clarkson, Cox and Thelwell 2019). This pattern is also mirrored in coach education practices (Lewis, Roberts and Andrews 2018) as there appears to be a systemic problem in the football workplace, with 66% of women experiencing discrimination (Women in Football 2020). This issue is widely reflected in sport more generally, with Didymus and colleagues (2020) discussing the lack of diversity in sports coaching and commenting specifically on the workload stressors on women. In football, Norman, Rankin-Wright and Allison (2018) reported that women needed clear pathways for development with an associated 'learning culture', along with inclusive leadership and positive relationships with those senior and equivalent to them. There are patterns of social change emerging in the governance and political management of women's football; however, alongside these positive changes run the familiar pattern of cultural stagnation. The next section will examine micro-level experiences of players participating in football.

Women's football: A micro analysis

An approximate 30 million females play football globally (FIFA 2016), and the pattern of increased participation is a worldwide occurrence (FIFA 2019). Players' daily experiences are influenced and shaped by gender politics which are framed by the social patterns in existence. There are many reasons as to why individuals seek to play and enjoy sport. Sport is a way to make friends (Themen and Van Hooff 2017), bring us pleasure (Pringle, Rinehart and Caudwell 2015) and is associated with physical and mental health benefits (Jenkin et al. 2018; Maier and Jette 2019).

Participation in sport can also serve to construct, develop and consolidate identities (Donnelly and Young 1988; Walseth, Aartun and Engelsrud 2017). Participation can be a form of 'identity work' (Vermeulen and Verweel 2009), and identity changes in football are pronounced at transitional life stages (Pielichaty 2021). The professionalisation of women's football presents significant identity challenges whereby women experience conflict relating to the need to prove they are legitimate footballers worthy of being recognised as deserving of professional status (Culvin 2021).

The gendered patterns surrounding women's football provide an interesting account of identity work. The identity work that takes place in and around football spaces is gendered due to the patriarchal history of the sport (Clayton and Harris 2004; Grundlingh 2010). Traditionally, it was boys and men who utilised football to emphasise and consolidate masculine identities (Swain 2000; Jeanes and Magee 2011), albeit they do now in more inclusive, contemporary ways (see Adams 2011). Whereas girls' and women's participation in football complicates this equation because conventionally, femininity is not associated with masculine activities, such as playing football (see Devonport et al. 2019). Football's historical connection with masculinity is reflected by the everyday experiences of women players who report derogatory labelling linked to their playing. This stereotyping includes references to lesbianism and *butchness* (Devonport et al. 2019; Pielichaty 2020), a gendered pattern of behaviour which has been prevalent for decades (see Caudwell 2003; Harris 2005). Such stereotyping has cross-over with sexual identities, and football for women has been described as a complicated space consisting of both safety and stigma (see Scraton et al. 1999; Drury 2011). This stereotyping is so extensively ingrained in British women's football that players have actively sought to distance themselves from it through 'self-policing' (Devonport et al. 2019). The following section focuses on appearance and bodies in football to extend these discussions further.

Women's football: Appearance and bodies

Much has been made of the 'look' of women's football. Caudwell (2000, p. 107) explains: '[w]omen must look like women', regardless of the type of sport they play. Many stakeholders are involved in the gender policing of women's football regarding appearance. The former FIFA President, Sepp Blatter, infamously claimed women's football could be better promoted if players wore tighter shorts (Christenson and Kelso 2004). Previous research has shown how players' body image and presentation in relation to hair style and length (Cox and Thompson 2000; Knijnik 2015), clothing (Pielichaty 2021) and body shape and size (see Devonport et al. 2019; Tomas 2020) have been monitored. The nicknaming of Marta Vieira da Silva, a Brazilian international, as 'Pelé in a Skirt' (Moreira 2014, p. 507) highlights how women's achievements can be devalued through references to physical appearance.

Women's football culture presents a uniqueness when examining gender performances which involve contradictions and meticulous surveillance through the mediating of physical representation. Devonport et al. (2019) reported on the careful balance of gender identities connected with the rejection or acceptance of conventional forms of femininity. A rejection can lead to butch lesbian stereotyping, but an acceptance of femininity may lead to tension in the football subgroup. These complexities are also seen in connection with cosmetics whereby excessive make-up application correlated to low footballing talent (Pielichaty 2021). This emphasises the challenging gendered milieu of football, whereby femininity needs to be moderated to ensure legitimacy. Surveillance was also discussed by Culvin (2021) who describes the players' discomfort with being constantly *watched*. In essence, elite women players felt pressured to look and behave professionally at all times and, in general, there was an 'expectation to be good professionals' (Culvin 2021, p. 8).

It appears that women footballers themselves are also directly involved in constraining the gender displays of one another in and around the sport. Devonport et al. (2019, p. 1137) highlight the 'perpetual cycle of body surveillance' that players are succumbed to alongside the reward of acceptance and male approval for 'successful self-policing' (Devonport et al. 2019, p. 1139). The gender patterns described in these examples present interlacing inequalities linked to sporting identities and body image that are encompassed by an approach to women's football that is gender policed by players and others alike. This policing causes perpetual challenges when aspiring for a more gender-just sporting world because football 'as work' for women presents inequalities that populate every facet of women's lives. As demonstrated so far, women footballers work in an environment which is different to elite men's football. Differences can be seen and understood in social, economic, financial, political and cultural terms. In other words, women's football has been plagued by historical (male) oppressions much of which are directly connected to its current circumstances and the ever-present need to play 'catch up'.

Conclusion: Gender patterns and gender justice in women's football

Women's football in England is currently sitting on a precipice of change. It is up to every individual and community connected with the game to be an advocate for the next stage in its development. We cannot wait for gender politics linked to football to dissipate; instead, we need to actively seek out a new, culturally significant advancement in football. In this light, this chapter has brought together the macro and micro experiences of women's football through a focus on gendered social patterns. In recent decades, football has made significant strides towards equality in terms of participation increases, invigorating the professional game, officiating and media representation. It is difficult, however, to capture whether these gains have led to corresponding socio-cultural shifts (see Pielichaty 2020).

Woodward (2017) highlights the simultaneous stories (or patterns) of progress and setbacks that occur in women's football. It is these patterns which have been presented in this chapter, and it is important to understand what we can do with and about them. Social change and cultural shifts cannot operate at discrete micro or macro levels, but rather, they must be tackled in unison across strata of football communities (see Pielichaty 2021). As Parry (2014) acknowledges, it is both the macro and micro level changes that can (and will) instigate social justice. Consequently, increased visibility and participation of women in and around sports alone does not always equate to real cultural change (Jeanes et al. 2020). As Dunn and Welford (2015, p. 92) write, 'inclusion does not equal equity; the presence of women is not enough', structural change must also follow.

These recurring patterns of gender injustice as documented in this chapter must be disturbed and remodelled. How can we unify the contradictory 'stories' concerning women's football to formulate a joint effort to tackle injustice? The answer is not simple, yet by harnessing key elements of gender justice, progress can be made. Nawaz (2013, p. 294) calls for women's voices to be heard and the need to empower women in this human rights issue, acknowledging that, 'we have to consider the human part of every policy'. A disturbance of unjust gender patterns in football and the need to empower women will therefore involve:

- Women footballers to be provided with an elite working environment to correspond with their professional status;
- Women to be actively included in policy making processes;
- Policies to be informed by both macro and micro experiences of women in sport;

- Experiences of girls and women footballers to be understood and related to wider levels of injustice across football communities;
- Governing bodies to work with past and current players to manage and govern the sport;
- Policies to directly address social and cultural challenges in sport;
- Women's football to be effectively resourced and funded;
- Social communities (clubs, schools, families) to be provided with tools and information to educate others about equality, acceptance and inclusion.

The gendered social patterns that are present in women's football reflect the complexities involved in playing a male-dominated sport. It is hoped, however, that through strategic macro and micro level changes, football will become a more equal, equitable and empowering space for women to thrive.

REFERENCES

Adams, A. (2011) '"Josh wears pink cleats": inclusive masculinity in the soccer field', *Journal of Homosexuality*, 58(5), pp. 579–596. doi: 10.1080/00918369.2011.563654.

BBC (2020) *Stephanie Frappart on being first woman to referee a men's Champions League game*. Available at: https://www.bbc.co.uk/sport/football/55417573 (Accessed: 8 January 2021).

Barclays (2019) 'It's all to play for: third of Brits now fans of women's football and 69% of these believe it deserves the same profile as the men's game'. Available at: https://home.barclays/news/press-releases/2019/09/third-of-brits-now-fans-of-women-s-football/ (Accessed: 21 September 2021).

Braun, V. and Clarke, V. (2019) 'Reflecting on reflexive thematic analysis', *Qualitative Research in Sport, Exercise and Health*, 11(4), pp. 589–597. doi: 10.1080/2159676X.2019.1628806.

Butler, J. (2004) *Undoing gender*. New York: Routledge.

Caudwell, J. (2000) 'Football in the UK: women, tomboys, butches and lesbians', in: Scraton, S. and Watson, B. (eds.) *Sport, leisure identities and gendered spaces*. Eastbourne: Leisure Studies Association, pp. 95–110.

Caudwell, J. (2003) 'Sporting gender: women's footballing bodies as sites/sights for the (re) articulation of sex, gender, and desire', *Sociology of Sport Journal*, 20(4), pp. 371–386. doi: 10.1123/ssj.20.4.371.

Caudwell, J. (2007) 'Queering the field? The complexities of sexuality within a lesbian-identified football team in England', *Gender, Place and Culture: A Journal of Feminist Geography*, 14(2), pp. 183–196. doi: 10.1080/09663690701213750.

Celis, K., Kantola, J., Waylen, G., and Weldon, S.L. (2013) 'Gender and politics: a gendered world, a gendered discipline', in: Waylen et al. (eds.) *The Oxford handbook of gender politics*. Oxford: Oxford University Press, pp. 1–26.

Christenson, M. and Kelso, P. (2004) 'Soccer chief's plan to boost women's game? Hotpants', *The Guardian*, 16 January. Available at: https://www.theguardian.com/uk/2004/jan/16/football.gender (Accessed: 6 May 2021).

Clarkson, B. (2019) 'There are plenty of female superstars in football, but very few women coaches – here's why', *The Conversation*, 27 November. Available at: https://theconversation.com/there-are-plenty-of-female-superstars-in-football-but-very-few-women-coaches-heres-why-126139 (Accessed: 11 January 2021).

Clarkson, B.G., Cox, E., and Thelwell, R.C. (2019) 'Negotiating gender in the English football workplace: composite vignettes of women head coaches' experiences', *Women in Sport and Physical Activity Journal*, 27(2), pp. 73–84. doi: 10.1123/wspaj.2018-0052.

Clarkson, B.G., Culvin, A., Pope, S., and Parry, K.D. (2020a) 'Covid-19: reflections on threat and uncertainty for the future of elite women's football in England', *Managing Sport and Leisure*. doi: 10.1080/23750472.2020.1766377.

Clarkson, B.G., Culvin, A., Parry, K., and Pope, S. (2020b) 'Coronavirus: the future of women's football is under threat', *The Conversation*, 15 June. Available at: https://theconversation.com/coronavirus-the-future-of-womens-football-is-under-threat-139582 (Accessed: 20 September 2021).

Clayton, B. and Harris, J. (2004) 'Footballers' wives: the role of the soccer player's partner in the construction of idealized masculinity', *Soccer and Society*, 5(3), pp. 317–335. doi: 10.1080/1466097042000279580.

Cox, B. and Thompson, S. (2000) 'Multiple bodies: sportswomen, soccer and sexuality', *International Review for the Sociology of Sport*, 35(1), pp. 5–20. doi: 10.1177/101269000035001001.

Culvin, A. (2021) 'Football as work: the lived realities of professional women footballers in England', *Managing Sport and Leisure*, epub ahead of print, pp. 1–14. doi: 10.1080/23750472.2021.1959384.

Dale, J. (2021) 'Birmingham City Women: PFA supports players over complaints to club board', *Sky Sports*, 8 April. Available at: https://www.skysports.com/football/news/11095/12268619/birmingham-city-women-pfa-supports-players-over-complaints-to-club-board (Accessed: 23 April 2021).

Devonport, T.J., Russell, K., Leflay, K., and Conway, J. (2019) 'Gendered performances and identity construction among UK female soccer players and netballers: a comparative study', *Sport in Society*, 22(7), pp. 1131–1147. doi: 10.1080/17430437.2018.1504773.

Didymus, F.F., Norman, L., Hurst, N., and Clarke, N.J. (2020) 'Job stressors, strain, and psychological wellbeing among women sports coaches', *International Journal of Sports Science and Coaching*, 16(3), pp. 456–464. doi: 10.1177/1747954120974345.

Donnelly, P. and Young, K. (1988) 'The construction and confirmation of identity in sport subcultures', *Sociology of Sport Journal*, 5(3), pp. 223–240. doi: 10.1123/ssj.5.3.223.

Drury, S. (2011) '"It seems really inclusive in some ways, but…inclusive just for people who identify as lesbian": discourses of gender and sexuality in a lesbian-identified football club', *Soccer and Society*, 12(13), pp. 421–442. doi: 10.1080/14660970.2011.568108.

Dunn, C. (2016) *Football and the Women's World Cup: organisation, media and fandom*. London: Palgrave Macmillan.

Dunn, C. and Welford, J. (2015) *Football and the FA Women's Super League: structure, governance and impact*. London: Palgrave.

FA (2020a) *Time for change: the FA strategy 2020-2024*. Available at: https://www.thefa.com/about-football-association/what-we-do/strategy#group-section-OUR-STRATEGY-iRH4tpTunF (Accessed: 12 January 2021).

FA (2020b) *Inspiring positive change: the FA strategy for women's and girls' football 2020-2024*. Available at: https://thefabrochures.co.uk/19268_WOMENS_GIRLS_FOOTBALL_STRATEGY_2020-24/index.html (Accessed: 12 May 2021).

FA (2020c) *Find out how we helped increase number of female refs by 72 per cent since 2016*. Available at: https://www.thefa.com/news/2020/jun/03/gameplan-for-growth-refereeing-030620 (Accessed: 8 January 2021).

FA (2021) *An introduction to the leagues and competitions of women's football*. Available at: https://www.thefa.com/womens-girls-football/leagues-and-competitions/introduction-to-womens-leagues-and-competitions (Accessed: 5 January 2021).

FIFA (2016) *FIFA 2.0: The vision for the future*. Available at: https://resources.fifa.com/mm/document/affederation/generic/02/84/35/01/fifa_2.0_vision_e_neutral.pdf (Accessed: 11 June 2019).

FIFA (2018) *Women's football strategy*. Available at: https://resources.fifa.com/image/upload/women-s-football-strategy.pdf?cloudid=z7w21ghir8jb9tguvbcq (Accessed: 10 June 2020).

FIFA (2019) *Women's football member associations survey report 2019*. Available at: https://img.fifa.com/image/upload/nq3ensohyxpuxovcovj0.pdf (Accessed: 8 July 2020).

FIFA (2020) *Women's football: minimum labour conditions for players*. Available at: https://resources.fifa.com/image/upload/women-s-football-minimum-labour-conditions-for-players.pdf?cloudid=f9cc8eex7qligvxfznbf (Accessed: 27 April 2021).

FIFPro (2020a) *Raising our game: women's football report*. Available at: https://www.fifpro.org/media/vd1pbtbj/fifpro-womens-report_eng-lowres.pdf (Accessed: 5 January 2021).

FIFPro (2020b) *COVID-19: implications for professional women's football*. Available at: https://www.fifpro.org/media/mybpsvym/fifpro-womens-football-covid19.pdf (Accessed: 23 July 2020).

Glass, A. (2020) 'From Finland to Japan, women in soccer are getting their due', *Forbes*, 29 February. Available at: https://www.forbes.com/sites/alanaglass/2020/02/29/from-finland-to-japan-women-in-soccer-are-getting-their-due/?sh=13adc94a2681 (Accessed: 8 January 2021).

Grindstaff, L. and West, E. (2006) 'Cheerleading and the gendered politics of sport', *Social Problems*, 53(4), pp. 500–518. doi: 10.1525/sp.2006.53.4.500.

Grundlingh, M. (2010) 'Boobs and balls: exploring issues of gender and identity among women soccer players at Stellenbosch University', *Agenda: Empowering Women for Gender*, 24(85), pp. 45–53.

Harding, S.N. (2021) '"Boys, when they do dance, they have to do football as well, for balance": young men's construction of a sporting masculinity', *International Review for the Sociology of Sport*, 57(1), 19–33. doi: 10.1177/1012690220987144.

Harris, J. (2005) 'The image problem in women's football', *Journal of Sport and Social Issues*, 29(2), pp. 184–197. doi: 10.1177/0193723504273120.

Hassan, D. and Acton, C. (2018) *Sport and contested identities: contemporary issues and debates*. London: Routledge.

Hofmann, A.R., Sinning, S., Shelton, C., Lindgrend, E-C. and Barker-Ruchtid, N. (2014) '"Football is like chess - you need to think a lot": women in a men's sphere. National female football coaches and their way to the top', *International Journal of Physical Education*, 51(4), pp. 20–32.

Hoffmann, R., Ging, L.C., Matheson, V., and Ramasamy, B. (2006) 'International women's football and gender inequality', *Applied Economics Letters*, 13(15), pp. 999–1001. doi: 10.1080/13504850500425774.

Jarvie, G. (2018) *Sport, culture and society: an introduction*. 3rd edition. London: Routledge.

Jeanes, R. and Magee, J. (2011) 'Come on my son! Examining fathers, masculinity and fathering through football', *Annals of Leisure Research*, 14(2-3), pp. 273–288. doi: 10.1080/11745398.2011.616483.

Jeanes, R., Spaaij, R., Farquharson, K., McGrath, G., Magee, J., Lusher, D., and Gorman, S. (2020) 'Gender relations, gender equity, and community sports spaces', *Journal of Sport and Social Issues*, 45(6), pp. 545–567. doi: 10.1177/0193723520962955.

Jenkin, C.R., Eime, R.M., Westerbeek, H., and Van Uffelen, J.G.Z. (2018) 'Sport for adults aged 50+ years: participation benefits and barriers', *Journal of Aging and Physical Activity*, 26(3), pp. 363–371. doi: 10.1123/japa.2017-0092.

Knijnik, J. (2015) 'Femininities and masculinities in Brazilian women's football: resistance and compliance', *Journal of International Women's Studies*, 16(3), pp. 54–70.

Lewis, C.J., Roberts, S.J., and Andrews, H. (2018) '"Why am I putting myself through this?" Women football coaches' experiences of the Football Association's coach education process', *Sport, Education and Society*, 23(1), pp. 28–39. doi: 10.1080/13573322.2015.1118030.

Long, J., Fletcher, T., and Watson, B. (2017) *Sport, leisure and social justice*. London: Routledge.

Maier, J.M. and Jette, S.L. (2019) 'Mental illness and identity intersections', in: Atkinson, M. (ed.) *Sport, mental illness and sociology*. Bingley: Emerald, pp. 45–62.

Mansbridge, J. and Flaster, K. (2007) 'The cultural politics of everyday discourse: the case of "male chauvinist"', *Critical Sociology*, 33(4), pp. 627–660. doi: 10.1163/156916307X210973.

McElwee, M. (2021) After "batters", where next for sports lingo? *The Daily Telegraph*, 28 April, p. 16.

Moghadam, V.M. (2010) 'Gender, politics, and women's empowerment', in: Leicht, K.T. and Jenkins, J.C. (eds.) *Handbook of politics. handbooks of sociology and social research*. New York: Springer, pp. 279–303.

Mohr, M., Nassis, G.P., Brito, J., Randers, M.B., Castagna, C., Parnell, D., and Krustrup, P. (2020) 'Return to elite football after the COVID-19 lockdown', *Managing Sport and Leisure*, doi: 10.1080/23750472.2020.1768635.

Monro, S. (2005) *Gender politics: citizenship, activism and sexual diversity*. London: Pluto Press.

Moreira, R.P. (2014) 'Marta past Messi: (re)definitions of gender and masculinity, patriarchal structures and female agency in international soccer', *Soccer and Society*, 15(5), pp. 503–516. doi: 10.1080/14660970.2013.828592.

Nawaz, F. (2013) 'Global gender justice in 21st century: lessons and the way forward', *The Social Sciences*, 8(4), pp. 290–294. doi: 10.36478/sscience.2013.290.294.

Norman, L., Rankin-Wright, A.J., and Allison, W. (2018) '"It's a concrete ceiling; it's not even glass": understanding tenets of organizational culture that supports the progression of women as coaches and coach developers', *Journal of Sport and Social Issues*, 42(5), pp. 393–414. doi: 10.1177/0193723518790086.

Parry, D.C. (2014) 'My transformative desires: enacting feminist social justice leisure research', *Leisure Sciences*, 36(4), pp. 349–364. doi: 10.1080/01490400.2014.916976.

Pavlidis, A. (2020) 'Being grateful: materialising "success" in women's contact sport', *Emotion, Space and Society*, 35, pp. 1–7.

Petty, K. and Pope, S. (2019) 'A new age for media coverage of women's sport? An analysis of English media coverage of the 2015 FIFA Women's World Cup', *Sociology*, 53(3), pp. 486–502. doi: 10.1177/0038038518797505.

Pfister, G. (2015) 'Assessing the sociology of sport: on women and football', *International Review for the Sociology of Sport*, 50(4/5), pp. 563–569. doi: 10.1177/1012690214566646.

Pielichaty, H. (2019) 'Identity salience and the football self: a critical ethnographic study of women and girls in football', *Qualitative Research in Sport, Exercise and Health*, 11(4), pp. 527–542. doi: 10.1080/2159676X.2018.1549094.

Pielichaty, H. (2020) 'Pleasure and the sanctuary paradox: experiences of girls and women playing soccer', *International Review for the Sociology of Sport*, 55(6), pp. 788–806. doi: 10.1177/1012690219857023.

Pielichaty, H. (2021) *Football, family, gender and identity: the football self*. London: Routledge.

Pringle, R., Rinehart, R.E., and Caudwell, J. (2015) *Sport and the social significance of pleasure*. London: Routledge.

Ratna, A. and Samie, S.F. (2018) *Race, gender and sport: the politics of ethnic 'other' girls and women*. London: Routledge.

Risman, B. (2004) 'Gender as a social structure: theory wrestling with activism', *Gender and Society*, 18(4), pp. 429–450. doi: 10.1177/0891243204265349.

Sajad, K. (2018) 'Football referees: Sian Massey-Ellis, Chris Kavanagh and others on being an official', *BBC Sport*, 21 December. Available at: https://www.bbc.co.uk/sport/get-inspired/46506154 (Accessed: 28 April 2021).

Scraton, S., Fasting, K., Pfister, G., and Brunel, A. (1999) 'It's still a man's game?: The experiences of top-level European women footballers', *International Review for the Sociology of Sport*, 34(2), pp. 99–111. doi: 10.1177/101269099034002001.

Swain, J. (2000) '"The money's good, the fame's good, the girls' are good": the role of playground football in the construction of young boys' masculinity in junior school', *British Journal of Sociology of Sport*, 21(1), pp. 95–109. doi: 10.1080/01425690095180.

Taylor, L. (2020) 'England women's and men's teams receive same pay, FA reveals', *The Guardian*, 3 September. Available at: https://www.theguardian.com/football/2020/sep/03/england-womens-and-mens-teams-receive-same-pay-fa-reveals (Accessed: 23 April 2021).

Themen, K. and Van Hooff, J. (2017) 'Kicking against tradition: women's football, negotiating friendships and social spaces', *Leisure Studies*, 36(4), pp. 542–552. doi: 10.1080/02614367.2016.1195433.

Tomas, F. (2020) 'Weight charts, 'fat clubs' and disordered eating: the hidden health crisis in women's football', *The Telegraph*, 23 October. Available at: https://www.telegraph.co.uk/football/2020/10/23/weight-charts-fat-clubs-disordered-eatingthe-hidden-health-crisis/ (Accessed 4 March 2022).

Vermeulen, J. and Verweel, P. (2009) 'Participation in sport: bonding and bridging as identity work', *Sport in Society*, 12(9), pp. 1206–1219. doi: 10.1080/17430430903137886.

Vitality (2020) *Vitality announces six new partnerships for the new 2020/21 football season and signals their further commitment to women's sport*. Available at: https://www.vitality.co.uk/media/vitality-announces-six-new-partnerships-for-the-new-football-season/ (Accessed: 5 January 2021).

Walseth, K., Aartun I., and Engelsrud, G. (2017) 'Girls' bodily activities in physical education. How current fitness and sport discourses influence girls' identity construction', *Sport, Education and Society*, 22(4), pp. 442–459. doi: 10.1080/13573322.2015.1050370.

Watson, B. and Scraton, S. (2017) 'Gender justice and leisure sport feminisms', in: Long, J., Fletcher, T., and Watson, B. (eds.) *Sport, leisure and social justice*. London: Routledge, pp. 43–57.

Waylen, G., Celis, K., Kantola, J., and Weldon, S.L. (eds.) (2013) *The Oxford handbook of gender and politics*. Oxford: Oxford University Press.

Women in Football (2020) *Women in Football launch new phase of growth as two thirds of members working in the industry report gender discrimination*. Available at: https://www.womeninfootball.co.uk/news/2020/10/08/new-phase-of-growth-as-66-per-cent-of-members-working-in-the-industry-report-gender-discrimination/ (Accessed: 12 January 2021).

Women in Football (2021) *Sian Massey-Ellis on the challenges of parenthood and working as an elite match official*. Available at: https://www.womeninfootball.co.uk/news/2021/03/08/sian-massey-ellis-on-the-challenges-of-parenthood-and-working-as-an-elite-match-official/ (Accessed: 28 April 2021).

Woodhouse, D., Fielding-Lloyd, B., and Sequerra, R. (2019) 'Big brother's little sister: the ideological construction of Women's Super League', *Sport in Society*, 22(12), pp. 2006–2023. doi: 10.1080/17430437.2018.1548612.

Woodward, K. (2017) 'Women's time? Time and temporality in women's football', *Sport in Society*, 20(5–6), pp. 689–700. doi: 10.1080/17430437.2016.1158471.

Wrack, S. (2020a) 'Hollow promises of equality are to blame if Women's Super League is cancelled', *The Guardian*, 23 May. Available at: https://www.theguardian.com/football/blog/2020/may/23/hollow-promises-of-equality-are-to-blame-if-womens-super-league-is-cancelled (Accessed: 1 July 2020).

Wrack, S. (2020b) 'FIFA says planned £800m investment in women's football will not be cut', *The Guardian*, 20 April. Available at: https://www.theguardian.com/football/2020/apr/20/fifa-says-1bn-investment-in-womens-football-will-not-be-cut (Accessed: 23 April 2021).

Wrack, S. (2021) '"A huge step forward": WSL announces record-breaking deal with BBC and Sky', *The Guardian*, 22 March. Available at: https://www.theguardian.com/football/2021/mar/22/a-huge-step-forward-wsl-announces-record-breaking-deal-with-bbc-and-sky (Accessed: 20 September 2021).

Yates, L. (2015) 'Everyday politics, social practices and movement networks: daily life in Barcelona's social centres', *The British Journal of Sociology*, 66(2), pp. 236–258. doi: 10.1111/1468-4446.12101.

30
Gender Participation in Decision Making Positions of Sport Federations

Amalia Drakou, Popi Sotiriadou and Dimitris Gargalianos

Introduction

Sociologists report an immense progress regarding gender equality in developed Western countries, sometimes labelled as "gender revolution" (England, Levine and Mishel 2017). Gender revolution may include the increase in women's employment, the proportion of women receiving postgraduate qualifications, and their entrance to traditionally male-dominated professions. Even the pay gap between men and women has been significantly decreased (Ellwood, Garcia-Lacall and Royo 2020). As opposed to developed countries, developing countries seem to engage in international conventions and agreements on women's empowerment and gender issues (Moyo and Dhliwayo 2019), but many of them still have great gender disparities (United Nations 2020). Gender inequities also exist in certain professional areas (e.g., politics) across the globe. Einarsdottir, Christiansen and Kristjansdottir (2018) mentioned that even in countries which score high in gender equality, like Iceland, the percentage of women holding top management positions is improving slowly. According to Statistics Iceland (2019), between 1999 and 2006, the proportion of women in boards of directors ranged from 21.3% to 22.3% and after the enactment of a law amending gender discrimination increased to 25.5% in 2014 and stayed at that percentage for the past years.

To improve the situation, the United Nations (UN) set as one of its *sustainable development goals* to achieve gender equality together with women's and girls' empowerment (Goal 5). This goal has urged nations to establish Institutes for Gender Equality. For instance, in 2018, the Canadian government established the *Women and Gender Equality Canada*, which emerged from the upgrade of the *Status of Women Canada* (SWC), an agency founded in 1972, under the umbrella of the Department of Canadian Heritage (SWC 2021). SWC advanced equality for women and aimed at diminishing violence against women and girls, increasing women's economic security and prosperity, and encouraging women's leadership and democratic participation (SWC 2011). In their 2018 two-year report, the SWC presented the steps they undertook to increase the representation of women in leadership roles. Some of the mechanisms used to achieve this goal included legislative amendments to encourage greater diversity in corporate leadership, funding research to improve knowledge, dissemination of it, and investment in projects aiming to mobilize women leaders and organizations across Canada. As a result of these efforts, in 2015, the representation of women serving as Government in Council appointees (individuals appointed by the Government to serve on boards, commissions, Crown corporations, agencies and tribunals, to ensure gender parity) was 34%, and by 2018, it reached 47% (SWC 2018).

In Chile, in 2016, the National Women's Agency, founded in early 1990s, was reconstituted as a completely developed Ministry under the name of Ministry of Women and Gender Equity (Law of Chile 2015). This upgrade came as no surprise, after two successful Equal Opportunities Plans that the Agency prepared and activated. The first Equal Opportunities Plan (1994–1999) acted as a fundamental tool to satisfy the accords that Chile accepted during the Fourth World Conference on Women, in Beijing, in 1995. It consisted of policies, initiatives, and programmes for women which resulted in changes in the legal framework of the country. Among the programmes and initiatives that transformed women's position in Chile's society during that period (1994–1999) are the "Programme for Low-income Female Heads of Household", the "Programme for Female Seasonal Workers in Export Agriculture", the "Information Centers on Women's Rights" and the "Interagency Commission on Family Violence". The second Equal Opportunity Plan (2000–2010) faced a key challenge: to fully integrate gender-focused policies into government ministries, departments, and enterprises. Some outcomes of the second plan regarding women included women's longer life expectancy, improved access to education, increase of participation in the labour market, and narrowing the salary gap between men and women (UN 2004).

These are only two, among many, examples of countries that recognized the strategic importance of gender equity and women's empowerment. Many countries over the world maintain a ministry for women's and/or gender affairs. Among them are Angola, Australia, Cameroon, Cote d'Ivoire, Denmark, France, Great Britain, Kenya, New Zealand, South Africa, and Sweden (European Institute for Gender Equality –The Commonwealth 2019; United Nations Developing Programme 2020).

Over time, women's sports participation has also increased, both in recreational participation and at the elite level (Sotiriadou and Pavlidis 2020). However, research shows that there is no significant increase in the number of women leading sport organizations from various positions (e.g., coaches, board members) (Burton and Leberman 2017; Sotiriadou, De Haan and Knoppers 2017). The European Commissioner for Innovation, Research, Culture, Education and Youth, Gabriel Mariya, stated that "…sport is an important source of health, skills, growth and jobs" (EU Office, European Olympic Committees, 2021, p. 5). In her interview with the Monthly Report, which is published by the EU Office of the European Olympic Committees, she argued that sport remains an important tool in the EU's 2020–2025 Gender Equality Strategy. Consequently, member states were called to ensure more women are involved in decision making positions. Ultimately, research on and related development around gender equity in sport leadership complements and advances the notion of "good governance" (Sotiriadou and de Haan 2019, p. 379).

Regarding the administration of sport, both genders contribute to organizational effectiveness in different ways (Adriaanse and Schofield 2014). The equal rights concept is important for sport organizations because it positively affects the organization, improves Boards' effectiveness, and strengthens the members' commitment and intention to stay in the organization (Spoor and Hoye 2014). Women have the tendency to explore issues concerning many and different stakeholders and ask interesting questions about issues that men do not easily talk about (Konrad, Cramer and Ercut 2008). Additionally, a gender-diverse Board of Directors can bring advantages to its performance (Gaston, Blundell and Fletcher 2020), which go beyond the sport arena and reach business goals and securing funding.

Despite the well reported benefits of gendered balance decision making in sport organizations, many studies reaffirm the continuous hegemony of the dichotomous thinking around gender in sport organizations and suggest that only a few women reach high level administrative positions (Albu and Fediuc 2018; Burton 2015; European Institute for Gender Equality 2017). Gaston, Blundell and Fletcher's (2020) study on gender diversity in US National Sport Bodies showed that among the 767 Board members of 45 National Sport Bodies that participated in the study, only 215 (28.03%) were women. Interestingly, only two of the National Sport Bodies had female CEOs, eight had a female chair, while 13 had less than 20% women's representation on their boards. A similar study on women's membership of Boards of Directors in Hellenic Sport Federations (Drakou, Gargalianos and Pertetzi 2019) revealed that women were less than 16% of the total number of Board members. Furthermore, 12 out of the 47 Federations included in the study had no female members at all and only three of them were run by female Presidents.

The European Institute for Gender Equality (2017) conducted a study on 28 European Olympic Sport Federations from 2010 until 2015 and concluded that women occupied only 14% of decision making positions with just one woman in a Presidential position. According to the European Olympic Committees' EU Office, which represents 50 European Olympic Committees, as of April 2020 in the 50 National Olympic Committees (NOC), there were 44 men Presidents and only six women. In the same report, it is mentioned that the proportion of women in NOCs Presidentship has doubled in the last decade. However, with this rate of increase, it will take approximately 50 years to reach gender balance (IOC 2020b). According to the European Parliament Resolution (21.01.2021) on the EU Strategy for Gender Equality, Member States rated less than 70 out of 100 on the EU Gender Index 2019, which is only 5.4 points higher compared to the ratio from 2005 (https://www.europarl.europa.eu/doceo/document/TA-9-2021-0025_EN.pdf). These statistics clearly indicate that the gender balance still requires further attention.

Barriers to women's participation in leadership roles in sport organizations

Women's underrepresentation at the top of the hierarchy of sport administration roles is alarming and contradicts the increasing rate of women sport management graduates and postgraduates since the early 1980s (Brassie 1989). This is not a trend exclusive to the field of sport management. For instance, in 2017, considering all scientific fields, US women earned more PhDs than men (World Economic Forum 2018). Therefore, women's marginalization in top sport management positions does not seem to be due to lack of qualifications. To understand the existing gap between the number of women who are educated and trained for leadership positions in sport administration and the actual number of women in such positions, we will focus on some of the reasons why women are excluded from leadership. Senne (2016) stated that the underrepresentation of women in sport derives from: (a) traditional gender discrimination methods embedded in the organization of sport (for example, there are separate men's and women's events), (b) the fact that historically sport has been created by men for men, and (c) skewed recruitment processes where women are often asked to meet more criteria and have higher qualifications than men do for the same position (for example, not to have young children, to have prior experience in high positions, and to have a high level of education).

Another explanation might be that women usually underestimate and conceal their achievements (Herbst 2020; Castaño et al. 2019). According to Evans and Pfister's (2021) review, women members of Boards of sport organisations often adopt stereotypically masculine behaviours to conceal their femininity, especially when they consider themselves as insignificant members. This self-perception may make them controllable, a characteristic which is undesirable for leaders. Furthermore, research (e.g., Aman et al. 2018) shows that women do not feel comfortable stepping into leadership roles, even if they have the same qualifications as men claiming the same position. In other words, women have the tendency to underplay their qualifications. While both genders browse jobs similarly, they apply to them differently. Research shows that to apply for a job, women feel they need to meet the criteria 100%, while men usually apply after meeting about 60% of the criteria (Ignatova 2019). Moreover, the relatively small representation of women in high positions within sport organizations may lead to lack of role models for other women or girls and, ultimately, preserving gender stereotypes (Turkel 2004). In their research on the representation of women in US sports, sports administration and team sport leadership, Aly and Breese (2018) surveyed people that had careers in sport leadership positions to investigate how they felt about women's representation and possible barriers for them. Most participants believed that there was a lack of female representation in team sport leadership and that sexism and lack of opportunities were responsible for this underrepresentation.

Similarly, Cosentino (2017) attributed the underrepresentation of women in sport administration to the fact that the majority of sport organizations cultivate and perpetuate values, types of behaviour and rules that reinforce male hegemony and stereotypes, which prevent women from rising to senior management positions. Aman et al. (2018, p. 1508) argued that "women face a disproportionate number of life challenges that reduces their ability to achieve their full potential". This argument is based on previous research (see Sartore and Cunningham 2007), which suggested that gender stereotypes related to social and sport ideology may act as barriers restricting women's capacity within sport contexts.

Establishment of institutes and committees for gender equality

The effort to reach gender equality demands methodical planning and organizing equity practices and policies (i.e., transparency in selection criteria, job allocation, law modifications). This section focuses on selected institutions that work toward this direction and their contribution to gender equality by examples of good practice.

There is an emerging trend at Universities and Research Institutions all over the world in relation to erecting committees for gender equality. Times Higher Education's (2020) annual report on Impact Rankings, which assesses and classifies universities using certain criteria, produced a list of top 100 universities for gender equality. Apart from conducting research on gender, some of the criteria used for the specific ranking were policies on gender equality, commitment to recruiting and promoting women, and the proportion of first-generation female students. Higher education can be the protagonist in this collective global effort to advance, protect, and disseminate diversity and gender equality. As Van Hiel et al. (2018, p. 1) argued: "education not only fosters the acquisition of skills and knowledge, but also sustains liberalization values in the form of autonomy and personal freedom" such as gender equality.

The International Olympic Committee (IOC) seeks to balance the number of female and male athletes who participate in the Olympic Games (OG), implements awareness campaigns on gender equality, and has created an online platform that helps women in any role (sports, coaching, administration) to network (IOC 2019). As a result, there is an emergence on gender equality committees at Olympic Movement organizations (e.g., the IOC's *Women in Sport Commission*). Gender equality constitutes one of the Fundamental Principles of the Olympic Charter (IOC 2020). The Olympic Movement has initiated significant gradual progress in promoting gender equality through adjusting the numbers of male and female athletes at the Olympic

Games. At the 1900 Paris Olympics, women constituted only 2.2% of the total number of the participating athletes. This percentage increased to 9.5% at the 1948 London Games and to 223% at the 1984 Los Angeles Games. At the 2020 Tokyo Olympics, held in 2021 due to the pandemic, female athletes represented 47.87% of all athletes (https://olympics.com/tokyo-2020/olympic-games/en/results/all-sports/entries-by-discipline.htm).

However, athletes' gender balanced participation is not the IOC's only concern. The IOC also focuses on leadership development, and this has resulted in more women taking up decision making positions within the administration and governance of sport (IOC 2020a; Sotiriadou, De Haan and Knoppers 2017). Since 2006, aiming to increase women's participation at the top levels of the Olympic Movement, the IOC, through its Women in Sport Commission, has organised leadership seminars and training programs addressed to women at mid- and senior-level positions in National Olympic Committees and International and National Sport Federations (IOC 2018b). The IOC has made progress in promoting gender equality within its own structure as well. For instance, in 1894 and for many of the following years, there were no female members at all within its Executive Board. The first woman was elected to be on the IOC Executive Board only in 1990, and in 1997, a woman was elected in the position of the vice-president. Three years later, in 2000, and during the second conference for Women in Sports, the IOC set a five-year goal that 20% of the decision-making positions should be held by women. By 2019, 33% of IOC members were women (IOC 2018a). On 28 May 2020, the IOC announced that women's membership of IOC's 30 Commissions had reached an all-time high proportion (47.7%). Additionally, two more women have been appointed to be Chairs of Commission Committees, raising the total number of commissions chaired by women to 11 out of 30 (36.7%) (IOC 2020b). According to the IOC's Gender Equality Review Project, coordinating efforts should focus on strategic mechanisms to increase the number of female candidates for decision making and executive board positions (IOC 2018a). All Olympic Movement Partners are recommended to review their electoral processes to develop strategies that would ensure gender-balanced representation in their governing bodies. Gradually, International and National Sport Federations seem to align to these recommendations (Gabriel 2021).

In another significant initiative, the International Paralympic Committee (IPC) adopted a motion to strive for women to hold 30% of leadership positions in all IPC, National Paralympic Committees, and International Organizations of Sport for the Disabled (IPC 2010). To increase the quantity and quality of women in leadership positions, the IPC suggested: (a) developing leadership training sessions and workshops for women, (b) educating women about the different types of opportunities in leadership, (c) promoting positive images of women in decision making positions to diminish societal stereotypes, and (d) creating the *Women in Sport Leadership toolkit*. The Women in Sport Committee, which was developed by the IPC, refers to helping increase women's participation in leadership across all levels of the Paralympic Movement as one of its strategic goals (IPC 2010). At its annual report (IPC 2020), the IPC devoted a section to women and leadership, giving women the stage to talk about their experiences as leaders in sport committees. This section featured two women Secretary Generals of National Paralympic Committee from Moldova and Tunisia and a woman member of IPC Medical Committee and detailed the ways they reached their positions and offered advice to encourage more women into leadership positions.

Despite all this, at its Governance Review on 27 April 2021, the IPC recommended adjustments to its proposal regarding gender proportion in sport committees. Specifically, it removed the primary target of 40% of each gender and retained the quota referring to non-mandatory 50% female members. These changes were justified on the basis of the committees' small size and existing members' expertise. It was assessed that replacing a male member with a female, or vice versa, might cause practical issues due to lack of knowledge and expertise by new members. This presents a good example of how policy does not necessarily translate into action or change. To achieve changes in mentality, it is suggested that the following are needed: (a) persistence in educating, (b) reminders of the benefits of women's presence in boards, and (c) evaluations of the costs and benefits that follow decisions regarding gender proportion in sport committees.

Research supported by the European Commission

In 2018, the European Commission, through its Erasmus+ funding program, commissioned a study on *Women's Empowerment in Sport and Physical Education Industry* (European Commission 2021). This was a one-year project among three European countries (Lithuania, Italy, Latvia) and was led by the Lithuanian Union of Sport Federations, followed by potential trainees, local/regional sport governing bodies, and sport clubs. Its aim was to empower women in sport management positions by adopting a sport management course to show women how to use their strengths and abilities more strategically, and become more confident in a competitive, male-dominated sport industry. Additionally, a network platform was set up where women leaders in sports would voluntarily counsel and mentor young women peers wishing to develop their sport management skills (European Commission 2021).

The UN Women Sports for Generation Equality (UN 2020) is another initiative implemented in cooperation with the IOC. It invites members of the sport ecosystem to share knowledge, learn from each other, and achieve gender equality in and through sport. So, sport, apart from becoming more gender balanced in all its aspects, also becomes a vehicle for advancing diversity and gender equality in wider society. According to the first principle of the initiative, members should "undertake efforts to promote women's leadership and gender equality in governance models" (UN Women 2018, p. 5). To achieve this, some of the propositions are to: (a) promote women in leadership roles in sport organizations, (b) offer organizational strategies that include gender equality principles, (c) develop policy documents related to the issue, (d) enable electoral processes that would protect gender balance, (e) advance women's capacities through training opportunities, (f) change the organizational culture to advance equality, and (g) remove any discrimination or bias against women from the criteria for board membership.

The Erasmus+ program and the UN Women initiative are good examples of how networking could foster solidarity and cooperation for gender equality within a sporting context. When networking, it is crucial to include a broad range of sports stakeholders, such as academics, practitioners, athletes, managers, and media representatives. This inclusion would facilitate dissemination of academic outcomes and could lead to empowerment of gender equality practices in sport organizations.

Governmental strategies

In addition to these international committees and initiatives, countries themselves have also taken action to address the situation. For instance, the Office of Sport of New South Wales (NSW) government in Australia has established a four-year project (2019–2023) under the name "Her sport – Her way" (NSW Government 2018). It includes a series of initiatives across four pillars: leadership, participation, places and spaces, and leveraging. The objective of this project is to develop sporting cultures that embrace diversity and increase the number of women in leadership positions. According to Sport Australia's *Mandatory Sports Governance Principles*,

National Sporting Federations for more than 30 Olympic sports are required to increase women's participation on their boards, reach a target of 40% representation and report back on the progress they make. Even though board and leadership training has been delivered to aspiring women leaders in past years, in 2018, more than half of NSW Boards (59%) did not have 40% female representation.

Governmental strategies may vary in policy style, from an imposition to a consensus/anticipatory style (Bali and Halpin 2021). Whatever the style might be, changes in mentality and culture require time and education to be solidified. Hence, for committees, institutions, and laws to make the difference, a stronger network and cooperation across stakeholders including citizens, communities, and ministries would be essential to not only enable a coordinated effort toward gender equity but to reduce red tape and duplications of resources in planning for change and consolidating the efforts toward long-term shifts and sustainable changes.

Recommendations

Based on the strategies offered across various sports organizations and countries that were described in this chapter and following the guidelines of international organizations that support and promote gender equality in political (UN) as well as sport organizations (IOC, IPC), we can summarise the following recommendations for narrowing the gender gap in decision making positions within sporting organizations.

- Women as *role models* could be used to counterbalance the male stereotype that still dominates in sport management. Women on Boards of popular sport clubs and women in decision making positions of national/international sport federations have the potential to motivate other women. Giving publicity to these women through television spots and national campaigns planned by the relevant governing bodies may help other women alleviate any constraints that hold them away from sport decision making positions.
- The creation of an *award system* adapted by national federations could recognize and reward sport organizations that meet national standards regarding gender equality in boards. This award system could help reach gender equality in the representation of women on Boards.
- A *backup system* for women in positions of high responsibilities could facilitate their daily routines as mothers and/or wives, beginning with childcare stations within federations' headquarters and training sites.
- *Recruitment interviews* should be without gender bias and controlled by an external appraisal agency.
- *Women's behavioural changes*. It is recommended that women's underestimation of their own achievements is a crucial constraint that is a matter of *behavioural change* and should be treated as such. Behavioural changes can take place at the universities where female students undertake sport management degrees. Using Stage-Based Theory, Brunton and St Quinton (2021) proposed some techniques to engage female students in participation at university sport. The same techniques could be used to bring about behavioural changes and engage female future sport managers to top management positions. These are:
  - Develop messages to target students' attitudes, barriers, and perceptions (informational approach).
  - Plan and reinforce leadership roles to all students for a sport event, for example, address roles of organizer, communication manager, site manager, etc. (social approach).
  - Create goals for self-evaluation (behavioural approach).

Conclusion

The literature on gender participation in decision making positions within sport organizations stresses the importance of gender equality and its positive connection to organizational effectiveness, organizational commitment, and economic prosperity. Even though there is considerable progress toward achieving gender equality, women are still underrepresented in decision making positions in sport organizations. The Olympic Movement has offered ways to reduce the gap regarding gender representation on Boards of sport governing organisations and other strategic positions that may influence the future of sports.

Among the main constraints women experience on their way to sport decision making positions are the existing male stereotypes, the unequal treatment in staffing process, the historical past of methods designed by men in sport, and the lack of a backup system that would facilitate women's multiple roles. Change needs time, and national and international sport organizations are aligning to the principle of gender equality. Sotiriadou and Pavlidis (2020, p. 252) concluded that "gender balanced leadership and an equal representation of women in the governance of sport may offer an enabler to collective leadership advancements in the world of sport". Strategies for empowering women's participation in top sport management positions focus on how these constraints could be successfully removed and could be summarized in the following: (a) using successful female sport managers as role models, (b) creating an *award system* adapted by national federations that would recognize and reward sport organizations, which meet national standards regarding gender equality in boards, (c) creating a backup system for helping women in their daily family responsibilities, (d) cooperating with universities, which have the duty and abilities to shape mentalities (they could help through research, policies on gender equality, commitment to recruiting and promoting women), and (e) reinforcing the networking among all stakeholders. Gender equality is a major challenge of our times, and sport organisations have the potential as well as the power to provide an inclusive model of equal participation between genders.

REFERENCES

Adriaanse, J. and Schofield, T. (2014) The Impact of Gender Quotas on Gender Equality in Sport Governance. *Journal of Sport Management*, 28(5), pp. 485–497.

Albu, S. and Fediuc, A. (2018) Women's representation in management positions in ten Romanian sport federations. *International Congress of Physical Education, Sports and Kinetotherapy: "Education and Sports Science in the 21stCentury"*, Bucharest, Romania.

Aly, E. and Breese, K. (2018) The Representation of Women in USA Sports, Sports Administrative, and Team Sports Leadership. *European Scientific Journal*, 14(5), pp. 55–70.

Aman, M.P., Yusof, A., Ismail, M. and Razali, A.B. (2018) Pipeline Problem: Factors Influencing the Underrepresentation of Women in the Top Leadership Positions of Sport Organizations. *Malaysian Journal of Movement, Health and Exercise*, 7(2), pp. 151–166.

Bali, A. and Halpin, D. (2021) Agenda-Setting Instruments: Means and Strategies for the Management of Policy Demands. *Policy and Society*, 40(3), pp. 333–344. doi: 10.1080/14494035.2021.1955489.

Brassie, P. (1989) Guidelines for Programs Preparing Undergraduate and Graduate Students for Careers in Sport Management. *Journal of Sport Management*, 3(2), pp. 158–164.

Brunton, J. and St Quinton, T. (2021) Applying Stage-Based Theory to Engage Female Students in University Sport. *Journal of Human Sport and Exercise*, 16(1), pp. 11–25. doi: 10.14198/jhse.2021.161.02.

Burton, L. (2015) Underrepresentation of Women in Sport Leadership: A Review of Research. *Sport Management Review*, 18(2), pp. 155–165.

Burton, L. and Leberman, S. (2017) *Women in Sport Leadership: Research and Practice for Change*. London and New York: Routledge.

Castaño, A., Fontanil, Y. and García-Izquierdo, A. (2019) "Why Can't I Become a Manager?"—A Systematic Review of Gender Stereotypes and Organizational Discrimination. *International Journal of Environmental Research and Public Health*, 16(10), p. 1813. Retrieved on 06.11.2020, from: http://dx.doi.org/10.3390/ijerph16101813.

Cosentino, A.B. (2017) *Women in Leadership Within Professional Sport in Canada*. Electronic Thesis and Dissertation Repository, 4761. Retrieved on 22.02.2019, from: https://ir.lib.uwo.ca/etd/4761.

Drakou, A., Gargalianos, D. and Pertetzi, C. (2019) Women's Participation in Boards of Directors of Hellenic Sport Federations. *Woman and Sport*, 11(1), pp. 40–54.

Einarsdottir, U.D., Christiansen, T.H. and Kristjansdottir, E.S. (2018) "It's a Man Who Runs the Show": How Women Middle-Managers Experience Their Professional Position, Opportunities, and Barriers. *SAGE Open*, 8(1). doi: 10.1177/2158244017753989.

Ellwood, S., Garcia-Lacall, J. and Royo, S. (2020) The Shattered Glass Ceiling and a Narrowing Gender Pay Gap in NHS Foundation Trusts: Gender and Salaries of Chief Executives. *Public Money and Management*, 40(1), pp. 1–31.

England, P., Levine, A. and Mishel, E. (2017) Progress Toward Gender Equality in the United States Has Slowed or Stalled. *Proceedings of the National Academy of Sciences*, 117(13), pp. 6990–6997.

European Commission (2021) *Women's Empowerment in Sport and Physical Education Industry. Erasmus + project*. Retrieved on 04.05.2021, from: https://ec.europa.eu/programmes/erasmus-plus/projects/eplus-project-details/#project/b206127c-b7a3-4641-ac2a-5168528786ca.

European Institute for Gender Equality (2017) *EIGE in brief 2017*. Retrieved on 04.05.2021 from https://eige.europa.eu › default › files › documents

European Union, Office of the European Olympic Committees (2021) *Monthly Report, January 2021*. Retrieved on 20.02.2021, from:. https://euoffice.eurolympic.org/files/EOC_EU_Office-Monthly-report_January_2021.pdf

Evans, A. and Pfister, G. (2021) Women in Sports Leadership: A Systematic Narrative Review. *International Review for the Sociology of Sport*, 56(3), pp. 317–342.

Gabriel, M. (2021) Interview in the Monthly Report of the EU Office, European Olympic Committees. Retrieved on 10.02.2021, from: https://euoffice.eurolympic.org/blog/new-edition-monthly-report-interview-commissioner-mariya-gabriel.

Gaston, L., Blundell, M. and Fletcher, T. (2020) Gender Diversity in Sport Leadership: An Investigation of United States of America National Governing Bodies of Sport. *Managing Sport and Leisure*, 25(1), pp. 1–16.

Herbst, T. (2020). Gender differences in self-perception accuracy: The confidence gap and women leaders' underrepresentation in academia. *SA Journal of Industrial Psychology*, 46 (1). Retrieved on 08.03.2022, from DOI: 10.4102/sajip.v46i0.1704

Ignatova, M. (2019) *New Report: Women Apply to Fewer Jobs Than Men But Are More Likely to Get Hired*. Retrieved on 04.05.2021, from: https://business.linkedin.com/talent-solutions/blog/diversity/2019/how-women-find-jobs-gender-report.

International Olympic Committee (2018a) *Key Dates in the History of Women in the Olympic Movement*. Retrieved on 11.02.2021, from: https://www.olympic.org/women-in-sport/background/key-dates.

International Olympic Committee (2018b) *IOC Gender Equality Review Project*. Retrieved on 10.02.2021, from: https://stillmed.olympic.org/media/Document%20Library/OlympicOrg/News/2018/03/IOC-Gender-Equality-Report-March-2018.pdf

International Olympic Committee (2019) *Promotion of Gender Equality in Sport*. Retrieved on 31.01.2021, from: https://www.olympic.org/gender-equality.

International Olympic Committee (2020a) *Olympic Charter*. Retrieved on 31.01.2021, from: https://olympics.com/ioc/olympic-charter.

International Olympic Committee (2020b) *Women's Participation in Olympic and Youth Olympic Games*. Retrieved on 07.04.2021, from: https://www.olympic.org/women-in-sport/background/statistics.

International Paralympic Committee (2010) *Women in Sport Leadership Toolkit - Increasing Opportunities for Women in Paralympic Sport*. Retrieved on 12.12.2020, from: https://www.paralympic.org/sites/default/files/document/130130154714620_2010_10_01++IPC+Women+in+Sport+Leadership+Toolkit.pdf.

International Paralympic Committee (2020) *IPC Annual Report 2019 – 2020. Redefining Leadership – the Future is Female*. Retrieved on 04.02.2021, from: https://www.paralympic.org/sites/default/files/2020-12/IPC_Annual_Report_2019_2020%20NEW.pdf.

International Paralympic Committee (2021) *IPC Governance Review, Appendix 1: Recommended Adjustment to the IPC Revised Proposal*. Retrieved on 04.05.2021, from: https://www.paralympic.org/sites/default/files/2021-04/2021_04_27%20IPC%20Governance%20Review%20Appendix%201.pdf.

Konrad, A.M., Cramer, V. and Ercut, S. (2008) Critical Mass: The Impact of Three or More Women on Corporate Boards. *Organizational Dynamics*, 37(2), pp. 145–164.

Law of Chile (2015) *Crea el Ministro de la Mujer y la Equidad de Genero, Y Modifica Normas Legales que Indica*. Retrieved on 14.02.2021, from: https://www.bcn.cl/leychile/navegar?idNorma=1075613.

Moyo, T. and Dhliwayo, R. (2019) Achieving Gender Equality and Women's Empowerment in Sub-Saharan Africa: Lessons from the Experience of Selected Countries. *Journal of Developing Societies*, 35(2), pp. 256–281.

New South Wales Government (2018). *Women's Strategy 2018-2022. Her Sport – Her way*. Retrieved on 08.03.2021, from https://www.sport.nsw.gov.au/hersportherway

Sartore, M. and Cunningham, G. (2007) Explaining the Under-Representation of Women in Leadership Positions of Sport Organizations: A Symbolic Interactionist Perspective. *Quest*, 59(2), pp. 244–265.

Senne, J.A. (2016) Examination of Gender Equity and Female Participation in Sport. *The Sport Journal*, 19, pp. 1–12. Retrieved on 23.02.2019, from: https://thesportjournal.org/article/examination-of-gender-equity-and-female-participation-in-sport/.

Sotiriadou, P. and Pavlidis, A. (2020) Gender and Diversity in Sport Governance. In Shilbury, D. and Ferkins, L. (eds.), *Routledge Handbook of Sport Governance*. NY: Routledge, pp. 366–380.

Sotiriadou, P. and De Haan, D. (2019) Women and Leadership: Advancing Gender Equity Policies in Sport Leadership Through Sport Governance. *International Journal of Sport Policy and Politics*, 11(3), pp. 365–383. doi: 10.1080/19406940.2019.1577902.

Sotiriadou, P., De Haan, D. and Knoppers, A. (2017) Understanding and Redefining the Role of Men in Achieving Gender Equity in Sport. *International Olympic Committee, Switzerland: Olympic Studies Centre*. Retrieved on 14.02.2021, from: https://library.olympic.org/Default/doc/SYRACUSE/171304/understanding-and-redefining-the-role-of-men-in-achieving-gender-equity-in-sport-leadership-popi-sot.

Spoor, J.R. and Hoye, R. (2014) Perceived Support and Women's Intentions to Stay at a Sport Organization. *British Journal of Management*, 25, pp. 407–424.

Statistics Iceland (2019) *Inform Society: Women 34.7% of Board Members of Medium and Large Companies*. Retrieved on 02.03.2021, from: https://statice.is/publications/news-archive/enterprises/managers-and-board-of-directors-2019/.

Status of Women Canada (2011) *Departmental Performance Report 2010 – 2011*. Retrieved on 12.04.2021, from: https://www.tbs-sct.gc.ca/dpr-rmr/2010-2011/inst/csw/csw-eng.pdf.

Status of Women Canada (2018) *Results: What We Achieved. Increasing the Representation of Women in Leadership Roles*. Retrieved on 13.04.2021, from: https://cfc-swc.gc.ca/trans/account-resp/pr/dpr-rmr/1718/02-en.html.

Status of Women Canada (2021) *Archived Information*. Retrieved on 12.04.2021, from: https://cfc-swc.gc.ca/index-en.html.

The Commonwealth (2019) *Gender Equality in the Commonwealth 2018/19*. Retrieved on 07.05.2021, from: https://thecommonwealth.org/sites/default/files/inline/WAMM%2819%294a%20-%20Gender%20Equality%20in%20the%20Commonwealth%202018%2019.pdf.

Times Higher Education (2020) *Top Universities for Tackling Gender Equality*. Retrieved on 10.02.2021, from: https://www.timeshighereducation.com/student/best-universities/top-universities-tackling-gender-equality.

Turkel, A.R. (2004) The Hand that Rocks the Boat: The Empowerment of Women. *Journal of the American Academy of Psychoanalysis*, 32(1), pp. 41–54.

United Nations (2004) *Chile – Report on Implementation of the Beijing Platform for Action Presented by the Government of Chile to the United Nations Division for the Advancement of Women*. Retrieved on 12.04.2021, from: https://www.un.org/womenwatch/daw/Review/responses/CHILE-English.pdf.

United Nations (2018). *Strategy for Gender Equality and the Empowerment of Women (2018-2021)*. Retrieved on 07.02.202, from: https://www.unodc.org/documents/Gender/UNOV-UNODC_Strategy_for_Gender_Equality_and_the_Empowerment_of_Women_2018-2021_FINAL.pdf

United Nations (2020) *Gender Inequality Index (GII)*. Retrieved on 10.02.2021, from: https://www.un.org/sustainabledevelopment/gender-equality/

United Nations Developing Programme (2020) *Factsheet: Sub-Saharan Africa*. Retrieved on 07.05.2021, from: https://www.undp.org › undp › library › km-qap.

Van Hiel, A., Van Assche, J., De Cremer, D., Onraet, E., Bostyn, D. and Haesevoets, T. (2018) Can Education Change the World? Education Amplifies Differences in Liberalization Values and Innovation Between Developed and Developing Countries. *PLoS ONE*, 13(6), e0199560. Retrieved on 12.02.2021, from: https://doi.org/10.1371/journal.pone.0199560.

World Economic Forum (2018) *Women Were Awarded More PhDs in the US Than Men Last Year*. Retrieved on 10.02.2021, from: https://www.weforum.org/agenda/2018/10/chart-of-the-day-more-women-than-men-earned-phds-in-the-us-last-year/.

31
Mamanet
Empowering Mothers Towards Sport

Riki Tesler, Kwok Ng, Daniel Gelber and Elina Hytönen-Ng

Introduction

The issue of women's involvement in activities, especially sport, traditionally considered "masculine" has been extensively discussed (Hargreaves 1986; Schultz 2018). The well-known feminist thinker and writer, Simone de Beauvoir (1989), distinguished between the biological tier of a woman and the cultural tier attributed to her. De Beauvoir (1989) explained that a woman is not born a woman, but rather learns to be one. De Beauvoir did not ignore the biological differences of the genders; rather she attributed culture as being the most significant factor for existing perceptions about women and their roles in society. Gender behavioural norms are dictated by culture and cut across a broad spectrum of society, including sport, which is deeply influenced by said perceptions (Alvariñas-Villaverde et al. 2017; Sartore and Cunningham 2007).

Since the 1960s and 1970s, liberal feminism has focused on equality of access and opportunity, socialization practices, elimination of gender stereotyping, and discrimination (Acker 1987; Scraton and Flintoff 2002). In the sociology of sports literature, the underlying assumption of liberal feminism is that sport represents a positive experience with limited access for girls and women (Scraton and Flintoff 2013). Differences between male and female sport participation are perceived as a result of key socializing agencies such as the family, the school, and mass media (Beamon 2010; Chinurum, OgunjImi and O'Neill 2014). This begins at a young age, where girls are socialized into activities seen as feminine, promoting female physicality, such as gymnastics, whereas boys are socialized into activities considered masculine, requiring excessive physical contact, such as football (Trolan 2013). Reduced access and discriminatory practices are common and prevent women from participating in sporting opportunities. The liberal feminist movement has already identified issues with the underrepresentation of women in decision-making positions, and this is the same for sport (Scraton and Flintoff 2013). Equal opportunities and freedom to choose are usually the values emphasized by liberal feminism. This is usually understood to mean personal autonomy (Mackenzie and Stoljar 2000).

Mothers and sport

Sport is recognized as a set of physical activities bounded by rules and competition (Malcolm 2008), influenced by the society in which it originates (King 2005). In other words, sport has a specific purpose and is governed by set regulations with zero-sum outcomes (McPherson et al. 1989). While physical activity is carried out with health benefits in mind, sport participation may incur risk of injury and pain (Malcolm 2008). Participation in sports that are perceived as safe has multiple benefits for the individual and, thus, can contribute significantly to a woman's wellbeing. Yet, much of the scientific literature notes several inhibitory factors to sport participation by mothers including lack of time, lack of resources, gender differences, body image, fertility impairment, moral commitment, and financial limitations (Dlugonski et al. 2017; Edwards and Sackett 2016; Fahrenwald and Walker 2003; Jones et al. 2010; Miller and Brown 2005).

In the scientific literature, several factors are noted to encourage team sport among women. Motivation for mothers to take part in sport is associated with a sense of belonging, body awareness, health and well-being, and identity (Hanlon, Taylor and O'Brien 2020). Brown and colleagues (2001) reported positive experiences commonly enjoyed by mothers participating in sport such as perseverance and enjoyment. Moreover, mothers who regarded sport activities as high importance for leisure developed strategies to overcome time management constraints. Such strategies included getting support and help from spouses as well as time management skills such as a schedule that would allow them to train and participate in group activities (Brown et al. 2001; Jones et al. 2010; Miller and Brown 2005). As such, team sports available were deemed as enjoyable and a good platform for mothers to partake. Group activities offer women a chance to get involved in social networks that are not related to work. This creates opportunities to build links that could support overall wellbeing and connections that go beyond their family or social status in the local community. Furthermore, participation in team sports may not reveal an individual's financial status as resources are shared (Schultz 2018).

One central issue for mothers of young children is the challenge of making time for sport participation. Pregnancy, childbirth, postnatal body changes, career demands, childcare, and home care are roles and tasks that are unique experiences to women who become mothers. According to Morris et al. (2020), the lack of time is the main barrier for mothers to engage in sport, which stems from a busy work schedule and childcare commitments. It has also been found that team sport requires adjustment to training times, making it difficult for mothers to incorporate training into their day-to-day lives (Paldi et al. 2021a). Researchers have indicated that further constraints that prevent female participation in recreational activities include, but not limited to, gender roles, body image concerns, cultural expectations associated with women, as well as women's anatomical and physiological structure (Jones et al. 2010; Scraton and Flintoff 2013; Sport Scotland 2008). Building on this insight about mothers in sports, this chapter focuses on how a mother-sports movement has liberated many mothers around the world. The sport is called Mamanet and was founded in Israel. This chapter reviews some of the key aspects of Mamanet in Israeli society.

Gender politics in Israeli sports

In Israel, women's sports were traditionally marginalized (Bernstein and Galily 2008). The Kazan Action Plan was developed to increase inclusive access for all to sport and eliminate all forms of discrimination against women. The plan has brought forth discussions about gender and sport.

However, despite the goals to create a global exemplar for women, sport, physical education, and physical activity, the gender equality in sport has been slow to meet set targets to reduce existing inequalities (Soysa and Zipp 2019). In Israel, the principles of gender equality are upheld via the Sports Law and the Convention on the Elimination of All Forms of Discrimination against Women that was adopted at the UN in 1979. Following ratification, these laws were also adopted in Israeli law, applied in the Ministry of Sports as well as in the rules of the various national sports associations (Israel State Comptroller 2013).

Despite the above, in reality, most of the sport budget and resources in Israel were allocated to fostering men's sports, and women's sports were marginalized. Even today, this remains largely the case. The "Constantini Committee" (2004), appointed by the Israeli sports minister Yitzhak Levy, declared that the Israeli government budget for women sport has suffered from lack of funds and the government operated with no clear goals, which led to the marginalization of women in Israeli sports for decades (The Knesset Research and Information Centre 2013). As seen through the lens of liberal feminism, the agenda of government, national, and international organizations is to include the delivery, provision, and development of sports and achieve a gender balance. The importance of sport and physical education for both girls and women has been declared in several policy documents (e.g., 1994 Brighton Declaration on Women and Sport; 1998 Windhoek Call for Action; 2008 IAPESGW "Accept Respect" Declaration, see Scraton and Flintoff 2013). At a national level, Israeli policy makers created the Public Committee for Promotion of Women's Sports between 2005 and 2012 to promote this agenda as well. However, the Israel State Comptroller's annual report (2013, pp. 1483–1488) stated that the Ministry of Culture and Sports did not sufficiently execute the women sport promotion project. These findings highlight the gap between the intention of a public committee to target this issue and the actual implementation of the aforementioned policy. The limited policy performance points to inefficiencies and non-compliance issues related to the promotion of women's sports.

Recently, COVID-19 has once again raised the issue of women sports in Israel. In October 2020, the Committee for the Advancement of Women and Gender Equality in the Knesset (Israeli Parliament) held an emergency discussion on discrimination against women in the re-opening of leagues and budget gaps in women sports. During the discussion, claims were made by Knesset members that there was still gender inequality in the field of sports to the detriment of women (Knesset 2020). Unfortunately, this contemporary evidence highlights the issue that women sports need further provisions to promote the implementation of policy supporting women sports in Israel.

To bring to fruition the proposed policies to support women sports, further budgetary investment is needed to carry out the stated objectives for the promotion of women sports in Israel. Resources for the sport budget in Israel are based on two agencies: Sports Administration (Ministry of Sport) and the National Lottery Board. Additional funding stems from sports associations, local authorities, and private sources. The Sports Administration included in its analysis of the 2019 budget that the percentage of women's sports teams was at 14.8%, whereas men's sports teams made up the remaining 85.2% (Elephant 2018). The budget gap still persists and, thus, it is little surprise that there is a lack of progress and low rates of women participation in sport in Israel.

One of the issues that affects the budgetary distribution is the low participation rates of women in Israeli sports. The basis for the budget is determined by the number of participants (Galily and Betzer-Tayar 2014). Thus, by increasing the percentage of women participating in sports, it will be possible to increase the budget. Unfortunately, according to the Adva Center (2012), the participation rate of women in Israel in sports is extremely low. This is reinforced by survey data carried out by the Sports Union in 2011 on school-aged children, where fewer female than male teams participate in leagues (Galily, Kaufman and Tamir 2015). Furthermore, in a study of sports professionals, the percentage of women who hold management positions within sports associations stands at 15%, only 8% of Israeli sports coaches are women, and only 8% of sports broadcasters are women. Moreover, in a review of sports media, a mere 5% of sport-focused articles detail women sports (Galily, Kaufman and Tamir 2015).

Therefore, initiatives such as the Olympic Committee program of 2020–2024 to increase the participation rate of women in Israeli sports are more relevant than ever. According to this program, the following targets were set: 30% women in the management of the Olympic Committee in Israel, 50% women in positions and senior management levels, 50% women on sports committees, and 40% participation of women in the Olympic Games' committees. An equal budget for men and women was also defined (The Israeli Olympic Committee 2020). It is through these programmes that equality between genders in sport may be achieved, which, in turn, will help women to thrive in sports that suit their needs. One such example is the rise of Mamanet, a sport played by women throughout Israel and worldwide.

The Mamanet sport model

The Mamanet League was established in Israel in 2005 by Ofra Abramovich and is the largest sports organization whose target audience is normally women approximately aged 30 years and above. There has been an emphasis on mothers of school-age children, because the activities are based around the schools. Through participation in Mamanet, many of the sustainable development targets such as health, education, empowerment of women, promotion of fair laws, striving for equal pay, and reducing violence, to name but a few, may be met. Mamanet prides itself on being an all-inclusive organization, therefore women of all ages, mothers or otherwise, may take part in the sport. The league has a unique and innovative model that combines sport, health, and community involvement to get women and their children (back) into sport participation. Specifically, Mamanet targets women who do not identify themselves as being athletic and who, for various reasons, have difficulties in accessing sports.

Since its establishment, the Mamanet League has spread across Israel and the world, including Austria, Canada, Cyprus, Finland, Germany, Greece, Italy, Singapore, and the United States, with more countries joining. The variety of countries involved led to the inclusion of the international Mamanet Championship as part of the 5th CSIT (International Workers and Amateurs in Sports Confederation) World Sports Games 2017 in Riga. "Mamanet has the potential to change the sports society and the life of women for the better", said Harry Bauer, President of CSIT (Mamanet 2020). Mamanet is the only sports league for mothers and helps women to either re-live their younger days as athletes or gain experience as a member of a sports league for the first time. However, the development and growth of Mamanet has not been without challenges. For the most part, the League consists of mothers, though this has been met with resistance. It has been argued that it is discriminatory to include only women who are mothers within the league, and, therefore, it has been opened up to include all women over the age of 30.

In 2018, the Mamanet League was made up of approximately 8,000 players in about 70 teams throughout Israel. For most participants, the teams are based near their children's school (or location of residence for non-mothers). These leagues are open to all women, most of them mothers, and previous experience is not necessary. As sport needs to have goals and purposes, there are different levels, such as the "premium league", which requires previous experience to play at a higher level, and participants can join any national team. Other variations include the "Golden League" for women over 65 years old, the "Kidnet" for children and "Abanet" for men ("aba" in Hebrew means "dad"). All variations of Mamanet focus on positive sports values, including fair play, open communication, social values, and supporting communities on the sports field.

The game played in the Mamanet League is called "Cachibol" and is also known as "Newcomb ball". The game was invented by Clara Gregory Baer in 1895, who studied physical education at Sophie Newcomb College in Louisiana, United States (Paul 1996). Cachibol is a team ball game based on volleyball rules and takes place on a court identical to that of volleyball (9x18 metres). Cachibol and volleyball have the same objective; to transfer the ball across the net into the opposing court. However, a fundamental difference is that in Cachibol, the players are allowed to catch and hold the ball rather than hit it as preferred in volleyball. Less impact leads to lower physiological demand for Mamanet participants, making it a physically safer sport. The nature of the game allows players of any age or fitness level to learn and participate. Each team consists of up to 14 players, with 6 members of each team on the court at a given time. The game's objective is to win 3-set matches, and are won by achieving 21 points per set by two clear points. Points are achieved when the serving team wins the rally. The game is not timed but generally lasts about 45 minutes. Each team has a coach and a team captain. Teams meet once a week for team practices and once a week for a league game. Cachibol has become increasingly popular and is currently the fastest-growing sport among women in Israel (Farkash et al. 2016).

Women's empowerment through Mamanet

A sports team can be used as a tool for empowerment (see Sadan 1997; Perkins and Zimmerman 1995). Perkins (2010) believes empowerment to be more of a collective rather than individual process, and that participatory empowerment has more of an impact when dealing with overcoming fears and obstacles, while also increasing one's wellbeing and satisfaction (Kim and James 2019). Empowerment has an impact on one's wellbeing by having a positive influence on health status (Cornwall 2016; Kim and James 2019). Mamanet players engage in an empowerment model of change as depicted in Figure 31.1.

Given the barriers to women in sport, the activities in Mamanet offer both short- and long-term outcomes. Through regular practices and competitions, the players can organize their

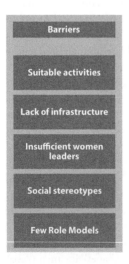

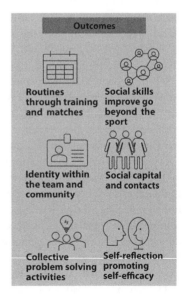

Figure 31.1 Mamanet sport empowerment model of change

routines with their families and friends to allow them to participate consistently. Team members form social circles which reach beyond the sport and encourage a set of skills that are atypical in a family setting. Belonging to a Mamanet League creates a sense of identity that enhances wellbeing (Paldi 2021b). The mother brings her family to the sport, and the families, in turn, develop a community. This strengthened community brings increased social capital and freedom in sports and beyond. Furthermore, Mamanet players are engaged in problem-solving when playing the game, creating more autonomy, thereby developing skills that may be used outside of the sport.

Mamanet and social capital

As depicted in the Mamanet sport model, the program has the tendency to contribute to the building of healthy and strong communities. Participation in the league focuses on positive social values, promoting fair play, team cohesion, improving communication skills, and building supportive communities around the sports arena and beyond. As such, the Mamanet League not only focuses on physical activity, but also the development and maintenance of community-based social capital and networks.

The theory of social capital that focuses on the development of community networks to support collective wellbeing can be helpful in contextualizing the cultural meaning of Mamanet. Putnam (1995, 2000) defines social capital as: "features of social organization such as networks, norms, and social trust that facilitate coordination and cooperation for mutual benefit". Putnam also argued that bonding, bridging, and linking social agents were important aspects of social capital. Bonding social capital, which is built on trust among like-minded individuals (Putnam 2000), is frequently associated with cognitive social capital. This type of social capital places an emphasis on psychological support as opposed to material support, which is especially important in participation in sports teams (Elmose-Østerlund and van der Roest 2017). As sports are traditionally viewed as a male domain (Forsdike et al. 2019; O'Neill and Gidengil 2013), studying the presence of social capital among women who are active in sports teams is of importance. Gaining and developing social capital has been viewed in association with participating in organized team sports, which is aligned with Putnam's view of social capital (Harvey et al. 2007; Welty Peachey et al. 2013). Participation in sports is seen as contributing to generalized trust and increased social connections via social activity. Team sports have the potential to provide a unique social dynamic, which is often expressed in group cohesion, as well as by mutual member support and a sense of belonging (Brown et al. 2001; Campo, Mackie and Sanchez 2019).

In Israel, the Mamanet League advocates community involvement and provides a platform for both social engagement and personal responsibility. The league aims to build a better, more active world for women, promote healthy lifestyle, and increase social capital in the community via activities in the sport arena and community. In addition to providing a platform for physical activity and participation in various leagues, Mamanet also supports initiatives around enhancing community engagement. For instance, Mamanet participants can and do train at-risk youth to be referees for games and to participate in their league. Mamanet is also highly involved in women's needs and holds annual national and international tournaments to raise breast cancer awareness. Additionally, Mamanet League works with local municipalities throughout Israel and the world to offer sports activities and sports spaces for sheltered women who experienced domestic violence, especially for mothers to have a safe place to play with their children. The league also provides a rehabilitation project for the inmates of the sole women's prison in Israel and assists refugees and asylum seekers' integration into local communities throughout Israel. Therefore, it is safe to say that Mamanet's reach and social capital extends well beyond the sport court.

Examples of Mamanet research

A comprehensive research study by Tesler and colleagues (2018) was conducted to analyse the impact of participating in a Mamanet Mother's League in Israel. The primary focus was to examine the differences in promoting health, wellbeing, and social capital. Using multiple research methods along with a comparison group, it was found that participation in the Mamanet League was associated with subjective wellbeing and physical activity among participants and their families as compared to participants in the control group. In addition, participation led to a sense of belonging with a supportive social network, trust in the environment, and social involvement among participants. Such findings confirm the success of Mamanet in allowing mothers and women to be empowered to participate in sport in an almost women-exclusive environment, unlike the male-dominated sport society in Israel.

Another study investigated levels of social capital, including social support, social involvement, and trust, and changes in those over time with Mamanet participants and non-participants (see Baron-Epel et al. 2021). The women were interviewed within three months of joining Mamanet and 13–15 months later. Initially, the participants had higher social capital and self-rated health scores, yet lower psychosomatic and depressive symptoms compared with the control group. Based on the second interviews, participation in the Mamanet League improves two of the three social capital measures: social support and social involvement. There was an increase among participants in the Mamanet group over time and no change in the control group. It is likely that participants are already socially engaged when they gain entry to Mamanet leagues and social capital is present. Based on these findings, this initial social capital is then maintained and extended through participation in Mamanet leagues. Participation in the league had no significant effect on wellbeing during this period and, thus, understanding the mechanisms of competitive opportunities requires further investigation.

Paldi and colleagues (2021b) further examined the association of participation in the Mamanet League with social capital, health, and wellbeing across two main ethnic groups in Israel, Jewish and Arab women. A cross-sectional survey was conducted among women aged between 30 and 64 years old. The sample included Jewish and Arab Mamanet League participants and compared them with Jewish and Arab non-participants. The findings revealed that Mamanet League participants from both ethnic groups reported higher social capital, better self-reported health, and lower psychosomatic symptoms compared to non-participants. Paldi et al. (2021c) also explored the emotional and social health behaviours of Mamanet participants and found two dominant themes: mental health centred (feelings of happiness, enjoyment, energetic, and social well-being) and citizenship centred (social skills, values, and community responsibility). Paldi et al.'s (2021b, 2021c) studies have revealed that participating in Mamanet offered multiple social, physical, and psychological benefits to women.

Based on the research noted above, it can be summarized that being part of Mamanet teams is perceived as a supporting resource that helps participants stay physically active on a regular and sustained basis in their everyday lives. Participants generally improve their quality of life as per findings by Hanlon and colleagues (2020). Mothers are often motivated to be involved in sport to improve their health, well-being, and body awareness as well as reflect on their identity and sense of belonging.

The proposed pillars are crucial to understand when devising implementations of policies and navigating the political landscape in sport and gender. A process that involves mothers and creates these types of opportunities can enact liberal feminism (Scraton and Flintoff 2013). On the social-integrative level, the combination of communalization with team sports activity has a positive effect on the participants' psychosocial wellbeing. The added benefit of social integration for women is to be physically active and emancipation within society (see Elling, Knoppers and De Knop 2001). The participants establish new relationships and expand their social networks beyond the sports they do, which assists them in transitioning out of social isolation, frequently associated with motherhood, and helps them (re)develop their social capital that reaches Mamanet.

Conclusions

Sport has traditionally been viewed as a male-dominated activity that excluded women and mothers. However, women can acquire valuable skills and benefits by taking part in sports. By (re)experiencing the concepts of fair play, winning, and losing, women can gain and develop invaluable social and cultural capital. Therefore, this chapter argues that creating more sport opportunities for women is essential to close the sport-based gender gap in Israel, which has a long history and broad social consequences. In Israel, despite being a modern, Western country, where women and men have equal rights (including in the military), women's engagement in sports remains very low to this day. Support from governments and sporting associations is in dire need to close existing gender gaps within sports. Mamanet was created to provide a solution to the aforementioned issues and aligns well with meeting sustainable development targets such as health, education, empowerment of women, promotion of fair laws, striving for equal pay, and reducing violence. Mamanet has spread rapidly in Israel as well as in many countries around the world. Mamanet offers women and mothers of all backgrounds and nationalities the opportunity to experience collaborative team sports, obtain all of the associated physical and psychological benefits, as well as being liberated from the inactive mother stereotype. Consequently, the infrastructure of Mamanet offers women the possibility to construct their own identity somewhat independent to that of family and work life. These opportunities offered by Mamanet network can enable growth in women's sport, which is of significance as there are still multiple barriers in existence. In essence, the case of Mamanet is an effective and promising working model to resist gender stereotypes associated with women (especially mothers) and skewed political resource allocation (mostly favouring men's sports) and to offer a broad range of opportunities for women to be part of a sports culture and to increase their social capital.

REFERENCES

Acker, S. (1987) 'Feminist theory and the study of gender and education', *International Review of Education*, 33(4), pp. 419–435.

Swirski, S., Konor-Attias, E. (2013) Adva Center, *'Israel: A Social Report 2012'*. Available at: https://adva.org/wp-content/uploads/2015/01/social-Eng_2012-12.pdf. (Accessed 10.9.2021).

Alvariñas-Villaverde, M., López-Villar, C., Fernández-Villarino, M.A. and Alvarez-Esteban, R. (2017) 'Masculine, feminine and neutral sports: Extracurricular sport modalities in practice', *Journal of Human Sport and Exercise*, 12(4), pp. 1278–1288.

Baron-Epel, O., Paldi, Y., Bord, S., Kadish, D., Guttman, E., Moran, D.S. and Tesler, R. (2021) 'Social capital and health among participants in the Cachibol league in Israel', *International Review for the Sociology of Sport*, 56(6), pp. 877–896.

Beamon, K.K. (2010) 'Are sports overemphasized in the socialization process of African American males? A qualitative analysis of former collegiate athletes' perception of sport socialization', *Journal of Black Studies*, 41(2), pp. 281–300.

Bernstein, A. and Galily, Y. (2008) 'Games and sets: Women, media and sport in Israel', *Nashim: A Journal of Jewish Women's Studies and Gender Issues*, 15, pp. 175–196.

Brown, P.R., Brown, W.J., Miller, Y.D. and Hansen, V. (2001) 'Perceived constraints and social support for active leisure among mothers with young children', *Leisure Sciences*, 23(3), pp. 131–144.

Campo, M., Mackie, D.M. and Sanchez, X. (2019) 'Emotions in group sports: A narrative review from a social identity perspective', *Frontiers in Psychology*, 29(10), p. 666.

Chinurum, J.N., Ogunjlmi, L.O. and O'Neill, C.B. (2014) 'Gender and sports in contemporary society', *Journal of Educational and Social Research*, 4(7), p. 25.

Cornwall, A. (2016) 'Women's empowerment: What works?', *Journal of International Development*, 31, pp. 293–313.

De Beauvoir, S. (1989) *The second sex*. New York: Vintage Books.

Dlugonski, D., Martin, T.R., Mailey, E.L. and Pineda, E. (2017) 'Motives and barriers for physical activity among low-income black single mothers', *Sex Roles*, 77(5), pp. 379–392.

Edwards, E.S. and Sackett, S.C. (2016) 'Psychosocial variables related to why women are less active than men and related health implications: Supplementary issue: Health disparities in women', *Clinical Medicine Insights: Women's Health*, 9(Suppl 1), pp. 47–56.

Elephant, L. (2018) *State Budget Analysis – Sport*. Available at: politicallycorret.co.il (Accessed: 14.8.2021).

Elling, A., Knoppers, A. and De Knop, P. (2001) 'The social integrating meaning of sport: A critical and comparative analysis of policy and practice in the Netherlands', *Sociology of Sport*, 18, pp. 414–434.

Elmose-Østerlund, K. and van der Roest, J.W. (2017) 'Understanding social capital in sports clubs: Participation, duration and social trust', *European Journal for Sport and Society*, 14(4), pp. 366–386.

Fahrenwald, N.L. and Walker, S.N. (2003) 'Application of the Transtheoretical Model of behavior change to the physical activity behavior of WIC mothers', *Public Health Nursing*, 20(4), pp. 307–317.

Farkash, U., Borisov, O., Hetsroni, I., Palmanovich, E., Zohar, E. and Nyska, M. (2016) 'Injuries in a developing sport, Cachibol (Newcomb Ball)', *Israel Medical Association Journal*, 18(2), pp. 85–89.

Forsdike, K., Marjoribanks, T. and Sawyer, A.M. (2019) 'Hockey becomes like a family in itself': Re-examining social capital through women's experiences of a sport club undergoing quasiprofessionalisation', *International Review for the Sociology of Sport*, 54(4), pp. 479–494.

Galily, Y. and Betzer-Tayar, M. (2014) 'Losing is not an option! Women's basketball in Israel and its struggle for equality (1985–2002)', *The International Journal of the History of Sport*, 31(13), pp. 1694–1705.

Galily, Y., Kaufman, H. and Tamir, I. (2015) 'She got game?! Women, sport and society from an Israeli perspective', *Israel Affairs*, 21(4), pp. 559–584.

Hanlon, C., Taylor, T. and O'Brien, W. (2020) 'Developing Sport for Women and Girls', in E. Sherry and K. Rowie (eds.), *Developing sport for mothers with dependent children*. Oxon: Routledge, pp. 34–46.

Hargreaves, J. (1986) 'Where's the virtue? Where's the grace? A discussion of the social production of gender relations in and through sports', *Theory, Culture & Society*, 3(1), pp. 109–121.

Harvey, J., Lévesque, M. and Donnelly, P. (2007) 'Sport volunteerism and social capital', *Sociology of Sport Journal*, 24(2), pp. 206–223.

Israel State Comptroller (2013) *Aspects of actions to promote women's sports in Israel*. Available at: https://www.mevaker.gov.il/sites/DigitalLibrary/Documents/63c/2013-63c-232-sport.pdf?AspxAutoDetectCookieSupport=1 (Accessed: 15.6.2021).

Jones, C., Burns, S., Howat, P., Jancey, J., McManus, A. and Carter, O. (2010) 'Playgroups as a setting for nutrition and physical activity interventions for mothers with young children: Exploratory qualitative findings', *Health Promotion Journal of Australia*, 21(2), pp. 92–98.

Kim, J. and James, J.D. (2019) 'Sport and happiness: Understanding the relations among sport consumption activities, long-and short-term subjective well-being, and psychological need fulfilment', *Journal of Sport Management*, 33(2), pp. 119–132.

King, S. (2005) 'Methodological Contingencies in Sports Studies', in D. Andrews, D. Mason, and M. Silk (eds.), *Qualitative methods in sports studies*. Oxford: Berg, pp. 21–37.

Knesset (2013) *Research and Information Centre*. Available at: https://m.knesset.gov.il/en/activity/pages/mmmabout.aspx (Accessed: 3.11.2021).

Knesset (2020) *The budgetary conduct of the Ministry of Sports is similar to economic violence*. Available at: https://m.knesset.gov.il/news/pressreleases/pages/press21.10.20a.aspx (Accessed: 17.8.2021).

Mackenzie, C. and Stoljar, N. (2000) 'Introduction: Autonomy Refigured', in Mackenzie and Stoljar (eds.) *Relational autonomy: Feminist perspectives on autonomy, agency, and the social self*. New York: Oxford University Press, pp. 3–34.

Malcolm, D. (2008) *The SAGE dictionary of sports studies*. London: SAGE Publications.

Mamanet (2020) *EFPM Fair Play green/white card research project*. Available at: https://www.mamanet.org.il/PDF/Mamanet_Green_Card_Case_Study_Final.pdf (Accessed: 10.10.2020).

McPherson, B.D., Loy, J.W., & Curtis, J.E. (1989) *The social significance of sport : an introduction to the sociology of sport*. Champaign (Ill.): Human kinetics.

Miller, Y.D. and Brown, W.J. (2005). 'Determinants of active leisure for women with young children—an "ethic of care" prevails', *Leisure Sciences*, 27(5), pp. 405–420.

Morris, K.A., Arundell, L., Cleland, V. and Teychenne, M. (2020) 'Social ecological factors associated with physical activity and screen time amongst mothers from disadvantaged neighbourhoods over three years', *International Journal of Behavioral Nutrition and Physical Activity*, 17(1), pp. 1–11.

O'Neill, B., & Gidengil, E. (2013). Gender, Social Capital, and Political Engagement: Findings and Future Directions. In *Gender and Social Capital* (pp. 385–396). Routledge.

Paldi, Y., Moran, D.S., Baron-Epel, O., Bord, S. and Tesler, R. (2021a) 'Ethnic disparities in social capital and health among Jewish and Arab participants in the Israeli Mamanet Cachibol League', *International Journal of Environmental Research and Public Health*, 18(1), p. 295.

Paldi, Y., Moran, D.S., Baron-Epel, O., Bord, S., Benartzi, E. and Tesler, R. (2021b) 'Social capital as a mediator in the link between women's participation in team sports and health-related outcomes', *International Journal of Environmental Research and Public Health*, 18(17), p. 9331.

Paldi, Y., Moran, D.S., Baron Epel, O., Bord, S. and Tesler, R. (2021c) 'The contribution of participation in sport team (Mamanet League) to the components of social capital and health measures among mothers', *The Spirit of Sport*, 7, pp. 89–105.

Paul, J. (1996) 'A lost sport: Clara Gregory Baer and Newcomb ball', *Journal of Sport History*, 23(2), pp. 165–174.

Peachey, J.W., Cohen, A., Borland, J. and Lyras, A. (2013) 'Building social capital: Examining the impact of Street Soccer USA on its volunteers', *International Review for the Sociology of Sport*, 48(1), pp. 20–37.

Perkins, D.D. (2010) 'Empowerment', in R. Couto (ed.), *Political and civic leadership*. Thousand Oaks, CA: SAGE, pp. 207–218.

Perkins, D.D. and Zimmerman, M.A. (1995) 'Empowerment theory, research, and application', *American Journal of Community Psychology*, 23(5), pp. 569–579.

Putnam, R.D. (1995) 'Bowling alone: America's declining social capital', *Journal of Democracy*, 6, pp. 65–78.

Putnam, R.D. (2000) *Bowling alone: The collapse and revival of American community*. New York, NY: Simon and Schuster.

Sadan, E. (1997) *Empowerment and community planning: Theory and practice of people-focused social solutions*. Tel Aviv: Hakibbutz Hameuchad.

Sartore, M.L. and Cunningham, G.B. (2007) 'Explaining the under-representation of women in leadership positions of sport organizations: A symbolic interactionist perspective', *Quest*, 59(2), pp. 244–265.

Schultz, J. (2018) *Women's sports: What everyone needs to know*. Oxford: Oxford University Press.

Scraton, S. and Flintoff, A. (eds.) (2002) *Gender and sport: A reader*. London: Routledge.

Scraton, S. and Flintoff, A. (2013) 'Gender, Feminist Theory, and Sport', in D.L. Andrews and B. Carrington (eds.), *A companion to sport*. Oxford: Blackwell Publishing, pp. 96–111.

Soysa, L. and Zipp, S. (2019) 'Gender equality, sport and the United Nation's system. A historical overview of the slow pace of progress', *Sport in Society*, 22(6), pp. 1–18.

Sport Scotland (2008) *Barriers to women and girls' participation in sport and physical activity*. Available at: https://www.funding4sport.co.uk/downloads/women_barriers_participation.pdf. (Accessed: 28.8.2021).

Tesler, R., Moran, D., Bord, S., Epel, O.B. and Harel-Fisch, Y. (2018) 'Participation in a Mamanet mothers' Cachiball League to promote health and social capital' (in Hebrew), *Movement: Journal of Physical Education and Sport Sciences*, 11(3), pp. 171–172.

The Israeli Olympic Committee (2020) *The Strategic Plan and Gender Standards as a Compass for Implementing Gender Equality 2024-2020*. Available at: https://www.olympicsil.co.il/wp-content/uploads/2020/11/The-Strategic-Plan.pdf (Accessed: 3.9.2021).

Trolan, E.J. (2013) 'The impact of the media on gender inequality within sport', *Procedia-Social and Behavioral Sciences*, 91, pp. 215–227.

32
A Strategy to Promote Gender Equality
The Number and Status of Women in Leadership and Decision-making Positions in Finnish Sport

Matti Hakamäki, Salla Turpeinen and Kati Lehtonen

Introduction

In Finland, there are around 10,000 sports clubs, and 69% of the population (total of 5.5 million) claim to participate in sport at least once a week (European Commission 2018). The characteristics of the Nordic sport model typically include sports organisations based on volunteerism and democratic decision-making structures inside the sport movement. The sport system is different in Finland than it is in other Nordic countries, because the state has a strong role as a coordinator, especially through funding. The Ministry of Education and Culture (OKM) is responsible for administering the distribution of state subsidies to sports organisations such as national governing bodies of sport (NGBs), not a central sport organisation like it is, for example, in Norway. The role of sports organisations is to implement the sport policy. Because the system is not clearly controlled by either the state or the sport movement, the Finnish system is regarded as a mixed model consisting of these two key governing entities (Henry 2009; Lehtonen and Mäkinen 2020).

While the sense of gender equality has deep roots in Finnish society, similarly to other North European countries, several sport policy initiatives around gender equality have been promoted, especially since the 1990s. One of these foci has been the proportion of women in leadership and decision-making positions. Both state and sport organisations have initiated several projects and strategic plans around the issue, aiming to increase the number of women in sport leadership positions. For example, Finland has been an active collaborator in the International Working Group (IWG) on Women & Sport, which was convened as an international conference organised in Helsinki in 2014. Due to this conference, the Brighton Declaration was updated by the IWG to become the Brighton plus Helsinki Declaration. According to the IWG Treaty (2021, p. 3), the aim was "to develop a sporting culture that enables and values the full involvement of women in every aspect of sport and physical activity."

In this chapter, we consider how the promotion of gender equality in Finnish sport policy has been actualised since the 1990s through the framework of policy process analysis. The emphasis is on the documentation of the proportion of women in leadership and decision-making roles in NGBs, which are traditionally the most male-dominant sport organisations in Finland (Särkivuori et al. 2020; Turpeinen and Hakamäki 2018). We analyse this progress by using numerical data, key informant interviews and policy documents. The policies and actions include recommendations, government programmes, gender impact assessments, the introduction of quotas and meeting requirements of gender equality policies to receive public funding. The chapter is structured as follows: after introducing some of the main concepts of policy process analysis – including focusing events, agenda setting and turning points – the methods section will detail data sets and analysis. The focus then turns to the results where statistical analysis is presented first, followed by interview analyses related to policy documents. The discussion section offers interpretations with future remarks on promoting gender equality in Finnish sport policy.

Framework for analysing gender equality promotion in the sport policy process

According to Sabatier (1991), those processes and practices in which governmental policies are formulated and implemented as well as the effects of those actions require an understanding of the behaviour of major governmental institutions. These behavioural dimensions include legislatures, courts and administrative agencies as well as the behaviour of interest groups such as public opinion, media and third sector organisations. Attention may be paid, for example, to those influences and agents of change that are the most prominent when looking at the policy process and its changes. From this point of view, key aspects to consider are the turning points during the policy process and the agenda-setting.

Turning points are also called focusing events, or, as per Atkinson (2019, p. 1), "triggering events." Conceptually, a focusing event is a large-scale event and can be defined, for example, as a large environmental disaster (Birkland 1998) as well as by the presence or absence of "policy entrepreneurs" both within and outside of governments or institutionalised events, such as periodic elections. Regarding agenda-setting, the focus is on the ways policy agenda is set up and, overall, on what issues are established as part of the policy agenda (Kingdon 1995). Policy process and policymaking is a complex, messy and contested process, involving negotiation and power play between diverse stakeholders over the control and use of limited resources (Springate-Baginski and Soussan 2002). The question of power arises in its most basic form, for example, when considering the institutional power relations between peoples and organisations, responsibilities to force or resist policy agenda or when the focus is on informal power structures controlling the policy process (Cairney 2020). When analysing the policy process, power is also one of the key influences affecting the process and its development.

Methods and data

The data sets for this chapter come from three sources: (1) six key person interviews to assess the turning points of promoting gender equality in sport policy context including its development, (2) four state policy documents to consider the overall progress of sport policy and (3) numerical data of positions and board memberships of NGBs between 1995 and 2019.

The interviews were conducted with representatives of the National Olympic Committee, the Ministry of Education and Culture (hereafter the Ministry) as the public sector authority of Finnish sport and stakeholder sport organisations. The interviewees were selected based on their current and leading managerial positions in sport organisations or in the Ministry or based on their expertise in gender equality issues. To retain the anonymity of the interviewees, detailed personal information such as working titles are excluded. The total duration of the interviews was six hours. The average duration of each interview was 60 minutes, usually lasting from 40 to 72 minutes. Catalysing questions guided interviewees towards (1) the main turning points of sport policy to increasing or decreasing the number of women in leadership positions, (2) overall issues of promoting gender equality in sport since the 1990s and (3) future aspects for promoting gender equality.

Three key policy documents on promotion and gender assessment in sport and the preparation of the national programme on sport were published by the Ministry of Education between 2005 and 2008. The Finnish Government report on sport policy was submitted to Parliament in 2018 and approved with parliamentary communication in 2019 (Finnish Government 2019; Finnish Parliament 2019).

In data sets 1 and 2, qualitative theory-oriented content analysis was used (Krippendorf 2013). In the first reading, data were grouped into three thematic areas suggested by theory: influences, agenda setting and focusing events. In the second round, we compared our findings to numerical data with an idea to understand how the progress of women in leadership positions has developed as a policy process. Third, we pinpointed the main influences and events as results.

The numerical data demonstrate the share of women and men in leadership positions in all NGBs and the longitudinal progress of gender equality development in Finnish sport. The data of NGBs from the years 1995–2017 have been compiled by the umbrella organisations such as Suomen Liikunta ja Urheilu (SLU), Valtakunnallinen liikunta ja urheiluorganisaatio (Valo) and the Finnish Olympic Committee (Turpeinen and Hakamäki 2018). The data consists of all Finnish NGBs, including the non-Olympic sports. Numerical data from the years 2018–2019 is compiled from the report "Equality in the national and regional sport organisations of Finland in 2019" (Särkivuori et al. 2020). The data are based on the information given by the respective organisations themselves in the application process concerning the general grants for national organisations promoting sport and physical activity in 2018 and 2019.

When summarising these three different data sets, the key informant interviewees form the basis for analysing the policy process. Interview data underline an interpretative frame for the numerical data, which demonstrates the overall progress of gender equality from the viewpoint of leadership. Documentary reviews are important to pinpoint the main documented policy goals and their background. In addition, the output of previous policy actions is presented in these documents. Therefore, sport policy documents complement both statistics and interviews.

Results

Gender distribution in national governing bodies

In this subsection, we present statistics that depict women's gradual increase in sport NGBs in Finland. According to the numerical data, decision-making and leadership roles in sport in NGBs have mostly been held by men for decades, but over the last 20 years, the number of women in leadership and decision-making positions has been gradually increasing. In total, the proportion of women on the boards of NGBs have increased between 1995 and 2019. Currently, the share of women is 28% (see Figure 32.1).

The lowest proportion of women is found among chairpersons. Chair positions remain firmly in men's hands in the NGBs. Only a few women serve as elected officials. In 1995, women accounted for 6% of chairs of all NGBs. In 2019, the share of women was 18% (see Figure 32.2).

Strategy to Promote Gender Equality

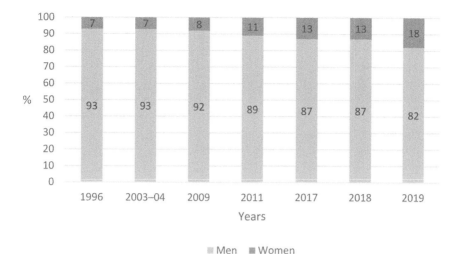

Figure 32.1 Gender distribution (%) in the boards of directors of national governing bodies, 1995–2019

The proportion of women in leadership positions is the highest in operative leading. The number of women in leadership positions in these bodies has increased notably from the 1990s. In 2019, approximately one out of three executive directors of NGBs were women (see Figure 32.3). The statistics presented here will be interpreted and combined with the other two data sets in the following sections.

1990s: A new era in sport gender equality promotion

From the viewpoint of sport policy actions, the 1990s was an abundant decade in Finnish sport: a new umbrella organisation, the Finnish Sports Confederation (SLU), was established in 1993

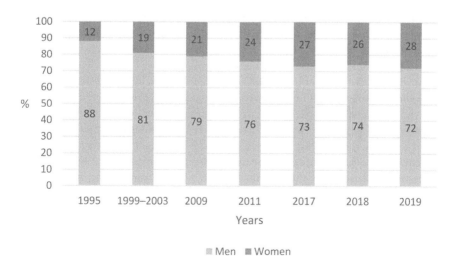

Figure 32.2 Gender distribution (%) among the chairs of the board of national governing bodies, 1995–2019

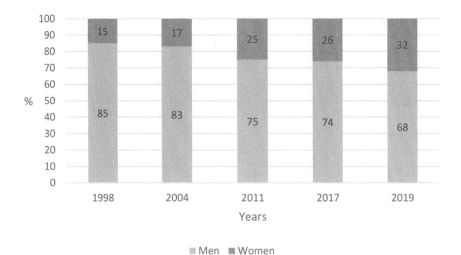

Figure 32.3 Gender distribution (%) in the Operative Lead of National Governing Bodies in 1995–2019

in the spirit of service production and in contrast to the bureaucratic sport system (Heikkala 1998). This structural change in the systemic level as institutional influence (see Sabatier 1991) opened the first window to set gender equality to a sports policy agenda. A representative of the Ministry stated during an interview: "SLU was looking for its identity and strategic goals. It gave us here in the Ministry the possibility to combine our policy actions with those of the SLU. Promoting gender equality was one of them." This possibility to set up a common policy agenda was supported by reform, where OKM renewed NGBs' subsidy system due to New Public Management practices that focused on results-based funding (Lehtonen 2017a). This subsidy system, as a new economic context, influenced and forced sport associations to target funding or working time to promote gender equality among certain sports (OKM 2005, p. 30). In addition, another governmental turning point of the 1990s was the revision of the Act on the Promotion of Sports and Physical Activity, where equality was listed among the objectives. The strengthening of the legal framework was therefore the key influence on the policy process together with economic and institutional ones.

The current Associations Act (503/1989) in Finland stresses the autonomy of associations. The umbrella organisation of Finnish sports, for example, the Finnish Olympic Committee, can issue recommendations to its member organisations if it wishes to steer gender equality in organisation and club Boards, as well as the Ministry of Education and Culture can set conditions to direct the funding/subsidies. From the viewpoint of sport associations' own policy agenda and political context (see Springate-Baginski and Soussan 2002), in 1998, SLU made a recommendation that the Boards of their member associations, including NGBs, should consist of minimum 40% of each gender. The recommendation was based on the Act on Equality between Women and Men (1986) with a statement that the proportion of both women and men in government committees, advisory boards and other corresponding bodies ought to be at least 40%, unless there were special reasons to the contrary (Turpeinen et al. 2012, pp. 25–27). This recommendation can be seen as the main turning point for increasing the number of women on Boards from 16% to 30% between 1995 and 2002 (see Figure 32.1). In addition, symbols and prizes as external influences were also used, as one interviewee from the Ministry explained: "In 1995, we started to award yearly recognitions to influential persons or organisations who have promoted gender equality in sport. It gave visibility to this issue."

One policy action to strengthen the policy agenda in gender equality was internationalisation. This viewpoint manifested in interviewees' comments and was mentioned especially as a strategic turning point made in the 1990s, thereby giving strong support to the Brighton Declaration (1994), leading to the IWG conference in Helsinki in 2014. However, most important was to systematically take part in international networks around global sport and combine national and international agents of change (see Springate-Baginski and Soussan 2002). Already in its early stage in the 1990s, this combination became a policy driver, as a representative of a stakeholder sport organisation explained: "Because we didn't get noticed here in Finland around gender equality and sport, we thought to create national sport policy throughout international sport policy. We networked, took part in conferences and acquired visibility. Little by little, it helped to bring gender equality stronger to national sport policy."

2000–2010: Increasing legislation and governmental agendas

At the beginning of 2000, promoting gender equality in Finnish society had reached the macro-policy level while the Government Programme of Prime Minister Matti Vanhanen's government included a section on gender equality, in which one objective was: "Methods for assessing gender effects will be developed and evaluation will be taken into account in the preparation of legislation and the central government budget" (Finnish Government 2003, p. 14).

The first decade of the 2000s was also an era of governmental agendas and guidelines – named institutional and legal influences of policy process (Springate-Baginski and Soussan 2002). The committee report "A draw: Promotion and assessment of the gender aspect in sports" was published by OKM in 2005. These reports were also important tools to "increase knowledge and awareness around gender and sport" – a representative of the Ministry stated. Therefore, we can note that information and knowledge started to be relevant influences in promoting gender equality. As it was already in the 1990s, financial support to policy-related measures for promoting gender equality through resource allocation and information-based guidance were seen to be relevant. In 2006, OKM appointed a committee to prepare and propose a national programme for sport and physical activity. The results were published in 2007 as an interim report: "Sport in the current of choices: Report of the committee preparing a national sport programme." Gender equality was discussed in one of the chapters and opened with a statement that for a long time, sport used to be an area specifically for men. In the text, it was noted that the majority of the decision-makers in sport federations and in the public sector were men, but the number of women participating in sport and volunteering has increased (OKM 2007).

In 2008, "A proposal for a national programme for sport and physical activity in view of public steering" was published. In it, sport policy was seen as part of a wellbeing policy. The committee proposed 43 measures to promote physical activity, enhance strategic work, provide equal opportunities and raise the level of professionalism in civic activities (OKM 2008). However, no specific recommendations to promote gender equality were given. This meant that promoting gender equality as a policy process did not proceed to the phase of agenda setting (Kingdon 1995). From the viewpoint of sport organisations and stakeholders, the main turning point occurred within the international sport policy context at the end of this period, when the IWG chair from 2010 to 2014 was appointed to Finland. This nomination linked the national sport policy to the international one, and through that, gender equality promotion became a more favourable policy agenda.

Summarising the first decade of the 2000s from the viewpoint of gender equality promotion in sport, a number of supporting regulations such as policy process influences were implemented and the overall political context became more favourable to improve gender politics (see Kingdon 1995). However, it seems that governmental sport policy actions provided only a frame and foundation to NGBs' own work, and they implemented the policy actions informally within their own organisational context and culture. Due to the autonomous status of the associations, the state as well as the National Olympic Committee have no power over how the NGBs operate. This lack of influence helps explain the numbers and the proportion of women, which were stable in the first decade of the 2000s (see Figures 32.1–32.3).

2010–2020s: What is gender?

Finnish sport re-structured itself again at the beginning of 2017 when the Finnish Olympic Committee started as a new central sport organisation. An eclectic reform process had started years before with the closing of several national sport organisations, ultimately resulting in the unification of both sport for all and elite sport organisations in the same organisation (Lehtonen 2017a, 2017b). The power structure was centralised, and the number of decision-making positions decreased overall (Lehtonen 2017c). As an institutional influence, this re-structuring could have signalled gender equality for stronger place on the policy agenda of sport organisations. However, the agents of change did not reach the institutional level, as a representative from the National Olympic Committee stated: "Promoting gender equality is still very personified and dependent on individuals interested in it. In addition, I have thought that when project funding ends, does the gender equality promotion drop away from our strategy?"

From the viewpoint of regulation and legislation as policy influences, the Act on the Promotion of Sports and Physical Activity was renewed in 2015, and today it gives to OKM the possibility to use incentives in encouraging associations to promote equality. When assessing eligibility for state aid, consideration shall be given to the type, extent and social impact of the activities in which the association is engaged, and the ways in which the association promotes equality and non-discrimination.

In addition, a new Non-discrimination Act was enacted in 2014. Adapting it to sport, everyone should be equally entitled to participate in sport and physical activity at all levels and in all roles. Based on the aforementioned legislation, the state's steering system tightened its grip on NGBs in 2020. The overall societal responsibility of NGBs' activities is considered when state subsidies are allocated. In practice, this means that NGBs must have updated strategic plans as to how to prevent, for example, sexual harassment, bullying and inequality, and promote good governance in order to gain state subsidies (OKM 2020). These plans and overall governmental guidance have been a policy driver, especially to the National Olympic Committee, as one of its representatives explained: "For my work, legislation and other governmental frames are important, it rationalises my work and it is easier to say that we have to consider gender issues also."

In the Finnish sport system, the state has had a strong role to push sport actors to implement the sport policy agenda (Lehtonen 2017a). In particular, it emphasises current practices as a representative of the Ministry stated: "Sometimes I feel that if we do not push them, they do not do anything [in OKM or NGBs]." Combining this view of person-dependent policy drivers with the Ministry's view that sport associations are not very active themselves, one remarkable strategic toolkit is missing compared to the 1990s: common goal setting and a strategic agenda to promote gender equality in sport. One interpretation of this situation is the long reform process of sport's organisational environment and the continual identity seeking of the country's central sport organisation (Lehtonen 2017a). Over time, this has led to a situation where sport's central organisation has lost its effectiveness to be an influential implementer of sport policy actions (Lehtonen and Mäkinen 2020). However, comparing these latest policy influences, agents of change and drivers that occurred in the 2010s to the numerical data, we notice a slight shift from policy development to policy implementation (cf. Springate-Baginski and Soussan 2002). Currently, the proportion of women in leading positions of chairperson and operative leader is at its peak (see Figures 32.2 and 32.3). However, the percentage of women on Boards has remained stable and has shown no change since 2002 (see Figure 32.1).

In the current decade, discussions have widened the perspective of ethical issues around sports, and today those are more large-scale than in the 1990s. The #MeToo movement in 2017 changed the world and generated discussion all around the globe, also in sport and sport research (Reel and Crouch 2019). As a global turning point, it also shaped Finnish sport policy, but more on the level of "overall worry," as the interviewees described the effect. All of the interviewees recognised that gender as a concept is changing, and in some cases, it seemed to be difficult – or even unnecessary as one of the Ministry representatives stated – to promote it anymore as a single issue: "We are speaking more about non-discrimination than gender equality… we are speaking of involvement. The upper concept is more and more abstract, and we are setting up many things inside one umbrella [concept]." These considerations are a mirror of society where gender in its different conceptual senses is under discussion in ordinary life, academic arenas and politics (Eagly and Sczesny 2019). At the same time, gender as a concept or the actualisation of it is filtered through an individual's own experience. It seems to be a part of identity politics, which might weaken the possibilities to share the common understanding of those practices which might promote gender equality in sport policy (Bernstein 2005).

Conclusions

We started our analysis of gender equality promotion as a sport policy process in the 1990s and concluded with its current state. Overall, societal development and related broader ethical questions along with the widening understanding of gender is an issue which goes beyond sport. The analysis shows that actors inside the sport system have realised the current societal frame with a diverse understanding of gender. This especially seems to have been happening since the IWG Helsinki 2014 conference. The current state and future seem to be less structured processes than was the progress from IWG Brighton 1994 to Helsinki 2014.

Brighton was a starting point to launch more systematic work towards gender equality in sport. Twenty years later, IWG Conference in Helsinki gave visibility to gender equality promotion in Finnish sport. However, looking backwards, it is worth considering the legacy of this 20-year journey. From the viewpoint of numerical data, the share of women in leadership positions in NGBs has increased, albeit slowly. Overall, the sport system at every level has cross-sectioned gender equality, mainly pushed by legislation or state funding criteria. In other words, as a policy agenda, it is not deeply rooted to the main values of the system and there seems to be no sudden, attention-grabbing focusing events, which could have changed the policy process (Birkland 1998).

Actions have been targeted and taken by a few individual agents of change interested in the issue. Therefore, one narrative during the decades has been the single active actors as policy drivers. The sport institutions acting as policy drivers have been in the minority, which has weakened the agenda setting when considering macro-policy and outcomes. Overall, as a policy process, gender equality promotion has remained more in the development phase than it has been applied in practice (Springate-Baginski and Soussan 2002).

From the viewpoint of power, institutions such as those that make up the sport movement could have been more active in using their institutional power to keep gender politics on their agenda more visible. In addition, using compulsory power has not been possible in the Finnish context where the autonomous status of associations like NGBs is high. As a Nordic society, the state has a guiding role that is often manifested through resource allocation and other soft power mechanisms (Norberg 1997). Moreover, as Lehtonen and Mäkinen (2020) have pointed out, even though the Finnish sport system is a mixed model of the state and the sport movement, the responsibility for implementing sport policy overall might have fallen into a desolate land without requirement to achieve specific goals.

Specifically, the last decade and present state of gender equality promotion in Finnish sport appear as a mixture of governmental regulation, conceptual interpretations and large-scale societal changes. However, the benefits of these are bound to be half-baked, partly because other societal developments in recent years have taken the basis of equality work towards broader societal responsibility. Therefore, the current situation and future in Finnish sport and gender equality promotion are unclear. It seems that in Finnish sport, gender equality has lost its identity. The promotion of it in Finnish sport is in a vacuum, where discussions around gender are amorphous without clear targets and aims. While gender remains within the conversation around inclusion, its obscurity has made both strategic thinking and any practical changes of implementation difficult. Therefore, if the policy agenda no longer recognises gender equality but rather a more generic approach of non-discrimination or, for example, human rights, is there a possibility that by removing certain words and concepts from the agenda, policy actions around gender equality will also go missing? To tackle this issue, the minimum starting point is that promoting gender equality should undergo a renaissance and achieve conceptual consensus among stakeholders within the sport system.

REFERENCES

Act on Equality between Women and Men (1986). Available at: https://finlex.fi/en/laki/kaannokset/1986/en19860609_20160915.pdf.

Act on the Promotion of Sports and Physical Activity (2015). https://finlex.fi/en/laki/kaannokset/2015/en20150390.pdf.

Associations Act (1989). Available at: https://www.prh.fi/en/yhdistysrekisteri/act.html (Accessed: 10 May 2021).

Atkinson, C.L. (2019) 'Focus Event and Public Policy', in Farazmand, A. (ed.), *Global Encyclopedia of Public Administration, Public Policy, and Governance*. Switzerland: Springer. Available at: https://doi.org/10.1007/978-3-319-31816-5_274-1 (Accessed: 14 January 2021).

Bernstein, M. (2005) 'Identity Politics', *Annual Review of Sociology*, 31, pp. 47–74.

Birkland, T.A. (1998) 'Focusing Events, Mobilization, and Agenda Setting', *Journal of Public Policy*, 18(1), pp. 53–74.

Cairney, P. (2020) 'Power and Public Policy', in Cairney, P. (ed.), *Understanding Public Policy: Theories and Issues*. 2nd Edition. London: Red Globe Press, pp. 1–18.

Eagly, A.H. and Sczesny, S. (2019) 'Editorial: Gender Roles in Future? Theoretical Foundations and Future Research Directions', *Frontiers in Psychology*. https://doi.org/10.3389/fpsyg.2019.01965

European Commission (2018) *Special Eurobarometer Sport and Physical Activity*. Special Eurobarometer 472 – Wave EB88.4 – TNS Opinion & Social. Brussels: European Commission.

Finnish Government (2003) *The Government Programme of Prime Minister Matti Vanhanen's Government on 24 June 2003*. Helsinki: Finnish Government.

Finnish Government (2019) *Report on sport policy. Finnish Government*, VNS 6/2018 vp. Available at: Valtioneuvoston selonteko liikuntapolitiikasta (eduskunta.fi) (Accessed: 20 May 2021).

Finnish Parliament (2019) *Finnish parliamentary communication on Government Report on sport policy*, EK 52/2018 vp. Available at: EK 52/2018 vp (eduskunta.fi) (Accessed: 20 May 2021).

Heikkala, J. (1998) *Ajolähtö turvattomiin kotipesiin: Liikunnan järjestökentän muutos 1990-luvun Suomessa* [Changes of the organised sport in the 1990's Finland]. PhD. Tampere University.

Henry, I. (2009) 'European Models of Sport: Governance, Organizational Change and Sports Policy in the EU', *Hitotsubashi Journal of Arts and Sciences*, 50, pp. 41–52.

IWG (2021) *International Working Group on Women and Sport. The Brighton plus Helsinki Declaration on Women and Sport*. Available at: Brighton-plus-Helsinki-2014-Declaration-on-Women-and-Sport.pdf (iwg-womenandsport.org) (Accessed: 4 May 2021).

Kingdon, J.W. (1995) *Agendas, Alternatives, and Public Policies*. New York: Longman.

Krippendorf, K. (2013) *Content Analysis. An Introduction to Its Methodology*. 3rd Edition. California: SAGE Publications.

Lehtonen, K. (2017a) *Muuttuvat rakenteet – Staattiset verkostot. Suomalaisen liikunta– ja urheilujärjestelmän rakenteelliset muutokset 2008–2015* [Changing structures – static networks. Finnish sport system´s structural changes in 2008–2015]. PhD. LIKES Research Centre and Jyväskylä University.

Lehtonen, K. (2017b) 'Building of the Legitimacy of a Sports Organisation in a Hybridised Operating Environment – Case Finland', *European Journal for Sport and Society*, 14(2), pp. 166–181.

Lehtonen, K. (2017c) 'Luolamiehet ja Suurlinkkaajat suomalaisessa liikunnan ja urheilun eliittiverkostossa [Cavemen and Big-linkers in Finnish Sport's Elite Networks]', *Yhteiskuntapolitiikka*, 82(2), pp. 127–140.

Lehtonen, K. and Mäkinen, J. (2020) 'The Finnish Sport System in Transition: From a Mixed Model Back to the Nordic Sport Movement?', in Tin, M.B., Telseth, F., Tangen, J.O. and Giulianotti, R. (eds.), *The Nordic Model and Physical Culture*. London: Routledge, pp. 117–130.

Non-discrimination Act (2014). Available at: 1325/2014 English - Translations of Finnish acts and decrees - FINLEX® (Accessed: 10 May 2021).

Norberg, J.R. (1997) 'A Mutual Dependency: Nordic Sports Organizations and the State', *The International Journal of the History of the Sport*, 14(3), 115–135.

OKM (2005) *Tasapeli – Sukupuolten välisen tasa-arvon edistäminen ja sukupuolivaikutusten arviointi liikunta-alalla* [A draw - Promotion and assessment of the gender aspect in sports]. Opetusministeriön raportteja 2005:3. Helsinki: Opetusministeriö.

OKM (2007) *Liikunta valintojen virrassa* [Sport in the current of choices – Report of the committee preparing a national sport programme]. Opetusministeriön raportteja 2007:13. Helsinki: Opetusministeriö.

OKM (2008) *Liikkuva ja hyvinvoiva Suomi 2010-luvulla* [A proposal for a national programme for sport and physical activity in view of public steering]. Opetusministeriön raportteja 2008:14. Helsinki: Opetusministeriö.

OKM (2020) *Liikuntajärjestöjen yleisavustus* [Subsidies for national sport organizations]. Available at: Liikuntaa edistävien järjestöjen yleisavustus - OKM - Opetus- ja kulttuuriministeriö (minedu.fi) (Accessed: 30 January 2021).

Reel, J. and Crouch, E. (2019) '#MeToo: Uncovering Sexual Harassment and Assault in Sport', *Journal of Clinical Sport Psychology*, 13(2), pp. 177–179.

Sabatier, P.A. (1991) 'Political Science and Public Policy', *Political Science and Politics*, 24(2), pp. 144–147.

Särkivuori, J., Vihinen, T., Lämsä, J. and Lehtonen, K. (2020) *Tasa-arvo valtakunnallisissa ja alueellisissa liikuntajärjestöissä 2019. Tiivistelmä* [Equality in national and regional sport organizations 2019. Summary]. LIKES Research Centre for Physical Activity and Health and Olympic Research Centre KIHU. Available at: Tasa-arvo valtakunnallisissa ja alueellisissa liikuntajärjestöissä 2019 (likes.fi) (Accessed: 30 January 2021).

Springate-Baginski, O. and Soussan, J. (2002) *A Methodology for Policy Process Analysis. Livelihood-Policy Relationships in South Asia*. Working Paper 9. York: Stockholm Environment Institute.

Turpeinen, S. and Hakamäki, M. (eds.) (2018) *Sport and Equality. An Overview of the Current Status of Gender Equality in Sports and Physical activity*. Publications of the Ministry of Education and Culture. Opetus- ja kulttuuriministeriö: Helsinki.

Turpeinen, S., Jaako, J., Kankaanpää, A. and Hakamäki, M. (2012) *Sport and Equality 2011. Current state and changes of gender equality in Finland*. Publications of the Ministry of Education and Culture 2012:13. Opetus- ja kulttuuriministeriö: Helsinki.

Index

Note: Page numbers in *italics* denote figures.

Aarhus (Denmark): 'Danishness' in 119–120; gender-segregated swimming in 119–120; women-only swimming programmes in 120
Abdelkader, H. 228
Abdel-Shehid, G. 95, 97, 102
Abelson, M.J. 242
ableism 219–220
Abukaram, Noor 230
Acker, J. 39, 85
Acosta, R.V. 73
activism: athlete 250–251; defined 249; political (*see* political activism); social (*see* social activism)
Act on Equality between Women and Men 348
Adams, Nicola 105
adaptivity: as political statement 208–210; in sports 203–204
Adidas 183
aesthetics: and self-objectification 293; and women athletes 308
A F L Women (AFLW) 126, 128–132
Ahmed, S. 6, 8
AKP (Adalet ve Kalkınma Partisi – Justice and Development Party) 227
Al-Ansari, M. 228
Alex, Marina 163
Al-Fadel, A. 225
Al-Ghasara, Ruqaya 228
Ali, Muhammad 250
Al-Khalidi, J. 226
Allen, K. 155
Al-Mutawaki, Nawal 228
Alternative for Germany 4
Aly, E. 326
Aman, M.P. 326
American Society of Human Genetics 51
Amy, Paul 126, 133
Anderson, E. 160, 161
Anthony, Carmelo 255
anti-LGBTQ bills 4

anti-male: community of shape, shaving, and symbolism 98–102; peloton 96–97; practicing 98–102
Antunovic, D. 255
Anzaluda, G. 6
Apelmo, Elisabet 207
Appleby, K.M. 74, 75
Aqeel, Najah 230
Arab world: discrimination against Muslim women 228; emancipation of women in 229
argumentative regimes 49
Arth, Z. 23
Ashton-Shaeffer, C. 220
Asiagate Scandal 259, 266
Association of Summer Olympic International Federations 146
Ataturk, Kemal 227
athlete activism 250–251
athlete mothers 184–187
athletes *see* men's sport; women athletes
Atkinson, C.L. 345
Australia: patriarchal politics of women footballers in 126–134; sports diplomacy activities 142–145
Australian Football League (AFL) 126, 128–133
Avalon, Frankie 282
Awamreh, M. 226

Baby Boomers 10–11
Baer, Clara Gregory 338
Banet-Weiser, S. 255
Barker, M.J. 235
Barlas, Asma 226
Barr body test 48, 50–51, 54
Barry, Michael 100–101
Bartali, Gino 95
Bartholomaeus, C. 240
Bass, J.R. 40
Beacom, A. 142
Beckham, David 96
Bekker, S. 61

Bell-Altenstad, K. 61
Benedict Anderson 120
benevolent sexism 127
benign sexism 131–132
Bentham, Jeremy 291
Bernstein-Sycamore, M. 237
Biden, Joe 238, 253, 254
Billings, A.C. 21, 23–24
binaries 31–34; rehabilitating 34–35
biological rationale: defined 5; and gender categories 6; gender-related 1; -informed arguments 7; and racism 6
Black Americans: racial bias by US justice system 250; racial injustices 252; and sports 250; treatment by police force 250
Black and minority ethnic (BME) women coaches 40
Black Lives Matter (BLM) movement 115, 120, 250, 254–255
Black Power Movement 250
Black women: on men's sport 303; racial stereotypes of hyper-sexuality 303
Blatter, Sepp 316
Bledman, R. 70
Blithe, S.J. 31, 33
Blundell, M. 325
body dissatisfaction: defined 291; and objectification theory 292; and self-objectification 292
body functionality: approaches in practice 294–298; defined 293; used for promoting physical activity 293
Bohuon, Anais 50
Bolsonaro, Jair 4, 8, 9
Bono, Chaz 106
Borders, L. 250
Bordo, S. 291
Borins, E.M. 89
Boulmerka, Hassiba 228
Bourdieu, Pierre 98–99
Boyd, J. 111
Boykoff, J. 251
Bratland-Sanda, S. 292
Braun, V. 313
Breese, K. 326
Brentin, D. 137
Brighton Declaration 59, 349
British university sport: as cultural and social activity 155; 'gender-collaborative' training opportunities in 152; gender politics in 149–158; 'lad culture' of 156
Brittain, I. 142
Brooke-Marciniak, B.A. 66
Brooks, D.D. 73
Brown, A. 139, 141
Brown, Mike 251
Bruce, T. 21

Buchbinder, D. 99
Bullen, E. 99
Bullingham, Rachael 1–14
Burton, L.J. 75
Bush, Billy 4
Bush, L. 288
Butler, Judith 4, 9, 29, 32, 34, 236–237, 241
Buzyn, Agnès 230

"Cachibol" 338
Cantwell, Lynne 65
capitalism 1, 8, 91, 255; industrial 170; state-organized 131
Carlos, John 250
Carpenter, L.J. 73
Carrington, B. 251
Cash, T.F. 293
Cathiness, Kate 144
Caudwell, J.C. 283
Cavalier, E. 254
Cervin, G. 139, 141
Chand, Dutee 52, 55
Channon, A. 164
Chaplin, G. 6
Chateauraynaud, Francis 49
Chile 324
Chiyangwa, Philip 263
Chizuzu, Hope 266
Choi, P.Y.L. 71
Christiansen, T.H. 323
cisgender: defined 236; and passing 236–237
cisgenderism 239, 240
Civil Rights Movement 250
Clair, Jill M. Le 207
Clarke, G. 151
Clarke, V. 313
Clarkson, B. G. 40
Clinton, Hillary 88, 253
coaches: Black and minority ethnic (BME) women 40; female S&C 71, 73–76; gendered qualifications for 40; women 40
Coceres, Jose 162
Cockburn, C. 151
Code, L. 130
Collegiate Strength and Conditioning Coaches Association (CSCCa) 72
Commonwealth Games Federation (CGF) 137
conflict: coach 217; and parasport 216–217; in regulation of female athlete eligibility 47–55; scientific 50–52
Connell, R.W. 150–152, 154, 157; gender in sport and university sport 151–152; hegemony and femininity 150–151
Connolly, Harold 141
Constantini Committee 336
control: coach 217; lack of voice 216; and parasport 216–217

Index

Cooky, C. 205, 208, 255
Cornelissen, Scarlett 138
Cosentino, A.B. 326
Coubertin, Pierre de 19
Court of Arbitration for Sport (CAS), Switzerland 47
COVID-19 pandemic 2–3, 186; and increase in golf participation 270; and professional footballers 314–315; restrictions 108; women sports in Israel 336
Cox, E. 40
Creak, Simon 195
The Creation of Patriarchy (Lerner) 84
Croston, A. 174
Cula-Reid, Penny 126–128
Culvin, A. 314, 316
Cummings, Dominic 3

D'Alonzo, K.T. 70
Damion, E. 264
dancers: non-binary 105–106; transgender 105–106
DanceSport 105, 107, 112
Dancing With the Stars (DWTS) 106
Danish Associationalism 122
Danish culture 12, 117, 119
Darby, P. 261
Darnell, S. 255
Das, S. 226
Davis, P. 32
Dawson, Peter 272–274, 277
de Beauvoir, Simone 291, 334
decolonial feminism 8
De Haan, D. 166
de la Chappelle, Albert 51
Delorme, N. 24
Demuth, S. 84
Denmark 115–123; gender-segregated swimming spaces in 12; Muslim community in 117; racism in 120
DePauw, K.P. 208, 210, 218
Desjardins, B.M. 138
Devaney, Bob 71
de Varona, D. 66
Devonport, T.J. 316
Dewar, A. 194
Dichter, H.L. 138
Differences of Sexual Development (DSD) 35
Diplomacy & Statecraft 139
disability: defined in medicalized world 204; in *Soul Surfer* 204–208; Tomasini's definition of 204
discrimination 97, 220–221; gender 59, 162, 205, 271, 323, 325; homophobic 152; and people with disabilities 204, 208, 212; social 6; systemic 131, 133; towards Muslim girls 230; and 'Western' societies

116; against women in sports 205–208, 212, 271–272, 315, 334–337
diversity 193–194, 199; of appearance in women 293; gender 12, 38–39, 42, 44, 65, 74, 105, 325; Gen Z and the Millennials 11
document analysis 263
Doerner, J.K. 84
Douglas, D. 33
Dreger, A. 36
Drinkell, P. 99
Dunn, C. 317
Dworkin, A. 70, 87
Dyer, Jack 128
Dyreson, M. 139, 141

Eason, C. 73–74
Eastman, S. 24
eating disorders: among women in UK 291; case study 294–295; defined 291; diet and exercise industry 291
Eating disorders: Recommendations for the fitness industry in Australia 297–298
Ebben, W.P. 73
Edmonds, S. 74
Edwards, Harry 250–251
Edwards, L. 32
Eichler, M. 89
Einarsdottir, U.D. 323
Elling-Machartzki, A. 43–44
Ellis, Jill 253
emphasised femininity 151, 154, 157
empowerment: and feminist theories 218; and parasport 218, 220; and storytelling 281; in wheelchair basketball 220; women, in sports study 328
Endocrine Society 51
Engh, M. 260
English, Jane 29–30
Ennis-Hill, Jessica 185
Epley, Boyed 71
equality: in exercise 180–187; in physical activity 180–187; in women's sport 180–187
Equality Act 2010 238
Equal Opportunities Plan 324
equity: gender 12; and women athletes 20–22, 24
Erasmus+ funding program 328
Erhart, I. 227–228
ethics of care 185; *vs.* excellence 174–177; and gendered sports experiences 171–173
ethnic politics 196
ethno-traditional nationalism 7
Europe: Islam in 115–118; and politics of exclusion 115–118
European Commission 328
European Court of Human Rights (ECHR) 52
European Institute for Gender Equality 325
European Same-Sex Dance Association (ESSDA) 105

exclusive male dominance 20
exercise: equality in 180–187; performance and sex differences 182
Expand Your Horizon 293

Facebook 11, 22
"fags" 43
Fair Play for Women 238
'False Hope Syndrome' 292
family: golf 274–275; and women para-athletes 213–214
fascistic habits 2
Felix, Allyson 184, 186
female athletes *see* women athletes
female inferiority, in university sport 153–155
female surfers *see* women surfers
femininity: contemporary perceptions of 149–158; control 50; emphasised 151, 154, 157; hegemony and subordination of 150–151
feminism 4, 85; decolonial 8; first wave 281; fourth wave 282, 288–289; and gender politics 282; 'lean-in' 5; mainstream 5; second wave 281–282; and surfing 282–283; third wave 282; trans-exclusive 5–6; and transversal politics 282; zero-sum 8
feminist views of patriarchy 85–88; household production 86–87; paid work 86; sexuality 87; 'the state' 88; violence 87–88
femmephobia 43–44
Fernández, Gigi 184
Ferris, Elizabeth 50
Fiani, C.N. 240
Fiji: civil society activism 197; gender equality 196; overview 196; physicality and postcolonial social order 196–197; postcolonial heteropatriarchy, and sport 198–199; women, sport and violent postcolonial heteropatriarchy 197–198; women rugby players 198–199
Fijian women: physical violence against 197; rugby players 198–199; sexual violence against 197; violent postcolonial heteropatriarchy 197–198
Fikotova, Olga 141
Finch, C.F. 61
Fink, J.S. 9
Finland 107; Rainbow dancing and transgender inclusion in 105–113; Rainbow dancing in 105–106; and transgender inclusion 105–106
Finnish Olympic Committee 350
Finnish sport: framework for gender equality in sport policy process 345; gender distribution in national governing bodies 346–347, *347*; and gender equality 344–352; gender equality promotion *347*, 347–349, *349*; legislation and governmental agendas 349–350
Finnish Sports Confederation (SLU) 347–348
Fischetti, N. 70
Fisher, L.A. 176
Fletcher, T. 325
Fluharty-Jaidee, J.T. 84
Foddy, B. 31
football: politics and gender in Zimbabwe 261–263; popularity in Zimbabwe 259; sexism 128–130; women in, administration 259
Francombe-Webb, J. 131
Franklin, Missy 35
Fraser, Nancy 127, 131
Fraser-Pryce, Shelly-Ann 31
Frederiksen, Mette 117
Frisby, C.M. 155
Fujimura, Joan 49
Fullagar, S. 282–283
funding: policy evaluations of 63–64; women's sport 64–65
Funicello, Annette 282
Furyk, Jim 164

Garland-Thomson, Rosemarie 207–208
Garn, A.C. 127
Gaston, L. 325
Gavron, S.J. 208
gender 2–9; cultural transformation of perceiving, in sports 205; defined 181; discrimination 59, 162, 205, 271, 323, 325; and football politics in Zimbabwe 261–263; identity 236; inequities 323; -informed privileges 12; navigating 304–308; norms, reinforcing 306–308; and patriarchy in Zimbabwe 260–261; pay gap 86; and physical activity 2–9; and politics 2–9; preferences 75–76; quotas 66; regimes 85, 312; revolution 323; roles in dance 107; *vs.* sex 181; in *Soul Surfer* 204–208; and sports 2–9, 151–152; and strength 70–76; in university sport 151–152
gendered behavioural expectations: for male surfers 287–288; for women surfers 287–288
gendered cultural beliefs 8
gendered inequality 180; in surfing 285–286
gendered patterns 313–314; and gender justice in women's football 317–318; sporting identities and body image 317; and women's football 316
gendered political activism, in sports 249–252
gendered separate spheres 185
gendered social activism, in sports 249–252
gendered transformations: 'barring' participation 50–52; overview 47–48; scientific

357

Index

conflict (1968-1991) 50–52; testosterone regulations 52–54; theorizing 49–50
gender equality 12–13; establishment of committees for 326–328; establishment of institutes for 326–328; IOC's initiatives 20; and the Olympics, 1984–2018 19–24; in sport organizations 329; strategy to promote 344–352; *see also* equality
gender justice: defined 313; and everyday experiences 313–314; and women's football 312–318
gender norms: male *vs.* female sport participation 182; and parents 182
gender politics 312–313; in British university sport 149–158; and feminism 282; and hegemony 150–152; in Israeli sports 335–337; of sex-integrated golf 163–165; of sex integrated sport 160–166; and sports 150–152, 302–304; in university sport 155–157
gender-segregated swimming 12, 118–120
gender stereotypes 182
generational change 9–11
generations: Gen Z 10–11; 'snowflake' 11; woke 9
Gentry, J.W. 162
Gen Z 2, 9–11
George, J. 271
Ghribi, Habiba 228
Gilligan, C. 171–172, 175, 177
Girls Can't Surf 287
"glass ceiling" 75
Global North 115, 193
Global South 3, 7, 47, 50, 53, 193–195
golf: family 274–275; golfer participant profile 270; men *vs.* women in 162–163; sex-integrated 163–166; women in 270–277
Gomez, E. 288
Goold, I. 184
Goucher, Kara 186
Gowin, Jarosław 4
Grabmüllerova, Aneta 19–24
Gramsci, Antonio 150; gender in sport 151–152; gender in university sport 151–152; hegemony and subordination of femininity 150–151
Great War 89
Green, R. 272
Greenwood, S. 75
Griner, Brittney 33
Grosz, Elizabeth 127, 204

Hacisoftaoglu, I. 227
hadith 225
Halberstam, J.J. 106, 110, 112
Haldar, D. 226

Hamiche, A. 226
Hamilton, Bethany: athletic achievements despite disability 203; inpiring story of survival 204; *Soul Surfer* based on 203–210; trip to Thailand 209
Hamstra, M.R. 90
Han, H.J. 240
Hanchey, J.N. 31, 33
Hanlon, C. 340
Hardin, M. 218
Hargie, O.D.W. 112
Hargreaves, J. 160
Harkness, G. 229
Harris, Tayla 129
Hartley, John 128
Hartshorn, M.D. 72
Hassan, D. 137, 145
Hay, Eduardo 50
health: mental wellbeing 215–216; and women para-athletes 214–216
Hearn, J. 7
hegemonic masculinity 7, 150–151; organized performance sport politics and 170–171; in university sport 153–155
hegemony: gender politics 150–152; and sport 150–152; and subordination of femininity 150–151
Henry, I. 166
"Her sport – Her way" (NSW Government) 328
Hess, R. 259–260
heteronormative masculinity 43
heteropatriarchy 3–5, 9
heterosexism 98–99, 102
heterosexual masculinity 43
heterosexual matrix 32
Hibberd, G. 130
Hills, L.A. 174
Hinault, Bernard 95
Hindman, L.C. 75
Hjelm, J. 260
Hofmann, A.R. 259
Holmes, M. 83
Holmgren, L.E. 7
homonegative speech acts 42–44
homophobia 107, 221
homosexuality 3, 4, 89
Hongsermeir, N. 229
Hoskin, R.A. 44
Hove, M. 266
Howe, P.D. 220
Huizing, Daan 162
Human Rights Watch (HRW) 47, 53

imagined communities 120
imperialism 8, 33
Indo-Fijian women: marginalisation 199; and postcolonial heteropatriarchy 198

358

Induráin, Miguel 95
industrial capitalism 170
inequality regimes 39
Inglehart, R. 7
injuries: and sex segregation in sports 303; and women para-athletes 214–216
Inspiring Positive Change 314
International Athletics Association Federation (IAAF) 32, 47
International Federation of Professional Footballers 312
The International Journal of the History of Sport 139
International Olympic Committee (IOC) 19, 29, 186, 301, 326–327; and 'femininity control' 51; Gender Equality Review Project 19, 24, 327
International Organizations of Sport for the Disabled 327
International Paralympic Committee (IPC) 327
International Triathlon Union (ITU) 169
International Working Group (IWG) on Women & Sport 344
intersectionality 40, 44, 193
in-vitro fertilisation (IVF) 184
Ireland 59; Irish Female Rugby Football Union 59; Irish Sports Council 60; Taskforce on Women in Sport 59
Islam 230; acceptable recreational and physical activities in 225–226; culture 116, 117, 119; in Europe and politics of exclusion 115–118; and sports 225–227
Islamic Feminism 226
Islamic laws *(fiqh)* 225
Islamic Ummah 226
Islamisation 227
Islamophobia 230
Islamophobic movements 227
Israel: Mamanet sport model 337–338; principles of gender equality 336; sports and gender politics in 335–337

Jablonski, N.G. 6
Jalal, Patricia Imrana 197
Jamal, Mariam 228
James, LeBron 250, 255
Jani, M. 226
Japajapa, Godfrey 266
Johns, A.L. 138
Johnson, Boris 3, 230
Johnson, Jack 250
Jordan, Michael 250
Journal of Applied Sport Science Research 72
Journal of Sport History 139
Journal of Strength and Conditioning Research 72
Joyner, Florence Griffith 33
Judaeo-Christian belief system 3
Juul Jensen, C. 101

Kaepernick, Colin 251, 252–253, 255
Kalman-Lamb, N. 95, 97, 102
Kamphoff, C. 74
Kandiyoti, D. 198
Kane, Mary Jo 30–31
Kanemasu, Y. 7
Kaplan, E.B. 9
Kaufman, P. 251
Kavanagh, E. 22
Kazan Action Plan 335
Kenny, Laura 184
Kenway, J. 99
Khan, Rafiq 263
Khupe, Thokozani 264
Kidd, Bruce 35, 36
King, Billie-Jean 251
Kirby, Carlton 95
Knoppers, A. 38–44
Knuttila, M. 97
Koca, C. 227
Kristjansdottir, E.S. 323

Ladies European Tour (LET) 161
Ladies Golf Union (LGU) 271–272
Ladies Professional Golf Association (LPGA) Tour 161
Lao National Games 195
Lapchick, R.E. 73
Laskowski, K.D. 73
Lawson Wilkins Paediatric Endocrine Society 51
leadership *see* sports leadership
'lean-in' feminism 5
Learmonth, Jess 169
Lee, Minjee 160
Lee, Min Woo 160
Legal Age of Majority Act 261
legitimacy, and women athletes 20–22, 24
legitimate football 259
leisure time physical activity (LTPA): gender-segregated 119–120; lived experience of politicised Muslim women 120–122; Muslim participation in 118–119; Muslim women in 115–123; and politics of exclusion 118–119; politics of minority ethnic women's 115–123
Lennard, Natasha 2
L'Equipe 22
Lerner, Gerda 84
lesbian, gay, bisexual, transgender, intersex, queer, asexual, allies and more (LGBTIQA+) activism *see* LGBTIQA+ activism
Lever, J. 172
Levine, Rachel 238
Lewin, Hannah 294–295, 296–297
LGBTIQA+ activism 105, 107
LGBTQ: LGBTQ+ 3, 10, 47; mental ill health 235; rights 4, 10; social and legal equality 87

Index

liberal feminism 334
Limpopogate fixing scandal 266
Lincicome, Brittany 162
Liston, K. 59, 60, 62, 63, 66
Litchfield, C. 22
Ljungqvist, Arne 51
Lochte, Ryan 35
Lock, R. 31–33
Lorde, A. 6
Lough, N.L. 172
Louis, Joe 250
Loy, J.W. 20

MacArthur, P. 23
MacKinnon, C.A. 34
MacLaren, Meghan 162
Macron, Emmanuel 230
Magnusen, M.J. 75–76
Magrath, R. 43
Maguire, Leona 164
male dominance: in Olympics (1984-1996) 20; in university sport 153–155
male surfers: gendered behavioural expectations for 287–288; perception of female surfers 283, 285–286
Mamanet League 337–338, 339
Mamanet sport model 337–338; examples of 340–341; and social capital 339; women's empowerment through *338*, 338–339
Mandatory Sports Governance Principles (Sport Australia) 328
Manipuri women footballers (India) 195
marginalisation 193, 218–219, 260, 272; heteropatriarchal 197–199; of Irish sportswomen 65; socio-political 196; women's, in sports 5, 196
Mariya, Gabriel 324
market demand, and coverage of sportswomen 23
Markula, P. 70
Martin, Dame Louise 144
Martinez, D.M. 73
Martínez Patiño, Maria José 51
masculine competitive sports cultures: and ethics of care 171–173; ethics of care *vs.* excellence 174–177; and gendered sports experiences 171–173; and hegemonic masculinity 170–171; lost voices of female athletes 171–173; organized performance sport politics 170–171; overview 169–170; reclaiming women's voice in 169–177
masculinity: contemporary perceptions of 149–158; hegemonic 7, 150–151, 170–171; heteronormative 43; heterosexual 43; meat eating and 14; practices of desirable 39; and professional road cycling 94–102; Western 5
Massey-Ellis, Sian 315

maternity 181, 183, 186–187, 314; *see also* motherhood
Mays, J. 40
Mazerolle, S. 73–74
McAllister, Laura 143
McCauley, Patrick 129
McCormack, M. 152, 155
McDonagh, E. 303
McGinnis, L.P. 162
McLachlan, F. 166
McNulty, Zoe 295–297
McQuillan, J. 162
media: discrimination against women athletes 182–183; and Olympics (1984–2018) 21–22; and women's sport 180
Meitei ethnic community 195
men: endurance *vs.* women endurance 181–182; institution controlled by 83–84; leadership advantages 90–91; medical advantages 89–90; patriarchy, and advantages of 89–92; sport development and sociocultural differences 181; sporting profits 91–92; on women athletes competitive nature 307; *vs.* women in golf 162–163
MENA (Middle East and North Africa) countries 229
men's sport: Black women on 303; forms of masculinity 303; *vs.* women's sport 303
mental wellbeing 215–216
Merckx, Eddy 95
Mernissi, Fatima 226
Messner, M.A. 152, 170, 172, 205
#MeToo 8, 115, 282, 351
Millennials 2, 9–11
Mills, James H. 195
Minimum Labour Conditions for Players 314
Ministry of Education and Culture (OKM), Finland 344, 348–350
Mocarski, R. 106, 112
Molnár, Győző 1–14
monitoring of women's sport 64
Montaño, Alysia 186
Moorabbin Saints Junior Football League (MSJFL) 127
Moran, Caitlin 7–8
Morgan, Alex 184
Morgan, Giles 273
Morris, Stuart 127
motherhood: Olympian athlete mother 184; and women athletes 181, 183–184
mothers: athlete 184–187; motivation for 335; and sports 335
Movement for Democratic Change (MDC) 262
Movement for Democratic Change – Tsvangirai (MDC-T) 264
Mugabe, Leo 263

Mujuru, Joyce 264, 265–266, 267
Mulready, M. 23
Munro, B. 33
Murray, Andy 250
Murray, S. 137
Muscular Christianity movement 224
muscularity: of Eastern bloc women 50; and women 70–71
Musika, Joseph 264, 265
Muslim participation in LTPA 118–119
Muslim women: athletes and fundamentalist groups 228; discrimination in Arab world 228; discrimination in West 230; and gender-segregated spaces 118; and gender-segregated swimming 119–120; lived experience of politicised 120–122; and sports 224–231; and Turkey 227–228; use of veil for 229; in West 229–230; *see also* women
Mutepfa, Mwandibhuya Kennedy 265
Mzembi, Walter 266

Næss, Hans Erik 19–24
National Coaching and Training Centre, Ireland 59
National Dance Council of America (NDCA) 105
National Football Association of Rhodesia (NFAR) 263
National Institute of Health 90
nationalism: ethno-traditional 7; nativism 7; and Olympics 23–24; primordial 7
National Olympic Committees (NOC) 325, 327
National Strength and Conditioning Association (NSCA) 72
nativism nationalism 7
Nawaz, F. 317
NBC 20–23
Ncube, L. 259, 265
necropolitics 2–3, 5, 7
negative integration 259
Newhall, K. 254
Nicholl, Liz 144
Nike 183, 186, 255
non-binary identities 236
non-binary people: dancers 105–106; participation in physical activity 234–235
Norman, L. 90
Norris, P. 7
Nyambi, O. 265

objectification theory: and body dissatisfaction 292; defined 292; and self-objectification 292
Ocasio-Cortez, Alexandria 253
Occupy Movement 288
O'Connor, M. 63, 66
Office of Sport of New South Wales (NSW) 328–329

Ogilvie, M.F. 152, 155
O'Gorman, J. 61
Olofsson, E. 260
Olympic Council of Ireland 59
Olympic Review 50
Olympics, 1984–2018: data and methods 20; exclusive male dominance (1984-1996) 20; new media and new vistas (2008-2018) 21–22; overview 19; sportswomen coverage (1996-2006) 21
Olympic World Library, Lausanne, Switzerland 20
O'Malley, L.M. 75
O'Neill, D. 23
Orban, Victor 3, 8, 9
Orientalist 116
Orloff, A.S. 133
Ormrod, J. 282, 286
Osborne, B. 156
overt sexism 127
Owens, Jesse 250
Ozbek, Aysum 227

Pacific Sport Partnerships 144
Paldi, Y. 340
Pannenborg, A. 265
Pappano, L. 303
'parallel society' 119
Paralympism 218
parasport: control and conflict 216–217; and empowerment 218, 220; experiences of women athletes 212–221; personal sacrifice 213–216; stories 218–221; tilting, in wheelchair basketball 212
Parsons, Vic 238
participatory action research (PAR) 107
passing: and cisgender 236–237; defined 236; impact of not 241–242; and transgender people 236–237
passing privilege: and cisgender 236; and participation in PA 239–240; and trans people 236
patriarchy: as commonly used 84; feminist views of 85–88; and gender in Zimbabwe 260–261; Holmes on 83; household production 86–87; institution controlled by men 83–84; and its discontents 83–92; men's advantages 89–92; paid work 86; philosophy of 84–85; politics of women footballers in Australia 126–134; rules and phallocentric constraints 130–131; sexuality 87; and sports 89; surveillance or objectification 291; 'the state' 88; violence 87–88
Paul, Chris 255
Pavlidis, A. 130, 282–283
Peers, Danielle 212, 214–216, 220

personal sacrifice: family and relationships 213–214; health and injury 214–216; parasport women athletes 213–216
Perumal, Wilson Raj 266
Pew Research Center 10–11
Phipps, Alison 2, 6, 8, 152, 155
physical activity (PA) 2–9; defined by World Health Organisation 235; equality in 180–187; and gender 2–9; men's *vs.* women's efforts, celebration of 180; motherhood and decline in 184; non-binary people participation in 234–235; and politics 2–9; and sports 2–9; transgender people participation in 234–235, 239–240
Physical Education Authority of Ireland (PEAI) 59
Pielke, R. Jr. 29, 31
Pieper, L.P 32–33, 35
PinkNews 238
Pleasure and Participation Model 169, 171, 173
policies: evaluations of implementation and funding 63–64; SMART objectives 62–63; timeframes 62
political activism: gendered 249–252; and social media 249
politics 2–9; ethnic 196; gender (*see* gender politics); and gender 2–9; populist 1; of positions of sport leadership 38–44; and sport leadership 38–44; transversal 282; of ZIFA 263–264
politics of exclusion: experiencing 118–119; Islam in Europe and 115–118
Pope Francis 3, 8
populist politics 1
pornography 87
Pornography: The New Terrorism (Dworkin) 87
postcolonial Global South 194–195; gendered relations of power 195; Manipuri women footballers 195; and women's sporting experiences 194
postcolonial heteropatriarchy: and Indo-Fijian women 198; resistance through sport 198–199; violent and Fiji women 197–198
postcolonial social order: ethnic politics 196; Fiji 196–197; masculine authority 197
post-structuralism 301, 308
Poulter, Ian 164
power 95–98, 101–102; as aspect of masculinity 70; cultural 150; gendered relations of 195; hegemonic 157; and introduction of quotas 41; and performance sports 170–171; physical 196–197; soft 141; of (white) women's emotions 8; and women surfers 281
Power and Performance Model 169
Poynton, Beverley 128

pregnancy: and competitive sport 183; exercising during 183; and practical advice 187
Pride Sports for Sport England 235
primordial nationalism 7
privilege: gender-informed 12; male 87, 161; of male violence 242; passing (*see* passing privilege); of race 6; Western 8; white 8, 118
production of content 23
professional: athlete 174; female 73, 75; golf 13, 160–166; organization memberships 72; road cycling 94–102; scientific communities 52
Professional Golf Association (PGA) Tour 161
professional road cycling: *anti*-male peloton 96–97; atrophying masculinity within 94–102; 'male' cyclist as antithetic 95–96; overview 94–95; practicing *anti*-male 98–102
protected categories, in sport 29–36
'public scandal' 54
public spaces: changing rooms and trans people 238–239; and transgender people 238–239
Pullo, F.M. 73

queer spaces: potential of 106–107; trans inclusion in sport 106–107
quotas: gender 66; size of 41–42; in sports 41–42

racial injustice, and athlete activism 251
racialisation of space 116, 119, 122
racism 8; and biological rationale 6; in corporate America 255; in Denmark 120; and Muslim women 230; scientific 7; systemic 116
Raducanu, Emma 1, 6, 7
Rainbow and Same-Sex dancing 106, 112; development of 107; events 107; in Finland 105–113; opportunities for transgender inclusion in 110; organizations 107; Santtu's story 108–110; and transgender inclusion 105–106
Rajten, Dora 35
Ramati Dvir, A. 172
Rampton, M. 282
Rapinoe, Megan 13; on Donald Trump 253–254; gendered political activism 256; social media use by 249, 255–256; sports accomplishments of 252
Ratna, A. 193
The Razor's Edge (Barry) 100
'rebellious dancing bodies' 107
Reed, R. 286
Reisman, A.L. 89
relationships, and women para-athletes 213–214
Rhea, D.J. 75–76
Richardson, N. 43

Riggs, Bobby 251
Riggs, D.W. 240
The Road Cyclist's Companion (Drinkell) 99
Robbins, R. 94
Robinson, Jackie 250
Robinson, Mark 129
Ronaldo, Cristiano 96
Roper, E.A. 74
Rowe, D. 133
Rowe, K. 138
Roy, G. 283
Royal and Ancient Golf Club of St. Andrews, Scotland 270–271; open championship and male-only golf clubs 272–274; and women's golf 274–276
Royal College of Obstetricians and Gynaecologists 183
Rubin, G. 85
The Rules: The way of the cycling disciple 99
Rushwaya, Henrietta 259, 263, 267; background 264; corruption scandals and scapegoating 266–267; as football administrator, narratives about 264–267; as moral misfit 264–265; as political pawn 265–266; and ZIFA 263–264

Sailors, Pam R. 29–36, 163, 166
Salafiyya 226
Salmond, Alex 272
Samaranch, Juan Antonio 51
Same-Sex dancing *see* Rainbow and Same-Sex dancing
Sanders, Bernie 253
Sanders, K. 130, 131
Savulescu, J. 31
Schaeperkoetter, C. 40
Scheele, J. 235
Schmidt, H.C. 252
School Strut 295–296
'scientific controversies' 54
segregation: sex 302–306; and sports 29–31
Sehlikoglu, S. 227
self-objectification: and body dissatisfaction 292; and fitness practitioners 291–299; non-aesthetic, body functionality approaches for 293; and women 13
Semenya, Caster 7, 33, 47, 51, 52
Semjen, Zsolt 3
Senne, J.A. 325
Serano, Julia 43, 237
sex: defined 181; -determining genes 49; differences 181–182; *vs.* gender 181; segregation 302–306
Sex Disqualification Removal Act 261
sex-integrated golf 165–166; competition 165; gender politics of 163–165
sex-integrated sports 303–304

sex integrated sports: gender politics of 160–166; gender politics of sex-integrated golf 163–165; men *versus* women in golf 162–163; overview 160–161; sex-integrated golf 165–166
sex integration: and gender politics 302–304; normalizing 305–306; and sports 302–304; and track-and-field 305–306
sexism 127, 130; benevolent 127; football 128–130
sex-segregated sports: binaries 31–34; overview 29; rehabilitating the binary 34–35; segregation 29–31; *see also* sports
sexuality 109; binary nature of 10; feminist views of patriarchy 87; fluidity 10; hyper- 303; LGBTQ social and legal equality 87; performative acts 237
sexual orientation 13, 75, 87, 102, 197, 249, 252, 282
sexual violence 87, 197
sex verification 31; binaries 31–35; segregation 29–31; in sports 29–36
Sfeir, L. 225
Sharuko, Robson 266
Shavit, U. 226
Sherry, E. 138
Shiff, T. 133
Shuman, K.M. 74, 75
Signs 88
Silva, C.F. 220
Simmel, G. 101
Sinning, S. 259
Sinnott, Ann 238
Sky Sports 314
Slumbers, Martin 274–275
SMART objectives 62–63
Smith, Ariyana 250–251
Smith, Tommie 250
Smits, F. 43–44
Smolak, L. 293
social activism: gendered 249–252; and social media 249
social capital: defined 339; and Mamanet sport model 339
social influences, and women athletes 182
social media 5, 11, 13, 22; and athlete activism 252; for political and social activism 249; use by black sportsmen 249; use by Megan Rapinoe 249; use by sportsmen 249; use by women 249
societal beliefs, and women's sport 180–181
Sociology of Sport Journal 193
Sorenstam, Annika 162
Sotiriadou, P. 166
Soul Surfer: based on Bethany Hamilton 203–210; gender and disability in 204–208
South African Football Association (SAFA) 260
South Carolina Sentencing Commission 84

Index

Spaaij, Ramón 38–44
Spork, Shirley 162
Sport, Statecraft, and International Relations since 1945 (Dichter and Johns) 138
Sport in Society 139
Sport Ireland Policy on Women in Sport (SIPWIS) 60–61
sport leadership: conceptual framework 39; gendered qualifications for coaching 40; homonegative speech acts 42–44; overview 38; politics of positions of 38–44; size of quotas 41–42; underrepresentation of women in 38–39
sport media, and Olympics, 1984–2018 19–24; *see also* media
sports 2–9; adaptivity in 203–204; binaries 31–34; and Black Americans 250; disability in 203; discrimination against women in 205; and gender 2–9, 151–152; gendered political activism in 249–252; gendered social activism in 249–252; gender inequality through false data 205; and gender politics 150–152, 302–304; governance 185–186; and hegemony 150–152; and Islam 225–227; labelling 187; leadership and politics 38–44; and mothers 335; and Muslim women 224–231; patriarchy and 89; political and social activism 249; and potential of queer spaces 106–107; protected categories in 29–36; quotas in 41–42; rehabilitating the binary 34–35; segregation 29–31; and sex integration 302–304; sex verification in 29–36; trans inclusion in 106–107; underrepresentation of women in leadership positions 38–39
sports diplomacy 139; activities (Australia and UK) 142–145; gendered review of 137–146; gendered review of literature 138–142; origins of term 137–138
Sports Diplomacy 2030 142
sportswomen *see* women athletes
Spracklen, K. 7
'the state,' defined 88
state-organized capitalism 131
Status of Women Canada (SWC) 323
Stayner, Emily 126–128
stereotypes/stereotyping 20–23, 302–308, 325–326; with Black activists 255; gendered 166; heteronormative 95; inactive mother 341; and liberal feminism 334; male 329–330; racial 33; societal 327; women and masculine traits 156–157; of women athletes 316
Storey, Sarah 184
Stout, James 95

strength and conditioning: barriers to 73–74; coaches, responsibilities of 72; experiences of women in 74–75; history of women's representation in 72–73; in the United States 71–72
Strittmatter, A.M. 61
Stuart, O. 261
Sundgot-Borgen, J. 292
surfing: gendered inequality in 285–286; male surfers' views of female surfers 285–286
sustainable development goals 323
Swedish Football Federation (SFF) 260
Swedish Golf Federation (SGF) 276–277
Swofford, Aleen 71

Tajeddine, Khadija 230
Taylor, Helen 126–128
Taylor, Katie 60
Taylor-Brown, Georgia 169
testosterone regulations 52–54
Thelwell, R. C. 40
Theorizing Patriarchy (Walby) 85
This Girl Can campaign 293
Thomas, Geraint 74, 97, 101
Thornton, Margaret 133
Thorpe, H. 11, 131
Tiller, N.B. 182
tilting, in wheelchair basketball 212
Time for Change 314
Title IX (United States) 149, 155, 301, 308
Todd, J. 73
Toffoletti, K. 11, 130, 131
Tomasini, Floris 204
track-and-field competition: sex-integrated training 301–302; and sex integration 304, 305–306; and sex segregation 304
traditional gender ideologies 185
trans-exclusive feminism 5–6
transgender inclusion: persisting challenges to 111–112; in Rainbow and Same-Sex dancing 110; in sports 106–107
transgender people: creating spaces in PA for 240–241; dancers 105–106; defined 236; and Donald Trump language 238; executive order in the US for 238; mental ill health 235; participation in physical activity 234–235, 239–240; passing 236–237; and public spaces 238–239; right to participate in PA and sport 238; and unwelcoming sporting spaces 235
The Trans Mental Health Study (McNeil, Bailey and Ellis) 235
transphobia 107
Trason, Ann 30
Tregoures, L. 137
"triggering events" 345

364

Trump, Donald 4, 88, 230, 251; Rapinoe on 253–254
Tucker, Ross 34–35
Turkey 227–228

UK Strength and Conditioning Association (UKSCA) 73
United Kingdom (UK): body functionality and physical activity 293; Clutch Pro Tour 161; eating disorders among women in 291; Office for National Statistics (ONS) 87; sports diplomacy activities 142–145
United Nations (UN) 137
United Nations Declaration of Human Rights 53
United Nations High Commissioner for Human Rights (UNHCHR) 53
United States: athlete activism 250; executive order for transgender people 238; history of strength and conditioning in 71–72; Sentencing Commission 84
university sports: female inferiority in 153–155; gender in 151–152; gender politics in 155–157; hegemonic masculinity in 153–155; male superiority in 153–155
UN Women Sports for Generation Equality 328
USA Dance 105
Usher, L. 288

Vail, S. 61
Valenti, Jessica 8
Vaughters, Jonathan 96
Velominati 99
Vieira da Silva, Marta 316
Vine, Jeremy 6
violence: feminist views of patriarchy 87–88; privilege of male 242; sexual 87, 197
Volatile Bodies: Toward a Corporeal Feminism (Grosz) 204

Wade, Dwayne 255
Wadud, Amina 226
Walby, Sylvia 85–87, 89
Walker, N.A. 75
Walters, Suzanna Danuta 88, 92, 153
Warren, Elizabeth 253
Wasatiyya 226
weaker/inferior sex narrative 180
Weaving, Charlene 29–36
Weber, M. 84
Web of Science 20
Weiner, G. 153
Welford, J. 317
Western: culture 116; femininity 5; Liberal Democracy 116; masculinity 5
Whaley, Suzy 162
Wheaton, B. 7
Whitten, E.J. 129

Wilde, K. 61, 65
Williams, J. 259–260
Williams, Serena 33, 184, 186, 250
Williams, Venus 250
Winmar, Nicky 129
Winter, O. 226
women: body dissatisfaction 291; emotionality 307; endurance *vs.* men endurance 181–182; and gendered cultural beliefs 8; in golf 270–277; identity issues 5; Israeli 13; leadership roles, barriers to 325–326; male violence against 87; marginalisation in sports 4–5; *vs.* men in golf 162–163; muscularity and 70–71; Muslim (*see* Muslim women); participation at Olympics 224; self-objectification 13; sport development and sociocultural differences 181; strength and conditioning 72–75; in strength and conditioning 74–75; transgender 8; Trump's attitude towards 4; underrepresentation in leadership positions 38–39; Victorian characterisation of 181; as the 'weaker sex' 161; white 8
Women and Gender Equality Canada 323
women athletes: and aesthetics 308; and binaries 32; eligibility in international sport 47–55; and equity 20–22, 24; and legitimacy 20–22, 24; lost voices of 171–173; mass media discrimination against 182–183; on men athletes ego 307; and motherhood 181, 183–184; in Muslim countries 227; Olympics, 1984–2018 21; parasport experiences 212–221; preference of women coaches 40; at Rio 2016 Olympics 224; and sex segregation 29–30; and sex verification 29, 34; and social influences 182; stereotyping of 316
women coaches: increase in number of 42; lived experiences of 39; women athletes preference of 40
women empowerment: in sports study 328; through Mamanet sport model *338*, 338–339; *see also* empowerment
women footballers: deconstructing benign sexism 131–132; patriarchal politics of, in Australia 126–134; patriarchal rules and phallocentric constraints 130–131; publicising women's football history 132–133; three steps to political discourse change 131–133
Women in Golf Charter 275
Women in Sport Leadership toolkit 327
Women in Sport Report (WISR) 60
Women's British Open 274
Women's Empowerment in Sport and Physical Education Industry 328

women's football: appearance and bodies 316–317; coaching in 315; and gender justice 312–318; and gender politics 313; leadership in 315; macro examination 314–315; micro examination 315–317; officiating in 315
Women's Gaelic Players Association (WGPA) 60
women's golf 270–277; inception to current day 271–272; and Royal and Ancient (R&A) 274–276
The Women's March of 2017 288
women's sport: characteristics of 303; consultation and development process 62–65; equality in 180–187; funding 64–65; government policy relating to 59–67; and mass media 180; *vs.* men's sport 303; methodology 60–61; overview 59–60; policy implementation and funding 63–64; policy SMART objectives 62–63; policy timeframes 62; societal beliefs 180–181; *see also* sports
Women's Super League (WSL) 314–315
Women's Tennis Association's (WTA) 186
women surfers: experiences, study of 283–284; gendered behavioural expectations for 287–288; growing culture of 284–285; inequality in 288; male surfers' perception of 283; narratives of 281–289; perceived differences in media depictions 286–287; representation of 282–283; sexualization of 283; sponsorship of 286–287; supportive culture of 284–285
Women's Victorian Football League 128
Wood, Z.C. 127
Woods, Tiger 250

Woodward, K. 317
World Athletics 29, 32, 47–48, 52–55, 301
World Dance Sport Federation (WDSF) 105
World Health Organization (WHO) 87; definition of PA 235
World Medical Association (WMA) 53

xenophobic nationalism 7
Xu, Q. 23

Yiamouyiannis, A. 156
Yoder, J. 181
Young, I.M. 34
Yuval-Davis, N. 120

Zaharias, Babe Didrickson 162–163
zero-sum feminism 8
Zimbabwe: colonialism, and male dominated acts 260; football popularity in 259; gender and patriarchy in 260–261; legitimate football 259; male dominated societies 260; Native Adultery Punishment Ordinance 260; women in football administration 259
Zimbabwe African National Union (ZANU) 262
Zimbabwe African National Union Patriotic Front (ZANU PF): formation of 262; political ideology of 265; and ZIFA administrators 263–264
Zimbabwe African People's Union (ZAPU) 262
Zimbabwe Football Association (ZIFA) 259, 262; affiliates 263; and Henrietta Rushwaya 263–264; origins of 263; politics of 263–264
Zimbabwe People's First (ZPF) 264
Zimbabwe Premier Soccer League (ZPSL) 263

For Product Safety Concerns and Information please contact our EU representative GPSR@taylorandfrancis.com Taylor & Francis Verlag GmbH, Kaufingerstraße 24, 80331 München, Germany

Printed and bound by CPI Group (UK) Ltd, Croydon, CR0 4YY
16/01/2025
01821405-0001